Marriage Breakdown
in Ireland

Marriage Breakdown in Ireland
Law and Practice

William R. Duncan
M.A., F.T.C.D.,
Barrister at Law (Middle Temple),
Associate Professor of Law, Trinity College Dublin,
Law Reform Commissioner.

Paula E. Scully
Diploma in Counselling, B.C.L., Solicitor.

with a
FOREWORD
by
The Honourable Mr. Justice Ronan Keane
Judge of the High Court of Ireland,
President of the Law Reform Commission.

with
ADDITIONAL MATERIAL
by
Cormac Corrigan, B.C.L.,
Barrister at Law (King's Inns)

Butterworth (Ireland) Limited
Dublin
1990

Republic of Ireland	Butterworth (Ireland) Ltd, 26 Upper Ormond Quay, DUBLIN 7.
United Kingdom	Butterworth & Co (Publishers) Ltd, 88 Kingsway, LONDON WC2B 6AB and 61A North Castle Street, EDINBURGH EH2 3LJ.
Australia	Butterworths Pty Ltd, SYDNEY, MELBOURNE, BRISBANE, ADELAIDE, PERTH, CANBERRA and HOBART.
Canada	Butterworths Canada Ltd, TORONTO and VANCOUVER.
Malaysia	Malayan Law Journal PTE Limited, KUALA LUMPUR.
New Zealand	Butterworths of New Zealand Ltd, WELLINGTON and AUCKLAND.
Puerto Rico	Equity de Puerto Rico, Inc, HATO REY.
Singapore	Malayan Law Journal Pte Ltd, SINGAPORE.
USA	Butterworth Legal Publishers, AUSTIN, Texas; BOSTON, Massachusetts; CLEARWATER, Florida (D & S Publishers); ORFORD, New Hampshire (Equity Publishing); ST PAUL, Minnesota; and SEATTLE, Washington.

© Butterworth (Ireland) Ltd.

British Library Cataloguing in Publication Data
Duncan, William R.
Marriage breakdown in Ireland: law and practice – (Irish Law Library).
1. Ireland (Republic). Families. Law
I. Title II. Scully, Paula E. III. Series 344.170615

ISBN 1–85475–046–1

First published 1990
Reprinted 1992, 1993

Phototypesetting by VAP, Kidlington, Oxford
Printed and bound in Great Britain by Antony Rowe Ltd, Chippenham, Wiltshire

FOREWORD

All happy families are alike. An unhappy family is unhappy after its own fashion. Tolstoy, *Anna Karenina*.

It has become the fashion to lump the untidy complex of laws which deal with marriage, divorce, the rights of children and related topics under the heading of "family law." The expression has a comforting resonance: it carries with it vague suggestions of disagreeable, not to say unseemly quarrels, which a wise father figure smooths away. Professor Duncan and Ms. Scully in deciding to give their new textbook the title "Marriage Breakdown" have faced uncompromisingly the reality which underlies this bland approach.

When I was called to the bar in 1954, the appearance of a matrimonial petition in the Master's list was sufficiently rare to provoke comment and, Ireland being a small and gossipy country, excited speculation as to whose identity was concealed by the discreet initials. All that has, of course, long since changed and it would be pointless to wonder why. Those who are understandably depressed by the huge growth in such cases might comfort themselves with the reflection that at least the grimmer manifestations of abuse, cruelty and neglect no longer remain concealed behind drawn curtains.

Irish law in these areas is a confusing mixture, some of it Victorian and deriving ultimately from the medieval jurisdiction of the "courts Christian", some of it representing the tentative essays in reform by the modern Irish legislator, some of it reflecting the influence in this area of the Constitution, sometimes baneful, occasionally ambiguous and rarely positive, and a great deal of it the fruits of the judges' struggle to make sense of the whole. The resultant problems for practitioners and students alike are compounded by the vast number of unreported decisions which have to be tracked down. (Even when they are reported, the lawyers' task is not eased by the fact that in the vast majority of cases he will search in vain for any report of counsel's arguments in the Irish Reports.)

Professor Duncan and Ms. Scully have provided in this book an authoritative guide through the labyrinth of the modern Irish law. They bring to their formidable task a blend of academic erudition and practical knowledge which makes the result uniquely valuable. Practitioners, in particular, will welcome the format of the book, in which a chapter setting out the legal principles which govern a particular topic is followed by an account of how the law operates in practice. Traps for the unwary are carefully signposted and the book derives an added value from the precedents and checklists hammered out, one can be sure, on the anvil of practical experience.

There was a time when practising lawyers and academics viewed one another with either hostility or indifference. That attitude, I hope, is on the wane: this book demonstrates repeatedly how important and rewarding the search for the rationale for a particular rule may be. To that sometimes challenging endeavour, both the practising lawyer and the scholar can contribute. And in this area of the law as much as any other – sometimes, indeed, more so – there is no substitute for a principled approach which rejects the easy pragmatism grounded in nothing more substantial than an intuitive sense of what may be "fair" in a particular context.

Inevitably, there is much citation of precedents from other common law jurisdictions, particularly England, in this book. But, as the authors are careful to remind the reader, such decisions although frequently valuable can also be misleading. It is not simply the factor of the Constitution: thus, it has to be remembered, when the recently enacted Judicial Separation and Family Law Reform Act, 1989 is being considered, that English decisions on the grounds for divorce are given in the context of a different definition of marital breakdown and of divorce jurisdiction which allows of the parties remarrying. It is indeed the absence of such a divorce jurisdiction, accompanied by as impressive an array of failed marriages as our European neighbours can boast, which gives Irish matrimonial law, seeking to accommodate the problems attendant on all manner of illicit cohabitation and "second tier" constitutional family units, its unique flavour. All concerned with the practical consequences in our law will be grateful to the authors for this comprehensive and lucid study, which reflects the greatest credit on their industry and learning.

Ronan Keane

Four Courts,
Dublin.

August 2nd 1990

PREFACE

The breakdown of marriage is no less a reality in Ireland than in other modern societies. The absence of a system of full divorce has not relieved the law of the need to confront the typical problems associated with breakdown – the regulation of the process of separation, the adjustment of maintenance and property rights as between estranged spouses, the adjudication of disputes over custody of and access to children, and the regulation of private agreements between spouses. In some respects, the absence of divorce has added to the law's complexity by, for example, giving rise to pressure for developments in the law relating to marriage annulment. The rules governing the recognition of foreign divorces also take on a particular significance in a country lacking a domestic divorce jurisdiction.

The purpose of this book is to provide a reasonably comprehensive description of the current principles governing the legal aspects of marriage breakdown, and of practice and procedure in the area. Where case law makes it appropriate, there is also reference to possible future developments. There has been considerable growth, dating from the mid-1970's, in legislation relating to marriage breakdown, culminating in the Judicial Separation and Family Law Reform Act 1989. The case law has developed apace, though the reduction of the High Court's jurisdiction effected by the Courts Act 1981 has resulted in fewer written judgments, especially in custody and maintenance cases. Many family law judgments unfortunately remain unreported. We have included coverage of those available up to June 1990. There are some matters which it was not possible to include in this edition. In particular, we regret the absence of a section on the social welfare aspects of marriage breakdown.

We have tried to maintain a balance between statements of principle and description of practice. We hope that the basic format of a chapter (or sections) dealing with legal principle followed by a chapter (or sections) dealing with practice and procedure will prove convenient to readers. One of the authors is an academic lawyer, the other a practitioner. The practitioner has naturally been primarily responsible for sections on practice and procedure while the academic lawyer has had primary responsibility for sections dealing with substantive law. The dividing line has, however, not been a rigid one and each author has learned from the other.

We would like to record our special debt of gratitude to Cormac Corrigan who not only took on the responsibility of writing chapters 10, 11 and 12, but also made numerous helpful comments on drafts of other chapters, particularly though by no means exclusively on matters of practice and procedure. He also provided the appendix on practice and procedure under the Judicial Separation and Family Law Reform Act 1989. Thanks are also due to Margot Aspell, Caroline Levis and Heidi Duncan for assistance with the typescript, to Heidi Duncan for help with the Tables and Index, and to Aedeen Boadita-Cormican for help in analysing some of the cases dealing with child custody and access.

William Duncan and Paula Scully

Dublin
August 1990

CONTENTS

TABLE OF CONTENTS

**CHAPTER 15: CHILD CUSTODY AND ACCESS DISPUTES:
PRACTICE AND PROCEDURE**

TABLE OF STATUTES

TABLE OF STATUTORY INSTRUMENTS

District Court

High Court and Supreme Court

TABLE OF THE CONSTITUTION OF IRELAND 1937

TABLE OF CASES

l

Chapter 1

JURISDICTION OF THE COURTS

Historical background

1.001 Until 1871 the ecclesiastical courts of the established Church of Ireland had exclusive jurisdiction in matrimonial causes and matters. They administered the king's ecclesiastical law which had its roots in the Roman Canon Law but which had developed independently from it from the time of the Reformation. The principal remedies provided by the ecclesiastical courts were divorce *a mensa et thoro*, nullity, restitution of conjugal rights and jactitation of marriage.[1] With the disestablishment of the Church of Ireland a new Civil Court for Matrimonial Causes and Matters was established, inheriting the jurisdiction of the ecclesiastical court. The Matrimonial Causes and Marriage Law (Amendment) Act 1870, which established the new court, provided in section 13 that:

> In all suits and proceedings the said Court for Matrimonial Causes and Matters shall proceed and act and give relief on principles and rules which, in the opinion of the said court, shall be as nearly as may be comfortable to the principles and rules on which the ecclesiastical courts of Ireland have heretofore acted and given relief.

Unlike its English counterpart, which had been established in 1857, by the Matrimonial Causes Act of that year, the new civil court was not given a jurisdiction to grant decrees of divorce *a vinculis*. Divorce by private Act of Parliament, the first of which had been granted to an Irish petitioner in 1729,[2] remained effectively available to the few who could afford it until 1922. The power of Parliament to dissolve marriages by legislation was formally abolished by Article 41.3.2 of the 1937 Constitution of Ireland.

---

1 The historical background is discussed in more detail in *R. v Millis* (1844) 10 Cl. & Fin. 534; *Ussher v Ussher* [1912] 2 IR 445; *McM. v McM. and McK. v McK.* [1936] IR 177; and *Mason v Mason* [1944] NI 134.
2 *Mr Austin's case.* See J. Roberts: *Divorce Bills in the Imperial Parliament* (Dublin, 1906).

1.002 The jurisdiction of the Court for Matrimonial Causes and Matters was merged into the High Court of Justice of Ireland on its establishment by the Judicature (Ireland) Act 1877, and was exercised by a Probate and Matrimonial Division of the High Court. By section 17 of the Courts of Justice Act 1924, the same jurisdiction passed in 1924 to the High Court of Justice of Saorstát Éireann. The present High Court, established under the Constitution of 1937, in turn inherited that same jurisdiction by section 2 of the Courts (Establishment and Constitution) Act 1961. The present High Court is thus the ultimate successor, in matrimonial causes and matters, to the ecclesiastical courts of the Church of Ireland. However, the only significant part of that jurisdiction still exercised by the High Court is the granting of annulments. Proceedings for the restitution of conjugal rights were abolished by section 1 of the Family Law Act 1981. The action for divorce *a mensa et thoro* was abolished by section 9 of the Judicial Separation and Family Law Reform Act 1989, and replaced by proceedings for judicial separation, jurisdiction for which was vested in the Circuit Court and High Court concurrently by section 31 of the same Act. In addition to the jurisdiction derived from the ecclesiastical courts, the High Court, prior to 1982, dealt with the great majority of disputes concerning matrimonial property, principally under the Married Women's Status Act 1957 and the Family Home Protection Act 1976. It also dealt with most disputes concerning the custody of, or access to, children. The High Court's jurisdiction was made concurrent with the Circuit Court by the Guardianship of Infants Act 1964, section 5, but in practice most cases were heard in the High Court. It could also grant injunctions and, from 1976, barring orders and maintenance orders, under the Family Law (Maintenance of Spouses and Children) Act 1976.

1.003 The involvement of the inferior courts in matrimonial disputes, apart from their criminal jurisdiction, began effectively in 1886 when Magistrates' Courts were given power to award maintenance to deserted wives under the Married Women (Maintenance in Case of Desertion) Act 1886. This limited maintenance jurisdiction, which was inherited by the District Court, was eventually reformed and expanded by the Family Law (Maintenance of Spouses and Children) Act 1976. Section 22 of that Act also gave the District Court power to grant barring orders of up to twelve months duration. Until 1982 the Circuit Court's role in matrimonial cases was limited. It could deal with certain property and guardianship matters, grant injunctions and hear appeals from the District Court, but in practice its family law jurisdiction was small.

1.004 The rapid expansion of family law litigation in the 1970s placed strain on the High Court and led to proposals to expand the jurisdiction of the inferior courts.[3] The result was the passing of the Courts Act of 1981

---

3 See the Report of the Committee on Court Practice and Procedure, *Increase of Jurisdiction of the District Court and Circuit Court* (Prl. 7459, 1978).

which came into force on 12 May 1982. This Act considerably increased the jurisdiction of the District Court and the Circuit Court. The District Court for the first time was given a role in custody and access disputes. The Circuit Court was given a wide range of new functions including the granting of decrees of divorce *a mensa et thoro* and maintenance and barring orders without limitation, and its jurisdiction with respect to property disputes was expanded. The new central role of the Circuit Court in matrimonial disputes has been further emphasised by the Judicial Separation and Family Law Reform Act 1989, which gives the Circuit Court jurisdiction, concurrently with the High Court, to grant judicial separations together with a wide range of ancillary orders. By section 31(1) of that Act the Circuit Court is now known as "the Circuit Family Court" when dealing with family law proceedings.

The District Court

The present jurisdiction of the District Court in relation to matrimonial disputes is as follows:

Maintenance

1.005 The Court has jurisdiction under section 23 of the Family Law (Maintenance of Spouses and Children) Act 1976 (as amended by section 12 of the Courts Act 1981) to award maintenance of up to £100 per week for the support of a spouse and up to £30 per week for a child. The Court may also order up to £30 per week maintenance for the support of a child under section 5 of the Guardianship of Infants Act 1964 (as substituted by section 15(a) of the Courts Act 1981).

Guardianship

1.006 The Court has jurisdiction (by virtue of sections 5 and 13 of the Guardianship of Infants Act 1964, as substituted by section 15 of the Courts Act 1981) to make orders under Parts II and III of the Guardianship of Infants Act 1964.

Barring and protection orders

1.007 The Court has jurisdiction under the Family Law (Protection of Spouses and Children) Act 1981 to make protection orders, and barring orders to last for a maximum period of twelve months. This Act came into force on 24 July 1981.

Disposal of household chattels

1.008 The Court has jurisdiction to make orders relating to the disposal of household chattels whose value does not exceed £2,500 under sections 9 and 10 of the Family Home Protection Act 1976. The value was raised from £1,000 to £2,500 by the Courts Act 1981, section 13(b).

3

Assault summonses

1.009 The District Court's criminal jurisdiction may be invoked in the course of a matrimonial dispute, particularly where there has been an assault by one spouse on the other. Assault summonses have been used less frequently since the introduction of barring orders in 1976.

The Circuit Court

The Circuit Court is known as the Circuit Family Court when exercising its jurisdiction to hear and determine family law proceedings or when transferring family law proceedings to the High Court. In relation to matrimonial disputes the Court's jurisdiction is as follows:

Judicial separation

1.010 By section 31(2) of the Judicial Separation and Family Law Reform Act 1989, the Circuit Court has concurrent jurisdiction with the High Court to hear and determine proceedings for judicial separation. Where, in proceedings for judicial separation, an order could be made in respect of land whose rateable valuation exceeds £200, the respondent is entitled to have the case transferred to the High Court.

Ancillary orders made pursuant to orders for judicial separation

1.011 The Court has power to make a wide variety of orders on granting a decree of judicial separation or at any time thereafter. These include a secured or unsecured periodical payment order, an order for the payment of a lump sum, a property adjustment order, an order relating to the occupation of the matrimonial home, an order for the sale of the matrimonial home, an order extinguishing succession rights and an order for the sale of property. The Court may in addition make orders under other legislative provisions as specified in **1.012** to **1.016**.

Guardianship

1.012 The Court has jurisdiction, concurrently with the District Court, to make orders under Parts II and III of the Guardianship of Infants Act 1964 (by virtue of sections 5 and 13 of the Act, as substituted by section 15 of the Courts Act 1981).

Protection and barring orders

1.013 The Court has jurisdiction, under the Family Law (Protection of Spouses and Children) Act 1981, to make protection orders, and barring orders for an unlimited duration.

Married Women's Status Act 1957

1.014 The Court has jurisdiction to make orders under section 12 of the Married Women's Status Act determining any dispute between spouses as to the title to or possession of any property. Under section 12(3) of the Act (as amended by section 3 of the Courts Act 1981), where the rateable valuation of land involved exceeds £200, the defendant or respondent may, before the hearing, require the proceedings to be transferred to the High Court.

Family Home Protection Act 1976

1.015 The Court has jurisdiction to make orders under sections 4, 5 and 9 of the Family Home Protection Act. By section 10(4) of the Act (as amended by section 13(a) of the Courts Act 1981) where the rateable valuation of any land involved exceeds £200, the defendant or respondent may, before the hearing, require the proceedings to be transferred to the High Court.

The Partition Acts 1868 and 1876

1.016 The Court has jurisdiction to order the partition of property under these Acts.[4]

Maintenance

1.017 The Court has jurisdiction, under the Family Law (Maintenance of Spouses and Children) Act 1976, to order a spouse to pay maintenance for the support of a dependent spouse or child. Section 12 of the Courts Act 1981 provides that there is no limit to the amount that may be ordered. It also has power to order maintenance for an infant under section 11 of the Guardianship of Infants Act 1964.

Wardship

1.018 The Circuit Court has a wardship jurisdiction which may occasionally be invoked in the course of a matrimonial dispute concerning an infant.[5] The jurisdiction is no longer dependent on the possession of any property by the infant.[6]

Injunctions

1.019 The Circuit Court has jurisdiction to grant injunctions in matrimonial cases, including an injunction excluding a spouse from the matrimonial home.[7]

Family Law Act 1981

1.020 The Circuit Court has jurisdiction to make orders under the Family

---

4 See chapter 12.
5 Sections 9 and 22(1) of the Courts (Supplemental Provisions) Act 1961 (as amended by sections 2(1) of the Courts Act 1981).
6 *The State (Bruton) v A Judge of the Circuit Court* (July 1984, unreported) High Court. Where the infant does possess property which includes lands with a rateable valuation exceeding £200 the High Court has jurisdiction.
7 See chapter 6.

Law Act 1981 which deals with disputes between engaged couples whose engagement has terminated.

1.021 Where an applicant or respondent in proceedings for judicial separation seeks certain preliminary orders, under section 12 of the Judicial Separation and Family Law Reform Act 1989 the Court may make such orders without the need for the institution of separate proceedings under the relevant Acts. The orders referred to are barring or protection orders, certain orders made under section 11 of the Guardianship of Infants Act 1964, and certain orders made under sections 5 and 9 of the Family Home Protection Act 1976.

The High Court

Nullity

1.022 The High Court continues to have exclusive jurisdiction to grant decrees annulling marriages. This jurisdiction, as already explained, derives ultimately from the ecclesiastical courts which exercised exclusive jurisdiction up to 1870. (see **1.001**).

Judicial separation and ancillary remedies

1.023 By section 31(2) of the Judicial Separation and Family Law Reform Act 1989, the High Court has jurisdiction, concurrent with the Circuit Court, to hear and determine proceedings for judicial separation.

Injunctions

1.024 The High Court's jurisdiction to grant injunctions may be invoked in the context of matrimonial disputes. The Court may, for example, order a spouse to leave or not to enter the family home.

Wardship

1.025 The High Court's wardship jurisdiction is occasionally used in matrimonial disputes relating to infants. As with the Circuit Court, the exercise of the jurisdiction does not depend on the possession of property by the infant.

Property disputes

1.026 The High Court has jurisdiction to make orders under section 12 of the Married Women's Status Act 1957,[8] under various sections of the Family Home Protection Act 1976,[9] and under the Partition Acts 1868 and 1876. It may also make ancillary property orders in proceedings for judicial separation.

---

8 See chapter 10.
9 See chapter 11.

Other matters

1.027 Until the operation of the Courts Act 1981 the High Court also had a statutory jurisdiction in matters of guardianship, under section 5 of the Guardianship of Infants Act 1964, and to hear applications for maintenance and barring orders, under section 23 of the Family Law (Maintenance of Spouses and Children) Act 1976. The Courts Act 1981, which vested jurisdiction in these matters in the Circuit and District Courts,[10] made no reference to any continuing jurisdiction in the High Court. However, there remained the possibility that the High Court might continue to exercise jurisdiction in these matters by virtue of Article 34.3.1 of the Constitution which invests the High Court with "full original jurisdiction in and power to determine all matters and questions whether of law or fact, civil or criminal."

1.028 The matter was considered by Gannon J. in *R. v R.*[11] He decided that, by reason of Article 34.3.1, it was not open to the Oireachtas to exclude the High Court from exercising original jurisdiction in matters of family law. On the other hand there was no constitutional right of access to the High Court at the choice of a litigant; where legislation conferred jurisdiction on inferior courts, it was open to the High Court to decline to entertain an application and to remit it for hearing in such courts. Following this decision, a practice direction (which is set out in full at **15.030**) was issued by the President of the High Court on 7 May 1982 indicating the procedure to be followed by applicants wishing to have certain family law matters[12] heard by the High Court. The procedure provided the applicant with the opportunity to submit evidence and arguments "as to whether the case is one appropriate for the High Court to exercise its jurisdiction . . . or whether it is a case which should be remitted to the Circuit Court or District Court." In the subsequent case of *O'R. v O'R.*[13] Murphy J. decided that, where legislation provided that an application could be made in the first instance to an inferior court, the High Court would be justified in departing from that procedure only where it was satisfied that in the particular case there was "a serious danger that justice would not be done" if the High Court declined to exercise its jurisdiction under the Constitution.

1.029 This line of authority is now in doubt following the Supreme Court's decision in *Tormey v A.G.*[14] The case concerned criminal jurisdiction in that the plaintiff was questioning the constitutionality of section 31 of the

10 Sections 12 and 15, amending respectively section 23 of the Family Law (Maintenance of Spouses and Children) Act 1976, and section 5 of the Guardianship of Infants Act 1964.
11 [1984] IR 296.
12 Under the Guardianship of Infants Act 1964, the Family Law (Maintenance of Spouses and Children) Act 1976, and the Family Law (Protection of Spouses and Children) Act 1981.
13 [1985] IR 367.
14 [1985] ILRM 375.

Courts Act 1981 which in effect abolished the previous right of a person sent forward for trial to the Circuit Court to have the case transferred to the Central Criminal Court. The judgment of the Court, delivered by Henchy J., dealt in general terms with the power of the Oireachtas to confer jurisdiction on the District Court and the Circuit Court. Henchy J. rejected a literal interpretation of Article 34.3.1 of the Constitution, and held that the Oireachtas may, in the exercise of its powers under Article 34.3.4,[15] either expressly or by necessary implication confer exclusive jurisdiction in some matters on the District Court or the Circuit Court. Where this has occurred the High Court will not hear and determine the matter in question. The High Court does, however, retain its full jurisdiction to review the proceedings in the lower court by way of judicial review to ensure that the hearing and determination will be in accordance with the law. As a result of the decision in Tormey's case it now appears that the High Court has no jurisdiction to make original orders under the Guardianship of Infants Act 1964, the Family Law (Maintenance of Spouses and Children) Act 1976, and the Family Law (Protection of Spouses and Children) Act 1981; the originating jurisdiction of the High Court under the Married Women's Status Act 1957 and the Family Home Protection Act 1976 was not abolished by the Courts Act 1981. The matter is not, however, clear beyond doubt. The decision of Gannon J. in *R. v R.*[11] has not been expressly overruled, and a further decision of the Supreme Court may be required to clarify the matter. In a later case *Mc.D. v McD.*[16] McKenzie J. accepted jurisdiction and having decided, in the terms of the practice direction, that the case was an appropriate one for determination by the High Court, made orders under the Guardianship of Infants Act 1964 and the Family Law (Maintenance of Spouses and Children) Act 1976.

Appellate jurisdiction of the courts

1.030 A District Court decision may be appealed to the Circuit Court.[17] The Circuit Court will conduct a full re-hearing, but once its decision is made, an appeal to the High Court will not lie. An appeal may be taken from a decision of the Circuit Court, where proceedings were initiated in that court, to the High Court. In that case, the High Court will conduct a full re-hearing. Its decision is final and conclusive and there is no further right of appeal.[18]

1.031 A decision of the High Court in the exercise of its original jurisdiction may be appealed to the Supreme Court. That Court is

15   The Article provides that the "courts of first instance shall also include courts of local and limited jurisdiction with a right of appeal as determined by law."
16   April 1986, unreported, High Court.
17   Section 84 of the Courts of Justice Act 1924, as amended by section 57 of the Courts of Justice Act 1936.
18   Section 39 of the Courts of Justice Act 1936, as applied to the High Court by section 48 of the Courts (Supplemental Provisions) Act 1961.

entrusted by Article 34.4.3 of the Constitution (with such exceptions and subject to such regulations as may be prescribed by law) with appellate jurisdiction from all decisions of the High Court. The appeal is generally based on the transcript of evidence of the High Court hearing, and on legal submissions. However, in exceptional circumstances, in particular in disputes under the Guardianship of Infants Act 1964, it has been held that the Supreme Court has inherent power to hear oral evidence. In *B. v B.*,[19] the oral evidence took place over five days, though the Court refused to receive as evidence an additional affidavit filed by the wife since the lodgement of the appeal. The Supreme Court also interviewed the children in chambers.

Walsh J. stated (at page 65): "If in the opinion of this court, on the hearing of any appeal, the examination of further evidence by this court is necessary or desirable, then in my view the court has ample jurisdiction within its appellate function to allow the appeal to be conducted on that basis." Walsh J. went on to indicate that if the case could have been remitted to the High Court to deal with the particular issue, it might be the better course. This was because "it would probably be both inconvenient and undesirable for this court, except in the most exceptional circumstances, to delay the other business of the court by conducting a time-consuming examination of oral evidence."

1.032 Order 58.8 of the Rules of the Superior Courts 1962 provides that, in an appeal from a final judgment, further evidence shall be admitted on special grounds only, and only with special leave of the court. However, where there is an interlocutory order, further evidence either by oral examination or affidavit may be given without special leave. The Supreme Court, in *B. v B.*, held that orders under section 11 of the Guardianship of Infants Act 1964 must be considered to be of an interlocutory nature and capable of being varied as the exigencies of the infants' welfare may require.

1.033 The discretionary nature of the Supreme Court's power to admit new evidence is well illustrated by the case of *E.K. v M.K.*,[20] in which a majority of the Supreme Court refused to hear medical evidence that had been tendered but not heard in the High Court. The Supreme Court stressed in another case, *K.E.D. (otherwise K.C.) v M.D.*,[21] which was a nullity appeal, that it was a fundamental principle arising from the exclusively appellate jurisdiction of the Supreme Court that, save in the most exceptional circumstances, the court should not hear and determine an issue which has not been tried and decided in the High Court. The arguments raised in the Supreme Court had not been made in the High Court, though they were included in the Notice of Appeal.

19 [1975] IR 54.
20 July 1974, unreported, Supreme Court.
21 December 1975, unreported, Supreme Court.

Chapter 2

NULLITY OF MARRIAGE

Description and sources

2.001 The law of nullity of marriage defines the conditions under which the High Court may declare a marriage to be invalid by reason of some fundamental defect relating to the form of the ceremony, or to the person or state of mind of either party to the marriage ceremony. The defect must have been present at the time the marriage was celebrated.[1] Subsequent acts or events cannot provide grounds, though they may be relevant to proving them. The decree declares that the marriage is not, and never was, valid. It is thus distinct from a decree of divorce (a vinculis) which dissolves an existing marriage, usually on the basis of facts or events occurring after the marriage ceremony. Article 41.3.2. of the Constitution provides that "No law shall be enacted providing for the grant of a dissolution of marriage." This prohibition on the enactment of laws permitting the dissolution of marriage obliges the legislature to maintain rigorously the distinction between the two. The judicial development of nullity law, even were it to tread dangerously close to the borderline between annulment and dissolution, is not constrained by this clause, which refers only to the "enactment" of laws. Despite several recommendations that it should do so,[2] the legislature has not yet addressed the issue of reform.

2.002 The jurisdiction of the present High Court to grant nullity decrees derives originally from the Matrimonial Causes and Marriage Law (Ireland) Amendment Act 1870, section 13 of which required the new civil court, established by the Act to

---

1 *S. v S.* (1 July 1976, unreported) Supreme Court, per Kenny J. at pages 4 & 5 of his judgment, citing *Napier v Napier* [1915] P 184.
2 See Office of the Attorney General. Discussion Paper on *The Law of Nullity in Ireland* (1976); Law Reform Commission, *Report on Nullity of Marriage* (LRC 9–1984), and *Report of the Joint Committee on Marriage Breakdown*, (Pl. 3074–1985), Chapter 7, section 1.

. . . proceed and act and give relief on principles and rules which . . . shall be as nearly as may be comfortable to the principles and rules which the Ecclesiastical Courts of Ireland have heretofore acted on and given relief.

The main source of the law is therefore the ecclesiastical law of the established Church of Ireland as it existed before 1870.[3] However, the law is not to be regarded as fossilised in its 1870 state. In *N. (orse K.) v K.* Henchy J. observed

> While section 13 of the 1870 Act did not fossilise the law in its state when the Act was passed, in that modern psychological, psychiatric and other advances in knowledge and understanding of human affairs may properly be applied today, nevertheless the basic principles and rules that are to be conformed to "as nearly as may be" are set in a pre-1870 mould.[4]

Just as the ecclesiastical law was in part judge made, so it has been accepted that the judges may continue to frame new rules[5] and develop the principles[6] to take account of advances in knowledge, especially in medicine, since 1870. The last ten years have seen the judiciary particularly active in this regard. Further developments are possible. However, there is a conflict of opinion within the High Court as to the role which it is proper for the judges to adopt in the evolution of nullity principles. While there is general agreement that existing grounds may be interpreted broadly in the light of advances in knowledge, there is disagreement as to whether new grounds may be recognised which are analogous to those which already exist. See **2.062** and Appendix A.

2.003 Although it is common for a petitioner to obtain a Roman Catholic Church annulment before seeking the civil remedy, neither this fact nor the rules currently employed in the Church's Regional Tribunals should have any direct bearing on the outcome of a civil case.

> Whilst . . . it is true that many of the principles and rules governing the decisions of these ecclesiastical courts coincide with the rules governing the decisions in the High Court and in . . . [the Supreme] . . . Court, the fact of such an ecclesiastical decree of nullity cannot of itself be a contributing factor to our decisions.[7]

---

3 See judgment of Finlay C.J. in *N. (orse K.) v K.* [1986] ILRM 75, at 82 and the judgment of Kenny J. in *Ussher v Ussher* [1912] 2 IR 445.
4 [1986] ILRM 75.
5 *S. v S.* supra, per Kenny J. at page 5 of his judgment, and accepted by Barrington J. in *R.S.J. v J.S.J.* [1982] ILRM 263, at page 265.
6 *D. v. C.* [1984] ILRM 173, per Costello J., at page 188.
7 Per Finlay C.J. in *N. (orse K.) v K.* [1986] ILRM 75, at page 82.

Void and voidable marriages

There is a basic distinction between defective marriages which are void and those which are voidable. The distinction has several legal consequences, as follows:

The need for a decree

2.004 As stated by Lord Green in *De Reneville v De Reneville*:

> A void marriage is one that will be regarded by every court in any case in which the existence of the marriage is in issue as never having taken place and can be so treated by both parties to it without the necessity of any decree annulling it: a voidable marriage is one that will be regarded by every court as a valid subsisting marriage until a decree annulling it has been pronounced by a court of competent jurisdiction.[8]

Although a decree is not strictly necessary in the case of a void marriage, in practice, especially where defective consent is relied upon, a decree is usually sought to confirm that the alleged grounds are in fact sufficient.

The validity of the marriage prior to the decree

2.005 The decree, whether made in respect of a void or a voidable marriage, declares that the marriage never existed. In the case of a voidable marriage this is a fiction. Such a marriage is in fact valid, and has all the legal consequences of a valid marriage, until such time as it is set aside. Thus as regards maintenance, property and succession rights, until a decree is granted, the couple enjoy the status of married persons, and their children are deemed legitimate. Any remarriage contracted by either party would be invalid for bigamy and may attract criminal prosecution.[9] None of this is true of a void marriage. It is invalid *ab initio*, and any decree made in respect of it simply confirms that fact. By contrast, the decree in respect of a voidable marriage retrospectively alters the status of the parties by deeming that the marriage never existed.

Who may petition?

2.006 In the case of a voidable marriage, only a party to the marriage may petition for a nullity decree, whereas any interested person may apply for a decree in respect of a void marriage.[10]

The time at which a decree may be sought

2.007 A voidable marriage must be annulled while both parties are alive.

---

8 [1948] P 100 at 110–111.
9 *F.M.L. & A.L. v Registrar General for Marriages* [1984] ILRM 667; *Mason v Mason* [1944] NI 134.
10 *D. v C.* [1984] ILRM 173 at 190, per Costello J., citing *A. v B.* (1868) LR 1 P & D 559.

A void marriage may be annulled at any time, even after the death of one or both parties.[10]

Approbation and ratification

2.008 A voidable marriage may be *approbated* by either party. That is to say, a decree may be refused to a petitioner who, while being aware that grounds for annulment exist, has acted in a manner which shows that he accepts the marriage as valid. The same doctrine does not apply to void marriages. However, a similar doctrine of ratification may be invoked where a marriage is alleged to be void for want of free consent. (See **2.147**)

2.009 There are at present only two grounds rendering a marriage voidable, namely, the inability of either party to consummate the marriage and the inability of either party, for various reasons, to enter into and sustain a normal marriage relationship.

2.010 A marriage may be void for any of the following reasons:

(a) The existence of a prior subsisting marriage,
(b) The non-age of either party,
(c) Non-observance of certain formalities,
(d) Absence of consent,
(e) Parties fall within the prohibited degrees of relationship, and
(f) Parties are not respectively male and female.

Onus of proof

2.011 "When a marriage has been celebrated in a proper form between apparently competent partners, there is a presumption of law in favour of its validity."[11] The onus is on the petitioner to prove invalidity. The High Court has traditionally approached claims for annulment with caution, it not being "a Court of convenience to release ill-sorted spouses from a marriage bond because it has become irksome to one, if not to both."[12]

2.012 The position under ecclesiastical law was that "the petitioner had to establish his or her case with a high degree of probability" or, as Lord Birkenhead expressed it in *C. (orse H.) v C.*,[13] "must remove all reasonable doubt."[14] In *McM. v McM.* and *McK. v McK.*,[12] Hanna J. (at 185) stated that petitions based on impotence are to be established "clearly, unequivocally and beyond reasonable doubt . . ." He also quoted,

---

11 Per Griffin J. in *N. (orse K.) v K.* [1986] ILRM 75 at 89, citing Haugh, J. in *Griffith v Griffith* [1944] IR 35 at 39.
12 Per Hanna J. in *McM. v McM. & McK. v McK.* [1936] IR 177, at 187.
13 [1921] P 399.
14 Cited with approval by Kenny J. in *S. v S.* (1 July 1976, unreported) Supreme Court, at page 4 of his judgment.

with approval, Lord Selborn L.C.'s dictum that "it is imperative to proceed only upon strict and thoroughly satisfactory proof."[15]

2.013 There is some evidence, in some of the more recent cases, of a less stringent approach towards the requirements of proof. In *N. (orse K.) v K.*, where absence of free consent was relied on, McCarthy J. said: "A petitioner must establish the case upon the balance of probabilities standard, but this must take into account the frequent absence of opposition, the possibility of collusion and so forth."[16] On the other hand, Keane J. in *U.F. (orse U.C.) v J.C.* disagreed with this statement and suggested that the law still required the removal of all reasonable doubt. In his opinion, the need to maintain this strict approach towards the granting of nullity decrees is emphatically reinforced by Article 41.3 of the Constitution.[17] See also Appendix A.

2.014 Whatever the position in theory, practice in many recent cases has indicated a more relaxed approach. For example, decrees grounded on impotence have in recent cases been granted on foot of evidence which might well not have proved sufficient in the past. In *S. v S.*,[19] a majority of the Supreme Court were prepared to find a husband psychologically impotent in relation to his wife in the absence of any medical or psychiatric evidence concerning the husband, without any direct testimony from him, and relying mainly on the uncorroborated evidence of the wife concerning the husband's unresponsive behaviour. This contrasts with the much earlier case of *R.M. v M.M.* in which O'Byrne J., after stating that the difficulty in discharging the onus of proof where psychological impotence is alleged may be "considerable", refused a decree despite medical opinion that the respondent's revulsion to the sexual act was invincible and incurable.[20]

Impotence

2.015 The inability of either party, at the time of the marriage, to have ordinary sexual intercourse with the other renders their marriage voidable, and either party may petition for a decree of nullity in respect of it. Inability to procreate arising from sterility is not relevant in this context. It is the ability to perform the mechanical function of intercourse, rather than the ability to have children, which is in issue, although deliberate concealment of sterility may be relevant to the issue of consent (see **2.067**). Once successful intercourse has taken place, even if only on one occasion, the marriage is consummated and no decree is available.

15   In *Cuno v Cuno* 2 HL Sc 300.
16   [1986] ILRM 75 at 94.
17   24 May 1989, unreported, High Court; pages 14 and 15.
18   See Duncan, *Sex and the Fundamentals of Marriage*. (1979–80) Dublin ULJ 29, at 31–2.
19   Supra, per Henchy & Griffin J.J., Kenny J. dissenting on this point.
20   (1942) 76 ILTR 165, which was confirmed on appeal to the Supreme Court.

Sexual intercourse

2.016 Sexual intercourse means "ordinary and complete intercourse; it does not mean partial and imperfect intercourse: yet . . . [not] every degree of imperfection would deprive it of its essential character."[21] In *M.M. (orse G.) v P.M.*,[22] the husband, though capable of erection and penetration, was unable to achieve emission. Evidence was given that, under the Canon Law of the Roman Catholic Church, ejaculation is essential to consummation. However McMahon J., applying principles long accepted by the ecclesiastical law of England and Ireland, at page 3 of his judgment refused a decree on the ground "that penetration is sufficient to amount to consummation and that emission of seed is not necessary." Penetration must be "full and complete." A failure to maintain erection immediately following penetration may provide grounds for a decree.[23]

2.017 Measures taken to avoid conception, such as the use of a contraceptive sheath, do not prevent consummation.[24] Equally, steps taken to induce conception, such as artificial insemination with the husband's semen *(fecundatio ab extra)*, do not amount to consummation.[25] It is therefore possible for a wife to obtain a decree grounded on her husband's impotence after having a child by him.

At the time of marriage

2.018 A fundamental principle of nullity law is that the defect relied on must have been present at the time the marriage was celebrated.[26] If the cause of impotence arises after the marriage, a decree ought not to be available. An example would be where a newly-married couple are involved in a serious accident on the way to their honeymoon, and impotence is a consequence of the injuries sustained by one of them.

2.019 However, the general principle appears not to have been applied in *A.O'H. (orse F.) v F.*[27] The wife initially suffered from vaginismus, an involuntary contraction of the muscles at the entrance of the vagina which makes penetration impossible. As a result, two attempts to have intercourse during the first year of marriage were unsuccessful. The couple continued to live together for thirteen years. Various efforts were made by the wife to overcome her problem, but the husband, while co-operating to some extent, made no real efforts on his own part to have the marriage consummated. He developed a psychological block which prevented him

---

21 Per Dr. Lushington, in *D-E. v A-G. (falsely calling herself D-G.)* (1845) 1 Rob. Eccl. 279, at page 298.
22 19 December 1985, unreported High Court.
23 *W. (orse K.) v W.* [1967] 3 All ER 178.
24 *Baxter v Baxter* [1948] AC 274.
25 *R.E.L. (orse R.) v E.L.* [1949] P 211.
26 Per Kenny J., in *S. v S.* (1 July 1976, unreported Supreme Court) at page 445 of his judgment.
27 19 December 1985, unreported, High Court.

from taking the steps which would have led to intercourse. Barron J. concluded at page 7 of his judgment that "as the marriage progressed . . . the husband contributed to the situation and ultimately became solely to blame." A decree was granted on the ground that "the husband has become unable to consummate the marriage because of impotence towards his wife."

2.020 Similarly, in *L.C. v B.C. (orse B.L.)*,[28] Lynch J. contemplated the possibility of a decree in a situation where a husband's impotence has followed an operation on his wife to remove her incapacity. In the particular circumstances, Lynch J. found it unnecessary to determine whether the husband had become impotent, because the wife's incapacity had remained, and a decree was granted on that basis.

2.021 There must remain some doubt as to whether the concept of subsequently-arising impotence will be accepted as a ground in future cases. Any relaxation of the general principle, which limits relief to cases involving defects which existed at the time of the marriage, risks breaching the dividing line between annulment and dissolution of marriage.

2.022 Because impotence must be proved from the time of the marriage, evidence that the parties engaged in sexual intercourse prior to the marriage will not necessarily preclude a decree. In *S. v S.*, a decree was granted on the basis of the respondent husband's impotence despite the fact that, before their marriage, the couple had intercourse on twenty five occasions. Some weeks before the marriage the respondent had begun a relationship with another woman. As a result, his attitude to his wife after the marriage was cold and unaffectionate. Although they slept in the same bed and lived together for six months, the marriage was never consummated. On one occasion the wife tried to have intercourse, but the husband proved unresponsive. Shortly after the marriage he told her that he had no affection for her, that she revolted him, that he had no interest in founding a family and that the only reason he had gone through with the marriage was that he lacked the courage to break off the engagement when arrangements for the marriage were so advanced.

2.023 In *R. (orse W.) v W.*,[29] the parties had sexual intercourse on three occasions before their marriage, though on each occasion the petitioner wife had found the experience increasingly distasteful. The wife wanted the marriage to succeed and hoped that her attitude towards intercourse would change. The husband's attempts to have intercourse, which diminished in frequency with the passage of time, were unsuccessful and the parties separated. The wife subsequently began a relationship with another man by whom she had a child. Psychiatric evidence was given by a doctor who had examined the wife after the separation but before the beginning of

28 18 November 1985, unreported, High Court.
29 1 February 1980, unreported, High Court.

her second relationship. In his opinion the wife suffered from a personality disorder resulting in her being able to accept and co-operate in sexual intercourse "on her own terms and without what she would perceive as the obligation of matrimony", but she could not do so at a particular stage in her development within the confines of matrimony. Finlay P. granted a decree to the wife on the ground of her own incapacity. This resulted from what he described at page 9 of his judgment as "an insurmountable repugnance" to having intercourse with her husband, "due probably to a psychosexual disorder."

Relative impotence

2.024 It is not necessary to prove general impotence, but only inability to have intercourse with the specific wife (*quoad hanc*) or the specific husband (*quoad hunc*). The cases of *S. v S.* and *R. (orse W.) v W.*, described above, illustrate this principle. In both, the impotent partner had a successful sexual relationship with someone other than his or her spouse. In *S. v S.*, Henchy and Griffin J.J. cited (at pages 6 and 3 to 4 respectively of their judgments) with approval the judgment of Lord Birkenhead L.C. in *C. (orse H.) v C.*, in which the authorities are reviewed and where it is pointed out that ecclesiastical law admitted and enjoined nullity in cases of relative impotence. Another example is *L.C. v B.C. (orse B.L.)*,[28] in which a wife underwent a minor gynaecological operation in order to overcome difficulty in achieving intercourse with her husband. The marriage nevertheless remained unconsummated, the parties separated and each subsequently formed a second relationship in which sexual intercourse was successful. The wife had a child by her second partner. A decree was granted by Lynch J. on the ground of the wife's incapacity relative to the husband.

Psychological impotence and wilful refusal

2.025 The inability to achieve complete sexual intercourse may derive from a physical cause or it may have psychological roots. Where psychological impotence is relied on, a distinction has been drawn in law between cases of genuine psychological disability, involving an invincible repugnance to having intercourse (or a paralysis of the will), and cases where the failure to consummate the marriage is a result of an act of will—a wilful refusal to consummate.

2.026 In *McK. v McK.*, during the two years in which the parties lived together following their marriage, the respondent husband made repeated attempts to have sexual intercourse with his wife, but was met on each occasion by a refusal on her part. The wife petitioned on the ground of her own impotence. Medical inspection revealed that she had no physical impediments, and there was no evidence of hysteria or neurosis. Hanna J. refused to grant the decree. Non-consummation had resulted, not from any incapacity in the petitioner, but from her wilful and persistent refusal to have sexual intercourse with the respondent.

17

2.027 In *R.M. v M.M.*,[30] intercourse was attempted by the petitioner, but the wife was physically revolted. Further attempts led to increasing nausea on her part. In the High Court, O'Byrne J., after stating that the onus of proof was high in cases of psychological impotence refused a decree. On the wife's attitude, he commented (at 172):

> I am satisfied that she was genuinely shocked and disgusted by the attempt. I am also satisfied that she had and continued, during her matrimonial life with the petitioner, to have a strong and real aversion to the sexual act. I am, however, asked to say that this aversion was of such an invincible character as to produce a paralysis and distortion of the will . . . I am far from being satisfied as to this. The respondent, when in the witness box, though over-wrought and suffering from severe nervous and emotional tension, struck me as being to some extent a rather self-willed and determined girl.

The Supreme Court dismissed the Appeal, Sullivan C.J. (for the Court), emphasising that there had been no initial consent to intercourse by the wife.

> Although the subject of their marital relations was discussed by the parties on several occasions there was no indication by the respondent that she would yield to her husband's wishes. Her reply to his re-monstrances was that she could not do it, that she did not like it at all and that people could live together without intercourse.

2.028 The distinction between impotence and wilful refusal, which is no longer accepted in the jurisdiction in which it originated,[31] seems likely to be retained because of the general principle which insists that annulment is only appropriate where the relevant defect existed at the time of the marriage.[32] A wilful refusal to have intercourse will usually only reveal itself after the ceremony. If it can be proved that there was an unrevealed intention, at the time of the marriage, not to engage in intercourse, a decree may possibly be available on the basis of absence of consent.[33] However, cases decided in recent years indicate clearly that the judges are less likely than they were in the past to attribute failure to consummate to a wilful refusal, and are more ready to accept a plea of psychological impotence. In addition, the heavy burden of proof which the earlier cases suggest rests on the petitioner where psychological impotence is relied on has not been applied in practice in the more recent cases.

---

30 (1942) 76 ILTR 165, High Court and Supreme Court.
31 See *Napier v Napier* [1915] page 184. Wilful refusal was made a statutory ground in England by the Matrimonial Causes Act 1937.
32 See Law Reform Commission, *Report on Nullity of Marriage* (LRC 9–1984), at page 146, where it is suggested that "to make wilful refusal to consummate the marriage a ground for annulment might well raise difficulties under Article 41 of the Constitution.
33 Per Kenny J. in *S. v S*. See **2.110.**

2.029 In *S. v S.*, a majority of the Supreme Court were prepared to make a finding that the husband was psychologically impotent relative to his wife in the absence of any medical or psychiatric evidence concerning him, and in the absence of any direct testimony by him. Kenny J. dissenting from Henchy and Griffin J.J. did not think that the evidence justified a finding that the husband was impotent when with the wife. The only pointer to the husband's condition came from the wife who gave evidence that he had not attempted intercourse with her, and that on the one occasion that she tried to persuade him to make love, he had proved unresponsive. The Court thus inferred the existence of a psychosexual disorder from the uncorroborated testimony of an interested party, and this in a case where the husband's potency vis à vis his wife prior to the marriage was demonstrated, as was his capacity in relation to a second partner both before and after the marriage. Also, there was no evidence of any initial consent or willingness to yield on the husband's part, which had been thought so important in *R.M. v M.M.* It is possible to distinguish the two cases by reference to a view expressed by Hanna J. in *McM. v McM.* and *McK. v McK.*, that for biological reasons the role of the male in the act of sexual intercourse is more likely to be affected by psychological factors than that of the female. A more likely explanation is that the Supreme Court, in *S. v S.*, was applying a less exacting standard of proof.

2.030 In *R (orse W.) v W.* the evidence was stronger than in *S. v S.* The petitioner, who was relying on her own impotence testified, and a professional psychiatric opinion was available to the Court. But again, it is doubtful whether the evidence would have been sufficient in the days of *R.M. v M.M.* The petitioner had not been examined while she was living with her husband, and, apart from consulting a member of the staff of a family planning clinic in the hope that a change of contraceptive pill would revive her sexual desire, she had done nothing to explore the possibility of a cure for her condition.

2.031 In *A.M.N. v J.P.C.*[34] all efforts by the wife to have intercourse were repulsed by the respondent. He became aggressive when she suggested that they should have intercourse, and he refused to see the local priest or a marriage guidance counsellor. She left him two and a half years after the marriage. Medical inspection established that she was *virgo intacta*, but no medical or psychiatric evidence relating to the husband was offered. Barron J. concluded at pages 3–4 of his judgment that:

> the reason for the failure to consummate the marriage was that the respondent regarded the act of sexual intercourse as being wrongful and something which he found repugnant. He was unable to bring himself to perform the act and was unable psychologically to overcome this attitude.

---

34   10 December 1985, unreported, High Court.

2.032 There was no suggestion by the learned judge that the husband's conduct might be characterised as wilful refusal to consummate. Nor was there any such suggestion by the same judge in *A. O'H (orse F.) v F.*, where the husband's mind "prevented him from taking the steps which would have led to . . . [intercourse]."[27]

Incurability

2.033 The incapacity must in theory be incurable,[35] but this requirement is not applied strictly in practice. Where an operation is available which might effect a cure, the impotence is still regarded as incurable if the operation involves danger,[36] or even if the person affected refuses to submit to it.[37] The requirement of incurability is, in fact, sometimes glossed over or ignored, particularly where psychological impotence is relied on. The absence of any serious attempt to overcome the incapacity by therapy appears not to raise judicial eyebrows. In a case where there is no direct medical evidence relating to the respondent's condition (for example *S. v S.*), or where the respondent refuses to undergo a medical examination (e.g. *N.F. v M.T. (orse F.)*),[38] it may be very difficult for a judge to reach an informed view about the prospect of a cure. This did not preclude the grant of a decree in the cases instanced.

2.034 In *N.F. v M.T. (orse F.)*, the parties had, before marriage, associated on intimate terms and had engaged in sexual contact falling short of intercourse. After the marriage, despite repeated attempts by the husband, sexual intercourse proved impossible. Medical inspection showed him to be capable of consummating the marriage. The wife refused to undergo medical inspection and denied that the failure to consummate was due to her incapacity. O'Hanlon J. was satisfied that she was incapable of consummating the marriage "by reason of difficulties referable to her physical make-up and also by reason of psychological problems which affected her." He admitted that it was impossible to forecast whether the wife's physical problems could be resolved by medical intervention. He was, however, prepared to accept that there was and would remain a complete psychological incapacity quoad the petitioner.

Repudiation by the respondent

2.035 A petitioner is entitled to rely on his or her own incapacity. It is now uncertain whether, in such a case, it is necessary for the petitioner to show that the respondent has repudiated the marriage. The older cases support such a rule, on the basis of avoiding injustice to the respondent.

2.036 In *McM. v McM.*,[39] the parties, both Roman Catholics, married in

35 *Dickinson v Dickinson* [1913] P 198.
36 *W. v H.* (1861) 2 Sw & Tr 240.
37 *G. v G.* (1908) 25 TLR 328.
38 [1982] ILRM 545.
39 [1936] IR 177.

1927 and lived together until 1931 when the respondent wife left as a result of the petitioner's persistent violence. In 1934 he petitioned for a decree of nullity based on his own impotence. The respondent entered an appearance, but refused to defend the proceedings. She was content that the petitioner should obtain a civil decree but, for reasons of conscience, she was not willing to repudiate the marriage until it had been set aside by an ecclesiastical court. Although psychological impotence in the petitioner was established, Hanna J., relying in part of the authority of *A. v A.*,[40] refused a decree because the petitioner had failed in his duty to "satisfy the Court that there has been, and is, conduct on the part of the respondent which has destroyed the *verum matrimonium*, for example, by a genuine and deliberate repudiation of the marriage contract and its obligations."

2.037 It was argued in *R. (orse W.) v W.*[29] that, following the decision in *Harthan v Harthan*,[41] in which the older decisions are analysed, the requirement of repudiation is unnecessary, although there may be other circumstances which disqualify a petitioner from relying on his own impotence, such as knowledge of the defect at the date of the marriage. In view of his finding that the respondent had unequivocally repudiated the marriage by instituting church annulment proceedings, Costello J. found it unnecessary to decide the issue, and expressly reserved his view on it. However, in the subsequent case of *L.C. v B.C. (orse B.L.)*,[28] Lynch J., in an obiter remark at page 4 of his judgment, implied the need for repudiation. The requirement was also accepted by Barrington J. in *R.S.J. v J.S.J.*,[42] and extended by analogy to cases where the petitioner relies on his own incapacity to enter into and sustain a normal marriage relationship. In the same context, the same principle was later applied in *D.C. v D.W.*,[43] but disapproved of in *P.C. v V.C.*[44] In the latter case, O'Hanlon J. gave obiter approval to the decision in *Harthan v Harthan*, the rationale being that, where both parties enter a marriage without any knowledge that a defect exists, it is unfair that the petitioner should be denied a decree merely because the respondent wishes to hold him to the marriage bond. It appears that a decision of the Supreme Court will be needed to resolve this issue.

2.038 What constitutes repudiation has not been clearly laid down. Desertion probably suffices. The initiation of church annulment proceedings by the respondent may be sufficient, but, as illustrated by *McM. v McM.*, not where the respondent takes the view that the marriage continues to subsist until the decree is granted.

---

40 19 LR Ir 408.
41 [1949] P 115.
42 [1982] ILRM 263, at 268.
43 21 February 1986, unreported, High Court, at page 8 of Blayney J.'s judgment.
44 7 July 1989, unreported, High Court. O'Hanlon J. also thought there was a good deal of substance in criticism of the repudiation requirement made in A. J. Shatter, *Family Law in the Republic of Ireland* (2nd ed.) pages 73–75. See further **2.062** below.

Medical inspection

2.039 It is not an absolute requirement that the parties should be medically inspected. There may be sufficient alternative proof of impotence. But it has, since the days of the ecclesiastical courts, been a general practice to require medical inspection. Detailed provision for the appointment of medical practitioners is made in the Rules of the Superior Courts (see **3.007**). Where a respondent refuses to undergo a medical inspection, and medical evidence shows that the petitioner is properly formed and capable of consummating the marriage, a decree may be made. Such was the case in *E.M. v S.M.*,[45] in which Maguire J. accepted that the refusal of the wife to submit to a medical examination resulted from an operation undergone during adolescence. A decree was similarly granted in *N.F. v M.T. (orse F.)*,[46] though no reason was alluded to for the wife's refusal to be inspected.

Inability to enter into or sustain a normal marriage relationship

2.040 In 1982 it was first judicially acknowledged in *R.S.J. v J.S.J.* that a decree of annulment might be available on the ground that one of the parties was, at the time of the marriage, "incapable through illness of forming a caring or considerate relationship."[47] (This development came six years after the publication by the Office of the Attorney-General of *The Law of Nullity in Ireland* (Prl. 5628, 1976), in which it was recommended (at page 7) "that legislation should be introduced to deal with unfitness for marriage arising from mental disorder existing at the date of the solemnisation of the marriage.") It appeared until 1989 that this new ground of annulment had become well established in the jurisprudence of the High Court. However, in *U.F. (orse U.C.) v J.C.*,[48] Keane J. questioned the juridical basis of the development and refused to accept the new ground. The Supreme Court has recently delivered judgment reversing on appeal, the decision of Keane J. The judgments of the court are discussed in Appendix A.

2.041 The juridical basis for accepting the new ground was the analogy with sexual impotence. In the leading case of *D. v C.*,[49] Costello J. stated:

> . . . Marriage is by our common law (strengthened and reinforced by our constitutional law) a life long union, and it seems to me to be perfectly reasonable that the law should recognise (a) the obvious fact that there is more to marriage than its physical consummation and (b) that the life long union which the law enjoins requires for its maintenance the

45 (1942) 77 ILTR page 128.
46 [1982] ILRM page 545.
47 *R.S.J. v J.S.J.* [1982] ILRM 263, per Barrington J. at page 265.
48 24 May 1989, unreported, High Court.
49 [1984] ILRM 173, at page 189.

creation of an emotional and psychological relationship between the spouses. The law should have regard to this relationship just as it does to the physical one.

2.042 The analogy with impotence has a number of consequences. The marriage is voidable, it is capable of being approbated, and the inability may relate to the particular partner. Again, as is the case with impotence, there is a doubt as to whether a petitioner who relies on his own inability must show that the respondent has repudiated the marriage.

Psychiatric illness and other disorders

2.043 There is "considerable disagreement among psychiatrists as to the 'proper' definition of mental illness."[50] Nevertheless, where the inability to enter into and sustain a normal marriage relationship results from a psychiatric illness, a decree may be available.

2.044 In *D. v C.* the couple had been married nine years and had two children. Before and after the marriage the respondent husband had experienced extreme changes in mood and periods of depression, and had shown little affection or warmth towards his wife. After being diagnosed as a manic depressive, a drug addict and an alcoholic, he underwent treatment but his condition deteriorated further. He attempted suicide and subsequently spent a period of 10 months in a psychiatric hospital. After two serious and terrifying assaults on her, the wife obtained a permanent order barring him from the matrimonial home. After carefully reviewing the medical evidence, Costello J. concluded that the respondent was, at the time of the marriage, suffering from "a cyclical manic-depressive disorder which resulted in disturbance in mood states which affected his personality and behaviour", and that the disorder was "sufficiently severe as to impair significantly his capacity to form and sustain a normal viable marriage relationship with the petitioner."

2.045 In *R. v R.*,[51] after a happy courtship, engagement and honeymoon, the respondent husband's attitude to his wife underwent a dramatic change. He became cold and distant and began to accuse her of having an affair with his best man and of putting drugs in his food. The relationship deteriorated. The wife then discovered for the first time that he had been diagnosed five years before their marriage as suffering from paranoid schizophrenia and had been hospitalised for two months. He had been receiving drug treatment for his condition which he had discontinued shortly before the marriage. He had since regressed and now required further hospitalisation. Costello J. accepted medical evidence to the effect that the husband was not capable of entering into a stable marriage relationship with the petitioner, and that it was the relationship with the petitioner which had caused his paranoia to deteriorate.

---

50 Law Reform Commission, *Report on Nullity of Marriage* (LRC 9–1984), at page 97.
51 21 December 1984, unreported, High Court.

2.046 In *D.C. v D.W.* the wife had contracted, about a year before her marriage, a psychotic disorder which was diagnosed as "schizophrenia-paranoid sub-type."[52] She was advised against marriage but, having become pregnant, saw the marriage as the only way of surviving. She separated from her husband, after living with him for only two weeks, following a row during which she had been struck by him. Blayney, J. was satisfied that, at the time of the marriage, she was incapable of entering into and forming a normal marriage relationship with the respondent.

Immaturity

2.047 It was originally thought that personality disorders or inadequacies falling short of psychiatric illness, such as immaturity, would not provide grounds. In *E.P. v M.C.*,[53] Barron J. rejected the claim that a wife, who had married only to avoid the shame of having an illegitimate child and to provide the child with a name, had never intended to enter into a proper and lasting marriage. She was spoiled and unprepared to accept the obligations of marriage, but her attitude did not spring from any illness. It is possible that the facts would now justify a decree on the grounds of defective consent (see **2.074**). In *P.C. (orse O'B.) v D.O'B.*,[54] Carroll J. refused a decree to a wife who had married at 18 years of age and who, at the time of her marriage had a variety of behavioural problems including soft-drug abuse and a tendency to react impulsively to situations. She had, prior to the marriage, spent two brief periods in hospital for psychiatric treatment for her drug addiction. Carroll J. stated at page 84 of the judgment:

> The petitioner at the time of the marriage did have an inadequate or immature personality, which to me is a mental condition rather than a mental illness. On one view, anyone who is immature is unsuited to marriage. But as long as the law permits people as young as the petitioner to marry it cannot be a ground for nullity unless it exists to an abnormal decree.

2.048 However, in *W. v P.*,[55] Barrington J. was prepared to accept that "emotional disability or incapacity", as well as psychiatric illness, would provide grounds. The respondent husband's immature personality was regarded as a relevant factor, but the degree of emotional disability to which it gave rise was much more profound than in *P.C. (orse O'B.) v D.O'B.* Also the immaturity was not a consequence of youth; the husband

---

52 21 February 1986, unreported, High Court. See also *M.E. v A.E.* (8 May 1987, unreported, High Court) where the respondent was diagnosed as suffering from paranoid schizophrenia.
53 13 March 1984, unreported, High Court.
54 2 October 1985, unreported, High Court.
55 (7 June 1984, unreported) High Court. See also *D. v E. (orse D.)* (1 March 1989, unreported) High Court, in which Barr J. granted a decree on the ground that the respondent by reason of "gross immaturity", lacked capacity to maintain "a meaningful marriage relationship".

was in his early thirties at the time of the marriage. The marriage was celebrated only after considerable emotional pressure, including two suicide threats, had been placed on the petitioner by the respondent. Following the marriage, the husband's behaviour became childish and dependent. When the wife became sick during their honeymoon, he refused to go by himself to the chemist to obtain medicine because it was a strange town. He cried at the possibility of her going to hospital. Subsequently, after taking drink, he began boxing his head violently and crying. The tantrums continued on a regular basis. On one occasion he hit himself with a poker; on another he put his head over a gas ring. He would sometimes lock himself in his bedroom, stamp on the floor and cry. The wife also discovered that the respondent's mother, with whom he had a strangely intense relationship, had written love letters on his behalf prior to the marriage. After two years the wife left the respondent following a double suicide attempt by him. Medical and psychiatric evidence was given to the effect that the respondent's degree of underdevelopment and immaturity was such as markedly to impair his capacity to sustain a normal and viable marriage relationship.

2.049 Keane J., in *U.F. (orse U.C.) v J.C.*[56] at page 28 of his judgment expressed the opinion that *W. v P.* involves a finding that mental illness is no longer a necessary precondition for relief. He further observed that, as a consequence, the influential dictum of Kenny J. in *S. v S.* concerning the need for judges to take account of advances in psychological medicine in exercising the nullity jurisdiction, ceases to provide a foundation for the new ground.

2.050 In *B.D. v M.C. (orse M.D.)*[57] it was for the first time explicitly recognised that proof of illness as such is not essential. There the main allegation was that the wife was emotionally immature. Barrington J. granted a decree on the basis that the petitioner and respondent were unable to enter into and sustain a normal marital relationship because of the incapacity of the respondent resulting from emotional immaturity and because of the respective states of mind and mental conditions of the petitioner and the respondent. Referring to the reasons for the failure of the marriage, Barrington J. stated at page 34 of the judgment:

This was because M. (the respondent) at the time of the marriage and at all times material to this case, was suffering from such a degree of emotional immaturity as to preclude the formation of a normal marriage relationship. I do not know if M.'s condition can be described as an illness. It is apparently a "disorder" which requires and may be susceptible to psychotherapy. But whether it is an illness or a disorder, it is equally incapacitating so far as the formation of a marital relationship is concerned.

56   24 May 1989, unreported, High Court. See also Appendix A.
57   March 1987, unreported, High Court.

2.051 *B.D. v M.C. (orse M.D.)* was approved and followed in *P.C. v V.C.*[58] in which O'Hanlon J. at page 27 of the judgment granted a decree on the ground that both parties

> were unable to enter into and sustain a normal marital relationship with each other by reason of incapacity deriving from lack of emotional maturity, and psychological weakness and disturbance affecting both parties to a greater or lesser degree.

The husband and wife were respectively 31 and 26 years of age when they married. Both were well educated. There was one child of the marriage. The marriage suffered from serious strains from the outset. The principal source of friction was the wife's deep attachment to her parents and grandmother, which resulted in the husband feeling excluded and developing an "obsessive pre-occupation with his own place in his wife's affections contrasted with that of her original family, and particularly her mother." A final separation occurred after about three and a half years of cohabitation which had been interrupted by a lengthy period during which the wife went to stay with her parents. After reviewing the evidence of two consultant psychiatrists, the family doctor and the Priest who officiated at the wedding, O'Hanlon J. at page 18 of the judgment came to the following conclusion about the relationship between the parties.

> There appears to have been a lack of capacity on each side to compromise, to give way, to adjust to the emotional needs of the other partner, and to reach a *modus vivendi* where a reasonable and tolerable marital relationship could evolve between them. . . . what would have been required on the part of the wife would have been a submission to unreasonable demands on the part of the husband that she should curtail her association with her parents. . . .
>
> I think there were some less obvious, but also unreasonable expectations on the part of the wife. She felt that husband and wife should fulfil distinct and separate roles which would have resulted in a virtual exclusion of the husband from taking part with her in household chores, shopping, caring for the child, whereas the husband professed a wish to be actively involved in all these spheres.
>
> On each side, but particularly on that of the husband, there was an obsessive secrecy and lack of openness, and trust, and an inability to sit down and talk things over in a calm and rational manner. Each retired into an entrenched position whenever any disagreement, however trivial, arose, and thereby perpetuated a state of conflict.

O'Hanlon J. concluded that the case went well beyond temperamental incompatability *simpliciter*, and brought into play other profounder factors of want of capacity.

---

58   7 July 1989, unreported, High Court.

Homosexual orientation

2.052 In *M. (orse O.) v O.*,[59] Hamilton J. at page 3 of the judgment held obiter that the homosexual orientations of one spouse may be a basis for a decree where it renders the spouse incapable of "entering into the relationship which should exist between married couples if a life long union is to be possible." The husband had engaged in a homosexual relationship before the marriage, but there was no evidence that he had done so since the marriage, and the sexual relationship between husband and wife had for some time continued on a satisfactory and normal basis. There being no evidence of incapacity, a decree was refused.

2.053 In *F. v F.* the respondent "was at all material times not only homosexual but a man who engaged in continual promiscuous activities, of which the respondent was totally ignorant."[60] The marriage lasted only five weeks. There was evidence of psychological disturbance in the respondent which prevented him from having the capacity to relate to others. Barron J., following *M. (orse O.) v O.*, granted a decree on the basis of the respondent's incapacity to maintain the life long relationship required of marriage. The incapacity was expressly stated by Barron J. at pages 12–13 to arise from psychiatric illness, rather than merely from the respondent's homosexual orientation. Strictly speaking the judge's finding that the respondent lacked capacity to maintain a life long relationship was obiter dictum. The marriage was in any case void for absence of full and free consent on the part of the petitioner. Once it has been determined that a marriage is void, it cannot in logic be regarded as voidable.

2.054 The question arises whether homosexual orientation as such, without proof of psychiatric illness or psychological disturbance or immaturity, may suffice to ground a decree where it leads to an inability to form or sustain a normal relationship with the respondent. It now seems clear that in *M. (orse O). v O.*, Hamilton J. was not necessarily viewing a homosexual orientation as a form of psychiatric illness or disorder. In a subsequent extra-judicial statement,[61] he agreed with the conclusion reached by the Law Reform Commission at page 106 of the *Report on the Nullity of Marriage* that "It does not seem to us necessary or appropriate to require practitioners to make the case that such orientation is an illness."

2.055 Thus a homosexual orientation appears to have been accepted as offering an alternative and independent basis on which to found an argument that a respondent lacks capacity to enter into and sustain a normal marriage relationship. Such has also now been accepted by the Supreme Court in *U.F. (orse U.C.) v J.C.* (11 July 1990, unreported). The petitioner alleged that the respondent's homosexual nature and tempera-

---

59   26 January 1984, unreported, High Court.
60   *F. v F.* 22 June 1988, unreported, High Court, at page 9 of Barron J.'s judgment.
61   The O'Dálaigh Lecture, *Some Aspects of the Law of Nullity*, delivered at University College Dublin on 21 February 1985, at page 12.

ment had made it impossible for him to form or maintain a normal marital relationship with her. It was proved that, at the time of the marriage, the respondent was a practising homosexual, that he concealed his condition from the petitioner, that shortly after the marriage he resumed his homosexual practices and that as a result the marriage had irretrievably broken down. The Supreme Court allowed the appeal against Keane J.'s refusal to grant a decree. See Appendix A.

Normal marriage relationship

2.056 The incapacity must be such as to render the relevant spouse incapable of forming or sustaining a normal marriage relationship with the other spouse. Although the incapacity must be shown to have existed from the time of the marriage, the subsequent history of the relationship will usually play a vital part in determining the nature and extent of the original incapacity. If the relationship which develops is abnormal, this may suggest that the original incapacity was sufficiently serious to justify a decree. However, the concept of "normality" is not an easy one to apply in the context of marriage relationships. As well as the difficulty of determining objectively the constituents of a normal relationship, there may also be disagreement among psychiatrists as to whether, in a particular case, the illness suffered by the respondent does make a normal relationship impossible.

2.057 In *R.S.J. v J.S.J.*,[62] a forty-seven year old farmer from a family with a history of psychiatric illness, married the respondent, a nurse at the top of her profession. The marriage failed and, after eight months the respondent left the matrimonial home, believing that the petitioner did not want her there. Before and after the marriage the petitioner had been suffering from a form of personality defect or illness similar to schizophrenia. This resulted, inter alia, in bouts of depression and some impairment in his ability to have emotional relationships with other people. Evidence was given by three psychiatrists. The first did not consider the petitioner incapable of having a successful marriage. The second thought that the petitioner would have great difficulty in marriage. The third, who did not see the petitioner until after the marriage, felt that he would not be able to have a meaningful relationship with any other person. Barrington J. refused a decree on the basis that, although the marriage had broken down and the petitioner's condition made it difficult for him to have a successful marriage, his incapacity at the date of the marriage did not make it impossible for him to do so.

2.058 The presence or absence of a "normal" sexual relationship will be a relevant, but not necessarily a decisive factor. In both *R.S.J. v J.S.J.* and *M. (orse O.) v O.* the presence of such relationship following the marriage

---

62   [1982] ILRM 263. See also *R.T. v V.P. (orse T.)* 30 July 1989 unreported, High Court.

in each case influenced the decision to refuse a decree. In *M.E. v A.E.*[63] it did not have the same effect. The respondent was shown to have been suffering from a psychiatric disorder at the time of his marriage O'Hanlon J. at pages 6–7 of the judgment was, "not without a good deal of hesitation", prepared to grant a decree despite the "long periods of normality" which prevailed during the three years following the marriage. This case also indicates that while the development of an abnormal relationship may tend to confirm incapacity, periods of normality in the relationship between the spouses do not necessarily rule out incapacity.

2.059 In *W. v P.* Barrington J. at pages 20–21 of the judgment, echoing the words he had used earlier in *R.S.J. v J.S.J.*, conceived of a normal marriage as "a caring and considerate relationship." He spoke also of the capacity of each party "to live in society with the other." In *D. v C.*,[64] Costello J. spoke of "the relationship which should exist between married couples if a life long union is to be possible." This type of language suggests that the basic questions to be asked in each case are, "Is it clear that a continuation by the two parties of their relationship has become impossible?" and, if so, "Does this impossibility arise from a recognised incapacity in one of the parties?" The more abstract questions about the meaning of a normal relationship are thereby avoided.

Relative incapacity

2.060 It is not necessary to prove general incapacity, that is, an inability to form and sustain a normal marriage relationship with any person of the opposite sex. It is necessary only to prove incapacity in relation to the particular spouse. In *W. v P.*,[65] a decree was granted despite medical evidence suggesting that the respondent might be capable of having a successful marriage with a woman "who would be content to mother the respondent and to manage him as one might a child."

2.061 In *D.C. (orse D.W.) v D.W.*,[66] the petitioner was granted a decree on the ground that she had been, at the date of her marriage, suffering from a psychotic illness as a result of which she was unable to enter into and sustain a normal marriage relationship with the respondent. Two years after her marriage she had begun a relationship with another man by whom she had two children. They had gone through a form of Church marriage, and by the time of the hearing their relationship had lasted for approximately six years. Blayney J. at pages 8–9 of the judgment considered that none of this was relevant to the question of the petitioner's capacity in relation to her husband at the time of the marriage:

---

63   8 May 1987, unreported, High Court.
64   [1984] ILRM 173 at 189.
65   7 June 1984, unreported, High Court.
66   21 February 1986, unreported, High Court.

The Court is concerned solely with the effect of the petitioner's illness at the date of her marriage to the respondent. It is not concerned with the state of her mental health at any other time to form a normal marriage relationship with any other person.

Repudiation by the respondent

2.062 The decision in *R.S.J. v J.S.J.* suggested that, where the petitioner is relying on his or her own incapacity, it is necessary to show that the respondent has repudiated the marriage.[67] In *D.C. v D.W.* the respondent had done so by seeking and obtaining a decree of nullity from the ecclesiastical courts. *R.S.J. v J.S.J.* also showed that acceptance by the respondent that the marriage has broken down does not of itself constitute repudiation, nor does a decision for good cause to leave the matrimonial home.

2.063 The requirement of repudiation has now been thrown into doubt by the decision in *P.C. v V.C.* There, O'Hanlon J. at page 25 of the judgment expressed the view, *obiter*, that where both parties enter into a marriage contract innocently, in the sense of being unaware that it could be impossible for them to sustain a normal marriage relationship for any length of time, "the petitioner should not be denied a decree of nullity because the respondent wishes to hold him to the marriage bond." He also approved, obiter, the decision of the English Court of Appeal in *Harthan v Harthan*.[68]

Recent developments

2.064 In *U.F. (orse U.C.) v J.C.*, Keane J. at page 30 of his judgment acknowledges that if previous judgments correctly state the law,

we have moved with remarkable abruptness to a position where a decree of nullity can now be granted in any case where the court concludes that a spouse because of an emotional disability or incapacity at the time of the marriage was unable to enter into and sustain a normal marital relationship.

He, however, is satisfied that "no such ground of nullity exists in our law."

2.065 His objections to the new ground of nullity begin with the contention that Section 13 of the Matrimonial Causes and Marriage Law (Ireland) Amendment Act 1870, from which the jurisdiction of the High Court in nullity matters derives, does not authorise "the addition by the courts of new grounds for nullity which the legislature has failed to create." He finds the analogy between physical impotence and the new ground

---

67 Per Barrington J. in *R.S.J. v J.S.J.*, supra, at page 265, citing *McM. v McM.* [1936] IR 177, and *A. v A. (sued as B.)* (1887) 19 LR (Ir) 403.
68 [1948] 2 All ER 639. See **2.037**.

unconvincing. The function of the court in relation to the former is described as "narrow and precise"[69] whereas the latter involves the "impalpable area of the emotions," giving rise to problems of definition and legal proof. Also, although the central issue is the state of the respondent's mind at the time of the marriage, a court will inevitably be influenced by his conduct after the marriage and will therefore be drawn into an enquiry akin to that conducted in cases involving judicial separation rather than nullity. He objects to the uncertainty as to whether mental illness is a pre-requisite to relief under the new ground, and refers to numerous other conditions which may be said to give rise to a lack of capacity to form a proper relationship.

2.066 In addition Keane J. regards the formulation of new grounds for nullity as an impermissible assumption of the legislative function which Article 15.2.1 of the Constitution vests exclusively in the Oireachtas.[70] Ad hoc development of the law of nullity is in any case inadvisable because it may lead to uncertainty in an area, that of marital status, where certainty is important. Finally, the change in the Constitutional and legal status of children effected by a nullity decree in respect of a voidable marriage must be considered. Keane J.'s decision has now been reversed by the Supreme Court. See Appendix A.

Consent

Introduction

2.067 Marriage is a "voluntary"[71] union. The free consent of both parties to the marriage has always been regarded as a fundamental requirement of a valid marriage. However, the judicial approach to the application of the consent requirement has undergone considerable change in recent years. Until the early 1970's a strict approach was adopted. Duress was, but undue influence was not, accepted as a basis for annulment. Only a high degree of duress would suffice, and it might be ignored where its imposition was regarded as justifiable.[72] English case law had suggested that an objective standard should apply, which concentrated, not on the actual state of the mind of the petitioner, but on the manner in which a reasonable person might have been expected to react in the petitioner's circumstances.[73] Mistake and fraud could be relied on only in limited circumstances,[74] and misrepresentation would not in general found a suit.[75] In effect, it was not enough for a petitioner to prove that he did not freely consent; it was necessary, in addition, to show that the factor

---

69 At page 23.
70 At page 31.
71 Per Lord Penzance in *Hyde v Hyde* (1966) LRI P & D 130, at page 133.
72 *Griffith v Griffith* [1944] IR 35.
73 See, for example, *Szechter v Szechter* [1970] 3 All ER 905.
74 *Moss v Moss* [1897] P 263.
75 *Swift v Kelly* (1835) 3 Knapp 257.

negativing consent was one known to the law. This strict approach was based on the public policy of protecting marriage, and the means employed was to make it difficult for parties to avoid an apparently valid marriage. The firm judicial view was that a decree of nullity should not be seen as an easy escape route for a discontented spouse, and that the rules should be framed in a manner which discourages collusive or speculative petitions.[76]

2.068 Over the last two decades judicial attitudes have relented. A more subjective approach to the issue of consent has been adopted, which places more emphasis on the reality of consent, and there is more inclination to accept that the factors which may in law negative consent do not constitute a rigid or closed list. The policy basis for this new more liberal approach remains the protection of marriage, but the perception of how that policy should be pursued has changed. The very indissolubility of marriage is seen as a special reason for insisting on the genuineness of consent. The judgment of Finlay C.J. in *N. (orse K.) v K.* may be regarded as indicating the fundamental principles of the modern law:

> The entry into a valid marriage is not only the making of a contract but is also in law the acquisition of a status. The status thus acquired and the related concept of a family receives special protection from the provisions of the Constitution. Furthermore, the provision of the Constitution prohibiting the enactment of legislation permitting the dissolution of a valid marriage makes the contract of marriage absolutely irrevocable.
>
> Consent to the taking of such a step must, therefore, if the marriage is to be valid, be a fully free exercise of the independent will of the parties. Whilst a court faced with a challenge to the validity of a marriage, based on an absence of real consent, should conduct its enquiry in accordance with defined legal concepts such as duress or . . . "the related topic of undue influence", these concepts and the legal definition of them must remain subservient to the ultimate objective of ascertaining, in accordance with the onus of proof, whether the consent of the petitioning party was real or apparent.[77]

This radical approach to the issue of consent, which has already affected the rules relating to duress and undue influence, may signal further changes in the law. In particular, the narrow scope at present given to the concepts of fraud, misrepresentation and mistake appears likely to come under review.

Incapacity to consent

2.069 The Marriage of Lunatics Act 1811[78] renders void a marriage contracted by a person who has been certified as a lunatic "by Inquisition",

---

76   See, for example, the judgment of Haugh J. in *Griffith v Griffith*, supra, at pages 399–42.
77   [1986] ILRM 75 at 82.
78   51 Geo. 111, c.37.

or as a "Lunatic or Person under a Phrenzy", whose person or estate has been committed to the care or custody of trustees, unless that person has been declared sane. The provisions of the Act apply even where a marriage has been contracted during a lucid interval.[79] The Act is of little practical relevance, and may even be unconstitutional in part in that according to Kenny J. in *Ryan v Attorney General*[80] the right to marry has been held to constitute an "unspecified personal right" protected by Article 40.3 of the Constitution.

2.070 Under common law a marriage is void if either party lacks the mental capacity to understand the nature of the marriage contract and the responsibilities which normally attach to marriage.[81] Various factors may affect a person's capacity to consent, including mental illness or retardation, alcohol or drugs. Want of the capacity to consent should be distinguished from incapacity to enter and sustain a normal marriage relationship. Both may derive from the same cause, such as mental illness, but while the former relates to an individual's understanding of marriage and its obligations, the latter concerns the individual's ability to undertake those obligations. Incapacity, in the former sense renders a marriage void, in the latter sense, it renders a marriage voidable. For a marriage to be regarded as valid the law does not require a high degree of intelligence or a sophisticated understanding of the implications of marriage. All that is required is a broad understanding of the responsibilities which normally attach to marriage.[82]

2.071 It has been rare in the past for a nullity decree to be granted on the basis of incapacity to consent, though the plea is often made alongside a plea that one party lacks the capacity to form and sustain a normal relationship.[83] However in *M.E. v A.E.*, O'Hanlon J. granted a decree based in part on the fact that the respondent was suffering from a psychiatric disorder at the time of the marriage which prevented him from giving a full, free and informed consent to the marriage. Evidence had been given that the respondent suffered from paranoid schizophrenia. In *D. v E.*,[84] Barr J. granted a decree where the respondent wife was grossly immature. As a result not only did she lack the capacity to maintain a meaningful marriage relationship, but also her apparent consent to the marriage was not full, free or informed. Strictly speaking a decree should not be granted on alternative grounds, one of which renders the marriage void and the other voidable. The question of whether the marriage is void

---

79 *Turner v Meyers*, (1808) 1 Hag. Con. 414, at 417 (per Sir W. Scott).
80 [1965] IR 294 at page 312.
81 There are many 19th century authorities. See, for example *Turner v Meyers*, supra, and *Durham v Durham* (1885) LR 10 PD 80.
82 *In re Park* [1954] P 89.
83 Examples of such cases where the plea failed are *R.S.J. v J.S.J.* [1982] ILRM 263, *D. v C.* [1984] ILRM 173.
84 (1 March 1989, unreported) High Court (Only a stenographer's note of the judgment is available.)

ab initio should be addressed first. If the marriage is void ab initio, the question of its voidability does not arise.

2.072 The idea expressed in the above two cases, that consent to marriage must be "informed" possibly suggests the development of a broader approach to the requirement that the parties understand marriage and the responsibilities attaching to it. The idea of "informed consent" is different from the notion of minimal understanding preferred in the earlier cases. This new approach also finds support in the judgment of McCarthy J. in *N. (orse K.) v K.* Having referred to the constitutional prohibition on divorce and the durability of the marriage contract, he speaks of "the consequent need for a full appreciation of what that contract entails . . ."[85] This implies that in future it may become easier to maintain that a marriage is void by reason of one party's failure to understand the full implications of marriage.

2.073 It is clear that drunkenness and other forms of intoxication may render a person incapable of understanding the nature or implications of the marriage ceremony.[86] In *Legeyt v O'Brien*,[87] the deceased had remarried a year before his death "during the Donnybrook fair". The curator of the children of his first marriage alleged that, at the time of the marriage, the deceased was suffering from delirium tremens. There being insufficient evidence at the time of the ceremony, the court refused to hold the marriage void. The principle was, however, accepted that drunkenness may give rise to unsoundness of mind sufficient to vitiate a marriage. The crucial question is whether the individual's condition created "a want of reason or volition amounting to incapacity to consent."

Duress and indue influence

2.074 Finlay C.J. has summarised the modern approach to duress and undue influence, in the context of consent to marriage, as follows

> If . . . the apparent decision to marry has been caused to such an extent by external pressure or influence, whether falsely or honestly applied, as to lose the character of a full free act of that person's will, no valid marriage has occurred.[88]

It is the reality of consent, rather than the degree of pressure, which has now become the focus of inquiry in cases involving duress, and undue influence. A subjective approach is adopted which asks, not whether the will of a reasonable person would have been overborne in the circumstances, but whether the will of the particular individual, having regard to

---

85 *N. (orse K.) v K.* [1986] ILRM 75, at page 93. Both McCarthy J. (at page 94) and Hederman J. (at page 91) use the word "informed" when describing the consent required.
86 See *Sullivan v Sullivan* (1818) 2 Hag. Con. 238; 161 ER 728.
87 (1834) Milw. Rep. 235.
88 *N. (orse K.) v K.* (supra) at page 82.

his or her psychological or emotional condition, was in fact overborne. The pressure may emanate from any source, not necessarily the respondent. It may take many forms ranging from emotional blackmail to fear of economic hardship. It is unnecessary to show that the pressure was wrongfully imposed. However, it is necessary to prove that the duress or undue influences was the predominant influence on the decision to marry. As noted in the introduction, many of these principles are of recent origin and derive from the broad approach to consent favoured in recent judgments.

The degree of pressure and the acceptance of undue influence

2.075 In *Griffith v Griffith*, Haugh J. stated that "Duress must be a question of degree and may begin from a gentle form of pressure, to physical violence, accompanied by thoughts of death."[89] Threats to life, limb or liberty have always been accepted as negativing consent. *Griffith v Griffith* is itself an illustration.

In July 1925 the petitioner Cyril Griffith a 19 year old apprentice in the leather trade who lacked a full knowledge of the facts of life, first met the respondent by chance on a camping trip on Howth Hill. He was intimate with her, but full sexual intercourse did not take place. They did not meet again until November when the respondent and her mother confronted him at his place of work, informed him that the respondent was pregnant, and accused him of being responsible. When the petitioner denied the allegation, the mother told him that only he could have been the father, that her daughter was under age (i.e. under 17), and that if he did not marry her daughter, she would refer the matter to a lawyer. The petitioner took this to mean that he would be prosecuted and go to gaol. The petitioner consulted his father and a priest both of whom expressed the view that he was bound to marry the girl. His father also repeated that he could go to gaol for what he had done. A week later the petitioner and respondent married. When, during a brief period of cohabitation some weeks after the marriage, the petitioner for the first time engaged in full sexual intercourse, he realised that he could not have been responsible for the respondent's pregnancy, and she admitted deceiving him. They separated. On his father's instructions the petitioner sent the respondent 10s. a week until 1935 when the marriage was annulled in Rome. The petitioner instituted proceedings for a civil annulment in 1942 and was granted one on the basis that his consent had been obtained by a combination of fraud and fear.

2.076 The facts of *K. v K.*[90] are similar. Prior to their marriage the parties engaged in sexual intercourse on two occasions. On each occasion intercourse was interrupted before completion. About six months after the second act of intercourse, the respondent wrote to the petitioner alleging that she was pregnant by him. At a later meeting during which the

89 [1944] IR 35 at page 52.
90 16 February 1971, unreported, High Court.

petitioner denied paternity, considering it impossible, the respondent told him that she had not had intercourse with any other man and insisted that he was the father. She threatened that, if he did not marry her, she would inform his parents and a sister of his who was a nun, and that she would bring legal proceedings against him which would result in adverse publicity. As a result he agreed to marry her. The marriage was not consummated. Shortly after its celebration the petitioner realised that he had been deceived. The parties continued to occupy the same house for a number of years, though not as husband and wife, and were still living there when the petition for nullity was presented. O'Keeffe P. granted the decree.

2.077 Haugh J., in his judgment in *Griffith v Griffith* stated that the fear inspired must be "real and grave". Modern English cases have gone even further by confining relief to cases where there exists a threat to life, limb or liberty. See *Buckland v Buckland*[91] where a decree is granted to a petitioner who had been charged in Malta with corrupting a minor and faced a possible two year prison sentence. *Singh v Singh*[92] involved an arranged marriage within the Sikh community in England. It was held that the seventeen year old bride, who met her husband only on the day of the ceremony and who married out of a sense of duty to her parents, had not been coerced. In *Szechter v Szechter*[93] a decree was granted in respect of a marriage celebrated in Poland, the sole object of which was to secure the release of the petitioner from prison where her health had been at grave risk. This particular line of authority has now been expressly rejected, first in the judgment of O'Hanlon J. in *McK. (McC.) v F.McC.*,[94] and more recently by the Supreme Court in *N. (orse K.) v K.* Supra,[85] at page 81, where Finlay C.J. approves the principles laid down in *M.K. (McC.) v F.McC.* Indeed, to limit relief to cases where there has been a threat to life, limb or liberty would be inconsistent with the subjective approach to consent which is now preferred by the Irish judiciary. That approach focuses less on the nature of the pressure, and more on its impact on the particular individual affected by it. It follows that pressure, which amounts only to "undue influence" rather than duress, will also vitiate consent, provided that its effect is to overbear the will of the individual. The expression "undue influence" is employed by O'Hanlon J. in *McK. (McC.) v F.McC.*, and its use there is referred to with approval by Finlay C.J. in *N. (orse K.) v K.* Thus, despite the objections of Henchy J. in his dissenting judgment in the same case, and his statement (at page 88) that "no influence short of duress can produce a nullity,"[95] it now appears that undue influence may indeed vitiate consent and provide a ground for annulment. Some of the cases referred to below, particularly those in

91 [1967] 2 All ER 300.
92 [1971] 2 All ER 828.
93 [1970] 3 All ER 905. See also *Parojcic v Parojcic* [1959] 1 All ER 1.
94 [1982] ILRM 277 at page 282.
95 The judgment of Palles C.B. in *Ussher v Ussher* [1912] 2 IR 445 at page 505 is cited in support of this proposition.

2.083–2.088, show that annulments have in fact been granted on the basis of undue influence. The present position is summarised by Carroll J. in *D.B. (orse O'R.) v N.O'R.* "If a person is induced or forced to go through a ceremony of marriage by fear of threats, intimidation, duress or undue influence of another person such a marriage is invalid."[96]

The subjective approach

2.078 The subjective approach adopted by the courts in recent cases again involves a clear rejection of modern English case law which prefers an objective test, requiring proof that the will of one party "has been overborne by genuine and reasonably held fear."[97] The subjective approach is not, however, new and is reflected in nineteenth century dicta. In *Scott v Sebright* Butt J. said:

> Whenever from natural weakness of intellect or from fear, whether reasonably entertained or not, either party is actually in a state of mental incompetence to resist pressure improperly brought to bear, there is no more consent than in the case of a person of stronger intellect and more robust courage yielding to a more serious danger.[98]

The first of the modern Irish cases in which the subjective approach was employed is *B. v D.*, (see **2.079**) decided in 1973. Since that time it has become commonplace in consent cases for the judge to analyse the character and disposition of the petitioner, as well as the nature of his or her relationship with the person said to have applied the pressure. This is illustrated by a number of the cases set out below.

Cases of emotional pressure arising out of the relationship with the respondent

2.079 In *B. v D.*, the petitioner and respondent, who were both national school teachers, met in November 1965. The relationship that developed was not based on love or affection. The respondent began to assume that the petitioner was his property. He used her car as if it were his own. He borrowed, and later demanded, money from her. He spent his leisure time gambling and, from February 1968, began drinking heavily. They married in August 1970. A week before the marriage the petitioner informed her family of the impending marriage and told them that she did not want to go through with the marriage and that the respondent was forcing her. The day before the wedding the parties met in Ennis and drove to Dublin. On the way the petitioner telephoned her sister and said that she was afraid of the respondent who was very aggressive. She decided to go to her sister's house but had no opportunity to do so. The respondent, without telling the

---

96 29 July 1988, unreported, High Court.
97 Per Sir Jocelyn Simon in *Szechter v Szechter* [1970] 3 All ER 905. See also *Buckland v Buckland* [1967] 2 All ER 300.
98 (1886) 12 P & D 21, at page 24.
99 20 June 1973, unreported, High Court.

petitioner brought forward the time of the wedding from 11 a.m. to 7 a.m. to ensure that no member of the petitioner's family would be present. Murnaghan J. described the respondent as "very forceful, mentally arrogant, and disinclined to take no for an answer", and said of the petitioner that she "found herself in her relationship with the respondent in a groove, which as time went on got deeper and deeper and out of which she was constitutionally unable to extract herself, and in which perhaps she was prepared in the circumstances, if not content, to remain". Murnaghan J. adopting a subjective approach, granted a decree. He considered that, cumulatively, the influence exercised by the respondent amounted to duress.

2.080 In *S. v O'S.*,[1] the parties, who were normal young people, became unofficially engaged and planned to marry when the respondent completed his medical studies. The respondent developed an illness known as Munchaus periodic Syndrome which resulted in him projecting with elaborate detail bizarre medical conditions, and convincing the petitioner that, in order to be cured, he needed her constant presence. Subsequently he persuaded her that, unless she married him, he would either go into rapid decline or commit suicide. The respondent, though intelligent and well advised by her father, believed the respondent and was in a state of emotional bondage to him. A marriage followed in June 1974. Finlay J. granted the decree and stated at pages 2–3 of his judgment:

> Essentially, it seems to me that the freedom of will necessary to enter into a valid contract of marriage is one particularly associated with emotion and that a person in the emotional bondage of another person couldn't consciously have the freedom of will. I am quite satisfied that, in effect, what was applied to the petitioner was a form of duress. . . .

2.081 In *C.O'K. (orse C.P.) v W.P.*,[2] the petitioner, a "quiet and unaggressive" woman, was 16 years of age when she met the respondent, an "introverted, determined and insensitive" man, who was then 18 years of age. The respondent was, from an early stage in the relationship extremely jealous, possessive and domineering. He insisted on having sexual intercourse. He was unsociable and, when with the petitioner, avoided contact with her friends. There was an informal engagement in 1972 but the respondent's conduct continued to be oppressive and there were frequent rows. The petitioner felt an obligation to stay with the respondent because of their sexual relationship. The respondent carried on a process of watching and besetting the petitioner at her work place, threatened to reveal their sexual relationship to her parents and work-mates, destroyed gifts given to him by her, treated her with occasional acts of violence not of a serious kind, and caused her to fear him as a person capable of great violence. An attempt by the petitioner to break off the

1   10 November 1978, unreported, High Court.
2   11 April 1984, unreported, High Court.

engagement in November 1983, was followed by an intensive campaign of watching and besetting and by a threat of suicide on the part of the respondent which resulted in the petitioner giving in and agreeing to restore the engagement. They were married in November 1974. After the marriage the relationship continued as before with frequent rows and no real communication. They had sexual intercourse for some years until the respondent lost interest. There were no children. In March 1981 the petitioner returned to live with her parents. McMahon J. was satisfied that the methods employed by the respondent to obtain the petitioner's consent amounted to duress and undue influence. A decree was therefore granted.

2.082 In *F. v F.*[3] the respondent, who was a practising homosexual, actively concealed his true nature from the petitioner. According to Barron J. (at page 13 of the judgment) he "deliberately set out to bind the petitioner to him emotionally and . . . succeeded in this design." In the circumstances the judge granted a decree in part on the ground that the petitioner's consent was defective. However, the element of deceit appears to have played a more significant role than undue influence (see **2.106**). The inability of the respondent, by virtue of psychiatric illness, to maintain the life-long relationship required of marriage, was another ground for the decree.

Cases involving pregnancy before or at the time of marriage

2.083 It has been common in many societies that, when an unmarried woman becomes pregnant, pressure will be placed upon her and the man thought to be responsible to marry one another. *Griffith v Griffith* and *K. v K.* (**2.075** and **2.076**) established that, where a threat of prosecution is directed against a man who is wrongly accused of causing a woman to become pregnant, their subsequent marriage may be void if it can be shown that the threat induced his consent. More recent cases have established that other lesser forms of pressure, applied either to the man or to the woman, may have the same consequence. Moreover, the principle established in *Griffith v Griffith*,[4] that justifiable duress (as when it is based on a true allegation of paternity) does not vitiate consent, has been abandoned.

2.084 In *M.K. (orse M.McC.) v F.McC.*,[5] the petitioner, when aged 19, had been associating with the respondent, then aged 21, as part of a group when, after a single act of intercourse, the petitioner became pregnant. The petitioner's parents were distressed and agitated at the news of the pregnancy and the mother told the petitioner that she would have to marry the respondent or leave home altogether. The petitioner was a shy, reserved and very sensitive girl closely attached to both her parents and very dependent on them. The respondent was of a tougher mould but still

---

3   22 June 1988, unreported, High Court.
4   Supra, per Haugh J. at page 43.
5   [1982] ILRM 277. Judgment was delivered by O'Hanlon J. on 16 March 1982.

immature. He encountered stormy scenes in his own household. His father refused to have anything to do with him. He was told that he had no option but to marry, and he had to leave home to live with a friend. Without consulting the parties the two sets of parents met and decided that a marriage should take place as quickly as possible. The petitioner then followed her mother's instructions in arranging the marriage. The marriage was celebrated in September 1972. The petitioner miscarried her child two weeks later. There were no subsequent children. The parties lived together until February 1975. Although they had a sexual relationship, their relationship otherwise deteriorated during their time together. A Roman Catholic Church annulment was granted in November 1980. O'Hanlon J. (at 279) concluded that, "An unwilling bride and a resentful husband were dragged to the altar and went through a ceremony of marriage which neither of them wanted and without any genuine feeling of attraction or affection which might have led to a happy union in the course of time."

2.085 A decree was granted on the ground that the will of each party was overborne by the compulsion of their respective parents. A subjective approach to the question of consent was adopted. O'Hanlon J. was influenced by the fact that the petitioner was little more than a schoolgirl at the time of the marriage. The respondent in turn was stunned and shocked and under so much pressure from his parents that he was unable to think coherently or make rational decisions about the future.

> In both cases I believe the will was overborne by compulsion by persons to whom they had always been subject in the parent and child relationship and that the duress exercised was of a character that they were constitutionally unable to withstand.[5a]

2.086 In reaching this conclusion, O'Hanlon J. expressly rejected the more stringent approach to duress illustrated by the English and American cases. He also rejected some of the comments of Haugh J. in *Griffith v Griffith*, in particular those which suggested that it is permissible to apply pressure on a man where the allegation made against him is well founded. He also expressly approved of the decision in *B. v D.* and *S. v O'S.*, (**2.080**) and "the broader application of the principles of duress" evident therein.[6] These statements of principle were subsequently approved of by Finlay C.J. in *N. (orse K.) v K.* He did not, however, approve O'Hanlon J.'s reference to decisions (relating to reverential fear) of the ecclesiastical courts of the "Catholic Church" as being some indication of the meaning of duress under canon law. In fact the law applied by the ecclesiastical courts prior to 1870, and carried over to the civil courts by section 13 of the Matrimonial Causes and Marriage Law (Amendment) Act 1870, was not the canon law of the Church of Rome, but the canon law of the established Church of Ireland.

5a *M.K. (orse McC.) v F. McC.* supra, at page 283.
6   Id., at 282.

2.087 In *N. (orse K.) v K.*[7] the petitioner, a quiet, unassertive and unsophisticated girl of 19, married the respondent, aged 20, in February 1979. Prior to the marriage the parties had only a casual relationship. After the petitioner had been persuaded by the respondent to have intercourse in November 1978, the relationship had petered out. The petitioner told her family at Christmas that she thought she was pregnant. There were meetings between the parents of the two parties and, as a result, it was agreed that a marriage should take place. The parties lived together only intermittently after the marriage and finally separated. Carroll J. was satisfied that

(1) The parties would not have got married but for the pregnancy.
(2) The respondent was completely immature and unsuited for marriage. He had no job and no means of supporting a wife and child.
(3) The petitioner was little more than a schoolgirl. She did not see any alternative to getting married. She would not consider an abortion. If she did not get married she believed she would get no support from her parents and would have to leave home.
(4) She acquiesced in her parents's wishes from the start. They said marriage was the best thing and she thought they knew what was best.
(5) She got no counsel or advice on what alternatives she did have, such as adoption or bringing up the child as a single parent.
(6) The shock of discovering she was pregnant probably put her into a state where she could not think clearly.

2.088 Carroll J. refused to grant a decree. She accepted that the parties were driven to marriage because of the pregnancy. On the other hand, they intended to marry. It was not a case in which the petitioner definitely did not want to marry. "She had no clear idea what to do and her father made up her mind for her." An appeal to the Supreme Court was successful. The general principles enunciated by Finlay C.J., in particular his acceptance of a subjective approach and his preparedness to entertain the concept of undue influence, have already been referred to. (**2.068, 2.074**) His conclusion, on the facts as found by Carroll J., was that the petitioner's consent to the marriage was apparent only. Griffin J., also adopting a subjective approach, agreed and emphasised the petitioner's sense, in the absence of any impartial advice, that no choice other than marriage was open to her. Hederman J. thought that the decision concerning marriage was made by the parents and that the young couple had acquiesced in a docile way. A valid marriage requires, in his opinion, "a personal and full internal and informed consent." McCarthy J. referred to the "need for a full appreciation of what the contract entails." "The test whether or not each party to the contract brought an informed and willing consent to it . . . is a subjective one . . . The only dissenting voice was that of Henchy J. who citing Palles C.B. in *Ussher v Ussher*[8] refused to accept undue influence as a basis for nullity.

7 [1986] ILRM 75.
8 [1912] 2 IR 445 at 505.

Cases of pregnancy where decrees were refused

2.089 Pressure applied as a result of pregnancy will not always negative consent. If it can be shown that, quite apart from the pressure, a bond of affection existed between the parties and that they were planning to marry in any event, the consent given may be effective and binding. The same may be true where there is evidence that the petitioner was psychologically and emotionally strong and therefore unlikely to have given in to pressure.

2.090 In *E.P. v M.C.*,[9] the parties began going out together in February 1979 when they were aged 21 and 20 years respectively. The respondent became pregnant and told the petitioner that, if they didn't marry, she would have an abortion. They married in November 1979. The evidence established that the parties would not have married when they did but for the respondent's pregnancy. The marriage was consummated, a child was born in April 1980, and the couple lived together for some months after the marriage. The petitioner alleged that the respondent continued to behave as if she were single. Three days after moving into their own home in August 1980 the respondent wanted to terminate the relationship. Her attitude was that, having got what she wanted out of the marriage (that is to avoid the shame of pregnancy outside marriage and to provide a name for her child), the marriage was over. She left six weeks later.

2.091 Barron J. refused to grant a decree because of collusion between the parties. In addition he held that duress had not been established. If the petitioner had given consent solely for the purpose of saving the life of his unborn child the marriage would have been void. As it was, the parties had what he described at page 8 of his judgment as "a normal engagement followed by a normal marriage and held themselves out as being a married couple. . . ." The marriage ceremony was not therefore a sham.

2.092 However, this case was decided before the Supreme Court's decision in *N. (orse K.) v K.*, to adopt a broad approach to the issue of consent. In view of this, some doubt now attaches to Barron J.'s insistence on an *exclusive* causal link between the fear induced and the consent given. A less stringent approach would be to require proof that the fear was the predominant, if not necessarily the exclusive, influence on the decision to marry.

2.093 In *A.C.L. v R.L.*,[10] the petitioner and respondent, aged 28 and 32 respectively, met in 1975 and began living together in 1976. The petitioner became pregnant. The respondent had wished to marry the petitioner and was pleased when she became pregnant. The petitioner was reluctant to marry and concealed her condition from her family. The parties moved to London, where the child was born in December 1976, and shortly afterwards they returned to live in Ireland. Upon being informed of the

9 13 March 1984, unreported, High Court.
10 18 October 1982, unreported, High Court.

birth, the petitioner's parents made it clear that they expected her to marry as soon as possible. Her brothers and sisters took the same view and pressed her to marry for the parents' sake. The parties married in March 1977. The petitioner alleged that she had not wanted to marry and only did so as a result of pressure from her parents. She sought an annulment on the ground of duress. Barron J., refusing to grant a decree, found that when the parties returned to Ireland they intended to live together as a family and to get married sometime in the future. In effect the parental and family pressures had merely served to precipitate a marriage which would probably have taken place in any case.

2.094 In the course of his judgment, at page 1, Barron J. suggests that pressure imposed from good motives cannot constitute undue influence, which involves "fastening on to another's weakness and seeking to obtain a benefit from such behaviour." This has now been contradicted by McCarthy J. in his judgment in *N. (orse K.) v K.*, supra, at 93 where he indicates that pressure "however bona fide . . . however well meaning the sources . . ." may prevent the exercise of true free will. Also Barron J.'s obiter dictum to the effect that, even where duress is established, a decree may be refused if the respondent was not aware that the will of the petitioner was overborne, seems contrary to the principle. The issue is not the respondent's, but the petitioner's, state of mind at the time of the marriage. If, unknown to the respondent, a petitioner is subject to a threat to his life which induces him to marry, it is scarcely conceivable that a decree would be refused.

2.095 In *J.R. (orse McG.) v P.McG.*[11] the petitioner had a particularly bigoted and intolerant mother who detested Roman Catholics and was totally intolerant about matters of sex. When she was 20 years of age the petitioner began going out with a fellow employee who was a Roman Catholic. They had sexual intercourse twice, induced, according to the petitioner, by alcohol. She became pregnant. When the mother learned of the situation she told the petitioner to pack her things and go. Although the petitioner did not immediately leave, she knew that she could not stay at home to have her baby. She unsuccessfully sought assistance from relatives. She lacked the financial resources to fend for herself. The respondent, when informed of the pregnancy, was non-committal but, realising the petitioner's difficult home circumstances, offered to marry her. There was also some bond of affection between them. They married in 1964 and remained nominally living together for 16 years. The marriage was always unstable and for half of the 16 years the respondent was absent, deserting the petitioner on many occasions. They had two children. They separated finally in 1980. The petitioner, in seeking a decree of nullity, claimed that the attitude of her mother and her financial position were her main reasons for marrying. Barron J., accepted that the attitude of the mother and her economic situation were "compelling" factors, but not the

11   24 February 1985, unreported, High Court.

only factors, influencing her decision to marry. The petitioner had not been wholly averse to the idea of marriage. The marriage could not be said to be a mere sham or device to avoid a particular threat. He refused to grant a decree.

2.096 As in his decision in *E.P. v M.C.* Barron J.'s insistence on the need to show the marriage was a sham or device to escape pressure or threats, may now, since the decision of the Supreme Court in *N. (orse K.) v K.*, be regarded as too restrictive. It would appear that the correct question to be asked is whether the threats or pressures were the predominant influences on the decision to marry. If such was the case the consent may be defective despite the existence of other subsidiary motives for marrying. This would accord more with the view expressed by Hederman J. at 91 (and by McCarthy J. at 93) in *N. (orse K.) v K.* that consent should be "full" as well as free.

2.097 In *J.R. (orse McG.) v P.McG.*, Barron J. at pages 7–8 drew a distinction between two types of duress. The first creates a form of emotional bondage of which the victim may be aware, with the result that he or she fails to apply his or her mind to the question of giving consent. With the second type, the person subject to duress knowingly consents, but does not do so from a desire to marry, but in order to escape from a particular threat. In either case, Barron J. suggests, a decree may be available, but in the second case proof is needed that the marriage was a sham or device to procure a particular result. While the distinction suggested by Barron J. is theoretically sound, it may in practice be difficult to classify all cases of duress so that they fall neatly into one or other category. Where, for example, a young impressionable and highly-dependent daughter becomes pregnant and is told by her parents that it is her moral duty to marry and that, if she refuses, she must leave home, her submission to such pressure and her consequent decision to marry may be the product both of her emotional dependence on her parents and of her wish to avoid the consequences of being cast into the streets. It may be too much to describe the daughter's mental state as one of emotional "bondage"; nor is it wholly accurate to describe the marriage as a "sham". Nevertheless, the combination of pressures operating on the daughter may be sufficient to negative her consent. It is submitted that the proper question to be addressed in such a case is whether the combination of pressures operating on the young person was or was not the predominant influence on her decision to marry.

2.098 Where a pregnant woman is found to have a strong and independent personality, or where she is self-willed, it may be more difficult to prove that pressures operating on her were instrumental in her decision to marry. The subjective approach to the issues of consent requires a judge to take account of strengths as well as weaknesses in the petitioner's psychological make-up and constitution. Two cases decided by Carroll J. provide illustrations.

2.099 In *P.C. (orse O'B.) v D.O'B.*[12] the petitioner was 17 years old when she became engaged to the respondent. Not long after, she became pregnant by him. Despite advice to the contrary given by a doctor and a priest, she decided to (and did) marry the respondent. Carroll J. at page 7 of her judgment described her as a self-willed girl, and did not accept her allegations that she was in fear of her parents and that they had pressured her into marriage. "While she was concerned for her parents and the worry and upset she was going to cause when she told them of her pregnancy, there was no evidence of any harrowing scenes or pressure being brought to bear." The petitioner's argument that she had been completely under the control of the respondent was also rejected, as was her contention that duress had been self-imposed.

> While I accept that the petitioner may well have got married when she did because she could not see any other solution to her problems, and in that sense she was forced to marry because of her pregnancy, it is relevant that she had already made a commitment to the respondent by becoming engaged to him . . . Her "self-imposed duress" comes down to the fact of pregnancy. On the state of the law at present, marriage because of pregnancy *per se* is not a ground for annulment.

The judgment was delivered one month before the decision of the Supreme Court in *N. (orse K.) v K.*, supra.

2.100 In *D.B. (orse O'R.) v O'R.*,[13] the petitioner had been brought up in an orphanage and did not meet her parents until she was thirteen. When she was 15 years old, while visiting her parents, she met the respondent who was then aged 25. They became engaged and subsequently, after one act of sexual intercourse, she became pregnant. She was sent back to the orphanage and, shortly after, at the age of 16, married the respondent. The marriage was to survive for 20 years, and there were five children. The marriage eventually broke down and the petitioner began living with another man. She sought an annulment on the ground of duress, but Carroll J. found no evidence that duress was applied by the respondent, by the petitioner's parents or by the sister in charge of the orphanage. Refusing to grant a decree, Carroll J. at page 6 of the judgment noted that the marriage had lasted more than 20 years, and accepted the sister's assessment of the petitioner as being, at the time of the marriage "an independent child with a mind of her own."

Pressure from third parties, or external circumstances

2.101 The pressure operating on the petitioner need not be shown to emanate from the respondent nor from the petitioner's family. Pressures from many different sources have been taken into account in determining whether the petitioner's consent was real or apparent. An extreme

12 2nd October 1985, unreported, High Court.
13 29 July 1988, unreported, High Court.

example is provided by the English case of *Szechter v Szechter*[14] in which a nullity decree was granted to a young Polish girl who had married in order to embarrass the Polish authorities into releasing her from prison. She had been detained without trial in appalling conditions for a long period, she had a weak constitution and there was a danger that, if she remained incarcerated she might become seriously ill. The marriage was arranged by the respondent, a noted historian, whose only motive was to save the petitioner. A decree was granted.

2.102 The question arises whether it needs to be shown that the pressure is the product of human agency, or whether pressure arising from circumstances for which no one bears any particular responsibility will be sufficient. In the course of her judgment in *D.B. (orse O'R.) v O'R.* (see **2.100** at pages 1 and 2) Carroll J. suggested that duress must emanate from a person or persons, and cannot be generated by circumstances alone.

> The pressure must be pressure from a person, not pressure of events such as unwanted pregancy, or fear of being poor or of having nowhere to live or of being unable to cope on one's own—such events or anticipated events might explain the motive for getting married, but events alone cannot constitute duress or undue influence. That must come from a person.

While Carroll J. may be literally correct to insist that both duress and undue influence must have an author, her approach to the fundamental issue of consent appears different in emphasis from that of the majority of the Supreme Court in *N. (orse K.) v K*. For Finlay C.J. concepts such as duress and indue influence, "and the legal definitions of them must remain subservient to the ultimate objective of ascertaining, in accordance with the onus of proof, whether the consent of the petitioning party was real or apparent" at page 82. And McCarthy J. (at page 93) clearly contemplates the possibility that consent may be defective in the absence of any outside agency, when he refers to "ignorance itself" as a possible source of fear leading to marriage.

2.103 In *W. (orse C.) v C.*,[15] Barron J. took account of strains arising from the circumstances of the petitioner at the time of her marriage. She was a primary teacher and had become pregnant by the respondent before marriage. He was a cruel and sadistic man who treated her shamefully both before and after the marriage. The Principal of her school made it clear that, unless she married, there was no future for her in the teaching profession. She decided to marry in order to recover her self respect and work again as a teacher. Barron J. concluded at page 6 of his judgment on the issue of consent, that, "Her decision in the circumstances to marry the respondent could only be regarded as one brought about by the strain of

14 [1970] 3 All ER 905.
15 17 February 1989, unreported, High Court.

her circumstances and the lack of ability for normal thought which she was manifesting at the time." The consent given was not therefore a true consent. It seems, following *N. (orse K.) v K.*, that the primary focus in cases involving claims of duress and undue influence, must be on the quality of the consent given. Contrary to the opinion of Carroll J. in *D.B. (orse R.) v O'R.*, the source of the pressure appears to be of only secondary importance.

Fraud, misrepresentation and mistake

2.104 Until recently it was possible to state with confidence that fraud, misrepresentation and mistake would only in very exceptional circumstances be accepted as giving rise to defective consent sufficient to justify a decree of nullity. In particular, it was never enough simply to prove that a fraud, misrepresentation or mistake had induced consent. In *Swift v Kelly*[16] Lord Brougham stated at page 29 that, ". . . no marriage shall be held void merely upon proof that it had been contracted on false representations and that, but for such contrivances, consent would never have been obtained." In *Moss v Moss*[17] Sir F.H. Jeune stated at page 268: "But when in English law fraud is spoken of as a ground for avoiding a marriage, this does not include such fraud as induces consent, but is limited to such fraud as procures the appearance without the reality of consent . . ." Proof that the petitioner would never have married had he or she known the truth was not sufficient. Thus, if one partner induced the other to marry on the basis of a dishonest claim that he was rich, or that he had a particular profession or that he had never been married before, or that his health was sound, the other partner was not entitled to a decree even though it may have been obvious beyond doubt to the court that she would not have married had she known the truth. In *Moss v Moss*, the wife had concealed from the husband that she was, at the time of their marriage, pregnant by another man. In *Ussher v Ussher*[18] the parties celebrated a marriage which was civilly valid, but which they also mistakenly believed was valid in the eyes of the Roman Catholic church. In neither case was a decree granted. There have, however, always been two exceptional cases where consent may be regarded as defective. The first is where there is a mistake as to the nature of the ceremony; the second is where the mistake is as to the identity of the other party.

2.105 It may be that the above restrictive principles still accurately represent the law. The reason why this cannot be stated with confidence is two-fold. First, in *S. v S.*[19] Kenny J. suggested that fraud may negative consent where it relates to a fundamental feature of the marriage. This proposition is discussed at **2.110**. Second, the radical and broad approach to the question of consent in marriage adopted by the Supreme Court in

16 (1835) 3 Knapp 257.
17 [1897] P 263.
18 [1912] 2 IR 445.
19 1 July 1976, unreported, Supreme Court.

N. (orse K.) v K. may possibly herald a re-appraisal of the restrictive role traditionally applied to fraud, misrepresentation and mistake. It is true that the judges in that case were speaking in the context of duress and undue influence. But a number of broad statements were made, concerning the general importance of the consent requirement, which may well influence the judicial approach to other factors which impinge on consent. Griffin J. (at page 90) spoke of the need for "full and free consent". Hederman J. (at page 91) stated that, "A personal and full internal and informed consent is essential to a valid marriage." McCarthy J. (at page 94) spoke of "an informed and willing consent," and warned that analysis of concepts such as duress, undue influence or fraud are likely to lose sight of the key question "was there a voluntary consent?" The general thrust of the majority judgments in *N. (orse K.) v K.*, is to shift the emphasis away from the categorisation of factors which may vitiate consent, and towards an analysis of whether the consent in the individual case was in reality free and informed. If this same approach is adopted generally, then arguments based on fraud, misrepresentation or mistake may become admissible. Consent to marriage based on a tissue of lies may come to be seen as no more free or informed than a consent induced by emotional blackmail.

2.106 The decision of Barron J. in *F. v F.*[20] offers further evidence of a movement away from the restrictive approach. In that case the respondent had concealed from the petitioner, by a series of tricks and lies, that he was a homosexual who engaged in continual promiscuous homosexual activities. Barron J. was satisfied "that the petitioner was totally taken in and would not have married the respondent had she even known a part of his true nature." He had "no doubt that her consent to the marriage was apparent only and was not a true consent." It is difficult to reconcile this decision with earlier cases such as *Moss v Moss* and *Swift v Kelly*. On the other hand, it conforms very well with general principles laid down in *N. (orse K.) v K.*

Mistake as to the person

2.107 *Swift v Kelly* is authority for the proposition that deceit as to the person may negative consent. If Paul, masquerading as Tom, marries Mary, who is taken in by the deception the marriage will be void. In the Australian case of *Allardyce v Mitchell*[21] the respondent had passed himself off as another man, whose family was known to the petitioner. She would not have agreed to the marriage had she now known the family.

2.108 The concept of personal identity poses problems of definition. It seems clear that identity is not simply equated with name or title. It has also been assumed that mistake or deceit in relation to the status, fortune or prospects of the respondent will not provide grounds for annulment.[22] A

20 (22 June 1988, unreported) High Court.
21 (1869) 6 W.W. & A'B (I.P. and M.) 45.
22 See the New Zealand case of *C. v C.* [1942] NZLR 356.

distinction has thus been drawn between mistake as to the *persona* and mistake as to attributes. However, it may be argued that identity is constituted by the sum total of an individual's attributes, and that a point may be reached where there has been deceit as to so many attributes of the respondent that in reality it is his *persona* which has been concealed. Moreover, Barron J.'s decision in *F. v F.* suggests that it may be sufficient to show that the deceit had the effect of concealing from the petitioner the "true nature" of the respondent.

Mistake as to the nature of the ceremony, or the effects of marriage

2.109 If either party to a marriage ceremony is unaware that it is in fact a ceremony of marriage the marriage is void. In the English case of *Mehta v Mehta*[23] the petitioner was deceived into believing that the ceremony which took place in Bombay was one of conversion to the Hindu faith. A decree was granted. A similar case is *Valier v Valier*[24] where an Italian with little knowledge of the English language went through a register office marriage in England without being aware of the nature of the ceremony. On the other hand, mistake as to the effects of a marriage ceremony may not justify a decree. In *Ussher v Ussher*,[25] a decree was refused to a petitioner who mistakenly believed that his marriage, which was valid under civil law, would be recognised as valid by the Roman Catholic church. In the English case of *Kassim v Kassim*,[26] the husband who mistakenly thought that his marriage was polygamous, and that he would be entitled to take further wives, was refused a decree.

Intention not to fulfil a fundamental feature of marriage

2.110 In *S. v S.*, the respondent had, some weeks before marrying the petitioner, begun a relationship with another woman. The petitioner was not aware of this. Following the marriage the respondent was cold and unaffectionate and, despite cohabitation for six months, the marriage was not consummated. A majority of the Supreme Court held that the marriage was voidable by reason of the respondent's psychological impotence *quoad hanc*. (see **2.024, 2.029**) Kenny J., however, concluded that the only reasonable inference from the evidence was that the respondent did not intend to consummate the marriage at the time of the marriage. The question was whether in such circumstances, the consent of the petitioner was valid, and Kenny J. stated at page 5 of his judgment

> It seems to me that the intention to have sexual intercourse is such a fundamental feature of the marriage contract that if *at the time of the marriage* either party has determined that there will not be any during the marriage and none takes place and if the parties have not agreed on this before the marriage or if the ages of the parties make it improbable

23 [1945] 2 All ER 690.
24 (1925) 133 LT 830.
25 [1912] 2 IR 445.
26 [1962] P 224.

that they could have intercourse (*Briggs v Morgan*[27]), a spouse who was not aware of the determination of the other is entitled to a declaration that the marriage was null. The intention not to have or permit intercourse has the result that the consent which is necessary to the existence of a valid marriage does not exist.

2.111 The above principle was neither approved nor rejected in the majority judgments. While Henchy and Griffin J.J. thought that there was no evidence that the husband had practised deceit, their judgments do not exclude the possibility that a marriage born of fraud may be annulled. There has been no subsequent case in which Kenny J.'s principle has been applied. On the other hand, it has not been disapproved of in any case. In *E.P. v M.C.*,[28] there was evidence that the wife had never seriously intended to live permanently with the petitioner, but that she had married to avoid the shame of pregnancy and to give her child a name. The petitioner claimed inter alia that his wife had never intended to enter into a proper and lasting marriage. Barron J. refused to grant an annulment because of collusion. The issue of deceit was not addressed.

2.112 It is impossible to say whether Kenny J.'s principle is likely to be accepted in future cases. All that can be said is that its acceptance would accord with the broad approach to the issue of consent adopted by the Supreme Court subsequently in *N. (orse K.) v K.*, and with the tendency to concentrate on the central question of whether consent is real. If the principle is accepted, the problem will arise of defining the fundamental features of a marriage. Kenny J. regarded an intention to have intercourse, with certain exceptions, as fundamental. Would an intention to cohabit or to have children also be regarded as fundamental? Is there a determinate number of objective fundamental features of marriage to be revealed by judges on a case by case basis? Or, can subjective factors, arising from the pre-marriage understanding or promises of the parties *inter se* or their special circumstances, be taken into account in determining what they believed to be fundamental? The latter seems unlikely in view of the possibility which would be opened up for collusive claims.[29]

Prior subsisting marriage

2.113 In *Hyde v Hyde* Lord Penzance described marriage as understood in Christendom, "as the voluntary union for life of one man and one woman, to the exclusion of all others."[30] A marriage celebrated between persons, one of whom is already party to a valid subsisting marriage, is absolutely

---

27 (1820) 3 Phill. Ecc. 325.
28 [1985] ILRM 34.
29 These matters are discussed further in W. Duncan, *Sex and the Fundamentals of Marriage* (1979–80) *Dublin University L.J.*, 29. See also Paul A. O'Connor, *Key Issues in Irish Family Law* (Round Hall Press, 1988), Chapter 3; Law Reform Commission, *Report on Nullity of Marriage* (LRC 9–1984).
30 (1866) LR 1 P & D 130, at page 133.

void. This will be so even though both or either of the parties honestly believed that there was no prior subsisting marriage. Thus, where one of the parties has been previously married and divorced abroad by a decree which is not entitled to recognition under the law of his ante-nuptial domicile (that is the law governing his capacity to marry), the marriage will be void,[31] despite the fact that both parties to the second marriage may have genuinely believed that the divorce was entitled to recognition. Similarly a marriage will be void where one of the parties has obtained an ecclesiastical annulment in respect of a prior marriage, unless circumstances exist which also render that prior marriage void, or it has been validly dissolved according to the civil law. If the first marriage is absolutely void at civil law, or has been dissolved by a foreign divorce which, in the circumstances, is entitled to recognition, the second marriage will be valid.

2.114 There is one situation in which a marriage, which is void for bigamy at the time of its celebration, may subsequently be validated. If one of the parties to the second marriage is already party to a marriage which is voidable, but has not yet been avoided at civil law, the second marriage is at the time of its celebration void. However, if a civil decree is subsequently obtained annulling the voidable first marriage, the retrospective effect of the decree results in the validation of the second marriage with effect from the date of its celebration.[32] Where a marriage is absolutely void at civil law the parties are entitled to re-marry without the need to first obtain a civil decree of annulment.[33]

Parties of the same sex

2.115 A marriage between persons who are not respectively male and female is void. A decree of nullity is unnecessary in such a case. There is no record of one being granted by an Irish court. In the English case of *Talbot (orse Poyntz) v Talbot*[34] where both parties were female, Ormrod J. granted a decree on the basis that there was plainly no marriage.

2.116 The position of marriages involving transsexuals is uncertain. In *Corbett v Corbett (orse Ashley)*[35] Ormrod J. applied chromosomal, gonadal and genital criteria in determining that a person who had been born with male characteristics and had subsequently undergone a sex-change operation, remained a male. In the United States, on the other hand, the effects of a sex-change operation may be recognised by law where anatomical or genital features are made to conform with a person's

---

31 See, for example *K.E.D. (orse K.C.) v M.C.* (26 September 1984, unreported) High Court (Carroll J.), affirmed by Supreme Court (13 December 1985).
32 *F.M.L. & A.L. v Registrar General of Marriages* [1984] ILRM 667.
33 *De Reneville v De Reneville* [1948] P 100.
34 111 Sol. J. 213 (1967, PDA).
35 [1971] P 83.

psychological sex.[36] The prohibition on marriage between persons of the same sex is not contrary to "the right to marry and to found a family" guaranteed by Article 12 of the European Convention of Human Rights.[37]

Non observance of formalities

2.117 The civil law prescribes different formal requirements for marriages celebrated within different denominations of the Christian religion, within the Jewish religion and by means of a secular civil ceremony. Within the Christian denominations, a sharp distinction is drawn between marriages celebrated according to the rites of the Roman Catholic church and others. Recognition of the former by the civil law is subject only to their compliance with the minimal requirements of the common law[38] whereas the latter are regulated by a complex web of statutory provision dating from 1844.[39]

2.118 It should be emphasised that not all formal defects will render a marriage void. Some formal requirements, for example those relating to parental consent, are of a directory nature only, in the sense that a failure to comply with them may justify a refusal to allow a marriage to go ahead, but will not, if the marriage is celebrated, result in its invalidity.[40] Failure to comply with some formal requirements, such as the requirement for the registration of Roman Catholics marriages, is sanctioned by a criminal penalty rather than nullity of the marriage.[41] Even in those cases where the Marriage Acts impose nullity as the sanction, it will not apply unless the parties have acted "knowingly and wilfully."[42] Finally, it is possible that some of the existing formal requirements relating to non-Roman Catholic religious marriages may be unconstitutional in that, by imposing stricter standards on certain religious denominations, they result in discrimination on the grounds of religious belief or profession contrary to Article 44.2.3 of the Constitution.[43]

36 *M.T. v J.T.* 140 N.J. Super. 77, 335 A. 2d 204. See further, Law Reform Commission, *Report on Nullity of Marriage* (LRC 9–1984), 4–8, and 90–92.
37 *Rees* judgment, 17 October 1986.
38 See generally W. H. Faloon, *Marriage Law of Ireland, R. v Millis* (1844) 10 Cl. & Fin. 534, and *Beamish v Beamish* (1861) 9 HL Cas 274.
39 The provisions of the 1844 Marriages (Ireland) Act, which remains the basic statute regulating formalities, did not extend to Roman Catholic marriages. Marriage Law (Ireland) Amendment Acts were passed in 1863 and 1873. Further amendments were made by the Marriages Act 1972. See also Registration of Marriages (Ireland) Act 1863.
40 See Marriage Act 1972 section 7. The section uses the formula: "A marriage shall not be solemnized . . .", which is similar to the formula used in the Act of 1844. That formula was interpreted as being directory. See *R. v Inhabitants of Birmingham* 8 B & Cr 29.
41 Registration of Marriages (Ireland) Act 1863.
42 See, for example *I.E. v W.E.* [1985] ILRM 691.
43 See *Report of Committee on the Constitution* (1967), 45–46. See also *I.E. v W.E.* above where the question was raised but not pursued. See **2.118**.

2.119 No attempt will be made here to set out in detail the formal requirements of marriage. What follows is an outline of the circumstances in which failure to comply with formal requirements will render a marriage void.

Marriages celebrated according to the rites of the Roman Catholic Church

2.120 Failure to comply with any of the common law requirements will invalidate a marriage celebrated according to the rites of the Roman Catholic church. The common law requires simply that the parties accept each other by words as man and wife in the presence of an episcopally ordained priest.[44] Because the Church's own requirements, deriving from the decree of the Council of Trent in 1563, are far more strict, it is extremely unlikely that a marriage which is formally valid in the eyes of the Church will be invalid under the civil law. Indeed the opposite is more likely to occur, as in *Ussher v Ussher*[45] where the absence of a witness invalidated the marriage in the eyes of the Roman Catholic church, but did not affect its validity under the common law. Although requirements relating to registration[41] and parental consent[46] now extend to Roman Catholic marriages, it seems that failure to comply with them does not render a marriage void.

Other marriages

2.121 Section 49 of the Marriages (Ireland) Act 1844 specifies a number of circumstances in which a non-Roman Catholic marriage will be void for non observance of formalities, but only if the parties have acted "knowingly and wilfully." The section covers marriages occurring—

> . . . in any place other than the church or chapel or certified presbyterian meeting house in which banns of matrimony between the parties shall have been duly and lawfully published, or specified in the licence, where the marriage is by licence, or the church chapel registered building or office specified in the notice and registrar's certificate or licence as aforesaid or without due notice to the registrar or without certificate of notice duly issued or without licence from the registrar in case such notice or licence is necessary under this Act or in the absence of a registrar where the presence of a registrar is necessary under this Act or if any persons shall knowingly or wilfully after the 31st day of March intermarry in any certified presbyterian meeting house without publications of banns or any licence, the marriage of all such persons except in any case hereinbefore excepted shall be null and void.

2.122 In *I.E. v W.E.*,[42] a Lutheran marriage was celebrated in Dublin in

---

44 *R. v Millis*, supra; *Beamish v Beamish*, supra.
45 [1912] 2 IR 445. Only one witness was present. The church requires two, but the common law requires none.
46 Marriages Act 1972, section 7.

1963 without publication of banns and without the issue of any licence or statutory certificate. Murphy J. refused to hold that the marriage was void under section 49 because the parties had not acted knowingly and wilfully in breach of its provisions. For a marriage to be void under that section, "it is necessary to establish not only that there should have been a conscious disregard of the provisions of the section but that both parties to the apparent marriage should have been aware of the defect."[47]

2.123 Section 25 of the Act of 1844 makes invalid a marriage celebrated more than three months after the notice of the intended marriage has been entered by the registrar prior to his issuing a registrar's certificate or licence.

2.124 Section 39 of the Matrimonial Causes and Marriage Law (Ireland) Act 1870 renders void a marriage solemnized by a protestant episcopalian clergyman between a person who is protestant episcopalian and a person who is not, or by a roman catholic clergyman between a person who is a roman catholic and a person who is not, where the parties to the marriage have "knowingly and wilfully" married (a) without due notice to the registrar, or (b) without a certificate of notice duly issued, or (c) without the presence of two or more witnesses, or (d) in a building not set apart for the celebration of divine service according to the rights of the religion of the officiating clergyman. In the case of the many other formal requirements set out in the Marriage Acts it is not made clear whether their breach renders a marriage void. One theory is that, in the absence of an express statement to that effect, such a marriage must be regarded as valid.[48]

Marriages celebrated abroad

2.125 Where a marriage is celebrated abroad, the general principle is that it must conform with the formal requirements of the country or jurisdiction in which it is celebrated (the *lex loci celebratonis*), regardless of the domicile or nationality of the parties.[49] If, however, it is impossible for the parties to comply with the local law, the marriage may be regarded as valid in this country if it complies with the common law requirements for a valid marriage.[50] In *Conlon v Mohamed*,[51] Barron J. considered the possibility of upholding as valid at common law an Islamic religious marriage which

---

47 *Templeton v Tyree* (1872) LR 2 P & D 420, and *Greaves v Greaves* (1872) LR 2 P & D 423 are cited in support.

48 See A. Shatter, *Family Law in the Republic of Ireland* (3rd edition), 94. See also Law Reform Commission, *Report on Nullity of Marriage* (LRC 9–1984), 13.

49 *Steele v Braddell*, 6 Milw. 1 (1838): *Du Moulin v Druitt* 3 ICLR 212 (1860); *Conlon v Mohamed* (25 July 1986, unreported) High Court.

50 In this context (i.e. for marriages celebrated outside Ireland) it appears that the presence of an episcopally ordained priest is not required. See *Preston v Preston* [1963] P 411.

51 (25 July 1986, unreported), High Court.

took place in South Africa, but which could not comply with the formal requirements of South African law because of the prohibition operating in that country on marriages between persons of different colour. In the event Barron J. held that, because the marriage was potentially polygamous, it did not satisfy common law requirements. See also section 2 of the Marriages Act 1972 which deemed retrospectively valid certain marriages celebrated by a religious ceremony prior to 20 December 1972 in the department of *Hautes* Pyrenees, France, between persons one at least of whom was an Irish citizen on the date of the marriage. This rather extraordinary provision was designed to meet a problem which had been caused by a number of marriages celebrated in Lourdes by Irish visitors in accordance with the rights of the roman catholic church, but without compliance with the civil requirements of French law.

Prohibited degrees

2.126 A marriage between persons who are within the prohibited degrees of consanguinity (relationships by blood) or affinity (relationships through marriage) is void. Prior to Lord Lyndhurst's Marriage Act 1835, such marriages were voidable only. The legislative history of the prohibited degrees is complex, "which raises some degree of uncertainty as to their precise scope."[52] The most recent changes were made by the Deceased Wife's Sister's Act 1907, when a marriage between a man and his deceased wife's sister was allowed, and by the Deceased Brother's Widow's Act 1921 when a marriage between the woman and her deceased husband's brother was permitted. The Adoption Act 1952, which introduced adoption for the first time in 1953, is silent about the effects of adoption on prohibited degrees. Section 24 of the Act provides that an adopted child "shall be considered with regard to the rights and duties of parents and children in relation to each other as the child of the adopters born to him, her or them in lawful wedlock," and implicitly brings the child within the prohibited degrees in relation to his adoptive parents. However, there is nothing in the Act to suggest that the adopted child may not marry other relatives by adoption.[53] At the same time the Act does not remove an adopted child from the prohibited degrees in relation to members of his natural family.

---

52 Law Reform Commission, *Report on Nullity of Marriage* (LRC 9–1984), at 46. The principal source is the Old Testament book of Leviticus. The earliest statute applicable to Ireland appears to be 28 Hen. 8 c. 2 (1537).
53 Proposals for reform are made in the Report of the Review Committee on Adoption Services, *Adoption* (Pl. 24 67, 1984), para. 13.11.

2.127 The existing prohibited degrees are as follows:

A man may not marry his
1. Grandmother
2. Grandfather's wife
3, Wife's grandmother
4. Father's sister
5. Mother's sister
6. Father's brother's wife
7. Mother's brother's wife
8. Wife's father's sister
9. Wife's mother's sister
10. Mother
11. Stepmother
12. Wife's mother
13. Daughter
14. Wife's daughter
15. Son's wife
16. Sister
17. Son's daughter
18. Daughter's daughter
19. Son's son's wife
20. Daughter's son's wife
21. Wife's son's daughter
22. Wife's daughter's daughter
23. Brother's daughter
24. Sister's daughter
25. Brother's son's wife
26. Sister's son's wife
27. Wife's brother's daughter
28. Wife's sister's daughter

A woman may not marry her
1. Grandfather
2. Grandmother's husband
3. Husband's grandfather
4. Father's brother
5. Mother's brother
6. Father's sister's husband
7. Mother's sister's husband
8. Husband's father's brother
9. Husband's mother's brother
10. Father
11. Stepfather
12. Husband's father
13. Son
14. Husband's son
15. Daughter's husband
16. Brother
17. Son's son
18. Daughter's son
19. Son's daughter's husband
20. Daughter's daughter's husband
21. Husband's son's son
22. Husband's daughter's son
23. Brother's son
24. Sister's son
25. Brother's daughter's husband
26. Sister's daughter's husband
27. Husband's brother's son
28. Husband's sister's son.

Lack of age

2.128 A marriage solemnised after 1 January 1975 between persons either of whom is under 16 is in general void for want of capacity by section 1(1) of the Marriages Act 1972. Prior to 1975 the marriage age was 12 for females and 14 for males. There is an exception where the President of the High Court, or another High Court judge nominated by him, has granted an exemption on the basis that, by section 1(3), it is "justified by serious reasons and is in the interests of the parties to the intended marriage." A marriage celebrated abroad and involving a person below the age of 16 may be recognised as valid provided that the parties had capacity to marry by the laws of their respective domiciles at the time of the marriage.[54]

2.129 At common law an under-age marriage was regarded as voidable rather than void, and could be affirmed by the parties after reaching full age. Although the Marriages Act 1972 does not use the term void, the

---

54 *Pugh v Pugh* [1951] 2 All ER 680: there is no specific Irish authority, but the general principle that a person's capacity to marry is determined by the law of his ante-nuptial domicile is supported by Carroll J. in *K.E.D. (orse K. C.) v M.C.* (26 September, unreported) High Court.

expression "shall not be valid" used in section 1(1) seems to import that meaning.

Bars to relief

Approbation and delay

2.130 A nullity decree in respect of a voidable marriage may be refused if there is evidence that the petitioner has approbated the marriage. Approbation is conduct which clearly shows that the petitioner has accepted the marriage as valid at a time when he knows that he has a right to have it set aside. The bar of approbation seems to be primarily based on the equitable doctrine of estoppel, according to which relief will be refused to a person who denies what he has previously asserted, especially where he has derived an advantage from that assertion.

2.131 In *D. v C.*,[55] Costello J. approved the following passage from Lord Selborne's judgment in *G. v M.*[56] as expressing the underlying principle:

There may be conduct on the part of the person seeking this remedy which ought to estop that person from having it; as, for instance, any act from which the inference ought to be drawn that during the antecedent time the party has with a knowledge of the facts and of the law approbated the marriage which he or she afterwards seeks to get rid of, or has taken advantages and derives benefits from the matrimonial relation which it would be unfair and inequitable to permit him or her having received them to treat as if no such relation had ever existed.

Awareness of facts and of the remedy

2.132 Approbation cannot occur when the petitioner is unaware of his or her right to apply for an annulment. In *D. v C.*, the marriage had been celebrated in 1974, two children were born, and it was not until 1983 that the wife's petition was heard in the High Court. The husband claimed that the petitioner had thus by her conduct approbated the marriage. Dismissing this claim, Costello J. (at 191) stated that a defence based on approbation

can only succeed where it is shown that the petitioner acted not only with knowledge of the facts which entitled her to a nullity decree but also with the knowledge that those facts would, as a matter of law, have entitled her to the right she now seeks to enforce.

In this case the petitioner had not become aware that the respondent was suffering from a psychiatric illness until several years after the marriage was celebrated, and she had not realised that his illness entitled her to a nullity decree until she obtained legal advice shortly before instituting the

55 [1984] ILRM 173, at page 191.
56 (1885), 10 App. Cas. 171, at page 186.

proceedings. The latter was not surprising, as the ground upon which her decree was based—the inability of the respondent by reason of psychiatric illness to enter into and sustain a normal marriage relationship with her—had not been mentioned in the case law as a possible ground until 1982[57] and, indeed, hers was the first case in which a decree was granted on that basis.

2.133 While in *D. v C.* the petitioner could not have known of her legal right to petition, in *N.F. v M.T.*,[58] the petitioner, who was relying on his wife's inability to consummate the marriage, might have known that he could petition, but was given incorrect legal advice. The parties had lived together for three and a half years before separating, and there was a lapse of a further two years before the proceedings were instituted. The petitioner had been wrongly advised by a solicitor, at the time of separation, that he had no real prospects of success and that he should do nothing until a change in the law had taken place. Later that same solicitor admitted that he was not sufficiently expert in family law and advised the petitioner to take advice from a more experienced firm. The petitioner did so and, as a result, instituted proceedings. O'Hanlon J. decided that approbation had not taken place. In doing so, he approved Donovan L.J.'s statement in *Pettit v Pettit*[59] to the effect that, where a petitioner is ignorant of the possibility of a decree, it will be natural for him to act as if the marriage were valid and to behave "like any ordinary decent husband", but that it would be unfair to deny him a decree unless he continues to do so after learning of his right to seek relief. In *N.F. v M.T.* both parties had "allowed the marriage to drift along, hoping against hope that it would come right in the end, but the petitioner had moved with reasonable expedition when life together became intolerable for both of them."[60]

2.134 Other cases in which delay was wholly or partly explained by the petitioner's unawareness of the possibility of relief are

(1) *W. v P.*,[61] where the delay was three years. In this case the decree was based on the husband's incapacity through psychological or emotional disability to enter into and sustain a normal marriage relationship with the petitioner.

(2) *D.C. (orse D.W.) v D.W.*,[62] where the delay was nine years but co-habitation had lasted only for a few months. Here the decree was based on the petitioner's own inability, by reason of psychotic illness, to enter into and sustain a normal marriage relationship with the respondent.

(3) *W. (orse C.) v C.*,[63] where the delay was approximately eleven years

57 *R.S.J. v J.S.J.* [1982] ILRM 263.
58 [1982] ILRM 545.
59 [1962] 3 All ER 37, at page 41.
60 Supra, per O'Hanlon J. at page 548.
61 7 June 1984, unreported, High Court.
62 21 February 1986, unreported, High Court.
63 17 February 1989, unreported, High Court.

and co-habitation had lasted approximately one and a half years. In this case the decree was based in part on the respondent's inability by reason of gross personality disorder to form a proper marriage relationship.

2.135 While it seems clear that approbation as such cannot occur until the petitioner is aware of the right to seek a decree, there may, nevertheless, be circumstances in which, despite his ignorance of the right to proceed, a petitioner may be refused a decree because it would otherwise be inequitable or unjust to grant it. In *Pettit v Pettit*[64] the English Court of Appeal refused a decree to a petitioner whose reason for a delay of 20 years was that he did not know until one year before commencing proceedings that he was entitled to rely on his own impotence. A child had been born to the respondent as a result of artificial insemination; she had carried the financial burden of keeping the house going during the war years, and there was evidence that an annulment would cause her financial and social embarrassment. The petitioner had fallen in love with another woman whom he now wished to marry. Had the same petition been brought in Ireland it would, until recently, have been rejected on the basis that a petitioner cannot rely on his own impotence unless the respondent has repudiated the marriage. The uncertainty which now surrounds this rule (see **2.035, 2.062**) gives added importance to the decision in *Pettit v Pettit*. Possibly the principle that a decree may be refused where in all the circumstances it would be unjust to grant it, is confined to cases where the petitioner is relying on his or her own incapacity.[65]

Attempts to rectify the defect

2.136 Where a petition is grounded on impotence, evidence that the parties have attempted to overcome sexual difficulties, by seeking medical psychiatric or other help, usually indicates that they have not become reconciled to an unconsummated marriage. It will not therefore constitute approbation. In *L.C. v B.C. (orse B.L.)*,[66] Lynch J. granted a decree based on the respondent wife's impotence. The couple had lived together for seven years, and the decree was sought three years later. The delay was explained by attempts to overcome the difficulties in consummating the marriage, which included the respondent undergoing a minor gynaecological operation. In *A.O'H. (orse F.) v F.*,[67] the parties had been married for fourteen years when the wife petitioned successfully on the ground of her husband's psychological impotence. The couple had lived in a happy relationship for nine years and had shared the same bedroom for 13 years. Although the question of approbation was not expressly addressed by Barron J. in his judgment, it is clear from the facts that the petitioner had continued unsuccessfully throughout their relationship to seek a solution to

---

64   [1962] 3 All ER 37.
65   See *Harthan v Harthan* [1948] 2 All ER 639.
66   18 November 1985, unreported, High Court.
67   19 December 1985, unreported, High Court.

their sexual problem. Had she not done so, it might have been suggested that she had become reconciled to an unconsummated marriage and thus approbated it.

The seeking of other matrimonial relief

2.137 Where a petitioner has, prior to seeking an annulment, applied for other forms of matrimonial relief, the question arises whether this may constitute approbation. An application, for example, for a barring order or for spousal maintenance, can only be made by a spouse, and therefore involves an implicit or explicit assertion that the marriage is valid.

2.138 In *D. v C.*[68] the respondent claimed that the petitioner was estopped *per res judicata* from seeking an annulment because she had previously successfully applied to the High Court for barring and custody orders. Costello J. (at 194) concluded that the plea of *res judicata* failed because the validity of the marriage was not an issue and not determined in the earlier proceedings. "It is true that the court acted on the assumption that the plaintiff in those proceedings was the 'spouse' of the defendant in them but the court was not asked to determine the validity of the marriage . . ." However, the question of whether a plea of *res judicata* is ever admissible in respect of a voidable marriage was left open.

> In the case of a marriage absolutely void (for example on the ground of bigamy) the inquisitorial nature of the court's jurisdiction in nullity would prevent it from accepting as true facts which on grounds of estoppel would otherwise be found false (see Walsh J. in *Gaffney v Gaffney*,[69] and Hailsham L.C. in *Vervaeke v Smith*[70]). Whether a similar rule applies in the case of a voidable marriage like the present one is a matter I am not now required to determine.[71]

2.139 In *W. (orse C.) v P.*,[72] Barron J. granted a decree of nullity on the dual grounds of lack of consent by the petitioner and the respondent's inability to sustain a proper marriage relationship. The fact that the petitioner had previously "sought the protection of the courts", and that there had been a saga of applications to the Court mostly commenced by the respondent, was mentioned but not discussed. These decisions contrast with the English case of *Tindall v Tindall*,[73] in which a wife who had taken proceedings against her husband in a Magistrate's Court alleging desertion and persistent cruelty, was held thereby to have approbated the marriage. Morris L.J. said that it would be unfair as between the parties and unseemly, from a public point of view, to allow the wife a decree.

68 [1984] ILRM 173.
69 [1975] IR 133, at page 152.
70 [1982] 1 WLR 855, at page 865.
71 *D. v C.* supra, at 195, referring to Tolstoy "*Marriage by Estoppel*", 84 *Law Quarterly Review* 258.
72 17 February 1989, unreported, High Court.
73 [1953] P 63 (Court of Appeal).

Long delay

2.140 The longer the period of time that elapses between the date of the marriage and the time of the institution of proceedings, the more difficult it becomes for the petitioner to resist the defence of approbation. However, the courts have been prepared to accept a variety of explanations for delay. As already explained, ignorance of the fact that grounds may exist for a petition, or continued attempts to overcome the defect in the marriage, may be accepted as good reasons for delay. Other reasons which are not the fault of the petitioner may suffice.

2.141 In *W. v P.*[74] part of the reason for a delay of three and a half years was that the petitioner could not afford the cost of proceedings. She was eventually referred to the Legal Aid Board who required counsel's opinion on the prospects of success before agreeing to undertake the case. Similarly in the English case of *Clifford v Clifford*,[75] where a husband was petitioning, after a delay of 27 years, on the ground of the respondent's impotence or wilful refusal to consummate the marriage, the Court of Appeal was prepared to accept that for the last ten years of that period he had been saving up the money necessary to bring proceedings. For the first seventeen years, during which the parties cohabitated, the petitioner had without success tried every proper method of persuasion to bring about consummation. He had never acquiesced in his wife's disability, and had therefore not approbated the marriage.

2.142 In *A.M.N. v J.P.C.*,[76] the wife obtained a decree on the ground of the respondent's psychological impotence. She had lived with the respondent for two years and nine months, during which time all efforts by the petitioner to overcome the respondent's inability were rejected. There was then a delay of approximately fourteen years before proceedings were begun. The reason for the delay was that the petitioner, having obtained an ecclesiastical annulment five years after her separation from the respondent, believed that it was unnecessary to obtain any further civil decree, and indeed remarried in the following year in a roman catholic church ceremony. Two children were born of that marriage. It was only when that second marriage broke down, and the petitioner sought legal advice, that she became aware that her first marriage had not been annulled under civil law. Once she became aware of the need for a civil decree, she acted promptly. She had not therefore by the delay approbated the marriage.

Public policy and the rights of third parties

2.143 The doctrine of approbation operates principally to avoid injustice as between the parties to a nullity suit. The question arises whether the doctrine may also be invoked to protect innocent third parties, particularly

---

74 (7 June 1984, unreported), High Court.
75 [1948] P 187.
76 [1988] ILRM 170.

children, likely to be adversely affected by a nullity decree. In *G. v M.*,[77] Lord Watson referred to "public policy", in addition to equity, as a basis for the doctrine. This might justify a court in considering the wider implications of a decree.

2.144 The most obvious case is one where the parties to an unconsummated marriage adopt a child, and subsequently one of them applies to have the marriage annulled on the ground that the other is impotent. In such a case the petitioner might seem to have approbated the marriage by holding himself out, for the purpose of the application to adopt, as a married person.[78] However, if at the time of the application to adopt, the petitioner was not aware of his right to apply for a nullity decree, the usual principles would suggest that approbation would not have occurred. To hold otherwise might appear unjust to the petitioner. Yet, if a decree is granted, the repercussions for the adopted child are very serious. Because a decree of nullity in respect of a voidable marriage operates retrospectively, the adoption order would presumably be retrospectively invalidated on the basis that, at the time of its making, the applicants were not validly married. The status of the child would in this way be fundamentally changed by the nullity decree. His rights in respect of his adoptive parents would be diminished, as would their rights in respect of the child.

2.145 Where a natural child has been born within a voidable marriage, the decree of nullity also has a profound affect on his status. This situation may arise where the decree is based on the incapacity of one party to form or sustain a normal marriage relationship; it may also occur where a decree is grounded on impotence, but a child has been conceived by artificial insemination, as in *Pettit v Pettit* (see **2.135**). The impact of a decree on the status of the child is not generally alluded to in such cases. The only exception is *U.F. (orse U.C.) v J.C.*[79] in which Keane J. at page 32 of his judgment referred to the undesirable consequences for the child as one reason for not recognising the new ground (that is incapacity to form or sustain a normal marriage relationship) rendering a marriage voidable.

> The legal status of such children [i.e. children of a non-marital union] has been happily eased by the Status of Children Act 1987: it remains the fact that as a result of a decision arrived at in proceedings in which they are not heard children may find themselves relegated to being members of a family which no longer enjoys the privileged status accorded by the Constitution to the family based on marriage: see the *State (Nicolaou) v An Bord Uchtála*[80]

---

77 (1875) 10 AC 171, at 197, cited with approval by O'Hanlon J. in *N.V. v M.T.* [1982] ILRM 545, at page 549.
78 Such was the decision in *W. v W.* [1952] P 152.
79 24 May 1989, unreported, High Court.
80 [1966] IR 567. Compare the comments of Henchy J. in his dissenting judgment in *N. (orse K.) v K.* [1986] ILRM 75 at 86.

2.146 It remains an open question whether, in the context of a claim that a voidable marriage has been approbated, the courts will be prepared to consider as a relevant factor the impact of a decree on the constitutional status of a child of the marriage. It is of some interest to note that in *A.M.N. v J.P.C.*[81] Barron J., in rejecting a claim that the petitioner had approbated her first marriage, expressed the view that it was in the public interest that a decree of nullity should be granted because, by retrospectively validating her second marriage, it would also establish the two children of that marriage as being, and as always having been, legitimate.

The possible ratification/validation of void marriages

2.147 There is some authority for the proposition that a doctrine of ratification, similar in its operation to that of approbation, applies to marriages which are alleged to be void by reason of the defective consent of one of the parties.[82] In *Ussher v Ussher*,[83] Lord O'Brien acknowledged the possibility that a marriage which is void *ab initio* may be validated in this way, but admitted that the concept has no basis in reason. His remarks were obiter because no ratification had in fact been attempted.

2.148 In *B. v D.*,[84] where the petitioner alleged duress, the respondent argued that, because there had been acts of intercourse subsequent to the date of petition, the petitioner had condoned the marriage. Murnaghan J. did not suggest that such a defence could not be raised, but (at page 9 of his judgment) rejected it in the particular circumstances because the intercourse had taken place "under the same duress as compelled the petitioner to marry the respondent".

2.149 In *N. (orse K.) v K.*,[85] Henchy J., in a dissenting judgment, suggested obiter that, even in a case where duress is proved, "requirements of basic fairness or natural justice, and other dictates of constitutional propriety" may preclude a judge from issuing a decree. His particular concern was for a six year old child of the marriage who, if a decree were granted (as it was), would inexorably "lose her status of legitimacy and be condemned, unheard, to illegitimacy, with all the legal disability and social stigma attaching to that state." However, McCarthy J., in the same case, at 94 reserved for further consideration "whether or not there can be a valid and enforceable approbation of what was initially an invalid contract of marriage."

2.150 It is appropriate to point out that the concept of an absolutely void marriage being made valid has been accepted twice in other contexts in recent years. The Marriages Act 1972 retrospectively validated certain

---

81 [1988] ILRM 170, at page 173.
82 See *Ellis v Bowman* (1851) 17 LT (OS) 10.
83 [1912] 2 IR 455, at page 480.
84 (20 June 1973, unreported) High Court.
85 [1986] ILRM 75, at page 88.

marriages celebrated in Lourdes prior to the passing of the Act. (see **2.125**) And in *F.M.L. and A.L. v Registrar General of Marriages*,[86] it was accepted that a bigamous marriage may be retrospectively validated by the grant of a nullity decree in respect of a prior voidable marriage.

Collusion

2.151 Collusion "means essentially an agreement between the parties so that the true case is not presented to the Court."[87] Where such an agreement has been made, the court may refuse to grant a nullity decree. The court is not entitled to conclude that collusion has occurred where the issue has not been raised at trial and the parties have not been given an opportunity to retract the allegation.

2.152 In *M. v M.*,[88] the petitioner sought a nullity decree on the ground of her husband's psychological impotence. The evidence was that, despite living together for six and a half years and seeking professional help, the marriage was not consummated. Medical evidence was given to the effect that the petitioner was still a virgin. The medical reports of a consultant psychiatrist, to whom the respondent had been referred, were referred to. The respondent also gave evidence admitting that, despite their best efforts and due to his own non-physical incapacity, the marriage was not consummated. The possibility that there may have been collusion or perjury was not raised, nor referred to by the judge, in the course of the proceedings. Two weeks after the hearing the judge delivered a reserved judgment in which he refused to grant a decree on the ground that he was not satisfied that the parties had not acted collusively or given perjured evidence. He had little doubt that the parties had mutually agreed to have their marriage annulled, and he was not satisfied that consummation had not taken place. On appeal to the Supreme Court, the petitioner was awarded a decree on the basis that the trial judge, by casting aside the corroborated and unquestioned evidence of witnesses and by imputing collusion or perjury to them without giving them any opportunity to refute the accusation, had not acted in accordance with the proper administration of justice. A decree of nullity had been the only verdict that was open on the evidence given, and it was therefore unnecessary to refer the case to the High Court for rehearing.

2.153 In *E.P. v M.C.*, (see **2.090**) the petitioner sought a decree on the grounds of duress and the respondent's incapacity to accept the obligations of marriage. The respondent's attitude to the petitioner was that she would co-operate provided that the petitioner maintained her child. This was made clear in two letters from her solicitors. The second letter contained the following passage:

---

86 [1984] ILRM 667. See **2.166**.
87 Per Barron J. in *E.P. v M.C.* [1985] ILRM 34, at page 37.
88 (8 October 1979, unreported) Supreme Court. (Henchy, Kenny & Parke JJ.).

. . . our client instructs us that she is prepared to co-operate with your client and agrees that it was not her intention at the time of the alleged marriage to your client to cohabit with him. Clearly a consultation would need to take place to allow your counsel to clearly understand the nature of our client's proposed evidence.

The reference to the respondent's intentions in the letter was inaccurate. No consultation did subsequently take place and the petitioner made no attempt to follow up the suggestion in the letter. The respondent did not defend the petition and was not called to give evidence. Barron J. (at 748) refused to grant a decree on the ground that there had been collusion. He stated

In the present case, there is no specific agreement nor has any specific fact been concealed. Nevertheless, the two letters . . . show clearly the mind of the respondent which was to ensure that the relief sought . . . was obtained on terms agreeable to her. This attitude must and does lead me to have a suspicion that if the respondent had given evidence the case might well have appeared differently. The onus of proof is on the petitioner to establish that there are no reasonable grounds for thinking that the true case has not been presented to the Court. In my view this onus has not been discharged.

2.154 The test of collusion laid down by Barron J. places a very heavy burden on the petitioner. The judgment implies that collusion may exist in the absence of an agreement between the parties and that it may be constituted by the unilateral statements of the respondent or the respondent's solicitors. Thus a petitioner, who might otherwise be entitled, may be refused a decree for no fault of his own and a respondent who wishes to avoid a decree being granted may achieve that end by promising to co-operate. Can Barron J.'s decision be reconciled with that of the Supreme Court in *M. v M*? It is not clear from his judgment whether the issue of collusion was raised at the time and, if so, whether the petitioner was given an opportunity to refute the allegation. Barron J.'s statement that the petitioner has the onus of establishing that there are no reasonable grounds for thinking that the true case has not been presented to the court, could be interpreted as placing on the petitioner, rather than the court, the obligation of raising any possible issue of collusion. This would appear to be in conflict with the Supreme Court's decision in *M. v M*.

2.155 The Law Reform Commission has suggested that the present law relating to collusion is in some respects uncertain and difficult to justify.[89] Where false evidence is fabricated a decree should be refused, not because of any agreement or conspiracy between the parties, but because no ground for annulment has been made out. Also, where a marriage is in fact void, a court's refusal to grant a decree because of collusion is a futile

---

89 *Report on Nullity of Marriage* (LRC 9–1984), 157–159.

exercise, because the parties are in any case entitled to treat the marriage as a nullity without the need for a decree. The Commission proposes the abolition of collusion as a ground for refusing to grant a decree.

Effects of a nullity decree

2.156 In the case of both a void and a voidable marriage, a nullity decree pronounces the marriage to have been (and to be) absolutely null and void. The marriage is thus declared to have been invalid from the moment of its celebration. In the case of a void marriage, which the parties are entitled to treat as void without obtaining a decree, the decree does not operate retrospectively; it is merely declaratory of an existing fact—that the marriage was absolutely void *ab initio*. In the case of a voidable marriage the declaratory form of the decree is something of a fiction, in that the decree does effect a change in the status of the parties, albeit retrospectively. A voidable marriage is for all purposes a valid marriage until it has been set aside by a nullity decree.

The rights and duties of spouses inter se

2.157 The parties to a void marriage, or to a voidable marriage which has been annulled, are not spouses and are therefore not entitled to the various remedies, protections and benefits which the law confers on a married couple. Neither may apply for maintenance, unless it be for the support of a dependent child, under the Family Law (Maintenance of Spouses and Children) Act 1976, nor for a barring or protection order under the Family Law (Protection of Spouses and Children) Act 1981. The various protections afforded by the Family Home Protection Act 1976, in respect of the family home and other matrimonial property, are not available, nor are the rights of succession afforded to spouses by the Succession Act 1965.

2.158 The question arises whether a person is entitled to retain any financial benefits, for example under a maintenance order, derived from the above legislation prior to obtaining a nullity decree. In the case of a voidable marriage, the doctrine of concluded transactions (see **2.162**) suggests that the benefits may be retained (see also **8.002**). In the case of a void marriage, the matter is unclear, though it would in most cases be impractical for the party who has paid maintenance to seek recovery. Where a marriage is void, any separation agreement entered into by the parties as husband and wife will also be void because it is based on a mistake of fact.[90] In the case of a voidable marriage, English authority[91] suggests that a nullity decree will not end a spouse's liability to pay maintenance under a separation agreement.

---

90   *Galloway v Galloway* 30 Times LR 531 (1914). *Law v Herragin* 33 Times LR 381 (1917).
91   *Adams v Adams* [1941], KB 536 (Court of Appeal). The decision relied on an analogy between a nullity decree and a decree of divorce. See Law Reform Commission, *Report on Nullity of Marriage* (LRC 9–1984), 84–85.

Parents and children

2.159 The children of a void marriage, or of a voidable marriage which has been annulled, are technically illegitimate, although, since the passing of the Status of Children Act 1987, the term "non-marital" is preferred. In the case of a voidable marriage, but not a void marriage, the decree actually alters the status of any children—a fact explained by Henchy J. in *N. (orse K.) v K.*[92] and by Keane J. in *U.F. (orse U.C.) v J.C.*[93]

2.160 The Status of Children Act 1987 has to a large extent equalised the rights of marital and non-marital children. However, some distinctions remain. For example, under section 46(1) of the Act, a married mother who is applying for a maintenance order for the support of her children may, if she is married, rely on a presumption that her husband is the child's father. Under section 46(4) that presumption does not apply where the marriage is void, though it does apply where the marriage is voidable and subsequently annulled. Where the presumption of paternity does not apply, the mother has the burden of establishing paternity by other means.

2.161 The Status of Children Act 1987 distinguishes between the parental rights of married and unmarried fathers. In the case of the former (whose rights arise automatically by section 6(1) of the Guardianship of Infants Act 1964); the father regarded as joint guardian of his child as from the moment of the child's birth. Unmarried fathers do not enjoy automatic parental rights, but are entitled (under sections 6 and 11 of the 1964 Act)[94] to apply to the court for them in the form of a guardianship, custody or access order. However, special provision is made in this context for a father who has been party to a void or voidable marriage. He will have automatic guardianship rights in respect of his child, in the case of a voidable marriage, where the decree of nullity was granted at, or at some time during the period of ten months before, the birth of the infant.[95] Where the marriage is void, the father will have automatic guardianship rights if he reasonably believed that his marriage was valid at the relevant time.[96] There is a presumption that he did so believe. Thus, for most practical purposes, the fact that a marriage is void or has been annulled will not diminish the father's rights under legislation. However, the father's constitutional rights and duties are affected, in that being unmarried he does not enjoy the inalienable right to educate his child under Article 42.1 of the Constitution.[97]

---

92 [1986] ILRM 75, at 88.
93 (24 May 1989, unreported) High Court, at pages 31 and 32 of Keane J.'s judgment. See **2.064**.
94 As amended by Status of Children Act 1987, sections 11, 12 and 13.
95 Guardianship of Infants Act 1964, section 2(3)(a)(i), as amended by section 9 of the Status of Children Act 1987.
96 Id., section 2(3)(b).
97 See *The State (Nicolaou) v An Bord Uchtála* [1966] IR 567.

Property transactions

2.162 The retrospective operation of a nullity decree in respect of a voidable marriage creates particular difficulties in relation to property transactions. The general principle appears to be that where a person is entitled to, or excluded from, an interest in property by virtue of the existence of a marriage, that entitlement or exclusion will cease when the marriage is annulled. However, where money has already been paid, or property already distributed on an assumption, which is correct at the time, that a marriage is valid, the court will not order that transaction to be undone. The distinction is well expressed by Harman J. in *In re Dewhirst*:

> It is one thing to say that a person is entitled to property or rights after the annulment of the marriage, but it is quite another thing to upset transactions, completed or made permanent, while the marriage was current. There is no doubt that, during that time, the whole world is bound to accept the fact that the spouses have the status of married people, and all the results which flow from that necessarily follow.[98]

2.163 In *re Eaves*[99] provides an example of a concluded transaction. A testator had bequeathed property to his son subject to a life interest in his widow so long as she maintained that status. Six years after the testator's death, the widow remarried, and immediately before doing so she gave her son permission to sell the property and use the proceeds for his own purposes. Twelve years later the second marriage was annulled on the ground of the husband's impotence, and the widow claimed a life interest in the proceeds of sale of the property. The Court of Appeal rejected the widow's claim. Goddard L.J. stated that "transactions which have taken place during the marriage on the footing that it is subsisting, or in direct contemplation of a marriage which afterwards takes place, cannot be affected by a subsequent decree of annulment."[1] He also emphasised that different considerations would apply were the marriage void rather than voidable.

2.164 In *Re d'Altroy's Will Trusts*,[2] a testatrix had willed her residuary estate on protective trusts to her daughter's widower so long as he retained that status. Before the testatrix's death, he had remarried but, shortly after her death, the marriage was annulled on the ground of impotence. The trustees had not transferred the property or its income to the next of kin. They had retained it pending a determination of the widower's entitlement. Because a transfer of the property had not been effected before the annulment had been granted, it was possible to recognise the retrospective effect of the decree, and the reinstated widower was held to be entitled to the property.

98 [1948] Ch. 198, at page 205.
99 [1939] Ch. 1000; affirmed, [1940] Ch. 109.
 1 [1940] Ch. 109, at page 122.
 2 [1968] 2 All ER 191.

Prior invalid marriage

2.165 Where a mariage is void, the parties are entitled to re-marry without the need first to obtain a decree of nullity. Where a marriage is voidable, it remains valid until a decree in respect of it is granted, and therefore a re-marriage by one of the parties prior to the decree is bigamous and void. Nevertheless, it has been held that the subsequent annulment of the first voidable marriage has the effect of retrospectively validating the second bigamous marriage.

2.166 In *F.M.L. and A.L. v Registrar General of Marriages*[3] the plaintiff married his first wife in August 1972. Six years later a papal dispensation was obtained in respect of the marriage. In September 1979 the plaintiff married his second wife in a roman catholic church ceremony in Dublin. No attempt was made to have the marriage registered. In October 1980 the High Court granted the plaintiff a decree of nullity in respect of his first marriage on the ground of the impotence of his first wife. He then applied to the registrar general of marriages to have the second marriage duly registered. The registrar general refused on the ground that, at the time of the celebration of the second marriage, the plaintiff was properly registered as being married to his first wife. The plaintiff successfully sought a declaration that the second marriage was valid and lawful, and an order requiring the registrar general to register the marriage accordingly.

2.167 In recognising the full retrospective effect of the decree made in respect of the first marriage, Lynch J. relied on *P. v P.*,[4] *Newbold v Attorney General*[5] and *Mason v Mason*,[6] in preference to a line of contrary English authorities.[7] The result was that a marriage (the second) which was absolutely void at the time of its celebration, the parties to which might have been prosecuted for bigamy, was retrospectively validated. Indeed Lynch J. noted the undesirability of acting as the plaintiff had done.

> I must point out however that the chronology of the steps taken by the first named plaintiff in this case is, so far as the civil and criminal law of the land is concerned, very undesirable and may give rise to many problems and is indeed very risky from the point of view of a person in the position of the first named plaintiff.
>
> A marriage which is voidable for impotence is not known to be voidable nor consequently void *ab initio* unless and until the High Court shall have pronounced it to be so. In the meantime the spouse remains apparently validly married and open to prosecution for bigamy under Section 57 of the Offences Against the Person Act 1861 . . . If a trial for bigamy should pre-date the decree of nullity the accused spouse would

3 [1984] ILRM 667.
4 [1916] 2 IR 400.
5 [1931] P 75.
6 [1944] NI 134.
7 *Inverclyde v Inverclyde* [1931] P 29, *De Reneville v De Reneville* [1948] P 100, *R v Algar* [1954] 1 QB 279, and *Wiggins v Wiggins* [1958] 2 All ER 555.

be liable to conviction and penalty. I express no views as to what would then happen or follow in law if a decree of nullity were subsequently to be granted . . .[8]

2.168 It is clear also that, besides validating retrospectively a second bigamous marriage, a nullity decree in respect of a first voidable marriage will have the effect of legitimising retrospectively any children born of the second marriage. In *A.M. v J.P.C.*,[9] the petitioner, having obtained an ecclesiastical annulment of her first marriage, remarried and several years later petitioned successfully for a civil decree in respect of her first marriage on the ground of her first husband's impotence. Barron J. (at 173) stated that, the decree established that two children of the second marriage "are and have always been legitimate".

Constitutional implications

2.169 A voidable marriage is valid until set aside by a decree of nullity. If no decree is sought or obtained during the joint lives of the parties the marriage remains good for all time. During the validity of the marriage, it presumably attracts those special constitutional protections which are reserved for marriage, marriage-based families and the members of such families. Under Article 41.1.1 of the Constitution, the family, if based on marriage, is recognised as having inalienable and imprescriptible rights. The Supreme Court has consistently held that the family referred in Article 41 is exclusively the family based on marriage. See *The State Nicolaou v An Bord Uchtála*[10] and *G. v An Bord Uchtála*.[11] In Article 41.3.1 the State pledges itself to guard with special care the institution of marriage, and Article 42.1 guarantees respect for the inalienable right and duty which married parents have to provide for the education of their children. The Supreme Court has also held that a child has a right to be a member of and to be brought up and educated within his constitutionally recognised (that is, his/her marriage-based) family.[12]

2.170 If it is true that the members of a family based on a voidable marriage enjoy these various constitutional guarantees,[13] it follows that the effect of a decree of nullity is retrospectively to extinguish them. A child of the family finds himself or herself withdrawn from a constitutionally recognised family, "and categorised as a member of a unit which does not enjoy the same status in our constitutional hierarchy of values".[14] The mother ceases to enjoy the "inalienable" right and duty which is accorded to her as a parent under Article 42, and instead enjoys only the

---

8 [1984] ILRM 667, at page 670.
9 [1988] ILRM 170.
10 [1966] IR 567.
11 [1980] IR 32.
12 *K.C. and A.C. v An Bord Uchtála* [1985] ILRM 302.
13 Keane J. certainly took this view in *JF (orse U.C.) v JC* (24 May 1989, unreported) High Court.
14 Id., per Keane J., at page 32 of his judgment.

more limited alienable rights implicit in Article 40.3.[15] Most affected is the father who loses all constitutional protection for his parental rights.

2.171 It must be said that the courts have not yet considered these matters in any detail, and an alternative view is possible. This is that a voidable marriage, because it has once been valid, has full constitutional protection, and that once the various constitutional rights have vested in the members of the family, they cannot, because they are variously described as imprescriptible and inalienable, be removed by judicial decree. The difficulty with this theory is that the decree of nullity in respect of a voidable marriage maintains the fiction that the marriage never was valid and therefore, presumably, that it never attracted constitutional rights. To hold otherwise would be to accept that the decree effectively dissolves, rather than annuls, the marriage. What emerges is an impossible dilemma. If a decree in respect of a voidable marriage is genuinely an annulment, then it is difficult to see how the constitutional guarantees for the family can survive it; if some constitutional rights do survive, this can only be based on a recognition that the marriage did in fact exist, and hence the annulment begins to look more like a dissolution.

15 See *G. v An Bord Uchtála*, supra.

Chapter 3

NULLITY OF MARRIAGE: PRACTICE AND PROCEDURE

Documents

Order 70

3.001 Order 70 of the Rules of the Superior Courts sets out the complicated procedure for nullity which must be complied with. It is therefore recommended that reference be made to the rules for each procedural step.

Petition

The petition is the grounding document. A draft petition is set out in Appendix L, Form No. 1 of the Rules (see **3.024**). This draft petition is not very helpful, as it deals with an issue of adultery, arising in a petition for a decree of divorce *a mensa et thoro*, which is dealt with also under Order 70. The petition must state certain facts:

(1) The present domicile of the parties and their domicile at the date of the ceremony of marriage.
(2) The place and date of the ceremony of marriage, together with exact location of the church, if any, or Registry Office. Often the denomination of the church is specified.
(3) The addresses where the parties resided together during the marriage and their present address (or addresses if not residing together).
(4) A description of the occupation of each party, or if unemployed the last occupation, for example, "unemployed carpenter".
(5) If there are children, a statement as to whether they were born before or after the ceremony of marriage and the names and dates of birth of each child.
(6) The petition should simply set out the facts grounding the application for nullity; for example, if the ground is non consummation, a

statement is inserted indicating whether there was any physical impediment which prevented the consummation. If the ground relied on is duress, the facts grounding the alleged lack of consent, and a statement as to the source of the alleged duress should be inserted. When the grounds are based on psychological or psychiatric disability, a typical insertion would be: "I say that, by reason of my (or his/her) mental disability and state of mind at the time of the marriage, I was unable fully to understand the nature, purposes and consequences of the marriage contract, and I was incapable of forming and sustaining a normal marriage relationship".[1]

(7) The title of the petition is important, the usual form being "Mary Single, falsely called (or otherwise known as) Mary Married v David Married". Clients do not like the designation "false". It is helpful to explain that it is not meant to cast aspersions on his or her character.

(8) The petition must be dated and signed by the petitioner, preferably with the use of single names. Counsel must next sign the petition, and then the solicitor for the petitioner. The date of filing in the Central Office must be inserted. It is stamped.

Affidavit

3.002 At the same time as the petition is signed, an affidavit must be sworn by the petitioner. It verifies the facts that are set out in the petition distinguishing between facts which are, and those which are not, within the petitioner's personal knowledge. It must contain an averment that there is no collusion and connivance between the petitioner and respondent. This must be clearly explained to the petitioner. The petition (and copy petition) and grounding affidavit are lodged in the central office of the High Court. The registrar of the central office initials the original petition. The copy petition is certified to be a true copy of the original petition, and is sealed. The original and attested stamped copy petition are then available for collection. A sample affidavit is shown at **3.025**.

Citation

3.003 The citation will probably be drafted by counsel, at the same time as the petition and affidavit. It sets out the grounds relied on and commands the respondent to answer the petition. An *ex parte* application is made to the master of the High Court, in his family law list, for "Leave to extract a citation". The application is usually made by counsel. The solicitor should have the sealed copy petition, a certified true copy of the affidavit, the original citation and an *ex parte* docket duly completed, setting out the name of the case and the nature of the application. The master will examine the documents to ensure that the affidavit is correctly sworn, and that the grounds set out in the petition fall within the limited grounds available. Leave to extract the citation will be granted. In a case of

---

1 See *D. v C.* [1984] ILRM 173.

urgency, the original citation can be initialled by the master's registrar, and signed, "Issued pursuant to Order of the Master" and dated. But usually one waits until the order is drawn up. It is collected when it appears in the master's order index with the original citation. The latter is lodged in the pleadings section of the central office, so that it can be signed by the registrar of the central office. When it is signed, the solicitor for the petitioner also signs the original citation. A sample citation is shown at **3.026**.

Service

3.004 Service of the petition, affidavit and citation takes place in accordance with rules 7 to 15 of Order 70. The sealed copy of the petition, a true copy of the affidavit and the citation are served personally on the respondent. Under rule 7, service must be personal. If service cannot be effected personally an application, under rule 10, can be made for an order for substituted service, for example, by advertisement. An affidavit of service is filed, in which the original citation has been endorsed with a certificate of service which recites: "This Citation was duly served by the undersigned on the within named Respondent of —— address, at ——, on the ——day of —1989", and it is then signed, and witnessed by the Commissioner for Oaths. Since the citation is an exhibit in the affidavit of service, the following must be endorsed on the back of the citation: *Exhibit "A" referred to in the affidavit of Mr Summons Server, sworn herein on the ——day of—1989*. The affidavit of service is filed with the original citation.

The respondent

Time and mode of trial

3.005 An appearance may be entered, within eight days by prepaid post to the petitioner's solicitors, or may be left at their office. Rule 17 provides for an appearance to be entered at any time before a proceeding has been taken in default. The respondent has a further 28 days from the date of service of the citation on him to file an answer in accordance with rule 20. The answer may vary from a simple denial of the facts alleged by the petitioner, to detailed cross allegations. If the latter is proposed, rule 22 provides for an affidavit to be prepared, in addition to the answer, verifying such additional matters, and this will be filed with the answer. Under rule 23 the affidavit must state that there is no collusion or connivance with the petitioner. Under rule 24 it is open to the petitioner to file a simple denial of the averments of the respondent, by filing a reply. The petitioner has 14 days from the date of filing and delivery of the answer to file the reply.

3.006 A notice of motion to fix time and mode of trial is issued, in accordance with the usual motion rules (rule 71). It is very common for the respondent to have failed to lodge an appearance or answer at this stage. The respondent should be served personally in sufficient time for him to obtain legal advice, even at this late stage (rule 66). Rule 79 provides that where the respondent has not lodged an appearance, and an affidavit of service of the citation has been filed, the case may proceed, but any notice of motion or other pleadings shall be filed with the proper officer in the central office, in lieu of service. This is a provision which is not always complied with, and the judges will usually seek affidavits of personal service of each document, before allowing the cases to proceed on the date for hearing. Advice should therefore be sought from the Central Office regarding the procedure. Even if the officer insists on compliance with this rule, a courtesy copy of each document can be served upon the respondent. It is generally in the interests of the petitioner that the respondent attends at the hearing so that any charge of collusion can be resisted.

Counsel will have prepared the questions that are to be tried and these are read out to the master. It is taken for granted that it is to be a trial without a jury. The master will then make the order, which will encompass the issues to be tried.

Medical inspection

3.007 If the petition is grounded on impotence, an application to appoint medical inspectors will be made. It is helpful if both parties have agreed to undergo inspection, and that the medical inspectors have been agreed, and contacted and provisional appointments been given. The dates of the inspection are put into the order. If the respondent is not legally represented, and does not turn up in the master's court, the master may still make the order for medical inspection. It is usual for a gynaecologist to examine the woman, and an urologist or endocrinologist to examine the man. The registrar of the central office may be contacted for a list of medical inspectors. Where non consummation is based on the psychological incapacity of the respondent, an application may be made to appoint a medical inspector, which in this case will be a psychiatrist (Rule 32). When the appointment date for medical inspection comes up, it is necessary for the solicitor for each party being examined to be present initially to identify the client to the doctor and the registrar. An oath must then be administered to the medical inspector. After the medical inspection, which takes place in private the report is sent to the registrar. A copy of it can only be obtained on payment of a fee to the central office.

3.008 The master's order fixing the time and mode of trial will have been obtained and served on the respondent's solicitor (rule 68) or lodged in accordance with rule 79, or served on the respondent prior to medical inspection. The books of pleadings (including all pleadings filed in court) must be prepared in duplicate and attached to a setting down docket together with an index of pleadings. If the respondent has not entered an appearance, then each affidavit of service should be included in the books. The master's order fixing time and mode of trial must be included.

The High Court

3.009 Once the books of pleadings are lodged, the registrar will arrange to have the case listed the following Friday, or the Friday thereafter, to fix a date for hearing. It is the responsibility of the solicitor for the petitioner to monitor the legal diary, to see when it appears on the list. If the respondent is not represented, it is usual to undertake to the court to notify him by letter (or personally) of the date for hearing. The court will expect to be told whether it is a Dublin case, or a case with the parties out of Dublin, or out of the jurisdiction, and how long it is likely to take. It is helpful to have ascertained the availability of professional witnesses before a date is set for hearing. Otherwise there is the inconvenience of seeking an adjournment of the case at the date for hearing, or in the Friday list. Once the date is fixed, if the respondent has not entered an appearance, he may be notified by registered letter (to be exhibited in an affidavit of service) or personally, of the date. The court may request the person who informed the respondent to attend personally, to give evidence of the response. It is essential that the respondent be notified of the particular High Court in which the case is to be listed. High Court family law cases are not always heard in Arus Ui Dhálaigh, Inns Quay, Dublin 7, and one does not know the court until the legal diary appears that morning. The respondent should be told to ring the registrar, or else a meeting should be arranged.

3.010 On the date of hearing, it is not uncommon for the respondent to turn up without having entered an appearance. A judge may nevertheless hear him in evidence. Respondents frequently indicate that they want to get out of the marriage and though disputing some of the allegations of the petitioner, their behaviour may in fact confirm the petitioner's evidence. In *K. v K.*[2] the respondent did not appear. She had entered an appearance by a firm of solicitors who afterwards withdrew from the case, by leave of the court. They appeared before the master when the issues to be tried were fixed, but did not appear at the hearing. O'Keefe, J. noted:

> I think that the attitude of the respondent in entering an appearance in proceedings and instructing solicitors up to a point, is indicative of there being no collusion between the petitioner and the respondent. Viewed in this light her absence from the trial is almost an admission of the truth of the facts set out with considerable detail in the petition.

He then followed the precedent set in *Griffith v Griffith*[3] and adjourned the case for 14 days. He directed the registrar to write to the respondent informing her that in default of special application by her within that period he intended to grant the decree sought. Alternatively, respondents have appeared and given evidence even though they are not strictly contesting the making of a decree. They may be concerned at a decree

2   16 February 1971, unreported, High Court.
3   [1944] IR 35.

being made against them based on allegations which they do not completely agree with.

Checklists to ascertain whether there are grounds for taking nullity proceedings

3.011 The following information should be obtained from a client to check whether there are, in fact, grounds for nullity proceedings:

1. Client's full married (and maiden) name.
2. The other spouse's full name.
3. The present address of client and the other spouse, and all previous addresses where they resided together.
4. The date and venue of the marriage ceremony.
5. Information on client's employment, and that of the spouse, at the date of marriage.
6. Client's present employment, and that of the spouse.
7. Nationality and domicile of the spouses at the time of the marriage, and at the present time.
8. A full history of the relationship between the parties, both before and after the marriage. Their experience of other relationships prior to their own relationship may be relevant.
9. The names of the children of the relationship, whether born before or after the marriage, and any other children born to either of them by another person.
10. The level of education and social background of each spouse.

Specific information necessary for each ground of nullity

Impotence

3.012 The following information should be obtained to see if there are grounds for a claim based on impotence:

1. The client's knowledge and experience of his sexuality, prior to the relationship.
2. A similar question as regards the other spouse's sexuality.
3. Any attempts at sexual intercourse during the courtship prior to marriage.
4. Information, in detail, on attempts made to have intercourse after marriage, and the reasons for the failure to consummate, for example, inability to have an erection, inability to penetrate the vagina due to vaginisimus, refusal to engage in intercourse arising from the particular spouse being the victim of child sexual abuse, or from some other reason.
5. Details of attendance by either spouse with a doctor, psychiatrist, psychologist, marriage guidance counsellor, sex therapist, counsellor at a family planning clinic or other specialised agency,

concerning the sexual difficulties. The level of co-operation given by each spouse to such attendance.

6. Distinguish between wilful refusal to consummate and inability to consummate due to a physical or psychological problem.

If neither spouse has sought professional assistance, if the client is the wife, it will be necessary to have her examined by a gynaecologist to find out if the hymen is intact. If it is, this will be clear evidence corroborating the non-consummation. If it is not intact, there may be other explanations for this, besides intercourse. If the client is the husband he will be examined by an endocrinologist, or urologist to ascertain if there is a physiological reason for his inability to consummate the marriage. If there is no physical reason for either spouse, as to why the marriage has not been consummated, then the client will have to be referred to a psychiatrist, preferably one specialising in psycho-sexual disorders. A problem arises where the inability lies with the other spouse who fails to cooperate in attending a psychiatrist. The psychiatrist who has seen the petitioning client may not be prepared to speculate as to the reasons for non-consummation based solely on interviewing one of the spouses. If the respondent spouse has attended a psychiatrist or other specialist but now refuses to re-attend for the purposes of the proceedings, the psychiatrist will not disclose details of his file to the other spouse without his own patients consent, which will probably not be forthcoming. One is left with the option of summonsing the doctor to the court and hoping that the court will reject any claim of privilege and force disclosure of the relevant medical records which may or may not be of assistance to the petitioner.

Duress

3.013 The following information should be obtained to check whether there are grounds for duress:

1. Was the alleged consent a fully free exercise of the independent will of the parties?
2. The social and educational background of both spouses, including their experience of other relationships with members of the opposite sex.
3. The reasons why the client married.
4. The nature of the pressure exerted on the client to get married. Was the client blackmailed, threatened, or was it a more subtle pressure, was the client in the emotional bondage of the person exerting the pressure?
5. By whom was the pressure exerted—the other spouse, the parents or other relatives of the client or other spouse, or other third parties? Was there pressure of circumstances?
6. A personality profile of client—extrovert, shy, easily influenced, of weak character, strong-willed, stubborn, and so on.
7. The names and addresses of witnesses who can corroborate what the client says.

8. It is relevant whether sexual intercourse took place before and since the marriage. Was a premarital pregnancy the reason for the marriage?
9. Details of the day of the marriage and the honeymoon.
10. The history of the marriage and whether the parties are residing together or are on good terms. It is relevant if the client is in another relationship particularly where client wishes to remarry.
11. Has an annulment in the roman catholic church been sought or obtained?

It is recommended that the witnesses be interviewed prior to the issuing of the proceedings. It may be helpful to have client examined by a psychologist or psychiatrist.

Psychiatric or psychological disability

3.014 The following information should be obtained to see whether an argument may be based on the fact of psychiatric or psychological disability:

1. A full history of any behaviour of the client, or/and the other spouse, which could be considered to amount to a psychological or psychiatric disability.
2. Did this behaviour make the client or the other spouse unable to fully understand the nature, purpose and consequences of the marriage contract, at the time of the marriage and since then?
3. Did this make either of them unable to maintain and sustain a normal marriage relationship with their spouse and the children?
4. A list of any doctors, paramedics, psychologists, psychiatrists, counsellors, therapists, social workers, clergy or ministers of religion, consulted by either spouse, who can confirm treatment of the respondent or the client.
5. A list of other witnesses—relatives, neighbours or friends who can corroborate any strange behaviour.
6. If possible, a check of any criminal record, by eliciting the date of conviction and the venue of the court (assault or malicious damage or arson may be relevant).

Practical guidelines for nullity cases

General

3.015 When interviewing a family law client for the first time, the first issue that needs to be addressed is whether there are grounds for nullity. This is because of the risk of approbation, ratification and delay (see **2.130** to **2.135**). The consequences of applying for other matrimonial relief before seeking an annulment are discussed at **2.137**. There is also the risk of being accused of collusion. If the client wishes to separate from the other spouse, there is no point securing a deed of separation only later to discover that there were good grounds for nullity although it may be possible to word a deed of separation so that it does not approbate or ratify the marriage (see chapter 16). At that stage one may be facing the risk of being sued by an irate client.

3.016 The practical benefits and disadvantages of a nullity decree need to be outlined to a client at the earliest opportunity so that the appropriate legal redress is sought. A decree may be appropriate where the client is in a second relationship and has children by it. Another client may wish to forego the benefits of nullity so that maintenance can continue to be paid. This is of particular relevance to the older client who has little opportunity of employment outside the home. A client who has a particularly violent spouse may prefer the protection of a barring order rather than relying on the less effective methods of enforcing an injunction. The Family Law (Protection of Spouses and Children) Act 1981 provides for criminal penalties for breach of a barring order and gives the Gardaí a power of arrest. Breach of an injunction constitutes contempt of court in which further pleadings need to be served on the respondent and it is rare for offenders to go to prison as they usually undertake to comply with the order. Problems associated with the children of the marriage becoming illegitimate have diminished considerably following the passing of the Status of Children Act 1987 section 3 of which provides that "the relationship between every person and his father and mother shall . . . be determined irrespective of whether his parents are or have been married to each other." Section 9 of the Act, inserting a new definition of father into section 2 of the Guardianship of Infants Act 1964, provides that a father who is party to a voidable marriage, or a void marriage, where he reasonably believed that it resulted in a valid marriage, is still guardian of any child born of that marriage. The property issues need to be addressed in that the protection of the Family Home Protection Act 1976 will not be open to a person who has obtained a decree of nullity, though equity may mitigate some of the harshness of the law. (See chapter 00).

Maintenance

3.017 If the client is a spouse with dependent children with no independent means, it is necessary to secure maintenance or alimony pending the hearing of the nullity proceedings. Once the applicant spouse is aware that she can issue nullity proceedings under Order 70 rule 47 (and has instructed the solicitor to do so) it is more appropriate that an application for alimony pending suit is made in the High Court, rather than an application for maintenance in the District Court. The difficulty is that the rule 47 provides for the application to be taken after the citation has been served on the husband. The court may dispense with such service, on application, provided an affidavit has been previously filed establishing "the factum of the marriage". If the court does not so dispense the wife may have to be supported by maintenance, by agreement with the husband, or in default, by supplementary welfare. Supplementary welfare, in practice, may not be given unless a copy of a summons or other court document (or letter from the solicitor) is exhibited, to prove efforts to obtain maintenance. The health boards also have power to recover sums paid from the spouse of the applicant.

3.018 The wife applies by notice of motion, supported by a grounding affidavit. Even if the wife is the respondent, under rule 48 she may apply for alimony. The husband can file a replying affidavit. If the wife is not satisfied with the information contained therein, she may apply under rule 5 by motion to the court for an order for a fuller affidavit or for his attendance for cross-examination. The alimony will be paid until the pronouncement of a decree annulling the marriage. Alternatively, an application for maintenance can be made in the District Court or the Circuit Court for the maintenance of the children only, under section 18 of the Status of Children Act 1987 which inserted a new Section 5A into the Family Law (Maintenance of Spouses and Children) Act 1976, allowing maintenance applications by a parent who is not married to the other.

Possible problems for the solicitor

3.019 The involvement of a solicitor with his client may come under scrutiny. In *N.F. v M.T. (otherwise known as F.)*[4] there was a delay of two years in issuing the petition. The petitioner swore that he had consulted a solicitor who had advised him that he had no real prospect of success in taking nullity proceedings. The solicitor later conceded that he was not sufficiently expert in matrimonial matters and referred the petitioner to another firm, who then issued the proceedings.

3.020 There is also the problem of collusion. In *E.P. v M.C. (otherwise P.)*[5] Barron J. refused a decree on the ground of collusion. Letters written between solicitors were produced to the court, indicating that the respondent would not be contesting the petition for nullity, provided proper arrangements were entered into for maintenance of the child of the relationship. Even though there was no specific agreement, nor was any specific fact concealed, the court declined relief. The respondent had not attended the hearing.

3.021 A solicitor may have to deal with two "spouses" of the client. In *A.M.N. v J.P.C.*,[6] the petitioner had already obtained a roman catholic church annulment and had undergone a ceremony of marriage with C.S., her present "spouse". Her "marriage" had difficulties and C.S. had issued proceedings for bigamy.[7] At the hearing of her nullity petition, the court

---

4   [1982] ILRM 545.
5   [1985] ILRM 34. See **2.151**.
6   December 1985, unreported, High Court.
7   The director of public prosecutions has not initiated prosecutions for bigamy for some years, though there have been several private prosecutions. These are rarely returned for trial, and even if they are, it is rare for a conviction to be recorded.

adjourned the case to give C.S. an opportunity of being heard. This was because his status would be affected by the granting of the decree. He did appear. The decree was granted against the respondent, who had not appeared.

3.022 A solicitor may have to defend his client against a private prosecution for bigamy. It may be possible, if the client is of limited means, for a solicitor to be assigned under the Criminal Legal Aid Scheme to defend him. Every effort should be made to have the prosecution dismissed at the stage of preliminary examination, rather than let the matter go forward for trial. The defendant is entitled to be served with a book of evidence, which will have to be prepared by the solicitor for the private prosecutor. As it is a criminal matter, the case against the defendant must be proved beyond a reasonable doubt. It may be necessary to delay the prosecution as long as possible, so that nullity proceedings may be initiated and heard first. Advice should, if necessary, be sought from a specialist criminal lawyer.

3.023 The last important point is that every possible ground for nullity should be pleaded in the petition and argued before the High Court. There is no point trying to introduce a new ground at the appellate stage, as is seen from the judgment of the Supreme Court in *K.E.D. (otherwise K.V.) v M.C.* The Supreme Court stated that it was a fundamental principle arising from the exclusively appellate jurisdiction of the court that, save in the most exceptional circumstances, the court should not hear and determine an issue which had not been tried and decided in the High Court.

Forms and precedents

3.024 The Petition

THE HIGH COURT
MATRIMONIAL

Between/ MARY SINGLE
(falsely called Married) PETITIONER
AND
DAVID MARRIED RESPONDENT
PETITION.

To the High Court.

The humble Petition of Mary Single (falsely called Married) of [insert her current address], Solicitor, showeth as follows:

1. Your Petitioner on the 10th day of November 1979 went through a ceremony of marriage with the Respondent David Married according to the rites of the Roman Catholic Church at Adam and Eve Church, 3 Happy Street in the City of Dublin.
2. At the time of the said ceremony of marriage your Petitioner and the Respondent were and still are citizens of Ireland.

3. Your Petitioner and the said David Married are respectively domiciled in Ireland and were at the date of the said ceremony of marriage domiciled in Ireland.
4. After the said marriage your Petitioner lived and cohabited with the Respondent at [here insert the address of the family home].
5. Your Petitioner has been employed as a solicitor in the ——firm at —— address and is aged 30, having been born on the 1st day of April 1959.
6. No child has been born of the said marriage.
7. The said marriage has not been consummated despite numerous attempts at consummation by the Petitioner with the Respondent, due to the Respondent's impotence.
8. Sexual intercourse has not taken place between the Petitioner and the Respondent due to the Respondent's inability to sustain an erection.
9. Your Petitioner resides [here insert her current address] and the Respondent resides at [here insert his current address] and is an accountant.
10. Your Petitioner therefore humbly prays that this Honourable Court will be pleased to decree;
    (a) that the marriage celebrated between the Petitioner and the Respondent is null and void.
    (b) that your Petitioner may have such further and other relief in the premises as to this Honourable Court may seem meet.

Dated this 14th day of October 1989.

Signed Mary Single (falsely called Married)
        Petitioner.
Signed Cathy Counsel
        Counsel
Signed Sally Solicitor
        Solicitor for the Petitioner
        Law Centre,
        Dublin 1.

This Petition was duly presented in the Central Office, on the 21st day of October 1989 by Sally Solicitor, Solicitor for the Petitioner, of the Law Centre, in the City of Dublin. It is intended to serve a copy of this Petition on the Respondent.

3.025 Petitioner's affidavit

THE HIGH COURT
MATRIMONIAL

Between [Heading as in **3.024**]
        Affidavit of Mary Single
        (falsely called Married).

I Mary Single (falsely called Married) of [here insert her current address] solicitor, aged 18 years and upwards, MAKE OATH AND SAY AS FOLLOWS:

1. I am the Petitioner herein and I beg to refer to my Petition herein dated the 14th day of October 1989.
2. The matters referred to in paragraphs 1, 2, 4, 5, 6 and 9 of the Petition herein are within my personal knowledge and are true to the best of my knowledge and belief. The matters referred to in paragraphs 3, 7 and 8 of the Petition herein are true to the best of my information and belief.
3. No collusion or connivance exists between this Deponent and the Respondent.
4. I therefore pray this Honourable Court for the reliefs in the terms sought in my Petition and for such further or other relief as this Honourable Court may seem fit.
5. I make this Affidavit from facts within my own knowledge, save where otherwise appears, and where so appears I believe same to be true.

Mary Single

Sworn at
(here insert venue of swearing)
in the City of Dublin

this 14th day of October 1989
by the said Mary Single (falsely
called Married) before me a
Commissioner for Oaths and I
know the Deponent.
Commisioner for Oaths

This Affidavit is filed on behalf of the Petitioner by Sally Solicitor, Law Centre, in the City of Dublin.

3.026 Citation

[Heading as in **3.024**]
To David Married
[insert current address] and occupation.

WHEREAS Mary Single (falsely called Married) of [insert her address and occupation], claiming to have been lawfully married to you according to the rites of the Roman Catholic Church has filed her Petition against you in the High Court wherein she alleges that the marriage has at no time been consummated due to your inability to have sexual intercourse.

Now this is to command you that within eight days after service hereof on you inclusive of the day of such service you do appear in the High Court then and there to make answer to the said Petition a copy whereof sealed with the seal of the High Court is herewith served upon you.

And Take Notice that in default of your so doing the High Court will proceed to hear the said charge proved in due course of law and to pronounce sentence therein your absence notwithstanding.

And Further Take Notice that for the purposes aforesaid you are to attend in person or by your solicitor at the Central Office, Four Courts, Dublin, there to enter an Appearance without which you will not be allowed to address the Court either in person or by Counsel at any stage of the proceedings.

Dated this 20th day of October 1989

Signed ————————————————
        Registrar.

Signed ————————————————
        Sally Solicitor,
        Solicitor for the Petitioner,
        Law Centre,
        Dublin 1.

3.027 Answer

[Heading as in **3.024**]

Delivered the 20th day of November 1989 by Richard Solicitor, Solicitor for the Respondent, of [insert the address].

  1. The Respondent admits the averments contained in paragraphs 1–4 in the Petition herein and each of them.
  Or "The Respondent admits the averments contained in the Petition herein and each of them".
  2. There is not and has never been any connivance or collusion between the Respondent and the Petitioner.

If the Respondent wishes to contest the Petition for Nullity, he should insert the following "Wherefore this Respondent humbly prays that this Honourable Court will be pleased to reject the prayer of the said Petition and decree."

Dated the 20th day of November 1989.

Signed ————————————————
        Richard Solicitor
        Solicitor,
        (insert address)
        Solicitor for the Respondent.

3.028 Affidavit

[Heading as in **3.024**]

This Affidavit is filed on behalf of the Respondent by Richard Solicitor, Solicitor of [here insert address] this 30th day of October 1989.

I, David Married of [here insert his home address, or if he does not wish to disclose same, his work address] aged 18 years and upwards MAKE OATH AND SAY AS FOLLOWS:

1. I beg to refer to the Answer herein dated the 30th October 1989. The facts referred to therein are true and accurate to the best of my knowledge, information and belief.
2. No collusion or connivance exists between me and the Petitioner.
3. Save where otherwise appears I make this Affidavit from facts within my own knowledge.

Sworn etc.

Filed etc.

3.029 Notice of motion

[Heading as in **3.024**]

TAKE NOTICE that an application will be made before the Master of the High Court at the Four Courts in the City of Dublin on the 10th day of December 1989 at 10.30 a.m. or at the first opportunity thereafter by Counsel for the Petitioner, for an Order for directions as to the time and mode of trial herein and for such further or other orders as shall seem proper and for the costs of this application.

WHICH SAID APPLICATION shall be grounded upon the Petition, the Affidavit of the Petitioner, the proceeding already had herein, the nature of the case and the reasons to be offered.

Dated this 4th day of December 1989

Signed ————————————————

Sally Solicitor,
Law Centre, etc.

To/Richard Solicitor
(insert address)

To/Registrar
Central Office
Four Courts
Dublin 7.

---

8 [1987] ILRM 189.

Chapter 4

BARRING AND PROTECTION ORDERS

The barring order

4.001 The Family Law (Protection of Spouses and Children) Act 1981 ("the Act") provides a system of barring and protection orders for the benefit of spouses and children whose safety or welfare is put at risk by the conduct of the other spouse. Barring, but not protection, orders were first introduced by the Family Law (Maintenance of Spouses and Children) Act 1976, section 22. A barring order is under section 2(1) of the Act one which (a) directs a respondent spouse, if residing at a place where the applicant spouse or the child resides, to leave that place, and (b) prohibits the respondent spouse from entering such place until further order by the court or until such other time as the court specifies.

4.002 The barring order under section 2(2) of the Act may also prohibit the respondent from using, or threating to use, violence against, molesting or putting in fear the applicant or the child, and the court may impose such exceptions and conditions as it thinks fit. An order not to use or threaten violence, etc., is not confined to any specific location, and may be of use where, for example, the respondent is harassing the applicant when out conducting business or the child when visiting school.

4.003 A spouse may thus be barred not only from the family home, but from any place at which the applicant spouse or the child resides. Moreover the respondent may under section 2(6) of the Act be barred from a place in which the applicant or child formerly resided if that residence came to an end as a result of the conduct of the respondent. The fact that the respondent carries on a business in part of the relevant premises does not preclude the making of a barring order. However the loss of income for a family resulting from an interruption of business may be taken into account in considering the question of welfare.

4.004 In *R.K. v M.K.*[1] the applicant wife, who had left the family home, applied for an order to bar the husband to allow her to return. One objection raised by the husband was that the premises were used in part for his business. Ground adjoining the house was used for storage, a shed adjoining the house contained woodworking machinery used in the business, and within the house was an office. Finlay P. held that, while there was no general principle forbidding the granting of a barring order in such circumstances it would not be in the interests of the applicant or her children to grant one in this case. The effect of an order would be either to place extra financial burden in the event of the business being moved, or to create a situation in which both spouses would have access to the same general premises, an undesirable situation having regard to the hostility between the parties. Notwithstanding this case, a barred spouse is sometimes allowed access to part of the family home separate from the living quarters. Examples include allowing him access to a self-contained garage adjoining the house to park, and work on, a vehicle used in his work, or allowing a husband general access to the farmyard and outbuildings next to the house to enable him to run the farm properly.

4.005 The District Court may grant a barring order for a period of not more than 12 months, renewable by application (see **5.045**). The Circuit Court, exercising original jurisdiction, but not on appeal from the District Court, may (under section 2(4) of the Act) grant an order of unlimited duration.

Spouses and children

4.006 Only a spouse may apply for a barring or protection order. A co-habitee is not entitled to apply. If a marriage is void or has been annulled by a civil decree, the remedies are not available. Where for example, there has been a "re-marriage" between persons one of whom has previously obtained an ecclesiastical annulment but not a civil annulment, no protection is afforded by the 1981 Act except in the unlikely event of the first marriage being void under civil law. The same is true in the case of a marriage between persons one of whom has previously been party to a foreign divorce which does not qualify for recognition. In such cases, if protection is needed, the appropriate remedy will be an injunction (see chapter 6).

4.007 A barring or protection order may only be made against a spouse. It is not possible to bar other relatives or members of the household. If for example a co-habitee, a lodger or an older child is abusing a mother or a younger child, the 1981 Act does not offer a remedy. Again an injunction may be appropriate.

4.008 A child, for the purposes of the Act, under section 1(1) means any child of either the applicant or respondent spouse, or of both of them, or a

1   24 October 1978, unreported, High Court.

child adopted by either in the Republic of Ireland, or a child in relation to whom either is or both are in loco parentis.[2] The child must be under the age of 18 or if older, suffering from mental or physical disability. A child has no standing to apply on his or her own behalf for a barring or protection order even where a parent is unwilling to take the necessary initiative. Although there is no specific mention of a child adopted abroad, such a child would in any case be included where his adoptive parent is in loco parentis to him and is married. Similarly, a third party such as a health board has no right to apply on the child's behalf.

Safety or welfare

4.009 A barring order may (under section 2(1) of the Act) be granted if the court is of the opinion that the safety or welfare of the applicant spouse or a child so requires. Proof that there exists a continuing risk to safety or welfare is therefore necessary but it is not always a sufficient condition to justify an order.

4.010 According to O'Higgins C.J. in *O'B. v O'B.*, "The use of the word 'safety' probably postulated a necessity to protect from actual or threatened physical violence emanating from the other spouse."[3] *D.C. v A.C.*[4] provides an example. The respondent husband was financially irresponsible and occasionally violent. He several times forcibly removed his wife when she attempted to control the volume on the television set which he had turned up. Resistance by her was met with further violence which included slapping her and banging her head against the wall. On one occasion he locked her in the bathroom and together with the children left the home. His conduct in other respects was characterised by selfishness and immaturity. The wife eventually persuaded him to move out of the house. Granting a barring order against the husband for a period of two years, Carroll J. was satisfied that there were "reasonable grounds for believing that incidents of physical force possibly coupled with violence might occur again unless he achieves some degree of maturity." An additional ground was that of the welfare of the wife and children. There was evidence of a considerable improvement in their well-being since the husband's departure.

4.011 A clear risk to the welfare of a spouse or child may justify a barring order in the absence of any evidence of physical violence or force. The word "welfare" is, in the opinion of O'Higgins in *O.B. v O'B.* "intended to provide for cases of neglect or fear of nervous injury brought about by the other spouse."[3] The Chief Justice also accepted that the practice of giving "welfare" a very wide ambit is correct, provided that the threat to the welfare of the spouse or child can be attributed to the conduct of the

2 Reform proposals are made in the Law Reform Commission, *Report on Illegitimacy*, (LRC 4–1982) page 162.
3 [1984] ILRM 1 at page 3.
4 7 May 1981, unreported, High Court.

respondent spouse. In his judgment in the same case Griffin J. at page 8 confirmed that a barring order is not confined to cases of violence or threatened violence, and added "'Welfare' ordinarily refers to health and well-being, and in respect of a spouse this would include both physical and emotional welfare. In the case of a child it would in addition include moral and religious welfare."

4.012 *McA. v McA.*[5] is a case where a barring order appears to have been granted exclusively on welfare grounds. The wife's main complaint was that the husband had deliberately over a considerable period of time, cut off communication with her except where absolutely necessary and then only in the most formal way. The couple had not had sexual intercourse for three years and were sleeping in separate bedrooms. The husband refused to cooperate in trying to find a solution. He refused to see the family doctor, a consultant psychiatrist, a marriage counsellor and a social worker. The wife's health suffered. She experienced anxiety and depression, and there was a risk of chronic neurotic depression should she continue living with her husband. Although these facts were addressed by Costello J. in the context of a successful petition by the wife for a divorce *a mensa et thoro* grounded on cruelty, they had previously justified the granting of a barring order by the same judge. It is worthy of note that Costello J. paid careful attention to the medical evidence and emphasised that the matrimonial problem had persisted over a considerable period of time.

4.013 It is more difficult and less common for a barring order to be granted on the welfare, as opposed to the safety, ground.[6] One reason is the general requirement laid down by the Supreme Court in *O'B. v O'B.*, and discussed in the next section, that the risk to the applicant or child must derive from serious misconduct on the part of the respondent. It is easy to construe violent behaviour as serious misconduct. Silence, neglect or coldness tend to attract less censure. Indeed, had *McA. v McA.* been decided after *O'B. v O'B.*, it is possible that the result in relation to the barring application would have been different. While there was sufficient evidence of a threat to the welfare of the wife and an infant daughter, a judge might now find it difficult to construe the husband's behaviour as serious misconduct.

4.014 The decision of O'Hanlon J. in *C. v C.*[7] is perhaps more typical than *McA. v McA.* O'Hanlon J. refused to grant a barring order against a husband who had caused his wife considerable distress and upset by insensitive behaviour and language, and by an inability to demonstrate affection. The wife was not submissive by nature and was therefore unlikely to be overborne by a stronger personality. The case was essentially one of incompatibility of temperament and stubbornness. There were

5 [1981] ILRM 361.
6 See Peter Ward, *Barring orders: A need for change.* Irish Law Times, April 1988, 90.
7 16 December 1982, unreported, High Court.

two grounds for refusing relief. Firstly, a barring order by reason of its "drastic and far-reaching nature", should not be granted except where the respondent

> has been guilty of serious violence or other cruelty, whether mental or physical, or other serious misconduct, which has jeopardised the safety or welfare of the other spouse, and has earned the penalty and stigma of exclusion from the family home by such misconduct (at pages 1 and 2).

Secondly, having regard to the interests of the children the existing situation in the home was preferable to one where the parents were living apart, with the attendant problems of custody and access.

Serious misconduct

4.015 To justify the making of a barring order it must be demonstrated that the risk to safety or welfare of the applicant or child arises from serious misconduct on the part of the respondent spouse. It is uncertain whether proof of serious misconduct is an invariable condition. It certainly is "ordinarily" a requirement. The requirement is not explicit in the 1981 Act. It is the decision of the Supreme Court in *O'B. v O'B.* which has confirmed the principle in particular. McCarthy J. stated at page 14, that the 1981 Act "ordinarily" clearly contemplates positive action or conduct on the part of the guilty spouse.

4.016 In *O'B. v O'B.*[3] the parties had married in 1972 and had two young children. The marriage had already been under strain when in April 1979 the husband left the family home. He remained away, paying a weekly visit to the children, until his return in September 1980. The tensions in the marriage revived and the wife obtained a District Court barring order against him in February 1981, which was set aside on appeal to the Circuit Court in June 1981. The husband returned to the family home, the same tensions arose and the wife once again applied for a barring order, this time in the High Court. Costello J. granted the order and the husband appealed to the Supreme Court. In setting out the causes of tension in the marriage, the judges of the Supreme Court differed in their emphasis. O'Higgins C.J. specified "rudeness by the husband in front of the children, a lack of sensitivity in his manner to her and efforts by him at dominance in running the house—none of which, in themselves, could be regarded as amounting to serious misconduct . . ." McCarthy J. (at 11) mentions bickering and finding fault with each other as well as sexual difficulties. "Living in the same house causes serious tension and matrimonial strain which is very undesirable for the children; the husband has contradicted and abused his wife in front of the children; the wife has taken a rather intractable view as to the marriage." Griffin J. (at 9) in his dissenting judgment, instanced a number of actions by the husband which he regarded as "abnormal in married life by any standard." These included the husband taking a holiday in Spain despite outstanding family debts, his failure to provide the wife with sufficient housekeeping money so that she was compelled to take "degrading" domestic employment, his constant abuse and humiliation of the wife in front of the children including disparaging remarks about her religion, and his undermining of the wife's authority over the children. It was accepted by all three judges that there had been no physical violence and that the marriage had irretrievably broken down. It was also common ground that the wife was suffering from serious nervous strain and that the situation was an undesirable one for the children.

4.017 By a majority the Court concluded that a barring order was not justified by the circumstances. It was not sufficient to prove that the safety or welfare of the wife or children was at risk, or that the marriage had irretrievably broken down. According to O'Higgins C.J. (at page 5) it had to be shown in addition that the husband was guilty of some "serious misconduct." All three judges agreed that there must exist a causal link between the defendant's conduct and the resulting risk to the spouse or children. They also agreed that the conduct complained of must go beyond that which may be expected as part of the ordinary wear and tear of married life. The reason for Griffin J.'s dissent was that he alone thought that the husband's conduct had gone beyond that point.

4.018 The Chief Justice viewed the requirement of serious misconduct as implicit in the 1981 Act for three reasons. First, the long title to the Act refers to the "conduct of the other spouse." Second, the consequences of a barring order are very serious; it is of potentially indefinite duration, and criminal sanctions operate if the order is broken. Third, the fact that a court has power to discharge an order when no longer required "indicates that the barring order . . . is intended to deal with a situation which is changeable and remediable by the act of the parties, or one of them, but not with a situation of complete marital breakdown which may be beyond the competence of either to remedy."[8] In addition, McCarthy J. thought that the ordinary requirement of "positive action or conduct" on the part of the guilty spouse gave a meaning to section 2(1) of the Act which recognised "the fundamental nature of the marriage contract as constitutionally recognised and, as indeed expressed in the words of the marriage service 'in sickness and in health.'"

Continuing or repetitive

4.019 In *O'B. v O'B.* O'Higgins further required that the serious misconduct of the offending spouse be "something wilful and avoidable which causes, or is likely to cause, hurt or harm, not as a single occurrence but as something which is continuing or repetitive in its nature." The requirement that the misconduct be continuing or repetitive in nature is consistent with

---

8 Each of these reasons is questioned, and the judgments further analysed, in W. Duncan, *He stepped out and he stepped in again.* (1983) 5 Dublin University LJ (ns) 155.

the need to prove that the risk to the applicant or child is a continuing one. On the other hand, it would seem to involve an unnecessarily, and perhaps dangerously, restrictive interpretation of the Act to refuse a barring order because there has been only one instance of misconduct. A single attack, if sufficiently vicious, might well justify an order if there is a real danger that it may be repeated. O'Higgins C.J.'s statement should probably be interpreted as meaning, not that a single occurrence of misconduct can never justify a barring order, but that, where a single occurrence is relied on, the risk of a recurrence must be clearly established.

Wilful and avoidable

4.020 In *O'B. v O'B.*, the need to prove that the respondent's misconduct is "wilful and avoidable" is stressed by O'Higgins C.J. This in his view, follows from the serious consequences of a barring order, including the criminal sanctions which may operate on breach of an order. The question arises, therefore, whether it is ever possible for a spouse to obtain a barring order to avoid a dangerous or threatening situation arising from the presence of the respondent in the family, but where there cannot be said to be any guilty intent or moral blame attaching to the respondent. The most obvious case is one where the respondent's misconduct results from a psychiatric condition over which he has no control. His behaviour may be "wilful" in the sense that his actions are directed by his own mind, but it may not be "avoidable." Another example would be where a spouse contracts an illness or disease which, for the protection of others, requires his isolation. The spouse's condition in such a case can scarcely be described as wilful or avoidable misconduct; yet the protection of family members may require a barring order.

4.021 In the different context of the definition of "cruelty", this same dilemma has been resolved in favour of protecting the vulnerable spouse by not requiring proof that the respondent intended to be cruel. Despite his reference to the words of the marriage service "in sickness and in health," McCarthy J., in *O'B. v O'B.*, clearly envisaged the possibility of granting a barring order, in extreme circumstances, against an innocent spouse.

> There may be circumstances—for example, mental disturbance of an aggravated kind or, even, infection with some highly contagious dis- order, in which a spouse, innocent of any serious misconduct towards the other spouse or any member of the family, may be subjected to a barring order (at page 14).

Whatever the position in relation to extreme cases, in the usual case the degree of "guilt" attaching to the respondent's conduct will be a matter of concern to the court. This is reflected in decisions in which the respon- dent's apparent misconduct has been excused on the ground of provocation by the applicant.

4.022 In *P. v P.*[9] the wife failed to convince Barrington J. that her husband was a cruel and violent man. In the case of one incident where it was accepted that the husband had behaved aggressively and others where he had accosted his wife, the judge was prepared to accept the husband's explanation that his behaviour was an understandable reaction to the wife's refusal to allow him access to their young child. The husband was described by the judge as "a hard-working excitable and difficult man" who according to his mother "had a bit of a temper." The wife was refused a barring order.

Protection orders

4.023 One of the defects in the original system of barring orders introduced by section 22 of the Family Law (Maintenance of Spouses and Children) Act 1976 was the inability of an applicant to seek the court's protection other than by injunction in the period between the taking out of a barring summons and the hearing of the case, sometimes a matter of several weeks. To help remedy this defect the Act of 1981 introduced the protection order. A protection order is available, under section 3(1) on the same conditions and grounds as a barring order on an *ex parte* basis. It may be applied for at any time between the making and determination of a barring application, or under section 3(2), before the barring summons has been served. Under section 3(3) it ceases to have effect when the application for a barring order is determined. The order does not exclude the spouse from any premises but orders that he shall not "use or threaten to use violence against, molest or put in fear the applicant spouse or the child." An injunction is the appropriate remedy if immediate exclusion is essential to protect family members (see chapter 6). Nevertheless, some judges have been prepared to grant barring orders on an interim basis, *ex parte*, and on an interlocutory basis in cases where immediate exclusion is essential to protect family members. The perceived reasoning appears to be that where the court has power to grant relief under statute, its general equitable jurisdiction allows it to grant such relief on an interim or interlocutory basis. The protection order is promulgated and enforced in the same way as a barring order (sections 5-7).

Operation and enforcement of barring and protection orders

4.024 Under section 4(1) a barring or protection order takes effect on notification of its making to the respondent spouse. The court, under section 5(1), when making varying or discharging a barring order, or when making or discharging a protection order, sends a copy of the order not only to the applicant and respondent but also to the local Garda station for the area in which the relevant place of residence is situated. A respondent spouse is deemed to have notification of the making of a barring or protection order if present in court at the time when it is made.

9   12 March 1980, unreported, High Court.

4.025 Under section 6(1) breach of a barring or protection order is an offence punishable on summary conviction, by a maximum fine of £200 and/or imprisonment for a term not exceeding six months. It may also constitute contempt of court (see **18.073**). Under section 7 a Garda has power to arrest without warrant a person whom he has reasonable cause to believe is committing or has committed a breach.

Variation, renewal, discharge and appeal

4.026 Under section 2(3) a barring order may be varied at any time on the application of either spouse. It may also be renewed (under section 2(5)) if it is not of indefinite duration, by application on or before its expiration. Either spouse may apply under section 11(1) for a barring and/or protection order to be discharged on the ground that the safety and welfare of the spouse or child for whose protection it was made do not require its continuation. Appeal from a barring order granted by the District Court is to the Circuit Court with a stay of action only if the court of first instance or the appeal court allows it, and subject to such terms as the court determines (section 10(1)). Under section 10(2) an appeal from a protection order to the Circuit Court cannot stay its operation.

Chapter 5

BARRING AND PROTECTION ORDERS: PRACTICE AND PROCEDURE

Jurisdiction

5.001 The Family Law (Protection of Spouses and Children) Act 1981 vests jurisdiction to grant barring and protection orders in the Circuit Court and the District Court. Barring orders made by the District Court may not exceed 12 months but may be renewed on application. Section 14 provides for the proceedings to be heard otherwise than in public. The Circuit Court, and the High Court, on appeal, have special provision for hearings in chambers. It is submitted that a justice has a right, even if implied, in his inherent jurisdiction to also hear his case in chambers with the public excluded.

The High Court

5.002 The High Court had jurisdiction to grant barring orders of an indefinite duration, under section 2(5) of the Family Law (Maintenance of Spouses and Children) Act 1976. Section 17(1) of the Family Law (Protection of Spouses and Children) Act 1981 repealed section 22 of that Act. Nevertheless section 2 of the 1976 Act still has relevance for indefinite barring orders, for example, if an application is made to vary. In particular, it provided in the definition section, that "court" would mean the Circuit Court and the District Court. It was silent on any High Court jurisdiction, except by way of transitional provision in section 17(3) for cases commenced but not determined before the date the Act came into force. Gannon J., in *R. v R.*[1] stated that this omission of the High Court showed a clear purpose of excluding the High Court from the scope of the 1981 Act. Yet later in the judgment he interpreted the wording of the Family Law (Protection of Spouses and Children) Act 1981 as not restricting or removing the jurisdiction of the High Court. The case of *O'R. v O'R.*[2]

1   [1984] IR 296.
2   [1985] IR 367.

clarified the practical implications of the judgment of *R. v R*. Murphy J. interpreted the Courts Act 1981 and the relevant sections of the Family Law (Protection of Spouses and Children) Act 1981 as meaning that proceedings should be initiated in the court of limited and local jurisdiction unless the High Court was satisfied that there was a serious danger that justice would not be done if the High Court declined to exercise the jurisdiction. It is clear that the High Court was not intended to have jurisdiction. The only provision for the High Court is section 17(3) of the Family Law (Protection of Spouses and Children) Act 1981 which states that an application for a barring order under section 22 of the 1976 Act which was not determined before the commencement of the Courts Act 1981 may be dealt with by the High Court under the new Act. This was seen only as a transitional arrangement. O'Higgins C.J. in the important judgment of *O'B. v O'B*.[3] stated that

> it will, I think, appear that this appeal probably constitutes the last occasion upon which the Court can consider the proper application of the statutory provisions to the making of such orders. He was more direct later in the judgment when he stated "Under this 1981 Act the jurisdiction to make barring orders is confined to the Circuit Court and District Courts . . .".

Taking account of the decisions of *O'B. v O'B, O'R. v O'R.* and *Tormey v Ireland and the Attorney General*[4] it is recommended that no attempt be made to initiate barring proceedings in the High Court. The only possible reason for attempting such proceedings would be if there were property proceedings about to be issued in the High Court, and ancillary relief for an injunction or barring order were also sought.

The District Court

5.003 The Family Law (Protection of Spouses and Children) Act 1981 came into force on the 23 July 1981. The relevant rules are the District Court Family Law (Protection of Spouses and Children) Act 1981 Rules 1981 (SI 246/1981) and they came into force on the same date. Section 12 (as implemented by rule 6) provides that the jurisdiction to make an order under the Act will be exercised by the justice of the district where the applicant spouse resides or where the relevant "place" is situate. If the place is outside a large urban area it is sometimes necessary to clarify the boundary of the area of the particular court district.

5.004 Residence is flexibly interpreted by the court, so that even temporary residence at, for example, a battered wives refuge has been accepted as founding jurisdiction. If for example, a woman ordinarily resides in Drogheda but she is staying with relatives in Dublin because of violence,

---

3 [1984] IR 182.
4 [1985] IR 289; [1985] ILRM 375.

she may issue proceedings in Drogheda or in Dublin. She may be treated as still residing in Drogheda by virtue of section 2(6) of the Act. There is an additional flexibility in that rule 6 provides for the application to be made at any sitting of the court for the district. This means that one is not confined to a family law sitting though in practice, it may be so confined for the sake of organising the lists. The Dublin hearings are listed separately as the Dublin Family Law Court is the only full time family law court in the country. It sits 5 days a week, and the office is open from 10 a.m. to 12.30 p.m. and 2 p.m. to 4 p.m. It deals with the extended Dublin Metropolitan District but excluding the Borough of Dun Laoghaire.

Checklist for an emergency application for a barring order or protection order

5.005 The following information should be obtained from the client when taking initial instructions for a barring order or protection order:

1 Full names and addresses of the husband and wife. If the husband is residing with the wife, obtain the address where he is most likely to stay if barred. Check whether the applicant spouse is residing at the family home or if she is temporarily residing elsewhere, so that the correct address from which the respondent is to be barred is inserted in the forms.

2 Date of marriage. Confirm that the register was signed in case it is a church marriage that may not be recognised by the civil law. Note that there is usually insufficient time to take a full history of the marriage to see if there are grounds for nullity but this information can be obtained at a later interview.

3 Dates of birth and names of children. Check if any child suffers from a mental or physical disability. Ensure that the child for whose protection the order is sought (especially if the violence or misbehaviour was directed at the child alone and not the spouse) falls within the definition of child.

4 List recent incidents of violence and if there is time any serious incidents over the years but particularly in the last year. If there has not been serious violence, check *O'B. v O'B.* to see whether there is a case for a barring order at all.

5 Try to establish the dates of all relevant incidents of misbehaviour. Clients may be too traumatised to remember but memory can be encouraged by asking whether an incident occurred in the summer, near a birthday, wedding, funeral, end of school year, or does she remember what she was wearing, etc. This is important as otherwise hospital and Gardaí reports may not be traceable.

6 Obtain a physical description of the respondent, which will be needed for personal service.

7 If the injuries of the applicant spouse are clearly visible, photographs should be taken while they are still fresh.

8 If the applicant has not attended a doctor or casualty department she

should be advised to do so so that a note of the injuries can be taken, especially if the injuries are in places of the anatomy that are usually clothed. She should be asked to obtain a written note of the injuries from the doctor. It is preferable to obtain a typewritten full report but if the barring hearing is going to be in a week it is unlikely that the doctor will have time to organise a typewritten report. There will be a fee for such a report, usually at the rate agreed between the Irish Medical Organisation and the Law Society. This should be paid in advance by the client.

9   Names and addresses of witnesses. If the Gardaí were called, but did not prosecute the respondent for assault it may be difficult to trace the names of the Gardaí (usually a team of two). If the time that they were called to the house is known and the approximate day it should be possible to trace the unit in the station that was on duty for that shift and to ask the sergeant in charge of that unit whether he remembers being called to that address. Gardaí cannot attend court without being served with a witness summons. In cases of emergency, where the case is coming for hearing quickly, they may agree to attend court and receive the summons that morning or accept service by post at the station. This saves the expense and time of the summons server. There is a difficulty with neighbours acting as witnesses, as they may be afraid of the respondent or may not want to get involved. They may cooperate if a witness summons is issued and served and they are assured that the respondent will be told that they did not want to get involved, but that they were compelled to attend court by virtue of the witness summons.

10 Check if there have been prior applications for barring, and whether the applicant took the respondent spouse back into the home during the currency of a barring order. Find out if any other orders exist and contact the family law office, quoting the reference number, to find out. Obtain the client's instructions as to the way the respondent spouse was allowed back into the home. This is important as the justice may refuse to grant a protection order if he sees this application for a barring order as an abuse of the court process. The justice may be familiar with the client's history from previous cases and a naive solicitor may be very embarrassed to discover that they have been led astray by a more experienced client.

11 Check if the client has had previous solicitors and obtain client's written authority to have the old file sent on provided the outstanding fees have been paid.

Emergency application for a protection order: Dublin

5.006 A protection order will help a client who is being subjected to violence, pending a barring order hearing. If a solicitor is unable because of other commitments to complete the necessary forms, the client should be sent to the District Court Family Law Office at Dolphin House, East

Essex Street, Dublin 1. The client will be interviewed in private and the necessary forms completed: Form 1 is the summons for a barring order, and Form 2 is the information. In an emergency it is easy to concentrate on the issue of barring. Before the protection order is applied for the possibility of listing other proceedings for the same date should be considered. If the respondent is financially supporting the applicant but is unlikely to continue to do so or has threatened not to support her, then a maintenance summons should be issued. An application will have to be made to abridge time and substitute service in order to have the matter dealt with on the same date. The justice may decline to do so on the basis that there will not be time to hear other applications on that date. If there has been a threat to take the children or if there are likely to be problems regarding access to the children the applicant may issue proceedings for custody and an order regulating access, or she may leave the question of access for the respondent to regularise. The applicant will be brought before the justice at a convenient stage in the list. The application for the protection order is *ex parte*, that is without notice to the respondent spouse. Every effort is made to apply for protection orders at the beginning of the list at 10.30 a.m. or at 2 p.m., or as soon as possible thereafter. It is a matter for each individual solicitor in consultation with the client, to decide whether the client should be legally represented. This matter should not be allowed to delay an application for a protection order, in an emergency.

The information

5.007 The information form does not have room to state fully why a protection order is being sought. The core reason for protection should be inserted. When the client is brought into the justice she must swear on oath that the facts set out in the information are correct. The justice may ask for clarification of some fact set out in the information but it is not a full hearing. If the justice is satisfied that a protection order should be granted the applicant must wait in court while the clerk draws up the protection order. The justice will sign and he may also sign the summons for the barring application. The District Court clerk will sign if a barring summons is issued without a protection order being granted, which is unusual. A date will have already been given by the office. The protection order is completed in quadruplicate by the clerk on special forms where only the identifying features of each case are entered. An order under section 2(2) of the Act of 1981 is included on the standard form of order, unless the justice specifically deletes it. A copy protection order is then handed to the applicant. She is advised on the need to show the order at the local Garda Station but not to hand it in as the Gardaí are sent out their copy by registered post that evening. The applicant is then free to leave the court. She should be advised to ask for the station sergeant when she visits the station, so that a note can be made in the "Barring and Protection Order" file. This could be very important if she has to seek enforcement of the order, prior to the Gardaí obtaining their own copy by post.

Application for substituted service

5.008 Section 13 of the Act gives power to make rules of court for the expeditious hearing of barring orders (though the protection order is not stated) and for the service of documents other than by section 7 of the Courts Act 1964, as amended by section 22 of the Courts Act 1971. An application for substituted service of the barring summons and protection order may be necessary where for example, the respondent spouse does not reside at the family home and has no fixed address. The barring summons must have been completed in duplicate and stamped on the back with the substituted service stamp. The court normally substitutes personal service or it may direct for example, that the documents be sent care of the Labour Exchange. (Rule 50 of the District Court Rules 1948 provides that the provisions of rules 46, 47 and 48 shall be in addition to and shall not be deemed to override or vary the provisions of any enactment authorising or requiring any other mode of service or authorising or requiring the substitution of service in particular cases).

5.009 The time for service need not be abridged as the rules only provide for seven days notice. But in the case of a risk to life or where physical or sexual abuse has just been discovered the court can be asked to abridge the time for service to say, four days, and the case put in for hearing at short notice. This facility should not be abused as every client thinks that "their" case warrants such emergency action.

Witness summons

5.010 Witness summonses can be issued in the family law office at this stage if the witnesses have been ascertained. This can be critical if the case is listed for hearing in seven days because it is usual to give a witness reasonable notice of approximately seven days. In the case of professional witnesses, it is unlikely that they will be able to re-arrange their diaries at such short notice. General medical practitioners do not welcome Monday listings as that is one of their busiest days, especially if they are sole practitioners, who may have to organise locum cover.

5.011 It must be stressed that a protection order may be obtained after a barring summons has been issued provided it is applied for and granted before the determination of the application for a barring order (section 3(1)). This may occur where the barring case has been adjourned and a protection order has to be applied for in the interim. The applicant may apply for a protection order in the court on the date of the adjournment in the presence of the respondent. If he is present, he will not be able subsequently to claim that he was not aware of the making of the order.

Service of protection order and barring summons

5.012 It is the responsibility of the District Court clerk, under rule 11 to serve the protection order and the barring summons. A solicitor cannot serve either of these documents. Rule 11 provides that a summons shall be served at least seven clear days before the date of the hearing. It is sent by prepaid ordinary post and is deemed to be served at the time at which the envelope would be delivered in the "ordinary course of post". It is useful to remind one's client of the importance of handing the envelope to the respondent's spouse if she takes charge of the post. If there is a past history of the respondent being forgetful it may help if a note of the date and time of delivery is taken. Rule 14 provides for a certified copy of the protection order being sent by prepaid ordinary post to the respondent.

5.013 The endorsement on the original summons of the time date and place of posting of the envelope is (under rule 12) prima facie evidence of service. Clients frequently ask if they have to inform the respondent that the protection order has been made, or if they should wait until he gets the documents in the post. Most applicants do not want to notify the respondent as they fear being assaulted. The main problem arises if a protection order is granted on a Friday and the post will not arrive until Monday. This is the danger time for alcohol related violence. There may be something to be said for telling the respondent about the order before he goes drinking though this may provoke a binge. If he disobeys the protection order he can be prosecuted as he had become aware of the order and yet ignored it. The Gardaí, if called to the scene of an alleged breach of a protection order will take the precaution of formally notifying the respondent of the order before arresting him or asking him to accompany them to the station.

Emergency application for a protection order: outside Dublin

5.014 Under rule 6 application for a protection order and the issuing of a barring summons, may be made at any sitting of the District Court provided that it is made in the relevant District Court area. However under rule 5 it must be heard otherwise than in public. This is done by the clerk listing such applications in the justice's chambers at the beginning or the end of the morning list, or at the beginning or end of the afternoon list. If the local court is sitting at a venue some distance from the solicitor's office, it may not be possible for a solicitor to travel there. It is important, with the distances involved and the lack of public transport in rural areas, to ensure the minimum disruption for an already traumatised client in securing such an order. If possible, definite plans should be made with the local clerk for the listing of the application for the protection order. It may not be possible for the client to visit her local Garda station and she may be embarrassed to do so. The solicitor should check with the client and, if necessary, contact the sergeant by telephone to notify him of the order before it is received by post.

The family home

5.015 At the stage of securing a protection order, and once the barring summons has been issued, the client should be advised that section 9 of the Family Home Protection Act 1976 forbids the disposal or removal of household chattels until the determination of the application for a barring order. This applies to the applicant spouse as well as the respondent spouse. If a client wishes to dispose of chattels urgently, for example to pay debts, an application may be brought to the court and time for service abridged. Chapter 11 provides a fuller discussion on this matter.

District Court procedure

Preparation for the hearing of a barring application

Witnesses

5.016 There may be difficulty in tracing a doctor in a hospital. The applicant may not have asked for the casualty doctor's name. If the solicitor is aware of the time and approximate date it may be possible to trace whether the doctor was the senior house officer, registrar or casualty consultant. A phone call to medical records may provide the name. A letter of consent to obtaining medical, social work and psychiatric reports should have been signed by the client at an early stage. The letter should be addressed to the casualty consultant, requesting a report, and checking the amount of fee. Hospitals and consultants usually require the fee to be paid in advance. Because of the time involved reports sometimes have to be collected the morning of the hearing. If the client can collect it it saves the solicitor's time but the hospital may have to be informed in advance. The medical witnesses find it hard to understand why the rules of evidence dictate that they must personally appear in court even though they have supplied the solicitor with a written report in advance. If possible, try and arrange with the solicitor acting for the respondent to send him the report and obtain his consent to it being admitted without the doctor appearing. Much depends on the practice of the local justice. He may insist on the doctor's presence and once there is an objection to the admissibility of the report he may accept such objection. A telephone call to the local clerk may be helpful.

5.017 Some hospitals have a policy whereby the casualty consultant is the only doctor who appears in medico-legal matters. The consultant will appear in court with the original file and the typed report and will read out what notes the junior doctor took. However, if there is a dispute about the nature of the injuries or if for example, there is a query as to whether the applicant had alcohol consumed at the time, the best evidence rule may dictate that the doctor who actually saw the demeanour of the applicant should be the one who attends court. It is best if this is clarified beforehand. Usually, respondents do not object to a simple statement of fact; that Mrs B. presented herself to casualty, that as a result of what she said it was apparent that she had been assaulted by someone, and that she alleged it was her husband. The report should then detail each bruise or cut and it should avoid jargon.

Gardaí are valuable independent witnesses. They may be able to indicate whether Gardaí had previously been called to that house regarding other domestic incidents. If the respondent has previous convictions for violence to his spouse or others the Gardaí can obtain a computer printout, and present it to the court. Only the Gardaí are allowed access to the criminal record office. If there was an assault which is/was apparent to the eye the Gardaí should be asked in advance of the hearing, whether they advised the applicant that she could prosecute and if so, what was the reaction of the applicant spouse. Some justices take the view that if a spouse is seriously assaulted a prosecution should be initiated. A spouse who has refused to make a formal complaint to the Gardaí so that a decision could be reached on prosecution, may find it difficult to explain her ambivalence.

5.018 The applicant may have been in contact with the local social worker at the health centre and s/he should be contacted as a potential witness. He may have made visits to the home and the applicant may have disclosed several previous incidents to the social worker. The social worker may have interviewed the respondent, who may have made admissions of violence, or of misbehaviour when drunk. The social worker may be able to give evidence of seeing the applicant very distressed, and that may appear consistent with the applicant's allegations. Any report prepared by the social worker should avoid hearsay and should concentrate solely on the social worker's own observations.

Acting for the respondent

5.019 Taking instructions from a respondent in a barring case is similar to taking instructions for an injunction case. The initial reaction of a respondent is anger, and he may wish to issue counter proceedings. There is no point in doing this unless there are grounds. If the respondent is not residing at the home from which application is being made to bar him, he may issue proceedings for access. This is because the court, if it bars him, will want to ensure that he still sees his children, and the applicant spouse may be reluctant to agree access. If the respondent strongly opposes the barring application, and he is residing in the same home as the applicant, he may not want to have access proceedings taken at this time. This is in case it is interpreted as a sign of weakness in the respondent's defence of the barring application.

5.020 If there are allegations of assault, particularly if a prosecution is being contemplated, care should be taken with instructions from the respondent. It is unlikely that the respondent will tell his solicitor how many times or how severely he assaulted his wife or whether he has done so. A solicitor should not adopt an accusing or condemnatory tone, as he is unlikely to secure cooperation or frankness. Each incident that is admitted should be recorded in writing with an outline of how the injury occurred, whether he was injured in return, when the first complaint was made and to whom. Care should be taken to distinguish between assaults which he denies and those which he admits, but whose details he disputes. The solicitor for the applicant may not cooperate in advance of the hearing in disclosing the nature of his case. Unlike the Circuit Court there are no affidavits to rely on. However it can be pointed out to the applicant that if there is a refusal to disclose the nature of the case in advance, an application may be made during the case, for an adjournment to give an opportunity to locate witnesses or prepare a defence. If the respondent's solicitor is generally aware of the nature of the allegations and it appears that there is not much of a defence the respondent may decide to offer an undertaking to the court to temporarily leave the house, without admission of any misbehaviour. He thus saves face and avoids putting either party through the ordeal of giving evidence. This may be especially important where the respondent wishes to reconcile with his spouse, or wants the opportunity of obtaining treatment for alcoholism, or drug or gambling addiction. Respondents often have an unrealistic hope of reconciliation, and underestimate the seriousness of the rift that has developed. If the respondent accepts that he may have a problem with drink or some other addiction, he should be referred in advance of the court date to the relevant agency (see **18.083**) for help. This may impress the applicant into agreeing on an adjournment for a month or so.

Hearing of the barring application

5.021 Rule 5 of the District Court Rules provides that witnesses are permitted to be present in court however, it is considered bad practice for witnesses in a family law case to be present throughout the hearing. The witnesses should be kept outside, called in individually to give evidence and then excluded. The following original documents need to be available, with copies for the justice and the respondent:

1 Marriage certificate and birth certificates of the children.
2 Doctor's reports.
3 Photographs (and their negatives) with duplicates or at least photocopies.
4 School reports on the children.
5 Any report from any other agency dealing with the children, for example a child guidance clinic, or if the child has a disability, a report from the relevant clinic.
6 Ensure the Garda has copies of the record of convictions from the criminal record office.

5.022 The information should be inspected if the solicitor for the applicant was not present when the protection order was obtained. The solicitor for the respondent should always inspect the information, to see if the grounds for barring correspond with the allegation made in the information. If professional witnesses have pressing business the court may be prepared to hear them first and release them. If there are ancillary proceedings, for example for custody or maintenance, the court should be asked at an early stage for directions as to whether the barring proceedings should be heard in isolation from the other proceedings, or whether each witness is to deal with each set of proceedings together.

5.023 It is not acceptable to bring children into the precincts of the court or the court itself, and a client should be advised in advance of the hearing not to do so. In some cases of violence, an older teenager may be heard by the justice, if he has directly witnessed an incident. If children do accompany the applicant or respondent spouse, any interview with a client should not take place in the hearing or presence of the children.

5.024 The focus of a District Court hearing will be on the recent past, particularly incidents in the previous year. They should be listed by the client in chronological order. The effect on the children and on each particular child should be stated by the client. Clients who are upset often forget to state how the children have been affected. This can be a deciding factor with a justice.

Acting for the respondent at the hearing

5.025 It is common for the respondent's solicitor to be taken by surprise at the hearing of a barring application. Allegations may be made by the applicant, with little opportunity to obtain instructions to defend them. The solicitor is often left whispering to his client in the court while the applicant continues to make more allegations. If the applicant's solicitor has failed to be cooperative, the respondent's solicitor may make an application, before cross examining the applicant, to take his client's more detailed instructions in order to cross examine properly. However, taking into account that this is not a criminal trial and that the District Court has insufficient time for each case justices may take the view that the respondent will have ample opportunity to defend himself when he goes into the witness box. This leaves a solicitor having to quickly decide what strategy to adopt in cross examination.

5.026 At the end of the applicant's case, the respondent's solicitor may submit that there is no case to answer. It is unusual in such a serious matter as barring to grant a dismissal at this stage. The respondent is then called to give his evidence. He should have been advised to be as frank as possible and not to appear evasive. He should be able to deal chronologically, with his solicitor's guidance, with each allegation of the applicant spouse. If he admits to assault and does so with remorse, he is likely to be treated more leniently by a justice.

When the evidence has been heard, if the justice appears reluctant to grant a barring order, he may be asked whether an undertaking by the respondent to leave for a short period, or to go for treatment and have the proceedings adjourned would be acceptable.

The making of a barring order

5.027 If the court grants a barring order, the justice has a discretion to decide its duration. Under section 2(4) of the Act of 1981 a District Court barring order automatically expires 12 months after it has been made. If it is the first application for a barring order, the justice may decide to give the respondent a warning that the misbehaviour will not be tolerated and bar him for three months. If there have been serious incidents the justice may bar him for the full twelve months. Submissions may be made by the applicant and respondent on the duration.

5.028 The order bars the respondent from a *named address*. If the applicant wants the respondent barred from a new address which she wishes to keep secret, it is unlikely that she will get a barring order. The courts take the view that a respondent cannot be barred from an unknown address. The applicant has the option of disclosing the new address and asking the justice to amend the summons at the initial stage of the case, or of not proceeding with the barring application, but reserving her right to re enter the proceedings or issue a fresh summons should the respondent find out the new address and harass her there.

5.029 The time from which the barring order is to commence should be specified. The applicant will want to have it effective from that evening, though the justice will usually allow the respondent to collect his personal belongings before the order becomes effective. The respondent's solicitor may want to postpone the operation of the order for a few days, depending on whether the respondent has a relative's house to move to or whether he has to obtain a flat. There are more difficulties encountered in rural areas, as the respondent may have to organise transport at a distance, and he may have difficulties getting accommodation locally near his place of work or farm. There are considerable difficulties with a farm. The respondent may be barred from the farmhouse but he needs access to the sheds and outhouses. It may be necessary for a map to be annexed to the order so that both spouses know exactly the extent of the barring order. Solicitors will be embarrassed if they have not already checked out the layout of the farmhouse and its access routes. If a workable arrangement is not feasible, the applicant may prefer to move back to her relatives, and have the respondent barred from approaching her there. The difficulty here is that if she moves out of the family home prior to a court application, she may have to defend an allegation of desertion which will have implications for maintenance and succession rights. On the other hand if she plans to move to her relatives and she is seeking a barring order from the new address, but she is not actually residing there at the time of the barring application, she may be unsuccessful, on a strict interpretation of section 2 of the Act. This is because the Act envisages that the respondent will be barred from entering the place where the applicant currently resides. Section 2(6) provides that an applicant spouse who would, but for the conduct of the respondent, be residing at a place, shall be treated as residing at that place.

(But that does not cover the situation outlined). If she has moved to a new address and the respondent has not approached her there, she may have difficulties persuading a justice to bar him from the new address until the respondent misbehaves there.

5.030 In making the barring order, the respondent should be reminded of section 9(2) of the Family Home Protection Act 1976, so that only personal belongings are removed. Section 9(1) of the 1981 Act provides for section 9 of the 1976 Act to apply, if a barring order is made while it is in force.

5.031 Since the barring order can be made subject to exceptions or conditions under section 2(2) the respondent should apply for access to be regulated if there is no access summons before the court. The solicitor for the respondent should ensure that this is recorded on the face of the order. A respondent may seek to exercise access in the house but this may lead to conflict. If this is likely the order may specify that the children are to be collected at the gate at a fixed time and date, and delivered back to the gate, or the nearest bus stop.

5.032 The respondent may under section 10 apply for a stay on the barring order pending an appeal. This is unlikely to be granted by the court that has granted the order. The time to apply for the stay and for recognisances to be fixed or waived, is when the barring order is being made. This should have been anticipated by the solicitor for the respondent. If an appeal is to be lodged, and a stay has been refused, the respondent can (at the time the order is made) ask for the barring order not to come into effect for a few days, to give time to apply to the Circuit Court for a stay. If this application is not granted, strictly speaking the respondent must move out of the home or risk being prosecuted. If he has moved out of the home by the time an application for a stay has been made he is unlikely to be allowed back unless it is because he is running a business from home or runs a farm, or because he is suffering from physical or mental disability.

Costs and witness expenses

5.033 Section 15 of the Act provides for costs being at the discretion of the court. The expenses of the professional witnesses can be ordered in accordance with rule 13 of the District Court Rules 1981. The order will be sent by ordinary post to the respondent and it is effective on notification being given to him. Under section 4(3) if he was in court when the barring order was made, that constitutes effective notice.

Consequential matters

5.034 If a maintenance order has not been made at the same time as the barring order, arrangements need to be made by the solicitors (preferably before they leave the precincts of the court) regarding the amount of maintenance and where the maintenance is to be paid. If the respondent is too distressed to discuss the matter the applicant's solicitor should get his own client's instructions and be in a position to sort out these problems later. Consideration should be given to the fact that the respondent may have to give one month's rent in advance with a deposit equivalent to another month's rent. The respondent may have no savings. So the applicant may have to accept that there will be no maintenance for a short period. She may need a letter from the solicitor to apply for supplementary welfare allowance from her local community welfare officer. The question of who is going to pay outstanding bills on utilities, hire purchase, mortgage or rent needs to be addressed. If the court lists are full, and the respondent does not pay maintenance, or else refuses to pay, the applicant may need a letter from the solicitor verifying the fact that the respondent has been barred and asking for extra time for the applicant to pay bills pending a maintenance order.

5.035 If there is a local authority tenancy, the applicant will usually want the tenancy transferred into her name. There is no point in doing this unless the respondent has been barred for the maximum 12 month period. The fact that he has been barred will reduce the rent payable, on the differential rents scheme, as the husband's income will not be taken into account. If the wife persuades the respondent to transfer the house into her sole name, she may then transfer to another area without the respondent's knowledge or consent. This is why most respondents do not agree to this. However the local authority can take proceedings against both spouses and after obtaining a token order of possession, proceed to allocate the tenancy into the sole name of the applicant spouse. This is in spite of section 16(1), which provides that a person is still deemed to reside at the address from which he has been barred, for the purpose of rights under the Landlord and Tenant Acts 1967 to 1980, the Statute of Limitations 1957, or the Rent Restrictions Acts 1960 and 1967. The respondent should leave a forwarding address for his post, so that bills can be sent to him.

Breach of a protection order or a barring order

5.036 Section 6 deals with breaches of protection and barring orders. It provides for criminal penalties. In effect there are five offences encapsulated into the one section:

1 A respondent contravenes a protection order.
2 A respondent contravenes a barring order.
3 He refuses to permit the applicant spouse, or any child, to enter and remain in the home.
4 He does any act for the purpose of preventing the spouse or child, from entering or remaining in the home.
5 He breaches an order made under section 2(2), which provides for a prohibition against using or threatening to use violence against, molesting or putting the spouse or any child in fear.

As section 2(2) is an inherent part of the standard barring order, made by the District Court, breach of its provisions should be regarded as constituting an offence under section 6. The Gardaí generally do not prosecute for a breach of section 2(2) of the 1981 Act. They see the breach section as relating to a respondent who tries to enter the family home, or refuses to leave.

5.037 A complaint of a breach of a protection order or barring order should be made to the local Garda station. Usually by the time the applicant does this, the respondent has gone to another Garda area. The Gardaí may prefer to take a written complaint from the applicant and prosecute by way of summons. This is because some spouses decide not to go ahead and give evidence against a spouse. They may fear that a prison sentence will result in loss of maintenance or that, when a husband is released, he will take revenge. In practice it is unusual to sentence a respondent to prison for breach, unless it is a flagrant breach, perhaps accompanied by an assault, or if there have been previous convictions for breach. This is a much slower method, but it gives the applicant time to weigh up the advantages and disadvantages of prosecuting the other spouse. The summons is served personally on the respondent, and he may apply in the local District Court office for criminal legal aid. A respondent has a greater chance of obtaining free criminal legal aid, than his spouse has of obtaining civil legal aid, which has a small fee. If his solicitor is already on the criminal legal aid panel, this makes it easier.

5.038 If however the Gardaí decide to arrest the respondent, as for example where he is found at the family home and refuses to leave, he may be released on station bail, and required to attend at the next convenient court, to face charge(s). He may find himself on a charge of breach of the peace, or of resisting or obstructing a peace officer in the due execution of his duty, or common assault on his spouse, apart from the charge of breaching the barring order. He is unlikely to stay in custody, as the only objection to bail that can be made is that he is not likely to attend for his trial. If he has threatened the applicant spouse or he is charged with a serious assault, in addition to the breach of a barring order, objections on the ground of likely intimidation of a witness can be made. A common condition of bail is that the accused agree not to remain in, or approach the family home, pending the hearing of the charge. The respondent should be advised that if there are further breaches of the barring order while he is on bail, the court will impose a consecutive sentence. (Section 8 provides for a sentence to be consecutive, if a further offence is committed on bail). If access is a problem, an access summons can be listed in the family court, so that he does not have an excuse to approach the home again.

5.039 The hearing may be adjourned because the respondent is applying for criminal legal aid or is seeking time to organise witnesses. The chief prosecution witness, that is the spouse, may think that her own solicitor is going to prosecute the case, when in fact this will be done by a state solicitor, a superintendent or inspector, or the prosecuting Garda. In practice, in rural areas, the local inspector or superintendent will prosecute criminal cases. In the Dublin Metropolitan district, the case will be prosecuted by the Garda who arrested the respondent unless a decision has been taken for it to be prosecuted by a solicitor from the chief state solicitor's office. The solicitor for the applicant spouse does not participate in the hearing as the spouse is merely a witness. However the solicitor may assist the prosecution in advance, for example, by furnishing copies of medical reports or other useful information.

5.040 Offence cases take place at the criminal sittings of the courts, and not at the family law sittings. However individual justices especially in a rural area may prefer to hear such prosecutions on the same day or time as family law cases. The case should be heard in public, unless the justice can rule that there is something of an indecent or obscene nature, which would allow him (under section 20 of the Criminal Justice Act 1951) to exclude the public. The press are entitled to be present. They can be politely asked not to report the case, if they seem interested in it. The prosecution must prove the breach beyond a reasonable doubt. The barring order should be produced in evidence. The prosecution should be confined to the facts relevant to the particular breach, and not stray into the continuing fray between the parties. A respondent may allege that the only reason he approached the house was to see the children and that access had been denied by the applicant. The applicant spouse will have to be ready with an explanation if this is true. If the applicant spouse has invited the respondent spouse back to live with her, and there was subsequent misbehaviour and he refused to leave at her request, he may be prosecuted. However, justices have occasionally dismissed such cases. Some clients assume that this means that the barring order no longer subsists. This is not the case, and the respondent should be written to, advising him of this, and requesting that he vacate the house, if he has not already done so and warning him not to return. If the Gardaí refuse to prosecute, a private prosecution can be initiated against the respondent, and the solicitor for the applicant spouse is the prosecutor. Private prosecution should not be attempted unless the solicitor familiarises himself with the relevant judgments on making a complaint in a criminal case, which have made the law more technical. (This area of law is outside the scope of this book). The prosecution must be initiated within six months, which is the time limit for making a formal complaint. It is possible to use the offence section of this Act to prosecute for a breach of a permanent barring order, made under the Family Law (Maintenance of Spouses and Children) Act 1976. The old section 22 of the 1976 Act stated that where a person contravenes a barring order or, while a barring order is in force, molests or puts in fear his spouse or a dependant child, he is guilty of an offence. It is no longer possible to prosecute under this section, as it has been repealed by section 17 of the 1981 Act. But the breach section of the 1981 Act applies to any permanent orders made under the old section 22 of the 1976 Act. Section 17(2) states "This Act shall apply to an order made under the said section 22 which is in force . . . as if it were a barring order which included the prohibition referred to in section 2(2) of this Act."

Variation, discharge, and renewal of a barring order

Variation

5.041 Under section 2(3) an application to vary a barring order may be made by either spouse. Under rule 9 it is made to the court where the barring order was made. A summons is issued, in accordance with rule 10 setting out how the order is proposed to be varied. Such an application may be made where the applicant is changing address, and wants the barring order to be applicable to the new address. Unfortunately, many applicants change their address to a secret location, and do not approach the court for a variation. If the respondent then tries to enter the new address, he cannot be prosecuted for a breach of section 2(1), but he can be prosecuted for breach of section 2(2), as he has put her in fear, and there is no territorial limitation on this offence. A solicitor should advise the applicant that if she proposes to change address, it is best to vary the order. Under rule 13 a copy of the variation order must be sent to the respondent sources. Section 4(4) provides that a variation order takes effect on the respondent spouse being notified of it, if he has not been present in court.

Discharge

5.042 Under rule 11 an application to discharge a barring order may also be made by either party. This may be made by consent. The court retains, under section 11(1), a discretion not to discharge the order, unless satisfied that the welfare or safety of the spouse or children does not require it. No minimum time is specified as to how soon after a barring order has been made, a discharge summons may be issued. If such an application were made within a matter of weeks, the court might dismiss it on the basis that the respondent should have appealed the barring order instead. The court would expect some change of circumstances to justify making such an application. The respondent may make such an application where he alleges that he was not aware that he was barred, as he never received the summons. It may be quicker to apply to the court under rule 9 to discharge the order, rather than wait a number of months for an appeal to come into the list. Alternatively, if the justice saw fit to dismiss such an application, and indicated that it would be more appropriate for the respondent to appeal, he could extend the time limit for lodging an appeal, and (under section 10) grant a stay on the operation of the barring order.

5.043 Spouses frequently reconcile without making an application to discharge a barring order. If the misbehaviour then starts again the applicant may seek to have the barring order enforced. The solicitor for the respondent should advise his client to obey the barring order in the interim, issue a discharge summons and abridge the time for service, so as to get the earliest time for a hearing. Under rule 13, the Gardaí must be notified if a variation order or discharge order is made.

5.044 A court determining any other matrimonial or guardianship issue between the spouses is given discretion under section 11(2) of the 1981 Act to discharge any barring or protection order made against either of the spouses. The applicant spouse may raise objections if the court purports to discharge a barring order in these circumstances, on the basis that an application to discharge could have been issued by the respondent, and that she had not been given sufficient opportunity to defend the retention of the barring order. In practice this is rarely used.

Renewal

5.045 Section 2(5) provides that on or before the expiration of a barring order, a further barring order may be made with effect from the expiration of the first mentioned barring order. It is therefore advisable to remind a client to contact the solicitor at least three months before the expiration of a District Court maximum barring order. This is necessary owing to the increasing delays in securing a date for hearing and in order to consider whether it would be more appropriate to issue proceedings in the Circuit Court. There are no guidelines in the 1981 Act as to whether the applicant must adduce fresh evidence of misbehaviour or whether the prior history is sufficient. If the respondent wants a reconciliation and has undergone treatment or counselling during the currency of the order, it certainly will be difficult to bar him again. It must be stressed to the client that a barring order is seen as a temporary remedy in the District Court, to deal with protection of her safety and welfare. If she has decided that there is no hope of reconciliation, then she may wish to apply in the Circuit Court for a judicial separation. She may alternatively have sufficient evidence to seek a permanent barring order.

5.046 If an application is being made in the District Court to renew the order then fresh evidence should if possible be adduced. The respondent may claim that he was attending an agency for help with his drink problem, the relevant counsellor will have to be contacted to see if this is true. The applicant should have kept a diary of any contact that she had with the respondent, and of any further misbehaviour, particularly when calling to collect or return the children. Difficulty arises where a respondent makes efforts to reform, and suffers remorse, but the applicant spouse decides that she cannot face repetition of past behaviour. The court may query why she refused to cooperate with the respondent in going for counselling to an agency dealing with reconciliation. If a spouse has decided (during the currency of the barring order) to separate it is best to tell the respondent (by letter) at that stage, rather than waiting until near the expiration of the barring order, when the respondent's hopes of returning to the home may have been raised.

5.047 If the respondent is prepared to negotiate on the terms of a deed of separation, but the barring order is about to expire the new barring case can be adjourned, on his undertaking to stay away from the family home. The case can then be adjourned for a period of two months, but with liberty to re-enter on four days notice if there is a breach of the undertaking. If he breaches the undertaking he is in contempt, but the only contempt that the District Court can punish is contempt in the face of the court. See **18.074**. The justice may proceed to bar him for a short period, to enable the applicant to issue Circuit Court proceedings.

Appeals from the District Court

5.048 Rules 190–198 of the District Court Rules 1948 apply to appeals from the District Court, and accordingly, they apply to appeals against a barring order, except with regard to a stay on the order. Usually the entering into of a recognizance operates as a stay on a District Court order (rule 192). Section 10 of the 1981 Act indicates that a stay will not operate unless ordered by the court that made the barring order, and the court may impose terms on a stay. If a stay is not imposed, the respondent's solicitor will want to have the appeal heard as soon as possible. This causes problems in the long vacation especially if it was a short barring order. There are particular difficulties with barring orders outside Dublin; in accordance with order 1 (rules 2–3) of the 1950 Circuit Court Rules, is unusual for vacation sittings to be held. Representations can be made to the local county registrar to have a vacation sitting and if this is not possible, the circuit judge may be requested before the end of the law term, or indeed by an emergency application in his home, to have a stay imposed on the operation of the District Court order. Such application will have to be made on notice to the other party.

5.049 The respondent's solicitor should ensure that the Circuit Court has an up to date address to serve notice of the hearing to the respondent, especially if he was not represented at the District Court. Witness summonses may have to be issued, because under Order 21, District Court summonses do not apply in the Circuit Court. A copy of the barring order, protection order and information should be bespoken if the respondent does not have copies. The appeal proceeds by way of rehearing. If the applicant tries to adduce fresh evidence s/he will be asked why this evidence was not produced in the District Court if it was available then. If there are any inconsistencies between the evidence given by the appellant or the respondent in the District Court, and that given in the Circuit Court these should be alluded to by each side as necessary.

5.050 The District Court appeal list is heard separately from the Circuit Court hearings of original proceedings. A situation can arise where a short barring order has been made in the District Court which is appealed and, in the meantime the applicant spouse decides to separate, and issues proceedings in the Circuit Court for a decree of judicial separation and a permanent barring order. If there is a long waiting list for a hearing in that Circuit Court, the applicant spouse will still have to defend her spouse's appeal against the barring order so that she has protection in the interim.

5.051 Under section 2(4) of the 1981 Act the maximum barring order that can be granted on appeal is 12 months. If a short barring order for say three months, has expired by the time the appeal comes up in the Circuit Court, in effect the appeal is spent, and no order can be made. Appellants are sometimes aggrieved at this, as they feel prejudiced by the fact that a barring order was made in the first place, and want the record of it expunged. The wording of the appeal order should be carefully examined. If an appellant wants to withdraw his appeal, the appeal can be struck out and the District Court order confirmed. That means that the barring order operated from the date of the District Court order not the date of the Circuit Court order. If an appeal is dismissed, this confirms the District Court order, and the order may specify that the District Court order is affirmed and the barring order operates from the date of the District Court order. If the Circuit Court decides to change the order made in the District Court, it may vary it by changing its duration, its location, or the date of its commencement. Costs of the District Court, and Circuit Court may be awarded, and the court can certify for counsel. The order made on appeal is final and it may not be appealed to the High Court. By section 84 of the Courts of Justice Act 1924, as amended by section 57 of the Courts of Justice Act 1936 the order may issue from the Circuit Court, or the District Court: Order 43 rule 7 provides that in cases in which jurisdiction has been conferred upon the District Court by paragraph A of Section 77 of the Courts of Justice Act 1924, the Court may issue the instrument necessary to enforce its decision, or may allow it to be issued by the District Court in accordance with section 23 of the Courts of Justice (District Court) Act 1946. If there is a breach of the barring order, which has been upheld by the Circuit Court, recourse is had to the District Court, and not the Circuit Court. Rule 198 of the District Court Rules 1948 provides that upon the return of the A5 form of appeal by the Circuit Court to the justices of the District Court, he may issue the necessary warrant and take all further steps requisite for the execution of the order, as confirmed or varied by the Circuit Court, where the Circuit Court judge shall not have caused the necessary warrant to enforce his order to issue.

Circuit Court procedure

Application for an indefinite barring order

5.052 The relevant rules are Circuit Court Rules (No. 3) 1982 Order 66 which came into force on the 27th May 1982. Under rule 2 the application is brought in the circuit in which the applicant spouse resides or where the subject matter of the application is situate. The originating document, the application, is prepared in accordance with form no. 1 of rule 3. It is recommended that an application for an order under section 2(2) of the 1981 Act be included in any standard barring application. This is because the standard order drawn up by the registrar does not include an order under section 2(2) of the 1981 Act, unlike the District Court. It is stamped and issued. Under rule 5, the original is entered in the office before it is served. The rules provide that a date for hearing is then obtained. However in the Dublin Circuit Court the practice has developed of a date "for mention only" being given. This is likely to be the following Monday or Monday week, on which date all applications and motions are listed. This is so that there is more control over the very busy lists, and urgent applications for barring will be facilitated. The rules also provide that for the purpose of a quick hearing, an application for a barring order can be set down for hearing at any sitting of the court within the circuit.

Application for a protection order

5.053 An *ex parte* application for a protection order may be made after an application has been prepared and issued. The *ex parte* docket and the affidavit grounding the application for a protection order are filed. The application for a protection order does not have to be made at a formal sitting of the Circuit Court. Rule 4 provides for urgent applications to be made, "at any time or place approved by the judge, by arrangement with the county registrar".

5.054 There are no guidelines in the rules as to the details required in the affidavit grounding the application for a protection order. The details of Form No. 1 in the rules can be used as a guideline. A protection order can be applied for by notice of motion (or by *ex parte* application), if an application for a barring order has already issued. Since a protection order is designed to protect the spouse from the respondent using or threatening to use violence, such an application is best applied for on an *ex parte* basis. If a notice of motion is issued seeking a protection order, the respondent may seek an adjournment to file a replying affidavit, thus delaying the matter. If a respondent spouse is dissatisfied with the making of a protection order on an *ex parte* basis, he may apply (again, under rule 4) by notice of motion to discharge same.

5.055 When a protection order is made, the rule provides that the registrar "shall cause a copy of the order to be given to the applicant spouse" and to be given or sent, as soon as practicable to the respondent spouse" In practice, a draft order may be prepared by the registrar, and the solicitor then has to have it engrossed and sent back for signature by the county registrar. This may take at least a day, depending on the circuit and how busy the registrar is. The solicitor may have to prepare a letter verifying the making of the protection order and have a copy delivered by the client to the local Garda station until the order is available.

Service

5.056 The application will be served, together with the protection order and grounding affidavit. It is helpful to send a copy of the protection order with the other documents, with a penal endorsement attached. This gives the option of trying to have the respondent attached or committed for contempt of court if the Gardaí do not prosecute. Section 6 of the Act preserved this right. Rule 8 provides for four clear days notice before the hearing. Service is personal, in accordance with Order 10 of the Circuit

Court Rules 1950 (as amended) or by leaving same at the respondent's residence. Order 10 of the Circuit Court Rules 1950 originally provided for service of any civil bill or other originating document to be personal, wherever the respondent was to be found, or at his residence. But it was amended to allow for registered post if there was no summons server. It is therefore unclear whether rule 8 of the barring rules was intended to allow for registered post. If that was the intention it was not clearly stated. The respondent will probably still be living at the same address as the applicant. The applicant should be advised not to accept service of the documents on behalf of the respondent. This is to avoid any allegation that he did not receive them. If there is no summons server for the relevant area, any one over the age of 21 years may serve. In accordance with rule 9 an affidavit of service must be filed (or at least handed up) at the hearing of the application. There is sometimes confusion over the method of service. Rule 11 provides that an application for a barring order may be joined together with any other application on the same notice of application. Thus an application for barring may be included in an application for custody or maintenance, whose rules provide for service by prepaid post. Strictly speaking such a composite application should be sent by ordinary post, in accordance with the rules for maintenance, and an identical copy of the application should be served personally, to comply with the rules on service of barring applications. Alternatively, if it is feared that the respondent will evade service once he gets an application by post, he can be served personally for the purpose of all the applications and an application to deem service good can be made with regard to the application for maintenance.

5.057 If there is difficulty serving the application personally, an application can be made to court on an *ex parte* basis for an order for substituted service. This is grounded on an affidavit setting out the difficulties and the proposed alternative method of service. Alternatively the application can be served in the best possible way, considering that it is an application for a barring order, and an application can be made under rule 10 on the date for hearing to deem service good and sufficient.

Hearing of an application for a barring order

Preparing for the hearing

5.058 The Circuit Court adopts a stricter approach to proofs and procedure than the District Court. An answer should be filed by the respondent, even though the rules, surprisingly, do not provide for same. A draft answer is provided by Circuit Court Rules (No 6) 1982 (SI 158 of 1982). Rule 8 allows a hearing within four days of service of the application which would not give the respondent time to file an answer. The respondent is unlikely to be ready to defend an application for a permanent barring order within such a short period. The court may adjourn the application and it may grant interim relief by way of a temporary barring order. The rules and the 1981 Act are silent on this matter but some judges have taken the view that it is possible to grant an interim barring order.

5.059 Witness summonses are issued in accordance with order 21 of the Circuit Court Rules 1950 and, in accordance with rule 8, they are served personally. The advantage of a Circuit Court hearing is that the applicant and respondent have notice of each other's allegations. If reference is made to assaults, where the applicant needed a doctor, a notice to produce can be served under rule 4 seeking production of the medical reports in advance. This may not be complied with on the basis of a claim of privilege. Such medical reports are usually marked "Private and confidential: not to be shown to anyone other than the person to whom it is addressed". However, if the doctor consents, it may be better to comply with such a notice. The respondent may not be denying that an assault took place, but may allege that he is not the person who assaulted the applicant. If that is the case the solicitors and counsel on both sides may be able to agree to the admissibility of the reports, as the doctor is unable to say who committed the assault. If the application is vague on incidents or dates, it may be helpful to serve a notice for particulars,[5] under order 14 rule 3.

5.060 Under order 28 rule 1 the applicant can serve a notice to admit relevant documents for example, District Court records of previous barring orders, or copy orders of convictions for assault on the applicant. If the respondent fails or refuses to allow their admission, the court can order the costs of proving such documents against the respondent.

Hearing of the application

5.061 Section 14 of the 1981 Act provides that proceedings in the Circuit Court may be heard in chambers. If they are heard in the court proper they must be heard otherwise than in public. Practices vary from circuit to circuit, but usually they are heard in the court with all members of the public excluded. Solicitors and counsel are generally allowed to attend.

5.062 Rule 10 provides for applications for barring orders to be heard on oral evidence save by special leave of the court. Since the applicant is looking for an indeterminate order, it is necessary to outline incidents of violence or other misbehaviour throughout the marriage with the emphasis on more recent incidents. There may have been previous barring orders in the District Court. If there is a composite application under rule 11 before the court claiming several family law reliefs, the court may prefer to hear the application for barring and judicial separation first. The court may then make a ruling on these matters before dealing with the more practical consequential matters of custody and access to the children, and maintenance. This is probably the best way of dealing with such a case, as otherwise the judge and the parties can become distracted by detailed financial matters from the central issue of protecting the applicant from violence.

5.063 The court has the power under section 2(1)(b) of the 1981 Act to make a barring order "until further order", or until such other time as the court shall specify. In practice the Circuit Court will make the order until further order. The judge should be asked to make an additional order under section 2(2) of the 1981 Act. Section 15 provides that costs are at the discretion of the Court.

5.064 The registrar will draw up a draft order which will be engrossed and signed by the county registrar as someone authorised on his behalf. Rule 12 provides that a copy of the order is to be sent to the respondent spouse and the Gardaí. It is helpful if the applicant's solicitor sends a letter to the inspector in charge of the station also stating that "until further order" means an order of indefinite duration, and that it does not mean a temporary order. The legislation does not use the term "permanent", though in effect the order is permanent unless the respondent succeeds in having the barring order discharged. The applicant may want to serve the barring order personally on the respondent with the penal endorsement on it, so that if necessary, he can be brought to court for contempt for breach of the order. Under rule 25 of order 33 the standard endorsement is as follows: "If you the within named A.B., neglect to obey this order by the time herein limited, you will be liable to process of execution for the purpose of compelling you to obey the said order".

Appeals from the Circuit Court

5.065 The respondent has 10 days to lodge an appeal against the whole or part of the order. The respondent must apply for a stay on the order as otherwise the court may not impose a stay. If the Circuit Court refuses a stay he may apply for a stay to the High Court under the provisions of rule 6 of order 61 of the Rules of the Superior Courts. The Circuit Court office may be asked to expedite sending the file to the High Court so that the case will come into the Friday list and dates may be fixed as soon as possible. The respondent will usually seek the earliest date for the hearing of the appeal if no stay has been imposed on the order. The appeal will be a rehearing of the case. In accordance with section 39 of the Courts of Justice Act 1936, as applied to the High Court by section 48 of the Courts (Supplemental Provisions) Act 1961, *there is no further appeal.*

Breach of a Circuit Court barring order

5.066 Section 6, the offence section, applies to breaches of barring orders made in the Circuit Court, as well as the District Court. Section 6(2) states that the offence section is without prejudice to the law regarding contempt of court (see **18.073–18.076**). It is difficult to decide whether a respondent should be prosecuted for breach or attached and committed for contempt. It is much simpler to have the Gardaí arrest the respondent if it is a serious breach, and have him charged, rather than come back to court for contempt. However if the Gardaí are reluctant to prosecute, or if they are proposing to proceed by way of summons, it may be quicker to issue a notice of motion for contempt. The court may be more willing to attach and commit for contempt of a barring order more than any other family law order, as it is clear that the legislature has already laid down criminal penalties for breach. If there is a breach of an order under section 2(2), and the Gardaí are reluctant to prosecute it may be is necessary to proceed for contempt.

5.067 Repondents are ingenious in finding ways of harassing the applicant without apparently breaching an order under section 2(1). It may be necessary to seek a variation of the barring order, for example cover the respondent approaching the road where the applicant resides. If the court is reluctant to interpret section 2(2) in a broad way, to include harassment at the applicant's place of work, or the children's school, it may also be necessary to seek an injunction.

5.068 It is possible to apply to the Circuit Court for breach of a High Court barring order granted under the old section 22 of the Family Law (Maintenance of Spouses and Children) Act 1976. This is because section 17(2) provides that the 1981 Act applies to an order made under the old section 22, as if it were a barring order which included the prohibition of section 2(2). However there was no obligation under the old Act for copies of barring orders to be sent to the local Gardaí. It is good practice, if there are difficulties, to send them a copy of such order. Section 17(5) goes on to state that an order made under section 22 shall be treated as if it had been made by the Circuit Court, if it is to expire more than 12 months after it has been made. The rules do not provide any forms for this type of case, but if it is just an application for contempt a motion and affidavit exhibiting the High Court order may be sufficient if the Circuit Court decides to make a contempt order, at that stage a copy of the High Court order should be attached to the new order and sent to the local Gardaí. If it is an application to vary the High Court order the rules provide for an Application to be filed.

Variation and discharge of a Circuit Court barring order

5.069 Rule 3 provides for an application to be drafted, in accordance with Form No 2, for a variation or discharge of a barring order. Rule 10 provides that such application will be heard on oral evidence. There is no requirement for filing an answer, but it makes it easier to defend if it is filed. If the court decides to make a variation discharge order, rule 12 provides for a copy of the order to be given to the applicant, the respondent, and the local Gardaí.

Forms and precedents

5.070 District Court: Summons for a barring order

AN CHUIRT DUICHE   THE DISTRICT COURT
Rule 6   Form 1

FAMILY LAW (PROTECTION OF SPOUSES AND CHILDREN) ACT, 1981
   section 2.
 SUMMONS FOR A BARRING ORDER.

District Court Area of   District No.
Dublin Metropolitan District.

Applicant: Mary Tough

Respondent: Terence Tough.

YOU ARE HEREBY REQUIRED to appear at the District Court No. 11 at Dolphin House, East Essex Street, Dublin 2, on the 12th day of May 1989, at 2 p.m., to answer the application of your spouse, the above named applicant, residing at 3, Inlaw Road, Inchicore, Dublin 8, for an order of the court directing you to leave the family home at 3, Terrible Row, Terenure, Dublin 6, in the court area aforesaid, and prohibiting you from entering that family home until the Court so orders, on the ground that the safety or welfare of your spouse, and/or a child/children so requires.

Dated this 1st day of May 1989.

      Signed _____
          Justice of the District Court, or
          District Court Clerk.

To Terence Tough
of 3 Terrible Row,
Terenure,
Dublin 6.
Repondent

5.071 District Court: Information

Rule 8   Form 2.

FAMILY LAW (PROTECTION OF SPOUSES AND CHILDREN) ACT, 1981
   section 3(1).
   INFORMATION.

District Court Area of   District No.
Dublin Metropolitan District.

Applicant: Mary Tough

Respondent: Terence Tough

The information of the above named applicant of 3 Inlaw Road, Inchicore, Dublin 8, who says on oath: On the 1st day of May 1989, I caused a summons for District Court No. 11, Dolphin House, East Essex Street, Dublin 2, on the 12th day of May 1989, to be issued against my spouse, the respondent, applying pursuant to the provisions of section 2 of the above Act for a barring order in respect of the family home at 3 Terrible Row, Terenure, Dublin 6.

I now request a protection order against the respondent pursuant to the provisions of section 3 of the Act on the grounds: "The respondent assaulted me last night, as a result of which I sustained a fracture of my wrist, and a black eye."

Signed _____
Informant.

Sworn before me this 1st day of May 1989.

Signed _____
Justice of the District Court.

5.072 District Court: Protection Order

Rule 16   Form 7.

FAMILY LAW (PROTECTION OF SPOUSES AND CHILDREN) ACT, 1981
    section 3.

PROTECTION ORDER.

District Court Area of   District No.
Dublin Metropolitan District.

Applicant: Mary Tough.

Respondent: Terence Tough.

THE COURT HEREBY ORDERS that the above-named respondent shall not use or threaten to use violence against, molest or put in fear the above-named applicant or any child of the applicant who resides at 3 Inlaw Avenue, Inchicore, Dublin 8, in the court district aforesaid, having caused a summons to issue for the Court at No. 11. Dolphin House, East Essex Street, Dublin 2, on the 12th day of May 1989, at 2 p.m. pursuant to the provisions of section 2 of the above Act applying for a barring order against the respondent in respect of the family home at 3 Terrible Row, Terenure, Dublin 6, in the court district aforesaid, which application has not been determined and the Court being of opinion that there are reasonable grounds for believing that the safety/welfare of the applicant, and/or a child/children so requires.

Dated this 1st day of May 1989.

Signed _____
Justice of the District Court.

To Terence Tough,
of 3 Terrible Row,
Terenure,
Dublin 6.

5.073 District Court: Barring Order

Rule 16.   Form 6.

FAMILY LAW (PROTECTION OF SPOUSES AND CHILDREN) ACT 1981.

section 2.

Barring Order.

District Court Area of   District No.
Dublin Metropolitan District.

Applicant: Mary Tough.

Respondent: Terence Tough.

THE APPLICATION of the above-named applicant of 3 Inlaw Avenue, Inchicore, Dublin 8, in the court district aforesaid, for a barring order against the above-named respondent pursuant to the provisions of section 2(1) of the above Act coming by summons duly served before the Court this day and the Court on the evidence given being satisfied that the applicant and children reside(s) for the purpose of the section at the family home at 3 Terrible Tow, Terenure, Dublin 6, in the court district aforesaid, and being of opinion that there are reasonable grounds for believing that the safety/welfare of the applicant and/or child/children so requires,
NOW THE COURT HEREBY DIRECTS YOU, the respondent, to leave the family home at 3 Terrible Row, Terenure, Dublin 6 on being notified of the making of the order, AND PROHIBITS YOU FROM entering that family home until the 14th day of May 1990, without leave of the Court SAVE AND EXCEPT

AND FURTHER PROHIBITS YOU from using or threatening to use violence against, molesting or putting in fear the applicant and/or any such child during the period aforesaid.

Dated this 12th day of May 1989.

Signed _____

Justice of the District Court.

To Terence Tough,
3 Terrible Row,
Terenure,
Dublin 6.

WARNING.

A person who disobeys this order may be arrested without warrant by a member of the Garda Síochána and, on conviction for a first offence, may be fined £200 or sentenced to six months imprisonment, or be both fined and imprisoned.
A copy of this order is being sent to the Garda Síochána Station at Terenure.

5.074 Circuit Court: Application for a barring order

THE CIRCUIT COURT.

DUBLIN CIRCUIT   COUNTY OF THE CITY OF
                                 DUBLIN.

FAMILY LAW (PROTECTION OF SPOUSES AND CHILDREN) ACT 1981.

SECTION 2(1).

APPLICATION FOR A BARRING ORDER.

BETWEEN:

Mary Tough.

APPLICANT

and

Terence Tough

RESPONDENT

TAKE NOTICE that the above named Applicant of 3, Terrible Row, Terenure, in the City of Dublin, hereby applies to the Court sitting at Court No. 21, Arus Ui Dhálaigh, Inns Quay, in the City of Dublin, pursuant to Section 2 Subsection 1 of the above Act for an Order requiring the Respondent to leave the premises (or, where the Respondent is no longer residing there, prohibiting the Respondent from entering the premises) at 3 Terrible Row, Terenure, in the City of Dublin, where the Applicant and/or a child/children within the meaning of the Act resides and (where the Respondent has been living there) and prohibiting the Respondent from entering that place until further Order by the Court or until such time as the Court shall specify, and for such further or other Order as the Court thinks fit, together with an Order providing for the costs of the application.

AND TAKE NOTICE that the Applicant will rely on the following matters in support of the application:

1. The applicant and the respondent were married on the 9th day of April 1975 at the Church or Our Lady of Refuge, Rathmines, in the City of Dublin.
2. The following children (within the meaning of the above Act) reside at the place described above, namely Brian born the 9th day of September 1975, Linda born the 12th day of November 1978, and Tony born the 15th day of May 1985.
3. The safety and/or welfare of the Applicant and/or of the child/children mentioned in paragraph 2 above require the making of a Barring Order in that throughout the marriage, from time to time the Respondent has been violence towards the Applicant.
4. The Respondent has been drinking heavily since the first child Brian was born. He has frequently threatened to assault the Applicant. He has terrorised the Applicant, coming home in an intoxicated state

every Friday, and has frequently assaulted the Applicant on these occasions.

5. In particular, on the 30th day of April 1989, the Respondent assaulted the Applicant causing her severe bruising on her arms and legs and a black eye. As a result of this incident the Applicant applied for a barring order in the District Court. The Respondent was barred for a period of twelve months as and from the 12th day of May 1989.

6. In or about the 29th day of December 1989, the Respondent arrived at the family home situate at 3 Terrible Row, Terenure, in the City of Dublin, in a very intoxicated state. He demanded to see the children and he forced his way into the said family home. The Respondent thumped the Applicant on the side of her head as a result of which she fell. He further used foul and abusive language. The children witnessed this incident and the Applicant's son, Brian, attempted to intervene, but the Respondent slapped him across the face. The Respondent then left the home.

7. The Applicant has suffered severe anxiety as a result of the Respondent's behaviour. The Applicant's General Practitioner has prescribed anti-depressants and sleeping tablets. The youngest child Tony insists in sleeping in the same bed as the Applicant as he is afraid of his father the Respondent. The applicant and the children remain in constant fear of the Respondent returning to the family home. It is not in the interests of the Applicant and the children that the Respondent be allowed to return to the family home.

(insert this paragraph, even though it is not contained in the Circuit Court Rules)

AND TAKE NOTICE that if you intend to dispute the Applicant's claim, or any part thereof, you must within four days of the service of this Application on you, file with the County Registrar, in the Circuit Court Family Law Office, at Arus Ui Dhálaigh, Inns Quay, in the City of Dublin, an Answer in the form prescribed in the Rules of the Circuit Court.

AND TAKE NOTICE that this Application will be mentioned before the Court at 11 o'clock on the 7th day of May 1990, and shall be heard on that day or on such date as the court may fix for the hearing thereof.

Dated the 27th day of April 1990

Signed _____

Sally Solicitor,
Solicitor for the Applicant,
Law Centre,
Litigation Quay,
Dublin 29.

To Terence Tough,
Salvation Army Hostel,
Mercer Street,
Dublin 1.

5.075 Affidavit grounding a protection order application

Insert the usual averments, and the background history, and continue, by way of a sample paragraph, as follows:

3. I say and believe that on account of the Respondent's behaviour, I have instituted proceedings under the Family Law (Protection of Spouses and Children) Act 1981. I say that I am also seeking a decree of Judicial Separation. I beg to refer to the Matrimonial Civil Bill (or Application, under the new Judicial Separation Act 1989)., and the Application, insofar as they are within my own knowledge, are true to the best of my knowledge, information and belief. I say that I fear for my safety and the safety and welfare of my children. I pray this Honourable Court for a Protection Order pursuant to Section 3(1) of the 1981 Act, that the Respondent shall not use or threaten to use violence against, molest or put in fear this Deponent, or the children of the marriage.

5.076 Circuit Court: Answer to an application for a barring order

[insert the same headings as the Application]

     ANSWER.

TAKE NOTICE that the above named Respondent of the Salvation Army Hostel, Mercer Street in the City of Dublin, disputes the claims made in the Application made pursuant to the Family Law (Protection of Spouses and Children) Act 1981, to the extent indicated hereunder:

The said Application was served upon the Respondent on the 1st day of May 1990.

AND TAKE NOTICE that the Respondent will rely upon the following matters in disputing the Applicant's said claims:

1. The Respondent herein denies that during the marriage he has been violent towards the Applicant or that he verbally abused her, whether as alleged or at all.
2. (Set out, in numbered paragraphs, the grounds upon which the Applicants claim is disputed, and whether the Respondent is denying them— this should occur in the same sequence as the Applicant has detailed her allegations.
3. The Respondent herein prays this Honourable Court to refuse the Applicant's claim herein, and is anxious to return to reside in the family home.

Dated the 4th of May 1990.

                  Signed _____

                  Richard Solicitor,
                  Solicitor for the Respondent,
                  Mercer Solicitors,
                  Dublin 2.

To Sally Solicitor,
Law Centre,
Litigation Quay,
Dublin 29.

Chapter 6

INJUNCTIONS

Uses of injunctions

6.001 An extensive exposition of the general law on injunctions could not be attempted in this Book. For a more detailed treatment, readers are referred to Chapter 15 of *Equity and the Law of Trusts in the Republic of Ireland* by Judge Ronan Keane (Butterworths, 1987). Injunctions are now used less frequently by spouses as the barring order is cheaper, the procedure is simpler, and it has criminal remedies for breach of its orders. In contrast, the injunction has only civil remedies for its breach and there are more complicated pleadings. However, injunctions can be used as necessary to compensate for the narrow scope of the Family Law (Protection of Spouses and Children) Act 1981. They are used most frequently where a spouse subsequently resides with another partner, who is violent, and whom she wishes to exclude. A barring order is not available in these circumstances. Injunctions may also be sought in the following circumstances:

1. A person who is seeking a decree of nullity, or who has already obtained one, may wish to have the former "spouse" removed from the home. An injunction may be sought in lieu of a barring order, in case the latter is regarded as approbation in subsequent nullity proceedings. The statement of Costello J. in *D. v C.* that since the validity of the petitioner's marriage was not put in issue in her earlier barring proceedings, there was no estoppel *per res judicata*, has to be weighed against his other statement' that the petitioner did not know that her husband's illness entitled her to a nullity decree until after the barring.
2. A spouse may seek an injunction to restrain watching and besetting where it occurs on the public highway adjacent to the family home. It may be thought that the wife should have sought an order under section 2(2) of the Family Law (Protection of Spouses and Children)

Act 1981 which states "The court may also prohibit a spouse from using or threatening to use violence against, molesting or putting in fear a spouse or any child of the marriage". This order is rarely sought in the Circuit Court, and the Gardai rarely prosecute breaches of it. This is because they take the view that section 6, the offence section, relates to breaches of barring orders proper, that is orders under section 2(1) ordering the respondent out of the family home.

3. An injunction may be sought to restrain harassment at the spouse's place of work or business, or on the public highway.

4. A spouse may seek to restrain communication by telephone or letter where these methods of communication are used as harassment.

5. Where a spouse has a barring order, but has allowed the respondent spouse back into the family home, the applicant spouse may have difficulties in enforcing it she may seek an injunction instead. This is where she revokes the prior invitation and seeks enforcement. Justices are reluctant to convict on such prosecution because of the issue of invitation and this deters the Gardai prosecuting such breaches.

6. An injunction may be sought to restrain a spouse who has been barred from molesting or harassing a child of the marriage, who is not residing with the applicant spouse. This is especially useful in cases of physical or sexual abuse where the child is residing with a relative or is a resident of a hostel or other institution.

7. An injunction may be sought on an *ex parte* basis in a case of extreme urgency to order a respondent spouse who has been violent to the applicant or the children where there would be undue delay in obtaining a date for hearing. This is useful in cases outside Dublin where the Circuit Court lists for family law are infrequent and where a judge may give more priority to an application for emergency equitable relief.

The situation before 1976

6.002 It is not easy to elicit clear principles from the cases. Their common thread is an allegation of violence. The usual equitable principles governing the granting of injunctions apply to matrimonial injunctions.

6.003 In *O'Malley v O'Malley*[2] the wife sought an interlocutory injunction restraining the husband from remaining in possession of the matrimonial home which was her property. She alleged that he had behaved in a violent and aggressive way and was terrorising the servants. The High Court refused to grant the injunction and this refusal was upheld by the Supreme Court. O'Byrne J. noted that there was no suggestion of any matrimonial offence by the husband which would justify her living apart from her husband. A conditional order of habeas corpus had been obtained by the

1 [1984] ILRM 173.
2 [1951] 85 ILTR 43.

husband, but the wife had already gone to the United States so the order was not served on her. She had left one child behind with the father. The court accepted an undertaking from him not to remove furniture or stock pending the hearing of the substantive action thus preserving the status quo. The court was not prepared to grant an order which would deprive him of his right to remain where he had lived for a number of years. There was no evidence that the wife would suffer irreparable damage if the injunction were refused. In the 1970's as the number of matrimonial cases in the High Court increased the courts became more willing to grant relief.

6.004 In *M.K. v U.K.*[3] the wife had to leave home with the children after a history of assaults by the husband on her and the children. She claimed that her husband was in constructive desertion as he had forced her to leave the home. Kenny J. ordered that the husband be restrained from molesting her or the children and that he vacate the home. He was further restrained from re-entering the home.

6.005 In *M.C. v L.C.*[4] the wife had also left the home. While the husband was away she returned and changed the locks. She then applied for an injunction *ex parte* restraining him from assaulting or molesting her. Kenny J. granted the order, and later granted an interlocutory injunction until the trial of the substantive procedings under the Guardianship of Infants Act 1964 and the Married Women's Status Act 1957.

6.006 In *Conway v Conway*[5], Kenny J. granted an injunction restraining the husband from entering the family home. The evidence before the court was of frequent assaults and insults; the Gardai had been called on several occasions. The husband disconnected the telephone and cut off the electricity. There was "coercive evidence" that the children were frightened of him and a social worker gave evidence that the children reacted badly to him. Kenny J. relied on Lord Denning's judgment in *Gurasz v Gurasz*,[6] to the effect that, in an extreme case, if his conduct is so outrageous as to make it impossible for them to live together, the court will order him to get out and leave her there. Lord Denning also referred to a husband's duty to provide a wife with a roof over her head and this was a personal right which the court will enforce by way of an injunction. It is available irrespective of the title to the home. Kenny J. concluded that the husband's behaviour in the case before him had been so outrageous and had such a bad effect on the children, that an injunction should be granted. The injunction was made restraining the husband from entering the home, although he was the owner of a half share of it.

3 1975, unreported, High Court. There was no written judgment.
4 1975, unreported, High Court. There was no written judgment.
5 [1976] IR 254.
6 [1969] All ER 822.

The situation after 1976

6.007 The introduction of the barring order remedy in the Family Law (Maintenance of Spouses and Children) 1976 diminished the need for injunction proceedings. In *R.K. v M.K.*[7] in which a barring order and injunction were refused, Finlay P. stated "there is no general principle which would inhibit me from making a barring order, or the equivalent, in the form of an injunction, merely because the spouse to be barred carried on business in portion of the premises concerned". (See **4.004**).

6.008 In *R. v R.*,[8] an injunction was granted by O'Hanlon J. restraining the husband from entering the family home, primarily in the interests of the children. O'Hanlon J. indicated that the particular case had circumstances which were less aggravated than *M.K. v U.K.*, and *Conway v Conway*. However the welfare of the children had been jeopardised in a significant manner by the matters complained of by the husband. The wife had left the family home with the 3 children some eight months prior to the court hearing. She resided with her mother in very cramped conditions. However the accommodation soon became inadequate and she decided that she had no alternative but to issue proceedings. She issued a special summons seeking, *inter alia*, an injunction restraining the husband from entering the home. Evidence was furnished of the husband's over-possessiveness and jealousy, his personal hygiene, his behaviour in the home, his personal habits, and constant arguments and rows. The husband denied the allegations and he argued that she was adulterous. There was no mention of any physical violence. O'Hanlon J. stated: "The combination of these factors had created a situation where there was tension and friction on a fairly constant basis, which, I conclude, was harmful to the wife and very detrimental to the children". The injunction was granted ordering the husband to vacate the family home pending the full hearing or until further order. A further injunction was made restraining him from attending at, or entering upon or attempting to enter the house. He was further restrained from molesting or interfering with her, and from watching or besetting her in the family home or in her place of work, or elsewhere.

6.009 The most recent written judgment is that delivered by Murphy J. in *F. v F.*[9] The wife sought orders of custody and maintenance, and an injunction restraining the husband from entering the family home. There is no explanation offered in the judgment as to why barring proceedings under section 22 of the Family Law (Maintenance of Spouses and Children) Act 1976 were not issued. The Family Law (Protection of Spouses and Children) Act 1981 came into force on 24 July 1981, though presumably the proceedings were issued prior to that date. The wife alleged violence, including being kicked on the floor, and an assault that resulted in a suspected fractured rib. She further alleged that sexual

---

7   24 October 1978, unreported, High Court.
8   16 December 1981, unreported, High Court.
9   20 May 1982, unreported, High Court.

intercourse had taken place against her will the week before the hearing. Murphy J. commented that the first incident was not mentioned in her affidavit. She had not complained to her doctor about the source of her injuries, but had pretended that she fell against a table. She also alleged adultery, that the husband was out most of the time and that he had threatened to take her life by giving her an overdose of insulin. Murphy J. refused to grant an injunction on the basis that he was not satisfied that the safety or welfare of the wife or children required the exclusion of the defendant from the family home. He adjourned the case to see if the parties could resolve their difficulties, or else enter into a deed of separation. If the husband did not try harder to build a more tolerable domestic relationship then he might grant the injunction. The principles that Murphy J. used, which he stated to be relevant to the granting of an injunction, were those applicable to barring orders. In other words, the court should be satisfied "That there are reasonable grounds for believing that the safety or welfare of that spouse or any dependant child of the family requires it". He further noted that there were no proceedings for a divorce *a mensa et thoro* before him. He did not state why this might be relevant though he may have been referring to the remarks of Porter MR in *Gaynor v Gaynor*[10] where an injunction was refused, where he stated; I have a great objection to do indirectly what could be done directly by proper proceedings, viz, to grant a judicial separation".

6.010 The principle laid down by Murphy J. of relying on the criteria applicable to barring orders, may result in the courts adopting the more stringent approach *O'B. v O'B.* in deciding whether to grant a matrimonial injunction. It is hoped that this will not be so, as the injunction is a flexible equitable remedy, which can be applied for in many circumstances. The facts outlined in *F. v F.* should have been sufficient to grant an injunction (or a barring order).

Jurisdiction of the courts to grant injunctions

Statutory basis

6.011 Section 28(8) of the Judicature (Ireland) Act 1877 empowered the courts to grant interlocutory relief where it was just and convenient to do so. The Courts (Supplemental Provisions) Act 1961 vested in the High Court the common law and equitable jurisdiction vested in its predecessor. The Circuit Court under section 22 of that act has power to grant injunctions though the rateable valuation of the property concerned should not exceed £200. Order 17 of the Circuit Court Rules 1950 regulates the power to grant ad interim injunctions. The District Court has no jurisdiction to grant injunctions.

6.012 Prior to the Courts Act 1981 most matrimonial injunctions were granted in the High Court. Now it is more usual to issue the injunction

10   [1901] IR 217.

proceedings in the Circuit Court as the substantive action in which the interlocutory relief is sought will be granted in the Circuit Court. However, in vacation, the Dublin Circuit Court is usually the only Circuit Court which has sittings, and applicants from other Circuits cannot move in Dublin. However, order 1, rule 2 of the Circuit Court Rules provides for no sittings of the Circuit Court in August and September. Under rule 3, the Dublin Circuit Court is usually the only Circuit Court which has sittings. As applicants from other Circuits cannot apply in the Dublin Circuit Court they may apply to the High Court vacation judge for an injunction. Nevertheless rule 4 allows urgent applications *at any time or place approved by a judge*. This power derives from section 22(11) of the Courts (Supplemental Provisions) Act 1961. Section 22(14) states that a Circuit Court judge may make, out of court, any orders which he may deem to be urgent.

The rules of equity

6.013 The general equitable principles govern the granting of matrimonial injunctions. The principle "He who comes to equity must do so with clean hands" means that the plaintiff must have conducted himself properly, and there must not have been *undue delay*. Plaintiffs often delay out of a sense of fear or powerlessness. If a reasonable explanation for the delay is offered in the pleadings it will probably be accepted, though the court may adopt a stricter view in relation to property injunctions. If for example, the plaintiff wife seeks an injunction to restrain her husband from putting the house up for sale, when she has been aware for some time that this was his intention and she only now seeks a share of the family home, the court may question why she has not issued proceedings earlier under the Married Women's Status Act 1957. He cannot in any event sell it without her consent, under the Family Home Protection Act 1976, though the consent to sale is usually endorsed at the contract stage. Delay was a factor in refusing relief in *O'Malley v O'Malley*[11] where the wife could have taken steps to obtain judgment if the defendant had not filed a defence, and she could have delivered her statement of claim when the appearance was entered.

Types of injunction

Prohibitory and mandatory

6.014 The most common matrimonial injunction is for an order restraining the defendant from entering the family home, and from molesting or assaulting the applicant and the children.

The same willingness of the courts to grant injunctions between husband and wife, did not always apply to injunctions sought by a spouse against a son or daughter. In *Cullen v Cullen*[12] Kenny J. refused to grant an injunction to restrain sons from interfering in the father's business and

11   [1951] 85 ILTR 43.
12   [1962] IR 268.

from trespassing on the family home. He stated that "relations between fathers and sons should not be govered by the heavy artillery of court orders, injunctions or the threat of committal to prison but by respect, affection, honour and the feeling of moral obligation". It is now not uncommon for a parent to obtain an injunction against a child of the marraige, who is usually over 18 years, from entering a family home, where he has been guilty of violence. Of course, the barring remedy is not available because it can only be obtained against a spouse.

6.015 The court will usually grant a prohibitory injunction and a mandatory injunction The mandatory injunction orders the defendant to do a particular thing, for example, to leave the family home. The prohibitory injunction restrains the defendant from doing certain things, for example, restraining him from entering the family home. In family law cases, it may be easier to obtain a prohibitory injunction than mandatory injunction especially if the mandatory injunction sought is akin to an order of specific performance of a contract. For example, there may be a clause in a deed of separation in which one spouse agrees to leave the family home and not to molest the remaining spouse, and not to enter or approach the home without the resident spouse's consent. If the defendant spouse refuses to leave or refuses to stop calling to the home, an injunction may be sought by way of a mandatory order, to force him to comply. A mandatory injunction may be granted, provided proceedings for specific performance are also issued. Alternatively an injunction could be sought based on the history of misbehaviour, rather than just relying on the deed of separation, to order the defendant out of the home. An injunction may be sought as a substantive remedy, for example, an injunction ordering a spouse to leave the home. After a full hearing a perpetual injunction may be granted in these terms. More usually an injunction will be used as a remedy to preserve the status quo pending the full hearing on contested issues of fact between the parties. This could be an issue of custody, access, child abduction, property or maintenance.

Interim or *ex parte* injunctions

6.016 Order 40 rule 20 of the Rules of the Superior Courts provides that the court has power to grant an interim or temporary injunction, on an *ex parte* basis, that is, without notice to the other party. This should only be applied for in cases of great urgency. Order 17 should be used for interim and interlocutory applications. The onus is on the plaintiff to set out all the facts of the case and in particular why the order should be granted on an *ex parte* basis.

6.017 In family law matters, this is usually sought on the basis that the plaintiff and the defendant are residing in the same house and that, if the defendant is to be served with proceedings in advance, he is likely to assault or intimidate the plaintiff. The ex parte procedure should be used only if relief is required *immediately*, rather than waiting four days for a

133

hearing by way of notice of motion. If the defendant is not residing with the plaintiff, but an injunction is sought to restrain him from coming to the family home, it may be advisable to await an application for an interlocutory injunction, on notice to him. Each case depends on its own facts, and it is from these facts, guided by the case law, that an objective assessment must be made as to whether the application should be made *ex parte* or on notice.

So for example, if a man threatens to set the family home on fire, and it is his first threat of that nature it may be decided that it was a threat made in the heat of the moment, and that an injunction on notice is preferred. If however, he had previous convictions for arson, or he had made previous attempts to set the house on fire, even in a half hearted way, such a threat would warrant immediate action on an *ex parte* basis.

6.018 The term "irreparable or serious mischief", as used in order 51 of the Rules of the Superior Courts is a guide to deciding whether action on an *ex parte* basis is warranted. The corresponding English rule was considered in *Hipgrave v Hipgrave*.[13] In that case the husband had already given an undertaking to the court not to assault or molest the wife and not to visit the home. He made an attempt to run her down with his car. An *ex parte* application was made to commit him to prison for contempt, for breach of his undertaking. The court heard the wife and a detective sergeant in evidence. The husband's solicitor and counsel were notified to attend though they had no instructions from their client. The court, noting that they could take no part in the proceedings, made an order to commit him forthwith to prison. However, he had the right to apply to set the order aside.

Interlocutory injunctions

6.019 An application for an interlocutory injunction is an application, on notice to the other party, to seek orders to preserve the status quo or to protect the plaintiff from further harm, pending the full hearing in which a perpetual injunction will be sought, and the trial of the substantive issues between the parties. An interlocutory injunction is important because it brings the litigation to an end. By the time the action comes on for trial, the position of the parties may have changed and court intervention is no longer needed. Some of the most frequent orders, at the interlocutory stage, are: ordering the defendant to leave the family home, restraining him from leaving the country, or restraining access to children, where there are allegations of abuse of the children.

6.020 The Supreme Court's decision in *Campus Oil Ltd v Minister for Industry and Energy and others (No2)*[14] clarified the principles on which a court should act in considering the granting of interlocutory relief:

13   [1962] All ER 75.
14   [1983] IR 88; [1984] ILRM 45.

1. Such relief will be granted where what is complained of is continuing and is causing harm or injury which may be irreparable, in the sense that it may not fairly or properly be compensated for in damages.
2. It is designed to keep matters in status quo during the period before the action comes for trial, and is a discretionary relief.
3. In disputed cases, the court must not only consider the action complained of, but also what inconvenience, loss or damage might be caused by the other party, and see where the balance of convenience lies between the two.
4. The plaintiffs have to establish that there is a fair question to be decided at the trial.
5. It is not necessary to establish a probability that the party seeking relief would succeed in his claim at the trial. That would amount to a determination, at the interlocutory stage, of an issue which properly arises for determination at the trial.

6.021 These principles were confirmed by the Supreme Court in *Irish Shell v Elm Motors*.[15] It was held that it was no part of the court's function at the interlocutory stage, to try to resolve conflicts of evidence on affidavit, nor to decide difficult questions of law which call for detailed argument and mature consideration. While reserving the question as to whether there are exceptional cases, in which it is proper to express a concluded view as to factual or legal issues, the determination of whether to grant an interlocutory injunction ordinarily lay only in answers to the two material questions (1) whether there is a fair case to be made and (2) where the balance of convenience lies. The Court concluded that the relevant date for the determination of the balance of convenience and the status quo which should be maintained, is the date the judgment of the court is delivered.

6.022 It is at the interlocutory stage that the plaintiff is expected to give an undertaking as to damages to the court. This is still frequently requested and given in family law cases, even if the applicant is legally aided. It is in the following terms; "that the plaintiff will abide by any order which this court may make as to damages, in case this court shall be of opinion that the defendant shall have sustained any, by reason of this order, which the plaintiff ought to pay".

Perpetual injunctions

6.023 The court may grant a perpetual injunction where there is no other remedy. In non-family law matters, damages are not usually relevant unless property or money is involved, or damages are sought for injury caused by the respondent.

6.024 The judge in a family law case may consider whether prosecution of the defendant for his acts of violence would be more appropriate, though usually this would not be seen as appropriate. The plaintiff may be asked

---

15   [1984] ILRM 595.

whether she has made complaints to the Gardai or other independent persons. However, judges are usually aware that spouses are reluctant to use the criminal law procedure.

Quia timet injunctions

6.025 Where there have been threats of violence, or threats to do something which will breach or damage the plaintiff's rights then a *quia timet* injunction may be sought. It is granted on the basis that there is a strong probability that damage will occur. The most appropriate use is where the defendant has made threats to take the children out of the country, but has not actually done so; or where threats of violence have been made, though not actually carried out. Since threats of violence are common in cases of marital disharmony, it is unlikely that an injunction will be granted on this basis alone, but, if accompanied by a background of past violence, especially of a serious nature, then it may be worth applying.

Checklist for injunction proceedings

Details needed

6.026 The following details should be obtained from the client before any proceedings are commenced:

1. Names and addresses, and telephone numbers of both parties. It is possible that an injunction will be sought against relatives of the respondent who may be party to the harassment of the petitioner. Their names and addresses should be obtained even if they are not to be named in the pleadings.
2. Names and dates of birth of any children.
3. Nature of ownership or possession of the accommodation that is relevant to the injunction.
4. The date the parties ceased living together, if applicable.
5. Full history of the relationship between the spouses, with particular relevance to the type of injunction that is likely to be applied for.
6. If the injunction applied for is to exclude the respondent from the home, details of all alternative accommodation available to him.
7. Names, addresses and statements of witnesses who can corroborate client's history.
8. Names and addresses of any potential professional witnesses, and any other independent witnesses.
9. Detailed physical description of the respondent, including a photograph if possible. Photographs should strictly be proved by having the person who developed the negatives attend at court. However, in some family law cases, photographs taken by relatives or by passport machines have been accepted.
10. Any other information as regards the respondent's movements, for example, the time and place of signing on at the local labour exchange, the address of any public house, or club that he frequents.

Steps to be taken

6.027 After the preliminary details have been obtained, the following steps should be taken:

1. Check out the allegations by telephone with any independent witnesses or professional witnesses, having secured a consent (preferably written) from the client.
2. Send instructions (preferably typed) to counsel for drafting of the relevant proceedings.
3. Telephone the valuation office (County Registrar for areas outside Dublin) to request a certificate of rateable valuation for the relevant premises, and arrange for it to be collected or posted.
4. Obtain medical reports and social work reports, or any other relevant reports.
5. Obtain photographic evidence, if the injuries are still clearly visible. There may be difficulties providing such evidence, and this must be weighed against the trouble of obtaining such evidence. (See **6.026** — note 9).
6. Obtain marriage certificate and childrens' birth certificates, if relevant.
7. If there has been such a serious assault that it is likely to result in a prosecution, then the client should be encouraged to make a separate complaint to the Gardai. The Gardai do not have a clear policy on domestic disputes. Much discretion is left with the individual officer, to weigh the facts of each case, and decide, in consultation with his superiors, whether or not to prosecute for common assault. There is no point in doing so unless the client is willing to give evidence in a public court against a spouse.
8. Check out that the correct circuit, where either party resides, or carries on their business, profession or occupation, has been identified.

Court documents and preparatory work

Note: the following discussion covers only the Circuit Court procedure as most applications are made in that Court.

Equity civil bill

6.028 An equity civil bill is the originating document; this is provided for by order 5 rule 4 of the Circuit Court Rules. It must set out in the indorsement of claim the facts grounding the application. Order 5 rule 2 provides that the civil bill must state such facts as may be necessary to show the jurisdiction of the court. The rateable valuation of the land or premises must not exceed £200. The civil bill must be signed by the solicitor.

Affidavit

6.029 A grounding affidavit must be filed setting out the facts grounding the civil bill in more detail. The facts should include those facts as give rise to seeking the substantive order; the facts grounding the interlocutory relief, and the application on an *ex parte* basis. The affidavit should set out any defence that is likely to be made, any facts that would be likely to lead the court to refuse relief on an ex parte basis, and the precise nature of the relief claimed. It may be helpful to put in a specific undertaking as to damages, so that the client understands the commitment requested. The client must check the affidavit before swearing it, and frequently it has to be amended, and perhaps engrossed, again.

Ex parte docket[3]

6.030 Order 17 rule 2 allows *ex parte* applications to be made. There is a standard form available from law stationers, otherwise entitled a "general requisition" form, which sets out briefly that an interim injunction is sought, and the names of the parties. The form is then signed by the solicitor.

Attendance at Circuit Court office

6.031 The registrar checks that the documentation is in order, after the relevant documents have been stamped. In Dublin stamping takes place at the Stamping Office in Arus Ui Dhálaigh, Inns Quay, adjacent to the Four Courts, and outside Dublin by posting an office cheque with the documents to the relevant Circuit Court office. The registrar will determine in what court the case will be listed and when. The urgency of the matter should be stressed, to ensure the earliest possible date. If the Circuit Court office is not accessible, the documents may have to be posted by express post, by arrangement, or by courier.

If the documents are in order as provided for by order 10 rule 1 the civil bill can be issued. It cannot be issued unless the civil bill is stamped. The affidavit is stamped and the original is lodged, and a copy can be franked with the stamp of the Circuit Court office. The *ex parte* docket is lodged with the original civil bill. A copy of all documents should be retained by the solicitor. The original civil bill will be retained until the interim order is granted, and it is then returned, as it is needed for service purposes.

Service of equity civil bill on an ex parte application

6.032 Under order 10 rule 1 a civil bill is deemed to be issued when it is served by registered post on the defendant at his place of business or home or, if it is a civil bill officer area, when it is posted or handed to him for service on the defendant. Section 7(6)(1) of the Courts Act 1964 provides that a civil bill is deemed to be issued when the envelope is posted. Usually the risk is not taken of posting the civil bill in advance, as the rationale of obtaining an order without the knowledge of the defendant is then lost. The defendant may further assault the plaintiff if he is aware of the proceedings prior to any order.

6.033 It is a copy of the civil bill that is posted to the defendant. Therefore, the civil bill can be posted prior to the application for an ex parte order, though the affidavit, the interim order, and notice of motion for an interlocutory injunction, can only be served personally. If the civil bill can only be served by an official civil bill officer, then the civil bill cannot be served in advance, as it is retained by the registrar until after the interim order is granted.

Circuit Court procedure

Privacy

6.034 Section 45(1) of the Courts (Supplemental Provisions) Act 1961 allows applications for an injunction to be heard in private. In addition, order 17 rule 1 of the Circuit Court Rules provides that applications which would be more conveniently disposed of in chambers may be so heard by the judge. If the application is being made in the family law list, it will be heard in camera. If it is on an equity list, then application can be made to clear the court. This can be difficult, especially in a crowded Circuit Court outside Dublin. It may not be necessary, at the interim stage, to clear the court as the plaintiff will usually not be present and the case is heard on affidavit. Judges usually read the papers privately and the parties may be referred to in court as the plaintiff and the defendant.

Interim relief

6.035 If interim relief is sought and the application is not in camera, the court can be asked to grant an interim injunction in the terms of paragraph 1, 2, (etc), of the civil bill. Service of the order or notice of the making of it should be clarified. Usually, if the address of then defendant is known, service will be personal on the basis of a return date of approximately 4 days hence for the motion for the interlocutory injunction. Notice of the making of the order, while one is awaiting the order, can be given by telephone, by registered or prepaid ordinary or express post, by courier, fax, or by telemessage. It is quite common not to notify the defendant personally in advance of service of the order, as the element of surprise is critical to the success of an injunction. If he is aware that an order has been made he may make efforts to evade service. The order is of little use if it is not served personally, because of the law on contempt. An order must be served personally with the penal notice endorsed, before a defendant can be attached or committed for contempt. However, each case depends on its own facts, and a solicitor must make the appropriate decision. Costs are usually reserved.

Obtaining an interim order

6.036 If the interim injunction has been granted, the registrar draws up a draft order as soon as possible. This will usually be on the same day, though that may not be possible in a court sitting on circuit. The order is engrossed and the draft and order lodged in duplicate, for signing by the county registrar. The original is stamped. In an injunction dealt with in the Dublin Circuit Court family law office it is usual to endorse on the back of the draft order that it has been compared with the original, and the solicitor certifies on the back that it is a true copy of the original draft order. The attested copy is left out for collection, duly signed by the county registrar. The next most important step for the solicitor is to endorse the penal notice at the end of the order. Order 33 rule 5 provides for the penal notice as follows: "If you the within named John Defendant neglect to obey this judgment or order by the time therein limited, you will be liable to process of execution for the purpose of compelling you to obey the said judgment or order". If the defendant has a low standard of education, or of understanding, it is helpful to accompany the order with a letter explaining this in plain English. The original civil bill will have been collected, so that it can be shown to the defendant, if it is being served personally.

Notice of motion

6.037 A Notice of Motion for an interlocutory injunction should be drafted and typed while the solicitor is awaiting the interim order. The notice of motion seeks an interlocutory order in the same terms as the civil bill, and in addition there may be a prayer to deem service of the civil bill and interim order good and sufficient. Where an interim order has been made under order 51 rule 3 the same affidavit grounds the notice of motion. If no interim order was applied for, then the motion is issued with the civil bill, and the grounding affidavit is filed in the office. Order 51 rule 2 deals with the length of the notice. The rules provide for four clear days between the service of a notice of motion and the date of hearing, unless a judge grants special leave to the contrary.

Service of the civil bill

6.038 The civil bill, affidavit, notice of motion and interim order may be served personally, in accordance with order 10 rule 4. Alternatively the civil bill may be served by registered post and the interim order, affidavit and notice of motion may be served personally, because of the shortness of time before the hearing. An affidavit of service of the affidavit, interim order and notice of motion should be lodged as soon as possible. The original civil bill is endorsed with service by the civil bill officer or the summons server, or if a true copy was sent by post, then a statutory declaration of service is sworn, but the top part of the third page of the civil bill must also be endorsed in accordance with order 10 rule 6. The original is usually lodged in the Circuit Court office prior to the hearing of the interlocutory injunction, despite the fact that order 10 rule 15 provides for it being lodged within 8 days of service. There is stamp duty on the entry and S.I. 202 of 1985 provides for it to be lodged within a period of not less than 10 days and not more than 18 days, if it has been served in accordance with the rules governing registered post provided by section 7 of Courts Act 1964.

Acting for the defendant in an injunction case

6.039 The defendant has usually been served with notice of the making of an *ex parte* injunction or with the order, when he first contacts a solicitor. A full background history should be taken *before* he is asked to comment on the civil bill or the plaintiff's affidavit. This makes for a more logical set of instructions. Then a separate statement should be taken, detailing his replies to the plaintiff's affidavit. This makes it easier for counsel to draft a replying affidavit and defence. It should be stressed to the client, that he should strictly comply with the order, until the matter comes up in the list. In particular, the order should be examined to see whether it contains a penal endorsement. If it does, the client should be told that non compliance could mean committal to prison. It usually takes a few days for the matter to appear on the list. Order 51 rule 4 provides for 4 clear days notice unless there is special leave to the contrary. If a mandatory injunction has been granted, ordering him to leave the family home he is obviously anxious to defend the allegations, and secure the quickest hearing. At this stage, the plaintiff may not be inclined to expedite matters. Instructions need to be clarified as to whether the solicitor is authorised to give an undertaking to the court and if so on what terms, and whether the defendant wants to defend the case to a full trial, or just to deny the allegations made, to retain as much dignity as possible. It may be the case that the relationship between the parties to the injunction will have deteriorated, and the defendant may decide that he does not wish to return home but yet does not want the stigma of an order continuing against him.

6.040 Order 51 rule 1 provides that any party affected by an *ex parte* order may apply to set aside such an order. This can be done by motion and affidavit but it is unlikely that it will be listed on a date earlier than the motion for the interlocutory injunction. The solicitor for the plaintiff needs to be contacted, to obtain his consent to adjourn the motion and to give time to enter an appearance, and to file a replying affidavit and a defence. It will make it easier to persuade him to agree if the defendant is prepared to consent to the continuance of the injunction in the interim, without prejudice, or to give an undertaking to comply with same. If there is a problem with the method of service or the time for service, the plaintiff may be more willing to consent, if no objection is raised by the defendant to service. Under order 12 rule 2 an appearance should be filed in the Circuit Court office and a copy sent to the other side, by post orlodging in the plaintiff's solicitor's office. There is then (under order 12 rule 4) a further 10 days to lodge a defence.

Interlocutory injunctions

6.041 Under order 22 rule 11 where a special time is limited for delivery or filing an affidavit, no affidavit delivered or filed after that time shall be used unless by leave of the judge. It is unusual for a defendant to have a replying affidavit filed by the time the motion for an interlocutory injunction first comes into the list. The court will not be concerned with the absence of a defence, as that is included in the pleadings for the trial. The plaintiff's counsel may apply to deem service good and sufficient. Order 11 rule 1 states that, in any case, the judge may declare the service actually effected sufficient. If the defendant's counsel objects, on the grounds of lack of notice, the court may prefer to deem service sufficient, but give the defendent time to file replying documents.

Personal undertaking

6.042 The court may take a personal undertaking from the defendant, on oath, to comply with the terms of the injunction and strike out the motion for an interlocutory injunction or continue the interim order until further order. It is preferable for the defendant to give the undertaking personally rather than through his counsel. This avoids any subsequent allegation by him that his legal advisers did not explain the nature of an undertaking. The judge usually explains the nature of the undertaking to him and asks him to confirm that he understands it. The plaintiff may apply to have the undertaking noted in the body of the order, so as to make it easier to commit him for a subsequent breach of the order. The Supreme Court made it clear in *Gore-Booth v Gore-Booth*[16] that every injunction, whether interlocutory or final, must be obeyed and that breach may be punished. If an undertaking is accepted by the court it may decline to award costs to the plaintiff. However costs should be sought, as the award of costs, whether or not eventually recovered, has a salutory effect on a defendant.

6.043 In the case of a defendant who is not legally represented, it will save court time if the plaintiff's legal advisers approach him in advance of the case being called, to explain the nature of the order requested.

6.044 If the motion for an interlocutory injunction is being vigorously defended, it is important for both sides to have their cases well prepared. If this means adjourning a case, to produce affidavits or witnesses to corroborate, this should be done. This is because this hearing may in effect become the determination of the case. This happens particularly if the injunction is sought as a remedy in itself. Despite motions usually being determined on affidavit it is not uncommon for oral evidence to be heard. If the defendant has left the family home in the interim efforts should be made to obtain an alternative address, so that he can be served with the order made at the interlocutory stage.

Appeal and further action

6.045 The judge may refuse an injunction, on the basis that it is not a suitable remedy. The plaintiff can appeal this decision to the High Court within 10 days of the Circuit Court order — see rule 2 of order 61 of the Rules of the Superior Courts. Alternatively if the injunction was for emergency relief, and there is a substantive claim involved the judge may

16   [1956] ILTR 32.

set the matter down for hearing as soon as possible. The function of the appellate court was considered by Black J. in *O'Malley v O'Malley*[17]. "The granting of an interlocutory injunction being discretionary, I should be unwilling to interfere with it, unless he exercised it upon an erroneous principle . . . or unless his exercise of it would probably cause injustice." Lavery J. in *Gore-Booth v Gore-Booth*[18] held that the Supreme Court had power to review the High Court decision, if there has been an error of principle and "a gross miscarriage". If an injunction has been obtained, the plaintiff may prefer not to proceed further in order to avoid expense and further distress. This may be reasonable provided that the defendant continues to obey the order, and does not himself want the matter set down for trial. If there is a liklehood that the order will not be obeyed, it is more appropriate to have a final order, to avoid having to take committal proceedings for breach of an interlocutory order.

Preparing for trial

6.046 Order 12 rule 16 provides for no appearance or defence to be lodged later than the appropriate time without leave of the judge. The defence should therefore be filed as soon as possible. A letter consenting to late filing may be required. If there is no progress in filing the defence a 14 day warning letter must be sent to the defendant. If the defence is still not filed a motion for judgment in default of defence can be issued, though there are restrictions imposed in the Dublin Circuit, arising out of the new practice direction of the Dublin Circuit Court of the 14th March 1989. This provides that a notice of motion for a default judgment shall not issue unless the plaintiff has at least 10 days prior thereto, given written notice to the defendant or his solicitor of his intention to issue same, and consenting therein to the late delivery of the appearance or defence, (as the case may be), within 14 days of the date of the letter. If within 10 days of the service of the notice of motion the defendant files the appearance or defence, having obtained an extension of time from the County Registrar, and delivers to the plaintiff's solicitor a copy thereof, then the plaintiff shall only be entitled to a sum of £100 (to include outlay) measured costs of the said notice of motion. The defendant will usually appear on the return date of the motion and seek permission to extend the time for filing. This is usually done for a further 10 days with costs of the motion or costs reserved to the hearing.

6.047 If judgment has been given in default of appearance or defence, in effect a perpetual injunction order has been made. The defendant may apply to set it aside within 10 days after he has knowledge of the order, but service of such a motion does not operate as a stay. The relevant order here is order 27 rule 1 deals with review of judgments in default of an appearance or defence. The application must set out why no appearance or defence was lodged, the nature of the "fraud, misrepresentation, surprise,

---

17 [1951] ILTR 53.
18 [1956] ILTR 32.

or mistake relied on and the grounds of the defence". In addition, order 27 rule 3 provides for costs of the motion for judgment to be lodged in court, before the motion to set it aside can be heard. If this is the case a stay may be applied for. Such an application is not common in family law cases as an order for judgment in default will not be made until the judge is satisfied of proper service of the motion. Problems may arise if the defendant is residing at the same address as the plaintiff especially if the plaintiff has signed for the registered letter which enclosed the motion. Alternatively the motion is posted by registered post to his last address but it may not be returned to the solicitor's office, uncollected, until after the motion for judgment has been disposed of. In those circumstances, the solicitor, as an officer of the court, should contact the Court registrar and arrange to have the motion re-entered as soon as possible. The judge should then be informed of the return of the registered letter unopened, and asked to vacate the order.

Notice of trial

6.048 This is usually served by the plaintiff within 10 days of the defence. Order 30 rule 5 provides that if it is not issued within six weeks of the defence, the defendant may apply to dismiss the case for want of prosecution. Order 30 rule 3 provides that notice of trial in the Dublin Circuit Court, specifying the date and time, be given. It is important to have checked out the availability of the client and professional witnesses before a date is chosen particularly during early summer. Outside Dublin (under order 30 rule 2) notice is for the next sittings of the Circuit Court after the expiration of the 10 day notice.

Costs

6.049 The court may reserve the costs of the interlocutory application. However if the plaintiff has been successful, then he should seek costs at this stage rather than await the trial. If costs are reserved this will be an added incentive to the plaintiff to proceed to trial, to secure a final order of costs. This is only worthwhile if the defendant is a mark for costs, though the fear of costs sometimes has a deterrent effect on defendants.

Enforcement of an injunction

Acting for plaintiff

6.050 A solicitor is more likely to have problems enforcing an injunction than any other family law order. This is because there are only civil remedies, as distinct from criminal powers, for breach of an injunction and it is in the nature of the case that the defendant is likely to be difficult. Before taking steps to enforce an injunction, it is necessary to establish that all relevant legal documents have been served properly on the defendant and that an affidavit (as set out in order 22 rule 15) of service has been prepared or filed in the Circuit Court office. The penal endorsement (as set out in order 33 rule 25) must have been added to the interim, interlocutory or perpetual injunction, whichever is the relevant order.

6.051 A notice of motion for attachment and committal is prepared, in a standard format (order 36 rule 3) with a grounding affidavit which sets out exactly each alleged breach of the order. This is a serious matter and the defendant is entitled to know exactly what is alleged against him. There may be difficulties obtaining instructions from a distressed client about the dates of breaches. Sometimes the Gardai may have been called, and the call may have been logged. The doctor may have seen the client, or the neighbour may have heard the client screaming and remember the date. Despite the pressure to get an early date for the hearing of the motion, the client should very carefully check the affidavit before swearing it.

6.052 The notice is issued at the Circuit Court office and the earliest date obtained. It must be served personally on the defendant, unless the court for good cause orders otherwise, even though he has a solicitor on record. Order 10 rule 21 provides for a solicitor to be served with any document except where the Rules provide for personal service. This means he must be given 4 days notice (order 51 rule 2) and the solicitor on record should be given a courtesy copy. The orders are probably exhibits in the affidavit grounding the motion. In case of doubt it is best to serve the orders with the motion and grounding affidavit. This will be helpful if there is a further breach of the order from the time of serving the motion and the date of court. The orders must have been served personally and not simply on the defendant's solicitor. If that has not happened as no breach of the order was anticipated, then at the first opportunity after the complaint of the breach the defendant should be served personally with the orders.

6.053 A motion can be issued for breach of an undertaking even if it was not embodied in the order as drawn up by the registrar, as reference to the fact that an undertaking was given will have been made in the order. The notice of motion must include the wording of rule 3 of Order 36, "To show cause why he should not be committed for this contempt in neglecting to obey such order".

6.054 If the plaintiff has failed to serve the defendant personally, because of his deliberate evasion of service, the court may, by request in advance, order service by post, or on the defendant's solicitor.[19] If the defendant still does not respond, the court can then proceed to make an order committing the defendant to prison for contempt, and a warrant will issue for his arrest. Order 36 rule 4 states that the party at whose instance an order for attachment or comittal has been obtained shall lodge it with the proper officer for execution.

---

19 Order 36 rule 3.

Acting for a defendant

6.055 The solicitor for the defendant needs to be careful when dealing with a client who is intent on disobeying the order, if the solicitor is aware that the plaintiff is trying to serve his client, he should not assist his client in avoiding service. The court will expect to be told by the defendant's solicitor what contact his client has had with him since the order was made or disobeyed and this may be received as sworn evidence. It is advisable to encourage the defendant to give instructions as to the alleged breaches and come into court and apologise to purge his contempt rather than evade the due process of law. If the defendant fails to accept his solicitor's advice the solicitor should apply to come off record having so informed his client. A solicitor should not become involved in the committal motion where he has not received clear instructions to do so especially if his client has not bothered to attend court. The solicitor is entitled to have a watching brief of the case.

6.056 If a defendant does attend court he will rarely have filed a replying affidavit defending the allegations. His counsel may seek an adjournment to file such affidavit but this is likely to be strongly resisted. The court may instead take oral evidence from the defendant, explaining his case. The lawyers for the defendant should anticipate this happening and have detailed instructions from him. He will be expected to apologise to the court and undertake that there will be no further breaches and to comply with the order in the future.

6.057 If the defendant is denying the plaintiff's allegations and the plaintiff has not made any complaint of violence to the Gardai or the doctor the plaintiff may find it difficult to prove the alleged breaches of the order. Even if the court accepts the allegations it is unlikely to commit the defendant on the plaintiff's word alone. On the other hand, the defendant may admit to misbehaviour but minimise what has actually happened.

6.058 If the injunction has ordered the defendant to leave the family home and he has failed to leave, the court may proceed to make the committal order but put a stay on the order, and give him 24 hours to vacate. The order should be very specific as to when the stay expires, whether or not the defendant can take his personal belongings with him, and whether he will be allowed pass the threshold again for any purpose, including access to the children. If the defendant is not in court, and the court proceeds to make an order, it may make an order of attachment, that is, ordering him to be arrested and brought before the court, or else it may make an order of committal, that is, that on arrest he will be brought to a specified prison and held there, either for a specified time, or until he purges his contempt. The order will be directed to the superintendent of the gardai for the district in which he resides or may be found, or to such other member of the Gardai as the court may direct (order 36 rule 2). A photograph of the defendant, and any other information on his movements should be sent to the Superintendent to assist in arresting him. In Dublin it is usual to send the order of committal to the Garda Depot at the Phoenix Park which will then arrange for it to be endorsed to a particular warrant officer at the local Garda Station. A copy of the order can be left with the warrant office at the Bridewell Station which is the station for the Four Courts.

6.059 When the defendant is committed, he may apply to have the order discharged under order 36 rule 5. He must do so on notice to the plaintiff. This should be by way of a notice of motion though the courts do not always insist on this as the defendant has been deprived of his liberty. If the defendant applies by way of a motion it can be served on the plaintiff's solicitor thus giving 2 days notice. The solicitor for the defendant may have to apply to have a body warrant issued by the court on an *ex parte* basis. This is because the prison is under no obligation to produce a prisoner on an oral request from a solicitor and security arrangements change from time to time. The prison office must be contacted prior to any date being fixed to find out their requirements. If a body warrant is required, an *ex parte* docket can be completed and application made to the court. The warrant should then be delivered to the prison or sent by express post. It is helpful for the court registrar to telephone the prison to confirm that it is a genuine request if the prison do not require a body warrant.

6.060 Where there is a very serious breach of an order it is helpful if a formal complaint is made to the local station sergeant. A defendant is more likely to comply with an injunction if there is a criminal prosecution contemplated or pending. There is no point wasting the time of the Gardai unless the plaintiff is agreeable to giving evidence in open court on a prosecution. Sometimes a prosecution is struck out, as the defendant has complied in the interim with the injunction.

6.061 Under Order 33 rule 26 where a mandatory order or injunction has not been complied with the court may in lieu of committal direct that the act ordered, which the defendant was supposed to have carried out, be done by the plaintiff and the expenses of same will be met by him, and execution may issue for this amount. This order may be useful where an order is made under the Family Home Protection Act 1976 to carry out repairs to make the house habitable.

Principles governing contempt

6.062 The courts are reluctant to commit for contempt in a family law matter, except as a last resort. It may lead to further danger for the plaintiff when the defendant is released from prison. One of the few written judgments relating to a contempt in a family law matter was in *Gore-Booth v Gore-Booth*.[19] The committee of the ward had obtained an interlocutory injunction restraining the defendants, who were the mother and sister of the ward from interfering with or obstructing the committee from taking control over livestock. It was alleged that the defendants had scattered cattle and done other acts to hinder the committee. The High Court refused to commit them and awarded them their costs against the committee.

6.063 The committee appealed to the Supreme Court. It reversed the High Court decision and held that there had been a serious breach of the order and contempt of court. The court made clear that the burden of proof was on the plaintiffs to show the breach of the order. Lavery J. stated that the sympathy he had for the defendants, in having their home broken up, must give way to the paramount consideration that orders of the court must be obeyed and that if deliberate action to obstruct the administration of the estate and to frustrate court orders is established the offence must be punished. The court also confirmed that every injunction order whether interlocutory or final must be obeyed. The injunction order was interpreted to include agents and servants of the committee though it did not specifically say so. The defendants were not in fact committed to prison.

6.064 A more recent judgment on the principles of contempt is *Ross Co. Ltd (in receivership) and Shortall v Swan and others.*[20] The defendants were deliberately disobeying the court order, which restrained trespass, and had no intent to purge their contempt in future. The plaintiffs applied for attachment or committal. O'Hanlon J. held that the power to commit to prison in civil proceedings is a jurisdiction that should not be exercised when it is unlikely to produce the desired result and when there is some reasonable alternative available. If no other reasonable course is open then an order to commit to prison for a fixed period may have to be made to vindicate the authority of the court. If some other reasonable course is open then it is preferable that it should be adopted. In the circumstances of this case, there was an alternative: a prosecution under the Forcible Entry and Occupation Act.

6.065 The significance of this decision for family law cases is that it relied on an English family law case *Danchevsky v Danchevsky.*[21] The facts of this case were that the husband had been ordered to give up possession of the house and an order for sale had been made. Lord Denning enunciated the principle that if there was a reasonable alternative method available of ensuring that a court order was obeyed which did not involve prison then it should be used. He noted that an order for possession could have been enforced by a warrant for possession and the court could have ordered that the conveyance be executed by a third party.

6.066 O'Hanlon J. in the *Ross* case took the view that the High Court had inherent power to prevent the abuse of its own process so that it could punish for contempt by a fixed period of imprisonment. He stated that it would be undesirable for the High Court to commit to prison for an

20   [1981] ILRM 416.
21   [1974] 2 All ER 561.

indefinite period a person who had no intention of obeying the order of the court and who may even welcome the publicity he gains by the making of such an order, as a means of furthering his own cause.

6.067 The difficulty with injunctions and indeed many other family law orders is that there is no other civil method of enforcing an order without recourse to contempt. The powers of the criminal law in this area are also limited. The Gardai have traditionally been reluctant to intrude on the privacy of marriage and wives are reluctant to involve the Gardai in prosecutions. However the Ross case helps to clarify the limits the exercise of the court's jurisdiction in relation to contempt. It is therefore necessary that the solicitor for the plaintiff and defendant explore any other remedy prior to issuing proceedings for contempt.

High Court procedure

Obtaining a High Court injunction

6.068 An injunction may be sought in the High Court instead of the Circuit Court, on the basis that there is only a property dispute to be resolved or where an injunction is sought as a substantive remedy. This is one of the difficulties of commencing non-property family law proceedings in the High Court, because of the effect of the Courts Act 1981 and the judgments of *R. v R.*, and *O'R. v O'R.* (See Chapter 1). It may be possible in a complex case to get a hearing more quickly in the High Court than in the Circuit Court. Where there are no vacation sittings (particularly outside of Dublin) it may be more convenient for an application to be made to the High Court.

Documents

6.069 There has been some confusion as to whether a plenary summons or special summons should be used. Until the Courts Act 1981 substantive remedies in family law were sought in the High Court and relief by way of injunction may also have been sought. It was therefore quite usual for a special summons to be used. Order 3 of the Rules of the Superior Courts 1962 had provided for a special summons to be used for cases under the Guardianship of Infants Act 1964 and the Married Women's Status Act 1957. The High Court Rules 1986 deleted the reference to the former, arising out of section 15 of the Courts Act 1981 which substituted a new definition of "court" in section 13 of the Guardianship of Infants Act 1964 as meaning the Circuit Court and the District Court.

6.070 If an injunction is sought as an emergency form of relief, where there are substantive proceedings issued under the Guardianship of Infants Act 1964, Married Women's Status Act 1957, Family Home Protection Act 1976, or the Family Law Act 1981, a special summons is used. An injunction may be sought under the Guardianship of Infants Act 1964 by using the special practice direction. (See Chapter 1) but the risk may be

149

taken that the court may refuse to hear it. However if it is sufficiently urgent and it is not possible to apply in the Circuit Court then one can proceed in the High Court.

6.071 If an injunction is sought as an equitable remedy in itself without substantive relief being sought, for example an injunction to exclude a spouse from harassment as the other spouses's place of work, then a plenary summons must be used. This is because order 1 of the Rules of the Superior Courts states, at rule 6, "In all proceedings commenced by originating summons, procedure by plenary summons shall be obligatory, except where procedure by summary summons or by special summons is required or authorised by these rules".

Proceeding by way of plenary summons

6.072 An affidavit grounding the application for an injunction must be filed in advance of the *ex parte* application or at least produced to the court with an undertaking given to file same. A further undertaking can be given to issue the plenary summons, if that has not issued, but this should only be done, in an emergency case. The family law registrar will give guidance as to the court in which the *ex parte* application can be made. Under order 4 rule 2 the plenary summons should state in its general indorsement of claim the relief claimed and the grounds. The original is issued in the central office and is handed back to the solicitor with the record number on it, (order 5 rules 7–12). A copy is kept by the central office. The grounding affidavit sworn by the applicant spouse should be filed at the same time. It should be sworn on the day the summons is issued or the day after but not beforehand. The affidavit should comply with order 50 of the Rules of the Superior Courts, which deals with motions.

6.073 Strictly under order 20 rule 2 a statement of claim should be prepared. It is to be served on the defendant though it does not need to be filed in the central office. Some judges do not expect a statement of claim to be filed in a family law matter but others do. Counsel should therefore be instructed to draft a statement of claim which may be delivered to the defendant within twenty-one days from the service of the plenary summons. The defendant has the right to seek a statement of claim, on filing an appearance. It must, under order 20 rule 7, specifically state the relief sought by the plaintiff.

6.074 Under order 52 rule 2 a notice of motion should be prepared at this stage to avoid delays subsequent to the grant of the interim relief *ex parte*. It is also useful to have the motion drafted at this time, as it must be served with the *ex parte* order. Order 52 rule 3 provides that; in any case the court, if satisfied that the delay caused by proceeding by motion on notice under this order would or might entail irreparable or serious mischief, may make any order *ex parte* upon such "terms as to costs or otherwise, and subject to such undertaking, if any, as the court may think just; and any party affected by such order may move to set it aside."

The family law list

6.075 A family law injunction should preferably be applied for in the family law motion list on a Friday. *Ex parte* applications are also taken then. The family law registrar should be notified in advance that an application is to be made and if the documentation is available he can check it. The application will be made in the 11 o'clock list after the call over of the list. As there is no Monday list for family law it may be necessary to apply instead in the Monday *ex parte* list. This will be in a public court. The court registrar should be notified of this in advance. This may result in the case being put back to the end of the *ex parte* list. The court should be asked to make the order returnable for the family law list that Friday or Friday week. It is possible to apply at the beginning of the family law list for an injunction between Tuesday to Thursday but again the registrar of the family law list or if he is not available, the registrar in charge of the central office should be contacted. This is because it is usual to have only one case listed per day, other than the motion day and if that case has collapsed, there will be no family law list. Application will then have to be made to the registrar dealing with family law for a direction as to which court the application should be made before.

6.076 If an *ex parte* order is granted the registrar will draw up the order. He should be asked how long approximately this is going to take. An *ex parte* order does not need to be typed thus saving valuable time. The order is made available at the appropriate counter in the central office, and stamp duty is payable.

Service of the summons

6.077 Order 9 rule 2 deals with service of the plenary or special summons. Service is personal on the defendant, "if it is reasonably practicable". A copy of the plenary or special summons, affidavit, and order is served, and the original of the summons and order are exhibited to him (rule 3). The order needs to be served personally in case it is later necessary to attach him for contempt. The summons server (under rule 12) should endorse on the summons, the day and date of service, and also complete an affidavit of service of the summons, affidavit, and order. If the defendant deliberately avoids personal service and service is effected in some other way, the court may under rule 15, upon just grounds, declare the service actually effected sufficient. Alternatively an order for substituted service may be applied for under order 10.

6.078 In accordance with order 52 a notice of motion for an interlocutory injunction should have been issued by this stage, and served at the same time as the other court documents. The motion must be served four clear days in advance of the hearing, as must it be served personally. If is is being served on the defendant's solicitor then two days is sufficient. The motion may be served even though an appearance may not have been entered by the defendant (rule 10).

Acting for a defendant: appearance

6.079 Appearances are dealt with under order 12. Under rule 3 a memorandum of appearance should be entered, within eight days, if a plenary summons has been served. It is marked with an official stamp, and the plaintiff is served with a marked duplicate. It should state whether or not a statement of claim is required. If a special summons has been issued, there is no time limit on the memorandum, but the defendant will not be heard in the case unless he has entered an appearance. The special summons will be made returnable to the master's court for the Wednesday family law list. This will be so even though there may be a motion seeking an interlocutory injunction listed for an earlier date.

6.080 The most urgent need is to defend the motion. A replying affidavit needs to be prepared and served on the plaintiff. If there is insufficient time before the motion, the plaintiff should be notified that there will be a request for an adjournment. This should not unduly prejudice the plaintiff, as the court can continue the interim injunction until further order. An application can be made to adjourn the case in the masters list, to give time to prepare a defence, if a statement of claim has been served. It is unlikely that the plaintiff will have served a statement of claim, by the time the case comes into the master's list. There is likely to be consent to adjourn the case in the master's list.

Hearing of a motion for an interlocutory injunction

6.081 Order 50 rule 6 provides that the court may grant an injunction by an interlocutory order in all cases in which it appears to the court to be just or convenient so to do. The order may be unconditional or upon such terms and conditions as the court thinks just. If the defendant fails to appear, under order 52 rule 12, the court may proceed in his absence. The court may grant an interlocutory injunction until the trial of the action after hearing the plaintiff and the defendant in evidence, and reading their affidavits. It will be in the interests of the defendant if he is unhappy with this outcome to get the case set down for trial as soon as possible. The plaintiff may delay at this stage.

6.082 The court also has power to direct an early trial, rather than hearing the matter in an interlocutory way. If it so orders it can make such order as the justice of the case may require in the interim. In effect, in many family law cases the hearing of the motion may dispose of the matter in dispute. If the court thinks that the hearing of the motion will not be suitable for a Friday motion list it may set aside a day to hear it. It is then in the interests of the parties that this day become the hearing of the action. The necessary documentation must therefore be in order.

Master's Court

6.083 The family law list is on a Wednesday, at 10.30 a.m. The master will ensure that each party has filed an affidavit verifying the claim on the summons. The Master has power (under order 38 rule 7) to extend the time for filing of an affidavit. When the proceedings are in order for hearing the master transfers the case into the judge's list for hearing. It usually appears in the Friday list to fix dates the following Friday or Friday week. A date for trial is then fixed if the matter has not been disposed of at the hearing of the motion for an interlocutory hearing.

Plenary hearing

6.084 If a statement of claim has been served under order 21 rule 1 the defendant has a further 28 days to file a defence. With the new rules it is not necessary to file the defence in the central office but it has to be served on the plaintiff. A reply is unnecessary where all the material statements of fact are merely to be denied and put in issue. A notice of trial, giving 21 days notice must be served in accordance with order 38 rule 7. The case is set down for trial by preparing two books of pleadings with each copy pleading being certified as a true copy, a setting down docket, and a proper index of the documents (order 36 rule 4). The case then comes into the family law list to fix dates. A plenary hearing takes place with evidence being orally given.

6.085 If an injunction is granted the order is drawn up by the registrar in the usual way. It must be served personally with the penal notice endorsed on it. Order 41 rule 8 sets out the penal endorsement as follows if you the within named A.B. neglect to obey this judgment or order by the time therein limited, you will be liable to process of execution including imprisonment for the purpose of compelling you to obey the same judgment or order. If an injunction is refused on an *ex parte* application, an application for an injunction may be made to the Supreme Court (under order 58 rule 13) within four days from the date of the refusal or within such enlarged time as the Supreme Court may allow. The notice of appeal shall be a two day notice (order 61 rule 9) and it is not necessary to serve any person. If either party is unhappy with the court order either after a plenary hearing or a hearing on an interlocutory basis, he may appeal in the usual way to the Supreme Court.

Forms and precedents

Circuit Court

Equity civil bill

6.086 The first page of an ordinary civil bill is completed having inserted the names and addresses of the plaintiff and defendant. The term "ordinary" is deleted and "equity" inserted. The solicitor must sign the front page. The indorsement of claim is on page 2. The standard form from the law stationers states, "The plaintiff's claim is for". This should be deleted.

6.087 Injunction where the plaintiff intends to take nullity proceedings

The names of the parties are Sheila Seconds and Sean Seconds.

INDORSEMENT OF CLAIM

1. The plaintiff is a Civil Servant and she resides at 10, Unhappy Avenue, Donnycarney, in the City of Dublin.
2. (where the plaintiff intends to take nullity proceedings) The Plaintiff went through a ceremony of marriage with the Defendant on the 13th May 1987. The said ceremony of marriage was in accordance with the rites of the Roman Catholic Church. The Defendant had previously gone through a ceremony of marriage with one Mary Froid, in respect of which he had obtained an annulment from the Roman Catholic Regional Marriage Tribunal.
3. There were issue of the said union, between the Plaintiff and the Defendant, namely Jason born on the 10th day of October 1987, and Pamela born on the 12th day of January 1989.
4. The Defendant resides at the dwellinghouse situate at 10, Unhappy Avenue, Donnycarney, in the City of Dublin. The Plaintiff and Defendant are joint tenants of the said premises, and they hold same by virtue of a tenancy agreement with the Corporation of Dublin.
5. On divers occasions within the past two years, the Defendant has wrongfully assaulted the Plaintiff. The Defendant has used foul and abusive language to the Plaintiff in the presence of the children, and has threatened to kill her.
6. The Defendant has, by his conduct, caused the Plaintiff to leave the said premises on several occasions and to seek shelter with her sister.
7. On or about the 13th day of February 1989 the Defendant assaulted the Plaintiff, by hitting her on the head and face, as a result of which she sustained a black eye and bruises to the face. The children witnesses the said incident, as a result of which they were terrified and have suffered nightmares on several occasions since.
8. The Defendant threatens and intends to assault, molest and annoy the Plaintiff unless restrained by this Honourable Court.
9. In consequence of the matters aforesaid, the Plaintiff has suffered physical injuries, great distress, fear, loss and damage.

AND THE PLAINTIFF CLAIMS:-

(a) Damages not exceeding £15,000 for assault.
(b) An Injunction restraining the Defendant from assaulting, molesting, annoying, threatening or putting the Plaintiff in fear or otherwise interfering with the Plaintiff, the children, her family or her relations.
(c) An Injunction directed to the Defendant requiring him to vacate forthwith the dwellinghouse situate at 10, Unhappy Avenue, Donnycarney, in the City of Dublin.
(d) An injunction restraining the Defendant, his servants or agents, from

being on or remaining on or entering upon or continuing on in occupation of the said dwellinghouse.

(e) An injunction restraining the Defendant from attending at or watching or besetting the Plaintiff's dwellinghouse, or any dwellinghouse where the Plaintiff may from time to time reside. Or

(f) An injunction restraining the Defendant, his servants or agents, and all persons having notice of these proceedings, from watching or besetting the Plaintiff, her servants or agents, at her residence, place of employment, or any place that the Plaintiff may be.

(g) Such further or other relief as to this Honourable Court deems meet and just.

(h) Costs.

The Rateable Valuation of the Plaintiff's dwellinghouse does not exceed £200.

Signed. ——————————————————

Solicitor for the Plaintiff

6.088 Where the plaintiff seeks an injunction to protect children who have been the subject of abuse or violence by the defendant spouse

THE CIRCUIT COURT

DUBLIN CIRCUIT   COUNTY OF THE CITY OF DUBLIN

BETWEEN/

Joan Foley (an infant) suing by the mother and next friend Mary Foley

Plaintiffs

and

Patrick Foley

Defendant

INDORSEMENT OF CLAIM.

After setting out the facts grounding the application, insert the Plaintiff's claim as follows;

1. Damages for civil assault by the Defendant on the infant Plaintiff;

2. Damages for trespass to the person by the Defendant on the infant Plaintiff;

3. An injunction restraining the Defendant from removing or attempting to remove the infant Plaintiff from the premises, 13, Unhappy Road,

Foxrock, in the County of the City of Dublin, or from the care, custody and control of her mother named in the title herein.

4. An Injunction restraining the Defendant from contacting or communicating with or approaching the Plaintiffs or either of them.

5. An Injunction restraining the Defendant, his servants and agents and all persons having notice of these proceedings, from assaulting, battering, molesting, threatening or placing in fear or watching or besetting the Plaintiffs, their servants or agents, at their place of residence or any place that the Plaintiffs may be.

6.089 Affidavit grounding an application for an injunction

Insert the usual title, and the names of the Plaintiffs and Defendant.

Affidavit of Mary Foley.

I, Mary Foley, aged 18 years and upwards, a civil servant by occupation, of 13, Unhappy Road, Foxrock in the County of the City of Dublin, MAKE OATH AND SAY AS FOLLOWS:-

1. I make this Affidavit from facts within my own knowledge save where otherwise appears and where so otherwise appears I believed same to be true to the best of my information, knowledge and belief.

2. (For next friend) I am the Mother and Next Friend of Joan Foley, the first named Plaintiff in these proceedings. The said Joan Foley is aged four years, having been born on the 2nd day of February 1985.

3. (For a Plaintiff who proposes to take nullity proceedings) I say and believe that I went through a ceremony of marriage with the said Sean Seconds herein on the 13th day of May 1987. I say and believe that the Defendant informed me at that time, that he had been previously married to one Mary Froid, but that the marriage had been declared null and void by the Dublin Regional Marriage Tribunal of the Roman Catholic Church. The Defendant stated that he was therefore free to marry again. I say and believe that I accepted what the defendant told me. I believe that our marriage was a true and valid marriage in the eyes of the Roman Catholic Church and the eyes of the State. I say and believe that I was greatly surprised to be told by my solicitor and counsel that the said marriage is not valid in accordance with the Civil Law.

(The facts grounding the application for the injunction should be chronologically set out, and be as specific as possible. The title or right of the Plaintiff to be in occupation of the premises should be set out. If a spouse is applying to have the owning spouse put out of the family home, then if she is likely to be taking subsequent proceedings under section 12 of the Married Women's Status Act 1957 or the Judicial Separation and Family Law Reform Act 1989 she should state that she is claiming a beneficial share of it.)

The affidavit should end as follows:
I pray this Honourable Court for the Reliefs set out in the Indorsement of Claim in the Equity Civil Bill herein.
The jurat and filing clause are then inserted.

6.090 Ex parte docket

A form called a general requisition, obtainable from a law stationers, can be adapted.

I desire to apply to the Court on the—day of—1989, for an interim injunction, on behalf of the Plaintiff to the following effect;

1. An interim injunction restraining the Defendant from entering into, attending at or residing in the Plaintiff's residence at 13, Unhappy Road, Foxrock in the County of the City of Dublin.
2. An interim injunction restraining the Defendant from interfering with assaulting, molesting, threatening or putting in fear the Plaintiff.
3. Such further or other order as to this Honourable Court deems meet and just.

Date this—day of—1989.

Signed _____
Sally Solicitor
Law Centre
Refuge Quay
Dublin 1.

6.091 An interlocutory injunction

NOTICE OF MOTION

TAKE NOTICE that on the—day of—1989, at 11 o clock in the forenoon or at the first available opportunity thereafter, Counsel on behalf of the Plaintiff will apply to this Honourable Court sitting at (the exact location and address of the court at which the matter is to be heard), for the reliefs set out hereunder:

1. An Interlocutory restraining the Defendant from assaulting, molesting, threatening or in any way whatsoever interfering with the Plaintiff (or the Plaintiffs or either of them).
2. Insert here all the other claims for relief, set out in the Equity Civil Bill.
3. An order providing for the costs of this Application.

Which said application will be grounded upon the Equity Civil Bill issued and served herein, the Affidavit of Service, the Affidavit of the Plaintiff sworn herein on the—day of—1989, the exhibits therein referred to, proof of service of this Notice of Motion and Grounding Affidavit, such further

or other oral evidence as may be adduced by or on behalf of the Plaintiff, the nature of the case and the reasons to be offered.
Dated this—day of—1989.

Signed _____
Sally Solicitor, etc.

To/Sean Seconds,
13, Unhappy Road,
Foxrock,
County Dublin.

And/The Circuit Court
Arus Ui Dhálaigh,
Inns Quay,
Dublin 7.

6.092 Draft orders

Generally the registrar will draw the order, but if the registrar is unable to do so with sufficient haste, it may be agreed that the plaintiff's solicitor should draft it and lodge it for approval.

ORDER

THIS MATTER coming before the Court this day on Motion ex parte on behalf of the Plaintiff, and on hearing Mr Barry Counsel for the Plaintiff and on reading the Affidavit of Mary Foley, the Plaintiff and the Civil Bill intended to be served, and the Plaintiff through her Counsel undertaking to abide by any order the Court may make as to damages in case the Court shall hereafter be of opinion that the Defendant shall have sustained any loss by reason of this Order which the Plaintiff ought to pay.

THE COURT DOTH GRANT an ad interim injunction as sought, in the terms of paragraphs 1,2,3, and 4 of the Indorsement of Claim in the Civil Bill and Doth Order:

1. That the Defendant by himself, his servants, or agents be restrained from molesting, assaulting, annoying or threatening or otherwise interfering with the Plaintiff, her family or her relations.
2. That the Defendant be restrained from watching and besetting the Plaintiff, or following her upon the public highway.
3. That the Defendant be restrained from residing at, entering into, or attending at the Plaintiff's residence at 10, Unhappy Avenue, Donnycarney, in the City of Dublin, or any other residence at which the Plaintiff may reside.

And the Court Doth grant leave to the Plaintiff to serve a Motion for an Interlocutory Injunction returnable for the—day of—1989, in (the exact location and address of the court to which the matter is returnable for interlocutory hearing) and the Court Doth Order that this ad interim injunction do continue until the said date And the Court Doth Further Order that the Plaintiff do notify the Defendant by telephone and letter of the making of this Order And the Court Doth Further Order that a copy of this Order, the Civil Bill and the Affidavit of the Plaintiff be served with the Notice of Motion for an Interlocutory Injunction and the Court Doth reserve the costs.

By the Court
County Registrar.
Endorsement on copy order to be served.
If you the within named Defendant neglect to obey this Order forthwith within the time limited you will be liable to process of execution for the purpose of compelling you to obey and said Order.

Sally Solicitor
Solicitor for the Plaintiff,
Law Centre,
Refuge Quay,
Dublin 1.

6.093 Order for an interlocutory injunction

ORDER

The Defendant having been duly served with an Equity Civil Bill herein and the same coming on for hearing the Court this day on Motion by the Plaintiff for an Interlocutory Injunction pending the hearing of this action. Whereupon and on reading the Pleadings, the Notice of Motion dated the—day of—1989, the Affidavit of Service at the (e.g Civil Bill), the Notice of Motion herein, the order made by this honourable Court on the day of—, and the Affidavit of Mary Foley duly filed and the exhibit referred to, and on hearing what was offered by Mr Barry of Counsel for the Plaintiff, there being no appearance by or on behalf of the Defendant (or—and Patrick Foley the Defendant appearing in person). The Court doth grant the Interlocutory Injunction as sought pending the hearing of this action and the Court doth Order:

1. That the Defendant his servants or agents be restrained from attending at or entering upon or attempting to enter upon the Plaintiff's place of residence situate at 10 Unhappy Road, Foxrock, in the County of the City of Dublin.

And the Court Doth reserve the costs. (or—the Court Doth make no further order).

High Court

6.094 Plenary summons; general indorsement of claim

1. The Plaintiff's claim is for an Injunction restraining the Defendant, his

servants or agents and all persons having notice of these proceedings, from assaulting, battering, threatening, or placing in fear or watching or besetting the Plaintiff, his servants, or agents at his residence at (insert the home address), place of work (here insert the place of work), or any place that the Plaintiff may be.
2. An Injunction restraining the Defendant from attending at or near or residing at the premises (here insert the address).
3. (See the Circuit Court precedents in relation to the other usual claims, for example, costs.).

6.095 Affidavit

The affidavit is similar to the affidavit, in the Circuit Court, except for inserting "Circuit Court".

6.096 Notice of motion

The Notice of Motion is similar to the Circuit Court Form, except for inserting "High Court", and the following:

"AND TAKE NOTICE that the said Application will be based upon the Plenary Summons (or insert "Special Summons"), the Affidavit of the Plaintiff, and so on.

Chapter 7

JUDICIAL SEPARATION

Introduction

Judicial separation and divorce

7.001 The law relating to judicial separation is contained in the Judicial Separation and Family Law Reform Act 1989, which, under section 46(2), came into force on 19 October 1989. Section 9(1) of the Act abolished the action for divorce *a mensa et thoro*, which was the old system of judicial separation inherited from the ecclesiastical courts (see **1.001**) and available on the limited grounds of adultery, cruelty and unnatural practices. Actions for divorce *a mensa et thoro* commenced before 19 October 1989 are excepted. Decrees made under the former procedure remain in force. As well as introducing new grounds and procedures for obtaining a judicial separation, the Act radically extends the ancillary orders which the court may make, especially in relation to financial provision, property adjustment and the occupation of the family home. These ancillary matters are dealt with in chapter 13.

7.002 The Act of 1989 began as a private member's Bill, based to a considerable extent on recommendations for reform made in the *Report of the Joint Committee on Marriage Breakdown*. (P1. 3074, 27 March 1985). The committee was a joint committee of both houses of the Oireachtas. The joint committee itself considered the Law Reform Commission, *Report on Divorce a Mensa et Thoro and Related Matters* (L.R.C.8—1983), but did not agree with the grounds for judicial separation recommended by the Commission. In its own report it recommended (at 7.3.8.1.) that "irretrievable breakdown" should be the "one overall ground for the grant of a decree of judicial separation," but that in considering whether or not a marriage has irretrievably broken down the court should be satisfied that such a breakdown has occurred on proof of a number of conditions, which included adultery, desertion, behaviour by the respondent making it

161

unreasonable for the applicant to co-habit with him, periods of separation, and other facts or reasons making it reasonable for the applicant to live apart from the spouse: paragraph 7.3.8.2.

7.003 This formula, linking a basic "no-fault" ground and a number of specific facts including some of the old matrimonial offences clearly owed much to the English Divorce Reform Act of 1969 (see now the Matrimonial Causes Act 1973 section 9). But the ground of "irretrievable breakdown" in the English Act is confined to divorce. The same Act makes judicial separation available on proof, not of irretrievable breakdown, but of any one of the facts which, in divorce proceedings, entitles a court to find that a marriage has irretrievably broken down (—See Matrimonial Causes Act 1973 section 17). The Judicial Separation and Family Law Reform Bill, as initiated in 1987, adopted a similar formula, which, during the Bill's tortuous passage through the Oireachtas, was eventually jettisoned when the Bill was recommitted to a special committee of the Dáil in December 1988. "Irretrievable breakdown" was removed as a ground, and instead a list of six separate grounds was preferred. The Government's objections to "irretrievable breakdown" as a sole ground for judicial separation were that the concept is inappropriate in the context of judicial separation and that it places on the petitioner an excessive burden of proof.[1]

7.004 The principal legal effect of a degree of judicial separation is that it releases the spouses from their normal duty to cohabit. For some petitioners, to have a formal legal statement to this effect may be important; but for most, this is unlikely to be the main reason for proceeding. There are a number of reasons for this. First, the duty to cohabit is, and has for many years been, unenforceable. Second, where a couple are already living apart, the decree does no more than formally acknowledge an existing state of affairs. Third, if a couple are living together, and one spouse wishes to enforce a separation, the decree of judicial separation does not achieve this. It releases spouses from the duty to cohabit; it does not compel separation (see **7.084**). Fourth, where spouses separate by agreement, there is little which a decree of judicial separation can achieve which cannot be achieved consensually by the more direct, and usually less expensive separation agreement. It seems likely that the principal motive which most applicants will have for seeking a judicial separation under the Act of 1989 will be to gain access to the very extensive range of financial and property orders which Part II of the Act makes available. Many of these ancillary remedies are not available through any procedure other than judicial separation. These are facts which may have some bearing on the manner in which the different grounds for judicial separation are interpreted. The significance for most applicants of a finding that grounds for separation do not exist will lie, not in their failure to obtain a decree of

1 See speech by Dr. Woods, on behalf of the Minister for Justice, during the Bill's second stage in the Dáil. *Dáil Debates*, Vol. 377 (2 February 1988) col. 895. See supra at **7.003**.

judicial separation, but in their inability to gain access to ancillary remedies. Judges interpreting the grounds will no doubt be aware of this.

7.005 The difference, in this context, between judicial separation and divorce needs to be emphasised. In those jurisdictions where divorce is available the usual reason why an individual makes application for a decree of divorce is to acquire a change of status and the capacity to re-marry. Ancillary remedies may also be needed, but in many divorce jurisdictions they are available through alternative procedures. Thus, a judge when interpreting grounds for divorce does so primarily in the context of a decision about whether the parties should be freed for re-marriage. This is very different from a decision about whether the parties should be released from their normal duty to cohabit, and whether they may have access to ancillary relief.

7.006 The reason for stressing these differences between divorce and judicial separation is a practical one. A number of the concepts employed in the Judicial Separation and Family Law Reform Act 1989 are identical or similar to concepts used in divorce legislation in other jurisdictions. For instance, the "living apart" provisions in section 2 of the Act have close analogies with provisions in the divorce laws of Australia, New Zealand, Canada, many of the United States, as well as England and Northern Ireland.[2] Because of this it is likely that the case law from some of these jurisdictions will be used as an aid in interpreting the Act of 1989. But a word of caution is necessary. Because of the different contexts—divorce and judicial separation—it is not safe to assume that interpretation of the Irish Act will necessarily follow the lines adopted in foreign divorce jurisdictions, even where identical concepts or phrases are used. In the case of English divorce law in particular, while some of its phraseology is reflected in the provisions of the Irish Act, there remains a major difference. In English law the one ground for divorce is "irretrievable breakdown" of the marraige. Some of the facts, which in the Irish Act are independent grounds for judicial separation, are in the English legislation facts which may evidence irretrievable breakdown, and interpretation of them has been affected by that context. By contrast it is clear that a deliberate decision was made in relation to the Irish Act not to require an applicant to prove irretrievable breakdown. It remains to be seen whether, as a consequence of these differences, interpretation of the grounds set out in the Act of 1989 proves to be less restrictive.

Circumstances in which an application may be made

7.007 Only a spouse may apply for a judicial separation. Where there has been a foreign divorce which is entitled to recognition in this country, or an

2 See, for example Matrimonial Causes Act (England and Wales) 1973, sections 1(2)(d) and 1(2)(e). The English provisions, which derive from the Divorce Reform Act 1969, were extended to Northern Ireland by the Matrimonial Causes (Northern Ireland) Order 1978. For Australia see Family Law Act 1975. For New Zealand see Family Proceedings Act 1980, section 39(2). For Canada see Canadian Divorce Act 1967–68.

annulment of the marriage which is effective in civil law, no application will be possible. Co-habitees cannot apply. The significance of these limitations lies in the fact that a former spouse or an unmarried partner can not avail of financial and property remedies made available by the Act.

7.008 It is not clear whether a spouse who has obtained a divorce *a mensa et thoro* under the pre-existing law, is entitled to apply for a judicial separation under the Act of 1989. Section 43 states that a decree of divorce *a mensa et thoro* should not be affected by the Act. Because a decree of divorce *a mensa et thoro* has the same effect as a decree of judicial separation in that it relieves the parties from the normal duty to cohabit, it may be argued that an applicant who already has a divorce *a mensa et thoro* is stopped *per res judicata* from applying for a judicial separation. The consequence would be that the applicant would not have access to the ancillary remedies provided by the Act.

7.009 Under section 31(4) of the Act jurisdiction to hear proceedings for judicial separation may only be exercised "where either of the spouses is domiciled in the State on the date of the application commencing proceedings or is ordinarily resident in the State throughout the period of one year ending on that date."

7.010 It appears that a spouse may be precluded by prior agreement, express or implied, from applying for a judicial separation. In *K. v K.*[3] the parties entered into a formal deed of separation in which, apart from agreeing to live apart, arrangements were made for the sale of the family home, for the division of the proceeds of the sale, and for the custody of the children. The husband subsequently petitioned for a divorce *a mensa et thoro* on the ground of adultery by the wife. His objective in doing so was to deprive the wife of her rights under section 120(2) of the Succession Act 1965 as amended by section 42(1) of the Act of 1989. MacKenzie J. held that the separation agreement was a bar to the husband's petition. The decision in *Courtney v Courtney*[4] was approved, in which the Court of Appeal had held that a separation agreement without an express covenant not to sue is a bar to subsequent proceedings for divorce *a mensa et thoro* if that can be shown to have been the real character of the agreement entered into by the parties. There is nothing in the Act of 1989 which precludes the application of the same principle to proceedings for judicial separation. However, it may yet be possible to argue that in some circumstances a covenant not to proceed for judicial separation should be void for reasons of public policy (see **16.013** to **16.016**).

Standard of proof

7.011 Section 3(1) of the Act requires proof "on the balance of probabilities" in relation to any of the grounds for judicial separation. This removes uncertainty which had existed under the previous law as to

3 12 February 1988, unreported, High Court.
4 [1923] 2 IR 31.

whether proof of a matrimonial offence, such as adultery, should be subject to a stricter standard than that normally applicable in civil actions.[5]

The grounds for judicial separation

Adultery

7.012 Section 2(1)(a) of the Judicial Separation and Family Law Reform Act 1989 provides that the first ground for judicial separation is "That the respondent has committed adultery".

7.013 Adultery occurs where there is consensual sexual intercourse between persons of the opposite sex, one at least of whom is married, but who are not married to one another. A person who is raped does not commit adultery.[6] Sexual intercourse in this context must involve some penetration by the male organ, no matter how brief.[7] This means that the artificial insemination of a wife by a donor other than her husband probably does not constitute adultery.[8]

7.014 There is seldom a witness to an act of adultery. The proof will often consist of evidence of opportunity combined with evidence of intent or inflamed passion. The typical example is of a couple who, having registered in false names, spend a night together in a hotel bedroom. The court may be prepared to infer the fact of adultery from such circumstances. In *J.M.H. v J.P.H.*, Ellis J. said that adultery may be "inferred from circumstances which lead to it by fair inference as a necessary conclusion, when adultery will be presumed, or taking all the evidence into account, the circumstances are sufficient to lead the guarded discretion of a reasonable man to the conclusion that adultery took place."[9] The expression "guarded discretion of a reasonable man" is taken from *Lovedon v Lovedon*[10] and was used also by Andrew L.C.J. in *Lyons v Lyons*.[11] In view of the principle that proof on the balance of probabilities is now sufficient to establish adultery (1989 Act, section 3(1)), the expression may be regarded as too cautious. In *B.L. v M.L.* MacKenzie J. was satisfied that the husband had committed adultery on the basis that "His failure to deny either adultery coupled with the uncontradicted evidence of the wife in relation to each episode leads to no other reasonable conclusion."[12]

5   See *Blyth v Blyth* [1966] 1 All ER 524 (HL). In *Lyons v Lyons* [1950] NI 181, Andrew L.C.J. supported a standard somewhere between the civil and the criminal, an approach subsequently approved in *Bastable v Bastable* [1968] 3 All ER 701 (CA). See also *J.M.H. v J.P.H.* January 1983, unreported, High Court.
6   *Redpath v Redpath* [1950] 1 All ER 600. Fraud, duress and possibly insanity would also negative consent.
7   *Dennis v Dennis* [1955] P 153.
8   *MacLennan v MacLennan* 1958 SLT 12. CF. *Orford v Orford* (1921) 58 DLR 251 (Ontario SC).
9   January 1983, unreported, High Court, at page 73 of Ellis J.'s judgment.
10 (1810) 2 Hag Con 1.
11 [1950] NI 181.
12 3 October 1988, unreported, High Court, at page 11 of MacKenzie J.'s judgment.

7.015 Section 44(1) of the 1989 Act provides that condonation is no longer a bar to an application for judicial separation. However, where the spouses have lived with each other for more than one year after it became known to the applicant that the respondent had committed adultery, the applicant is not entitled to rely on that adultery as a separate ground, but may rely on it as one of the factors going to prove, under section 2(1)(b) of the Act, behaviour by the respondent such that the applicant cannot reasonably be expected to live with him.

7.016 Section 44(2) provides that connivance in the adultery by the applicant is a discretionary bar to relief. Connivance has been described as conduct "consisting of a knowledge of the adultery and a failure to make any remonstrance concerning it or to take any steps to try and persuade a partner from continuing with it."[13]

Behaviour

7.017 Section 2(1)(b) of the Judicial Separation and Family Law reform Act 1989 provides that the second ground for judicial separation is "That the respondent has behaved in such a way that the applicant cannot reasonably be expected to live with the respondent."

This ground is identical to one of the facts which, under divorce legislation in England[13a] and Northern Ireland[13b], entitles a court to find that a marriage has irretrievably broken down. Its introduction as an independent ground for judicial separation was recommended by the Law Reform Commission. (See **7.002**).

Relationship to cruelty

7.018 Although there are differences between the new ground and the old ground of cruelty, there remain certain similarities and it seems likely that as a minimum, conduct previously characterised as cruelty will constitute "behaviour" under the new ground. One difference is that cruelty consisted of conduct which rendered co-habitation unsafe or which made it likely that co-habitation would be attended by injury to the person or health of the complainant.[14] Under the new ground the applicant is not required to prove that the respondent's behaviour rendered co-habitation "unsafe", but that as a result of the behaviour, it is no longer reasonable to expect the applicant to continue living with the respondent. No doubt conduct which previously constituted cruelty will be regarded as having this consequence; if continued co-habitation is attended by a risk of injury to health, bodily or mental, it follows that it is unreasonable to expect it to

---

13 Per Finlay P. in *L. v L.* 21 December 1979, unreported, High Court, at page 13 of his judgment.

13a Matrimonial Causes Act 1973, section 1(2)(b).

13b Matrimonial Causes (Northern Ireland) Order 1978. Article 3(2)(b). See also the Divorce (Scotland) Act 1976, section 1(2)(b).

14 See *Carpenter v Carpenter* (1827) Milw. Rep. 159, at page 160, and *Kelly v Kelly*, LR 2 P & D 59, both of which were cited with approval by Costello J. in *McA. v McA* [1981] ILRM 361, at page 362.

continue. Indeed this consequence was often stressed in cruelty cases. For example, in *Murphy v Murphy*[15] by reason of the husband's conduct a stage was reached "when common life became impossible" (per Davitt P. at page 81). In *B.L. v M.L.*[16] Barr J. (at page 13 of his judgment) described the husband's conduct as having "destroyed the marriage relationship and created a situation whereby it would be unreasonable to expect the wife to cohabit with him again". On the other hand it is possible that cases will arise where, although there is no established risk of injury, it may yet be unreasonable to expect the applicant to continue co-habitation. If, for example, a husband decides to ignore his partner and live an independent life, staying away from the family home frequently,[17] it may be difficult for a strongly-constituted wife to provide evidence of a threat to her health; it may nevertheless be unreasonable to expect her to continue living with him. For the same reason the requirement laid down by Butler J. in *D. v D.*,[18] of showing "the absolute impossibility that the duties of married life could be discharged", would appear not to be implicit in the new ground. In the example given it may not be absolutely impossible for co-habitation to continue, but again it may be unreasonable to expect the applicant to continue living with the respondent.

Cumulative effect of behaviour

7.019 No doubt the practice under the old law of having regard to the cumulative effect of the respondent's conduct over time will be continued. In *Murphy v Murphy*[15] unhappiness in the marriage had lasted for many years and arose from a variety of causes. Over several years the husband pursued a course of conduct designed and intended to compel the wife to his point of view. On occasions he ordered her out of the house and shut her out at night; he threw water over her; he spoke to her offensively in front of the children; he did not in general allow her to handle money; he objected to her friends; and he was mainly responsible for the constant quarrels. Davitt P. concluded that, while many of these matters taken by themselves were trivial, their cumulative effect was serious and such that her health was affected. See also *B.L. v M.L.*[16] where the husband's conduct included physical assault, violent behaviour, verbal abuse, wrongful allegations that the wife was mentally ill, and humiliating the wife by committing adultery in the family home while she was residing there.

The test of reasonableness

7.020 The applicant is not required to prove that the respondent's conduct is unreasonable, but rather that it is unreasonable having regard to the respondent's behaviour, to expect the applicant to continue co-habitation. In *Carew-Hunt v Carew-Hunt*, Ormond J. stated, in the context of the

---

15 [1962–3] Ir Jur Rep 77.
16 3 October 1988, unreported, High Court.
17 Cf. *Bannister v Bannister* (1980) 10 Fam. Law 240.
18 December 1966, unreported, High Court, at page 7 of Butler J.'s judgment.

similar English provision,[19] "The question is not whether the respondent has behaved unreasonably and the court is no longer required, except marginally, to pass judgment on whether a person's behaviour is right or wrong, good or bad."

7.021 It is perhaps less easy in practice to maintain a neat distinction between the reasonableness of the applicant's wish not to cohabit, and the reasonableness of the respondent's conduct. Whether the applicant's reaction is reasonable must necessarily depend in part on the court's view of whether the respondent has behaved unreasonably.

The test of reasonableness implies an objective standard but this does not mean that the court may not take into account factors which are particular to the applicant and respondent, and to their relationship. In *Ash v Ash*[20] Bagnall J. suggested that the proper question to be addressed was:

> . . . can this petitioner with his or her character and personality, with his or her faults and other attributes, good and bad, and having regard to his or her behaviour during the marriage, reasonably be expected to live with this respondent?

7.022 As an example, while refusal by the respondent to have sexual intercourse may in some marriages be regarded as relevant in deciding whether it is unreasonable to expect the applicant to continue cohabitation, in other cases it may not. In *Archard v Archard*[21] the parties were practising Roman Catholics. The wife insisted, for medical reasons, on the use of contraceptives, while the husband refused for religious reasons to have intercourse with their use. The court refused to find that in such circumstances it was unreasonable to expect the wife to continue living with her husband. Where the applicant is sick, insensitive conduct by the respondent, which the petitioner might normally be expected to tolerate, may provide grounds. The circumstances of *R.K. v M.K.*[22] provide an example. The wife suffered from a motor neurone disease and as a result became depressive, anxious and irritable. The husband was unsympathetic and insensitive to the wife's needs. Finlay P., stressing that matrimonial obligations may be heightened by the sickness of a spouse, characterised the husband's behaviour as cruelty, and found that the wife was justified in leaving him.

7.023 The application of a test of reasonableness, albeit having regard to the particular circumstances of the parties, necessarily involves the making of judgments about what does and what does not constitute a tolerable standard of behaviour within a modern marriage. In making this kind of judgment in the context of cruelty and constructive desertion, the tend-

19   (1972) Times LR, 28 June.
20   [1972] Fam. 135, at page 140.
21   [1972] The Times, 19 April.
22   24 October 1978, unreported, High Court. (see **7.043**).

ency of Irish judges in the past has been to apply the standards of ordinary men and women, rather than of the angels, and to expect married partners to put up with the ordinary wear and tear of married life. In *Counihan v Counihan*[23] the wife's principal complaints against her husband were his irresponsibility in financial matters, his recklessness in contracting large debts and his taking employment away from home. Kenny J. decided that folly about money and a failure to provide a wife with the amount which she requires to run the house according to her standards would not justify her in leaving the husband and complaining that he had committed constructive desertion.[24]

7.024 Whether the same approach will be adopted in interpreting the section 2(1)(b) ground is uncertain. On the one hand, it could be argued that to apply the standard of "ordinary men and women" fails to take account of any special characteristics, whether in the constitutions and personalities of the parties, or the history of their relationship, which might make it reasonable not to expect the particular applicant to continue co-habitation. However, an entirely subjective approach cannot be adopted, because to do so would ignore the requirement of reasonableness in relation to what the applicant can be expected to tolerate. A middle path seems likely.

7.025 One relevant factor is that of provocation. Where the respondent's behaviour has been provoked by the applicant, this will have a direct bearing on whether or not it is unreasonable for him or her to continue co-habitation.[25] As was the case with the concept of cruelty, a test of reasonable proportionality is likely to apply. In *B.L. v M.L.* Barr J. was not prepared to accept as a justification for the husband's cruelty the fact that the wife had left the matrimonial bedroom, had refused thereafter to provide for him, and had begun legal proceedings. The husband's subsequent cruelty was described as "out of all proportion" to the wife's conduct.[26]

The intention of the respondent

7.026 It appears that there is no need for the applicant to prove that the respondent's behaviour was intended to drive him away, or to force an end to co-habitation. Nor, under the old law relating to cruelty, was such proof required. In *McA. v McA.*,[27] the wife's petition for a divorce *a mensa et thoro* was based on the complaint that her husband had over a long period

23 27 July 1973, unreported, High Court. (see **7.049**).
24 Cf. *Gollins v Gollins* [1963] 2 All ER 966, where the House of Lords found that a husband, who was incorrigibly lazy and tended to build up large debts, was guilty of cruelty.
25 See *Stevens v Stevens* [1979] 1 WLR 885.
26 3 October 1988, unreported, High Court. per Barr J., at page 13 of his judgment, approving a direction to the jury given by Finlay P. in *O'Reardon v O'Reardon* (February 1975, unreported) High Court. See A. J. Shatter, *Family Law in the Republic of Ireland* (3rd ed.), 221, note 34.
27 [1981] ILRM 361.

refused to communicate with her except in the most formal way. They conversed only about the necessities of life. Otherwise messages from the husband were transmitted through their three-year-old daughter or by note. The husband appeared emotionally cold and insensitive to his wife's needs. Sexual intercourse had ceased and the couple were sleeping in separate bedrooms. The husband refused to co-operate in seeking a solution, and the wife's health deteriorated. She suffered anxiety and depression, and there was a risk of further deterioration in health if co-habitation were to continue. Costello J. granted the decree and said:

> In the present case I am satisfied that the defendant's conduct has been deliberate in the sense that it was consciously adopted by him. I should make clear, however, that the defendant . . . has not set out deliberately to injure his wife's health. But this does not disentitle the petitioner to relief as it has been established in *Kelly v Kelly*[28] and confirmed in the House of Lords in . . . *Gollins v Gollins*[29] that cruelty in matrimonial cases can exist in the absence of an intention to injure.

7.027 The English courts have held that behaviour resulting from the mental or physical illness of one spouse may in certain cases make it unreasonable to expect the other spouse to continue co-habitation. In *Katz v Katz* the husband's behaviour resulted from manic depression. In *Thurlow v Thurlow*[31] the wife's behaviour resulted from epilepsy.[32] A decree will not therefore be granted in every such case, and no doubt the courts, in interpreting section 2(1)(b), will bear in mind the usual marriage vows, and that it is reasonable to expect a spouse to take some rough with the smooth. In *Thurlow v Thurlow* Rees J. stated (at 44) that account should be taken of the obligations of married life which include "the normal duty to accept and share the burdens imposed upon the family as a result of the mental or physical ill-health of one member". Given the wording of section 2(1)(b), the central question in such cases is likely to be—what amount of strain is it reasonable to expect the applicant spouse to tolerate? Much may depend on the strength of the medical evidence relating to the risks for the applicant if a separation does not occur. In *Katz v Katz*,[30] for example, the wife suffered acute anxiety which resulted in a suicide attempt.[32]

7.028 Although it appears unnecessary to prove that the respondent's behaviour was intended to hurt or cause separation, it may nevertheless be necessary to show that the behaviour was deliberate in the sense that the respondent was consciously directing his behaviour. A purely passive condition may not suffice. If, after a serious accident, a spouse becomes

---

28 LR 2 P & D 59.
29 [1964] AC 644.
30 [1972] 3 All ER 219.
31 [1976] Fam. 32.
32 See also *Williams v Williams* [1963] 2 All ER 994, where the husband suffered from insane delusions.

permanently comatose, this can hardly be described as "behaviour".[33] On the other hand, if a spouse is himself responsible for bringing about a condition, such as a serious and communicable venereal disease, which renders co-habitation unsafe, this might well be regarded as "behaviour". See *O'B. v O'B.*[34] ILRM in which McCarthy J. (at 14) thought it possible that infection with some highly contagious disorder might justify a barring order, and this despite the fact that, in general, "serious misconduct" must be proved.

The relationship between the "behaviour" and other grounds

7.029 If an act of desertion by the respondent were to constitute behaviour making it unreasonable to expect the applicant to continue co-habitation, then the one-year desertion ground in section 2(1)(c) of the 1989 Act would become redundant. The "behaviour" ground would inevitably be preferred because it avoids the need to prove that separation has continued for one year. To leave a spouse without just cause has always been regarded as a serious matrimonial offence. It is difficult therefore, to envisage a clear case of desertion which would not make it unreasonable to expect the deserted spouse to remain living with the respondent. Nevertheless, the English decision of *Stringfellow v Stringfellow*[35] suggests that a simple act of desertion, in which the principal behaviour relied on is the act of separating without just cause, can only be treated under the desertion ground. The relationship between the behaviour ground and constructive desertion is dealt with below, at **7.048**.

7.030 Adultery has also always been regarded as a serious offence against the matrimonial state and it is likely that it would be regarded as behaviour which makes it unreasonable to expect the applicant to continue co-habitation. However it is unlikely where adultery alone is relied on, that the behaviour ground will be employed. Section 2(1)(a) requires proof of adultery simpliciter, and the bar of condonation has been abolished. If section 2(1)(b) were relied on, the respondent might argue that condonation by the applicant suggests that it is not unreasonable for him to be expected to continue co-habitation. Section 4(1), which bars relief under the adultery ground where the applicant continues to live with the respondent for more than a year after discovering the adultery, makes it clear that in such a case the adultery may be one of the factors taken into account under section 2(1)(b); the implication is that the adultery alone, in such circumstances, would not be sufficient to establish the ground.

Effect of subsequent cohabitation

7.031 Where the parties have continued to cohabit after the incidents relied on to establish the "behaviour" ground, under Section 4(2) the court is bound to ignore such cohabitation if it has continued for a period of, or

---

33 See *Smith v Smith* [1973] 118 SJ 184. The issue is discussed, but not resolved, in *Thurlow v Thurlow*, supra.
34 [1984] ILRM 1.
35 [1976] 1 WLR 645.

periods amounting to, less than six months. It does not follow that where cohabitation has continued for more than six months, the court must necessarily refuse relief; but it may then take account of the period of cohabitation in determining whether in all the circumstances the applicant cannot reasonably be expected to live with the respondent.

Desertion

7.032 Section 2(1)(c) of the Judicial Separation and Family Law Reform Act 1989 provides that the third ground for judicial separation is "That there has been desertion by the respondent of the applicant for a continuous period of at least one year immediately preceding the date of the application."

7.033 Desertion was never a ground for a decree of divorce *a mensa et thoro*. The remedy for desertion provided by the ecclesiastical courts was a decree for the restitution of conjugal rights. This was abolished by Section 1 of the Family Law Act 1988. As the principal effect of a decree of judicial separation is to release the parties from the normal duty to cohabit, it may seem strange to provide the remedy in circumstances where cohabitation has clearly already come to an end. On the other hand, the remedy does offer the deserted spouse an opportunity to clarify his or her status, and it offers access to a wide range of ancillary orders relating to financial provision and property. The Law Reform Commission[36] proposed the introduction of desertion as a ground to reduce the uncertainty in the position of a deserted spouse brought about by the fact that desertion may be terminated at any time by a *bona fide* offer from the deserting spouse to return. A decree will enable the deserted spouse to plan his or her life as a separate individual.

7.034 If the English experience is any indicator, it is unlikely that desertion will be relied on in proceedings for judicial separation in more than a small minority of cases. (In England and Wales in 1985, only 4.2% of petitions for divorce relied on the fact of desertion.[37] Under Section 1(2)(c) of the Matrimonial Causes Act 1973 the required period of desertion is two years.) Where there has been matrimonial discord prior to desertion, the applicant is more likely to rely on the "behaviour" ground, and where the respondent consents to a decree the petitioner will (under Section 2(1)(d) of the 1989 Act) use the simpler ground of a one-year period of separation. In the first case it is not necessary to establish that separation has continued for one year, and in neither case is it necessary to prove desertion.

7.035 The Irish case-law on desertion has been built up in the context, not of judicial separation, but of maintenance proceedings. Prior to 1976, proof of desertion was necessary for a wife to obtain a District Court

---

36 *Report on Divorce a Mensa et Thoro and Related Matters*, at pages 38–39.
37 *Judicial Statistics: Annual Report 1985* (Cmnd, 9864, 1986), 51.

maintenance order. The Family Law (Maintenance of Spouses and Children) Act 1976 section 5(2) made desertion by the applicant an absolute bar to his obtaining a maintenance order for his own support. There is no reason to suppose that the definition of desertion adopted in that context should not be applied in proceedings for judicial separation. The main principles are therefore set out here.

Ceasing to live as one household

7.036 "Desertion is not the withdrawal from a place, but from a state of things".[38] Although the typical desertion involves the departure of one spouse from the matrimonial home, this need not occur. Desertion involves a unilateral rejection of the obligations of marriage which results in a couple ceasing to share a common life. This may occur while the couple are living under the same roof. Whether desertion occurs in such a case depends on whether the couple are living as two households or as one.[39] In effect the test is the same as that which applies to the concept of living apart in sections 2(1)(d) and (e) of the Act of 1989 (see **7.060–7.065**). Section 2(3)(a) requires the court to treat a couple as living apart "unless they are living with each other in the same household". In *Walker v Walker*[40] the wife withdrew to a separate bedroom, refused to work or perform any household duties for her husband and communicated with him by notes. Although the couple were forced occasionally to use the same kitchen, the wife was held to be in desertion.

7.037 There must be a rejection of all matrimonial obligations, not merely of some. Refusal by one spouse to sleep with the other does not constitute desertion as long as the other aspects of common matrimonial life continue to be shared.[41] The refusal may, however, be taken into account under section 2(1)(b) in determining whether the respondent's behaviour makes it unreasonable to expect the applicant to live with him.

The intention to desert

7.038 A spouse is not guilty of desertion unless he intends permanently to desert the other spouse. Where separation is involuntary desertion does not occur, as for example where a spouse is imprisoned, compelled for reasons of health to remain in hospital, or compelled by reason of economic necessity to seek employment abroad. What begins as an involuntary separation may nevertheless convert into desertion if the separated spouse subsequently forms an intention not to resume cohabitation.[42]

38   Per Ld. Merrivale P. in *Pulford v Pulford* [1923] P 18 at page 21.
39   Per Ld. Denning in *Hopes v Hopes* [1949] P 227, at page 235.
40   [1952] All ER 138; see also *Naylor v Naylor* [1961] 1 All ER 129.
41   *Weatherley v Weatherley* [1947] 628. See also *Hopes v Hopes*, supra, where the husband, who had withdrawn to his own room, occasionally shared a common family meal and shared the rest of the house with his family. Bucknill L.J. held that the husband was not in desertion.
42   See, for example, *Beeker v Beeker* [1948] P 302.

7.039 A spouse may, by reason of mental incapacity, be incapable of forming an intention to desert.[43] In *Crowther v Crowther*,[44] the House of Lords held that where a deserting spouse subsequently becomes insane, the onus falls on the deserted spouse to prove that the intention to desert has continued. The Law Reform Commission has proposed[36] legislative amendment of this principle along the lines of section 2(4) of the English Matrimonial Causes Act 1973. This provides that, in determining whether a spouse is in desertion, "the court may treat a period of desertion as having continued at a time when the deserting party was incapable of continuing the necessary intention if the evidence before the court is such that, had that party not been so incapable, the court would have inferred that his desertion continued at that time". This proposal has not been incorporated into the 1989 Act.

The absence of consent by the applicant

7.040 If spouses are living apart by agreement neither can allege that the other is in desertion. The agreement may be express or implied,[45] written or oral. A formal separation agreement will usually have the effect of precluding desertion; though a court may interpret a particular agreement as being essentially a maintenance agreement to last while the parties are separated.[46] Where desertion has already occurred, the signing of a separation agreement will usually terminate the desertion.

7.041 The agreement to live apart must be voluntary. This may not be so where a spouse is pressurised into signing an agreement without receiving legal advice, as was the case in *Holroyd v Holroyd*[47] where the wife believed that it was necessary to sign the agreement to make her husband pay her maintenance. There is a difference between consenting to separation and being glad that the separation has occurred. "Desertion does not necessarily involve that a wife desires her husband to remain with her. She may be thankful that he has gone, but he may nevertheless have deserted her."[48]

The absence of just or good cause

7.042 A spouse does not desert where he has good or just cause to leave the other spouse. This may be so where the applicant has behaved in a way which justifies the other in leaving. In such a case the applicant would have no ground for judicial separation, while the respondent may have grounds, either under section 2(1)(b) of the Act of 1989 based on the "behaviour" of the other spouse, or under section 2(1)(c) of the Act based on constructive

---

43   See *Perry v Perry* [1963] 3 All ER 766.
44   [1951] AC 723.
45   *Joseph v Joseph* [1953] 2 All ER 710.
46   *Crabtree v Crabtree* [1953] 1 WLR 708.
47   (1920) 36 TLR 479.
48   Per Buckley L.J. in *Harriman v Harriman* [1909] P 123, at 148.

desertion. Whether just cause exists is a matter of fact to be determined in the light of the particular circumstances in each case.

7.043 In *R.K. v M.K.*[49] the wife was jealous and suspicious of her husband from the start of their marriage. She made an unfounded accusation of infidelity. The husband was extremely insensitive towards her and demanding in the standards he required of her. There were two short separations, during one of which the husband committed adultery which was legally condoned but not forgiven by the wife. The wife was diagnosed as suffering from a motor neurone disease. As a result she suffered depression and anxiety, became irritable and found the unhappy aspects of the marriage unbearable. The husband's reaction was unfeeling reflecting "his fundamental view of his wife as a housekeeper and minder of his children". As a result, the wife left the matrimonial home. Although the husband did not rely on desertion to contest the wife's claim for maintenance, Finlay P. said that he would have rejected any contention that the wife deserted her husband. The obligations of a husband or a wife are not obviated, but may be heightened by the sickness of a spouse. The husband's gross lack of attention to and sympathy with her real needs, as her illness progressed, amounted to cruelty, justifying her departure from the home.

7.044 In *M.B. v E.B.*[50] the husband was a heavy drinker, a habit which intensified after the birth of a child. He often returned home drunk at night causing the wife concern for the welfare of the child. The parties began sleeping in separate rooms. The wife left the matrimonial home together with the child, following a night during which the husband had returned home drunk with a bottle of whiskey, and had, after a scene, put on the tape-recorder full-blast. Barrington J. found that "objectively" the wife had just cause for leaving.

7.045 By contrast in *P.G. v C.G.*,[51] Finlay P. decided that the wife had no just cause for leaving her husband. The parties were young and immature at the time of their marraige. The husband admitted assaulting the wife, though not in a serious manner, on two or three occasions, and was described by Finlay P. as "probably uncaring and insensitive" during the marriage. After one and a half years of marriage the wife left and went to England where she lived with a married man, but returned to Ireland soon after. The husband showed some willingness to attempt a reconciliation; the wife was adamant that no purpose would be served thereby. Finaly P. regarded the immaturity of both parties as the fundamental reason for the failure of the marriage, and found that the husband's conduct did not amount to just cause for the wife's departure.

7.046 In *P. v P.*[52] the wife left and returned to the matrimonial home on a

49 24 October 1978, unreported, High Court.
50 19 February 1980, unreported, High Court.
51 12 March 1982, unreported, High Court.
52 12 March 1980, unreported, High Court.

number of occasions before her final departure. She was pregnant at the time and after the birth of her child her attitude to the husband was cold and withdrawn, and she excluded him from contact with the child. Instances of aggression by the husband were, according to Barrington J., to be viewed in the light of him being denied all formal access to the child. While accepting that the husband was an "excitable and difficult" man with, according to his mother, "a bit of a temper", Barrington J. was not satisfied that he was violent or vicious. In all these circumstances the wife had not made out her case that she had just cause for leaving.

Constructive desertion

7.047 Desertion for the purposes of section 2(1)(c) of the Act of 1989 includes what is described by section 2(3)(b) as "conduct on the part of one spouse that results in the other spouse, with just cause, leaving and living apart from that other spouse." This concept of "constructive desertion" is well known to the law.[53] A similar formula is used in section 3(1) of the Family Law (Maintenance of Spouses and Children) Act 1976. One slight difference is that the Act of 1976 refers to the other spouse "living *separately* and apart". The omission of the adverb "separately" in the Act of 1989 does not appear to have any special significance though it re-inforces the principle that desertion can occur while spouses continue to live under the same roof.

7.048 It seems unlikely that constructive desertion will be much relied upon in proceedings for judicial separation. Most instances of conduct constituting constructive desertion would also be regarded, under section 2(1)(b), as behaviour which makes it unreasonable for the applicant to be expected to continue living with the respondent. The advantage of proceeding under that section is that there is no need to prove that the spouses have lived apart for one year. The one situation that is perhaps not covered by section 2(1)(b) is where the respondent has simply ordered the applicant out of the home.[54]

7.049 Another reason why constructive desertion is unlikely to be much used in separation proceedings is that it requires proof that the respondent intended to disrupt the marriage or bring co-habitation to an end. How this intention may be proved has been a matter of controversy. A subjective approach, requiring proof that the respondent personally wished to bring about a separation, would place a heavy burden on the applicant. An entirely objective approach, asking whether a reasonable person in the position of the respondent would have realised that his conduct would be likely to bring about a separation would offer better protection for the applicant but might ignore any extenuating circumstances, such as illness, attaching to the respondent. In *Counihan v Counihan*[53] (at page 10 of his

---

53 See *Counihan v Counihan* (27 July 1973, unreported) High Court.
54 See *Morgan v Morgan* (1973) 117 SJ 223.

judgment) Kenny J. attempted to resolve the matter by accepting McDermott L.C.J.'s statement in *McLaughlin v McLaughlin*:

> To constitute constructive desertion an intention to disrupt the marriage or to bring the co-habitation to an end must be proved against the spouse alleged to have deserted and a presumption in favour of that intention based upon the conduct of such spouse and its natural and probable consequences, though rebuttable, will not necessarily be rebutted by showing that the offending spouse did not want the other to depart, it being possible for a person to wish one thing and intend another.[55]

7.050 In practice, the approach taken to constructive desertion appears little different from that of cruelty. The emphasis generally is on the question whether the conduct of the respondent was such, in the light of the history of the marriage and the particular circumstances of the parties, that the applicant could not be reasonably expected to continue to endure it.[56] This in effect was the approach taken by Kenny J. in *Counihan v Counihan*. The parties had chronic financial difficulties which resulted in them living apart, sometimes for long periods, in the early years of their marriage. The husband was irresponsible about money matters, gambling and contracting large debts. The wife, who was used to a high standard of living, wanted financial security and a settled life for herself and their young child. There were frequent quarrels about finances and about the husband's absences from home. The husband had to take employment in a different part of the country. The wife suffered "severe nervous trouble". The final separation occurred when the wife told the husband to leave. He did so. Kenny J. concentrated entirely on the question of whether the wife was justified in her action, and his conclusion was that she was not.

> Folly about money, an inability to give the wife an amount which she requires to run the home according to her standards, would not have justified her in leaving her husband . . . The standards to be applied in judging the conduct of husband and wife are those of men and women and not of angels. In my view, if the husband's conduct, though inconsiderate, was not such as would have justified the wife in leaving him, it follows that when she told him to leave and he followed her instruction, she cannot complain that he was guilty of desertion.

7.051 Whether a spouse, whose conduct is the result of psychiatric illness, may be held to be in constructive desertion is uncertain. The presence of such illness might be accepted in a particular case as rebutting the presumption that the respondent intended to bring about the natural and probable consequences of his conduct. In the context of separation proceedings the matter is only of theoretical interest, because in such a case the applicant is likely to rely on section 2(1)(b) or (f) of the Act of

55   [1956] NI 73, following *Lang v Lang* [1955] AC 402 (Privy Council).
56   See *Hall v Hall* [1962] 1 WLR 1246.

1989, neither of which grounds requires proof that the respondent formed any particular intention.

The length of desertion and attempts at reconciliation

7.052 Under section 2(1)(c) of the Act of 1989 desertion must have lasted for a continuous period of at least one year immediately preceeding the date of application. However, in determing whether the period of one year has been continuous, no account may be taken of any period or periods, not exceeding six months in total, during which the spouses resumed living with each other. The period or periods during which the spouses have resumed co-habitation do not count towards the one-year period of desertion, and under section 2(2) the spouses must not be living with each other at the time the application is made. The object of this provision is to facilitate attempts at reconciliation. If an unbroken period of separation were required, a spouse who is contemplating proceedings under the Act might be deterred from making any last attempts to salvage the marriage.

Termination of desertion

7.053 *Resumption of cohabitation* If spouses resume living together as one household this will normally bring desertion to an end. However if co-habitation is resumed for less than six months this is not taken into account in determining, for the purposes of the Act of 1989, whether desertion has been continuous. "A resumption of cohabitation must mean resuming a state of things, that is to say, setting up a matrimonial home together, and that involves a bilateral intention on the part of both spouses to do so."[57] A brief resumption of cohabitation, even when accompanied by sexual intercourse, does not bring desertion to an end if the deserting spouse has no intention of permanent cohabitation. The fact that the parties resume living together under one roof is not sufficient to terminate desertion; there must in addition be an intention to establish a single household.[58]

7.054 *Cessation of intention to desert* Desertion may terminate if the deserting spouse genuinely wishes to resume cohabitation. In the case of actual as opposed to constructive desertion, the deserted spouse must consider seriously any genuine offer from the deserting spouse to resume cohabitation; if he does not do so, he may be held to be in desertion.[59] An offer from the deserting spouse to resume cohabitation will be regarded as genuine if (a) it is communicated to the other spouse; (b) the deserting spouse is prepared and in a position to implement the offer;[60] (c) the offer

---

57   Per Ld. Merriman P. in *Mummery v Mummery* [1942] 1 All ER 553, at page 555.
58   *Bartram v Bartram* [1949] 2 All ER 270.
59   *Fraser v Fraser* [1969] 1 WLR 1787.
60   *Turpin v Turpin* [1965] 1 All ER 1051 n.

is not subject to unreasonable terms;[61] and (d) it is a reasonable offer in its terms and in its tone having regard to the previous relationship and dealings between the parties.

7.055 In the case of constructive desertion the deserted spouse may sometimes be justified in refusing an offer to resume cohabitation. This will be so where constructive desertion is based on adultery[62] or outrageous conduct by the deserting spouse.[63] In other cases the deserted spouse is entitled to seek assurance from the deserting spouse that the conduct which constituted constructive desertion will not be repeated.[64] Of course, in such cases it is unlikely that the ground of desertion will be used in separation proceedings. The constructively deserted spouse is more likely to employ section 2(1)(a), (b) or (f) of the Act of 1989.

7.056 *Subsequent consent*   Where, subsequent to desertion, the parties enter into a separation agreement the desertion is usually thereby terminated.

7.057 *Supervening insanity in the deserting spouse*   See **7.039** above.

7.058 *Other supervening events*   The grant of the decree of judicial separation will itself terminate desertion. But will any other type of separation order bring desertion to an end preventing the applicant seeking a judicial separation on the desertion ground? Where a barring order or an injunction excluding a spouse from the matrimonial home exists, the duty to cohabit is brought to an end; it is difficult to see how a spouse can be said to be in desertion where there exists no duty to cohabit. In England it has been found necessary to provide by legislation that a period during which spouses live apart under an exclusion order or injunction may be counted as a period during which the respondent is in desertion for the purpose of divorce proceedings.[65] The absence of such a rule in the Irish Law relating to judicial separation is of little consequence because in most cases where a barring order or matrimonial injunction is in force, an applicant will be able to rely on the grounding facts in applying for a judicial separation under sections 2(1)(b) or (f) of the Act of 1989.

Living apart for at least a year

7.059 Section 2(1)(d) of the Judicial Separation and Family Law Reform Act 1989 provides that the fourth ground for judicial separation is "That

---

61   *Slawson v Slawson* [1942] 2 All ER 527 (the wife's offer to return was conditional on there being no sexual intercourse). An offer to resume cohabitation, subject to unreasonable terms, from the deserted to the deserting spouse may terminate desertion, and possibly place the offeror in desertion. See *Barrett v Barrett* [1948] P 277.
62   *Day v Day* [1957] 1 All ER 848.
63   *Edwards v Edwards* [1948] P 268.
64   See *Thomas v Thomas* [1942] P 194.
65   See the Domestic Proceedings and Magistrates' Courts Act 1978, section 62, amending the Matrimonial Causes Act 1973, section 4.

the spouses have lived apart from one another for a continuous period of at least one year immediately preceding the date of the application and the respondent consents to a decree being granted".

Once again this provision is borrowed from English divorce legislation, the one difference being that the period of living apart is two years in the English Act.[66] The object of the provision is the admirable one of avoiding court-room hostilities or "mud-slinging" by permitting the parties to apply by consent for a separation after one year's separation without the need for one to establish that the other is responsible for the breakdown of the marriage. However, it seems unlikely that this ground will be much used in seeking judicial separation. A requirement is that the respondent consents to a decree being granted; where his consent is forthcoming it will usually be simpler and cheaper for the parties to enter into a separation agreement. If there is a dispute between the parties over matters of finance and property a separation agreement may prove impossible; but equally, where such a dispute exists the respondent is unlikely to consent to a judicial separation because by doing so he opens up to the applicant a wider range of financial provision and property orders than she would otherwise have available.

Living apart—the fact

7.060 The concept of living apart has already been discussed in relation to desertion (see **7.036**) and the approach is likely to be similar in this context. The idea that spouses may be living apart under the same roof if they maintain separate "households" is implicit in section 2(3)(a) which provides that

> . . . spouses shall be treated as living apart from each other unless they are living with each other in the same household, and references to spouses living with each other shall be construed as references to their living with each other in the same household.

7.061 The question is whether all aspects of a communal matrimonial life have ceased. In *Fuller (orse Penfold) v Fuller*,[67] the wife separated from the husband and began living with another man. When the husband became seriously ill he moved into his wife's new home as a lodger, sleeping in his own room, and paying a weekly rent. Although the wife provided her husband with food and did his laundry, the Court of Appeal held that they were not living in the same household as a husband and wife. They were therefore living apart. By contrast, in *Mouncer v Mouncer*[68] the parties, whose relationship had broken down, were living in the same home because the husband wanted to live with and help look after the children. He slept in a separate room, but meals were usually taken

---

66 Matrimonial Causes Act 1973, section 1(2)(d). See also the Matrimonial Causes (Northern Ireland) Order 1978, Article 3(2).
67 [1973] 2 All ER 650.
68 [1972] 1 All ER 289.

together. In this case sufficient elements of a common matrimonial life remained to justify a finding that the couple were not living apart. The fact that the couple were not having sexual intercourse was not by itself sufficient to justify a finding that they were living apart.

Living apart—the mental element

7.062 There is nothing in the Act of 1989 to suggest that anything more than the *fact* of living apart for a year need be proved. There is no mention of any intention in either spouse which must accompany the factual separation. A literal reading of the Act would therefore justify a finding that a couple have been living apart where separation is involuntary, as where one spouse is hospitalised through illness or is imprisoned, or forced by economic circumstances to find employment abroad. A separation which is voluntary and consensual, as where a spouse is serving for a period abroad in the armed forces or as a diplomat, would also literally constitute living apart.

7.063 The English Court of Appeal in *Santos v Santos*[69] was not prepared to adopt this literal approach and held that the concept of living apart involves more than physical separation. It also implies recognition by at least one of the parties that the marriage is at an end, although it is not necessary that this should be communicated to the other spouse. The spouses cannot be said to be living apart "whilst both parties recognise the marriage as subsisting".[70] In the New Zealand case of *Sullivan v Sullivan*[71] Turner J., adopting a less exacting standard, said that "living apart" must involve "a mental attitude averse to cohabitation on the part of one or both of the spouses". Although the imputing of a mental element into the concept of living apart has been criticised[72] there is a considerable body of authority from several jurisdictions which use the "living apart" concept in their divorce laws, that it is not sufficient to prove mere physical separation.[73]

7.064 If it is accepted that one party must at least assume a mental attitude averse to cohabitation, but that no communication of that attitude to the other spouse is necessary it becomes difficult in particular cases to determine exactly when living apart has begun. The matter is one of proof, as there would be obvious risks in accepting the applicant's word on the matter without some corroborative evidence.

---

69 [1972] 2 All ER 246.
70 Id., per Sachs L.J., at page 256.
71 [1958] NZLR 912 (CA), at page 924.
72 By e.g., S. M. Cretney in *Principles of Family Law* (4th ed., 1984), 157.
73 Per Sachs L.J. in *Santos v Santos* at 251. The jurisdictions include Australia, New Zealand, Canada, and the United States. See *Main v Main* (1949) CLR 636 (High Court of Australia), *Sullivan v Sullivan* [1958] NZLR 912 (New Zealand Court of Appeal), *Rowland v Rowland* [1969] 2 OR 615 (Ontario).

7.065 If one spouse is not in any position to form a mental attitude towards the separation, as for example where that spouse is hospitalised in a comatose state or with a psychiatric illness, it seems that living apart may nevertheless commence when the other spouse makes it clear that he regards the marriage as at an end. In the New Zealand case of *McRostie v McRostie*[74] the husband was a patient in a mental institution for some years and his wife had a child by another man. The spouses were treated as living apart even though the husband did not know and could not become conscious of her desertion. It is unlikely in such a case that the wife would under Irish law be able to rely on a one-year period of separation because that requires the consent of the respondent; but she might be able to rely on the three-year period in section 2(1)(e) of the Act of 1989.

The consent of the respondent

7.066 It is likely that the courts will require evidence of positive consent by the respondent not mere acquiescence. In particular a consent that is implied or given on behalf of the respondent is unlikely to be sufficient.[75] Where the respondent suffers from mental incapacity the test of whether he is capable of giving consent is likely to be the same as the test for determining whether a person is capable of consenting to marriage as laid down in *Re Park's Estate*.[76] Was the respondent capable of understanding the nature and effects of the consent given?[77]

The continuity of living apart

7.067 Section 2(1)(c) of the Act requires that the one-year period of living apart should be a continuous period lasting until immediately preceding the date of the application. In order not to discourage attempts at reconciliation section 2(2) provides that in considering whether the requisite period of living apart has been continuous no account may be taken of any one or more periods not exceeding six months in all during which the spouses have resumed living with each other. Such periods of living together may not be taken into account in calculating the period for which the spouses have been living apart, and any period of resumed co-habitation must have come to an end at the time the application is made.

Living apart for at least three years

7.068 Section 2(1)(e) of the Judicial Separation and Family Law Reform Act 1989 provides that the fifth ground for judicial separation is "That the spouses have lived apart from one another for a continuous period of at least three years immediately preceding the date of the application."

This ground enables a guilty spouse or one who has been responsible for the breakdown of the marriage, to obtain a decree of separation against

---

74 [1955] NZLR 631.
75 *McG. (formerly R.) v R.* [1972] 1 All ER 362.
76 [1954] P 89. [1953] 2 All ER 408.
77 *Mason v Mason* [1972] Fam. 302. [1972] 3 All ER 315.

the wishes of an innocent spouse. Its rationale is that there comes a point at which, regardless of the wishes of an innocent spouse, the law must recognise the fact of breakdown and make provision for it. The granting of the decree does little damage to the innocent spouse; it simply formalises the spouses' separated status. The more important issue from the point of view of the innocent spouse, is the extent to which s/he is protected in the provisions relating to the ancillary financial, property, custody and other orders; see chapter 13. This is not to say that every applicant employing section 2(1)(e) will be a guilty spouse nor that every respondent will be innocent. A respondent's consent to a decree of judicial separation may be refused for quite selfish motives.

7.069 The principles applicable to this ground are the same as those applicable to section 2(1)(d), as set out in the previous section, with the exception that the period of living apart is three years[78], and the respondent's consent to a decree being granted is not required.

No normal marital relationship for at least a year

7.070 Section 2(1)(f) of the Judicial Separation and Family Law Reform Act 1989 provides that the sixth ground for judicial separation is "That the marriage has broken down to the extent that the court is satisfied in all the circumstances that a normal marital relationship has not existed between the spouses for a period of at least one year immediately preceding the date of the application."

This ground for judicial separation was introduced at a late stage in the passage of the Judicial Separation and Family Law Reform Bill through the Oireachtas, on the Bill's recommital to the Special Committee. It represents a compromise between the original proposal that irretrievable breakdown of marriage should be the sole ground for judicial separation and the Government's view that irretrievable breakdown is an inappropriate concept for judicial separation as opposed to divorce.

7.071 The omission of the adverb "irretrievably" from the section is deliberate. There is no need for proof that the marriage has broken down without any prospect or hope of a reconciliation between the spouses. What is required is proof that a normal marital relationship has not existed for at least one year. How are the courts likely to interpret this requirement?

A normal marriage relationship

7.072 The concept of normality clearly invites a court to draw comparisons. But with what is the condition of the marriage over the last year to be compared? One possibility is for the court to compare the marriage in its

---

78   The Law Reform Commission, *Report on Divorce a Mensa et Thoro*, supra, at 48, recommended a five-year period. The three-year period was recommended in the *Report of the Joint Committee on Marriage Breakdown*, supra, at para. 7.3.8.

recent state to the condition which it previously enjoyed. If there has been a sudden change in the relationship it could be argued that the marriage is no longer in its normal state. While a sudden change in the nature of the relationship may certainly be relevant it can hardly be a decisive factor. The change may be for the better or there may be no basis for comparison, as where the relationship is abnormal from the start.

7.073 If an analogy with the "behaviour" ground is accepted (see **7.020**) the question likely to be asked by a court is this: bearing in mind the particular circumstances of the parties and the history of their marriage, does their relationship differ so markedly from what might reasonably be regarded as a normal relationship to justify the conclusion that the marriage has broken down? This formulation requires the application of an objective standard of normality but allows for account to be taken of any special characteristics within the particular marriage. Thus, if a couple have agreed from the outset to live together without having sexual intercourse and have done so for many years without protest from either party the fact that this situation has persisted for a further year could not reasonably be regarded as evidence that the relationship has become abnormal given the history of the marriage and the particular understandings on which it was based. On the other hand if a relationship has survived for many years in the absence of any real communication between the parties, apart from constant mutual abuse, it might be regarded as abnormal by any objective standard. The concept of a normal marital relationship is already being used within the law of nullity: see **2.056**. It seems likely that judicial interpretation of the concept will proceed along similar lines in the two branches of the law.

The mental element

7.074 Whether a marriage has or has not broken down is a matter of fact. The question of fault or responsibility for the breakdown appears to be irrelevant. The fact that a marriage has broken down due to circumstances beyond the control of a spouse (for example psychiatric illness or an accident which has affected the personality of the spouse) will presumably not preclude a decree. Although it may not be necessary to prove an intention to bring the marriage to an end, it is possible that a mental element will be implied in the concept of breakdown. By analogy with the concept of "living apart", it may be decided that a breakdown cannot be said to occur unless at least one party forms a belief that the marriage has broken down (see **7.062–7.065**).

The period of one year

7.075 Proof is needed that there has not been a normal marital relationship for at least one year immediately preceding the date of application. The one-year period is not expressed to be "continuous", as are the periods of desertion and living apart in sections 2(1)(c), (d) and (e).

Relationship with other grounds

7.076 Behaviour by the respondent making it unreasonable to expect the petitioner to continue cohabitation may well indicate the absence of a normal marital relationship. However, the "behaviour" and "breakdown" grounds are not indentical. The "behaviour" ground does not require proof of a one-year period of breakdown; and the "breakdown" ground does not require proof of intolerable behaviour by the respondent. Indeed the petitioner, under the "breakdown" ground, may be the one responsible for the breakdown of the marriage.

7.077 The "breakdown" and "living apart by consent" grounds differ in that, in the former the petitioner may rely on breakdown without proving that the respondent consents to a separation. If living apart is evidence that a normal marital relationship does not exist (and it is difficult to avoid that conclusion), it follows that, where the spouses have been living apart for a year it is safer for the petitioner to rely on the "breakdown" ground, in case he fails to prove consent by the respondent. Apparently the only case where it would be preferable to use the "living apart" ground, is where the one-year period of separation has been interrupted by periods of co-habitation not exceeding six months in all. They may be discounted under the "living apart" but not under the "breakdown" ground, though it is not clear, under the "breakdown" ground, that the one year period of abnormal relationship needs to be "continuous".

7.078 The relationship between the "breakdown" ground and the "three-year living apart" ground is the most problematic. The latter is clearly designed to prevent living apart being used as a ground, without the consent of the respondent, until three years at least have elapsed. Yet the breakdown ground seems to provide the means of circumventing the prohibition if, that is, it is accepted that living apart necessarily implies that a normal marital relationship does not exist. It may be that, in order to give meaning to section 3(1)(e), the courts will feel obliged to hold, somewhat perversely, that living apart is not per se evidence that a normal marriage relationship does not exist.

Provisions to encourage reconciliation

7.079 A solicitor acting for an applicant or a respondent in proceedings for judicial separation is required:

(a) to discuss with his client the possibility of reconciliation;
(b) to supply the names and addresses of persons qualified to help effect a reconciliation;
(c) to discuss with his client the possibility of engaging in mediation to help effect a separation on an agreed basis;
(d) to supply the names and addresses of persons and bodies qualified to provide a mediation service;

(e) to discuss with the client the possibility of effecting a separation by the negotiation and conclusion of a separation deed or written agreement. (Sections 5(1) and 5(2)).

7.080 The solicitor acting for the applicant must satisfy these requirements before the making of the application; the solicitor acting for the respondent must do so as soon as possible after receiving instructions. In both cases the solicitor must certify to the court that he has complied with the requirements. Where he fails to do so, under sections 5(2) and 6(2), the court may, but is not bound, to adjourn proceedings for a reasonable period to allow discussion of these matters to take place.

7.081 The court is also under a duty in all proceedings for judicial separation to "give consideration to the possibility of reconciliation", and under section 7(1) it may adjourn proceedings at any time if both spouses so wish to afford them an opportunity to consider a reconciliation. Section 7(2) provides that, if during an adjournment for this purpose the spouses resume living together, no account may be taken of that fact in the proceedings. The court may also under section 7(3), if both spouses so wish, adjourn proceedings to allow the parties an opportunity to reach agreement on the terms of separation in so far as is possible. Where an adjournment is granted under section 7(4) either party may at any time request that the application be proceeded with, and the court is then bound to resume the hearing as soon as is practicable.

Circumstances in which a decree may be refused

7.082 Many of the circumstances in which a court may refuse to grant a decree of judicial separation have already been described. The following is a summary:

1. It seems that a spouse may be precluded by prior agreement, express or implied, from applying for a decree of judicial separation.
2. Where the petitioner is relying on the adultery ground—(a) under section 4(1) co-habitation for more than one year after the petitioner becomes aware of the respondent's adultery is an absolute bar to relief and (b) under section 44(2) connivance is a discretionary bar; (see **7.013–7.016**).
3. Where there are dependent children, a court must not grant a decree unless (a) it is satisfied that proper provision has been made for the welfare of the children, or (b) the court itself intends by order to make such provision: section 3(2); see **14.001**.
4. Failure to supply the court with certificates that the applicant and respondent have been made aware of alternatives to separation proceedings and that the possibility of reconciliation has been discussed may result in proceedings being adjourned, but does not operate as a bar to relief: section 5(2) and 6(2).

7.083 The Act expressly provides in section 44(1) that collusion between the spouses in connection with an application for judicial separation or any conduct (including condonation or recrimination) by the applicant shall not bar the grant of a decree. The one exception is connivance in proceedings grounded on adultery.

Effects of a decree of judicial separation

7.084 Under section 8(1) the grant of a decree of judicial separation terminates the parties' obligation to cohabit. The obligation to cohabit has for long been unenforceable and the proceedings for the restitution of conjugal rights have now been abolished by section 1 of the Family Law Act 1981. It does not, however, follow that a decree of judicial separation has no real effect; see **7.001–7.006**. It clarifies the status of the parties. It makes available a range of ancillary remedies relating to financial provision and property. Once the decree has been granted neither party can be held to be in desertion.

7.085 The decree releases the parties from the duty to cohabit, but it does not compel separation. A separate order is required to exclude one spouse from the matrimonial home. Where the respondent has been guilty of serious misconduct, a barring order or an injunction is the appropriate remedy. It has been common practice in the past for the Circuit Court to make exclusion orders pursuant to decrees for divorce *a mensa et thoro*, and this practice has been approved by the High Court.[79] Where there has been no serious misconduct by either spouse, a procedure for determining who should remain in occupation of the family home to the exclusion of the other is provided by section 16(a) of the Act of 1989 (see chapter 13). The grant of a decree of judicial separation no longer automatically excludes a "guilty" spouse from sharing in the estate of the other spouse by way of legal right or on intestacy.[80] The court may, however, under section 17 of the 1989 Act, make an order extinguishing such rights.

---

79 *E.W. v K.W.* (26 January . . ., unreported), High Court, where the husband was an alcoholic and had committed acts of serious violence against the wife.
80 Succession Act 1965, section 120(2), as amended by the Act of 1989, section 42(1).

Chapter 8

MAINTENANCE PROCEEDINGS

Introduction: The different maintenance proceedings

8.001 There are three forms of proceeding by which a spouse may obtain a maintenance order for his or her support or for the support of a dependent child:

a) The Family Law (Maintenance of Spouses and Children) Act 1976 gives the District Court and Circuit Court, jurisdiction to make a maintenance order against a spouse for the support of the applicant spouse and/or any dependent child of the family, in circumstances where the respondent spouse has failed to provide proper maintenance. At present the District Court is limited to a maximum order of £30 per week for the support of a dependent child and £100 per week for the support of a spouse. There is no limit on the amount that may be ordered by the Circuit Court. (On the question of whether application may also be made to the High Court, see **1.027–1.032**). The principal determinants of maintenance under the Act of 1976 are the needs of the dependent spouse and children and the means of the liable spouse. Proceedings under the Act may be brought independently of any other legal proceedings. A legal separation need not be applied for, nor is it necessary that the spouses should be living apart.

(b) Under section 11 of the Guardianship of Infants Act 1964 the District Court and Circuit Court have jurisdiction on the application of a guardian, to order maintenance for the support of a child (see **1.027–1.032**). There is a difference in the definition of a child qualifying for maintenance under the 1964 and 1976 Acts. Also, those qualified to bring proceedings differ under the two Acts. Otherwise the principles applicable are broadly similar. Such differences as exist are summarised in **8.056–8.059** below.

(c) The Judicial Separation and Family Law Reform Act 1989 provides a much broader basis fr the making of financial provision orders than the 1964 or the 1976 Acts. One of those available under section 14 of the Act of 1989 is an order for the making by one spouse of periodical payments

188

(secured or unsecured) to the other spouse or a dependent child. Although such an order will normally be sought to obtain maintenance for the necessary support of the applicant spouse or dependent child, the order appears to have a broader function than a simple maintenance order. Proof is not required that the respondent spouse has not been providing proper maintenance, and the factors which the court must, under section 20, take into account in determing periodical payments go far beyond the measurement of the means and needs of the respective parties, which is the basis for assessment under the 1976 Act. An order for periodical payments under the Act of 1989 may only be made on the grant of a decree of judicial separation. Because of the special nature of an order for periodical payments and its possible inter-relationship with other orders relating to financial provision and property under the Act of 1989, it will be described, along with those other orders, in chapter 13. In this chapter the "Act of 1976" refers to the Family Law (Maintenance of Spouses and Children) Act 1976.

The Family Law (Maintenance of Spouses and Children) Act 1976

Maintenance for a "spouse"

8.002 To qualify under the Act of 1976 to apply for maintenance for his or her own support under section 5(1)(a) of the Act of 1976 the applicant must be a "spouse" of the respondent. A co-habitee has no right to apply nor does a party to a marriage which is void at civil law. In the case of a voidable marriage, until an annulment is granted, the marriage is treated as valid and either party may apply for a maintenance order. Once a decree has been granted, neither party may orginate maintenance proceedings. However if a maintenance order is already in force when the decree is granted, it is arguable that it remains in force until set aside or varied by the court. This matter has not been ruled upon by the courts, but there is an analogy with the case of a foreign divorce which is discussed at **8.052– 8.055.**

8.003 Where a foreign divorce which is entitled to recognition has been granted by a foreign court neither party any longer has the status of a "spouse" and neither, it appears, may originate maintenance proceedings. See *M(C) v M(T)*[1] in which Barr J. (at page 11 of his judgment) states that the Act of 1976 requires "that the applicant shall be the spouse of the respondent at the time when the application to the court is made." See also *L.B. v H.B.*[2] where the wife, whose French divorce was not entitled to recognition, succeeded in her claim to maintenance. The inference was that, if the divorce had been recognised, the wife's claim would have failed.[3] However, the fact that divorce proceedings are pending abroad,

1 30 November 1989, unreported, High Court.
2 [1980] ILRM 257.
3 Per Egan J. in *M(C) v M(T)* [1988] ILRM 456, at 461.

even though they may be well advanced, does not bar a spouse's right to apply for maintenance. In the earlier hearing of *M(C) v M(T)*[3] the husband had already obtained a decree *nisi* of divorce in England (which was to become absolute in a few weeks), when the wife applied for an interim maintenance order. Egan J. refused the husband's application to stay the proceedings and awarded the wife interim maintenance. The question of whether an *existing* maintenance order lapses on the granting of a recognised foreign divorce is discussed at **8.052–8.055**.

In subsequent proceedings in *M(C) v M(T)*[3] Barr J. discussed the doctrine of "divisible divorce", which has been accepted in some other jurisdictions[4], according to which a foreign divorce though recognised as altering the status of the parties, may be regarded as having no effect on separable personal rights including the right to maintenance. If the doctrine were accepted in full a qualifying spouse validly divorced abroad would not only continue to enjoy rights under an existing Irish maintenance order but would also be able to bring original maintenance proceedings under the Act of 1976 even after the foreign divorce has been granted. Barr J. neither accepted nor rejected the doctrine but found that it would be inapplicable in the instant case because the wife had participated in the English divorce proceedings. The doctrine operates only where the non-petitioning spouse plays no part in the divorce proceedings. It remains uncertain therefore whether the doctrine of "divisible divorce" would be applied in an appropriate case.

8.004 The fact that a spouse has willingly petitioned for, or co-operated in obtaining, a foreign divorce does not prevent him or her from subsequently claiming that the divorce should not be recognised in this country for the purposes of a maintenance application. In *L.B. v H.B.* the wife had been a a willing party to a French divorce obtained on the basis of collusion. In maintenance proceedings brought against her "husband" in this country many years later, if was held by Barrington J.[5] that she was not estopped from denying the validity of the French divorce. This she successfully did and was awarded maintenance. However considerable injustice might result if the same principle were to apply in a case where a husband seeks to avoid paying maintenance to second wife by claiming that the divorce which he obtained from his first wife is not entitled to recognition.

Maintenance for a "dependent child of the family"

8.005 Maintenance may be sought by one spouse against another for the support of a "dependent child of the family," which includes the following:[6]

---

4 The cases cited were *Estin v Estin* 334 US 451, *Lynn v Lynn* 302 NY 193 in the USA, and *Wood v Wood* [1957] P 254 in England.

5 Following *Gaffney v Gaffney* [1975] IR 133. And see *C. v C.* (27 July 1973, unreported) High Court.

6 Act of 1976, section 3(1), as amended by the Status of Children Act, section 16(b).

(a) a natural child of both spouses;
(b) a child adopted by both spouses under the Adoption Acts 1952 to 1988;[7]
(c) a child in relation to whom both spouses are *in loco parentis*;
(d) a natural child of one spouse, or a child adopted by one spouse under the Adoption Acts or a child in relation to whom one spouse is *in loco parentis*—provided, in each case, that the other spouse, being aware that he is not the parent of the child, has treated the child as a member of the family.

8.006 Maintenance is payable in respect of a dependent child up to the age of 16, or, if the child is or would be receiving full-time education, up to the age of 21, or indefinitely where the child is suffering from mental or physical disability to such an extent that it is not reasonably possible for him to maintain himself fully. The reduction of the age of majority from 21 to 18 by Age of Majority Act 1985 has not affected these principles. See section 2(4)(b) of the Act of 1985.

Where married parents have obtained a foreign divorce which is recognised in the state, it appears that neither may apply as a "spouse" for maintenance for the support of a dependent child per Egan J. in *M(C) v M(T)*[3] (see **8.003**). An *existing* maintenance order made on the application of a spouse for a dependent child does not automatically lapse when the parents' marriage is dissolved by a foreign divorce, per Barr J. in *M(C) v M(T)*, at a later hearing. However, application may be made by either parent under section 5A(1) of the Act of 1976, as amended by section 18 of the Status of Children Act 1987. This refers to "a dependent child whose parents are not married to each other," and would include divorced parents. In addition a divorced parent may apply as a "guardian" for a maintenance order in respect of a dependent child under the Guardianship of Infants Act 1964. However, the range of dependent children covered by the Act of 1964 is narrower than that encompassed by the Act of 1976. For example, children in respect of whom the parents are *in loco parentis* are not covered by the Act of 1964.

8.007 The right to bring maintenance proceedings for the support of dependent children vests in the parents. An exception to this general principle is made by section 5(1)(b) of the Act of 1976 which allows "any person" to apply for maintenance for a dependent child within a family where a spouse (a) is dead, or (b) has deserted or been deserted by the other spouse, or (c) is living separately and apart from the other spouse. An application under the section can only be made where the child is not being fully maintained by either spouse, and it is made against the surviving spouse or as the case may be, either spouse. "Any person" would include a person such as a relative, caring for the child, and may arguably include the child himself. For example, an 18-year-old college student, one of whose parents is dead, might apply for an order for his own support

---

7 A child adopted abroad is not included. In most cases such a child would be one in relation to whom both spouses are *in loco parentis*.

against the surviving parent. Where both spouses are alive and living together, third party proceedings are not possible under the Act even though the spouses may not be fully maintaining their child.

Purpose of the Act of 1976: Meeting present needs

8.008 The primary function of the Act of 1976 is to ensure that proper and adequate maintenance is available to a dependent spouse or child from a spouse who has failed to provide reasonable maintenance for their support.[8] It is not necessary for the applicant to prove the commission of any matrimonial offence; under section 5(1)(a) the ground for application is simply the failure of the respondent spouse to provide such maintenance as is proper in the circumstances. The purpose of the Act is "to deal with the situation of the parties at the time the proceedings were brought."[9] Appropriate maintenance is determined more on the basis of the current needs and resources of the parties than on any past dealings between them.[10]

8.009 Because a maintenance order is designed to meet current needs, it is not available to provide compensation for past losses arising out of the marriage. In *J.S.J. v R.S.J.*[11] the spouses had separated eight months after their marriage. There were no children. The wife's claim for maintenance was based principally on the losses she had suffered, estimated at £8,636.00, as a result of the marriage. She had given up her employment as a clinical teacher in a hospital and had been unable to secure identical employment after the separation. She suffered a reduction in salary and losses incurred in the purchase of a home at her new place of employment. She did not offer evidence indicating an existing need for support. On the contrary, the evidence indicated that she had sufficient means to support herself. Ellis J. dismissed the wife's application for maintenance under section 5, concluding that the real substance of her claim was to recover by way of maintenance past and apprehended financial losses or expenses and that the Act of 1976 was not intended to provide the means of recovering such losses.

No waiver of rights under the Act of 1976 permitted

8.010 The policy of ensuring that family dependants have adequate support overrides any pre-existing agreement between the parties. Neither party can waive his or her right to bring proceedings under the Act. Section 27 makes void an agreement "in so far as it would have the effect of excluding or limiting the operation of any provision of this Act . . ." The

8   See judgment of Walsh J. in *H.D. v P.D.* 8 May 1978, unreported, Supreme Court.
9   Per Walsh J. in *H.D. v P.D.*, supra, at page 7 of his judgment.
10 See *R.H. v N.A.H.* (20 June 1983, unreported) High Court; *O'S v O'S.* 18 November 1983, unreported, High Court.
11 26 June 1980, unreported, High Court.

words "in so far as" indicate that, if the agreement to exclude the Act is part of a wider agreement, other elements in the agreement remain valid and binding on the parties. This provision applies to any agreement, oral or written, express or implied, and regardless of the consideration provided. Monies paid or property transferred under such an agreement will be relevant only in considering the applicant's current needs in proceedings under the Act. Section 21 is excluded from the provision. It is possible, therefore, for spouses to contract out of the normal principle that an allowance made for meeting household expenses is joint property.

8.011 These principles were underlined by the Supreme Court in *H.D. v P.D.*[8] The respondent wife had begun proceedings for divorce *a mensa et thoro* in 1972, and had applied for alimony *pendente lite*. The proceedings were settled in 1973 on the basis of a written consent signed by both parties, and made part of the order of the court. The consent included a term that the husband should pay the wife "in full satisfaction of all claims in the petition" the sum of £10,000. He also agreed to pay for the education of each of the two younger (of four) children until each reached the age of 18. In 1977 the wife applied to the High Court for a maintenance order for the support of herself and her two younger children. The husband argued that she was estopped from making such application by reason of the 1973 consent. Rejecting the husband's appeal, Walsh J. stated at page 7 of his judgment

> In my view it is not possible to contract out of the Act by an agreement made after the Act came into force or by an agreement entered into before the legislation was enacted . . . It appears to me that in a case such as the present one, the function of the Court under the Act of 1976 is to determine whether or not there is a financial need justifying the making of the order sought under the Act. Therefore, if by reason of a previous arrangement between the parties, either in the form of a separation agreement or in some less formal type of agreement, one spouse makes payments to the other spouse or may have already made a lump sum payment, the income of which or other use of which may be sufficient to alleviate in whole or in part the financial need complained of, the Court shall have regard to such payments in deciding what order should be made in a claim for maintenance pursuant to section 5 of the Act.

It is not clear why Walsh J. made no mention of section 27. The section appears broad enough to encompass agreements entered into before the passing of the Act.

8.012 The decision in *H.D. v P.D.* is clearly opposed to any idea of a "clean break". The parties cannot by agreement make final and irrevocable arrangements relating to financial provision and property. The possibility of either spouse making application under the Act of 1976 is ever present. The absence of divorce also militates against the idea of a clean break. Cf. the position in England: in *Minton v Minton*[12] it was decided that, where a consent order is made which does not stipulate periodical payments or under which periodical payments are to come to an end on the happening of a specific event, the order represents a final settlement between the parties.

Assessment of maintenance

General principles

8.013 There is no magic formula for assessing appropriate maintenance in a given case. Section 5(4) of the Act, as substituted by the Status of Children Act 1987 section 17(b), requires the court, in deciding whether to order maintenance and what amount to order, to have regard to "all the circumstances of the case" and in particular, the following matters:

    (a) the income, earning capacity (if any), property and other financial resources of—
        (i) the spouses and any dependent children of the family, and
        (ii) any other dependent children of which either spouse is a parent,
        including income or benefits to which either spouse or any such children are entitled by or under statute, and
    (b) the financial and other responsibilities of—
        (i) the spouses towards each other and towards any dependent children of the family, and
        (ii) each spouse as a parent towards any other dependent children, and the needs of any such children, including the need for care and attention.

8.014 The assessment of maintenance therefore turns on the balancing of two principal determinants:

    (a) the needs of the dependent spouse and children, taking into account any actual or potential resources available to them, and
    (b) the resources of the liable spouse, taking into account his current and expected expenses and liabilities.

Where, as is frequently the case, combined needs exceed combined resources, standards of living are necessarily reduced. How the losses should be apportioned between the parties is not always easy to determine. One principle is clear: the resources of the liable spouse should not be reduced to a point where he has insufficient to meet his own current basic needs. This principle is explicit in Part III of the Act dealing with attachment of earnings. Section 10(4)(b) requires an attachment of earnings order to specify a "protected earnings rate," i.e., the rate below which the maintenance debtor's earnings should not be reduced. Thus if there is a serious shortfall the greater loss is likely to fall on the dependent spouse and children. The principle operating here is one of practicality rather than

12 [1979] 1 All ER 79. See also Matrimonial Causes Act 1973, s. 25A(3) as inserted by the Matrimonial and Family Proceedings Act 1984, s. 3.

fairness. If the income of the liable spouse is reduced too far there will be little incentive for him to continue working. The practical consequence is that where social or supplementary welfare payments are needed to augment family income, it is the dependants rather than the wage-earner who will generally be obliged to apply for them.

8.015 The broad principles applicable to the fixing of maintenance under section 5 have been expressed by Finlay C.J. as follows:

> The Court . . . must first have regard to the somewhat pathetic fact that upon the separation of a husband and wife and, particularly a husband and wife with children, it is inevitable that all the parties will suffer a significant diminution in the overall standard of living. The necessity for two separate residences to be maintained and two separate households to be provided for makes this an inescapable consequence of the separation. Subject to that overriding consideration a court must, of course, ascertain the minimum reasonable requirements of, in this case, the wife and the children for whose upkeep she is responsible; it must then ascertain income earned or capable of being earned by the wife, apart from the maintenance for which the husband is responsible; its next task is to ascertain the true net take-home pay or income of the husband, bearing in mind the general consideration of economy affecting all the parties concerned, but leaving him with a reasonable standard of living.[13]

8.016 Because the respondent must be left with "a reasonable standard of living", the bottom line in fixing maintenance is the respondent's capacity to pay. *R.H. v N.H.*, the case from which the above quotation is drawn, illustrates this principle. The husband was successful in his appeal to the Supreme Court because the trial judge had over-estimated his net take-home pay and as a result had fixed maintenance at a level which was "not properly related to his capacity to pay and provide for his own living expenses."

8.017 Leaving the respondent with a reasonable standard of living does not entail maintaining it at its present level. Where it is possible to do so, without reducing the respondent's income to a level which makes it impossible for him to live at a reasonable standard, the tendency is to make an order which will require all parties to reduce their standard of living somewhat. This policy of "equal misery" is illustrated by *C.P. v D.P.*[14] At the time of the wife's application for maintenance for herself and her two children, she was living in rented accommodation while her husband occupied the matrimonial home. The husband had business and other debts amounting to approximately £24,000. He also owned some antique furniture and *objets d'art* valued at approximately £12,000. In making an

13   *R.H. v N.H.* 24 October 1985, unreported, Supreme Court, at pages 7 and 8 of Finlay C.J.'s judgment.
14   [1983] ILRM 380.

order of £150 per week in favour of the wife, Finlay P. (at 386 and 387) recognised, on the one hand, "that the overall lifestyle of the children and wife, whilst in no sense extravagant or irresponsible, exceeds what in my view under any circumstances the husband is able to pay," and, on the other hand, that "the husband must accept a limited standard of living and economic accommodation in order to try and meet the long-term financial obligation of maintaining his wife and children." The order was made on the assumption that both parties would make necessary adjustments in their lifestyles and in the management of their assets. In *O'K. v O'K.*[15] Barron J. applied a policy of equal misery by splitting 50/50 between the parties the husband's net resources after deduction of the husband's necessary expenses. The wife, who was looking after the two children, had her own income which was approximately half that of her husband. See **8.033**.

8.018 The conduct of the spouses may occasionally result in modification of the policy of equal losses. Where for example, the respondent's behaviour is viewed as irresponsible, and particularly where he is in desertion, greater emphasis may be placed on the need to safeguard the financial position of the dependent spouse, particularly if she has children in her care. In *E.D. v F.D.*[16] the husband had deserted his wife after twelve years of marriage. There were three children being cared for by the wife. The husband had not complied with a previous order, made in interlocutory proceedings, to pay his wife £130.00 per week maintenance. He had for some time been living above his means, and had contracted substantial debts. In fixing maintenance for the wife and children at £746.00 per month, Costello J. stated:

> . . . I do not accept the view . . . that because the overall family expenses rise when a husband deserts the family home, the extra burden should be borne equally by the husband and the wife and children who are living with her, and that all must be prepared to accept a reduction in their living standards. When a husband deserts his wife and children the court should be concerned to ensure that their financial position is protected, even if this means causing a drop in the husband's living standards.

The relevance of the conduct of the spouses is discussed further at **8.035– 8.038**.

Calculating the needs and resources of dependants

8.019 The practical details involved in calculating the needs and resources of dependants are dealt with in the next chapter. What constitute "reasonable needs" depends in part on the lifestyle formerly enjoyed by the dependent spouse, provided always that the resources of the liable spouse are sufficient to meet such a level of need. In *L.B. v H.B.*[17] the wife was

15 16 November 1982, unreported, High Court.
16 23 October 1980, unreported, High Court.
17 31 July 1980, unreported, High Court.

living in a stately home in the West of Ireland and receiving £50.00 per week alimony. She had the right to buy groceries and other goods at shops where her husband kept credit accounts. Each year she was given a ticket to fly to London for the sales. She alleged that the facilities in her present home were unsatisfactory and that her husband was a "very mean man". The husband owned two other substantial properties in Ireland as well as other assets in Ireland and the U.S.A., including 200 acres of land near Washington, D.C., valued at between four and nine million dollars. Barrington J. fixed maintenance at £300.00 per week and stated (at page 38 of his judgment):

> I am satisfied that [the husband] has not maintained his wife in the style to which the wife of so wealthy a man may reasonably aspire and which she formerly enjoyed . . . I am satisfied therefore that the defendant has not maintained the plaintiff in the manner which is proper in the circumstances. I accept the evidence of the plaintiff that she cannot live with any measure of comfort in a house the size of the family home without, at least, the services of a housekeeper and a gardener.

8.020 A spouse's poor health may give rise to additional needs. In *R.K. v M.K.*[18] Finlay P. accepted that a wife who was suffering from a motor neurone disease, which resulted in depression and anxiety, would require hired help in addition to the other essentials of life.

8.021 Section 5(4) of the Act of 1976 has been modified by section 17(b) of the Status of Children Act 1987 to make it clear that responsibilities towards, and the needs of, all dependent children (including non-marital children) of the spouses must be taken into account. Thus, although one spouse cannot in general[4] be required to pay maintenance for the support of an extra-marital child of the other spouse, the needs of that child, and the responsibility which the parent has towards it, must be taken into account in assessing what that spouse's needs and resources are. (A spouse may, under section 3(1), be required to pay maintenance for the support of an extra marital child if, being aware that he is not the parent, he has treated the child as a member of the family).

8.022 The needs of a spouse or dependent child are of course reduced where he or she has an income or other resources. As well as actual earnings the court is required by section 5(4)(a) to consider "earning capacity,"[19] that is the income "capable of being earned"[20] by the applicant spouse. Where a dependent spouse has an earning capacity which is not being realised, the court may make a short-term award at a higher level with the prospect of it being reduced at a later stage when she obtains employment. It is accepted that the earning capacity of a spouse will be less

---

18 24 October 1978, unreported, High Court.
19 The earning capacity of the wife was one of the factors taken into account in *L. v L.* 21 December 1979, unreported, High Court.
20 Per Finlay C.J. in *R.H. v N.H.*, supra, at page 8 of his judgment.

where she has the care of young children. In *C.P. v D.P.*[21] Finlay P. accepted that the wife's "capacity to take employment . . . is obviously circumscribed by the obligations of looking after two children . . ." He thought, nevertheless, that "The wife must make . . . realistic if less pleasant plans towards obtaining worthwhile employment bearing in mind the limitations which are imposed upon that."

8.023 Where there are no children and the wife is in receipt of an income sufficient to meet her needs, an order may be refused, as in *J.S.J. v R.S.J.* (see **8.009**) where the wife, who was in employment, offered no evidence to indicate an existing need for support. On the other hand, if the dependent spouse has insufficient resources, she may be entitled to maintenance even though there are no children and co-habitation has lasted a relatively short period. In *J.C. v J.H.C.*[21a] the couple lived together for less than four years and there were no children. The husband established a model photographic agency and a hairdressing salon, but the wife took no part in their running. The matrimonial home was held on a joint beneficial tenancy. The husband's violent conduct had led to a separation. Maintenance was fixed by Keane J. at £82.00 per week. This case is further evidence of a tendency to grant maintenance more readily where the defendant is at fault.

8.024 Any property at the disposal of the applicant which is a potential source of income, may be taken into account. In *L. v L.*[22] because the house in which the wife lived without children was too large for her needs, maintenance was fixed at a level which took account of the capital likely to be raised by her selling and renting alternative accommodation. However, less will be required of the dependent spouse where the liable spouse has substantial resources. In *L.B. v H.B.*[17] where the husband was very wealthy and the wife was living in a stately home owned by him the question of alternative cheaper accommodation was not raised. It may also be that less is expected of the applicant spouse where the liable spouse is judged to have been responsible for her predicament. In *E.D. v F.D.* (see **8.018**) the wife who had young children and was deserted by her husband was not expected to raise additional income by taking in a lodger.

8.025 In fixing appropriate maintenance for a child, the court may find it necessary to include a sum to enable a parent to care for the child. This is relevant where the parent is for some reason not entitled to maintenance in her own right. In *P. v P.*[23] the mother's desertion disqualified her from obtaining maintenance. However it was asserted that, in order to look after a young child, she would not be able to work for some years. Barrington J. therefore included in the maintenance for the child a sum sufficient to enable the mother to look after the child. Similarly in *A.H. v*

---

21 [1983] ILRM 380 at 386 and 387.
21a 4 August 1982, unreported, High Court.
22 21 December 1979, unreported, High Court.
23 12 March 1980, unreported, High Court.

A.H.[24] where the wife had deserted, the sum of £50.00 per week to be awarded for each of three children included, according to Lynch J. at page 13 of his judgment, "a sufficient sum to make some reasonable provision for the care and attention which they will have to be given either by the wife their mother, or, if she was not available, then by some paid help."

Effect of applicant's entitlement to maintenance under an agreement

8.026 It has already been explained that a dependent spouse retains the right to apply for maintenance under the Act of 1976, even though she may be in receipt of maintenance under the terms of a settlement or agreement, and even though she may have purported expressly to waive her right to apply for maintenance, See **8.010–8.012**. In *H.D. v P.D.*[25] Walsh J. indicated that payment of maintenance under an agreement or settlement is relevant, in proceedings under section 5 of the Act, in determining what are the applicant's needs and what if any, is the appropriate level of maintenance to be ordered. Proceedings under section 5 do not discharge a contractual obligation to pay maintenance. Notwithstanding the existence of an agreement or settlement, the court may make an order for the full amount of maintenance to be paid by the liable spouse, that is, for the agreed sum plus any additional amount which the court deems appropriate. In such a case maintenance paid under the order can be treated as satisfying *pro tanto* the contractual obligation. Such an order has the advantage for the dependent spouse of simpler enforcement.

8.027 Some of these principles are illustrated by *O'S. v O'S.*[26] The spouses, who had seven children, had executed a separation agreement in 1973 under which the husband was to pay the wife £1,400.00 per annum for the children's support, subject to annual adjustments by reference to the official cost of living index. There was no provision for payment of maintenance to the wife, though she was to be paid a salary of £20.00 per week for managing a business. In 1980 the husband discontinued payments under the agreement, and the wife obtained a maintenance order in the Circuit Court for £379.40 per month in respect of six of the children who were still infants. This was equivalent to the adjusted amount due under the separation agreement. The husband was now earning approximately £10,000.00 per year and owned a valuable residential property in England. The husband argued that the original agreement for the payment of maintenance was rendered void by section 27 of the Act of 1976 in that by providing for a fixed sum of maintenance, it purported to exclude or limit the provisions of the Act. This argument was rejected by Murphy J. The husband's contractual obligation still subsisted. At the same time the court was entitled to entertain the wife's application for maintenance under section 5 of the Act, and would treat the maintenance agreement as one of the many "circumstances of the case" to be considered in deciding whether

24 19 December 1985, unreported, High Court.
25 8 May 1978, unreported, Supreme Court.
26 18 November 1983, unreported, High Court.

to make an order and, if so, for what amount. There was no reason why the contractual obligation to pay maintenance should not remain alongside a duty to pay further maintenance by virtue of an order made under the Act. In the particular circumstances, however, Murphy J. chose in effect to incorporate the contractual obligation into a maintenance order. He ordered that the husband pay £75.00 per week to the wife, and that that sum, as and when paid, should be credited against the sums which the husband was contractually bound to pay. A particular reason for making the order in this form was that the court would have statutory powers to ensure payment.

8.028 A similar approach may be adopted by the court where there is difficulty in interpreting the terms of a maintenance agreement, or where circumstances have changed since the agreement was made. In *R.H. v N.H.*[27] there was a dispute between the spouses over the interpretation of a review clause in a settlement and the husband had suffered an unexpected reduction in his tax-free allowances. On the wife's application, Costello J. decided to fix maintenance under section 5 of the Act of 1976 "by reference to the parties' needs and actual means," rather than on the basis of the agreement. In a subsequent appeal to the Supreme Court, this approach was approved.[28]

Calculating the resources, expenses and liabilities of the liable spouse

8.029 In *R.H. v N.H.* Costello J. stated at page 15 of his judgment: "I have regretfully to say that the defendant has not been entirely candid in the disclosure of his means." This statement points to the problem in maintenance cases of determining the liable spouse's real income and other resources. The practical problems are discussed in chapter 9. Costello J. assessed the husband's income on the basis of actual income over the past twelve months rather than a forecast of probable future income. The dangers of relying solely on past income were exposed in the husband's successful appeal to the Supreme Court. He had in the year prior to the proceedings in the High Court, earned a significant additional income by way of overtime bonus payments. There was no evidence of any expectation of similar overtime payments for the future. As a result the High Court had over-estimated the net take-home pay likely to be earned by the husband.

8.030 Although the courts do not have powers under the Act of 1976 to order lump sum payments nor to order the sale of property, capital assets are considered in assessing the resources of the liable spouse and it is common for maintenance to be fixed at a level which will require that spouse to realise certain assets. In *C.P. v D.P.* an order was made which represented a charge on certain antique furniture and objets d'art owned

27 20 June 1983, unreported, High Court.
28 See *R.H. v N.H.* 24 October 1985, unreported, Supreme Court, per Finlay C.J., at page 5 of his judgment.

by the husband. In *R.K. v M.K.* it was recognised by the court that, in order to pay the maintenance ordered, the husband might have to borrow against future realisation of some building land. In *J.C. v J.H.C.*[29] Keane J. ordered a husband with a present income of £97.00 per week to pay a maintenace of £82.00 per week to his wife. The judge was satisfied that a re-arrangement of the husband's assets would enable him to produce sufficient income to support his wife at that rate.

8.031 *R.F. v M.F.*,[29a] a case where the capital assets of both parties were considered, shows that a liable spouse is not entitled to arrange his financial affairs in such a way that this income is diminished at the expense of the dependent spouse. Loan repayments of £120.00 per month to a credit corporation were, for that reason, ignored by D'Arcy J. in assessing the husband's available resources.

Relevance of obligations (or benefits) deriving from an extra-marital relationship

8.032 In assessing the liable spouse's current obligations and expenses, account must be taken of his responsibilities in respect of all his dependent children, including any that he is now supporting within an extra-marital relationship.[30] On the other hand, any other benefits or obligations arising out of a relationship with a second partner are, it seems, to be ignored.

8.033 In *O'K. v O'K.*[31] following the breakdown of the marriage, the husband was living with a third party who was contributing to a common pool, used for their joint living expenses. The husband's net average earnings in the previous year were £112.00 per week. The wife was earning £46.00 per week and receiving £22.50 per month in children's allowances. The wife argued that the earnings of the third party should be taken into account in assessing the husband's means from which maintenance should be paid. Addressing the question of principle, Barron J. states at pages 6–7.

> Neither the fact that the husband is living in an adulterous association nor the fact that the third party is earning or not earning is a consideration which should be taken into account. The wife should not be entitled to any greater maintenance from her husband because he has the benefit of earnings of a third party with whom he is living, nor should the wife suffer because the third party with whom her husband is living is not earning and has to be supported by him.

Nevertheless, "as a matter of practicality", Barron J. went on to take account of the third party's contribution of £68.00 per week in assessing the

29 4 August 1982, unreported, High Court.
29a 1 December 1982, unreported, High Court.
30 Act of 1976, section 5(4)(b)(ii), as amended by section 17 of the Status of Children Act 1987.
31 16 November 1982, unreported, High Court.

husband's overall resource situation. The wife's, the husband's and the third party's incomes were totalled up, necessary expenses were deducted, and the maintenance order made in favour of the wife represented one half of the balance. Barron J. (at page 8) thought that an equal division of the balance was reasonable, "having regard to the fact that part of it is being provided by the lady with whom he is now living."

8.034 It is not possible to reconcile Barron J.'s statement of principle with the manner in which he in fact assessed maintenance. However, he did indicate that, adopting an alternative method of assessment, which took no account of the third party's income, maintenance would be fixed at the same level. In practice it is not unusual for judges or justices to take account of any help that the liable spouse is receiving from third parties in meeting his current expenses. In the subsequent case of *M.McG. v D.McG.*[32] Barron J. himself did so once again, but "only on the basis of what is factual." The husband had set up home on a permanent basis with another partner and as a result the level of the husband's expenses after tax was less than it might otherwise have been. Barron J. (at page 5) saw "no reason why he should not act upon the basis of that state of affairs." On the other hand it appears not to be general practice to reduce the maintenance payable to a spouse by reason only of the fact that the liable spouse has accepted an obligation to support his co-habitee.

The effect of conduct on maintenance rights and obligations

Desertion by the applicant

8.035 Section 5(2) of the Act of 1976 requires a court not to make a maintenance order in favour of a spouse who has deserted and continues to desert the other spouse, "unless, having regard to all the circumstances (including the conduct of the other spouse), the Court is of the opinion that it would be repugnant to justice not to make a maintenance order." The quoted words were inserted by the Judicial Separation and Family Law Reform Act 1989, section 38(2)(a). Where a maintenance order is already in existence it may be discharged on the same basis.[33] Under section 3(1) desertion includes "conduct on the part of one spouse that results in the other spouse, with just cause, leaving and living separately and apart from him," that is constructive desertion. Desertion does not affect a spouse's right to apply for maintenance for the support of a dependent child.

8.036 The case-law on desertion has already been considered in detail at **7.033–7.058**. The proviso that desertion does not act as a bar to maintenance where, in the court's opinion, it would be "repugnant to justice" not to make an order, was introduced by the Judicial Separation and Family Law Reform Act 1989. Previously desertion had been an absolute bar. It is

---

32 February 1985, unreported, High Court.
33 Section 6(2) of the Act of 1976, as amended by the Judicial Separation and Family Law Reform Act 1989, section 38(3)(b).

not easy to predict how the proviso will be interpreted in practice. Where desertion is raised as a defence the court's first duty is to determine whether desertion has in fact been established. In making this determination certain principles of justice are relevant, for example the principle that a spouse is not in desertion where she has just cause for leaving the other spouse. Once desertion is established, the court will presumably consider whether there are any other circumstances relating to the parties, the history of their marriage or the circumstances of its breakdown, which suggest that it would do a serious or grave injustice to the applicant spouse to deny her maintenance.

8.037 The "conduct" of the other spouse is mentioned as a relevant factor in deciding the question of justice. However if that other spouse is guilty of misconduct prior to the applicant's departure from the matrimonial home, it is unlikely that the applicant will be found to be in desertion[34] unless the misconduct is no more than is to be expected as part of the wear and tear of normal married life. In *P. v P.*, a young wife had left a husband who was an an excitable and difficult man but not violent or vicious. He had reacted aggressively, but in Barrington J.'s view understandably, to the wife's attempts to deny him access to their young child. She therefore had no just cause for leaving him and was held to be in desertion. It might be thought that in such a case it would be regarded as "repugnant to justice" to refuse the wife any maintenance for her own support, particularly in view of the fact that she had the care of a young child and was not therefore readily able to take paid employment. In fact Barrington J. overcame this problem by including in the maintenance awarded for the support of the child a sum sufficient to enable the mother to look after the child. See also *A.H. v P.H.*[35] and *P.G. v C.G.*[36] in which a young mother deserted her husband to have a brief affair with a married man in England. The maintenance ordered for the child was £12.00 per week, and no mention was made of including a sum to enable the mother to rear the child. The husband's means were, however, very slender.

8.038 The situation in which it might perhaps be regarded as repugnant to justice to refuse a wife all maintenance is where she deserts following long and loyal service as a wife and mother. A wife who leaves her husband after thirty years of marriage, when all the children have become independent, might well claim that in justice she deserves some recognition of the contribution she has made not only in providing a home for her husband and children, but also in enabling her husband to develop his career and therefore his capacity to generate an income. She herself, because of her long absence from the labour market, might well find it very difficult to earn a reasonable income.

---

34 See, e.g., *M.B. v E.B.* 19 February 1980, unreported, High Court; *R.K. v M.K.* 24 October 1978, unreported, High Court, discussed in **7.043**.
35 14 December 1985, unreported, High Court.
36 12 March 1982, unreported, High Court.

Other "conduct" of the applicant

8.039 Section 5(4)(c) of the Act of 1976 requires the court, in deciding whether to grant maintenance, and if so what amount, to have regard to "the conduct of each of the spouses, if that conduct is such that in the opinion of the court it would in all the circumstances be repugnant to justice to disregard it." This clause was inserted by section 38(2)(c) of the Judicial Separation and Family Law Reform Act 1989. The Act at the same time, sections 38(2)(b) and 38(3)(c), removed section 5(3) and 6(4) from the Act of 1976 by thus removing the discretionary bar of adultery.

8.040 The objective of the new provision is that misconduct, including adultery, should play a less prominent role in determining entitlement to maintenance. The same provision applies to financial provision and property-related orders made in proceedings for judicial separation under section 20(2)(i) of the Act of 1989. The rationale for according less prominence to misconduct is that this helps to avoid the "bitterness, distress and humiliation,"[37] which may arise when a court attempts to ascertain the relative responsibility of the parties for the breakdown of their marriage. The approach adopted by the English courts to the making of financial provision after divorce, since the 1969 Divorce Reform Act, has been based on the same philosophy. In *Wachtel v Wachtel*[38] Lord Denning M.R. considered the implications of the requirement under section 25(1) of the Matrimonial Causes Act 1973, that the court should have regard so far as was practicable, to the conduct of the parties in making financial provision.

> Does this mean that the judge in chambers is to hear their mutual recriminations and go into their petty squabbles for days on end, as he used to do in the old days? Does it mean that, after a marriage has been dissolved, there is to be a post mortem to find out what killed it? We do not think so. In most cases both parties have contributed to the breakdown.

8.041 He then went on to consider exceptional cases of misconduct which could not be ignored, employing in part phraseology similar to that contained in the new Irish provisions.

> There will no doubt be a residue of cases where the conduct of one of the parties is . . . "both obvious and gross,"[39] so much so that to order one

---

37   See the Law Commission (England and Wales), *Reform of the Grounds of Divorce, the Field of Choice* (1966, Cmnd. 3123), para. 15.

38   [1972] Fam 72.

39   Excessive emphasis in subsequent cases on the words "obvious and gross" was criticised as unduly restricting a court's discretion. (See Law Commission, *The Financial Consequences of Divorce*, etc., Law Com. No. 112, para. 38). The present statutory formulation requires a court to have regard to conduct, "if that conduct is such that it would in the opinion of the court be inequitable to disregard it." (Matrimonial Causes Act 1973, section 25(2)(g), as amended by the Matrimonial and Family Proceedings Act 1984).

party to support another whose conduct falls into this category is *repugnant to anyone's sense of justice* . . . But, short of cases falling into this category, the court should not reduce its order for financial provision merely because of what was formerly regarded as guilt or blame. To do so would be to impose a fine for supposed misbehaviour in the course of an unhappy married life.

Three preliminary points may be made concerning the new Irish provisions. The first is that the respective conduct of the spouses (with the exception of conduct that amounts to desertion) is in general to be ignored in maintenance proceedings. The second is that the court is required to have regard to conduct where it would be repugnant to justice to disregard it. The third is that, even where there has been conduct which cannot be disregarded, it is only one of the circumstances to be taken into account alongside all the other relevant considerations set out in section 5(4) of the Act of 1976. Bearing in mind this context, how will a court decide whether conduct is such that in all the circumstances it would be repugnant to justice to disregard it?

8.042 It does not follow, from the removal of adultery by the applicant as a discretionary bar to relief, that adultery by the applicant may now in all circumstances be disregarded. However the removal of any specific mention of adultery does suggest that adultery by the applicant should be given less prominence than in the past, and that adultery is not conduct which *per se* it would be repugnant to justice to ignore. It may also safely be predicted that adultery which under the pre-1989 law, would have been ignored because it had been condoned, connived at or by wilful neglect or misconduct conduced to by the other spouse, will also be ignored under the new provisions.[40]

8.043 In *L. v L.*[41] the husband had in a flagrant manner begun an adulterous relationship which was continuing at the time of the maintenance proceedings. A separation followed and, soon after the wife had an adulterous relationship which lasted about one month followed by a second long-term relationship. At the time of her application for maintenance the wife was not living with or being maintained by the other man, but he was from time to time staying overnight with her, and they were sharing a social life. Finlay P. found that the husband had by wilful misconduct conduced to the adultery of the wife and that under the then section 5(3)(a) of the Act of 1976, he had no option but to ignore it in deciding the question of maintenance. It seems very likely that a similar approach will be adopted under the new section 5(4)(c), though the new provision does in fact leave more to the discretion of the judge.

---

40 Act of 1976, section 5(3)(a), now removed, along with the rest of section 5(3), by the Judicial Separation and Family Law Reform Act 1989, section 38(2)(a).
41 21 December 1979, unreported, High Court.

8.044 In *O.C. v T.C.*[42] the wife, after fifteen years of marriage, left her husband to live with another man in a relationship which was to continue for five years. McMahon J. viewed the marriage as seriously deficient in affection and trust from an early stage. However, the wife's adultery was due, not to wilful neglect on the part of the husband, but to the wife's infatuation with the other man. In addition the terms of a separation agreement entered into by the husband and wife, and the terms of a custody order made by the Supreme Court, were flagrantly breached by the wife. In those circumstances McMahon J. at pages 7–8 of his judgment held that "it would . . . clearly be unfair to the husband to revive the obligation to support his wife which was extinguished by her adultery." Again it is possible that a similar decision would be made under the new provisions relating to conduct. It might be regarded as "repugnant to justice" to ignore the wife's conduct in *O.C. v T.C.*, where the misconduct was primarily one-sided, but not so in *L. v L.* where misconduct was bi-lateral.

8.045 Examples of misconduct which have been taken into consideration by the English courts in making financial provision and property adjustment orders since 1970 include the[43] firing of a shotgun at a husband, the slashing of a wife's wrist with a razor with the result that she could not pursue her career as a nurse,[44] extreme financial irresponsibility by a husband,[45] refusal *ab initio* by a wife to join her husband in a new house,[46] and cases where all the responsibility for the breakdown of a marriage is borne by one party.[47] Where there has been misconduct by both spouses, it is generally disregarded.[48]

8.046 Whether it would ever be regarded as "repugnant to justice" to ignore conduct for which a spouse bears no moral blame is uncertain. Arguably the test implies an element of fault, so that conduct which is brought on by physical or psychological illness should be ignored. Examples are *West v West*[49] and *J. (H.D.) v J. (A.M.)*,[50] where the court held that persistent persecution of a husband (who had re-married), and of his second family, by a wife suffering from chronic schizophrenia could not be ignored. It may also be "repugnant to justice" to disregard meritorious conduct by a spouse, as in *Kokosinski v Kokosinski*[51] where the wife had been "faithful, loving and hard-working" both during five years of marriage and a previous twenty years of co-habitation.

---

42   9 December 1981, unreported, High Court; noted in [1983] ILRM 375.
43   *Armstrong v Armstrong* [1974] 118 SJ 579.
44   *Jones v Jones* [1975] 2 All ER 12.
45   *Martin v Martin* [1976] 3 All ER 625.
46   *West v West* [1977] 2 All ER 705.
47   See *Robinson v Robinson* [1973] 2 FLR 1.
48   For example *Leadbeater v Leadbeater* [1985] FLR 789.
49   [1978] Fam 1.
50   [1980] 1 All ER 156.
51   [1980] 1 All ER 1106.

"Conduct" of the defendant spouse

8.047 The conduct of "each of the spouses" is referred to in the amended section 5(4)(c) of the Act of 1976. Prior to the amendment of this section in 1989, the defendant's conduct was relevant in a number of circumstances. In the context of a claim by the defendant that the applicant was disentitled to maintenance by reason of desertion, the defendant's conduct was relevant in determining whether the applicant had just cause for leaving or living apart. Where adultery by the applicant was raised, the court was obliged to ignore it where the defendant had by his conduct condoned, connived at or by wilful neglect or misconduct conduced to the adultery. There were also some cases in which serious misconduct by the defendant affected the level of maintenance awarded, as in *E.D. v F.D.*[52] where the husband's misconduct led Costello J. to reject an argument that losses arising from the breakdown of the marriage should be borne equally by the husband and the wife and children who were living with her.

8.048 The misconduct of the defendant will continue to be relevant where the bar (now discretionary) of desertion is pleaded. In other contexts it will now be treated as relevant only where in the opinion of the court it would in all the circumstances be repugnant to justice to disregard it. No doubt the courts will try to avoid maintenance proceedings becoming an arena for the rehearsal and dissection of petty domestic squabbles; only serious forms of misconduct are likely to be considered relevant. However where the defendant raises the issue of the applicant's misconduct the court may not be able to avoid looking also at the conduct of the defendant, if only for the reason that the defendant's conduct is relevant in deciding whether in all the circumstances it would be "repugnant to justice" to disregard the applicant's conduct.

The conduct of a dependent child

8.049 Although the Act of 1976 does not specify that the conduct of a child, for whose support maintenance is being sought, should be a relevant consideration, it might in an extreme case be regarded as one of the circumstances of the case to which the court should have regard, for example, where an application is made for an order against the mother of a twenty-year-old college student who has persistently abused her.

Other relevant circumstances

8.050 Section 5(4) of the Act of 1976 requires the court to have regard to "all the circumstances of the case." There then follows a list of particular matters to which the court must have regard (see **8.013–8.018**). This list is narrower in range than that embodied in section 20(2) of the Judicial Separation and Family Law Reform Act 1989 which applies to the making of financial provision and property-related orders in proceedings for

---

52 23 October 1980, unreported, High Court.

judicial separation. The two lists have certain common features, and they are not mutually incompatible. There seems no reason therefore why a court, considering an award of maintenance under the Act of 1976, should not in addition to the specific matters mentioned in the Act, have regard to some of the matters specified in the Act of 1989. There is no obligation on the court to do so, but it would help to avoid the development of an unhealthy rift between two sets of proceedings which have similar objectives.

Interim orders

8.051 Section 7 of the Act of 1976 enables the court to make an interim maintenance order where it appears proper to do so "having regard to the needs of the persons for whose support the maintenance order is sought and the other circumstances of the case." The application for interim maintenance may be made at any time before the application for a full order is determined, and the order for interim maintenance will last either for the period specified in the order or until the application for the full order is adjudicated upon.

Discharge, variation and termination of maintenance orders

8.052 Under section 6(1)(a) of the 1976 Act a maintenance debtor may apply to have a maintenance order discharged, provided that one year has elapsed since the order was made, on the basis that having regard to his record of payments under the order and the other circumstances of the case, the person supported under it will not be prejudiced by the discharge of the order. In addition under section 6(1)(b), either party may at any time apply for a discharge or variation of the order on the basis of a change of circumstances or new evidence coming to light since the order was made or varied. The granting of a foreign divorce does not *per se* justify variations or discharge—see **8.002–8.004**. Under section 38(3)(a) of the Judicial Separation and Family Law Reform Act 1989 the changed circumstances may include "conduct" of either party where it would be repugnant to justice to disregard it. The maintenance debtor may apply for the discharge of an order made in favour of a spouse at any time where that spouse is in desertion, unless the court, having regard to all the circumstances (including the conduct of the other spouse) is of the opinion that it would be repugnant to justice to discharge the order.[53] Desertion by, or conduct of, a spouse is not however, a ground for discharging or varying any part of a maintenance order which provides for the support of a dependent child of the family.[54]

8.053 Any part of a maintenance order providing support for a dependent child stands automatically discharged when the child reaches the age of 16

---

53 Section 6(2), as amended by the Judicial Separation and Family Law Reform Act, section 38(3)(b).
54 Section 6(5), as amended by the Judicial Separation and Family Law Reform Act, section 38(3)(d).

or 21, as the case may be. The maintenance debtor may also apply to have such order discharged on the ground that the child has ceased to be a dependent child for the purposes of the order.[55]

8.054 A difficult question is whether a spouse who has already obtained a maintenance order under the Act of 1976 loses the right to maintenance when a recognised foreign divorce is finally and absolutely granted. In *M.T.T. v N.T.T.*[56] the wife obtained a District Court maintenance order, and a subsequent variation order increasing the level of maintenance. Her husband who, though resident in the State, retained his English domicile, then obtained an English decree of divorce absolute, and applied to have the Irish maintenance order terminated. The Supreme Court held that the English divorce decree was entitled to recognition. Although the Court did not comment expressly on the effect of recognition on the Irish order, by inference it appears to have accepted that it relieved the husband from his obligation to pay maintenance to his wife. The husband did not contest his obligation to continue paying maintenance for the support of his children. This interpretation of *M.T.T. v N.T.T.* was adopted by Egan J. in the later cases of *M(C) v M(T)*[57] though he did point out that no argument to the contrary had been raised in *M.T.T. v N.T.T.*

8.055 In *M(C) v M(T)*, Egan J. was able to grant the wife interim maintenance on the basis that her husband's English divorce had not yet been made absolute. The case subsequently went before Barr J. for a decision on whether that divorce now made absolute, was entitled to recognition. He held (at page 462) that it was but later considered further arguments relating to the effect of the divorce on the "wife's" maintenance rights.[58] He concluded that the maintenance order already made under section 5 of the Act remained valid and enforceable until varied or rescinded by the court on the application of either party. Section 5 should not be interpreted in a way which would result in a maintenance order, made during a subsisting marriage for the benefit of a spouse and/or child of the marriage, automatically lapsing on the granting of a recognised foreign divorce. Such a construction might lead to hardship for the dependent spouse and children, and would be incompatible with the Constitution. Emphasis was placed on the fact that, while the husband had a domicile in England where the divorce was granted, the wife had a domicile and was resident in the State. Barr J. at pages 11–12 of the judgment stated that if the contrary view were taken, the wife and the children, though domiciled in the State, would be deprived of the benefit of the maintenance order made in the State.

Being so deprived, and without any alternative maintenance order or agreement in lieu thereof, it would follow that the wife and children

---

55 Section 6(3), as amended by the Status of Children Act 1987, section 19.
56 [1982] ILRM 217; [1983] IR 29.
57 [1988] ILRM 456; at 460.
58 These subsequent High Court proceedings (30 November 1989) are as yet unreported.

were thereby deprived of equality with the husband before the law, and the wife to a basic right in marriage (that is, maintenance) which may continue even after final dissolution. A statutory provision which could bring about that result would seem to me to be incompatible with Article 40, sub-articles 1 and 3(1) and Article 41 of the Constitution.

Barr J. expressed the further opinion that the granting of the English divorce would not *per se* be a reason for varying the Irish maintenance order in subsequent proceedings. The practical implications of seeking a discharge or variation of a maintenance order under the Act of 1976 are discussed at **9.086–9.096**, **9.106** and **9.110**.

The Guardianship of Infants Act 1964

8.056 Section 11(1) of the Guardianship of Infants Act 1964 gives the court power, on the application of a guardian of an infant, to order the father or mother to pay towards the maintenance of the infant such weekly or other periodic sums as, having regard to the means of the father or mother, the court considers reasonable. (Section 11(2)(b)). Both the District Court and Circuit Court have jurisdiction (see **1.005–1.021**) to make orders under section 11 but the District Court may not order more than £30.00 per week maintenance in relation to each qualified child.

8.057 Applications for maintenance under the Act are usually made by married parents, but since 1987 it has been possible for the mother of a child born outside marriage, as the child's guardian, to apply for an order against the child's father where (a) the child's father has been appointed a guardian or (b) subject to certain provisos, the parents were parties to a void marriage or one which has been annulled.[59] The father of a child born outside marriage may apply under section 11(1) for an order against the child's mother only if he is a guardian of the child.

8.058 The class of children who may benefit by a maintenance order made under the Act of 1964 is in some respects more narrowly defined than under the Act of 1976 (See **8.005–8.007**). Only natural or adopted children of both partners qualify. There is no provision for children in respect of whom one or both parents is or are merely *in loco parentis*. On the other hand children adopted under a recognised foreign adoption order, though omitted from the Act of 1976 are now included in the Act of 1964, following the amendment of section 2(1)(b) of that Act by section 9 of the Status of Children Act 1987. Section 2(4) of the Age of Majority Act 1985 preserved at 21 the age up to which a maintenance order may be made, while reducing to 18 the age at which a child ceases to be an infant for other purposes under the Guardianship of Infants Act 1964. Section 6 of the Age

---

59 See the change in the definition of father in section 2(1) of the Act of 1964 effected by the Status of Children Act 1987, section 9.

of Majority Act 1985 inserted a new section 11(5) into the 1964 Act which provides that a maintenance order may continue indefinitely in the case of a child who is suffering from mental or physical disability to such an extent that it is not reasonably possible for him to fully maintain himself.

Section 6 of the Age of Majority Act 1985 also amended sections 11(3) of the 1964 Act to provide that an order for the maintenance of a child under the Act of 1964 is effective notwithstanding the fact that his parents continue to cohabit.

Taxation

Taxation of married couples: general principles

8.059 A husband and wife may elect to be assessed jointly, separately or as single persons.[60] This treatment of married couples is provided for by sections 192–198 of the Income Tax Act 1967 which were inserted into the Income Tax Act 1967 by section 18 of the Finance Act 80 (with effect from 6 April 1980) following the decision of the Supreme Court in *Murphy v Attorney General*.[61] The plaintiffs argued that the earlier sections 192–198 were unconstitutional, in that, in certain circumstances, the tax treatment of a married couple was financially more severe than that of two single people. In finding for the plaintiffs, Hamilton J. on 12 October 1979 confirmed the decision of the High Court stating "the nature . . . of . . . [the relevant sections] is such that in the opinion of the Court it is breach of the pledge by the State [in Article 41] to guard with special care the institution of marriage and to protect it from attack." The new sections 192–198 operate to ensure that married couples *automatically* received double tax allowances and rate bands.

Joint assessment

8.060 A husband and wife living together are deemed to have elected for joint assessment under section 194 of the Income Tax Act 1967, unless either spouse has given written notice before the end of the tax year that he or she wishes to be assessed as a single person for that year. Under joint assessment, a married couple is assessed on their combined total income, that is their incomes are aggregated. Joint assessment will apply even where one spouse has no income. The advantage of joint assessment is that the couple are entitled to twice the personal allowances and reliefs available to a single person, and the tax rate bands are double those applicable to a single person. Under joint assessment, the husband is charged to tax on the combined income of the spouses, and under section 194(1) his wife's income is deemed to be his income. It will be obvious that joint assessment is of special value where only one spouse is in receipt of an income, or where the income of one spouse would be too low to attract tax

60 For a comprehensive account see *Judge: Irish Income Tax* (Butterworths) **3.221** et seq.
61 [1982] IR 241.

under single assessment. For example, where spouses are paying interest on a mortgage of the family home, they are entitled to twice the (interest paid) allowance of a single person, even where only one of the spouses has an income.

Separate assessment

8.061 Where a married couple wish to retain the benefits of joint assessment, but want at the same time to maintain some independence by being treated separately, they may elect under section 197 for separate assessment. In this case, the allowances are apportioned between the spouses so that each spouse pays tax in proportion to his or her income. This is usually on the basis that the personal allowances and the double tax rate bands (those below the highest rate), are divided equally between them. If one spouse has a surplus income which is liable to tax at the top rate, any unused part of a lower rate tax band will be transferred to him from the other spouse. This reduces the amount of income subject to tax at the top rate. Life assurance relief and interest relief are divided in proportion to the amount paid by each spouse. The net tax effect of separate assessment is that the total tax paid by a husband and wife is *the same as if they had opted for joint assessment.*

Single assessment

8.062 Under single assessment (section 193) each spouse is taxed as if each were a single person. Each spouse receives only the allowances and reliefs accorded to a single person. There is no right to transfer surplus allowances or relief from one spouse to the other. The relevant tax rate bands are similarly those applicable to single persons. The combined tax paid by spouses, assessed singly, is unlikely to be less than under joint assessment, and will often be more. Notice of application for single assessment may be made by either spouse before the end of the year of assessment. Single assessment will then continue until the spouse who requested it withdraws from it by a notice in writing to the inspector. Single assessment should *not* be opted for by married persons without consulting a tax advisor. (See **8.069**).

Taxation of separated spouses: general principles

8.063 Separated spouses are in general taxed as two separate single persons, unless they opt for joint assessment. For this purpose, spouses are regarded as separated if they are living apart under a court order or by deed of separation, or otherwise if they have separated in such circumstances that the separation is likely to be permanent. A court order would include a barring order, a decree of divorce *a mensa et thoro* or a judicial separation. Treatment as single persons will begin immediately in the tax year in which separation occurs. The effect is that the separated spouses become responsible for their own tax returns; their incomes are computed separately, personal allowances and reliefs for single persons apply to each, and tax for each is assessed on a single person basis.

Maintenance payments made by a separated spouse on single assessment after 9 June 83.

8.064 Where one separated spouse is ordered by the court to pay maintenance for the benefit of the other spouse or a child of either party, there is said to exist a "maintenance arrangement", and payments under the order are subject to the provisions of section 3 of the Finance Act 1983. The same is true of certain other legally enforceable maintenance payments, for example those made under a deed of separation, a trust, a covenant or other legally enforceable agreements. The "maintenance arrangement" may be made not only pursuant to a separation but also where there is a dissolution or annulment of the marriage. Three essential ingredients, if maintenance payments are to fall within the provisions of section 3, are (a) that they are made at a time when the spouses are living apart, (b) that they are legally enforceable and (c) that they are annual or periodical.

Section 434 of the Income Tax Act 1967 imposes an obligation on persons makings "pure income" payments to other persons by way of interest (except to commercial banks) royalty, covenant etc to withhold tax at the standard 30% (from 6.4.90) rate from the payment and pay over that tax to the Revenue Commissioners. The 1983 Finance Act specifically exempts maintenance payments from one spouse to another from this provision.

8.065 *Payments for the benefit of the other party* Where a maintenance payment which is subject to section 3 is made for the benefit of the other spouse, such payment may be deducted in computing the payer's total income for the tax year in which the payment is made. The payer does not withhold tax at the standard rate from such maintenance payments; he makes gross payments. But he is able to reduce his tax liability by setting off the maintenance against his taxable income. On the other hand, the maintenance payment is treated as income in the hands of the recipient spouse who is chargeable for income tax under Case IV, Schedule D. The recipient, however, is entitled to a single person's allowances and reliefs and, if she has no other source of income, may find that her income is small enough to be exempt from tax: £3250 for a single person from 6 April 90, increasing by £300 for each dependent child. Section 3 is particularly beneficial to the payer where the amount of maintenance is high, and exceeds the amount which he would have received as a married man by way of allowance.

8.066 *Payments for the benefit of a child* In the case of maintenance payments falling within section 3, made directly or indirectly *for the benefit of a child*, a different approach is adopted. The payer is not entitled to deduct such payments in computing his income for tax purposes. In other words, he makes the payments out of his (net) taxed income. At the same time, the payments are not treated as income in the hands of the child or any person receiving the payments on behalf of the child. The person making the maintenance payments is entitled to claim any child allowance in respect of the child, if the child is physically or mentally handicapped.[62] If the recipient is also contributing to the maintenance of the child, any child allowance will be divided *pro rata*. Where there is doubt as to whether a particular maintenance payment is for the support of a child or a spouse, it will usually be deemed to be the latter. For this reason, it is important that a "maintenance arrangement" specify the purpose for which payments are to be made, and indicate the amount of maintenance which is to be paid for the benefit of a child.

Maintenance Orders made before 9 June 1983

8.067 Where a maintenance order (or other maintenance arrangements) was made before 9 June 1983, and steps have not been taken to bring it within the 1983 regime, the old rules continue to apply. Maintenance paid under a court order for the benefit of a spouse were, under the old rules, payable in full and could not be deducted by the payer in computing his income. They were not regarded as income in the hands of the recipient. In the case of maintenance paid under a court for the benefit of a child, the payer likewise was entitled to no deduction and the payments were not treated as taxable income of the child. The old rules continue to apply to maintenance orders made before 9 June 1983, only where the maintenance arrangements has not since been varied or replaced by another maintenance arrangement. It is also possible for the parties jointly to elect that the new provisions of section 3 of the Act of 1983 should apply. Consequently, there are probably very few maintenance orders still subject to the old rules.

Joint assessment under section 4 of the Finance Act 1983

8.068 Section 4 of the Finance Act 1983 allows separated spouses to elect to be assessed jointly, on the following conditions:

(a) both spouses must be resident in the State in the year of assessment;
(b) legally enforceable maintenance payments must be made by one spouse to the other in the year in which joint assessment is to apply;
(c) the marriage must not have been annulled or dissolved;
(d) election must be made jointly in writing, before the end of the tax year for which it is to apply.

Where separated spouses have elected for joint assessment, they are taxed jointly, but the separate (not "single") assessment procedure, described above, applies. The advantage is that the spouses are able to enjoy the full effects of the married person's double rate bands, together with the double allowances and reliefs. If, for example, one spouse only is making substantial interest payments on a mortgage of the family home, his allowance will be double that which would apply, were he and his spouse not to elect for joint assessment. Maintenance payments made by one

---

62 Income Tax Act 1967 section 141; Finance Act 1986 section 4.

spouse for the support of the other are not taken into account in computing the respective incomes of the spouses.

The single parent allowance

8.069 This allowance is provided for by section 138A of the Income Tax Act 1967, which was inserted by section 4 of the Finance Act 1985, for 6 April 85 et seq. The existence of a single parent allowance may influence the decision by a separated couple whether or not to elect for joint assessment. The purpose of the allowance is to give the same personal relief to a taxpayer who has care of a child, as is usually available to a married person. It is available to (a) a separated spouse, (b) a divorced person who has not remarried, and (c) a person whose marriage has been annulled provided in each case that the child is a "qualifying"[63] child who is resident with him for the whole or any part of the relevant tax year. The parent is entitled to only one allowance, regardless of the number of children living with him. Where the child has overnight access to the non-custodial spouse, this may be sufficient for that spouse to claim the allowance. The allowance is not available where the separated spouses have elected for joint assessment. A separated couple may therefore have to weigh carefully the advantages of joint assessment against the loss of the single parent's allowance.

63   The definition of a "qualifying child" is set out in section 138A.

Chapter 9

MAINTENANCE PROCEEDINGS: PRACTICE AND PROCEDURE

Taking instructions for maintenance

Procedure

9.001 A client will rarely come to a solicitor on the sole issue of maintenance. It must not be forgotten that a client is entitled to seek maintenance against the other spouse even though the spouses continue to live under the same roof and do not intend to separate. Different lists of expenditure should be completed for parties still living together, and those who are separating. The wife seeking maintenance may not be proposing to pay all the bills out of maintenance, as the husband may insist on continuing to pay certain items, such as the mortgage. The question of who pays what bill should be sorted out at an early stage. The reasonable minimum requirements of an applicant spouse should be estimated. The current needs of a spouse can be difficult to estimate until the respondent has actually left the house. The client should be advised that an interim maintenance order may be more flexible for her needs.

9.002 The respondent's reasonable living expenses whether he is still residing in the home or not should be estimated. This will include, if he has left, the cost of renting a flat/house, running a car, food and so on.

9.003 Because it will take a number of weeks to have a hearing, a client who is receiving no housekeeping money should be referred to the local community welfare officer. This may require a letter from the solicitor verifying that an application for maintenance is being sought, or the client may produce the maintenance summons to the officer. The officer may grant supplementary welfare pending the hearing. Supplementary welfare is administered by the health boards, under the Social Welfare (Consolidation) Act 1981. Experience has shown that once the respondent spouse leaves home, particularly if he is barred, he will cease to pay bills.

Accusations may be made that the applicant spouse is deliberately running up the bills. The responsibility for outgoings of this kind is often not clarified in court, though in *E.D. v F.D.* the court made a specific order that a husband was not liable for any outgoings.

Self employed respondent

9.004 If a respondent is self-employed it may be difficult to estimate his income. His lifestyle may reflect his disposable income. If that includes an expensive car, frequent holidays abroad, membership of expensive clubs, or ownership of non essential leisure items, the court may question any large discrepancy between his certified income and the lifestyle.

Debts

9.005 A list of debts and hire purchase commitments needs to be made particularly if incurred in the purchase of household goods. The ownership of a motor vehicle should be checked. A search in the Motor Registration Office at River House, Chancery Place, Dublin 7, or the local registration office, if one has the registration number of a car, will elicit the age and make of the car, and clarify whether the car is in the respondent's name, or his company's name. The respondent may want to continue to pay life insurance, mortgage protection insurance, mortgage, Voluntary Health Insurance, as he is claiming tax relief on them.

9.006 All expenditure items must be vouched well in advance of the date of hearing. It should be remembered that a wife who is a home maker may have income, or earnings from another source such as Disability Benefit, Disabled Persons Maintenance Allowance in respect of a handicapped child, and perhaps, Constant Care Allowance for the child, as well as the usual Child Benefit.

Applicant's earning capacity

9.007 An applicant spouse must be asked about her earning capacity, even if she is fulltime looking after children. She may be asked this in court, and if she is unprepared her answers will appear evasive. She may be capable of looking after other children, home baking, crafts, dressmaking, typing from home, setting up her own business, taking in lodgers, and so on.

Farm

9.008 If there is a farm, the acreage must be noted, the extent of farm buildings, the number of dry cattle, or dairy cattle, or other animals. The source of cash income needs to be ascertained—whether it is seasonal, or based on a monthly creamery cheque, and whether the respondent is in receipt of farmer's dole that is, unemployment assistance at the non urban rate. Is he affected by the superlevy, does he receive headage payments.

1   23 October 1980, unreported, High Court.

Are there borrowings from the Agricultural Credit Corporation or other financial institution? Are the title deeds lodged in the bank? It may be necessary to get a copy of the folio, and a map would be helpful.

Effect of a separation on maintenance

9.009 The most important point to get across is that in practice a separation usually results in a drop in the standard of living of both spouses. The dependent spouse cannot expect to be maintained at the same level as before, unless the couple are very wealthy.[2] The client must be advised that she cannot recover financial losses, nor will maintenance be awarded, unless there is financial need justifying the order.[3]

Documents

9.010 All expenditure claimed needs to be vouched as follows:

1. Recent bills for electricity, gas, telephone, oil, water rates, or other utilities.
2. Payslips of the respondent, if available. Seek his last P60. Check payslips for credit union deductions, tax deductions, overtime, commission or other "hidden earnings". Check for the tax free allowance certificate, which will indicate what personal allowances he is claiming. Is he claiming all the possible allowances? If there is a lack of documentation, witness summonses will need to be issued, to establish the respondent's income and assets. Over-enthusiastic clients should be deterred from seeking to obtain documentation illegally. In *O.C. v T.C.*,[4] the court ruled as inadmissible letters obtained by a wife by breaking into her husband's house.
3. List earnings from undisclosed sources, commonly known as "nixers". It will be impossible to prove such income unless it was diligently put into a separate bank account, but the client may be able to estimate it. The respondent would then have to rebut such estimate in the witness box.
4. If the respondent is self employed, it is still unusual to summons his accountant to court to give evidence. This is partly because of the expense of the witness. If the financial affairs are complicated, it may be better to take proceedings in the Circuit Court, even if the maintenance order is unlikely to exceed the maximum of the District Court (£100 for a spouse, £30 for a child). There is no provision in the District Court Rules for the service of a notice to produce although this is commonly used in practice. Further there is no power to make an order for discovery. On the other hand if a company official such as a wages clerk or the financial controller is summonsed to court to give evidence of the respondent's earnings the justice may adjourn the case and order more financial information to be produced by the

2 See *R.H. v N.H.* [1986] ILRM 352 and **8.013–8.018**.
3 See *J.S.J. v R.S.J.* 26 June 1980, unreported, High Court.
4 December 1981, unreported, High Court.

witness and the respondent. The justice may threaten contempt, if they are uncooperative, or he may order a high amount of maintenance, on the basis that the real income has not been disclosed. It is arguable that the District Court has no power to commit for contempt of court except if the contempt is committed in the face of the court. The court will also look at devices designed to avoid liability as, for example, where the respondent arranges with a third party for payments to be made to the respondent's company, rather than to him personally. The court will interpret that emolument as being personal.

Third parties

9.011 It is difficult to predict what view judges will take towards a third party or cohabitee. If a husband has left home to set up home with his girlfriend and they have a child, the child is taken into account in assessing maintenance for the children of the marriage and the wife. The courts have not laid down clear guidelines as to whether it is relevant that the cohabitee is or is not earning. However, in practice judges often do, whether expressly or implicitly, take such earnings into account. A wife will probably find her own maintenance discharged or at least varied, if she left home to set up house with a third party. The court will regard this man as having a "moral" obligation to support her even if there is no child of the relationship. If the client has a cohabitee, the latter should if possible be interviewed to check on her contribution to the joint household expenses. It is helpful to have her available as a witness to clarify an aspect of income or expenditure just in case the court sees it as relevant.

Desertion adultery and conduct "repugnant to justice"

9.012 A client's full instructions should be taken with a view to establishing whether an allegation of desertion or adultery may be made. If this appears likely, full details must be taken as, despite the changes made by the Judicial Separation and Family Law Reform Act 1989 the Court may still adopt a conservative approach, and refuse maintenance to a "guilty" spouse. There are separate proofs necessary if there is an allegation of desertion by the applicant. Inevitably a full history of the marriage has to be taken, focussing on the circumstances leading up to the parties living apart. This is made easier if the application for maintenance is accompanied by an application for a barring order or judicial separation.

9.013 In the District Court, in the absence of any pleadings, it is difficult to know in advance if allegations of desertion or adultery are likely. One of the best ways of telling is to ask the client what sort of allegations the respondent spouse has made against her, and to whom. He may allege that she has left home because of an affair with a named man. If it is likely that her conduct will present difficulties it may be better to take proceedings in the Circuit Court. There the maintenance for each child will not be limited to £30 per child, and the court may be prepared to award a sufficient sum to make reasonable provision for the care and attention which the children would have to be given either by the wife or by some other paid help.[5]

Taking instructions from a respondent

Procedure

9.014 With rare exceptions, the average respondent is the husband. He may not wish to oppose maintenance in principle but rather to pay less than the sum requested by his wife. Nevertheless a history of the marriage should be taken, to exclude the possibility of nullity or to determine whether there is sufficient misconduct to act as a bar to maintenance by the applicant spouse. With the new requirements of "conduct repugnant to justice", a full history needs to be taken of all aspects of behaviour.

9.015 The respondent should be encouraged to be as frank as possible in the disclosure of his assets. There is no point in him being evasive with his solicitor when the other spouse may disclose his assets in the middle of a court case. A P60 and a letter from the wages section, indicating the income to date, gross and net, separately itemised should be obtained where appropriate. If bonuses or other emoluments are not paid they should be specifically excluded. This may save the embarrassment of a wages clerk being summonsed to attend court, which may put his/her promotion prospects, or indeed employment in jeopardy. It is helpful for the employer to include a reference to projected earnings and projected overtime pay for the next 12 months. If overtime is seasonal, there should be an indication of the average overtime pay and whether it is likely to be similar in the coming year.

9.016 Respondents sometimes think that the less information they disclose, the less maintenance they will have to pay. If anything the converse can be true. If a court decides that there is deliberate lack of disclosure, or a wilful failure by the respondent to sort out his financial affairs, for example, his tax affairs, the court may order a large sum of maintenance, or order a sum based on his gross income.

The validity of the marriage

9.017 The respondent may dispute that the petitioner is his lawful spouse because he alleges that the marriage is null and void, or that a recognised foreign divorce has been obtained. Documentary evidence as to the latter, such as the divorce pleadings, decree nisi, or decree absolute, needs to be examined. The petition should indicate the domicile which the parties believed they had at the time the divorce proceedings were issued. It will also contain the address of both spouses. There is a heavy onus on a respondent who seeks to establish that he acquired a foreign domicile of choice. Any proofs which establish employment abroad, the purchase of a house, an application for citizenship abroad, the disposal of all assets in

5 *P. v P.* 12 March 1980, unreported, High Court.

this jurisdiction, the remarriage of the respondent to a national of that foreign jurisdiction, and the birth of children there etc are helpful. The plaintiff may have sworn an affidavit in relation to the arrangements for the children, which may disclose their residence and schooling, which may be helpful in relation to domicile. It is useful if there can be some disclosure of documentation in advance. This may avoid having to contact witnesses from a foreign jurisdiction, or going to the expense of preparing notarised affidavits. The difficulty in the District Court is the lack of power to order disclosure or serve a notice to produce or to admit. In the Circuit Court or High Court there is a stricter requirement of proofs. Egan J. in *M.(C.) v M.(T.)*[6] concluded that he would not decide the question of domicile on evidence confined to affidavits and correspondence. It would have to be resolved by a full plenary hearing with the benefit of oral evidence. Witnesses may have to be called to corroborate an intention to retain a domicile of origin or to acquire a new permanent residence. Where a foreign divorce has been obtained the petitioner may issue a maintenance summons in the normal way if s/he proposes to argue that the divorce should not be recognised. A summons may also be issued if foreign divorce proceedings are still pending, or where only a conditional decree of divorce has been granted. Where a final and recognisable decree has been granted the "ex spouse" probably cannot originate maintenance proceedings under the Act of 1976 for her own support, but she may seek maintenance for the children under section 5, as amended by section 18 of the Status of Children Act 1987, or under the Guardianship of Infants Act 1964: see **8.002–8.004** and **8.052–8.055**. The summons issued under Rule 8, Form 3, of the District Court (Status of Children Act 1987) Rules 1988 (S.I. No 152 of 1988).

Checklist: applicant's expenditure

9.018 The checklist should be completed by the applicant and with appropriate modifications, by the respondent spouse. It may also be helpful if each party completes a separate list of the expenses likely to be claimed by the other.

	£ per week
Food	
Milk	....
Meat	....
Groceries	....
Special diet (for example for a coeliac or allergic child) ...	....
House	
Rent/Mortgage	....
House Contents Insurance	....

6   [1987] ILRM 262.

House Structural Insurance ....

Mortgage Protection Insurance ....

Telephone ....

Gas (Bottled, or natural gas) ....

E.S.B. ....

Heating—*E.S.B.* ....

    Gas ....

    Oil ....

    Coal ....

    Turf Briquettes ....

    Logs ....

    Sticks and firelighters ....

Television *Licence* ....

    Cable ....

    Rental/Purchase ....

Video Rental/Purchase ....

Hire-Purchase-household goods ....

Repairs, including bank loan repayments ....

Transport

Bus/DART/Train ....

School bus ....

Separate bus fares for children (other than above) ... .

Motor Vehicle—*Petrol/Diesel* ....

    Insurance ....

    Tax ....

    Repayments ....

    Maintenance ....

    Automobile Association membership ....

Clothes and shoes

Clothes for self ....

Clothes for children ....

Department Store charge card-repayments ....

Shoes for children ....

School uniforms ....

School/College expenses

School fees ....

University/College/Business or Language School fees .. ..

Extra tuition costs ....

School books and other writing material ....

School outings (for example, swimming, holidays,
excursions) ....

School lunches ....

Other expenses for the children

Swimming ....
Boy/Girl Scouts ....
Dancing/Music lessons ....
Other sports ....
Presents/birthdays/Christmas/Christmas savings club ....

Medical expenses

Medical expenses for self ....
Medical expenses for children ....
Special medical needs, for example, for an
asthmatic child ....
Drugs/chemist bills ....
Voluntary Health Insurance ....
Other health insurance schemes ....
Private special expenses for example, child psychiatrist ... .

Insurance

Life insurance for self ....
Life insurance for children ....
Life insurance for respondent spouse ....
Any other insurance ....

Debts

Credit union repayments (and savings) ....
Bank loan ....
Moneylender ....
Private debts to friends/relatives ....
Debts to shopkeepers, milkman, coalman ....

Miscellaneous

Babysitting ....
Child minder during the day ....
Creche ....
Holidays ....
Cigarettes ....
Drink ....
Membership of Ladies' Club, Sports' club, etc ....
Newspapers/Magazines ....
Night classes ....
Church contributions ....
Other miscellaneous ....

Checklist: applicant's income

9.019 The following checklist should be completed by the applicant so that his or her income can be ascertained:

Income	**£** **per week**
Employment income	
Income from part time employment (official)	....
Income from part time employment (unofficial)	....
Income from full time employment (official)	....
Income from full time employment (unofficial)	....
Dividends and interest	
Income from company dividends	....
Income from government stocks etc	....
Interest from savings account: Bank	....
Interest from savings account: Building Society	....
Interest from savings account: Post Office	....
Interest from savings account: Commercial Bank	....
Company benefits	
Has the applicant a company car? (Yes/No)	....
Does the company reimburse petrol, insurance, car tax etc?	....
Does the company pay the applicants' VHI, life assurance etc?	....
Does the company provide low interest loans or other benefits?	....
Property income	
Income from letting of a house	....
Income from letting of an apartment	....
Income from letting of a holiday home	....
Income from letting of land	....
Income from letting of a commercial building	....
Trade and professional income	
Income from a trade carried on by the applicant (eg shop)	....
Income from a profession carried on by the applicant	....
Trust income	
Income from a trust of which the applicant is a beneficiary	....
	———
TOTAL	———

Checklist: applicant's assets

9.020 The following checklist should be completed by the applicant in order to ascertain the total of his or her assets:

	£ **per week**
Assets	

Cash

Cash in hand	. . . .
Housekeeping money	. . . .
Cash in current account	. . . .
Cash in savings account: Bank	. . . .
Cash in savings account: Building Society	. . . .
Cash in savings account: Post Office	. . . .
Cash in savings account: Commercial Bank	. . . .

Securities

Government stocks etc held by the applicant	. . . .
Share in public or private companies held by applicant	. . . .
Prize bonds held by the applicant	. . . .

Property

Does the applicant own a second or third house (let)?	. . . .
Does the applicant own an apartment or holiday home?	. . . .
Does the applicant own land?	. . . .
Does the applicant own a farm (or have the use of a farm)?	. . . .
Does the applicant own any commercial property	. . . .

Valuables

Does the applicant own a boat or caravan?	. . . .
Does the applicant own any antiques or paintings?	. . . .
Does the applicant own any jewellery or furs?	. . . .
Does the applicant own any valuable books?	. . . .
Does the applicant own any silver?	. . . .

Unrealised assets

Does the applicant have any life policies which are near maturity?	. . . .
Is the applicant awaiting an inheritance from a deceased relative?	. . . .

TOTAL

Checklist: respondent's assets

9.021 The following checklist should be completed *on behalf of* the respondent, in addition to a checklist as in **9.020**:

	£ **per week**
Additional assets	

Hidden assets

Does the respondent have property or cash placed in the names of cohabitees or relatives to avoid disclosure?	. . . .
Does the respondent have property or assets owned via	

shares in offshore companies, for example, shares in a
Channel Islands or Cayman Islands company? ....

Illegal earnings
Does the respondent have income, for example from
handling stolen goods or selling drugs? ....

Assets which are easily disposed of
Does the respondent have a second car, TV or stereo? ... .

TOTAL

General jurisdiction

9.022 Section 23(1)(a) of the Family Law (Maintenance of Spouses and Children) Act 1976, as amended by section 12 of the Courts Act 1981, provides for the Circuit and District Courts having jurisdiction to hear maintenance and ancillary applications. Ancillary proceedings include variation, discharge, interim orders, and orders to transmit payments through the District Court Clerk's office. Section 12 increased the limit on the District Court, and the Circuit Court on appeal, to £100 per week for a spouse, and £30 per child. The Circuit Court has no limit on the maintenance it may order.

9.023 It is no longer recommended that maintenance proceedings be issued in the High Court. (For reference, see chapter 1.) The High Court retains jurisdiction over maintenance orders that it made prior to the implementation of the Courts Act 1981 which came into effect on 12 May 1982. Section 23(2)(b) of the Act of 1976, as amended; provides that the District Court and the Circuit Court have as a general rule no jurisdiction to make maintenance or ancillary orders, in relation to an order which the High Court has already made. However section 23(2)(d) gives the District Court and the Circuit Court jurisdiction to vary or revoke[7] a High Court order, if

1. the order would have been within their new jurisdiction, under the Courts Act 1981, and
2. the circumstances under which the order was made have changed. So, for example, if a maintenance order was made in the High Court, in 1981, for £60 per week for a wife and £20 for a child and the husband was promoted in 1984 the wife may now apply for variation in the District Court as the order is now within the limit of the District Court's jurisdiction, and the circumstances have changed.

9.024 In practice, the District Court should entertain a variation even if the only change in circumstances is the increase in the cost of living as measured by the consumer price index. Section 23(2)(d)(ii) provides that if

---

7 The Courts Act 1981 uses the term "revoke" instead of "discharge", which is used in the 1976 Act.

a variation or "revocation" is applied for in the District Court (not the Circuit Court), the District Court only has jurisdiction over the High Court order, if (a) the circumstances have changed, and (b) the original order would have been within the District Court's jurisdiction had section 12 of the 1981 Act been in force at the time of the making of the original order. The above example is within the rule. But if the original maintenance order had been £70 for the wife, and £40 for each child, the variation would now have to be taken to the Circuit Court. This is because the District Court, even with its new limits may not award a sum in excess of £30 per child.

9.025 Provided circumstances have changed, the Circuit Court can grant a variation or discharge of a High Court order, made prior to the 12th May 1982, where the order exceeds the District Court limit, or indeed where it is within that limit. It may be preferable to apply in the Circuit Court, if the husband is self employed, and it is difficult to ascertain his assets. The Court's powers of discovery may be needed.

District Court procedure

Jurisdiction of the Court

9.026 The relevant rules are the District Court (Family Law (Maintenance of Spouses and Children) Act 1976) Rules 1976 (S.I. No. 96 of 1976), and the District Court (Family Law (Maintenance of Spouses and Children) Act 1976) Amendment Rules, 1980 (S.I. No. 268 of 1980). Section 23(3) of the 1976 Act provides that proceedings can be heard in the district where either party ordinarily resides or carries on any profession, business, or occupation.[1] This is implemented in rule 5 of the 1976 Rules. In effect this section gives a choice of up to four venues, if the parties are not living together. The applicant is likely to choose the most convenient venue, from the point of view of distance and frequency of court sittings. In addition, if the court clerk certifies that the case is urgent the summons may be listed for any court in the district.

Issue of summons

9.027 The following persons may issue proceedings:

    (a)   a spouse.
    (b)   a parent of a child, where the parties had been married to each other, and their marriage is validly dissolved,[9]
    (c)   a parent where the High Court has made a declaration that the "marriage" is null and void,
    (d)   where a spouse is deceased, deserted or living apart, and either

---

8 Section 6 of the 1976 Act deals with discharge, variation and termination of a maintenance order.
9 Section 5A(1) of the 1976 Act.

spouse has failed to provide proper maintenance, then a third party, on behalf of the child.

9.028 A summons may be prepared by a solicitor and given to a client to issue, or it may be issued by the solicitor, or by the District Court Clerk. Rule 41 of the 1976 Rules states.

A summons may be signed by a justice, a peace commissioner, or a district court clerk and shall be served on the person to whom it is directed seven clear days at least before the sitting of the Court to which the summons is returnable. The original of every such summons with a statutory declaration as to service endorsed thereon shall be lodged with the district court clerk four days at least before the date fixed for hearing.

The summons may be signed by the justice or the clerk. If an application is being made to abridge time under rule 51 of the 1948 Rules or for substituted service under rule 46(2) of the 1948 Rules the Justice may sign the summons. Since there are so few areas that have an official summons server it is more likely that the appropriate method of service is prepaid registered post: see section 7 of the Courts Act 1964. Under 42 of the 1976 Rules the registered slip should be affixed to the original maintenance summons. Then within three days, the time, date, and place of posting must be endorsed on the back of the original. A date cannot be obtained until at least twenty one days hence, if registered post is the method of service. At the same time as the summons is issued it is helpful if the respondent is reminded to furnish details of his earnings, within a certain time. If this is not complied with, a witness summons can be issued subsequently against a named wages clerk, or other person, who is competent to give evidence on earnings.

9.029 The statutory declaration of service must be completed not earlier than 10 days after the day on which the envelope is posted. It must be lodged at least four days prior to the hearing, in the appropriate District Court office. If there is no one in a household to sign for a registered post letter, the person has to collect same, within two days, at his local sorting office. If that is not done, it is sent back to the returned registered letter section, where it is opened and readdressed to the sender. If the registered envelope is returned in this way prior to the hearing, an application for substituted service and perhaps to abridge time, on a new summons will have to be made because the summons has not been served, the case cannot proceed, and a new summons has to be issued and a new date, if there is insufficient time, obtained. However, if service is directed other than by registered post, for example to his place of employment, seven days notice only is required. The order of substitution and abridgement must be endorsed on the back of the original and the copy to be served, on the respondent.

The hearing

Contested issues of fact

9.030 There are most likely to be contested issues of fact in relation to the following matters:

1. an allegation of misbehaviour, that is desertion, adultery, or "conduct repugnant to justice",
2. an allegation that a person is not the lawful spouse, or that a child is not a dependent child,
3. a dispute as to the amount of monies available, or the amount of expenditure claimed by either party, or their earnings.

9.031 If a respondent alleges for the first time at a hearing, that the applicant is guilty of adultery, desertion or other similar misconduct, and the applicant is unprepared for this, she may seek an adjournment to call witnesses in rebuttal. This may be refused, where the respondent has all his witnesses available. However, the applicant can reserve her right to apply again for an adjournment at a later stage in the hearing, before she closes her case, if it is apparent that it would not be just to decide the case, on the basis of the evidence presented. On the other hand, the justice may award an interim maintenance order under section 7 of the 1976 Act for the applicant spouse, without prejudice to the respondent's claim that she is not entitled to such, or the justice may award monies for the support of the children only, without prejudice to the applicant's case.

Adultery and paternity

9.032 It may be alleged that adultery is "conduct such that it would be repugnant to justice to disregard it".[10] The respondent may have served a witness summons on the alleged boyfriend of the applicant wife. There may be an allegation that the respondent is not the father of one of the children. With regard to the latter, the respondent may (under section 38 of the Status of Children Act 1987) seek the court's direction on blood testing. The District Court (Status of Children) Act 1987 Rules 1988 (S.I. No. 152 of 1988) deal with the complicated procedures. A notice in Form 9, is sent seven days in advance to each party to the proceedings, by prepaid ordinary post. The court can adjourn the hearing, if the direction for testing is made. The direction is in Form 10, and is also served on each party to the proceedings. The rules relating to the taking and preparation of the samples, are contained in the Blood Tests (Parentage) Regulations, 1988 (S.I. No. 215 of 1988). He must give notice to the applicant in advance, that he intends making such application: section 42(3) of the Status of Children Act 1987. If the court gives such direction, even where there is a presumption under section 46 that the respondent is the father, the court may dismiss the applicant's claim for maintenance, if she fails to cooperate. The court may under section 42(1) if it does not dismiss the

---

10   Section 38(2) of the Judicial Separation and Family Law Reform Act 1987.

claim, draw such inferences from the fact of failure to comply with the direction for blood testing, as appear proper in the circumstances.

Desertion

9.033 In trying to rebut an allegation of desertion (see **8.035–8.038**) the focus will be on establishing sufficiently serious misconduct which justified the applicant in leaving.[11] If there was violence, medical evidence, or evidence as to previous barring orders, or calls to the Gardaí will be necessary. Mental cruelty is more difficult to prove. Evidence from a doctor, psychiatrist, psychologist, social worker, counsellor or other professional may be needed to establish that there was just cause in leaving the home. Section 3 of the 1976 Act, in defining desertion, includes constructive desertion. The applicant may allege this, in response to the respondent's allegation of desertion by her. If the court rejects his allegation, and proceeds to award maintenance, it may be helpful, to have the court indicate whether it is holding, as a matter of fact, that there was constructive desertion by the respondent. This can be raised in a subsequent application for a decree of judicial separation[12] by the applicant, or to bar the husband from claiming maintenance from the wife in the future.

9.034 If the court decides to refuse maintenance for the wife, then the maximum figure for the children should be sought. In preparation, an expenditure list for the children only should have been prepared. It should separately detail the rent, and utilities, or other expenditure, which though "circumstantial", go towards ensuring a certain standard of living for the children. The court will usually be eager to maximise the amount awarded to the children, by way of compensation for the loss of maintenance to the spouse. However, it is still bound by the limit of £30 per child. Thus, unless there is a large family, the amount will be small and will have to be supplemented by earnings of the applicant spouse, or by social welfare.

Disputes relating to income, resources and expenditure

Acting for the applicant

9.035 The applicant should have duplicates of her expenditure and income sheet available and a calculator should be brought into court, if necessary, to save time.The justice should be asked for leave to admit it in evidence, and for the applicant to be able to refer to same in the course of giving evidence. The respondent is unlikely to object if there is a copy for the solicitor and the respondent, and the justice. Each item of expenditure referred to should be vouched by the production of exhibits of bills. Copies of these should be available for the respondent, and the originals should be handed into the justice. If the applicant's solicitor has not shown these in advance to the respondent's solicitor, the latter will insist on inspecting each document, before indicating whether he will object to its admission.

11 *P. v P.* (March 1980) High Court, unreported, relying on Lord Asquith in *Buchler v Buchler* [1947] 1 All ER 319.
12 Section 2(1) of the Judicial Separation and Family Law Reform Act 1987.

A lot of time will thus be wasted. An explanation of any unusual item of expenditure should be offered to the justice, to reduce the prospect of being cross examined vigorously on it.

9.036 The applicant should be ready to support allegations relating to the husband's income and expenditure by, for example, production of bank statements or other evidence of hidden earnings or assets.Even if the husband is paid on a monthly basis, the court is more familiar with working on a weekly computation. The expenditure or income figures should be adjusted accordingly. If the husband is still in the house, but is about to leave, the amount should be calculated by which this will reduce the weekly expenditure of the applicant.

His expenditure will increase, because of rent, higher metered utility charges, laundry, and the higher cost of catering for a single person. It is often, perhaps unfairly, assumed that men who are separated have to eat out, as they cannot cook.

9.037 The applicants' solicitor should be familiar with the cost of renting a flat in case the figure claimed by the respondent seems exorbitant. The recent payslips should be scrutinised for unusual deductions, or any sudden drop in overtime, as should any new loan from the credit union, with perhaps a high ratio of savings to the loan. The credit union loan is given on the basis that a certain sum is saved every week, but the husband may be saving more than the minimum. The respondent should also be asked whether he has income from investments, or the letting of property or land, or dividends from shares. The court will focus on the present, and if the respondent has a lot of debts, no matter that he was extravagant, he will probably be allowed take money out of the "kitty" to discharge them. If the wife has had a baby recently, she can now claim the birth expenses for the child, which can be considerable, particularly if she went privately to a consultant. These expenses should be vouched separately, including items like the purchase of a cot, the layette, and a buggy. Section 21 of the Status of Children Act 1987 inserts a new section 21A into the 1976 Act, which provides that the court can make a lump sum order in relation to a dependent child of the family where the other parent has failed to make such contribution as is proper in the circumstances towards the expenses incidental to the birth, or the funeral expenses of a child. The maximum is £750 each. The expenses include the first batch of nappies, clothes, bedclothes, babygrows, sterilising equipment and so on.

Acting for the respondent

9.038 The applicant should be cross examined on her earning capacity, if she is not engaged in work outside the home. If she is in part time work, the respondent should have already calculated the cost of child minding, to see if she is justified in not working full time. If the marriage has only just broken up, and there are young children, the court will probably not expect a mother to obtain outside work. The usage of the utilities may have been high, when economies might have been possible. The figure for clothing for the wife and children should be examined closely. She should be asked about the possibility of using her home-making skills in running a small business from home, or at least taking up a night class to brush up on her skills. The question of whether it is feasible to take in students or lodgers can be looked at. If the children have part time employment, there may be no need for pocket money. If the children are grown up and in receipt of a reasonable income, contributions of less than £30 per week should be queried. Parents should not be expected to subsidise young adults. The emphasis should be on querying the non essentials.

The maintenance order

9.039 Section 4 of the 1976 Act provides for a maintenance order not to commence earlier than the date the order is made. If payment is not to be on a weekly basis, the order should clarify whether it is payable every four weeks or every calendar month, and if the latter, what day of the month. The frequency of payment should coincide as far as possible with the payment of the respondent's salary. The day of the week is important. If a respondent is paid on a Thursday, it is usual to have the payment due that day.

9.040 It is recommended that the payment be made through the office of the District Court Clerk. Cash payments directly to the applicant, should be discouraged, no matter how convenient. Disputes usually arise as to how much cash was in fact received. If the payment is through the clerk's office, he is available, in the vicinity of the court to give evidence of arrears. Under section 5(1)(c) the order must specify what part of the order is attributable to each child. Sometimes payments for an older child, or a child with special needs may be larger than for a younger child.

9.041 The periodical payments order is for a gross sum out of which the applicant is expected to pay all household bills. An order for a lump sum payment is not possible under the 1976 Act—see **8.008**. The standard form of order does not allow for payment of arrears on utilities or mortgage, nor does it specify who is to pay the mortgage. If the court has made a ruling on these issues, then the court should be asked to draw it up in the form of an order, and the clerk to take a special note of it. Alternatively the issues can be clarified by agreement and an exchange of letters between the respective solicitors. The District Court seems reluctant to make orders for discharge of bills, and it is questionable whether it has such a power. Certainly, if a maintenance order is made by a justice on the basis of the applicant taking over responsibility for utilities, then from that date she is so responsible, even if the court-appointed date falls in the middle of a bill cycle. The E.S.B. meter reading can be taken, to ascertain the amount due. Telecom may give a closing account, if the account is being changed into her name. If the husband is about to leave the house, then the court may clarify that he is to discharge the utilities up to the date of leaving. All these outstanding matters should be sorted out in court, for the sake of reducing hardships and confusion to both spouses. The justice may give guidance on them, even though it does not form part of his order. An alternative way of resolving these outstanding bills, is to seek an interim order under section 7 of the 1976 Act—see **8.051**. The court may make an order in relation to specified arrears, and current utilities and mortgage, for a specified period. If the arrears are not discharged by the time the matter comes into the list for final disposal, the court can order increased maintenance to the applicant, on the basis that she has had to make arrangements to discharge arrears on a weekly basis, which can become part of the periodical payments order. Then if the interim order has not been complied with, an attachment of earnings summons can be issued: see **9.047–9.049**.

Payments through the District Court Clerk

9.042 Once the order is drawn up, in accordance with rule 11 of the 1976 rules the clerk sends a copy to the respondent, now known as the maintenance debtor, setting out the address where the maintenance is to be paid. Rule 12 provides for the clerk to send a notice, in form 10, notifying the debtor of the hours and places at which payments are to be made. Rule 13 provides for a receipt to be given to him. The applicant should be given the address and telephone number of the clerk and told to check directly with him, if the maintenance does not arrive. If the respondent is not paid until Friday, and he posts a cheque then, it will not arrive into the Family Law Office until Monday. The maintenance creditor will not receive her money until Tuesday, at the earliest. There is no remedy if this happens, as the payments are not strictly in arrears, and the Act does not provide a remedy for accidental or deliberate delay of payment. The maintenance creditor may have to call and collect the cheque, to ensure having it before the weekend.

9.043 If payment is made by cheque, the cheque should be made payable to the maintenance creditor. Otherwise the cheque has to be lodged for clearance, and the office may not be prepared to issue their own cheque for two weeks, in case the cheque "bounces". The cheque should be accompanied by the office reference number and all queries on payments should quote the reference number.

9.044 If payment is ordered through a bank account, and this proves unsatisfactory, because of delays caused by the maintenance debtor, an application can be made, under section 9(1)(b) of the 1976, by the maintenance creditor, to have the order paid through the District Court Clerk. Rule 14 provides for an application for a direction that payments be made to the district court clerk, to be made ex parte. Notice, in form 11 must be signed by the creditor or his solicitor, and lodged with the clerk, and the order of the court must be in form 12. If the maintenance debtor wishes to make the payment, other than through the District Court Clerk, he may apply under section 9(3) to discharge that method payment. Rule

15 provides for a summons in form 13 to be issued, on notice to the creditor. The court may do so if it is satisfied with his record of payments. In practice this application is rare. The spouses may agree themselves to alter the method of payment, or the creditor may start accepting direct payments, without informing the office. This can cause problems, if payments fall into arrears: See **9.047–9.051** and **9.071–9.076**.

Appeal to the Circuit Court

9.045 If either party is dissatisfied with the amount of maintenance ordered, or the making of the order itself, an appeal lies to the Circuit Court. If recognizances have been fixed and entered into, in accordance with rule 192 of the District Court Rules 1948, the order will be stayed pending appeal. This will prevent the maintenance creditor taking proceedings for arrears. However, the respondent should be advised to put aside the amount (or as near as possible to the amount) in a bank account. Alternatively, if he is only disputing the amount, he may pay what he alleges he can afford to the creditor and the children, even though the order has been stayed. If the recognizances have been waived the order of maintenance must be complied with pending appeal. This causes confusion, as it is the practice to waive recognizances in family law cases. The debtor quite innocently may not realise that he must comply with the order in the interim. It has been known for enforcement or attachment of earnings summonses to be issued, even though there is an appeal against the substantive order.

9.046 The appeal involves a rehearing. It is helpful to have clarified in advance whether the appeal is limited to the issue of the amount, or whether it is a full appeal. The court may uphold the order, in which case the maintenance order is backdated to the date of the District Court order. This can be a considerable bill for the respondent. If the creditor succeeds in recovering the arrears, she is obliged to repay the amounts obtained from the community welfare officer, pending the appeal.[13] If the maintenance order is neither dismissed nor upheld, and a new order is made, the order may be effective from either the date of the District Court or the Circuit Court orders. This should be clarified as there is much confusion on this point in practice.

Enforcement of maintenance orders

Attachment of earnings

Advantages and procedure

9.047 Part III of the 1976 Act deals with attachment of earnings. When there are arrears on a maintenance order, a decision must be made at an early stage whether an attachment of earnings summons or an enforcement

---

13 Social Welfare Consolidation Act 1981, section 317, as inserted by Social Welfare Act 1989, section 12.

summons is to be issued. An attachment of earnings order cannot be obtained if the maintenance debtor is self employed. The advantage of an attachment of earnings order, which is made payable through the District Court, is that only a request form need be completed, asking the District Court clerk to take such steps as he considers reasonable to recover arrears. Rule 16 of the 1976 Rules provides that the request form, in form 15 be completed. The clerk may then issue an attachment of earnings summons. This can be posted with a note stating the respondent's current address, and employer. This ensures that an attachment of earnings summons, rather than an enforcement summons is issued. The clerk can issue it provided the payments are made through his office. The usual rules relating to the issue and service of summonses apply. Alternatively, the solicitor may complete the summons, and ask the clerk to give a date, and the clerk signs the summons. If payments have not been directed by the court, to be made through the court clerk, rule 18 provides for a summons, in form 16, to be issued by the creditor, or her solicitor. In the latter case, the original summons must be lodged with the clerk, four days before the hearing, with the statutory declaration of service.

9.048 The other advantage of payments of the "antecedent order"[14] being made through the District Court clerk, is that the High Court[15] and Circuit Court orders can be enforced by way of an attachment of earnings summons in the District Court.[16] This is not possible if the higher court ordered payment through a bank account or directly. Section 9(2) of the 1976 Act allows the clerk to issue an attachment of earnings summons when payments due to him are in arrears. However, in the case of the latter, it may be possible to obtain an order for the maintenance to be paid through the court clerk, under section 9(1)(b) of the 1976 Act. This applies where the court has not given a direction under section 9(1)(a), for payments to be made through the clerk. The court was defined, in section 23 of the 1976 Act, prior to the Courts Act 1981, as the High Court, Circuit Court and District Court. Since the implementation of the Courts Act 1981, the Court is defined as the District Court and the Circuit Court only. It would seem therefore, that a High Court order of maintenance made prior to the 12th May 1982, which did not direct payment through the clerk, can be made payable through the clerk, on an application under section 9(1)(b) of the 1976 Act. But this can only be done in respect of Circuit Court or District Court orders made subsequent to the 12th May 1982, and not of any High Court maintenance orders made since that date.

---

14 Section 3(1) of the 1986 Act, defines "antecedent order" as a maintenance order, variation order or interim order, an order under section 8 of the Act, a maintenance order under section 11(2)(b) of the Guardianship of Infants Act 1964, an enforceable order under the Maintenance Orders Act 1974, and an order for alimony.
15 See section 10(1)(a) of the 1976 Act.
16 This is because section 9(1) states: Where the Court makes a maintenance order, the court shall . . . (b) in a case in which the court has not given a direction, under paragraph (a), direct, at any time thereafter, . . . that the payments shall be made to the District Court clerk.

9.049 Once the order directing payment through the District Court clerk is made by the District Justice, them a summons for attachment of earnings can be issued. Obviously, a copy of the High Court or Circuit Court order should be lodged in the District Court.

9.050 *Statement of earnings* The summons contains a detachable statement which requires the maintenance debtor to provide information relating to his employer, or any other person who pays earnings to him, his earnings, and expected earnings, his resources, his needs, information on his reference or pay number, within 14 days. If he does not do this, it may be difficult to trace the correct employer. Rules 16 to 18 deal with the relevant summonses.

9.051 Unfortunately there is no penalty if the statement is not furnished, except that, if it results in the creditor not obtaining her monies, he may be sued under section 20(1) for a simple contract debt. But if the information form is completed in a way that is, to the debtor's knowledge, false or misleading, he is guilty of an offence, and under section 20(2) he can be fined and imprisoned. The authors are not aware of any prosecution ever having been initiated. Under section 13(3) the statement, if completed, is regarded as admissible evidence of the facts stated in it. If the creditor is not happy with the information contained therein under section 13(1)(b) she can seek an order of the court directed to the employer, to furnish a statement of particulars of the debtor's earnings and expected earnings. Alternatively, the court may, before or at the hearing, order the debtor in accordance with section 13(1)(a) to furnish a written statement of his earnings, and employer. This order may be obtained subsequent to the making of an attachment of earnings order, where, for example, the debtor leaves his employment, and the creditor is trying to have the order enforced against the new employer.

Hearing of attachment of earnings summons

9.052 The applicant must establish, to the court's satisfaction, that the debtor has, without reasonable cause, defaulted in complying with the order. Section 10(3) provides that an attachment of earnings order shall not be made without the consent of the maintenance debtor, unless the Court is satisfied that the maintenance debtor has, without reasonable excuse, defaulted in the making of any payment under the relevant antecedent order. Usually the order has to be in arrears for a minimum of two weeks before the clerk is willing to issue the summons as it is the practice of the district court not to issue a summons for two weeks, in case there is a problem in clearing a cheque, or a postal delay. If the debtor is in steady employment, the court may decide that he had no reasonable excuse. However if the debtor was on strike or lost his employment, or was out sick, then the court may decline to order attachment of his earnings. If it dismisses the summons, he still remains liable for the arrears. It may be helpful to ask the court to certify the arrears, or get the debtor to agree the amount of arrears. This makes it easier to sue in the future, if the arrears are not discharged. It is possible to raise the matter again, if there is further default in the order. The court can include former arrears, in making an attachment of earnings order, even though the original summons was dismissed on the grounds that at that time there was a reasonable excuse as to why the order was not paid, provided that the court accepted that there were arrears. The respondent may plead *res judicata*. It is possible to sue for a contract debt within a period of six years. If he does not clear the arrears within a reasonable time, the creditor may issue enforcement, or sue by way of a simple contract debt. Alternatively, the court may adjourn the hearing, to give him time to issue a variation (section 6) and discharge the arrears over a period of time. Some justices may order him to discharge the arrears at a certain rate, and adjourn the case with liberty to re-enter. Such an order is not an attachment of earnings order, nor is it an enforcement order. Nor can the debtor be brought to court for contempt if he fails to discharge the arrears. This order is difficult to enforce. An advantage of the attachment of earnings order is that the arrears continue to accrue up to the date of the hearing of the application.

9.053 The first witness will be the court clerk, or the clerk who actually deals with payments. He will give evidence of the date of the court order, and the amount of payments due, and actually made. It is helpful to have discussed these figures in advance with the clerk, and the debtor's solicitor, to try and agree the figures. If payments have been made directly, the creditor will have to give evidence. She is likely to be cross examined, as it is unlikely she has kept proper records of payments, unless they were made by cheque, and were lodged to her Bank. Even if the payments were made through the office, it is usual to call the creditor to state that no payments were received directly by her. She may give evidence of any matter relevant to whether or not he had a reasonable excuse for defaulting with the payments.

The maintenance debtor is then called to state whether or not he agrees with the the amount of arrears and to furnish his excuse. Unfortunately debtors who get into financial difficulties often disregard the order, or start paying reduced amounts, instead of issuing a variation. The debtor will be expected to discharge the arrears, even if a variation order is made. The variation order will reduce the original maintenance order, as and from the next payment. The attachment of earnings order will be effective 10 days after service of the order on the employer.

Making of attachment of earnings order

9.054 The relevant legislation is contained in section 10(2). The attachment of earnings order directs the employer "to deduct" such amounts (specified in the order) as may be appropriate. This makes possible deduction of an additional sum for arrears (section 10(2)(a)). The monies will usually be paid to the District Court clerk, for transmission to the creditor. Alternatively the order may direct the payments to the creditor.

In making the order the court must fix the "normal deduction rate" (section 10(2)(b)), that is the rate at which it is reasonable that his earnings should be applied, in meeting the maintenance order as well as arrears and costs. The court must also fix the "protected earnings rate", that is, the amount below which the earnings should not be reduced, by a payment made under the attachment order. In doing this, the court must have regard to the resources and needs of the maintenance debtor (section 10(4)(b)). The object is to cushion the debtor against any unexpected reduction in income, by ensuring that his disposable income is not reduced to such a level that he cannot provide for his basic needs.

9.055 The definition of earnings, as set out in section 3 of the Act, includes any fees, bonus, commission, overtime or other emoluments. The protected earnings rate should, if possible have regard to the average wage or salary of the debtor, rather than be based on a figure inclusive of expected overtime or commission. This is because of unexpected fluctuations in income, which may cause problems in the administration of the order. But if the additional emoluments are substantial and regular, then they should be included in calculating the normal deduction rate, and protected earnings rate. The order can also be made against a pension or other like benefit in respect of employment. (Section 3(1)(b)).

Consequences of an attachment of earnings order

9.056 When an attachment of earnings order is made section 19(1) of the 1976 Act provides an enforcement order made under section 8 of the Enforcement of Court Orders Act 1940 ceases to have effect. It is not clear whether, under section 19 of the Act of 1976, the court has a discretion to include in the attachment order arrears owing under the discharged enforcement order.

9.057 Section 19(2) provides that an attachment of earnings order ceases to have effect when an order has been made under the Enforcement of Court Orders Act, 1940. This is more common. Take, for example the case of maintenance debtor who is out sick, and is only in receipt of social welfare (occupational injury or disability benefit) and who claims for his wife and children, not disclosing that there is a maintenance order in existence. The creditor since the attachment of earnings order is of no use, obtains an order, under section 8 of the 1940 Act, for him to discharge arrears at the rate of £5 per week. The social welfare is then sorted out and he resumes work. Because she has obtained an order under section 8, strictly speaking in accordance with section 20(1) her attachment of earnings order has ceased to have effect. Alternatively, she can issue a fresh attachment of earnings summons, and the order of £5 per week will then cease to have effect. The Act is silent as regards what an employer should do during temporary cessation of employment.

9.058 According to section 11 of the 1976 Act, the attachment of earnings order comes into effect 10 days after service of the order on the employer.

Rule 19 of the 1976 Rules provides for the order to be served on the employer, and on any subsequent employer. Section 11(1) states: "where an attachment of earnings order is made . . . the employer shall, if it has been served upon him, comply with it; but he shall be under no liability for non compliance therewith before 10 days have elapsed since the service". Rule 20 provides that the order is served by registered prepaid post, and also on the debtor. If the employer fails to comply with it, he can be sued. The maintenance creditor and debtor should be advised of the lapse of 10 days, so that alternative arrangements can be made for the first week.

9.059 If the debtor is a civil or public servant section 16 sets out who is the appropriate official and who is to be regarded as having the debtor in his employment. Section 16(2) provides that if there is any doubt as to which department employs the maintenance debtor, the Minister for Finance (formerly Public Service) at the request of the court, may make a determination on the issue. Such a determination, made in writing by an officer of the minister is admissible in evidence in accordance with section 16(3) without further proof. It is very important, with a large organisation, to have clarified who is the actual employer, so that the correct wages office is identified.

9.060 Under section 20(3) the employer is obliged to give a note of deductions to the employee. If he fails to do so, he is guilty of an offence. There is an interesting provision in section 12, that any payments from the employer must meet the maintenance order, before any costs are paid. The District Court clerk gives the receipt for payment to the employer (rule 21). The clerk transmits the payment to the creditor (rule 22). If the proper amount is deducted, then the clerk may send the costs separately to the solicitor, provided the client has authorised the clerk in writing to do this. Otherwise the cases are transmitted in the usual cheque to the creditor, who may not realise that the costs are included, and who is happy to receive a bonus!

Change of circumstances affecting an attachment of earnings order

9.061 A change of circumstances may occur as follows:

1. A maintenance debtor leaves his employment, to take up a new post.
2. A maintenance debtor leaves his employment, but becomes self-employed.
3. There is a change in wages or salary, for example, a loss of 'guaranteed' overtime, loss of travelling expenses, bonus or commission.
4. The maintenance debtor is on strike, or on sick pay for a relatively long period.

9.062 Under section 14(a) there is a legal duty on the maintenance debtor to notify the District Court office, in writing, of cessation of employment, within 10 days. The employer is also obliged under section 17(3) to notify the court office. The amount of the order will be deducted from holiday pay, or pay in lieu of notice. In effect if the debtor does not obtain new employment, the attachment element of the order lapses, but the obligation to pay the order reverts to the maintenance debtor. There is also a duty imposed on the debtor by section 14(b) to notify the office if he becomes employed again. The order then revives, and the District Court clerk serves the order on the new employer in accordance with rule 19. This provision is not well known or well used. If a new employer becomes aware that there is an order in force, he is required by section 14(c) to notify the office within 10 days. He must inform the office of the debtor's earnings. The section does not state that the employer must start making deductions from earnings. However, section 11 will apply which states that, where an attachment of earnings order is in force, the employer shall comply with it, if is served on him. If there is any doubt about the interpretation of these provisions, an application can be made to vary the order in accordance with section 17. If the new employer fails to cooperate, it may be possible to sue him, under section 20, for the amount of monies lost by the creditor. The attachment of earnings provisions are only of use if a maintenance creditor keeps up to date with the debtor's employment situation. However, where a husband fails to notify the office of a change of employment, diplomacy is needed as the new employer may discharge the new employee when he discovers his marital difficulties. A discreet contact by the solicitor of the maintenance creditor may be needed.

9.063 If the maintenance debtor's earnings are reduced as a result, for example, of sickness, the employer must pay him his protected earnings rate. This may result in a shortfall to the wife. The debtor may issue a variation of attachment summons, to reduce the normal deduction rate. This would spread the arrears and costs over a longer period.

What payments constitute "earnings"?

9.064 Section 15 of the 1976 Act refers to "payments to the maintenance debtor of a particular class or description". It is particularly relevant where a large bonus or commission is to be paid to the debtor. If the debtor is likely to dissipate a lump sum, an application may be made to determine if the attachment of earnings order applies to such a sum. The employer who is about to pay over the lump sum can be joined as a third party, or can issue the proceedings himself. The difficulty is that section 15(2) allows an employer to pay over any such sum while he is awaiting a decision of the court, or when an appeal is pending. If the debtor were about to collect such a sum, and leave the country, the creditor may have to seek an injunction in the Circuit Court to restrain him from disposing of the sum, pending a decision by the District Court, on whether the attachment of earnings order applies to the lump sum.

9.065 In the case of *E.B. v F.B.*[17] an attachment of earnings order had been made. The maintenance debtor was made redundant and became

17   20 July 1981, unreported, High Court.

entitled to a lump sum payment in lieu of statutory notice and holiday pay. The District Court clerk issued the summons under section 15, to determine whether these sums were "earnings". The justice stated a case to the High Court to determine whether the sum of £5347 was "earnings". The wife argued that the relevant paragraph of the earnings definition was designed to deal with compensation when employment ceased. She also argued that redundancy payments were calculated on previous service with the company, and that the lump sum represented future earnings, as if the employee had continued working. The husband conceded that the "notice" pay and holiday pay were "earnings". He argued that the redundancy pay was a once-off payment to compensate him for loss of employment. It was not in the nature of a pension. The court only had power to attach periodic payments. Ellis J. held that the lump sum was not "earnings" within the Act. The Act only covers periodic payments.

Discharge, variation and lapse of an attachment of earnings order

9.066 Section 17 of the Act of 1976 deals with discharge, variation and lapse of an attachment of earnings order. Such an order may be discharged on application by the maintenance debtor, the maintenance creditor, or the District Court clerk. If the original maintenance order is discharged due to desertion or conduct repugnant to justice (section 38)[18] section 18(1) provides that the attachment of earnings order ceases to have effect, with the exception of payments still due. In accordance with section 18(2) the employer must be notified of the discharge. If part of the maintenance order is discharged, or in effect, varied (as, for example, where a child ceases to be a dependent child) then a variation of attachment should be issued, so that the correct reduced order can be deducted by the employer. Section 6(3) of the 1976 Act states that the part of the order attributable to a dependent child, ceases when the child is no longer dependent. However, the rest of the maintenance order relating to other children, and the spouse stands.

The court has a discretion, if it thinks fit, to vary or discharge. In practice, a maintenance debtor should try and have the arrears discharged prior to such an application. An attachment of earnings order may be discharged if the arrears are paid off (see **9.061–9.063**) and the maintenance debtor undertakes to comply with the original order.

9.067 A variation of attachment of earnings order is applied for where earnings or employment change. In most circumstances, a variation of the original maintenance order is also needed. A variation of both may be needed if the maintenance debtor is being paid on a monthly basis but the wages clerk is paying the order monthly despite the order being weekly. If a compromise cannot be worked out, the court may have to decide the frequency of payments. If a variation of attachment is made, the employer must comply with it.

---

18 Section 5(2) as amended by section 38 of the Judicial Separation and Family Law Reform Act 1989.

9.068 If the maintenance debtor leaves employment section 17(3) provides that the attachment of earnings order lapses as regards that specific employer. It may cover holiday pay or pay in lieu of notice. Section 17(4) provides that the lapse of the order does not prevent the order remaining in force "for other purposes". This in effect means that the obligation under section 14 on the employee and the employer to notify changes in employment, and earnings continue. The section only covers notification of earnings, when there is a new employment. The employee is not obliged to notify the creditor or the court office, if there is an increase in his earnings.

Penalties

9.069 If a false or misleading statement is made by the maintenance debtor or an employer, the maintenance creditor may sue them for a simple contract debt (section 20(1)) provided the creditor has failed to obtain monies under the attachment of earnings order. The authors are not aware of any such action. There is no provision in the 1976 Rules for it. Presumably a civil process would be issued, and the action would take place in the ordinary civil list, in a public court. This acts as a deterrent to the maintenance creditor.

9.070 If the statement that is made is false or misleading, to the knowledge of the person making it, then that person commits a criminal offence (section 20(2)). The authors are not aware of any such prosecutions. The Rules are silent as regards the procedure. A private prosecution by way of summons would be appropriate if it were decided to proceed in this way. The penalty is a fine of £200 or six months imprisonment, or both.

Enforcement of Court Orders Act, 1940

Procedure

9.071 Section 8 of the Enforcement of Court Order Act 1940, as amended, deals with the enforcement of maintenance orders. It provides for a justice to levy arrears of maintenance by distress and sale of the goods of the "defaulter" or, unless he shows to the satisfaction of the justice that the failure to pay was due neither to his wilful refusal nor to his culpable neglect, sentence him to imprisonment for up to the three months.

9.072 In practice the distress powers are rarely, if ever, used. There would be difficulty ascertaining which household goods were the property of the defaulting spouse, as distinct from the applicant spouse. Nevertheless, section 8 offers the only way to collect arrears from an unemployed, or self-employed person. The relevant Rules are the District Court Rules (No. 2) 1962 (S.I. No. 8 of 1962), and the 1976 Rules—the District Court (Family Law (Maintenance of Spouses and Children) Act 1976) Rules 1976 (S.I. No. 96 of 1976).

9.073 *Maintenance paid direct to an applicant* Rules 26(2) of the 1962 Rules provides that an information form is completed, setting out the amount of arrears, and this is sworn by the applicant spouse before the justice. The application is made to the Justice, in the area where either the defaulter, or the applicant ordinarily resides, or carries on a profession, business or occupation, or where the original maintenance order was made, (rule 26(1)(i). By rule 26(2) it is at the discretion of the justice whether to issue warrant or a summons. Usually a summons is issued in the first instance to give the debtor the opportunity of stating his case, rather than the more dramatic method of a warrant.

9.074 An enforcement summons (form 52) is served by registered post, if there is no summons server, in accordance with rule 27 on service. If the debtor does not appear for the hearing of the maintenance summons, or is likely to evade service of the registered letter containing the summons, it may be more appropriate to issue a warrant in the first instance. Rule 29 of the 1962 Rules provides that in any case in which the defaulter is evading service, the Justice may order that the summons be served in the manner provided by Rule 46 and 47 of the District Court Rules 1948, as substituted by Rule 5 of the District Court Rules (No. 1) 1962. The warrant is prepared by the clerk, and signed by the justice. If the payments are to be made direct to the applicant, she must swear the information (Form 51) grounding the issuing of the warrant in accordance with rule 26(4) of the 1962 rules. The justice may endorse on the warrant an order allowing the defaulter to be released after entering a recognizance, with or without sureties, before the station sergeant. This will be on the basis of the defaulter agreeing to appear before a particular district court on a fixed date. If the warrant is in the Dublin area, it may be addressed to the warrant office in the Bridewell, which then transmits it, duly endorsed, to the local Garda station.

9.075 It is very important that the most up to date address of the defaulter, both at work and at home, is submitted to the Gardaí. Many warrants have gone astray where the defaulter has left his address with no forwarding address. It is also helpful to supply a photograph or physical description and to indicate where and when the defaulter is most likely to be found, and any other information which will save the time and expense of the warrant officer. If there has been no endorsement as regards bail, the defaulter, once he is arrested, is to be brought to the court as soon as possible. The court will then decide whether to remand him in custody, with or without bail fixed, or allow him to be released on bail, on his own surety or independent sureties, or proceed to hear the case. The applicant should be notified by the office of the date for hearing, especially where the payments are made direct to her. The defaulter should be advised of his right to apply for criminal legal aid if the court takes the view that it is a serious default, likely to lead to imprisonment.

9.076 *Maintenance payable through the District Court Clerk* Section 9(2) of the 1976 Act provides that where payments, to the clerk, are in arrear, the clerk shall, if the maintenance creditor so requests in writing (rule 16 provides for a form 15 to be completed) take such steps as he considers reasonable, in the circumstances, to recover the sums in arrear, whether by proceeding in his own name for an attachment of earnings order or otherwise. Rule 16 provides that this includes an order under section 8 of the 1940 Act. The applicant signs a request form to the clerk, asking him to take such steps as he considers reasonable in the circumstances to recover the arrears. The clerk will apply to the justice by way of information. The justice will listen to the views of the clerk, as to whether a summons or warrant is the more appropriate method of enforcement Rule 32 of the 1976 Rules provide that a justice may, if he thinks fit, instead of issuing such warrant as provided by section 8, issue a summons (form 30) on foot of the information sworn by the clerk. Rule 44 of the 1976 Rules states that the provisions regarding the addressing and execution of warrants in criminal proceedings contained in the District Court Rules 1948, shall apply to warrants issued under the 1976 Rules, with the proviso that warrants of distress shall be addressed to and executed by the several sheriffs and county registrars. The clerk therefore needs to be given as much background and up-to-date information as possible, to help him make recommendations to the justice. In accordance with rule 33 if a summons is issued either by the clerk or the applicant directly a warrant can be issued in lieu at any time thereafter. This may be done where the summons is returned uncollected. A warrant may also be issued if the applicant has no up-to-date address for the defaulter. The warrant may be addressed to the superintendent or inspector for the area where the warrant is issued, who will transmit it to the Garda station nearest to the employment exchange where the defaulter collects his payments. Alternatively it can be sent to an address where he is likely to call regularly for example, care of his parents address. A warrant is appropriate where the defaulter is likely to leave the jurisdiction, or a large sum of money has come into his possession which will be dissipated, if the applicant does not move quickly. If the defaulter pays the exact sum owed to the warrant officer, then the warrant will not be executed (rule 70 of the 1948 rules). The warrant officer may give a warning to the defaulter that he is about to arrest him and give him a few days to discharge the arrears. The warrant remains in force for six months, before execution. If he cannot be located within that time, the warrant is returned. Rule 78 of the Rules of 1948 provides for the return of unexecuted warrants, and their reissue.

Hearing of application for enforcement

9.077 Rule 40 of the 1976 Rules provides that on the hearing of an application under section 8 of the 1940 Act, the clerk, to whom the payments are payable shall tender as evidence the maintenance order, interim order, variation order, the request of the maintenance creditor, and any other relevant document. He shall also prove the amount of arrears for 6 months (26 weeks) up the date the information was sworn (section 8(7)of the 1940 Act). The clerk may indicate the arrears up to the Friday prior to the day of the hearing, but the court cannot include these when it certifies the arrears. The only way of collecting these arrears is by issuing a fresh enforcement summons prior to leaving the precincts of the court, when the present case is disposed of. The new summons will be listed for three weeks hence, and another hearing takes place. The applicant will give evidence of any payments made directly to her, even if the original order directed payment through the district court.

9.078 The applicant (or the clerk) needs to establish wilful refusal or culpable neglect in paying before the justice can impose a sentence of imprisonment (section 8(1) of the 1940 Act). The clerk will rely on information given by the applicant to establish these facts. If the payments are made through the office, the maintenance creditor need not be contacted, as the proceedings are issued by the clerk. This is because the clerk is the applicant, as distinct from the spouse. However the creditor should insist on being notified of the hearing so that the maximum information is presented to the court. If the defaulter has been made redundant, or has left his employment involuntarily, the court may dismiss the summons, or strike it out. This is on the basis that there has not been wilful refusal or culpable neglect. However, he may have obtained a lump sum, which could be used to discharge the arrears. The court cannot attach a lump sum.[19] A clerk from the former employment of the defaulter may need to be summonsed to ascertain the amount received by the defaulter. If the defaulter is in receipt of pay related benefit (part 2, chapter 6 of the Social Welfare (Consolidation) Act 1981) as distinct from a flat rate unemployment benefit (part 2, chapter 4) or assistance (part 3, chapter 2), the arrears may be discharged at a small rate per week. The summons may then be adjourned for a number of weeks. This may be helpful to the applicant, as she has no right to any share of his pay related benefit.

9.079 If the defaulter is brought to the court, on foot of an enforcement warrant, and the payments are made through the court office, the hearing will sometimes proceed in the absence of the applicant. This is because there may not be time to notify the spouse, especially if she has no telephone. The summons is more likely to be dismissed on the basis of the defaulter's inability to pay, as any knowledge of hidden resources will not be available to the court. There is some doubt as to whether the court is entitled to proceed in the absence of the applicant, as the section refers to the hearing by the justice of evidence adduced by the applicant and the defaulter. If the clerk is regarded as the "applicant" then the case can proceed in the absence of the spouse. If the spouse is aware of hidden assets, she could make that known to the clerk, with the name and address of her solicitor, when she first signs the request form. If the solicitor for the

---

19   See *E.B. v F.B.* 20 July 1981, unreported, High Court.

applicant spouse is present, even though it may not be possible to notify the spouse, the solicitor can cross-examine the defaulter, and put questions to him in relation to such assets that is provided that the solicitor already has instructions from the spouse to proceed in her absence. The costs of the maintenance order may now be obtained by using section 8. This is contained in section 3(5) of the Courts (No. 2) Act 1986. If the court decides to sentence him, a warrant of committal is prepared in accordance with rule 68 of the 1948 Rules. He may be committed to prison forthwith for the certified arrears. The warrant is addressed to the superintendent or the inspector for the area where the warrant is issued (rule 70). In Dublin, he will be brought to the Bridewell Station before being brought to Mountjoy Prison. Alternatively the justice may order committal, but put a stay of execution on it for, say, two months, and then the warrant will only issue if the arrears are not cleared by then. He may issue the warrant, stating the date on which it is to be issued, or he may issue the warrant after the time fixed for the stay has expired (rule 68). The solicitor for the applicant should keep a record of the expiry date, to remind the office to have the committal warrant issued, if the arrears are not discharged.

9.080 If the defaulter does not appear the justice may issue a warrant for his arrest in accordance with rule 31. He will then be brought before the court, and a hearing will ensure. Alternatively the justice, on being satisfied of the service of the original summons, may proceed to hear evidence. If he is satisfied that there has been wilful refusal or culpable neglect, the justice may sentence him to imprisonment for a period of up to three months. The warrant will issue, and when he is arrested, he will be brought straight to prison to serve his sentence. The District Court clerk will be notified in accordance with rule 68(5) of the 1948 rules.

9.081 Rule 193 of the 1948 Rules provides that a person wishing to appeal from an order committing him to prison under the 1940 Act shall, within seven days, in addition to lodging the notice of appeal, enter into a recognizance (Form A4), with two sufficient sureties, in such sum as the justice may determine, conditioned to reside at a certain address, and to attend at the Circuit Court, and prosecute his appeal, and to pay such costs of the appeal as may be awarded against him. The defaulter's solicitor may apply for extension of time by virtue of rule 13 of the 1948 Rules, as substituted by rule 5 of the 1955 Rules. Notice must be given to the applicant spouse. If the sureties are accepted by the court, the defaulter will be released on signing the recognizance, at the prison. If he discharges the arrears and costs when he is in prison, he will be released. Section 8(3) provides that the sums outstanding are to be paid either to the Governor or the District Court office. It is important to note that if he serves the full sentence without discharging the arrears, the imprisonment does not operate to extinguish the debt (section 8(5)). Nor does it deprive the applicant spouse of any other remedy for enforcing the debt. Proceedings in debt may be initiated in a civil court for up to six years. However it would seem that it may not be possible to apply for the grant of an examination order.[20]

An order under section 8 for imprisonment cannot be made against a member of the permanent defence forces, or a reservist on permanent service. Instead a copy of the original maintenance order should be sent to the Minister for Defence, and the appropriate sum of maintenance, arrears and costs may then be deducted.[21]

9.082 It is important to check the amount of arrears on each warrant issued, and to ensure that the sum on each warrant is discharged in full, prior to discharge from prison. Where an order for imprisonment of a defaulter has been made but not yet executed, acceptance by the creditor of a payment on account of the arrears due will be taken to be a waiver of the right to enforce the order for imprisonment.[22] In the case of *Credit Finance Bank Ltd v Healy*[23] on a case stated it was held that as the warrant had been executed, it could not be reissued, or a new warrant issued. This was because the period during which the debtor could have been imprisoned had expired. He had been committed for one month from the date of arrest, under section 6 of the Enforcement of Court Orders Act 1940, unless he paid certain fixed sums. He was released on payment of certain sums. Subsequently it transpired that there had been a mistake on one warrant involving an under estimate of £1000. The Governor of Cork Prison applied for a new warrant when the mistake was discovered. The justice stated a case to the High Court, as to whether he had jurisdiction to reissue a warrant. Neither the defaulter nor the creditor appeared. The Governor relied on *(Shields) v Justics of Tyrone*[24] which was authority for the proposition that a court had power to make execution effective by issuing a fresh warrant. The High Court distinguished this case, on the basis that the facts of that case dealt with a warrant which had been returned unexecuted.

Appeal against an order made under section 8 of the Enforcement of Courts Orders Act 1940

9.083 If the defaulter is present in court when he is ordered to be committed to prison, recognizances can be applied for. Rule 193 of the 1948 Rules provides that two sureties are needed. If potential sureties are not present in the vicinity of the court, the court may still fix recognizances, and the sureties may be approved later. If recognizances are not fixed and entered into, he will start serving his sentence. This also happens

---

20 *Faley v O'Mahony* [1929] IR 1.
21 Section 98 Defence Act 1954, and section 30 of the 1976 Act, and section 2 and 5 of the Defence (Amendment) (No. 2) Act 1979 (which extended the deductions provision to women).
22 67 ILTR 54.
23 19 January 1987, unreported, High Court.
24 [1914] 2 IR 89.

if the recognizances are waived. A stay, in accordance with rule 192, only applies if a recognizance is entered into. It is important to remind the sureties to bring a bank, post office, or building society book, to prove their assets, or alternatively proof of ownership of a house, or the log book of a motor vehicle. The court has to be satisfied that in the event of the appellant not presecuting his appeal, or not appearing to it the recognizance can be estreated (see rule 82). The defaulter will be held in custody in the nearest cell, until the sureties are approved (rule 68(7)) if they have come to the court at a later stage. These Form A1 (Notice of Appeal) and Form A4 (recognizance) need to be completed forms, and the notice of appeal will be signed. The notice of appeal will be sent to the applicant, by registered post. It is recommended that the statutory declaration of service be completed, exhibiting the registered slip, and sworn before the justice as soon as possible. This facilitates the file being sent to the Circuit Court as soon as possible. Rule 197 provides for the relevant documents to be sent to the County Registrar.

9.084 Hopefully the defaulter will make some effort to lodge some of the arrears in the court office pending appeal. He is not under an obligation to do so, in the sense that the committal order is suspended (rule 192) pending appeal, because he entered into a recognizance. But he must still pay the weekly maintenance order. If, when the appeal comes up, he has got into further debt, it will not help his case before the Circuit Court. He may apply for a variation of the original maintenance order in accordance with section 6 of the 1976 Act which should be heard in the interim in the District Court, or the same day as the enforcement summons.

9.085 A rehearing will take place at the Circuit Court. As the appeal is a rehearing, the judge has power to vary the District Court order, by increasing or decreasing a sentence, or substituting any order, within his powers. The defaulter will probably play for time, by seeking an adjournment to give him a chance to save the money owed. In the meantime, if he has run into further arrears, as the original maintenance order is not suspended, he may find himself back in the District Court on a further enforcement summons. If he has not made further efforts, he may be sentenced afresh on the new arrears. If he does not succeed in having both appeals listed together, he may end up serving two separate consecutive sentences of three months each. If instead, both are listed together, and the Circuit Court decides to commit him, his solicitor may ask for the sentences to run concurrently. The other risk of an appeal is that if the justice has not imposed the maximum sentence, the Circuit Court has a discretion to increase each sentence to the maximum, and order them to run consecutively. This is only likely to happen where there is a blatant disregard of the orders and where the defaulter has sufficient assets to discharge the arrears, but will not do so out of spite or bitterness. The Circuit Court Judge may either order that he be taken into custody pending the issue of a warrant by the county registrar in accordance with Order 43 rule 6 of the Circuit Court Rules 1950. Alternatively s/he may allow the warrant to be issued by the District Justice in accordance with Order 43 rule 7. The applicant spouse may prefer the former option if it is a blatant case. If she thinks that the defaulter has been frightened into obeying the order, she may allow it to issue from the District Court. This will allow him further time to pay, but the warrant officer will have to locate him, and he may try to evade service. The Circuit Court order is final and not appealable. The appellant has the option, if he fears an increase in his sentence, to withdraw his appeal before the hearing commences. If he does so, the District Court order is affirmed, and the judge decides whether the committal warrant issued or whether it should be issued from the District Court.

Variation of a maintenance order

9.086 Section 6 of the Family Law (Maintenance of Spouses and Children) Act 1976 deals with variation. The court may vary the order, if it thinks it proper to do so, having regard to

1. any circumstances not existing when the original maintenance order, or the last variation order was made, or
2. to any evidence not available when themaintenance order was made.

The range of circumstances which the court can rely on is not limited to financial circumstances.This is because the section goes on to deal with variation based on conduct. The relevant section has been considerably amended by section 38(3)(b) of the Judicial Separation and Family Law Reform Act 1989.

Financial circumstances

9.087 A common change justifying a variation is the increase in inflation, which can be ascertained by looking at the consumer price index, published quarterly by the Central Statistics Office in February, May, August and November. It is calculated on the mid Tuesday of those months, but the index does not become available to the public until approximately six weeks later.

Most maintenance creditors do not come back every year to seek an increase in accordance with the increase in the consumer price index. However, when inflation was in the region of 10% or more, then an application to vary on an annual basis was essential.

9.088 If a maintenance debtor is promoted, or changes employment with an increase in his earnings, a variation may be justified. The fact that children are getting older, and more expensive to feed, educate and clothe may also ground an application to vary. The Economic and Social Research Institute (ESRI) published a report in December 1988[25] in which it was estimated that in 1987 it cost £19.60 per week to keep one small child, £28.20 for an older child, £24.30 for two younger children, and

---

25 *Equivalence Scales and Costs of Children* (authors Denis Conniffe and Gary Keogh).

£33.40 for one younger and one older child. This was by way of comparison with what parents actually received from social welfare.

An application to increase maintenance, where there has been another baby in or around the time of a separation, may provoke an allegation of adultery. Adultery, as a ground in itself, for discharging or varying a maintenance order, has been removed by section 38 of the 1989 Act, but conduct is still relevant. A lot depends on the date of the actual separation. If a child is born more than ten months after a separation order is granted or a deed of separation executed, then the husband is presumed not to be the father, unless the contrary is proved on the balance of probabilities. Section 46 of the Status of Children Act 1987 deals with such presumptions of paternity and non paternity. The birth certificate of the child should be inspected to see if the husband has been registered as father. There is a presumption that the person named on a birth certificate is the father, but this can be rebutted.[26] If the child is born within the period of ten months after the formal separation, under section 46(3) of the Status of Children Act 1987, the husband is presumed to be the father. The wife should be advised that the husband may seek an adjournment of her variation proceedings to ask for the court's direction on blood testing. Sections 38 to 43 of the Status of Children Act 1987 deal with blood testing. If she refuses to cooperate, the court may, under section 42(3), dismiss her application even if the child was born in the period giving rise to a presumption of paternity.

Proofs

9.089 The maintenance creditor will need to prove that there has been a change in the maintenance debtor's income. She may have to summons a wages clerk from his employment. If the net increase in his wages is the same percentage as the increase in the consumer price index she may get a small increase. For example, if his net wages increase by £4 per week she will probably be given half of that. However, there are no guidelines laid down, so it is at the discretion of the court. If the solicitors can cooperate on the information received from the debtor's employment this reduces the expense of bringing the witness from the debtor's employment.

9.090 A fresh list of expenditure and income needs to be prepared by the creditor and the debtor. It is helpful to compare it with the original list on which the maintenance order was based if available. It is usual to wait at least a year before issuing a variation, unless there has been a material change in circumstances.

Variation by creditor, seeking an increase in maintenance

9.091 Rule 9 of the 1976 Rules provides for a summons in Form 7. The standard summons contains a choice of variation or discharge. The discharge part will be deleted by the creditor. The usual rules of service of

26 *Brierly v Brierly and Williams* [1918] P 257.

the summons apply. The clerk may issue the summons if the payments are paid through the office, or the solicitor may issue it on the creditor's behalf. The debtor should have been written to in advance seeking his consent to an increase with the creditor setting out the grounds. If it has been a number of years since the original maintenance order was made, it is helpful to seek information from the Central Statistics Office on the amount of increase in the index over the years. The creditor will often find that she has been looking for too small an increase, taking the index into account. On the other hand, if she wants an increase out of line with the index, the debtor may use this against her. She needs to establish why she should receive an increase over and above the index. This may be because of the extra expense of children attending secondary school, teenage children, or special medical needs for a child who has developed a chronic illness. Proofs, in the nature of letters from a school setting out the charges, the extra classes, or payments for school activities, a letter from a doctor setting out the nature of an illness, and the medication and a letter from the pharmacist, explaining the usual charges, and how much can be recovered from a Health Board (under the refund scheme for medicines) are all helpful. Creditors sometimes fail to understand that a debtor may not be aware of expenses of this kind as they have only arisen since he left the home. If all of this is shown to him in advance, the variation may well be settled. He may agree to compromise, by increasing the amount of maintenance attributable to a particular child. If it is settled, it is better if a consent variation summons is issued, particularly if an attachment of earnings order is in force. If such an order is in force, a variation of attachment summons will be also required. Rule 27 provides for form 25 to be issued to vary an attachment of earnings order. His employer will not be able to deduct more than the order unless the court so directs.

Variation by maintenance debtor: change in his financial circumstances

9.092 The maintenance debtor, if he issues a variation, needs to show that there is a reduction in his earnings or an increase in his liabilities. It is helpful if he produces a letter from his employer setting out the reduction in earnings and the reasons for it. The court may be suspicious of any sudden drop in bonus, commission, or overtime. It may seek a witness from his employment to verify the situation. If the debtor is self-employed if is more difficult for a creditor to oppose the application. On the other hand, the debtor will find it more difficult to convince the court of the drop in earnings, if it is based on his accounts. Ideally the debtor's accountant should be present to explain the accounts.

9.093 It is quite common for debtors who have been made redundant and who are now in receipt of unemployment pay related benefit, to seek a variation. This may be opposed on the ground that the lump sum paid on redundancy and invested in a financial institution should be taken into account in ascertaining his means. On the other hand if a lump sum is used to purchase a house or help him set up a business, the court may decline to take it into account as it is no longer available as a weekly supplement, to the maintenance order.

9.094 It is also quite common for those who have retired and who now have a pension to seek a variation. They will usually have obtained a lump sum in addition. It may be that though their gross income is half what it was, the net income is two thirds the old income as a result of having less tax to pay. That, supplemented by a lump sum, may result in the court refusing a variation, or varying it slightly. If the creditor has a pay slip, or the solicitor for the creditor was in court on the previous maintenance application, a comparison between the old and new income may show how big or small the difference is. If a variation is refused, and later the lump sum is invested in the purchase of a home, a further variation can be issued.

9.095 The fact that the maintenance debtor is cohabiting and has a child in that relationship, may justify a variation order as, under section 16 of the Status of Children Act 1987 which inserted new provisions into section 5 of the 1976 Act, a dependent child includes a child of either spouse. Section 17 of the Status of Children Act 1987 (which substituted a new section 4(b)(i) in the 1976 Act) allows the court to have regard to expense of looking after that child, as one of the circumstances to be taken into account. If the maintenance debtor was not in court, at the time the maintenance order was made, he may apply to vary the order in accordance with section 6(1)(b) on the basis of evidence not available at the time. However, a variation should not be applied for, unless some time has elapsed. Otherwise the more appropriate remedy may be for him to lodge an appeal.

9.096 The standard summons contains variation and discharge, and the choice is with the applicant which to delete. This can be a problem if the summons is issued by a debtor who is alleging desertion by the creditor. If the only change sought is in the amount of maintenance, whether because of desertion or conduct repugnant to justice, then a variation can be issued. The justice may reduce maintenance for the creditor to nil, but leave the order for the children untouched. For example, if there is a maintenance order of £100 per week, £70 for the wife, and £10 for each of three children the court may vary the order, by varying the maintenance for the wife down to nil, and increasing the maintenance for the children to £30 each, making a total of £90, thus effecting a reduction of £10 only. However, the loss of the order will have an impact, as the children cease to be dependent children. Alternatively, where the intention is that nothing should be paid for the support of the creditor, a summons to discharge can be issued, and section 6(5) can be brought to the court's attention. This provides that desertion by (or conduct of) a spouse shall not be a ground for discharging or varying any part of a maintenance order that provides for the support of dependent children of the family'. A court (sometimes) will amend a discharge summons to a variation, before making its order, and vary the payment to the creditor to nil, possibly increasing the amount for the children. The court may increase the latter amount to the maximum, so that the children do not suffer as a result of loss of maintenance by the creditor. The same criteria that apply to establishing desertion or misconduct in a maintenance case also apply to a variation. Rule 11 of the 1976 Rules provides that when the court makes the variation order a copy is sent to the debtor. If the original order specified that the payments were to be made directly, she may subsequently apply for the payments to be made through the office of the District Court. Rule 14 of the 1976 Rules provides that an attachment of earnings order, or enforcement summons may be issued to enforce payments under a variation order.

Discharge of maintenance order

Statutory basis

9.097 Section 6 of the Act of 1976 provides for various methods of discharge:

(a) The debtor may apply to discharge the order after one year, subject to establishing his record of payments, provided that the maintenance creditor and the children are not prejudiced. This is rarely invoked unless the debtor feels very strongly that the making of the original order was a judgment that he had failed to provide such maintenance as was proper, and he feels that he did provide proper maintenance. In practice, most courts will grant maintenance when parties are separating without the need to establish that there was such a failure.

(b) The order may be discharged by the court, if it thinks it proper to do so, having regard to any circumstances not existing when the order was made. This includes a case where evidence was not available to the applicant when the maintenance order was made. This will apply where there is a change in the debtor's financial circumstances, such as loss of employment, or where he becomes ill or suffers an accident having long term consequences. The maintenance order may be discharged on the basis that the financial circumstances of the creditor are such that an order is no longer justified. Where a debtor becomes unemployed, and fails to secure re-employment he may need to prove efforts to obtain re-employment. Both spouses will then be supported by social welfare. Alternatively if she secures employment which is sufficiently well paid that she no longer needs his financial support the court may discharge the order in her favour, on the basis that she is able to support herself, and allow both parties to share the financial burden of supporting the children. There may be tax advantages to the latter: see **8.060–8.069**.

(c) The court may discharge the order, on the basis of desertion or misconduct. Section 6(2) makes clear that subsequent desertion, may lead to discharge of the order.

Discharge of maintenance for children

9.098 Section 6(3) provides for that part of an order attributable to a child to be discharged, when the child ceases dependency. This is at the age of 16, or 21 if the child is undergoing further education or training. However a maintenance agreement and deed of separation may provide for maintenance to continue to be paid to a child up to the age of 18 years if the child remains unemployed but is not in full time education or training. The creditor may not realise that the debtor is entitled to apply to discharge that part of the order even though a child reaching 16 years may not go on to further education and may be unemployed. That child will not be eligible for social welfare until he reaches 18 years and then it is means tested. So a creditor may be left supporting a child aged between 16 and 18 years without support from the debtor or the State. However, many debtors neglect to issue a discharge summons at this time and continue to pay the full order. If the maintenance order runs into arrears the debtor may set off the overpayment of the order against arrears. The debtor should have issued a discharge summons listed for a date after the attainment of the 16th birthday, or the date that the child ceases further education. However, on a strict interpretation of the section there is no need for a discharge application to court. All the debtor needs to do is notify the creditor that as and from the date that the child ceases to be a dependent child, he is entitled to deduct the sum in the order that is attributable to the child. However, he will be obliged to continue supporting a child into adulthood, who is suffering from a mental or physical disability, to such an extent that it is not reasonably possible for him to maintain himself fully. "Dependent child" is defined in section 3 of the Act of 1976.

Circuit Court procedure

Application for maintenance

9.099 Proceedings in the Circuit Court are usually issued in conjunction with proceedings for barring or/and custody, and perhaps, property proceedings. This may be so, even though the respondent's income is such that he cannot pay in excess of £100 for his spouse, nor in excess of £30 per child, per week. It may save legal costs to have all the matters in dispute between the parties sorted out in one forum, rather than taking separate proceedings in the District Court for maintenance. On the other hand, outside Dublin, if the Circuit Court is not going to sit locally for a number of months, and it is not possible to have the case listed somewhere relatively accesible for the parties, even for an interim maintenance application, it may be best to take proceedings in the local District Court. The question of whether to issue proceedings in the District Court becomes complicated, when there are allegations that the dependent spouse has been guilty of desertion, adultery, or conduct repugnant to justice (see section 33 of the Act of 1989).

9.100 The relevant Rules are the Circuit Court (No. 6) Rules of 1982, S.I. No 158/1982. The application is drafted in accordance with rule 7. It should set out full particulars of the failure to maintain, the income and expenditure of the applicant, and any details available as regards the income and expenditure of the respondent. There is an advantage over the District Court, in that there are written pleadings, and the provisions of the Circuit Court Rules can be used to maximise the information available to the court. This is especially so if the respondent is self employed or has complicated financial ventures or assets.

9.101 The rules provide for the application to be issued for the date of the commencement of the sittings of the Circuit, or, outside Dublin, there may be a fixed date allocated to family law cases, though practice varies. It is important to check with the registrar what is the actual date, and the usual time, that family law matters are dealt with. The solicitor for the applicant must ensure, particularly if the respondent is not legally represented the respondent is notified of the actual date and time, preferably by registered post or by letter personally delivered. An affidavit of service should be filed or if there is not enough time the solicitor will have to give oral evidence. If the case is in Dublin, a date for mention is allocated. On that date, a date for hearing will be fixed. A hearing for maintenance if listed on its own, is never given the same urgency in the lists as a barring application. It may be necessary particularly coming up to a vacation to issue a motion grounded on an affidavit, seeking interim maintenance. This can be heard in the Monday list, though it may be adjourned on its first date, to give the respondent time to file a replying affidavit. An answer should be filed by the respondent in accordance with rule 15.

9.102 Rule 14 provides that the application is served by ordinary prepaid post. If it is issued with an application for barring, there may be an issue as to whether the maintenance application should have been served personally. This is because an application for barring should be served by registered post, or personally in accordance with the Circuit Court (No. 3) Rules of 1982 (S.I. 152/1982). It may be better practice to serve a composite application personally. It is unlikely that an answer will be filed within the requisite four days. The respondent will apply on the mention date to have time extended but a time limit of, say ten days should be placed on its filing.

9.103 If the answer appears vague or evasive, it is possible to serve a notice requiring further and better particulars. There is no provision in the family law rules for this request. Order 14 of the Circuit Court Rules 1950 is relied on, even though it refers to a defendant requesting such particulars after service of the civil bill, and the plaintiff making a similar request after delivery of the defence. However if the other party objects the applicant may seek the courts direction under rule 16 of the Circuit Court (No. 6) Rules 1982. Order 28 of the 1950 Rules may be used to file a notice to admit documents of a straightforward nature for example, rent or

255

mortgage receipts, usage of utilities, pay slips, P60, tax free allowance certificate, or similar matters. If the other party is being particularly obstinate and evasive an application for discovery can be made under Order 29 of the Circuit Court Rules 1950.

9.104 The application for maintenance will be heard on oral evidence. Copies of all financial documentation which the parties intend to rely on, should be available for the Judge, and opposing solicitor and counsel and if possible the other party. This shortens the hearing as counsel can refer to the documents when the parties are giving evidence. It is also possible to lead clients on such matters as lists of expenditure and income if the other party consents. They are more likely to consent if they have seen copies before the hearing, and have copies available to them. If either party is uncooperative, and refuses to show any documentation until the hearing commences this may appear to the court to be evasive. It can prolong the hearing and lead to confusion.

Witnesses

9.105 Accountants or finance staff may be called in evidence. The accountant should be warned in advance that he is giving evidence to the court and should be seen to be as objective as possible. It is also important that the accountant directly dealing with the client's affairs be the one to give evidence to the court. He or she should be warned that it is not simply a matter of reading financial figures contained in accounts to the court. A tax inspector may need to be called if there have been complications with regard to either party's tax affairs. Tax inspectors usually object to being called and try to claim privilege. This is on the basis that the individuals's tax affairs are private and confidential between the individual and the tax inspector. A witness summons may need to be issued.

Variation or discharge of a Circuit Court order

9.106 An application to vary or discharge a maintenance order is made under rule 7(c) of the Circuit Court (No. 6) Rules 1982. The rule specifically states that the application shall contain a brief statement of the matters intended to be relied on. Thus, if an application is being made to discharge or vary on the ground of misconduct the application should not go into undue detail of each item of misconduct in accordance with rule 14 of the 1982 rules. The application is issued in the usual way and sent by ordinary post. Service is deemed to be effected on the second day following the date of postage. An affidavit of service is lodged. It should be lodged before the return date. Under rule 15 of the 1982 rules an answer must be filed within four days. An extension of time will probably be sought by the respondent, and should probably be granted. This is because of the advantage of knowing something of the case one has to meet. The hearing of a variation is similar to an application in the District Court (see **9.086–9.098**). There will be more formality in the Circuit Court and stricter proofs are required. If an order is being varied and if the prior order did not order the payments to be made through the District Court the opportunity may be taken to have the order amended accordingly.

The variation or discharge order will take effect from the date of the court order or the next payment that is due. The order will not be retrospective.

Enforcement of a Circuit Court order

9.107 The Circuit Court maintenance order may be enforced by way of a motion for arrears, which includes an application for attachment or committal of the respondent, and for an attachment of earnings order. The motion should also seek an order setting the protected earnings rate of the respondent, and the rate of repayment of the arrears. The motion should follow the wording of section 10 of the Family Law (Maintenance of Spouses and Children Act 1976, or guidance may be sought, in the wording of the District Court attachment of earnings summons and order. The motion is grounded on an affidavit which should exhibit proof of the arrears for example by way of the bank account records of the applicant. It is assumed that if the Circuit Court order was made payable through the District Court Clerk an application for an attachment of earnings order will be made to the District Court. However if the respondent is self employed an application for arrears may be dealt with either in the District Court, if payments are made through it, or in the Circuit Court, by way of a motion for attachment or committal. The court will probably adjourn the motion on the respondent's undertaking to discharge the arrears at a weekly rate or by way of lump sum before the adjourned hearing. The Circuit Court can be more innovative in its approach by ordering discharge of specific bills, repayment of monies owed to the community welfare officer, discharge of mortgage arrears etc. If such orders are required the motion should specifically seek them.

Appeal

9.108 Either party may appeal against the making of an order for maintenance, variation or discharge of the order, or attachment or committal, or indeed, refusal to make such orders. The Circuit Court order will not be stayed, unless the Circuit Court Judge allows an application for a stay, or the High Court makes such an order. (See order 61.6 of the Rules of the Superior Courts 1986.). The time to apply for a stay in the Circuit Court is when the order has just been made. Alternatively a stay can be applied for when the case comes up in the High Court list to fix a date. However, if the respondent is not making an effort to discharge the payments the court may be reluctant to entertain his application. It is the duty of solicitors to ensure that their client, particularly the respondent, understands his duty towards the court with regard to payments and the risk of committal for failure to pay. When the High Court makes its order, if it affirms the Circuit Court order, that order is effective from the date of the Circuit Court order. If it varies the order it may make it effective from either date. The date that an order is to take effect has particular importance in a maintenance case as there may later be difficulty in computing payments and arrears. The court should be asked to be specific as regards the operative date of the order. The costs of the Circuit Court and the High Court should be sought if the appeal by the respondent is unsuccessful.

9.109 If an appeal from the Circuit Court fails in full or in part the order takes effect from the date of the Circuit Court order. For example, where the debtor appeals against an order varying maintenance upwards, and a stay is granted pending appeal, he may, if the appeal is unsuccessful, have to pay a lump sum to cover arrears.

Variation and discharge of a High Court order

9.110 Section 12 of the Courts Act 1981 allows the Circuit Court to vary or discharge (the word "revoke" is used) a High Court order, provided that the circumstances have changed, other than by reason of the Courts Act 1981. The Circuit Court does not have the limitation imposed on the District Court, that is, that the order should have been within the District Court's jurisdiction, if the section 12 limits had been in force at the time of the making of the original order. An example, in the Circuit Court, would be if the maintenance order exceeded £100 per week for the wife, or exceeded £30 for each child. The Circuit Court would then have to be the venue for a variation, not the District Court.

Maintenance under the Guardianship of Infants Act 1964

Procedure

9.111 The District Court (Guardianship of Infants Act 1964) Rules 1982, S.I. No 141/1982, apply to an application for maintenance under the Act of 1964. Rule 10 sets out the form of an application for the court's direction on a question affecting the welfare of an infant. This includes maintenance, which should be specifically stated on the face of form 11. The summons is signed by the solicitor or the applicant. Rule 4 provides that it is issued in the area where either party ordinarily resides, or carries on any profession, business, or occupation.

9.112 The summons must (under rule 10) be served on all other guardians of the infant. This can cause problems if the woman has had the child by a previous relationship. For example, where a child is born to a relationship outside marriage, the father may obtain an order under section 6(a) of the 1964 Act (as inserted by section 12 of the Status of Children Act 1987) appointing him a guardian. If the mother subsequently marries another man who acts *in loco parentis* to the child she may proceed against him for maintenance for the child's support under the Act of 1976, as the definition of "dependent child" in section 3(1) of the Act of 1976 includes a child *in loco parentis*. She cannot use the 1964 Act against her husband as he is not a guardian of the child. She can however bring the natural father to court for maintenance under the 1964 Act.

9.113 The hearing of a maintenance application under the 1964 Act is similar to that under the 1976 Act except that the proceedings will be more clearly focussed on the welfare of the child including the costs of his education. If a spouse is employed outside the home and only wants maintenance for the child when he is a teenager undergoing expensive schooling it may be more appropriate to issue proceedings under this Act. It will not be necessary to prove that the respondent spouse has failed to make proper provision for the child as required under section 5 of the 1976 Act. It may be that adequate provision has been made but the other spouse will not agree to the educational expenses. The maximum amount is £30 per week in the District Court for each child. The maintenance order is drawn up in accordance with the practice of the District Court and is similar to an order under section 5 of the 1976 Act except that the words "the welfare of the infant so requires" are inserted.

9.114 If a maintenance order under the Act has been made it is possible subsequently to apply to vary or discharge the order under section 12 of the Act. No criteria are laid down. The court may look to the 1976 Act (section 6) for guidelines. Section 15(2) of the Courts Act 1981 provides that the District Court is unable to make an order where the High Court or the Circuit Court has already made an order, with the exception that it may vary or revoke a High Court order, made prior to the 12 May 1982 if the circumstances have changed (other than by reason of such commencement) and the order would have been within the District Court jurisdiction if the 1981 Act had been in operation at the time of the making of the original order. The District Court may not vary or revoke an order made in the High Court, or Circuit Court after the 12 May 1982. However the District Court can make an attachment of earnings order provided the maintenance order was made payable through the District Court Clerk.

9.115 The Courts (No. 2) Act 1986 filled a gap in the enforcement legislation extending reference to an order in section 8(1) and (7) of the Enforcement of Court Orders Act 1940 to include an order made under section 11(2)(b) of the Guardianship of Infants Act 1964, or a variation order under the Act. It does not deal with arrears due prior to an order being discharged. This is unlike section 18 of the 1976 Act which provides that an attachment of earnings order shall cease to have effect upon the discharge of the relevant antecedent order except as regards payments under the order in respect of any time before the date of the discharge.

Maintenance order under section 7(6)

9.116 Section 7(6) of the Guardianship of Infants Act 1964 provides for a testamentary guardian who has been appointed to act to the exclusion of the surviving parent to obtain a maintenance order for the infant against the surviving parent, having regard to his means, and as the court thinks reasonable. This may be where the mother of the children, who had custody of them, dies and has appointed a relative as testamentary guardian of the children. The relative has the children living with him and wishes to obtain maintenance against the estranged spouse of the woman who has died.

The application is based on an adaptation of form 1 of the 1982 Rules and the application for maintenance should be stated on the form. The order is drawn up in accordance with rule 6 in form 4. The application can only be made where the testamentary guardian succeeds in establishing that the surviving parent is unfit to have custody, and the surviving guardian objects to acting jointly with the testamentary guardian.

Application for maintenance order in the Circuit Court

9.117 The Application is taken under rule 6 of the Circuit Court (No. 6) Rules 1982. It should be drawn up in accordance with form no. 2, or such modification as may be appropriate. Each child's full name and date of birth should be stated. If there are specific maintenance, and particularly education requirements these should be set out. The application must state that he or she is the father or mother. Service is personally or by prepaid post. An answer must be filed in the usual way. It may be brought in conjunction with any other application such as for custody. Section 40 of the Judicial Separation and Family Law Reform Act 1939 gives a court power to procure reports when there is a section 11 application before it. Since this covers an application for maintenance for children it is conceivable that a court could order a social worker, either from the Health Board or from the Probation and Welfare Service, to inspect the homes of either parents, to ascertain the physical needs of the children, and how they were being looked after. This would help the court to decide more accurately the maintenance necessary for the children. It may be helpful for a handicapped child whose parent is seeking extra maintenance, to instal aids in the home. The social worker could get the help of a social worker from a specialist agency dealing with the needs of the handicapped, so that a comprehensive report is put before the court.

Chapter 10

MARRIED WOMEN'S STATUS ACT 1957

Introduction

10.001 In the nineteenth century the common law position was such that a married woman was regarded as subservient to her husband, and the husband had proprietary rights over her. She had no contractual capacity. Any property owned by a woman at the time of her marriage automatically became that of her husband, as did property acquired by her subsequent to the marriage, although the husband only had a life interest in the wife's freehold property. Certain exceptions came into being, largely through the intervention of the courts of equity. These exceptions concerned items of personal property appropriate to the woman's station in life, for example, jewellery and personal clothing. The unfavourable position of married women extended beyond the grave in that the rules of succession to property of spouses were biased in favour of husbands.

10.002 The latter half of the nineteenth century brought with it a more enlightened attitude which resulted in significant legislative change. Section 1 of the Married Women's Property Act, 1882[1] altered the common law position thus: "A married woman shall, in accordance with the provisions of this Act, be capable of acquiring, holding and disposing by will or otherwise, of any real or personal property as her separate property, in the same manner as if she were a femme sole, without the intervention of any trustee." Section 17 provided that either party to the marriage could apply in a summary manner to court for the determination of any dispute affecting the title to, or ownership/possession of, property as between the spouses. The court was empowered to make any order it thought fit. Further changes in the legal position of spouses in relation particularly to their property culminated in the passing of the Married Women's Status Act, 1957. The Act is entitled "An Act to Consolidate

1   45 & 46 Vict. c. 75.

With Amendments The Law Relating to The Status of Married Women and The Liabilities of Husbands".

Secondary provisions of the Act

10.003 It was envisaged during the debate preceding the introduction of the Act that this legislation would improve the status of a married woman in addition to effecting change in the law relating to married women and property.[2] The Act by virtue of section 1 applies to all persons whether married before or after the commencement of the Act. Section 2(1) places a married woman in the same position as an unmarried person in relation to torts, contracts and the ownership and disposition of any property. This revised status of a married woman was to apply as between a married woman—and her husband in like manner as it applies between her and any other person. The remaining sections 2(3)–2(5) make appropriate changes in relation to a married woman's position as a trustee or personal representative, and in relation to the applicability of the Settled Land Acts 1882 to 1890 and the law of settlements. Section 3 of the Act provides that all property beneficially owned by a married woman prior to the commencement of the Act, or which she owns at the time of her marriage after such commencement, or which, subsequent to such commencement, devolves upon her or is acquired by her, shall belong to her as if she were unmarried and may be disposed of accordingly. The relationship between a husband and wife in respect of ownership of property, contract, tort and the exercise of a joint power, shall, by virtue of section 4, exist as if they were unmarried. A married woman is also to be treated, for the purposes of the acquisition of any property under a disposition made (or coming into operation) after the commencement of the Act, as a separate person from her husband. Thus the spouses took property as two persons in contrast to the prior position—section (5).

10.004 One of the more invidious distinctions in the law relating to the property of a married woman, as compared with that of an unmarried woman or a man, was the doctrine of Restraint upon Anticipation.[3] This restricted the right of a married woman to deal with or dispose of her property as she saw fit. This doctrine, to the extent that it could apply to the property of a married woman more so than that of a man, was abolished by section 6 of the Act. A restraint upon anticipation or alienation may still attach to property; however, such restraint will affect the property of spouses without distinction as to sex.

10.005 Section 7 concerns itself with contracts of insurance which are to benefit a spouse or child. In short, it is provided in subsection 2 that the

---

2 See Dáil Debates, 1956, at cols. 833–849 and, further, cols. 1558–1560, 1568–1571, 1585–1587.
3 See, further, Wylie, *Irish Land Law*, Professional Books, 2nd Ed. 1986, paragraphs 4.054, 9.083, 25.13–4.

policy shall create a trust in favour of the objects named in the policy. The remaining subsections provide, *inter alia*, for the appointment of trustees and the distribution of the proceeds of the policy. The following section provides that where a contract, other than one to which section 7 applies, is for the benefit of a third person, being the spouse or child of one of the contracting parties, that contract shall be enforceable by the third person in his or her own name as if he or she were a party to it. The remainder of section 8 is ancillary to the right just referred to. Section 9 equalises the position of the spouses with regard to the protection of their separate property by way of criminal proceedings both as regards third persons and as regards each other. Under section 10 the debts and liabilities of a married woman, both tortious and contractual, incurred prior to her marriage, remain her responsibility upon marriage, and she may be sued in respect of any such debt or liability. A husband of a woman shall not by reason only of his being such husband be liable in respect of any tort committed by her, or be liable in respect of any contract entered into, debt or obligation incurred by her either before or after the marriage—section 11(1). The section also provides that a husband shall not be sued or made a party to any proceedings brought in respect of any such tort, contract, debt or obligation. There is an exception in respect of necessaries supplied for the use of the wife. If a court has ordered the payment of alimony and it has not been paid, the husband is liable for such necessaries purchased on his credit.

10.006 Section 13(1) provides that settlements concerning the property of a married woman, already made or to be made, and made either before or after marriage, are not affected by the provisions of this Act. It is also provided that a married woman is in the same position in respect of the force or validity of a settlement or agreement for a settlement against her creditors as a man would be against his. Section 14 provides that a married woman's liabilities extend to any breach of trust committed by her, whether before or after marriage. A husband may not be sued on foot of such a breach by his wife by reason only of his being her husband. Section 24 of the Wills Act, 1837[4] providing that a will speaks from death, is extended to the will of a married woman, and it is not necessary to re-execute or republish the will after the death of her husband. The disability which prevented a married woman appointing an attorney to execute any deed or do any thing which she herself may do is ended by section 16, which provides that the legislative provisions governing powers of attorney apply to any such instruments executed by a married woman. The last substantive provision, section 18, provides that the Act shall not have any effect on the law relating to fraudulent gifts made between spouses or on the entitlement of creditors to trace any moneys deposited or invested by a spouse in the name of the other spouse.

4   7 Will. 4 & 1 Vict. c. 26.

Property disputes between spouses

10.007 Section 12 of the Act allows spouses to apply to the courts to determine disputes between them as to the ownership of any property. In practice the provisions have mainly been used in relation to family homes. However, disputes as to the ownership of other property of the spouses have been determined under the section, for example, claims to be entitled to a share in farmland, property set in flats, leaseholds and partnerships. The 1957 Act is silent on the principles to be applied. It was always likely that an approach similar to that adopted under section 17 of the Act of 1882 would be followed.[5] The terms of section 12 do not give the courts a general discretion to do what is just between the parties. Rather, the courts have applied established principles of law. The Judicial Separation and Family Law Reform Act, 1989 now gives the courts a much wider and more flexible jurisdiction to achieve justice between the spouses.

10.008 Immediately following the enactment of the Act of 1957 there was little increase in the number of court applications under its provisions compared with applications under section 17 of the 1882 Act. The first reports occur in the mid 1970s. A note is available of an earlier decision in a dispute concerning property owned by spouses.[6] It is not clear if this was an application under section 12 or if it was an application in which the fact that the parties were spouses is incidental. Whether the case was decided under section 12 or on common law principles, it remains instructive to consider the principles which Judge McWilliam felt were applicable. Having considered the cases cited, he decided that the following principles were established:

1. Where two people provide the purchase price for property which is conveyed to one of them only, prima facie the person into whose name it is conveyed will hold the property on trust in shares proportionate to their contributions to the purchase price.
2 This presumption may be rebutted by evidence of a contrary intention.
3. As between husband and wife, a court must take into consideration the nature of the mutual relationship between them. This does not however mean that, in the case of property in the sole name of a spouse, a court is entitled to presume an agreement, without evidence to support it.
4. Where there is a joint account between a husband and wife, into which they put all their resources, it should be assumed, unless there is compelling evidence to the contrary, that the account was intended as a joint account, with equal rights over it to each party.

5 Bromley, *Family Law*, 7th Ed., 1987, pages 506–8; Cretney, *Principles of Family Law*, 4th Ed., 1984, pages 649–50, 691–2. There are few reported cases on this topic. In addition, the respective provisions in the different jurisdictions are now quite altered.
6 See the Gazette of the Incorporated Law Society of Ireland, September, 1976, notes of recent Irish Cases, page 25, the case of *Galligan v Galligan*, Judge McWilliam, Circuit Court.

10.009 It is worthwhile taking care to consider the first reported judgments in some detail as these form the basis of subsequent developments. The case of *Heavey v Heavey*[7] decided by Kenny J. on 20 December 1974 marked out the future course of the law. There were a number of properties purchased, at various times by the defendant husband. Three of the properties were conveyed into his name and one into the wife's. The plaintiff wife had contributed substantial capital sums at various times during the marriage to the husband in addition to giving him the income she received from an interest in a business. Some of the money donated by the wife was used directly to assist in the purchase of the properties and the majority of the remaining purchase costs had come from a joint account of the parties on which each was entitled to draw. The properties, aside from the family home, were all converted into luxury flats at considerable expense over and above the purchase price. The conversion of one of the houses was financed by a mortgage secured by the title deeds of another property. The parties' marriage broke down and proceedings were instituted by the wife. She claimed ownership of all four houses which the husband had bought. Kenny J. took the view that it was a presumption of law that when a person makes a purchase of property in the name of his wife alone, it is intended as a gift to her at once and there is no resulting trust. This principle was also to apply where a husband expends his own money on the property of his wife, even if the property has been transferred by him to her. The learned judge went further to lay down that in the absence of a proved contract, the question whether a husband has a claim for improvements carried out to his wife's property should be solved by the concept of a resulting or constructive trust. He said that generally speaking, a husband has no claim to be repaid the amount spent on such property.

10.010 The decision in *Heavey v Heavey* provides the first unequivocal indication that the concept of the trust (and particularly the resulting trust) is applicable to this area of the law. It should be noted at this stage that there are two presumptions which are of major significance in this area of law. The first of these is the presumption of a resulting trust: where ownership of property is transferred to one person, but the purchase money is provided by another, a presumption arises that the transferee holds the property on trust for that other person. This is a resulting trust, which arises by implication.[8] This presumption of a resulting trust is rebuttable in the circumstances of each case. The second presumption is the presumption of advancement. In the present context, where property purchased by a husband is transferred into the name of his wife, a presumption arises that he intended to make a gift to his wife.[9] This presumption is also rebuttable.

---

7 [1974] 114 ILTR 1.
8 See *Redington v Redington* (1794) 3 Ridgew PC 106, and *O'Brien v Sheil* (1873) IR 7 Eq 255.
9 See *Alleyne v Alleyne* (1845) 8 Ir. Eq. R. 493, *Irwin v O'Connell* [1936] IR 44.

10.011 Because these presumptions are important in the determination of marital property disputes, some further elaboration is needed. The nature of the presumption was considered in the modern context by Keane J. in *J.C. v J.H.C.*[10] The pertinent issues in the case concerned the family home which, it was agreed, was purchased entirely out of monies provided by the defendant husband. The family home was held in the joint names of the parties. The defendant had established a business in which the plaintiff also worked. Keane J. wrote as follows with respect to the presumptions:

Where property is taken in the joint names of two or more persons, but the purchase money is advanced by one of them alone, the law presumes a resulting trust in favour of the person who advanced the money. This presumption may however be rebutted; and in particular the circumstances of the person into whose name the property is conveyed being the wife of the person advancing the money may be sufficient to rebut the presumption under the doctrine of advancement. However, it has been said in one English decision (*Pettit v Pettit* (1970) AC 777) that these presumptions are inappropriate to transactions between husbands and wives today and are readily rebuttable by comparatively slight evidence.

In the circumstances, Keane J. held that the presumption of a resulting trust was rebutted by reference to the presumption of advancement in favour of a wife. Whether this case can be taken as decisive authority for the general proposition that this will always be the position is not clear. It may be argued that either of these presumptions may, in given circumstances, be of greater probative value than the other, and that one presumption may be availed of to set off the effects of the other.

10.012 The decision in *R.F. v M.F.*[11] again considers the presumption as it applies in more recent times. D'Arcy J. set out the matters in clear terms.

The ordinary law of simple facts is that if a husband purchases either a house or any other property whether real or personal in the name of his wife or joint names of himself and his wife the law will presume an advancement and the wife will either be presumed to take it all or take one-half. That is based on a rebuttable presumption of advancement and the presumption is based on the fact that the courts presume the husbands to have natural love and affection for their wives. But it is a presumption and it is rebuttable. In fact nowadays "across the water" it is so easily rebutted that it has ceased to exist altogether, except in exceptional circumstances. The House of Lords based their decision on the changed nature of social conditions. I don't think social conditions here have changed yet to justify the view of the House of Lords. I think

---

10 Unreported, 4 August 1982, High Court.
11 Unreported, 1 December 1982, High Court.

the law of the presumption of advancement still exists, but it has been whittled down in this country.[12]

An interesting conclusion was reached on the facts of the case. D'Arcy J. found that the husband purchased the particular property in the joint names of the spouses with the intention that they would both reside there; that the conveyance was made on this definite condition and that the wife failed to comply with it. Therefore, he found that the wife held her one-half share in the property as a trustee for her husband. On appeal to the Supreme Court[13] Henchy J. giving the unanimous judgment of the Court, stated:

The equitable doctrine of advancement, as applied to transactions between husband and wife, has the effect that when a husband (at least where the circumstances show that he is to be expected to provide for the wife) buys property and has it conveyed to the wife and himself jointly, there is a presumption that the wife's paper title gives her a beneficial estate or interest in the property. Unless the presumption is rebutted by evidence of a contrary intention on the part of the husband at the time of the transaction, he will be deemed to have entered into the transaction for the purpose of conferring a beneficial estate or interest on the wife. That estate or interest is treated in law as an advancement, that is to say, a material benefit given in anticipation of the performance by the husband of his duty to provide for the wife. The presumption of advancement in those circumstances is, of course, rebuttable. For a rebuttal to be made out, it is for the husband to show, by reference to acts or statements before or around the transaction, that a beneficial interest was not intended to be conveyed in the circumstances relied on. As to subsequent acts or statements, the authorities show that they are admissible against the party making them, but not in his or her favour. Thus, subsequent acts or statements on the part of the wife are admissible in evidence to rebut the presumption of advancement.

10.013 Henchy J. agreed with D'Arcy J. in holding that as the husband's intention that the property should be enjoyed by the parties as a family home was not realised the presumption was rebutted. It appears that the presumption may not operate in circumstances where the wife is economically independent of her husband. Certainly, if there is a suggestion that the presumption of advancement is intended to protect an economically weaker spouse, usually the wife, it may well be that the presumption should not apply in certain cases. The difference between inapplicability of the presumption as opposed to allowing the presumption to be easily rebutted may not be readily appreciated. However, it could be important given certain circumstances.

---

12 See Cretney, op,. cit., footnote 3, at pages 640–3.
13 Unreported, 24 October 1985, Supreme Court.

10.014 The next reported case, following *Heavey v Heavey* was *C. v C.*[14] which laid the modern foundation for applications under section 12 of the Act of 1957. Shortly after the marriage the spouses purchased the family home which was conveyed into the sole name of the husband. The wife had given her husband a sum of money to pay the deposit and the expenses of purchase. In addition, on a number of occasions during the marriage the husband had found himself unable to meet the mortgage instalments. The wife had accordingly given him some of her own money to pay the instalments due. In total, the wife had contributed approximately one half of the purchase price of the house. In time the marriage broke down and the wife applied to the High Court pursuant to section 12 claiming a right to one half of the beneficial interest in the property Kenny J., adverting to the situation in which spouses usually find themselves, stated

> When the matrimonial home is purchased in the name of the husband either before or after the marriage, the wife does not as wife become entitled to any share in its ownership either because she occupies the status of wife or because she carries out household duties. In many cases however, the wife contributes to the purchase price or the mortgage instalments. Her contributions may be either by payment to the husband of moneys which she has inherited or earned or by paying the expenses of the household so that he has the money which makes it possible for him to pay the mortgage instalments.

The judgment proceeded to outline the principle to be adopted in cases where the spouses have not agreed on the ownership of the family home and where the property is in the sole name of the husband:

> I think that the correct and most useful approach to these difficult cases is to apply the concept of a trust to the legal relationship which arises when a wife makes payments towards the purchase of a house or the repayment of mortgage instalments when the house is in the sole name of the husband. When this is done, he becomes a trustee for her of a share in the house and the size of it depends upon the amount of the contributions which she has made towards the purchase or the repayment of the mortgage.

10.015 The plaintiff wife in this case obtained a declaration that she was entitled to one half of the beneficial interest in the family home. This case and judgment set the parameters for all subsequent applications under section 12 of the Act of 1957. It laid down the principle of treating such applications under the law of trusts and of applying the relevant equitable doctrines to such applications. The learned judge also referred to the legal authorities in England on equivalent issues.[15] A number of issues were left

14   [1976] IR 254.
15   *Pettitt v Pettitt* [1970] AC 777; *Gissing v Gissing* [1971] AC 886; *McFarlane v McFarlane* [1972] NI 59; *Kowalczuk v Kowalczuk* [1973] 1 WLR 930; *Hazell v Hazell* [1972] 1 WLR 301.

open by this decision as the judgment was restricted to the straightforward question of direct contributions made by a wife, who was not on the title, to the purchase price and mortgage instalments.

10.016 Before turning to consider specific problems it is helpful to set out the other major statement of principle which has become fundamental to the interpretation of section 12. This is the decision of Finlay P. in the case of *W. v W.*[16] At the time of the marriage of the parties a farm was transferred to the defendant husband subject to certain encumbrances. The plaintiff wife contributed to the farm activity by engaging in a prosperous bloodstock undertaking and generally doing whatever was required to help out. In addition, she had paid a significant sum into the farm bank account. A subsequent mortgage taken out on the farm to effect improvements was ultimately redeemed due to the endeavours of both spouses. The wife claimed to be entitled to a beneficial interest in the farm. It fell to the court to determine the question on the basis of the principles of law then applicable. Finlay P. referred specifically to *Heavey v Heavey*, *C. v C.* and *McGill v S.*[17] and set out the broad principles of law as follows:

1. Where a wife contributes by money to the purchase of property by her husband in his sole name in the absence of evidence of some inconsistent agreement or arrangement the court will decide that the wife is entitled to an equitable interest in that property approximately proportionate to the extent of her contribution as against the total value of the property at the time the contribution was made.
2. Where a husband makes a contribution to the purchase of property in his wife's sole name he will be presumed by a rebuttable presumption to have intended to advance his wife and will have no claim to an equitable estate in the property unless that presumption is rebutted. If it is, he would have a claim similar to that indicated in respect of the wife with which I have already dealt.
3. Where a wife contributes either directly towards the repayment of mortgage instalments or contributes to a general family fund thus releasing her husband from an obligation which he otherwise would have permitting him to discharge liabilities out of that fund and . . . to repay mortgage instalments she will in the absence of proof of an inconsistent agreement or arrangement be entitled to an equitable share in the property which had been mortgaged and in respect of which the mortgage was redeemed approximately proportionate to her contribution to the mortgage repayments: to the value of the mortgage thus redeemed and to the total value of the property at the relevant time. It is not expressly stated in the decisions to which I have referred but I assume that the fundamental principle underlying this rule of law is that the redemption of any form of charge or mortgage on property in truth consists of the acquisition by the owner or mortgagor of an estate in the property with which he had parted at

16 [1981] ILRM 202.
17 [1979] IR 283.

the time of the creation of the mortgage or charge and that there can be no distinction in principle between a contribution made to the acquisition of that interest and a contribution made to the acquisition of an interest in property by an original purchaser.

4. Where a husband contributes either directly or indirectly in the manner which I have already outlined to the repayment of mortgage charges on property which is in the legal ownership of his wife subject to the presumption of advancement and in the event of a rebuttal of that presumption he would have a like claim to an equitable estate in the property.

5. Where a wife expends monies or carries out work in the improvement of a property which has been originally acquired by and the legal ownership in which is vested solely in her husband she will have no claim in respect of such contributions unless she establishes by evidence that from the circumstances surrounding the making of it she was led to believe, or it was specifically agreed, that she would be recompensed for it. Even where such a right to recompense is established either by an expressed agreement or by circumstances in which the wife making the contribution was led to such belief it is a right to recompense in monies only and cannot and does not constitute a right to claim an equitable share in the estate of the property concerned.

6. A husband making contributions in like manner to property originally acquired by and solely owned as to the legal estate by his wife may again subject to a rebuttal of a presumption of advancement which would arise have a like claim to compensation in similar circumstances but would not have any claim to any equitable estate in the property.

Direct contributions

10.017 Direct contributions to the acquisition of the matrimonial home have been dealt with in a relatively straightforward manner according to the above principles. Accordingly, consideration will only be given to some of the decisions. One of the earliest instances of a claim based on direct contributions only was the case of *P. v P.*[18] There were a number of issues in dispute before the court. The evidence was that the family home was purchased for a sum of £8,100 and was transferred into the joint names of the parties. The money for the purchase was raised partly by a mortgage of £6,000, partly by a sum of £1,300 representing savings of the couple and a bank loan for the remainder. The husband contributed the greater part of the savings and during the marriage the wife earned considerably less than him. Nevertheless, Barrington J. determined that as the house was put into their joint names, and bearing in mind the direct contribution of the wife by means of her portion of the savings, the property was owned by them legally and beneficially in equal shares.

---

18 Unreported, 12 March 1980, High Court.

10.018 In *E.R. v M.R.*[19] the plaintiff wife inherited money on the death of her mother and she prevailed upon the owner of certain lands which the couple had rented to sell the property to them. She paid one third of the purchase price as a down payment and gave her husband the entire of the remainder out of monies earned by her from farming in a small way, to pay the balance of the purchase price. The lands were transferred into the husband's sole name, but, as Carroll J. put it, "the money he had received from his wife was impressed with a trust to pay the balance of the purchase money." Accordingly, having found that the plaintiff gave this money to the defendant for the specific purpose, these amounted to direct contributions and the plaintiff was beneficially entitled to the entire lands. A second point in the case concerned the ownership of the family home subsequently erected on the lands. This was financed by a local authority loan and a loan from a bank. Difficulties arose with the builder engaged which the defendant did nothing about. The plaintiff by means of her farming enterprise, savings and borrowings effected the completion of the house. Carroll J. found that one third of the cost of the house was financed by the plaintiff and two thirds by loans. The plaintiff contributed significantly to the repayment of the loans; the evidence on the ratio of the parties' contributions to the repayments was uncertain. Accordingly, the learned judge held that the plaintiff should receive full credit for the amount she contributed and that the plaintiff would be entitled to two thirds of the proceeds after first deducting the site value from the purchase money. The order of the court recited the register and substituted the name of the plaintiff as full owner in place of the defendant on the folio. This was an interesting example of how the application of the accepted principles can resolve what initially appeared to be a complex problem. Admittedly, the evidence as determined in the case was generally decisive in the plaintiff's favour.

10.019 The decision in *N.D. v A.D.*[20] is an example of how the courts will follow contributions and property as occasion demands. The parties were married in 1955 by which time they had obtained work in New York. The parties pooled their resources from that time forward. The plaintiff wife was earning substantially less than the husband. The husband's father died and left him the family holding in Kerry. The parties returned, bringing with them savings of about £3,000. In 1958, the farm was sold for about £2,000 and a larger holding bought for £5,000. The purchase price was provided to a large extent by the proceeds of sale of the smaller holding and by means of a bank loan. O'Hanlon J. was of the view that any contribution derived from the wife's earlier assistance in building up a joint savings fund was too obscure to support a claim to a share or interest in these lands. The parties, some years later, let the lands out and emigrated to London. A sale of farm stock and machinery realised about £3,500. A house was purchased in the husband's sole name for about £6,500, being paid for with the moneys brought from Ireland and a mortgage to make up

19   Unreported, 26 January 1981, High Court.
20   Unreported, 10 December 1982, High Court.

the balance. The wife claimed that her earnings were sufficient at this time to meet the mortgage repayments and were used for that purpose. This property was sold yielding a net £4,000. A licensed premises, with residential accommodation in Kerry had been bought the previous year in the husband's sole name. In addition to the purchase price of £4,380, a good deal of money had to be spent before it could re-open for business or could be used as a family home. The running of the premises was left largely to the wife. The premises were extended and the adjoining property was purchased in the sole name of the wife. Again a good deal of work was required on this property. The main source of income of the parties during the 1970s was derived from the licensed premises which had prospered due to the significant efforts and hard work of the wife which enabled the parties to extend the public house itself, pay off the mortgage on it, buy and re-furbish the adjoining property and clear off the loan on that premises.

10.020 O'Hanlon J. looked at the overall picture created by the evidence and firstly had no hesitation in holding that the entire beneficial interest in the adjoining property, its furniture and other contents was vested in the wife. With regard to the licensed premises, the business carried on therein, its furniture and fittings, she was held to be entitled to a 60% interest therein "having regard to her initial contribution through her earnings to the original purchase of the premises, and the later express or implied agreement between the parties whereunder it was left to the plaintiff to create and develop the business in the premises by her own unaided efforts and business expertise." The defendant was entitled to the full beneficial interest in the farm lands, stock and machinery.

10.021 This case demonstrates that a spouse can make direct contributions to the acquisition of business property not merely through money contributed to the purchase price, but also through his or her work in the business. It is perhaps a moot point whether the result would have been the same had the evidence been such as to deny any agreement, express or implied, about the work in and development of the licensed premises. Could it have merely been that the plaintiff was more suited to this type of work and the defendant more suited to the farm work without any form of agreement on the matter? Would the plaintiff then have only been entitled to a claim, if any, for work done and services rendered in excess of that for which she was paid? In either event the case illustrates the approach taken to a dispute involving a long series of property transactions.

10.022 The question of a wife's contributions to the acquisition of the family home was considered by the Supreme Court in *McC. v McC.*[21] A previous family home, in which it was accepted the wife had a one-third interest, was sold and produced a net sum. The wife never received her entitlement but allowed her husband, the defendant, to use it. The family home, the subject matter of the proceedings, was purchased by means of a

21 [1986] ILRM 1.

mortgage for the full amount. The total net proceeds from the sale of the previous family home were applied to furnishing and fitting the new home. The wife claimed an interest in the family home based on her one-third share of this net sum. The High Court held that she was only entitled to a one-third interest in the furnishings and fittings of the new home. The wife appealed. Henchy J., giving the judgment of the court, gave the following view of how the law recognises contributions to the acquisition of a home:

> Since the decision of Kenny J. in *C. v C.* . . ., it has been judicially accepted that where a matrimonial home has been purchased in the name of the husband, and the wife has, either directly or indirectly, made contributions towards the purchase price or towards the discharge of mortgage instalments, the husband will be held to be a trustee for the wife of a share in the house roughly corresponding with the proportion of the purchase money represented by the wife's total contribution. Such a trust will be inferred when the wife's contribution is of such a size and kind as will justify the conclusion that the acquisition of the house was achieved by the joint efforts of the spouses.

This puts the methodology of the decision-making process in everyday language and gave the imprimatur of the Supreme Court to Kenny J.'s approach. However, in the instant case, the court dismissed the appeal, holding that the wife was merely entitled to a one-third interest in the furniture and fittings.

Indirect contributions

10.023 The question of indirect contributions coupled with direct contributions arose for determination in a series of judgments given by Finlay P., as he then was. The first of these was *M. v M.*[22] The defendant wife purchased a house in her sole name as an investment. She obtained a loan in respect of the deposit from her sister and from a bank in respect of the remainder of the purchase price. The deposit was approximately one quarter of the total purchase price. The property was converted into a number of units for letting and this work was financed by the proceeds of sale of a business in which the spouses both had an interest in the rough proportions, one fifth in the husband's name and the remainder in the wife's. The loans were paid off out of the income received and, at the time of the hearing, both loans had been discharged. The defendant wife admitted at the hearing that she would not have been in a position to discharge fully the loans had it not been for money received from her husband who was working outside the jurisdiction. The first issue for determination was whether the monies paid by the husband were a gift or advancement to her. Finlay P. concluded that they were not a gift but were intended as a contribution towards the purchase of the property. Applying the principles laid down by Kenny J. in *C. v C.*, above, he determined that the monies paid by the husband were a clear indirect contribution to the

22   (1978) 114 ILTR 46.

discharge of the loans. The parties contributed equally to discharging the loans. Allowing for the disparity of interest between the spouses in the proceeds of their business, the property the subject matter of the application was held as to 60% of its beneficial interest in favour of the wife and as to 40% in favour of the husband.

10.024 In *K. v K.*[23] the defendant husband was the sole legal owner to three properties, namely the family home and two leasehold interests in retail premises. The question of the interest in the family home was resolved easily on the basis of the principles laid down in *C. v C.* in that the wife had contributed towards the household expenses and mortgage repayments. Finlay P. declared that the wife was entitled to a 50% share of the beneficial interest in the family home. The issue of the leasehold interests raised interesting points as this was the first instance of section 12 being applied to property other than residential property. No consideration was paid for the leasehold interests by the spouses. The rent reserved was paid out of the profits of a limited company in which the wife had a 50% interest. No other money was paid to the spouses in respect of their work in the leasehold businesses. Accordingly, the court determined that the leasehold interests were acquired by virtue of the payment of rent, which was in effect paid equally by the spouses, and the observance of the covenants in the leases. Finlay P. concluded that the wife was entitled to a one-half share in the property. Would it have been more correct to hold that the defendant husband held the leasehold interests in trust for the limited company, a separate legal entity from the shareholders in it?

10.025 The case of *R.K. v M.K.*[24] concerned a claim of indirect contributions made by a wife to the acquisition of the family home. The property was purchased by the husband without recourse to any loans or mortgages and was transferred into his sole name. He carried on the business of a builder and payment for the property came from the proceeds of the building business. Finlay P. (at pages 8–9) could not hold that the wife was entitled to any share in the property, and appears to have reached this conclusion on the basis that the wife's contributions to the business were of a minor nature and were not wholly unconnected with her management of the household.

10.026 The question of indirect contributions was also in issue in *R. v R.*[25] a decision of McMahon J. Subsequent to their marriage, the parties lived in a mobile home owned by the husband. This was later sold to provide a deposit for the purchase of a house. The remainder of the purchase price was supplied by means of a mortgage and a credit union loan. The property was transferred into the husband's sole name. The wife based her claim on the fact that during the marriage she worked an average of 33 weeks per year; that the money thus earned was spent on her own

23   (1978) 114 ILTR 50.
24   Unreported, 24 October 1978, High Court.
25   Unreported, 12 January 1979, High Court.

necessaries and in meeting the expenses of the household which the husband would otherwise have had to meet. McMahon J. found that, had the wife not been earning, the husband would not have been able to keep up with the mortgage repayments, run a car and maintain their standard of living. He saw no difference between money expended by the wife on household expenses and on necessaries exclusively for herself: "In either case there is a saving to the husband and if that enables him *pro tanto* to meet the mortgage repayments the wife should be regarded as contributing towards those repayments." Interestingly, McMahon J. then took account of the fact that the husband had received the appropriate tax allowances as a married man, with the result that the wife had been taxed on all her earnings, and decided that the fairest approach was to assume that their respective contributions to the family purse, and therefore to the mortgage repayments, were in the same proportions as their respective gross earnings before tax.

10.027 Another decision of Mr. Justice Finlay sets out in detail the manner of making calculations where indirect contributions found a claim to an interest in property. In *L. v L.*[26] the parties were married in 1971 and purchased a house in 1973 in the name of the defendant husband. The court was satisfied that up to that time the wife had contributed a high proportion of her earnings to the joint household. The purchase was financed by a mortgage and a bank loan guaranteed by the wife's father. The wife worked until 1976 during which time the husband discharged the mortgage repayments. Subsequent to this, the mortgage repayments were made but the bank loan was not serviced. The defendant's fortunes then fluctuated until 1979 when a second mortgage was raised with the consent of the wife, and was used to pay off the mortgage arrears. No repayments were made after this time, and at the time of the hearing the building society concerned had indicated that proceedings would be taken for possession. Finlay P. decided that he had first to determine the amount of the mortgage that had been repaid, then the amount of the equity of redemption, then what was the relationship between the gross earnings of the parties during the relevant period, and, finally, what proportion of those gross earnings went in by way of contribution to a joint family fund out of which the mortgage repayments were met. Having made these calculations, the court declared the wife to be entitled to a beneficial share in the family home of 35%.

10.028 In *M.B. v E.B.*[27] the court had, *inter alia*, to consider the question of a "kind of agreement" between the parties. Barrington J. referred to the authorities up to this point and distinguished *C. v C.*, *R. v R.* The judge was satisfied that the wife had made a substantial contribution towards the setting up of the matrimonial home, but had made no direct contribution towards the repayment of the mortgage. The court accepted the wife's

26 Unreported, 21 December 1979, High Court.
27 Unreported, 19 February 1980, High Court.

evidence that there was a "kind of an agreement" between the spouses that the husband would meet the mortgage repayments and the ESB bills and that she would pay for virtually everything else for the house. Reference was made to the comment of Kenny J. in *C. v C.* that spouses do not usually enter into formal agreements. However, Barrington J. was of the view here that there was an understanding between the spouses and that

> the subsequent conduct of both parties does . . . cast light on what the basic understanding or "kind of agreement" between them was and on the nature and interest of the trust which they created for each other. It appears to me to be quite clear on the facts of this case that the understanding between them was by their joint efforts to buy and furnish a home.

Mr. Justice Barrington then referred to the dicta of Lord Denning, M.R. in *Hazell v Hazell*[28] to the effect that if a husband accepts the contributions of a wife, where he is able to make mortgage repayments out of his own earnings, he thus is enabled to use more of his own money as he pleases. The conclusion was that the wife was entitled to an undivided one half share of the household goods and furniture other than those items personal to one or other party; in addition, the wife was entitled to a beneficial one half share in that proportion of the house that was acquired by means of the mortgage.

10.029 A major review of the authorities was conducted by Keane J. in *M.G. v R.D.*[29] The matrimonial home was purchased in the name of the defendant husband, being financed by a staff loan from his employers of £8,000 and two further loans of £1,000 from his mother and a bank. The plaintiff wife paid her salary into a separate bank account and out of it bought some of the housekeeping items; in addition she bought a car which was used by both parties. The mortgage repayments, loan repayments and other normal outgoings directly referable to the house were paid by the husband. There was no evidence that the payments made by the plaintiff were made on foot of any arrangement or agreement, "even of the loosest character". The judge determined that the plaintiff's contributions to the joint expenses of the household over the period of the marriage amounted to one-fifth. He also determined that the defendant would have been able to meet those expenses even if the plaintiff had made no contribution. Accordingly the wife's claim was on the basis of her indirect contributions. Keane J. then reviewed the following authorities at length: *C. v C., R. v R., McGill v S., M.B. v E.B., McFarlane v McFarlane, Gissing v Gissing, Falconer v Falconer,*[30] *Hargrave v Newton,*[31] *Hazell v Hazell, Kowalczuk v Kowalczuk, M. v M., K. v K.* and *L. v L.* He concluded that it was well established that, where the matrimonial home was purchased in the sole

28 [1972] 1 WLR 301.
29 Unreported, 28 April 1981, High Court.
30 [1970] 1 WLR 1333.
31 [1971] 1 WLR 1611.

name of one spouse, a constructive trust, as a result of which the contributing spouse becomes entitled to a share in the matrimonial home, will be implied where the contributing spouse makes payments directly towards the purchase of the home or the repayments of the mortgage.

10.030 Keane J. referred to indirect contributions specifically and felt there was some divergence of view as to the requirements necessary to create a constructive trust and he indicated that he considered the better view was that there must be some clear evidence of the common intention of the parties that the indirect payments made by the contributing spouse should give that spouse a beneficial interest in the matrimonial home. In the circumstances, there is a distinction between a direct contribution towards the acquisition of the matrimonial home and the indirect payment of other household expenses; the one supports the claim that it was intended that the payor should acquire some beneficial interest in proportion to the contribution made, whereas the latter situation requires further evidence that the payments were made in pursuance of a common intention that the contributor should acquire a beneficial share. In this case there was no such intention and accordingly the plaintiff was not entitled to succeed.

This case raises the question of the intention of the parties. A considerable portion of the judgment, particularly where it discusses the English authorities, is devoted to this issue. Keane J. refers with emphasis to the intention of the parties; and yet he speaks of constructive trusts. A constructive trust arises by operation of law whereas a resulting trust is imposed to give effect to the intention of the parties. Admittedly, many other judges have engaged in similar reasoning. This judicial confusion has appeared in many decisions in this jurisdiction and in England. Two decisions by Barron J. discuss the circumstances in which each form of the trust is applicable.[32]

10.031 The decision in *F.G. v P.G.*[33] considered the issue of contributions of a spouse which assisted the retention of property rather than its acquisition. The defendant purchased a house in Dublin in his sole name, financed largely by a mortgage, in addition to moneys of the defendant which paid the deposit. Some time later the family went to America, renting out the house. At all times the Dublin house was self-financing in that the income from it paid the mortgage repayments. The plaintiff wife obtained employment in America. The parties engaged in a series of property deals in America financed by a joint family fund, with the aid of various borrowings including a loan secured on the Dublin property. Finlay P. found that had the plaintiff not contributed her earnings to the general family fund, there was no way in which the defendant could have avoided disposing of the Dublin property to service and finance the general

---

32 See *N.A.D. v T.D.*, [1989] ILRM 153 and *C.M.C.B. v S.B.*, unreported, High Court, 17th May, 1983, Barron J.
33 [1982] ILRM 155.

family expenses and the American property deals. Accordingly, the plaintiff was entitled to a beneficial interest amounting to 30%. Finlay P.'s reasoning, following the principles in *Nixon v Nixon*,[34] was that the Dublin property and the other properties were all part of family assets, the retention and acquisition of which was achieved by the joint family fund.

10.032 Two more recent decisions provide interesting views on indirect contributions. In *C.R. v D.R.*[35] the wife based her claim on contributions she made to the family funds by keeping calves and supplying milk to a creamery. The defendant husband's occupation was that of a vet, and the wife also helped him by accompanying him on journeys in connection with his work. Lynch J. held that her contribution was so small as to be insignificant when compared with those made by the husband. He found that the wife had greatly assisted the husband in the veterinary practice during the period of his alcoholism. The wife asserted that this enabled him to earn money which was used to acquire the family home. This was rejected by the court as there was no evidence and no implication that the husband would have been unable to earn the money necessary to acquire the property in the absence of such assistance. Mr. Justice Lynch remarked on the issue of indirect contribution thus:

> Moreover if a wife indirectly and significantly assists in the acquisition of property by paying out of her own savings or out of monies earned by her from third parties family expenses which would otherwise have to be paid by the husband thus increasing the funds available to the husband to pay for the acquisition of the property, she will thereby become entitled to an interest in the property to be calculated on a similar basis to that already indicated in the absence of any express or implied agreement to the contrary.

10.033 There would not seem, as a matter of principle, to be any sound basis for making a distinction between "significant" and other contributions. However it is possible that Lynch J. was merely recognising that in a marriage partnership there will always be a certain amount of cross-contributions. It may be reasonable to suppose that if a spouse makes a significant contribution to the other spouse, or to a joint family fund, that some *quid pro quo* is intended by the contributor and that this amounts to the requisite intention to establish a claim. It is interesting to note at this point that Henchy J. in *McC. v McC.* also referred consistently to a trust being inferred when the wife's contribution is of such a size and kind as to justify the conclusion that the acquisition of the house was achieved by the joint efforts of the spouses. Admittedly, he was referring at this point to direct contributions; however, the observation made above is equally applicable.

---

34 [1969] 1 WLR 1676.
35 Unreported, 5 April 1984, High Court.

10.034 In *B. v B.*[36] the parties lived for a time in rented accommodation after the marriage. A family home was then purchased in the defendant husband's name financed by way of a loan and mortgage, the repayments in respect of which were met by the husband. This home was later sold and a second house bought. It was paid for out of the net proceeds of the first home and a mortgage which was discharged in full by the husband. In addition, substantial sums were expended on improving this home, all provided by the husband. The wife asserted her claim on the basis of buying all the furniture, and devoting all her earnings, which were not insignificant, to the family housekeeping and her own clothing. Accordingly, this made available to the husband sums which he would otherwise have had to pay. MacKenzie J. was referred to many, though not all Irish authorities. He felt constrained to distinguish *C. v C.* and *W. v W.*[37] as they concerned direct contributions. He then referred to Keane J.'s analysis of the law on indirect contributions in *M.G. v R.D.* He felt that this was the applicable law and was undistinguishable in the circumstances. Dismissing the wife's claim, he commented: "I am obliged to follow the judgment of Mr. Justice Keane which as I have said represents the law as it presently stands in this country, which as far as the wife is concerned, is Victorian and unjust."

10.035 In addition to support by Lynch J. and the reluctant support by MacKenzie J. above, Keane J.'s views on the requirement of an intention, above, were also supported by Murphy J. in *S.D. v B.D.*[38] He found on the evidence that the plaintiff wife had made contributions to the household expenses but that these were not made as a result of any agreement or understanding between the spouses. Murphy J. said that he considered the law as enunciated by Keane J. to be correct, and he applied it in the instant case. Support was expressed by Ellis J. in *S.W. v F.W.* for McMahon J.'s view of the principles stated in *R. v R.*

10.036 It is interesting to note the divergence of views among the judiciary as regards the question of intention being necessary to substantiate a claim to a beneficial interest in a family home based on indirect contributions. On the one hand, there is the view adopted by Keane J. supported by Murphy J., Lynch J. and MacKenzie J. And on the other hand there is the view adopted by Ellis J. and McMahon J. Given these differing judicial approaches, it is perhaps unfortunate that the Supreme Court did not resolve the problem in the *McC.* decision referred to. There was only one authority referred to by Henchy J. in his short judgment. It would appear despite the views of Keane J., that the question of intention is not the all-decisive issue where indirect contributions are concerned. For example, it would not take much legal ingenuity to hold that the law implies such an intention and that the onus is on the "owner spouse" to disprove such an intention.

36 Unreported, 22 April 1986, High Court.
37 [1981] ILRM 202.
38 Unreported, 19 March 1982, High Court.

The nature of the trust availed of to resolve these disputes

10.037 As has been seen in the cases considered, disputes which have arisen under section 12 of the 1957 Act have been resolved under trust law principles. There had been little or no discussion of the exact form of trust that was availed of by the courts in these matters. Indeed, in *Heavey v Heavey*[39] Kenny J. did not distinguish between constructive, resulting or implied trusts. This may have been as a consequence of the then recent English authority on the matter, when in *Gissing v Gissing*[40] it was clearly indicated that the court did not consider it necessary to distinguish between the three classes of trust in this type of case. Given the circumstances of that case, the approach may have been correct. This may be the correct approach in most cases, and may have been so in all of the cases discussed thus far, with the exception of *M.G. v R.D.* In *C.M.C.B. v S.B.*[41] the facts of which are not particularly noteworthy, Barron J. at page 5 commented on the plaintiff's claim for a share in the family home:

> Clearly the contributions made by the wife towards the purchase of the home in [England] and towards the purchase of the home here were made with the intention to provide a home for both of [the spouses] and with the intention of having a common ownership in it. Now even if I am not right in my view that a resulting trust would have been created it seems to me that it would be unfair to deny the wife a beneficial interest having regard to all the circumstances merely because her husband's name appeared solely on the title documents. It seems to me that the circumstances would be sufficient to create a constructive trust in her favour.

This suggests that the first question is whether a resulting trust is appropriate and, if not, the second question is whether the circumstances are sufficient to create a constructive trust in her favour. There was no discussion in the case of the nature of the various classes of trust.

10.038 The distinction between the resulting and constructive trust was clarified by Barron J. in *N.A.D. v T.D.*[42] The defendant husband supervised the building of the family home and assisted in its construction. It was built on a site purchased by him. The property was in the sole name of the husband. The court held that the real contributions of the parties, after making necessary adjustments on the basis of the evidence, to the cost of building the home were £1,950 by the husband and £1,200 by the wife. The wife's contribution was a lump sum of £900 and her indirect contribution was £300 as adjusted. Barron J. considered the *Heavey* and *C. v C.* decisions and concluded that:

39   (1974) 114 ILTR 1.
40   [1971] AC 886.
41   Unreported, 17 May 1983, High Court.
42   [1985] ILRM 153.

Where the property is being acquired the claimant wife must establish a resulting trust in her favour; whereas where the property already has been acquired by her husband before the contribution upon which she relies the trust to be established is a constructive trust. While the cases do not say so specifically, this is the conclusion which must be drawn from the fact that a contribution in one case gives an interest proportionate to the value of such contribution having regard to the total value of the house, whereas in another it gives no right whatsoever in the absence of an agreement or circumstances which led the party contributing to believe that a benefit would accrue.

He went on to comment on the manner in which each trust arises:

The resulting trust arises from the unexpressed but presumed intention of the parties where both contribute to its purchase either directly or indirectly and it is put in the name of one of them alone. Once each contributes, it is presumed in the absence of any expression or indication of contrary intention that the unexpressed but common intention of the parties arising from the fact of contribution coupled with its acceptance shall be held in the same proportion as their contributions. . . . The constructive trust is imposed by operation of law independent of intention in order to satisfy the demands of justice and good conscience. Its imposition is dependent upon the conduct of the person upon whom the trust is imposed and prevents him from acting in breach of good faith. There is no fixed set of circumstances in which such a trust is imposed.

10.039 This is a good example of the essential differences between these two classes of trust. In identifying that the trust imposed in *Heavey* was a constructive trust, Mr. Justice Barron set out that the essential prerequisite for the imposition of a constructive trust of this type is that there is an element in the conduct of the person upon whom the trust is imposed which would make it inequitable for him to assert his legal rights. Particular attention was paid to the fact that Kenny J. in *Heavey* specifically rejected an approach upon a finding of an implied agreement.[43]

10.040 This judgment of Barron J. is a reasonable analysis of the differing classes of trusts which may arise in matrimonial property disputes. Virtually all of the other cases which identify the particular class of trust refer to a resulting trust. However it would appear reasonable to conclude that, in strict terms, the constructive trust has been used to resolve the matter even though not always identified as such. In practice, the constructive trust is used quite often by the judiciary in precisely the circumstances that Barron J. identified as being the essential prerequisite of the constructive trust, namely, that it would be inequitable to allow one party assert his legal rights.

43 See Keane, *Equity and the Law of Trusts in the Republic of Ireland*, 1988, Butterworths, Chapters 7, 8, 12 and 13.

10.041 *N.A.D. v T.D.* also shed light on an issue which arises from time to time in practice. It concerns the question of improvements which would appear to offer the opportunity for the use of a constructive trust if the facts support the claim. In the circumstances Barron J. rejected the claim that the wife had assisted in the acquisition of the house thereby entitling her to an interest, but accepted an argument that her contributions improved the property. The issue therefore was whether this entitled her to an interest in the premises. Barron J. was of the view that there was a considerable difference between minor decorative improvements and payment for the erection of a dwelling house, and stated:

> In each case, since the legal and beneficial ownership of the property was already vested in her husband he is entitled at law in the absence of a contrary agreement to take the entire benefit of the improvement. In equity he is entitled to such benefit unless by his conduct he has in effect led his wife to act to her detriment. In the absence of such element, equity does not impose a trust in favour of the wife. At first sight, it might look as if the husband must be taken to have led his wife to act to her detriment whenever the improvement is so substantial having regard to the property as it originally stood that no stranger would have contemplated making such contribution without recompense. If so, then a line should be drawn somewhere. Should it be when the improved property is substantially a different thing as where a site is converted into a home; or should it be where an addition is made to a house as by building over the garage; or should it be whenever any substantial sum has been expended? No doubt in each of these cases reasonable spouses would be taken to have agreed that the wife should have either some interest in the property or some recompense following upon such expenditure. But the question is not what was the nature of the improvement nor what reasonable spouses would have agreed nor even what is fair, but whether or not the conduct of the owner of the property has been such that equity ought to impose a trust for the benefit of the contributor.

He concluded that the result depended on the particular facts of each case. Barron J.'s views are significantly different from the views expressed by Lord Denning M.R. and to a lesser extent by other judges in England. In *Hussey v Palmer*[44] for example, Lord Denning wrote that a constructive trust

> is a trust imposed by law whenever justice and good conscience require it. It is a liberal process, founded upon large principles of equity, to be applied in cases where the legal owner cannot conscientiously keep the property for himself alone, but ought to allow another to have the property or the benefit of it or a share in it.

---

44 [1972] 1 WLR 1286.

Constitutional developments

10.042 A number of judgments recently considered claims under the 1957 Act relying on the provisions of the Constitution to ground same. The fundamental decision was that of Mr. Justice Barr in *B.L. v M.L.*[45] This was the first case in which an argument based on the provisions of the Constitution, and in particular, Article 41, was advanced on behalf of a plaintiff. In brief, the facts of the case were that the plaintiff wife worked in the family home after the marriage and was almost exclusively engaged in and responsible for the care and upbringing of the two children of the marriage. The husband engaged in farming an extensive holding of a mixed nature. In addition he was involved as an agent or advisor of foreign nationals concerning land purchase and speculation. Barr J. reviewed many of the authorities[46] and wrote: ". . . the conclusion is inescapable that the wife is not entitled to a beneficial interest in the family home or farm because she has made no contribution in money or monies worth, directly or indirectly, towards the acquisition of either property." Barr J. proceeded to consider the constitutional argument and referred to a number of cases which had discussed this particular Article. He outlined his view of the nature of Article 41:

> Article 41 contains two fundamental concepts which are inter related. First, the family is recognised as the natural primary and fundamental unity group of society which is the necessary basis of social order and it possesses inalienable rights that are superior to all positive law. Secondly, it is recognised that woman's life within the home gives to the State a support without which the common good cannot be achieved. It seems to me that Article 41, in so far as it relates to woman, underscores the pivotal role which she has within the family and recognises that in the day-to-day life of the unit group she plays a crucial role in weaving the fabric of the family and in sustaining the quality of its life. The strongest possible emphasis is placed on woman's role within the home. Having regard to the terms of sub-article 2, which casts a specific duty on the State to endeavour to ensure that mothers will not be obliged by economic necessity to engage in labour to the neglect of their duties in the home, it is evident that the Constitution envisages that, ideally, a mother should devote all her time and attention to her duties in the home and that it is desirable that she ought not to engage in gainful occupation elsewhere unless compelled to do so by economic necessity. It follows that, if the Article is to be given flesh and meaning in practical terms, a mother who adopts that concept and devotes herself entirely to the family after marriage, has a special place in society which should be buttressed and preserved by the State in its laws. In my view the

45 Unreported, 3 October 1988, High Court.
46 *C. v C.* [1976] IR 254; *McC. v McC.* [1986] ILRM 1; *W. v W.* [1981] ILRM 202; *H.D. v J.D.*, Unreported, High Court, July, 1981. Finlay, P.; *R.K. v M.K.*, unreported, High Court, 24th October, 1978. *De Burca and anor. v Attorney General*, [1976] IR 385; *W. v Somers*, [1983] IR 126.

judiciary has a positive obligation to interpret and develop the law in a way which is in harmony with the philosophy of Article 41 as to the status of woman in the home. It is also in harmony with that philosophy to regard marriage as an equal partnership in which a woman who elects to adopt the fulltime role of wife and mother in the home may be obliged to make a sacrifice, both economic and emotional, in doing so. In return for that voluntary sacrifice, which the Constitution recognises as being in the interest of the common good, she should receive some reasonable security within the marriage. That concept can be achieved, at least in part, by recognising that as her role as full-time wife and mother precludes her from contributing directly or indirectly in money or money's worth from independent employment or avocation towards the acquisition by the husband of the family home and contents, her work as home-maker and in caring for the family should be taken into account in calculating her contribution towards that acquisition—particularly as such work is of real monetary value.

10.043 A number of issues arise out of the views of Barr J. For present purposes, and assuming for the moment that this reasoning will ultimately be upheld, one of the more interesting ones is that Barr J., appears to have laid some emphasis on the fact that in the case the plaintiff was a mother as well as a wife. This is in accordance with the philosophy of Article 41. Does this mean that a married woman without children who was a full-time wife is not included in the ambit of this reasoning? In so far as the case was concerned, Barr J. did not feel able to extend his views that far, for he wrote "In terms of the matter under review it is not necessary for me to consider whether a woman has any constitutional right to a share in the ownership of a matrimonial home which a husband has acquired by inheritance or gift or otherwise prior to the marriage and not in contemplation of it. That may be a matter which should be dealt with by legislation." This does, however, leave open the possibility that a court might subsequently rule on this question. A second comment of Barr J.'s merits consideration. Having set out his reasoning above, he concluded that such work as home-maker and in caring for the family is of real monetary value. This would seem to be a reversion to the generally accepted principles, in that by her work, a wife (mother) earns her interest. And what of a wife (mother) whose work in the home is limited to assisting an employed housekeeper and or nurse? Indeed, is a woman debarred from availing of this reasoning by her inability to carry out her "duties in the home", or by her inefficiency in carrying them out?

10.044 Accordingly, the terms of the judgment, while far-reaching, are open to interpretation. The narrowest view of it at present is that a wife and mother is entitled to earn a beneficial interest in property owned or acquired by her husband and used as the family home by virtue of her work in the home; such entitlement does not, however, extend to other property used for family purposes, such as a farm. The case is under appeal to the Supreme Court and it remains to be seen whether it will be upheld. There is a comment by Mr. Justice Finlay in an earlier case which may throw some light on the attitude of at least one member of the Supreme Court. In *R.K. v M.K.* he wrote: "The extent of her work in the household and in the care of her children was very considerable but our law does not recognise so far at least a right arising from that type of work to a part ownership of any family or marriage property."

10.045 There are more immediate reservations about the reasoning of Barr J. In *J.F. v B.F.*[47] which was heard very shortly after Mr. Justice Barr's decision, the argument based on the provision of Article 41 was again advanced. The parties were married in 1972 and lived in rented accommodation for a short period. The wife ceased work shortly after the husband qualified as a medical doctor. In time, the parties built a house which was financed by means of a mortgage in the husband's name and which was at all times funded out of the husband's income. The couple now had two children who were cared for by the wife. From 1979 a housekeeper was employed to do virtually all the housework. Mr. Justice Lardner set out the effect of the settled principles in relation to the acquisition of an interest in property bought in the name of another. In the case it was not contended that the wife was entitled to any interest under these principles. The argument for the wife rested squarely on Article 41 of the Constitution. Lardner J. agreed that Article 41 may well be read as being protective and supportive of the family unit. He referred to various legislative provisions which he considered as being directed towards this end.[48] He then wrote at page 11 "So far the Oireachtas has not thought fit to enact provisions giving the wife an interest in the family home during the husband's life by reason of her domestic work in the home." Turning to consider the constitutional argument. Mr Justice Lardner dealt with it as follows:

Having carefully considered the terms of Article 41, it cannot in my view be read as itself making any specific provision either expressly or by necessary implication in regard to how recognition by the State of the wife's position and life within the home should be given by law nor how the economic position of mothers who work in the home should be secured nor in regard to how the property rights of the husband or wife in the house in which the family lives should be regulated nor as conferring any specific jurisdiction to declare or alter those rights. It may be that the principle adopted in *L. v L.* would commend itself to the legislature. It seems to me a new legislative initiative and essentially to be concerned with matters of political and social policy relating to delicate and fundamental aspects of the family and of the relationship between husband and wife. These are matters which I do not find Article 41 gives any sufficiently clear guidance to be able to say that the

47 Unreported, 21 December 1988, High Court.
48 Family Home Protection Act, 1976; Succession Act, 1965; Family Law (Maintenance of Spouses and Children) Act, 1976; Social Welfare (Consolidation) Act, 1981; and the Married Women's Status Act, 1957.

application of this particular principle is required or is the way in which the relationship should be regulated. In my judgment whether it is to be adopted and applied as part of Irish law is properly to be considered as the province of Oireachtas, in whom the sole and exclusive power of making laws for the State is vested.

It may firstly be noted that the courts have on previous occasions dealt with issues of a delicate and fundamental nature involving the family without any difficulties.[49] If Lardner J. had felt that Article 41 gave guidelines on these matter, would he have remained steadfast in his view that it is a legislative matter? In this case the plaintiff wife did not succeed in her claim to a share in the family home.

10.046 The third case centering on this constitutional argument is probably the most inventive of all. In *E.N. v R.N. and anor*[50] Mr. Justice Barron was faced with this argument in interesting circumstances. The husband and wife were married in 1964 and on marriage the wife had given up her career to devote herself to looking after her home and the three children of the marriage. Until 1983 the wife worked in all, outside the home, a total of two months in two temporary jobs. From 1983 onwards she was employed part-time in her profession. The couple had purchased in 1964 in the husband's sole name a family home financed solely by the husband. The property was converted into a number of residential units in one of which the family lived, and the remainder of which were managed by the wife. The parties in the case were the wife as plaintiff and the executors of the deceased husband's will. In short, the husband's business had suffered badly in the latter years of his life and on his death there were significant debts and effectively this would have had the result that the plaintiff would have inherited very little. The plaintiff wife was claiming a share in the family home on two grounds: firstly, on the basis of the accepted principles by virtue of her work in managing the flats and by applying her earnings from 1983 onwards towards the family purposes, and secondly, through her work as wife and mother. On the basis of the accepted principles, the wife was entitled to a small interest in the property. The effect of this approach would have been to declare that some of the "husband's property" belonged beneficially to the wife at the date of his death, and therefore, would not have been part of his estate.

10.047 Dealing with the Article 41 argument and *L. v L.*, Mr. Justice Barron wrote

I do not feel that I can follow this decision. While I see the equity in recognising the contribution made by the plaintiff towards the welfare of her family, there does not seem to me to be anything in Article 41 of the Constitution to support her contention that she should become entitled

49 See, for example, *McGee v Attorney General* [1974] IR 284.
50 Unreported, 27 June 1988, High Court.

thereby to a share in the family home or any other property of any member of the family. The Article seeks to protect the family. The right granted is one whereby the State shall "endeavour to ensure that mothers shall not be obliged by economic necessity to engage in labour to the neglect of their duties in the home." Insofar as this provision may be construed as a guarantee of financial reward—and I express no view on this aspect of the matter—it seems to me that it must be a guarantee of reward from outside the family rather than a redistribution within the family.

This dismissal of Barr J.'s reasoning, in contrast to that of Lardner J., deals with the merit of the matter, if only in a cursory way. The interesting aspect of Barron J.'s view is that he views the effect of the *L. v L.* reasoning to result in a redistribution of finances/property within the family.

10.048 Accordingly, it appears that the approach adopted was to view the family property in strict legal terms in regard to ownership, rather than, as in many marriages, approaching the issue from the viewpoint that the property owned by either and both spouses is treated by them as "theirs" jointly. Given the "delicate and fundamental" nature of the issues, would this approach have been more appropriate, whatever the actual conclusion? Indeed, in the instant case, the spouses had reached agreement in relation to the wife obtaining a one-half interest in the family property. This had not been pursued by the spouses as, given the financial position of the husband at that time, such a transfer would have been open to challenge by the husband's creditors. This case has also been appealed to the Supreme Court.

10.049 There is one other judgment of relevance to this line of reasoning. In a decision given by Mr. Justice Barrington in the case of *A.H. v P.H.*[51] This argument was advanced primarily due to the fact that a number of financial institutions had mortgages over the property. The comments in the case on this aspect were *obiter*, as expressly recognised in the judgment. They are worth noting, however. The approach of Barr J. was approved of and on that basis

it would appear that the courts should recognise the contribution the wife makes by her work as a carer and rearer of the family within the home, because it appears to be quite inconsistent with the values in Article 41 in the Constitution that the wife, who leaves the home and has an independent income and is therefore able to make a financial contribution towards the repayments of the family mortgage, might, at the end of the day, be in a very much better position than the wife who fulfils the constitutionally preferred role and remains at home to rear

---

51 Unreported, High Court. The only written record is the true and accurate transcript of the stenographer's note of the ex tempore judgment. The transcript was approved by Barrington J. on the 13th of July, 1989.

the children. That seems to be an inconsistent conclusion and inconsistent with the principle in Article 41.

It is perhaps unfortunate that the case did not turn on this argument. If it had, Barrington J. would have been compelled to consider if it was a judicial function to recognise the argument or a legislative function. He had earlier in the judgment, having determined that the matter could be resolved on the straightforward principles, remarked that there "is no necessity to make new law." It is, accordingly, at least arguable, had it been been directly in point in reaching a decision, that Barrington J. would have followed *L. v L.* We are left, accordingly, with this line of reasoning still to be decisively accepted or rejected by the courts. The result, and possibly even more so, the reasoning of the Supreme Court is awaited with great interest.

Chapter 11

THE FAMILY HOME

Introduction

11.001 The Family Home Protection Act which came into force on the 12th of July, 1976, was hailed as a great advance in the law concerning the security of the family home. It is worth noting the comments cf the Minister for Justice introducing the Second Stage of the Bill.

> The primary purpose of the Bill is to protect the members of the family of a vindictive spouse from having their home sold or otherwise disposed of by him over their heads. The Bill is also directed towards actively encouraging spouses to place the family home in joint ownership by the abolition . . . of stamp duty, court fees and registration fees on transactions transferring ownership of the home from one spouse to both spouses jointly. The Bill, thirdly, proposes changes in the present law so as to give a spouse greater opportunity to clear off mortgage or rental arrears that the other spouse may have accumulated. Finally, the Bill provides for a wide-ranging protection for a family against the improper sale or removal of household chattels.

It will be seen from the discussion of the case law under the Act that the purpose of the legislation has largely been achieved. There was, however, some misunderstanding of the effects of several provisions, particularly in the immediate aftermath of its enactment.

The family home

11.002 The term "family home" is defined in section 2(2) of the Act as meaning primarily a dwelling in which a married couple ordinarily resides, and comprises in addition a dwelling in which a spouse whose protection is in issue ordinarily resides or resided before leaving. The definition covers situations where the spouses have no proprietary interest in the property and reside in the property as tenants or on foot of a licence. The terms dwelling is also defined in the Act as including any building, or any structure, vehicle or vessel, whether mobile or not, or part thereof, occupied as a separate dwelling and includes any garden or portion of ground attached to and usually occupied with the dwelling, or otherwise required for the amenity or convenience of the dwelling.

11.003 The question of the interpretation of the term "family home" has been considered in a number of cases. The first of these is *Hegarty v Morgan*.[1] The defendant vendor had included in the contract of sale a special condition to the effect that the premises, the subject matter of the sale, were not a family home within the meaning of the 1976 Act. It was also provided that the vendor would furnish a statutory declaration to this effect. The vendor furnished a declaration to this effect; however, the declaration recited facts and circumstances which indicated that the property could have been a family home. The vendor refused to take further steps to clarify the issue. The purchaser brought proceedings to rescind the contract for sale. McWilliam J. held that the statutory declaration was inadequate and stated that such a declaration should set out the facts establishing that the premises are not a family home. He also expressed the hope that a practice of providing a bald statement which purports to negate the application of the 1976 Act would not become the normal conveyancing practice.

11.004 In *Walpoles (Ireland) Ltd. v Jay*[2] the plaintiff limited company was the vendor of a property which it had owned for many years. In more recent years one of the directors of the company had resided for a period of two years in the property with his wife. A requisition raised concerning the property and the 1976 Act elicited the response that the property was not a family home as it was owned by a company. Correspondence ensued resulting in the defendant purchaser requesting the consent of the director's now divorced wife to the sale. The plaintiff contended that this was not necessary and McWilliam J. agreed that there was no provision in section 3 of the Act that could avoid a conveyance of the property by the plaintiff to the defendant. McWilliam J. did hold, however, that the premises were a family home. In this context he was of the view that there must be an investigation of the circumstances relating to the occupancy as a family home of any property, or any part thereof, being sold by a

---

1 15 March 1979, unreported, High Court. Noted at (1979) 113 LT & SJ 173.
2 (November 1980, unreported, High Court) McWilliam J. The earlier case of *L.B. v H.B.*, (July 1980, unreported) High Court, Barrington J. also discussed this point and had come to the same conclusion. The subsequent case of *B.M.C. v P.J.C.*, (May 1983, unreported, High Court) had a similar outcome. The husband and his wife occupied the property by leave and licence granted by a limited company owned and controlled by the husband's brother and sister-in-law. O'Hanlon J. determined that the property was a family home but that its transfer was not covered by the Act as the husband did not have any interest in the property as defined in section 1 of the Act.

company. In such circumstances the penalty would not be as great as in many cases as the "conveyance" transferring the company's interest is not avoided. The result would be that some other interest, that is, the interest of the occupants of the property would not necessarily have been terminated and may still subsist. As a result largely of this case, it has become recommended conveyancing practice to seek a declaration in relation to the 1976 Act when purchasing from a limited company. The remainder of this case discusses the issue of the interest in the property and the question of whether the director of the company was conveying any interest.

11.005 A case which has given rise to a number of difficulties is *Reynolds v Waters*[3] a decision of Costello J. In the course of the investigation of title the purchaser's solicitors requested that they be furnished with a draft statutory declaration verifying that the property was not a family home. The vendor's solicitors replied that such a declaration would be furnished on completion and would verify that the vendor had been separated from his wife who had deserted him prior to his taking up residence in the premises, and further that the wife from whom the vendor was now divorced had never resided in the premises. The purchaser's solicitors were not prepared to accept this and requested that the wife either furnish her consent or that a joint declaration of the spouses to the effect that the premises were not a family home be furnished. Costello J. held that this was unreasonable and that the facts as set out in the draft declaration, which was quite full, were a perfectly adequate answer to the concerns of the purchaser. Much of the decision is taken up with *obiter* comments leading Costello J. to the conclusion that there is no general principle to the effect that a prudent purchaser should not accept an uncorroborated statutory declaration of a vendor merely because the vendor is benefitting financially from the transaction. Costello J. also comments on the judgments of the Supreme Court in *Somers v Weir*.[4]

"Conveyance" of an "interest" in the family home without consent

11.006 The most important provision of the Act is contained in section 3(1) which makes void the purported conveyance by one spouse of any interest in the family home without the prior consent in writing of the other spouse. It is therefore necessary to consider the term conveyance as defined in the Act and the subsequent case law. The term "conveyance" is defined in section 1(1) as including for example a mortgage, lease, assent, transfer, etc. This envisages that the term may encompass transactions other than those specified. The section further provides that "convey" shall be construed accordingly.

11.007 Given the definition of conveyance in the Act and the requirement of prior written consent, the question arose as to whether there had to be separate consents to the contract for sale and the deed of conveyance. In

3 [1982] ILRM 335.
4 [1979] IR 94.

Kyne v Tiernan and anor.[5] the defendant spouses had determined to sell their family home. The property was held in the sole name of the husband, although both spouses were actively involved in the arrangements for the sale. The wife signed a letter drafted by her husband unequivocally consenting to the sale. Subsequent to the execution of the contract matrimonial difficulties arose between the spouses resulting in the wife refusing to endorse her consent to the sale on the deed of transfer in the ordinary manner. The purchaser brought proceedings for specific performance. Having determined that the letter signed by the wife was a sufficient consent for the purposes of the Act in relation to the contract for sale and that it demonstrated the wife's unconditional consent to the sale, the court had to consider whether a second consent was required from the wife for the valid completion of the conveyance? McWilliam J. stated:

> . . . it could be said on a strict interpretation of section 3 of the Act, that there must be a consent in writing to each conveyance, that is to say, both to the contract and to the final conveyance to the purchaser, but I cannot imagine that it can have been the intention of the legislature to require two consents for the completion of one transaction, namely, the sale of one house, and thus leave a purchaser in the position of conducting all the work and incurring all the expense necessary for the completion of a purchase only to find that a spouse had changed his or her mind about giving consent and require the whole transaction to be abandoned.

11.008 This is certainly the more practical answer to the problem posed. However it would have been open to McWilliam J. to interpret the provisions of the Act as necessitating two separate consents as this outcome would have been more in line with the definition of conveyance in the Act. Such an outcome may have resulted in purchasers being left in an unfortunate position through no fault on their part but the question remains whether this possible consequence was enough to influence the conclusion reached by McWilliam J.

11.009 There have been a number of judgments by the Supreme Court on the interpretation of section 3 of the Act. The first and possibly most important decision, is *Somers v Weir.*[4] The relevant transaction occurred shortly after the Act came into force. Property had been sold by a husband subsequent to the breakdown of his marriage. The purchaser wished to sell on and the second purchaser required proof that section 3 had not been breached. The wife had left the property in 1973 and had entered a separation agreement in 1974. Notwithstanding these facts the Supreme Court held that the property was a family home within the terms of the Act and that it was not possible for the husband to have validly sold the property without the prior consent of his wife.

---

5 15 July 1980, unreported, High Court.

11.010 A secondary point was whether the conveyance was saved by reason of being made to a "purchaser for full value" within the terms of section 3(3)(a) of the Act. The court determined that the enquiries made on behalf of the purchaser were inadequate given that the purchaser's solicitor had accepted a bare statutory declaration by the husband which averred that the spouses had executed a separation agreement, that the wife did not rely on the property as her family home, and that she had no interest therein. Accordingly, the Supreme Court held that if the necessary enquiries had been made the purchaser's solicitor would have been aware of the earlier non-compliance with the provisions of the Act, resulting in the purchaser by imputation having notice of the position at the time of the conveyance to him.

11.011 *Hamilton v Hamilton and anor.*[6] considered a situation which is unlikely to arise again in practice. This was whether the provisions of the Act apply to a conveyance of property in respect of which the contract of sale had been entered into prior to the commencement of the Act. Henchy J., writing the majority judgment in the Supreme Court held that the Act did not apply retrospectively although Costello J., sitting as an additional judge of the Supreme Court, wrote a strong dissenting judgment. Section 3(2) of the Act provides that subsection (1) of the section does not apply to a conveyance if it is made by a spouse in pursuance of an enforceable agreement made before the marriage of the spouses. Again, if the contrary were the position purchasers might be placed in difficulty through no act or omission on their part. However, it is arguable that the "evil" which the Act is designed to prevent, namely the sale by one spouse of the family home without reference to the other spouse, could, by virtue of the provisions of subsection (2), still occur. It is a value judgment whether a purchaser or spouse should suffer the consequences.

11.012 In *Nestor v Murphy and anor.*,[7] the defendants were a married couple and joint owners of property. Both spouses had signed a contract for sale of the property to the plaintiff. Subsequently, the defendants refused to complete the transaction claiming that the wife had not given her consent in writing to the sale prior to the signing of the contact. The plaintiff claimed specific performance of the contract. It was held that section 3(1) was not applicable. Henchy J. stated the purpose of the provision in the following terms.

> The basic purpose of the subsection is to protect the family home by giving a right of avoidance to the spouse who was not a party to the transaction. It ensures that protection by requiring, for the validity of the contract to dispose and of the actual disposition, that the non-disposing spouse should have given a prior consent in writing. The point and purpose of imposing the sanction of voidness is to enforce the right of the non-disposing spouse to veto the disposition by the other spouse

6 [1982] IR 466.
7 [1979] IR 326.

of an interest in the family home . . . an extension of that right of avoidance to spouses who have entered into a joint "conveyance" would not only be unnecessary for the attainment of that aim but also enable contracts to be unfairly or dishonestly repudiated by parties who entered into them freely, willingly and with full knowledge . . . the spouse whose "conveyance" is avoided . . . is a spouse who has unilaterally (i.e. without the other spouse joining) purported to "convey" an interest in the family home without having obtained the prior consent in writing of the other spouse.

In short, where both spouses join in the conveyance of the family home, the Act has no application.

11.013 This decision was followed shortly afterwards by the case of *Mulhall and anor. v Haren and anor.*[8] The facts of the case were slightly different in that the wife had not signed any contract. Keane J., however, held on the facts that the spouses had jointly authorised an auctioneer to conclude a contract. It being immaterial whether a spouse signed a contract personally or authorised some other person to do so on his/her behalf, it followed that there was no basis for availing of the 1976 Act to avoid the contract. Keane J. stated that the decision in *Nestor v Murphy* would have been no different if the wife's solicitor had signed the contract as agent on her behalf with her full authority if, for example, she had been away at the time.

Nature of rights conferred by the Act

11.014 The question of the nature of the rights created or conferred by the 1976 Act on a spouse has arisen in a number of decisions for differing reasons. In *Guckian v Brennan*[9] the plaintiff spouses were the joint owners of a leasehold interest in property which included the family home. After the enactment of the 1976 Act, the plaintiffs were registered as full owners of the property by virtue of transfer from the remainderman of his interest. The plaintiffs agreed to sell the property to the defendants and in the course of investigation of title the defendants required additional evidence to demonstrate that the transfer by the remainderman was unaffected by section 3 of the Act. The reply to this was in terms that the request was unnecessary in that the vendors had been registered as full owners of the property in the Land Registry and the register is conclusive. The Court was asked to determine whether the requisition was sufficiently answered. Given that the plaintiffs were joint owners of the property, the defendants were not concerned that section 3 may have applied to the transfer by them to the defendants. Gannon J. considered the terms of sections 55, 59 and 72 of the Registration of Title Act, 1964 and how various rights and burdens were dealt with thereunder. He then discussed the nature of the

8 [1981] IR 364.
9 [1981] IR 478.

right under the 1976 Act referring to *National Provincial Bank Limited v Ainsworth*[10] and to *Nestor v Murphy*[11] and stated:

> The Act of 1976 does not create, nor invest a married person with, any right affecting land or property in the nature of an interest in land which could fall within any of the classifications of burdens within section 72(1) of the Act of 1964. Such right as is conferred is a right which affects the instrument of transfer and its validity. If that instrument is invalid, the transfer is ineffective; but the spouse for whose benefit the transfer is rendered ineffective obtains no estate or interest which can affect the ownership or title to the property described in the transfer.

11.015 Gannon J. went on to refer to section 13 of the 1976 Act. This section provides that section 59(2) of the Registration of Title Act 1964 which deals with noting upon the register the provisions of any enactment restricting dealings in land, shall not apply to the provisions of the 1976 Act. He concluded: "In my opinion section 13 of the Act of 1976 says and means that in relation to registered land the provisions of that Act which are restrictive of alienation are not burdens created by section 59 of the Act of 1964 and do not come within section 72, sub-section 1 of that Act." Gannon J. concluded that the requisition referred to had been answered sufficiently by the vendors. Accordingly the nature and import of the right conferred by the 1976 Act is a right affecting the transaction as opposed to the property. In short, the right, when considered further in the light of the subsequent provisions of section 4 of the Act, is a right of veto.

The scope and limits of section 3

11.016 How may a spouse avail of the protection afforded by the Act and what are the limits of this protection? The "evil" which the Act was designed to counter usually results from actions of one spouse which have a detrimental effect on the other. There may be an attempt to injure economically that other spouse, or there may simply be financial mis-management. A number of spouses have attempted to avail of the provisions of section 3 to overcome difficulties of which they had no knowledge. In *Containercare (Ireland) Limited v Wycherley and anor.*[12] the defendant spouses were joint tenants of a leasehold interest in property which comprised the family home. Subsequently the plaintiff company obtained judgment against the husband. A judgment mortgage was registered against the family home in the Registry of Deeds. In the proceedings before the court, the plaintiff claimed a well-charging order over the husband's interest in the family home. The wife contended that the registration was void in that it amounted to a conveyance within the terms of the 1976 Act to which her prior consent in writing was not obtained. Carroll J. rejected this argument, stating (at 150): "A judgment

10 [1965] AC 1175, especially Lord Hodson at page 1220.
11 [1979] IR 326.
12 [1982] IR 143.

mortgage, if registered against a family home, is not a disposition by a spouse purporting to convey an interest in the family home. It is a unilateral act by a judgment creditor. . . ."

11.017 Barrington J. considered the same issue a short time later in *Murray v Diamond*.[13] He referred to section 6 of the Judgment Mortgage Act 1850, which deals with the registration of a judgment as a judgment mortgage and stated that it

> seems clear from this that it is the registration of the office copy of the affidavit which converts the judgment into a judgment mortgage. But while the section says that for the purpose of the entries made in the register the judgment creditor is to be deemed the grantee and the judgment debtor to be deemed the grantor it is clear that the judgment mortgage comes into existence by operation of the statute and not by virtue of any act of the judgment debtor.

It could well be suggested that in certain circumstances the registration of a judgment could come into existence by virtue of a positive act of the judgment debtor. See *O'N. v O'N.*[14] Barrington J. expressly followed the reasoning of Gannon J. in *Guckian v Brennan*[15] in agreeing that the rights of a non-owning spouse under the 1976 are valuable rights but are not an estate or interest in lands.

11.018 There are also instances where spouses unwittingly fall foul of the Act. *D. McCarthy and anor. (as Personal Representative of B. McCarthy, Deceased) v E. McCarthy*,[16] provides an interesting example. The plaintiffs were the personal representatives of A, deceased, who had been the joint owner with her husband, the defendant, of property comprised in Folio X. This property included the family home of A and her husband. By a deed of severance dated December 16, 1983, X transferred all the property in Folio X to the third-named plaintiff unto and to the use of herself. By her will of the same date, the deceased purported to devise her undivided half share in the lands as tenant in common to the first and second-named plaintiffs. In an administration suit, the defendant pleaded that section 3 invalidated the deed of severance. While other bases were put forward to undermine the transactions, the case was ultimately decided upon this issue. The learned Circuit Court Judge negatived any question of the matter coming under the "*donatio mortis causa*" exception in the definition of "conveyance" in section 1(1) of the Act and turned to consider the effect of the deed of severance. The terms of the relevant passage in the deed were as follows:

---

13 [1982] ILRM 113.
14 6 October 1989, unreported, High Court.
15 [1981] IR 478.
16 xxx ILT 216; 1 May 1984, Circuit Court

The said [deceased] is desirous of severing the joint tenancy. For the purpose of severing the joint tenancy the said [deceased] as registered owners in consideration of these presents hereby transfers all the lands described in Folio [X] . . . as specified in the schedule hereto to [the third-named Plaintiff] unto and to the use of herself the said [deceased].

11.019 Judge Sheridan stated at 217: "This is clearly a conveyance even though it was only a device for the purposes of an attempted severance of the joint tenancy. I have no doubt, therefore, that as far as the family home is concerned it is void." He went on to say that the harshness of the 1976 Act insofar as the position of joint tenancies is concerned may not have been appreciated. A novel argument was adduced by the plaintiffs in an attempt to salvage their position, namely that the void portion of the transfer, so far as it affected the family home, could be severed from that dealing with the lands in general. In aid of this argument, the plaintiffs cited the minority judgment of Costello J. in *Hamilton v Hamilton and anor.*[17] The full quotation from Costello J.'s judgment reads

Alternatively it was pleaded that if section 3 of the Act applies to the proposed conveyance it applies only to that part of "Hamwood House" which constitutes a dwelling within the meaning of section 2 of the Act. Section 2 defines a "family home" as meaning primarily a "dwelling" in which a married couple ordinarily reside and a "dwelling" as meaning any building including in the meaning of this word any garden or portion of ground attached to and usually occupied with the dwelling or otherwise required for the amenity or convenience of the dwelling. The purchaser does not deny that there is a "dwelling" on the property to be sold or that it is a dwelling in which a "married couple ordinarily reside", and he accepts that this dwelling and the garden attached to it is a family home within the meaning of the Act. But once this concession is made, as indeed it had to be made, it seems to me that the purchaser's argument must fail. The effect of the proposed conveyance will be to convey this "family home" and this will be the result even though there will be conveyed with the "family home" additional land which may not form part of it. Once a proposed conveyance includes a "family home" then, it seems to me, the provisions of section 3(1) apply to it and the written consent referred to in the subsection is required unless the transaction falls within one of the four exceptions set out in the section. No arguments were advanced to support the alternative plea that the court should, in effect, sever the property and decide that consent to part (the part comprising the "family home") of the proposed conveyance was required but not to the remainder. I do not think that such a contention is sustainable and I am satisfied that the court in these proceedings is concerned with a proposal to convey a "family home" within the meaning of the Act and that the written consent of the non-disposing spouse to this proposed conveyance is being withheld.

17 [1982] IR 466.

Sheridan J. afforded the views of Costello J. the greatest respect but stated that his own conclusion with considerable reluctance was to the same effect and that the entire transaction was tainted with illegality.

Equitable mortgages and the Act

11.020 The question of the relationship of the 1976 Act and equitable mortgages has arisen in a number of cases. In *Bank of Ireland v Hanrahan*[18] the plaintiff bank took an equitable deposit of the title documents to the defendant's lands. These lands included the family home of the defendant and his wife. The defendant brought the land certificate to the plaintiff bank with the intention of leaving it with the bank as security for a loan. It was pointed out to the defendant that his wife would have to give her consent to this transaction. The defendant left the certificate in the bank and later that day the wife called and signed the necessary consent under the 1976 Act. Subsequently, the plaintiff brought proceedings in relation to its security and the defendant raised the provisions of the 1976 Act as a defence. He contended that the consent was not a prior consent as required under the Act. O'Hanlon J. referred to the provisions of the Act and stated his conclusion in the following terms

> If the attempt by the defendant to effect a mortgage by equitable deposit of his land certificate was already complete before his wife called in to execute the consent, then it was not a "prior consent" as required by the Act, and the transaction should be regarded as void. However, in the particular circumstances of the present case, the bank and the defendant impliedly agreed to the retention by the bank of the land certificate as mere custodians thereof until such time as the defendant's wife came in to sign the necessary consent, and that a tacit agreement should be implied as between the bank and the defendant that as and from the time when Mrs. Hanrahan signed the consent, the character in which the land certificate was held by the bank should change and that from that time forward they should be entitled to retain it in the capacity of equitable mortgagees.

The question could be raised as to whether at the time the defendant appreciated the subtlety of his position.

11.021 The recent case of *Bank of Ireland v Purcell*[19] dealt with a more common situation. The case demonstrates the breadth of the 1976 Act's provisions and protection. The plaintiff held an equitable charge over the defendant's lands on foot of a deposit of the title deeds made in 1975 to secure liabilities then existing and future advances. The family home of the defendant and his wife was included in this property. Further advances were made by the plaintiff to the defendant subsequent to the enactment of the 1976 Act without the consent of the wife being sought or obtained. The

18 10 February 1987, unreported, High Court.
19 [1988] ILRM 480.

plaintiff bank was on notice at all times that the property comprised, *inter alia*, the family home of the defendant. The bank sought to realise their security. The general thrust of the plaintiff's submission was that the interest of the defendant passed to the plaintiff by virtue of the deposit of the title deeds and that accordingly when the further advances were made no further interest could have been (or was) passed to the bank. *In re O'Byrne's Estate*[20] was cited in support of this argument. This case had held, in short, that further advances were not a disposition of the estate which required registration for the purposes of section 4 of the Irish Registration Act, 1707. Barron J. distinguished this case by citing the comments of Naish C., distinguishing the security created by the execution of a deed and transactions effected on foot of the deed. A passage from the judgment of Kenny J. in *Allied Irish Banks Ltd. v Glynn*[21] was also cited. Kenny J. had stated that "The deposit, as security, of documents of title to land which is not registered gives the person with whom it is made an equitable estate in the lands until the money secured by it is repaid."

11.022 Barron J.'s reasoning dwelt largely on the definition of "interest" in the Act. He stated (at 482):

> The conveyance of the estate in lands is the conveyance of an interest for the purposes of the section, but the fact that the estate has already been conveyed need not prevent a subsequent transaction from conveying an "interest" in the lands. In the case of a mortgage the extent of the estate depends upon the amount which has been borrowed. Even in a case of a legal mortgage where there is a conveyance of the fee simple the interest of the mortgagor and of the mortgagee in the lands so mortgaged will depend at any given time upon the extent of the moneys lent and borrowed. No doubt so long as any moneys are charged on the lands the fee simple estate will be in the mortgagee. However, that of itself does not mean that thereafter the mortgagor cannot purport to convey a further interest to the mortgagee, because in that situation the value of the equity of redemption is being altered on the occasion of each further advance. The same situation arises in the present case.

He went on to say that the priority of the security is not affected by such further advances until the mortgagee has notice of any subsequent mortgage when the mortgagee's rights in respect of further advances are subordinated to the rights of the subsequent mortgagee. Barron J. also made it clear that if the bank had not had notice of the property being a family home, the rights of the spouse would have been subordinated to that of the plaintiff bank. The declaration in the case was that no security was created in favour of the plaintiff over the family home of the defendant in respect of advances made after the date upon which the Act came into force.

20 (1885) 15 LR Ir. 373.
21 [1973] IR 188 at 191.

11.023 It may be thought that Barron J. stretched the interpretation of the term "conveyance" beyond what was intended. However, while the interpretation was broad it is certainly tenable. In addition, there is no conflict with the decisions in *Containercare (Ireland) Ltd. v Wycherley*[22] and *Murray v Diamond*[23] although there might appear to be such on first sight. In the instant circumstances, the act which results in a conveyance of an interest in the family home is the positive act of the mortgagor in requesting and/or accepting each subsequent advance. On appeal to the Supreme Court[24] Barron J.'s reasoning was upheld. Walsh J., delivering judgment for the full court, approached the task of interpreting the 1976 Act on the basis that it was a remedial statute and should be construed widely and liberally, not as a conveyancing statute. He therefore felt entitled to emphasise the purpose of the Act, the "evil" at which the Act is directed. He also observed that in certain circumstances, similar to those in the instant case, the personal debt of the husband could give rise to the creation of a judgment mortgage. He went on to state at pages 8–9 that he did not "find it necessary to offer any opinion on the situation which would arise concerning the right of the other spouse in the event of a judgment mortgage being registered in respect of advances made after the coming into force of the 1976 Act." Two cases already referred to deal with this issue, concluding that a judgment mortgage is not a conveyance by a spouse within section 3 of the Act. This raises a question mark over the correctness of these earlier High Court decisions. A subsequent High Court decision[25] also appears to agree with the dictum of Walsh J., but admittedly the issue in this case varied slightly.

Dispensing with consent

11.024 Section 4 of the Act provides a procedure for dispensing with the consent of a spouse who omits or refuses to consent, or is incapable of giving consent or cannot be found, subject to certain conditions. The court must consider in each case whether it is unreasonable for the spouse to withhold consent. In reaching this determination the court must take into account all the circumstances. Subsection (2) of section 4 sets out that these circumstances include the respective needs and resources of the spouses and any dependent children, and the suitablility of any alternative accommodation offered. This has given courts a relatively wide discretion to consider all matters in any given case. In particular, the practice has developed whereby courts have decreed that a proportion of the proceeds of sale be set aside and used in the purchase of secure alternative accommodation for the other spouse. In *E.S.T. v C.A.T.*[26] in which the plaintiff wife sought relief under the Married Women's Status Act, 1957 in addition to section 4, Carroll J. ordered the payment into court of the

22 [1982] IR 143.
23 [1982] ILRM 113.
24 24 July 1989, unreported, Supreme Court.
25 *O'N. v O'N.*, 6th October 1989, unreported, High Court.
26 17 February 1982, unreported, High Court.

proceeds of sale of the family home to be availed of in the acquisition of a substitute home. In this case, the wife had been held entitled to a a one-half share in the family home.

11.025 However, in *O'M. v O'M.*[27] the defendant wife had no beneficial interest in the family home. The wife and children were, at the time of the application, living in a local authority flat, and the husband remained in the family home. The husband applied to dispense with his wife's consent to the sale. Finlay P. ordered that the consent of the wife should only be dispensed with provided that, following the sale, one-half of the net proceeds be lodged in court to be made available to the wife towards the acquisition by her of accommodation for herself and the children. There was no application for a barring order in this case; yet Finlay P. clearly took into account the fact that it was not possible for the wife and children to reside in the family home due to the attitude and conduct of the husband.

11.026 A clear example of the court taking account of the resources and needs of the spouses was provided by the case of *R. v R.*[28] The husband applied to the court to dispense with the consent of his wife to his raising an additional mortgage over the family home. The spouses were still living under the same roof but the clear intention of the husband was that he would use the additional money to discharge debts and assist in establishing another home for himself and the woman he had formed a relationship with. The wife for her part, was concerned that the only source of support for herself and their three dependent children should not be diminished. In these circumstances, McMahon J. decided to deal with the case by considering the claim for maintenance first. Having determined the maintenance he considered the potential repayments due on foot on the additional mortgage together with the amount required by the husband for his own support, and held that there would be a substantial risk that he would not be able to keep up with the mortgage repayments. Accordingly, he refused to dispense with the wife's consent.

11.027 *Somers v Weir*,[29] establishes that consent cannot be dispensed with retrospectively under section 4. Henchy J. stated as follows concerning the use of section 4

> The plaintiff moved by way of a special summons in which she asked for an order under section 4 of the Act of 1976 dispensing with the defendant's prior consent to the sale. This, in my opinion, was not the correct order to seek. If the plaintiff could be said to have been a "purchaser for full value", the proper order to seek would have been an order declaring the validity of the assignment which had been made without the defendant's prior consent in writing. An order under section

27 21 December 1981, unreported, High Court.
28 8 December 1978, unreported, High Court.
29 [1979] IR 326; see **11.009**.

4 of the Act of 1976 is intended to cover the position before conveyance when the spouse omits or refuses to consent. When the conveyance has been executed without the consent, it is either valid without that consent or it is void *ab initio*; in either event an order under section 4 would be inappropriate.[30]

11.028 In the dissenting judgment of Costello J. in *Hamilton v Hamilton* a number of important *obiter* observations are made about the interpretation of section 4 and, in particular, when it is reasonable or not reasonable for a spouse to withhold consent. In determining whether the withholding of consent was reasonable or not, the court will apply a subjective test rather than an objective test. One result of this, according to Costello J., is that the court is free to have regard to circumstances which the non-disposing spouse may have ignored, and may ignore, discount or take into account as it considers proper circumstances which may have motivated the non-disposing spouse. He interpreted the expression "all the circumstances" to be sufficiently broad to include non-financial aspects of the transaction, such as emotional factors.

11.029 Two further observations made by Costello J. are of interest as they concern matters which often arise in practice. The first of these is that the non-disposing spouse may well be unaware of the terms of section 3 and the effect of not consenting. Secondly, a refusal which was at the time reasonable may become unreasonable by the time of the hearing of any court application as a result of a change of circumstances. However, the contrary does not automatically follow.

11.030 These observations of Costello J. are important notwithstanding that his judgment was a dissent and his comments *obiter*. They are important because they reflect judicial practice. The circumstances in which a spouse is requested to give consent have a bearing on whether the refusal to give such consent is reasonable or not. In short, if a spouse is not given sufficient time to consider the request, refusal may at least temporarily be reasonable; if a spouse is not given adequate and exact details in relation to proposed alternative accommodation, a refusal may be reasonable. Indeed, it is submitted that there is a strong argument to be made that, if a spouse is not, for example, given sufficient time to consider a request or sufficient details of the transaction, there is no true refusal on foot of which a "disposing" spouse could apply to court. There is a further matter which arises frequently in practice. This concerns the practice of spouses issuing proceedings under section 4, and subsequently requesting the other spouse to give consent to the proposed transaction. The usual reason for this is to shorten the possible delay in getting into court, should the consent be refused. The non-disposing spouse might well argue either of the two points referred to above in relation to time or lack of detail. There is, however, a third argument which may yet be accepted to defeat a

30 [1982] IR 466.

section 4 application. It is arguable that the terms of the section and the form of pleading prescribed in the relevant rules posit a request and refusal prior to proceedings being instituted. The basis of this is that the applicant spouse should be in a position to demonstrate in the pleadings, or in the accompanying affidavit if one is used, the circumstances of the proposed transaction, the request for consent and the refusal of same. It is submitted that if the request was not made prior to the institution of proceedings, then such proceedings are premature and are an abuse of process of the court.

11.031 The provisions of subsection 3 and 4 of section 4 are widely used in practice. Under subsection 3 there is an obligation on the Court to dispense with the consent if the spouse whose consent is required has deserted and continues to desert the applicant spouse. Once there is desertion, the Court has no discretion in the matter, although application to Court is still necessary. Desertion includes "constructive" desertion. Subsection 4 provides that where the spouse whose consent is required is incapable of consenting by reason of unsoundness of mind or other mental disability, or has not after reasonable enquiries been found, the Court may give the consent on behalf of that spouse if it appears to the Court to be reasonable to do so. There was a question mark over the jurisdiction of the Court to dispense with the consent of a spouse under the age of twenty one years even if that spouse was willing to consent. The practice had developed of applying under the Guardianship of Infants Act, 1964, section 11 in respect of conveyances to which the consent of a minor spouse was required. The court could make any order that was in the best interests of the minor. The matter was clarified by section 10 of the Family Law Act, 1981. A practice direction of the President of the High Court states that where there is an application to dispense with consent in circumstances coming within these subsections, and where the spouse whose consent is required cannot be served as a party, the fact of desertion, unsoundness of mind or other mental disability, or of inability to trace should be corroborated by an affidavit of a disinterested third party verifying the averments in the applicant's affidavit. In such circumstances, while the practice direction does not expressly so state, the application is usually made on a *ex parte* basis.

Applications under section 5 of the Act

11.032 Section 5(1) empowers a court to make any such order as it considers proper to protect a family home in the interest of the applicant spouse or dependent child where the other spouse is engaging in such conduct as may lead to the loss of any interest in the home or render it unsuitable for habitation with the intention of depriving the applicant spouse or a dependent child of his residence in the family home. In *E.D. v F.D.*[31] Costello J. was of the view that the section conferred a very wide

31 23 October 1980, unreported, High Court.

discretion on the court including power to order a transfer of the matrimonial home to the applicant spouse. However, he went on to say that such discretion "can only be exercised when the Court is satisfied that the spouse is acting with the intention of depriving the applicant spouse or a dependent child of the family of his or her residence in the family home." It is necessary to prove that the defendant's conduct is wilful, in the sense of being consciously directed towards depriving the plaintiff of his/her residence. It is not enough simply to show that the defendant has acted irresponsibly or improvidently. He then reviewed the lifestyle of the defendant and noted that it was extravagant, including allowing arrears to build up on the mortgage and having judgments obtained against him. He determined that the defendant had not acted with the intention referred to in the section. However, liberty to renew the section 5 application was given, Costello J. having ordered the husband to enter various negotiations to resolve his financial difficulties. The matter came back to court a little over a year later[32] when it appeared to the court that the husband had failed to take any steps or enter any negotiations as previously ordered. In these circumstances, Costello J. concluded that the husband's conduct was deliberate. He accordingly ordered that the family home be conveyed to the wife, without prejudice to any equitable rights which the husband had in the property.

11.033 *D.C. v A.C.*[33] involved an application to transfer the family home, which was in the joint names of the parties, into the sole name of the wife. The family home was very suitable for the wife and the children; in addition, while an order for possession had been obtained by the mortgagee in respect of it, there would have been a considerable equity of redemption. Lastly, the plaintiff wife's father had offered to discharge the entire arrears provided the property was transferred into the wife's sole name. Carroll J. considered the terms of section 5 and determined that the expression "engaging in such conduct" covered inactivity as well as activity, and accordingly included the husband's failure to meet the mortgage repayments. The learned judge declined to transfer the property on the basis that the husband would be divested of a valuable asset at a time when both spouses had considerable debts incurred in the course of their marriage. In place of such an order, Carroll J. made a number of orders under section 5(2), recognising that such orders could be made only after a loss of residence in the family home. She indicated that if the building society proceeded with the sale of the property and if there were no change in circumstances, the wife should be refunded out of the balance of the purchase money her contribution towards the deposit together with such sum as represents a proportionate increase in the value of the house. Subsequent to this payment certain debts incurred during the marriage should be discharged out of the balance then remaining at the wife's option. Lastly, if there was any money remaining, any debts incurred in the

32 16 December 1981, unreported, High Court.
33 [1981] ILRM 357.

sole name of the husband should be discharged at the option of the husband. It was pointed out that such loss was imminent and that the order would take effect in the event of the sale by the building society.

11.034 The novel outcome to this case may indicate a means of surmounting a difficulty present in section 5. It is often the case that a spouse cannot prove the requisite intention necessary to obtain an order under subsection 1, and so must rely upon subsection 2 after the loss has occurred. This may not be in the best interests of the injured spouse. It may, on the reasoning of this case, be open to a spouse to apply for relief under subsection 1 and, in the alternative, under subsection 2 and thereby seek to obtain orders similar to those decreed in this case if the claim under subsection 1 fails.

11.035 O'Hanlon J. in *G.P.P. v I.H.P.*[34] held that the husband was engaged on a course of conduct designed to deprive his wife of the family home and to extract the maximum financial benefit for himself without any regard for the needs of his wife and children. On foot of earlier court proceedings the wife's consent to the raising of a loan by her husband using the family home as security for the loan was dispensed with. The husband did not use the loan subsequently raised for the purpose for which it had been obtained and the husband did not comply with the conditions which the earlier court order had imposed. In these circumstances, O'Hanlon J. was of the opinion that the husband was untruthful and untrustworthy. The order of the court was that the husband forthwith transfer the family home into the sole name of the wife and that no further money be raised by the husband on the security of the home. O'Hanlon J.'s order was comprehensive in that he stated that the wife

> shall be entitled to the entire beneficial estate and interest hitherto held by the [husband] in the house . . . to the intent that no further arrangement entered into by the [husband] with a view to encumbering the . . . property and no judgment registered against the [husband] which is sought to be converted into a judgment mortgage . . . and which has not been so registered . . . prior to the date of this judgment, shall take effect as a valid encumbrance against the property.

11.036 In *A.D. v D.D. and anor.*[35] there had been an agreement between the spouses that the husband would sell the family home and pay the balance, after discharge of the mortgage to his wife. In the event, the house was sold for less than the amount of the outstanding mortgage thus depriving the wife of her residence in the family home without any alternative accommodation. McWilliam J. held that the failure to implement the terms of the agreement arose through lack of finance, not through any action on the husband's part. Accordingly relief under section 5 was refused.

34 19 October 1984, unreported, High Court.
35 8 June 1983, unreported, High Court.

Orders under section 5 falling short of complete transfer

11.037 Some of the more recent decisions relating to section 5 emphasise that the complete transfer of the matrimonial home to the plaintiff is not always necessary to provide the protection envisaged under the Act. Where a complete transfer is not envisaged, there may be a tendency to interpret less strictly the requirement of "intent to deprive" on the part of the defendant. Indeed, in the light of the most recent decision on section 5, the following two cases may require re-examination. In *C.P. v D.P.*[36] the defendant carried on business in a partnership and later as a sole trader. Due to a recession in his line of activity, the dissolution of the partnership and the necessity of funding two households consequent on the separation of the parties, the defendant was substantially in debt, leading Finlay P. to comment that there was a significant danger of the loss of the family home. It was submitted on behalf of the wife that the word "intention" should be construed as not being equivalent to motive but rather with the intention which may be imputed to any person as to the natural and probable consequences of their conduct. Finlay P. stated that he could not

> construe the word "intention" in section 5(1) of the Act of 1976 as being equivalent to the implied or imputed intention which can arise from the natural and probable consequences of an act or omission. There must . . . be an element of deliberate conduct. I have come to this view as to the interpretation of section 5(1) largely by comparing the terms of that section with section 5(2) of the same Act. . . . It seems clear to me that if the legislature had intended by the use of the words "with the intention of depriving the Applicant spouse" in subsection 5(1) to involve only conduct the natural and probable consequences of which would be to deprive the Applicant spouse that having regard to the terms of subsection 2 where the conduct that has actually resulted in the loss of a family home gives rise to the discretion of the court that the word "intention" would also have been used in that subsection. To put the matter in another way having regard to the terms of section 5 subsection 2, if "intention" were to mean only a conscious or deliberate act the natural and probable consequences of which would be the loss of the family home in subsection 1 of section 5 it would be quite an unnecessary proviso and quite an unnecessary phrase.

In the circumstances, therefore, the relief sought was refused, although Finlay P. suggested that the most desirable thing for the family was for the earliest possible sale of the family home with the proceeds of sale being applied to provide a stable and secure family home for the wife and children and proper accommodation separately for the husband.

---

36 [1983] ILRM 380.

11.038 The second case which may require re-examination is *S. v S.*[37] The family home of the parties was in their joint name, some years previously, the business in which the defendant was involved collapsed and since that time the plaintiff had not known what the defendant was working at. All household bills were paid. However, in mid 1982 a representative from a bank called and informed the plaintiff that due to the defendant's severe financial difficulties the family home would have to be sold. Shortly after this the defendant left the family home and apparently left the jurisdiction. He took no part in the proceedings. McWilliam J. referred to the judgment in *E.D. v F.D.*[38] and the approach adopted by Costello J., the case of *O'M. v O'M.*[39] and *C.P. v D.P.*[40] Evidence was tendered by the plaintiff that there were considerable sums of money being claimed from the defendant by various creditors. McWilliam J. stated that in

> the present case the defendant appears to have looked after his wife and children to the best of his ability, possibly to a large extent with borrowed money. Although he may have acted improvidently and, possibly, dishonestly, and the natural and probable consequences of his actions may have been that the family home would be a target of his various creditors, it appears to me that it is unlikely that he formed any intention of depriving his wife and children of their residence in the family home and that it is much more likely that he left the country to escape the attentions of his creditors. . . .

11.039 Features of the above two cases are the thin line that is drawn between acts which do and those which do not involve the necessary intent, and the assumption which is made that the court must choose between the two alternatives of transferring or not transferring the family home to the plaintiff. These issues have been considered more recently by Barron J. in *O'N. v O'N.*[41] The family home was owned beneficially in equal shares. The respondent wife left the family home to live with another man, leaving the children of the marriage and the husband living in the family home. In previous proceedings taken by the wife the sale of the family home was refused on two separate occasions. In the meantime, the wife had judgment obtained against her in respect of a loan taken out by her subsequent to the breakdown. A judgment mortgage was then registered against her interest in the family home. The husband sought an order under section 5(1). Barron J. considered the following cases: *E.D. v F.D.*[38] *G.P.P. v I.H.P.*[34] and *A.D. v D.D. and anor.*[35] He was of the view that the wife clearly wished to realise her financial interest in the family home, but he also stated that the debt which resulted in the registration of the judgment mortgage was not incurred with the express intention of depriving the husband and children of their residence in the family home.

37 [1983] ILRM 387.
38 23 October 1980, unreported, High Court.
39 21 December 1981, unreported, High Court.
40 [1983] ILRM 380.
41 6 October 1989, unreported, High Court. This was a Circuit Court appeal.

In addition, as her conduct had not yet deprived them of their residence, the conditions for relief under section 5(2) had not been fulfilled. However, Barron J. went on to state:

> Nevertheless the [wife] is putting the residence of her husband and children in the family home at risk since she is making no effort to pay off the judgment mortgage. This may be owing to her poor financial circumstances, but does indicate a wish to retain the financial benefit of the loan at the expense of her family. Indeed, it is probable that the same financial circumstances will lead her to borrow again. If she does, there could be no doubt of her intention to obtain a personal benefit at the expense of her family.

11.040 Barron J. regarded the circumstances as coming within the terms of section 5(1) saying that the claimant spouse does not have to wait until there is a *fait accompli*, as, if this were so, much of the remedy provided by the section would be lost. Referring to the terms of the subsection he stated at page 5:

> The section does not require an absolute transfer of the interest of the errant spouse in favour of the claimant spouse or children. Regard must be had to the purpose of the Act. It is to prevent voluntary alienation of an interest in the family home by one spouse to the prejudice of the other or their dependent children . . . The order should be one which protects the family home for the benefit of the [husband] and the two children of the marriage. This can be done by transferring the restricted interest which the [wife] has in the premises by reason of section 3 of the Act. To do so in reality takes nothing from the [wife], but at the same time achieves the protection which the Act requires.

The order of the court was that the wife should transfer her interest to trustees so that her present beneficial interest vested in the husband or his personal representative until such time as the wife discharges the judgment mortgage or the parties otherwise agree.

11.041 The construction put on "intention" in section 5(1) of the Act by Barron J. is preferable to that adopted in *C.P. v D.P.* and *S. v S.*, above. It is certainly permissible to look to the purpose of the Act in construing the terms. In this regard, Barron J. has identified the purpose of the Act as being the prevention of the voluntary alienation of a family home by one spouse to the prejudice of the other spouse. Accordingly, if the conditions of the section are satisfied, the court is being asked to make any such order as it considers proper for the protection of the family home in the interests of the applicant spouse or the children. There is nothing in the section requiring a court, on finding that the conditions laid down are satisfied, to transfer the property into the sole name of the applicant spouse. This is a practice that has developed, nothing more. Yet it would appear from the approaches adopted by a number of judges that this is the order required to comply with the section. This is clearly not so; see in addition to the *O'N. v O'N.* case, Carroll J. in *D.C. v A.C.*[42] It is arguable that in the earlier cases there is an underlying view that the transfer of the family home into the sole name of one spouse is such a serious order that the question of "intention" should be construed strictly. Arguably the outcome in *C.P. v D.P.* and *S. v S.* might have been different if considered in light of the more flexible approach adopted by Barron J. in *O'N. v O'N.*

Chattels

11.042 Section 9 of the Act restricts disposal of household chattels in certain circumstances. "Household chattels" are defined in the section comprehensively; they include consumable stores and domestic animals. Significantly, the definition expressly does not include any chattels used by either spouse for business or professional purposes, money or security for money. Subsection 1 provides that if there are reasonable grounds for believing a spouse intends to sell, lease, pledge, charge or otherwise dispose of or remove the household chattels or a portion of them with the likely result that it would be difficult for the applicant spouse or dependent child to reside in the family home without undue hardship, the court may, on terms, prohibit the disposition or removal.

11.043 Subsection 2 prohibits the sale, lease, pledge, charge or other disposition or removal of the family chattels by either spouse where there are matrimonial proceedings between the spouses. There are two exceptions: where the other spouse consents, and where the court before which the matrimonial proceedings have been instituted grants permission to a spouse to so do. The definition of matrimonial proceedings is somewhat restricted. It has not been expanded to include proceedings under the Judicial Separation and Family Law Reform Act, 1989. It is an offence to contravene the terms of subsection 2(3).

11.044 Where a spouse contravenes an order under subsection 1 or the provisions of subsection 2, or has sold, leased, pledged, charged or otherwise disposed of or removed such proportion of the chattels as has made or is likely to make it difficult for the applicant spouse or dependent child of the family to reside in the family home without undue hardship, the court may order the other spouse to provide household chattels for the applicant spouse or a sum of money in lieu thereof. The purpose of this order is to place the applicant spouse or dependent child in a position as near as possible to that obtaining before the contravention, disposition or removal. The court may, where a third person has been informed in writing by a spouse of intention to avail of this section, make such order directed to that third person or other spouse as appears to it to be proper in the circumstances.

---

42 [1981] ILRM 357.

Miscellaneous provisions

11.045 Section 6 of the Act is designed to deal with the ordinary practicalities of the organisation of households. It provides, in short, that a payment by one spouse of liabilities of the other spouse in respect of matters affecting the family home shall be as good as regards the creditor as done or paid by that other spouse. In many households the discharge of the usual outgoings is shared, and the spouses may actually end up discharging bills in respect of which the other spouse is legally responsible. This can also be of importance where, taken in conjunction with subsection 2 of the section, the spouses have separated and the spouse remaining in the family home continues to discharge the mortgage repayments notwithstanding the other spouse's sole responsibility for same. Subsection 2 protects the rights of the spouse volunteering such payments. It provides that any rights the volunteer spouse may have to an interest in the family home by virtue of any such payment referred to in subsection 1 are not affected by the terms of subsection 1.

11.046 Sections 7 and 8 of the Act deal with arrears arising on foot of a mortgage or lease. Where it appears to a court, in proceedings claiming possession due to the arrears which have arisen, that the non-defaulting spouse is capable of paying the arrears due within a reasonable time in addition to the future periodical payments, and that spouse desires to pay the arrears and periodical payments, the court may adjourn the proceedings for such time and on such terms as appear to the court to be just and equitable. Under section 7(1) the court may only so adjourn the proceedings if, having regard to the terms of the mortgage or lease, the interests of the lessor or mortgagee and the respective interests of the spouses, it would be just and equitable in all the circumstances to do so. There is no provision in the section or in the rules enacted under the Act requiring the formal notification of the non-defaulting spouse. In practice proceedings can reach a hearing before a court without the non-defaulting spouse being made aware of them. This does not often occur due to the practice adopted by financial institutions of informing the non-defaulting spouse of the institution of proceedings.

11.047 Subsection 2 partially remedies this omission. It provides that in considering to adjourn the proceedings as allowed by subsection 1, the court shall have regard in particular to whether the spouse of the mortgagor or lessee has been informed of the non-payment of the sums. This ensures that the court may itself decide to consider the circumstances of a spouse of the mortgagor or lessee who does not appear initially. Section 11 of the Act also assists in this regard. It provides that each spouse may, by direction of the court or by the service on that spouse by an existing party to the proceedings of a third party notice, be joined in the proceedings.

11.048 Section 8(2) empowers the court to declare, on the application of a spouse after the adjournment of proceedings under the preceding section, that all arrears and all the periodical payments due to date have been paid. The advantage of such a declaration is that, if made, any term in the mortgage or lease providing that the default in payment under the terms of the lease or mortgage shall result in the capital sum advanced, or any other additional amount, becoming due, shall be of no effect for the proceedings then existing or in any subsequent proceedings in respect of the sum becoming due.

11.049 Section 12 provides for the registration by a spouse in the Registry of Deeds of a notice stating that he is married to any person, being a person having an interest in such property or land. To encourage such registrations, section 12(3) provides that no fees are payable. Subsection 2 of this section demonstrates the voluntary nature of this facility, as it provides that the absence of such registration shall not give rise to an inference of the non-existence of a marriage.

11.050 Further exemption from fees is provided in section 14. This concerns the creation of a joint tenancy in a family home which is immediately prior to the transaction owned by either spouse or by both spouses otherwise than as joint tenants. Again, this is intended to encourage the transfer of the family home into the joint names of the spouse without incurring great procedural costs in the process.

Chapter 12

MISCELLANEOUS PROPERTY PROVISIONS

Partition Acts, 1868–1876

12.001 In the absence of an agreement by joint tenants to sell their property and realise their interests, application must be made pursuant to the Partition Acts, 1868–1876[1] in order to divide or partition the property, or for an order for sale of the property *in lieu* of partition.[2] In *Byrne v Byrne*[3] it was held that a mere agreement by joint tenants to sell property does not of itself sever the joint tenancy; there must be an intention to sever. In the absence of this intention, an agreement by joint tenants to sell their property merely operates to convert their property from one species of property to another which will also be held jointly.

12.002 An order pursuant to section 2 of the Partition Act, 1868 has the effect of severing the joint tenancy by a partition of the property or by an order for sale thereof with the result that each joint tenant acquires a vested entire interest in one half of the original property as partitioned or in one half of the net proceeds of sale. This is subject to the outcome of the taking of accounts and enquiries which may reflect on the shares in the proceeds. In passing it should be noted that section 7 of the 1876 Act permits an application to court seeking a sale of the property without a claim for partition. A practical example is where the property market is buoyant and the joint tenants cannot agree to sell the property to take advantage of this. A joint tenant may apply to court for an order for sale without a severance of the tenancy, resulting in the joint tenants holding the net proceeds in the same proportions as they held the property.

---

1 31 & 32 Vict. c. 40 and 39 & 40 Vict. c. 17; section 2 c. 1868 Act. See generally, Wylie, *Irish Land Law*, 2nd ed, **7.35–7.36**.
2 Section 3 of the 1868 Act.
3 18 January 1980, unreported, High Court.

12.003 The jurisdiction of the courts to order partition or sale *in lieu* thereof was discussed in *O'D. v O'D.*[4] The right of joint tenants to seek to compel partition was conferred by the Act for Joint Tenants 1542[5] and was enlarged to provide for a sale *in lieu* of partition by section 3 of the Partition Act, 1868. Section 4 of the 1868 Act permitted an order for sale in a "suit for partition, where if this Act had not been passed, a decree for partition might have been made". This appeared to provide that an order for sale could only be made on the same basis as an order for partition. Murphy J. in *O'D. v O'D.* considered the basis of the jurisdiction. Having noted that the jurisdiction to order partition stemmed from the Act of 1542, he agreed that in former times the remedy of partition was considered to be a matter of right upon proof of title, citing case law which ordered single dwelling houses to be partitioned. Murphy J., however, went on to find that the existence of these precedents did not establish conclusively that such an order is of right or that the court is without discretion in the matter. In support of this finding he referred to an early authority and to the practice of the courts on such applications.[6] This practice included the giving of directions for the taking of accounts and enquiries as to the estates and shares of the parties, the existence of any agreement prohibiting sub-division, and the availability of any necessary consent of the landlord. This procedure confirmed to Murphy J. that the making of an order for partition does (and always did) require the court to be satisfied by evidence tendered to it (or to an officer of the court) that it was a proper case in which to make the order sought.

12.004 The matter was more complex than this as Murphy J. explained. The Act of 1542 had been repealed by the Statute Law Revision (Pre-Union Irish Statutes) Act, 1962.

In the circumstances, counsel for the [husband] was driven to argue that the jurisdiction to decree partition—as opposed to a sale *in lieu* of partition—is now exercisable in accordance with the principles which the authorities show as having been established by the decided cases in respect of the practice of the courts of Chancery. Whilst it is clear that a separate equitable jurisdiction arose . . .[7] I confess to having some hesitation in accepting that principles which evolved as to the manner in which a statutory jurisdiction might be exercised could survive the repeal of that statute . . .

Proceeding to assume rather than accept that jurisdiction exists, Murphy J. determined that, as the matter was of necessity part of the inherent equitable jurisdiction of the court, it is therefore subject in its exercise to the discretion of the court.

4 18 November 1983, unreported, High Court.
5 33 Hen. viii c. 10.
6 *North v Guinon* (1847) Beatty's Reports 342; Seton on *Decrees* and Babington's *County Court Practice*.
7 See *Mundy v Mundy* 2 Ves. Jnr. 122, referred to in the judgment.

12.005 Murphy J. then considered the question of the court's discretion stating that in an application for sale *in lieu* of partition the order would not be made where the court saw good reason to the contrary. Of major importance in what amounts to good reason were the rights conferred under the Family Home Protection Act, 1976. Murphy J. expressly rejected the contention that the Act of 1976 impliedly repealed the Partition Acts and also rejected the further contention that, accordingly, if a proper case was made out for partition and an order granted, the necessity of procuring consent under the 1976 Act was dispensed with. It seemed to him

> unthinkable that the court would direct a conveyance to be made under the 1868 Act without having regard to the right of a spouse to withhold his or her consent and indeed the express duty imposed on the court not to dispense with consent without taking into account all the relevant circumstances including in particular those specified in sub-section 2 of section 4 of the 1976 Act. . . . In my view a Court would be justified in concluding in the circumstances of our present times, under our Constitution and of the rights conferred by the Family Home Protection Act, 1976, that the loss of the statutory veto represented good reasons within the meaning of Section 4 of the Partition Act, 1968[8]

12.006 This view on the relationship of a claim under the Partition Acts and the Family Home Protection Act, 1976, was endorsed subsequently by Finlay P. in *A.L. v J.L.*[9] The wife was seeking to establish her interest in the family home, an order dispensing with the consent of her husband to the sale of the home and an order for sale *in lieu* of partition. Finlay P. did not refer to *O'D. v O'D.*, nor did he consider the jurisdictional basis of an order for partition. However, at page 6, he stated with regard to the relationship between the Acts that, having "regard to the provisions of the Family Home Protection Act, 1976, in the absence of an agreement between the parties, an order for sale cannot in my view be made under the Partition Acts unless the Court is also satisfied that it should dispense with the consent of the non-agreeing spouse under section 4 of the 1976 Act."

12.007 Murphy J's consideration of the jurisdiction to order partition or sale *in lieu* thereof on a "chicken before the egg" approach left the questionable basis of the jurisdiction unresolved. *F.F. v C.F.*[10] remedied this. The case came before Barr J. on appeal from the decision of the then President of the Circuit Court that he had power to make an order for sale *in lieu* of partition notwithstanding the repeal of the Act for Joint Tenants 1542 by the Statute Law Revision (Pre Union/Irish statutes) Act of 1962. This point of law was argued as a preliminary issue on the appeal. Barr J.

---

8 Presumably similar reasoning will apply to applications under the Judicial Separation And Family Law Reform Acts, 1989 seeking orders for sale in lieu of partition of the family home.
9 7 February 1984, unreported, High Court.
10 [1987] ILRM 1.

determined that there was no doubt that the Act of 1542 had indeed been repealed. The issue then was the construction to be placed on section 2(1) of the 1962 Act. This is in the following terms: "This Act shall not affect any existing principle or rule of law or equity, or any established jurisdiction, form or course of pleading, practice or procedure, notwithstanding that it may have been in any manner derived from, affirmed or recognised by any enactment hereby repealed." Barr J. stated that it "is evident that this provision is intended to be a safety-net to prevent, inter alia, the inadvertent extinction of any principle or rule of law or equity which is derived from any of the repealed statutes and which is not otherwise provided for in law." He then referred to the Dáil Debates on the second reading of the relevant bill and concluded that the Oireachtas had no intention of interfering with any legal right or principle of law which might have been created by or derived from any of the statutes which it was decided to repeal.

12.008 The point was raised on behalf of the appellant that the primary right to partition originating in the Act of 1542 had been repealed, and that as the right to seek a sale of the property *in lieu* of partition was ancillary to the right to partition, the right to seek a sale was dependent on the continued existence of the latter. Barr J. dealt with the argument shortly, having "no doubt that the right [to partition] is within the meaning and intent of the phrase 'any existing principle or rule of law or equity' therein contained and that it is a right derived from the repealed Act of 1542." Accordingly he held that the right of a joint tenant to partition, subject to the discretion of the court, was preserved.

12.009 The facility of applying under the Partition Acts remains useful in certain circumstances. Orders pursuant to the Acts may be made as an ancillary order to an order for judicial separation under section 16(f) of the Judicial Separation and Family Law Reform Act, 1989. In addition, this procedure may be appropriate where a decree of nullity has been granted in respect of the marriage of the parties. An application under the Married Women's Status Act, 1957, or under the Family Home Protection Act, 1976 is not then possible and the presumption of advancement does not apply. Accordingly, one method of resolving the property issues between the parties could be to apply under the Partition Acts, making use of the law of trusts, including the presumption of a resulting trust, and the taking of accounts and enquiries to establish the shares and estates and interests of the parties.

Vendor and Purchaser Act 1874

12.010 As the title of this Act[11] suggests, its provisions concern the relationship between vendors and purchasers. They are availed of to ask

---

11 37 & 38 Vict. c. 78. The discussion hereinafter is restricted to the relevance of this Act to matters relating to family property.

the High Court, by means of a special summons in accordance with section 9 to give its view of or direction on any requisition or objection, or in respect of any claim for compensation or any other question arising out of a contract. Questions as to the existence or validity of the contract are not referable to the court in this manner. The procedure under the Act was used in a number of cases following the enactment of the Family Home Protection Act, 1976 to clarify some of the conveyancing uncertainties which arose. There are two important cases which reflect on the continuing efficacy of the Act in family law matters.

12.011 In *Mulligan v Dillon*[12] McWilliam J. was asked to determine a number of matters arising out of requisitions raised. In order to substantiate the reply that the premises were not a family home, the vendor furnished not one but four draft statutory declarations for approval. The primary declaration was by the vendor herself and contained a full explanation of the circumstances of the acquisition of the property and of her subsequent residence in it, negativing any question of residence, visitation, occupation or accommodation therein by her husband. The other declarations were by the vendor's children and corroborated that of the vendor, varying only as to the periods referred to. The purchaser's rejoinder noted the contents of the drafts and stated that one or other course of action must then be followed. Firstly, a statutory declaration by the vendor's husband corroborating the vendor's declaration must be furnished or, secondly, a court order declaring the premises are not a family home must be obtained. The vendor replied by indicating that a special summons would be issued. McWilliam J. was asked to determine firstly whether the premises were a family home within the meaning of section 3 of the Family Home Protection Act 1976, and secondly, whether the defendant was a *bona fide* purchaser for value within the meaning of section 3. McWilliam J. was of the view that the parties were under a misapprehension as to the appropriate steps to be taken under an investigation of title on a sale and as to the function of the court. It was not the court's function, he said, to assume the onus of investigating title. It is for the court to decide the legal position, "whether good title has been shown or whether the vendor was bound to furnish further or better evidence of title." He further indicated that in the instant case it was for the defendant purchaser to consider the particulars furnished in the vendor's affidavit, make such further or better enquiries as she may be advised and then decide whether to refuse or accept the title. As no argument has been addressed on the law applicable to the rejoinder of the defendant, he declined to pronounce upon it.

12.012 Within the limits of the judgment there are strong indications of the usefulness of the procedure under the Act as it relates to family law. *Reynolds and anor. v Waters*[13] considered the matter further. The first-

12 7 November 1980, unreported, High Court.
13 [1982] ILRM 335.

named plaintiff had contracted with the defendant for the sale of his home. In reply to requisitions, the first-named plaintiff's solicitors set out that the premises were not a family home and gave the reasons for this. In addition, a draft statutory declaration was furnished to confirm the reply. The defendant' solicitors were not prepared to accept this and required either the consent of the first-named plaintiff's wife to the proposed sale or alternatively a joint declaration by the first-named plaintiff and his wife that the premises were not a family home. The vendor's solicitors replied to this that they were not prepared to furnish a consent by the vendor's wife and that the draft declaration of the vendor was perfectly adequate. Subsequently, the vendor obtained a court order dispensing with his wife's consent to the sale. Proceedings were then instituted by the vendor seeking interest from the purchaser due to his default in not completing in accordance with the contract. The purchaser submitted that he had not been bound to accept the vendor's declaration because the vendor's financial interest called into question his trustworthiness justifying a request for corroboration.

12.013 Costello J. stated the issue as follows. Should a vendor who has been furnished with a declaration stating that the premises is not a family home including an outline of the reasons for same accept this or seek a corroborating declaration or seek a court order that the premises are not a family home in the absence of a corroborative declaration.

Two of Costello J's comments are instructive. He stated at 338 that in this case "the purchaser's legal advisor's were excessively cautious and that the vendor's solicitor was correct in his view that the purchaser's requirement's were unreasonable." He further stated that there

is no general principle to the effect that a prudent purchaser should not accept the uncorroborated statutory declaration of a vendor merely because the vendor is gaining financially from the transaction. And it seems to me that if (a) the purchaser's solicitor has made all proper inquiries . . .; and (b) has been informed of facts which, if true, establish that the dwelling is not a family home and that these facts will be verified by statutory declaration; and (c) neither the purchaser nor his solicitor has any reason to doubt the accuracy or the veracity of the statements in the proposed statutory declaration; then it is not reasonable for the purchaser's solicitor to insist on corroboration of the vendor's declaration and in its absence to call on the vendor to obtain a declaration from the court. By accepting the draft declaration in such circumstances he will have done all that he can reasonably be required to do. Should it subsequently transpire that due to carelessness or fraud he had been misinformed and that the premises were in fact a family home, then the purchaser would have acquired the property in good faith and if full value was paid for it the conveyance will be protected by section 3(3)(a) of the Act.

This dictum of Costello J. is very useful in that it indicates what the legal position would be if there were a problem with the statutory declaration furnished.

Family Law Act, 1981

Property disputes between engaged persons

12.014 This Act provides (in section 3) that any property given to either or both of two persons who have agreed to marry each other by any other person is presumed to be given, in the absence of evidence to the contrary, to both of them jointly and subject to return at the request of the donor or his personal representative if the marriage does not take place for whatever reason. Where one of the parties to an agreement to marry gives the other a gift of property, including an engagement ring, it is presumed, in the absence of evidence to the contrary, firstly, that the gift was given subject to return at the request of the donor if the marriage does not take place for any reason other than the donor's death, and secondly, that the gift was unconditional if the marriage does not take place due to the death of the donor.

12.015 Section 5 of the Act is of great importance to the law of property. It provides in subsection 1 that the rules of law relating to the rights of spouses concerning property in which either or both of them has or have a beneficial interest shall apply in relation to any property in which they or either of them had a beneficial interest while the agreement was in force as they apply to spouses in similar circumstances. There is no definition of the expression "the rules of law relating to the rights of spouses in relation to property." It has been suggested that this might possibly involve the application of the Family Home Protection Act, 1976 and the Succession Act, 1965 to parties to an agreement to marry.[14] This might appear to stretch the interpretation of the provisions in that, if this was the intent, it would have been reasonable to expect such legislation to be specifically referred to. Nonetheless, this construction is possible using reasoning similar to that adopted by Barr J. in *F.F. v C.F.*[15] concerning the Partition Acts, 1868–76.

12.016 Subsection 2 specifically applies section 12 of the Married Women's Status Act 1957 to any dispute arising between persons who were party to an agreement to marry which has been terminated concerning property in which either or both of them had a beneficial interest while the agreement was in force. The result of this is, presumably, to apply all the case law under section 12 to this new context. There is as yet no judgment interpreting the effect of this subsection. Disputes involving the interpretation of the subsection are inevitable at some point, although, given the

---

14 See Power, *The Family Law Act, 1981—Yet Another Pandora's Box*, (1985) 79 Gazette of the Incorporated Law Society of Ireland 169. But c/f O'Donnell, *Conveyancing and the Family Home*, Lecture No. 146, Society of Young Solicitors.

15 1987 ILRM 1; see **12.007**.

unusual context, and the possibilities of resolution prior to or at hearing, the matter may remain unresolved for some time. It is interesting to note that the 1989 revised edition of the Incorporated Law Society's *Requisitions on Title* continue to refer to this Act notwithstanding the widespread view in the profession that the Act's provisions have no substantive effect. The Judicial Separation and Family Law Reform Act, 1989 may also have conveyancing implications given the wideranging ancillary property orders concerning the interest of one or other spouse in the property.

12.017 A practical difficulty arises from the terminology used in the provisions of the Act regarding the use of the expression "agreement to marry" rather than "engagement" and whether there is a difference between them. Certainly there can be no argument that the commonly used term is "engaged" or "engaged to be married". There is a difference in that there may be no formal engagement but there may be an agreement to marry, either express or tacit. This would then create difficulties as to the application of the 1981 Act.

12.018 The relevant sections of the Act only apply to persons who were "engaged" and whose engagement to marry has been terminated. One potential difficulty concerns the position of persons who remain "engaged" but who have a dispute about property in which one or both of them has a beneficial interest. It would appear that section 5 does not apply to them, and, accordingly, that the rules of law relating to the property of spouses do not apply. The matter is of some practical importance, as it very often occurs that "engaged" couples purchase a property/family home prior to the marriage. If a dispute arises in relation to the property at this stage, the non-spousal property rules will apply. This, it is submitted would be an illogical result of the legislation and must be considered to have been the result of an oversight. Indeed the terminology of the Act is confusing in that it refers to "agreements to marry" whereas the marginal notes consistently refer to "engagements to marry" and "engaged couples", as does the long title which refers to persons who have been "engaged to be married". The use of the term engagement, and its grammatical variations, would have firstly produced a more precise text as well as terminology which any layperson could readily understand and identify with.

12.019 The value of section 5 in allowing parties to a terminated agreement to marry to resolve property disputes under the section 12 procedure is outweighed by the vagueness of the term "rules of law" and by the fact that the section only applies to parties whose agreement to marry has been terminated. There are also difficulties in establishing proof that the agreement has been terminated and proof that the parties had a beneficial interest in the property while the agreement was in force.

Property disputes between cohabitees

12.020 Another difficulty of more practical consequence concerns property disputes between cohabitees,[16] as the provisions of the 1981 Act do not apply. The circumstances of any given case may be exactly similar to those occurring in the case of married persons, that is, one partner may have contributed to the purchase of the property in the name of the other, etc. What therefore is the legal position governing such claims? In *McGill v S.*[17] Gannon J. held that the presumption of advancement, does not apply to cohabitees. He went on to conclude that an indirect contribution by a cohabitee cannot generate a beneficial interest in the absence of an explicit agreement that it should do so. However, authority to the contrary is found in *Power v Conroy.*[18] McWilliam J. considering facts similar to those in McGill, with the addition that there were both direct and indirect contributions, stated:

> From these cases[19] it appears to me that the correct approach is to try and ascertain what sums have been paid by the parties towards the acquisition of the house and in doing this I must take into account such contributions towards the household living expenses made by either party as to enable the other party to make such payments as were made by him or her. Having done this I should treat the house as being held by the defendant on trust for the parties in the shares which they contributed either directly or indirectly towards it's purchase.

12.021 An assessment of the likely line of authority the courts might follow in such matters is very difficult; however, it is submitted that the increased attention being given in more recent times to constitutional rights of the family may have a bearing. The argument that a wife may, by virtue of her work as a home-maker, acquire a beneficial interest, insofar as it derives from Article 41, cannot apply to a cohabitee.

Checklist: instructions in property disputes

12.022 The following checklist should be used when taking instructions in property disputes:

1. *Full address of the family home.* This is important as the ultimate orders may affect the title and also if there is a suspicion that the other spouse may have debts which could be registered against the title and finally because it may at some point be necessary to lodge a *Lis Pendens* or register an inhibition.

---

16 See further Cooney: *Wives, Mistresses and Beneficial Ownership*, (1979) 14 Ir. Jur. (n.s.) 1. For a consideration of the relevant English authorities on property disputes between co-habitees, see Cretney, *Principles of Family Law*, 4th ed., (1984) at pages 660 et seq. See also the interesting case of *Calverley v Green* (1984) ALR 483, a decision of the High Court of Australia.
17 [1979] IR 283.
18 22 February 1980, unreported, High Court.
19 *Conway v Conway* [1976] IR 254 and *L. v L.* 21 December 1979, unreported, High Court.

2. *The estates and interests in the property.* It is often the case that a client may not know if she, more so than the man, has any estate or interest in the property and may often not know if the property is held as a tenancy in common or as a joint tenancy. Usually the client will be aware of matters such as the family home being rented or whether there is a mortgage over the property. Obviously the client should also instruct concerning the date of acquisition of the property.

3. *Similar details in respect of any other property* of the spouses as it may well be that a claim lies in respect of properties other than the family home. Also included here should be similar details in respect of a previous family home of the parties or any previous property owned by the spouses or either of them.

4. *Nature of the claim being made* (i) By this stage enough information should be to hand to give a sufficient outline of the circumstances of the property and its ownership. One should firstly enquire as to how the property was acquired and then seek full details of the basis for the claim, for example, a pattern of direct contributions to the mortgage repayments over a period of years, or a suggestion that the property was purchased in the joint names of the parties, yet transferred in the name of one spouse solely.

(ii) It is now essential to enquire as to *any improvements* made to the property by either spouse.

5. *Documentary evidence of the above matters.* The client should be asked to collect any documents which s/he has to support the basis of the claim s/he wishes to make. In this regard, matters of importance would be receipts of direct payments of the mortgage, receipts of the payment of other household bills which the other spouse was responsible for, invoices and receipts in respect of household improvements.

6. *Any agreement on matters relating to the property.* The client should be asked at this point if there ever was any agreement between the spouses in respect of matters affecting the basis of the claim. This is of particular importance where indirect contributions or improvements are concerned. This heading includes any agreement concerning previously owned property and any agreement by the spouses that one would work outside the family home in consideration of the other managing the home and family, if any.

7. *Family Law Act, 1981.* If the dispute concerns parties who are not married one should enquire if there ever was an "agreement to marry" and consider if the agreement has been terminated.

12.023 In addition searches should be carried out in the Land Registry and a copy of the folio or land certificate should be bespoken. If the property concerns a farm holding or other tract of land over and above the site containing the family home, it is advisable to attach a map of the property. If the property is known to be unregistered land, or if it fails to show up in the Land Registry search, a search in the Registry of Deeds bespeaking a copy of the memorial is needed. If searching fails to identify any property owned by the parties, it may well be that the party has an alias or popular name due to the common occurrence of that persons' proper name. If such is the case, the searches should be carried out again bearing the aliases in mind. There is a possibility that property may have been registered in or conveyed into the unmarried name of the wife.

12.024 Other matters on which detailed instructions should be sought include: list of items of household chattels over which there may be a dispute; ownerships of stocks or shares; details of directorships held by either party; other items of personal property not falling within the term household chattel, for example, racehorses, motor vehicles.

Forms and Precedents

12.025 Transfer of the family home to joint names with consent of building society

LAND REGISTRY

FREEHOLD

FOLIO _____   **COUNTY OF** _____

TO THE REGISTRAR OF TITLES

TRANSFER dated the   **day of**   **198**

WHEREAS:

1. X is the registered and absolute owner of the lands comprised in Folio   of the Register of Freeholders of the County of   subject to the charge in favour of the   Building Society registered as a burden at entry No.   in part Three of the said folio.

2. X is desirous of transferring the lands and premises comprised in the said folio into the joint ownership of himself and his lawful spouse Y.

3. The   Building Society (hereinafter called "The Society") has agreed to consent to the said Transfer on the terms hereinafter appearing.

NOW THIS INDENTURE WITNESSETH:

1. X in consideration of the natural love and affection he bears for his wife hereby transfers the entire property comprised in Folio   of the Register of Freeholders of the Counry of   to X and Y as joint tenants absolutely subject to all existing Charges thereon.

2. The address and description of the Transferees in the State for the service of notice are:

3. X and Y hereby jointly and severally covenant with the society to perform the Mortgagors Covenants contained in the Charge registered at Burden number in part Three of the said folio.

4. In consideration of the covenant contained in Clause 3 hereof, the Society hereby consents to the transfer of the property comprised in the said folio to the said X and Y jointly, subject to the aforementioned charge.

IT IS HEREBY CERTIFIED by the said X and Y that they being the persons becoming entitled to the entire beneficial interest in the said property hereby transferred that they are qualified persons within the meaning of Section 45 of the Land Act 1965 being both Irish Citizens.

IT IS HEREBY FURTHER CERTIFIED by the said X and Y that they are related to each other as lawful husband and wife and that the property hereby transferred is the Family Home within the meaning of Section 2 of the Family Home Protection Act 1976 and that exemption from Stamp Duty is claimed in respect of the within Transfer under the provisions of Section 14 of the said Act.

IN WITNESS WHEREOF the parties hereto have set their hands and affixed their seals the day and year first herein written.

SIGNED SEALED AND DELIVERED
by the said X
in the presence of:

SIGNED SEALED AND DELIVERED
by the said X and Y
in the presence of:

PRESENT when the Common Seal
of the   Building Society
was impressed hereon:

12.026 Draft voluntary conveyance/assignment of family home into joint names of husband and wife

THIS INDENTURE made the   day of   19

BETWEEN   of

(hereinafter called "the Grantor" which expression shall where the context so admits or requires include his executors and administrators) of the first part   of   (hereinafter called "the Trustee") of the second part and   of   (hereinafter called "the Grantees" which expression shall where the context so admits or requires include the survivor of them and their executors, administrators and assigns) of the third part.

WHEREAS: [Note: recite here the title of the Grantor, for example. . . .]

1. The Grantor is seised of the premises described in the Schedule hereto (hereinafter called "the premises") for an estate in fee simple in possession.

2. By Mortgage (hereinafter called "the Mortgage") dated the day of   19   and made between the Grantor of the one part and   (hereinafter called "the Mortgagees") of the other part the said premises were assured to the Mortgagees (subject to the proviso for redemption therein contained) and to secure payment of the principal sum therein specified with interest thereon at the rate therein and further subject as therein.

3. The Grantor is desirous of conveyancing/assigning the premises unto himself and his wife as joint tenants and the Trustee has agreed to join these presents for the purpose and in the manner hereinafter appearing.

NOW THIS INDENTURE WITNESSETH that in consideration of the natural love and affection which the Grantor bears for his wife the Grantor hereby conveys/assigns unto the Trustee **ALL THAT AND THOSE** the premises described in the Schedule hereto **TO HOLD** the same unto and to the use of the Trustee upon trust for the Grantees as joint tenants in fee simple (subject to the mortgage)/for all the residue now unexpired of the said term of   years granted by the Lease subject to the yearly rent thereby reserved and to the covenants on the part of the Lessee and conditions therein contained and subject to the mortgage and all moneys payable thereunder.

NOW THIS INDENTURE FURTHER WITNESSETH that the Trustee as Trustee at the request and by the direction of the Grantees hereby **CONVEYS/ASSIGNS UNTO THE GRANTEES** the premises described in the Schedule hereto/**TO HOLD** the same unto and to the use of the Grantees as joint tenants in fee simple subject to the mortgage and all moneys payable thereunder/**TO HOLD** the same unto the Grantees as joint tenants for all the residue now unexpired of the said term of years granted by the Lease subject to the yearly rent thereby reserved and to the covenants on the part of the Lessee and conditions therein contained and subject to the Mortgage and all moneys payable thereunder and the Grantees hereby covenant with the Grantor that the Grantees will henceforth pay the said yearly rent reserved by and perform and observe the covenants on the part of the Lessee and conditions contained in the Lease and will keep the Grantor effectually indemnified against all actions proceedings costs expenses claims or demands by reason or on account of the non-payment of the said rent or any part thereof or the breach, non-performance or non-observance of the said covenants and conditions or any of them and the second named Grantee hereby covenants with the Grantor that she shall jointly and severally with the first named Grantee pay all principal moneys and interest secured by and henceforth to become due under the Mortgage and perform and observe the other covenants and conditions expressed or implied therein on the part of the Grantor.

IT IS HEREBY CERTIFIED by the Grantees (and each of them) who become entitled to the entire beneficial interest in the property hereby assured that they are both Irish citizens and as such are duly qualified persons within the meaning of Section 45 of the Land Act 1965.

AND IT IS FURTHER HEREBY CERTIFIED that the premises herein assured are a "family home" within the meaning of the Family Home Protection Act 1976 and that the transaction hereby effected is within the meaning of Section 14 of the Act.

IT IS FURTHER HEREBY CERTIFIED by   that he/she the person entitled to the entire beneficial interest in the property hereby assured is related to the person heretofore entitled to the entire beneficial interest as a (lawful) spouse/child/father/mother.

IN WITNESS whereof the parties hereto have hereunto signed their names and affixed their seals the day and year first herein written.

SCHEDULE

ALL THAT AND THOSE premises comprised in folio   of the Register of Freeholders, County   , and known as and situate at 13 ABCD Road in

Sworn etc.

12.027 Draft affidavit of spouse seeking to have notice of the fact of the marriage registered on folio

THE LAND REGISTRY

FOLIO _____   **COUNTY OF** _____

TO THE REGISTRAR OF TITLES

I, C, B, Company Director of   , in the County of   aged 18 years and upwards make oath and say as follows:
  1. I am the lawful spouse of A B who is the registered owner of the lands and premises comprised in Folio   of the Register of the County

of   situate at   and known as

2. I say that I married the said A B on the   date of   19
   at   Church, in the County of
   and I beg to refer to the original of the marriage certificate recording
   the said marriage upon which marked with the letter "A" I have
   signed my name prior to the swearing hereof.

3. I say that the lands and premises comprised in the above Folio are a
   Family Home within the meaning of Section 2 of the Family Home
   Protection Act 1976 in that the premises was where the said A B and I
   resided together after our marriage.

4. Accordingly, I seek registration of the fact of my marriage to the said
   A B upon the said Folio pursuant to Section 12 of the Family Home
   Protection Act 1976.

Sworn etc.

**12.028 Draft High Court Summons and claim in respect of property
dispute between spouses**

THE HIGH COURT

In the matter of the Married Womens Status Act 1957 and in the matter of
the Partition Acts 1868–76 and in the matter of the Family Home
Protection Act 1976.

BETWEEN:

MARY SMITH	Applicant
and	
JOHN SMITH	Respondent

To: JOHN SMITH

of:

In the County of:

This Special Summons is to require you to attend before the Master at the
Four Courts, Dublin 7, on the   day of   at
O'Clock in the forenoon at the hearing of this Summons, issued on the
11th day of   and if you do not attend in person or by solicitor at
the time and place aforesaid, such order will be made and proceedings
taken as the Court may think just and expedient, and Take Notice that if
you wish to attend and to be heard, you should first enter an appearance.

By Order—The Hon. Thomas Finlay.

Chief Justice of Ireland the   day of   in the Year of Our
Lord One Thousand Nine Hundred and Ninety.

N.B. This Summons is required to be served not less than four days before
the return day mentioned therein (exclusive of the day of service).

SPECIAL ENDORSEMENT OF CLAIM
THE PLAINTIFF'S CLAIM IS FOR:

1. Pursuant to the Married Women Status Act 1957 and in particular Section 12 thereof for
   a) An Order that the Plaintiff is entitled to the entire beneficial interest in and the ownership of the dwellinghouse at   in the County of   and the contents thereof or alternatively such share or portion thereof as the Court may see fit.

2. Pursuant to the Family Home Protection Act 1976, Section 4, for an Order dispensing with the consent of the defendant to the sale of the Family Home at

3. Pursuant to the Partition Acts 1868/76 and in particular Sections 3 and 4 thereof for an Order for a Sale of the Family Home at   in, the county of   and a division of the proceeds of sale in such a proportion between the Plaintiff and the Defendant as the Court shall see fit.

4. If necessary, an Order that Accounts and Enquiries be taken.

5. Such further or other Orders as this Honourable Court may see fit.

6. The costs of these proceedings.

Signed _____
solicitor for the Plaintiff.

12.029 In relation to proceedings in the High Court, see further, S.I. No. 97 of 1990, Rules of the Superior Court (No. 1), 1990. This inserts a new Order, Order 70A, with the Rules of the Superior Courts. It deals generally with proceedings in the High Court in Family Law matters, and particularly with Judicial Separation.

12.030 Draft High Court affidavit in respect of property dispute between spouses

THE HIGH COURT

IN THE MATTER OF THE MARRIED WOMENS STATUS ACT 1957 AND IN THE MATTER OF THE PARTITION ACTS, 1868/76 AND IN THE MATTER OF THE FAMILY HOME PROTECTION ACT 1976.

BETWEEN

MARY SMITH

Plaintiff

and

JOHN SMITH

Defendant

327

AFFIDAVIT OF THE PLAINTIFF

I,   of
aged twenty one years and upwards **MAKE OATH** and say as follows:-

1. I am the plaintiff in the above entitled proceedings and I make this Affidavit from facts within my own knowledge save where otherwise appears and where so appears I believe same to be true.

2. I say that I married the Defendant John Smith on the   day of
    in

3. I say that there are two children of the marriage, A born on
    and B born on

4. I say that the proceedings herein relate to the family home at
    and to the contents of the
    family home.

5. I say that the property is comprised in Folio 1234 County
    , the title to which is vested in the sole name of the
    defendant, in fee simple.

6. (Please insert details of the money that was accumulated to enable the property to be purchased, e.g., the deposit, mortgage from Building Society, inheritance, loans from the family or relatives etc. If the finances involved the sale of a previous family home outline the circumstances of how that property was purchased, in whose name the legal title was vested, and how the proceeds of sale were divided and applied.)

7. (Detail the employment record and earning capacity of both spouses during the course of the marriage and prior to that and details of any financial assistance that either spouse may have been able to give to the family fund even though not fully employed e.g. part time work, help in the family business, gifts, inheritances, etc.)

8. (Please give a short history of why the application is being made, e.g. that the couple are separated and one is residing in the house with the children and the other spouse wishes to capitalise his/her interest in the property. Further, please state if it is possible to partition the property or that it would be more beneficial for all concerned for there to be a sale and division.)

9. (If the application relates to a family home application will have to be made to dispense with the consent of the other spouse to the sale.)

Sworn etc.

12.031 Draft Circuit Court claim in respect of property dispute between spouses

THE CIRCUIT COURT

_____ CIRCUIT   COUNTY OF _____

EQUITY CIVIL BILL

IN THE MATTER OF THE PARTITION ACTS, 1868–1876, AND IN THE MATTER OF THE FAMILY HOME PROTECTION ACT, 1976.

BETWEEN: **MARY CITIZEN**
                                                            Plaintiff

and

JOSEPH CITIZEN
                                                            Defendent

DRAFT INDORSEMENT OF CLAIM

The Plaintiff's claim is for

1. The Plaintiff's claim is as the wife of the Defendant and they were married to each other on the   day of   1983 at the . The Plaintiff and the Defendant herein are the owners as joint tenants of the dwellinghouse and premises situate at

2. Whereas the Plaintiff herein has instituted Proceedings against the Defendant herein for Judicial Separation on the grounds of the Defendant's adultery. The plaintiff is desirous of effecting a sale of the premises above referred to and claims that in all the circumstances of the case, a sale of the said premises and a distribution of the net proceeds of such sale is more beneficial to the Plaintiff and the Defendant herein, than a partition.

3. The rateable valuation of the dwellinghouse and premises situate at , does not exceed £200.

4. The Plaintiff's claim is for:-
   (1) An Order pursuant to the provisions of the Partition Acts 1868 to 1876 providing for the sale in lieu of partition of the dwellinghouse and premises situate at

   (2) If necessary, an Order for the taking of accounts and enquiries.

   (3) An Order providing for the distribution of the net proceeds of such sale   between the Plaintiff and the Defendant herein;

   (4) An Order directing the Defendant herein to execute all necessary documents to effect the sale as aforesaid;

(5) An Order pursuant to the provisions of Section 4 of the Family Home Protection Act 1976 dispensing with the consent of the Defendant herein to the said sale as aforesaid;

(6) Further and other relief;

(7) The costs of the proceedings.

Signed _____
Solicitor for the Plaintiff.

12.032 Precedent for Family Law Act, 1981

The Family Law Act 1981 refers to the Married Women's Status Act, 1957. There is no express reference in the 1981 Act to the format of the pleadings to be used. Section 5(2) provides for the application of section 11 of the 1957 Act to property disputes between persons whose agreement to marry has been terminated. This would appear to invoke the procedure/pleadings prescribed for the Married Womens Status Act, 1957. This interpretation is supported by the references in sections 6 and 7 of the 1981 Act to the application to Court being in a summary manner. There is no reference in S.I.s 158 or 244 of 1982 to the 1981 Act, and accordingly there is still some doubt on the point. The Circuit Court Family Law Office have ruled that such applications should be by way of Equity Civil Bill. Perhaps the appropriate approach would be to consult the local county registrar on the point prior to issuing.

12.033 If an application is ruled to be appropriate, it would be very similar to the precedent for section 12 of the Married Womens Status Act, 1957. The position would be very similar, with appropriate formal amendments, if an Equity Civil Bill was decreed appropriate. (See the precedent for a Partition Suit).

Chapter 13

SEPARATION PROCEEDINGS: FINANCIAL AND PROPERTY PROVISIONS

Introduction

13.001 This chapter is concerned with the financial and property orders which may be made ancillary to a decree of judicial separation under Part II of the Judicial Separation and Family Law Reform Act 1989. Some of the orders are not exclusive to separation proceedings. A periodical payments order made under the Act of 1989 is similar to a maintenance order which, as has been seen, may be obtained in separate proceedings. However, there are important differences between orders obtained under the Act of 1989 and orders made under the Family Law (Maintenance of Spouses and Children) Act 1976, especially as regards the factors which must be taken into account by the court in making awards. It is also possible to obtain, ancillary to a decree of separation, orders under section 12 of the Married Women's Status Act 1957 orders under sections 4, 5 or 9 of the Family Home Protection Act 1976 orders under sections 2 or 3 of the Family Law (Protection of Spouses and Children) Act 1981 orders for partition under the Partition Acts 1868 and 1876 and orders under section 11 of Guardianship of Infants Act 1964 all of which may also be obtained in separate proceedings. The criteria for making orders under these Acts are discussed in separate chapters.

13.002 In addition to these, the Act of 1989 introduces a number of ancillary orders which were not previously available in family proceedings. As a result, the court, in separation proceedings, now has available a wide range of options which it may employ, singly or in conjunction with others, to achieve a fair distribution of property and other resources between separated spouses. The new options include an order for secured periodical payments, an order for the payment of a lump sum, a property adjustment order, an order relating to the occupation of the family home, an order for the sale of the family home, an order extinguishing succession rights, and an order for the sale of property pursuant to the making of some of the aforementioned orders. The circumstances in which an application may be made under the Act of 1989 are discussed at **7.007–7.010** and the important question of whether a spouse may contract out of the right to apply for ancillary relief under the Act is discussed at **16.013–16.016**.

Preliminary orders and maintenance pending suit

13.003 Once the application for a decree of judicial separation has been issued, the applicant or the respondent may (without the need to institute separate proceedings) apply under sections 11/12 for preliminary orders which the court may make (where it appears proper to do so) before deciding whether or not to grant the decree itself. The preliminary orders are:

- (a) a barring or protection order under section 2 or section 3 of the Family Law (Protection of Spouses and Children) Act 1981,
- (b) a custody or access order or other orders on any question affecting the welfare of an infant, under section 11 of the Guardianship of Infants Act, 1964,
- (c) an order for the protection of the family home or of monies realised from conveyance of any interest in it under section 5 of the Family Home Protection Act 1976 and
- (d) an order for the protection of household chattels or any monies realised from their sale under section 9 of the Family Home Protection Act 1976.

13.004 Section 13 of the Act of 1989 provides for the making of a maintenance (i.e. periodic payments) order pending suit. Such orders may be made for the support of either spouse or of any dependent child of the family. The period during which such maintenance is to be paid may not begin earlier than the date of application and must end by the date the court determines whether or not to grant the decree. Although the court is empowered to order such periodical payments as it "considers proper", it must have regard to the wide ranging factors set out in section 20 which also apply to the various financial orders which may be made after a decree has been granted (see **13.020–13.038**). This is rather strange, as many of the factors set out in section 20 are obviously more relevant to the broader and longer-term exercise of determining financial provision following the grant of a decree, than to the necessarily more limited task of deciding what is needed for a spouse's or a child's support pending the decree.[1]

Periodicial payments and lump sum orders

Periodical payments

13.005 Once a decree of judicial separation has been granted, or at any

---

1 See section 22 of the (English) Matrimonial Causes Act 1973, which simply requires the court to make such maintenance order pending suit "as the court thinks reasonable".

time thereafter, the court may, on the application of either spouse, make a periodical payments order against one spouse in favour of the other and/or for the benefit of any dependent child of the family. A periodical payments order specifies the amount and times at which payments are to be made. The order may be backdated to the date when the separation application was issued, but no earlier. Any arrears of maintenance which arise from the backdating of the order may be ordered to be paid as a lump sum by a specified date. Under section 21(1) of the Act of 1989, a periodical payments order in favour of a spouse may be indefinite in duration, but it is subject to variation, discharge or suspension (under section 22 of the Act of 1989) in the event of changed circumstances or new evidence coming to light.

13.006 It is noteworthy that a periodical payments order is not described as an order "for the support of" the relevant spouse or child. This contrasts with a maintenance order pending suit made under section 13, or a maintenance order made under the Family Law (Maintenance of Spouses and Children) Act 1976. There is no need, as under the Act of 1976, to establish that the respondent has failed to provide such maintenance as is proper in the circumstances. Clearly, a periodical payments order will usually have the object of providing support for (in the sense of meeting the current needs of) the dependent spouse or children. However, the order may serve additional purposes. It may for example be made as part of an overall adjustment, in the interests of fairness, of the spouses' financial affairs following the breakdown of their marriage. The factors to be taken into account in making financial and property orders under the Act, which are set out in section 20, are wide enough to allow the court to employ periodical payment orders for this broad purpose. In the context, it should be noted that the discretionary bar of desertion (section 20(3)) only operates in the case of an order made for the support of a spouse. In the case of children see **13.022–13.046**.

Secured periodical payments

13.007 The court may order, pursuant to section 14(1)(b) of the Act, that specified periodical payments in favour of a spouse or dependent child should be secured "to the satisfaction of the court". This may involve the transfer of assets to trustees and the execution of a deed of security. The English courts have held[2] that security must be in the form of specific assets rather than a general charge on all of a spouse's assets, and that a covenant to make the payments is not an adequate form of security.

Lump sum orders

13.008 By sections 14(1)(c) and (d) of the Act the court may order the payment, in favour of a spouse or dependent child, of a lump sum or sums

---

2 See *Barker v Barker* [1952] P 184.

"of such amounts and at such time or times as may be so specified". Inter alia, by section 14(2)(a) of the Act a lump sum order may be made for the purpose of enabling a spouse to meet expenses and liabilities incurred in maintaining himself or herself, or any dependent child, prior to the making of the application. Similarly, where the lump sum order is made in favour of a dependent child, under section 14(2)(b) the court may take account of prior expenses or liabilities incurred by or for the benefit of the child. The court may order the lump sum to be paid by instalments and may, in such case, under section 14(2)(c) require the payments to be secured.

13.009 Presumably, the principal purpose for which the court will order the payment of a lump sum will be to adjust the capital assets of the parties, where such exist, in order to achieve a fairer distribution of assets in accordance with the considerations set out in section 20. Where, for example, the couple have been married for a considerable time and the husband has substantial capital, the court may take the view that the wife has earned a share in that capital. The English courts[3] have taken the view that a lump sum order should normally be regarded as a provision in its own right, rather than the capital equivalent of periodical payments. However, where a husband has capital but little income, the lump sum order may indeed be a better form of financial provision for the wife, than a periodical payments order. The lump sum order may also be appropriate where there is a danger that a spouse may remove assets from the jurisdiction[4] or where the enforcement of an order for periodical payments is likely to prove difficult.

Property adjustment orders

13.010 On granting a decree of judicial separation (or at any time thereafter) the court may, pursuant to section 15 of the Act, on the application of either spouse, make one or more of the following property adjustment orders:

A property transfer order

This is provided for in section 15(1)(a) and is an order that one spouse transfer to the other spouse any property to which the first spouse is entitled either in possession or reversion; or an order to transfer such property to any dependent child of the family, or to a named person for the benefit of such a child.

A settlement of property order

This is provided for in section 15(1)(b) and is an order for the settlement of property, as described above, for the benefit of the other spouse and/or any dependent child of the family.

---

3 See *Jones v Jones* [1971] 3 All ER 1201.
4 See e.g. *Brett v Brett* [1969] 1 All ER 1007.

An order to vary an ante or post-nuptial settlement

This is provided for in sections 15(1)(c) and (d) and is an order varying, for the benefit of the spouses and/or of any dependent child of the family, any such settlement made on the spouses, (including such settlements made by will or codicil); or an order extinguishing or reducing the interest of either of the spouses under any such settlement.

13.011 In relation to a property transfer order and a settlement of property order "property" probably includes income as well as capital.[5] It probably only refers to property which a spouse may claim as of right. This would seem to exclude income which may be paid to a spouse by trustees under a discretionary trust.[6] Also excluded may be property which the relevant spouse has no power voluntarily to transfer or settle.[7]

13.012 If English authority is followed regarding an order to vary an ante or post nuptial settlement the concept of such a settlement is likely to be broadly defined. Per Hill J. in *Prinsep v Prinsep*:

> The particular form of it does not matter. It may be a settlement in the strictest sense of the term, it may be a covenant to pay by one spouse to the other, or by a third person to a spouse. What does matter is that it should provide for the financial benefit of one or other or both of the spouses as spouses and with reference to their married state.[8]

The term "settlement" thus appears to include a separation agreement whether made orally or in writing.[9] This is a matter of some importance as the courts have not previously been given a power to vary the terms of separation agreements.[10] Provided that other conditions are met, a discretionary trust of which spouses are the subjects may constitute a "settlement", even though the spouses may claim nothing as of right.[11] A policy of life insurance taken out by a husband for the benefit of his wife may also be classified as a post-nuptial settlement.[12]

13.013 The power given to the courts to make property adjustment orders is one of the most radical under the Act of 1989. In particular, the power to order a transfer of property enables the court to achieve a fair distribution of property, including the matrimonial home, regardless of which spouse is legal owner of the property, and regardless of whether the other spouse has acquired an equitable interest by virtue of direct or indirect contributions. The courts are thus enabled to exercise much greater discretion

---

5 See *Style v Style* [1954] P 209.
6 *Milne v Milne* [1871] LR 2 P & D 295.
7 See *Hale v Hale* [1975] 2 All ER 1090.
8 [1929] P 225.
9 *Tomkins v Tomkins* [1948] 1 All ER 237.
10 In England a written separation agreement may be varied under section 35 of the Matrimonial Causes Act 1973. See also **16.010–16.011**.
11 Would this be the case where a spouse is simply included in a possible class of beneficiaries? See *Howard v Howard* [1945] 1 All ER 91.
12 *Gunner v Gunner* [1949] 2 All ER 771.

than is possible when dealing with applications under section 12 of the Married Women's Status Act 1957. These applications may consequently assume less significance in the context of proceedings for judicial separation.

13.014 It has yet to be seen how readily the courts will use their new powers. The tendency in England has been to regard property transfer and settlement orders as part of a final adjustment of property rights where a marriage has broken down irretrievably, typically in a divorce context. It may well be that the courts in Ireland will be reluctant to use such powers except when it is clear that the judicial separation represents a final break. However, the matters which the court is required to have regard to when exercising its power to make property adjustment orders generally are the same as those which apply in the case of periodical payments and lump sum orders. They are set out in section 20, and are discussed at **13.020–13.038**.

13.015 It is open to the court to consider and decide whether any property adjustment order or orders made in favour of a spouse should be made on one occasion only. Section 15(2) provides that this does not apply if, on the one occasion referred to, a spouse wilfully conceals information of a material nature relevant to the making of such an order (section 15(2)).

Miscellaneous ancillary orders

13.016 The court may, by section 16 of the Act, on granting a judicial separation or at any time thereafter (and on application by either spouse) make one or more additional ancillary orders. These include certain orders previously available in separate proceedings, which are discussed in separate chapters:

1. an order under section 12 of the Married Women's Status Act 1957, determining any dispute between the spouses as to the title to or possession of any property
2. an order under section 4, 5 or 9 of the Family Home Protection Act 1976
3. an order under section 2 or 3 of the Family Law (Protection of Spouses and Children) Act 1981
4. an order for the partition of property under the Partition Acts 1868 and 1876
5. an order under section 11 of the Guardianship of Infants Act 1964, concerning any dependent child of the family.

The factors relevant in making orders under the above Acts have not been altered, or added to, by the Act of 1989. In addition to the above ancillary orders, two entirely new orders have been introduced as follows:

An order relating to occupation of the family home

13.017 By section 16(a) of the Act the order is described as one "conferring on one spouse either for life or for such other period (definite or contingent) as the court may specify, the right to occupy the family home to the exclusion of the other spouse." The court is obliged to exercise this jurisdiction additional to that which arises under the Family Law (Protection of Spouses and Children) Act 1981 and section 19 of the Family Home Protection Act 1976. The court may, for example, make an order granting one spouse occupation, and excluding the other, in the absence of the proof of serious misconduct which is a normal prerequisite for a barring order made under the Act of 1981. In deciding whether to make an occupation order, the court must "have regard to the welfare of the family as a whole", and must take into consideration, in addition to the factors relevant to the making of financial and property orders which are specified in section 20, (a) that (under section 19(a)) where a decree of judicial separation is granted, it is not possible for the spouses to continue to reside together and (b) that (under section 19(b)) proper and secure accommodation should, where practicable, be provided for a dependent spouse and any dependent child of the family.

An order for the sale of the family home

13.018 Section 16(b) provides that the order may be made subject to such conditions as the court considers proper. This order is also additional to the jurisdiction of the Acts of 1981 and 1976, and, before making it, the court must take into account the same factors as in the case of an order relating to the occupation of the family home. The definition of "family home" in section 10 of the Act, (in relation to both of the above orders) is the same as that contained in section 2 of the Family Home Protection Act 1976.

Orders for the sale of property

13.019 These orders are provided for in section 18 of the Act. Where a court makes a secured periodical payments order, a lump sum order or a property adjustment order, it may by section 18(1) additionally thereafter at any time make a further order for the sale of any property in which either spouse has a beneficial interest. By virtue of section 18(3) the order for sale may include a provision requiring the making of a payment out of the proceeds of sale, and the court has power to attach other provisions as it thinks fit. However, by virtue of section 18(4) the power to order sale pursuant to a property adjustment order may not be exercised so as to interfere with a right to occupy the family home conferred by that order. Also, where a person, other than one of the spouses, has a beneficial interest in the property concerned, by section 18(b) the court must, before deciding whether to make an order for sale, give that person an opportunity to make representations, and take those representations into account.

Matters which the court must take into consideration

13.020 Section 20 of the Act of 1989 sets out the objective and matters which the court is required to have regard to, in deciding whether to make the following orders:

(a) an order for maintenance pending suit,
(b) a periodical payments order (secured or unsecured),
(c) a property adjustment order,
(d) an order relating to the occupation of the family home,
(e) an order for the sale of the family home.

In the case of the last two orders, additional matters must be taken into account, as set out at **13.017–13.019**.

General objective

13.021 The court is required by section 20(1) to "seek to ensure that such provision is made for any spouse or for any dependent child of the family as is adequate and reasonable having regard to all the circumstances of the case." Clearly, one of the objectives of the court, in making ancillary orders, is to try to cater for the basic accommodation and financial needs of the spouses and dependent children. Beyond this, the court is not given guidance as to its general objectives; rather it is given a list of particular matters to which it should have regard, (together with "all the circumstances of the case"), and it is left to determine for itself what weight should be attached to each. The particular matters to which the court must have regard vary slightly according to whether the court is exercising its powers in relation to spouses or dependent children. The position of dependent children is explained further at **13.041**. What follows is a list of the factors relevant to the exercise of the court's powers in respect of a spouse.

Financial resources

13.022 Section 20(2)(a) provides that the Court must have regard to:

the income, earning capacity, property and other financial resources which each of the spouses has or is likely to have in the forseeable future.

The task of determining the resources of the spouses is familiar in relation to maintenance applications made under the Family Law (Maintenance of Spouses and Children) Act 1976. The difficulties that the court may encounter in performing that task have already been discussed in that context; so too has the question of what types of resource may be taken into account. See **8.019–8.031**.

13.023 One important distinction between the above formula and that contained in the Act of 1976 is the reference to resources which a spouse is likely to have in the forseeable future. In maintenance applications under the Act of 1976, the courts have taken into account the earning prospects of either spouse under the heading of "earning capacity". However, they appear not to have taken into account prospects such as possible promotion or a likely inheritance. The English courts, in interpreting section 25(2)(a) of the Matrimonial Causes Act 1973 (as amended by the Matrimonial and Family Proceedings Act 1984) have taken the view that benefits to which a spouse may be contingently entitled in future may be taken into account, provided the contingency is not too uncertain or remote. In *Calder v Calder*[13] the order made in favour of the wife was increased by reason of the husband's prospects of succession under settlements contingent on him surviving his mother; the court ordered that the additional lump sum was not to be paid until after the mother's death.[14]

Financial needs and obligations

13.024 Section 20(2)(b) provides that the Court must also have regard to:

the financial needs, obligations and responsibilities which each of the spouses has or is likely to have in the forseeable future.

Once again, the assessment of needs, obligations and responsibilities of the spouses is familiar in the context of maintenance proceedings under the Act of 1976. (See **8.019–8.034**). Future needs have in fact been taken into account in such proceedings; though the Act of 1989 is different in that it expressly requires the court to do so.

Standard of living

13.025 Section 20(2)(c) provides that the Courts must also have regard to:

the standard of living enjoyed by the family before proceedings were instituted or before the spouses separated, as the case may be.

Usually, where a marriage breaks down and where as a result two households take the place of one, there are insufficient resources to enable the separated spouses to maintain their previous standard of living. This has been recognised in maintenance proceedings under the Act of 1976[15] and it is likely to be equally true in relation to proceedings for judicial separation. In rare cases decided under the Act of 1976, where the liable spouse has enjoyed considerable wealth, the courts have already made maintenance orders at a level which enabled the dependent spouse to live in the style which she formerly enjoyed.[15a]

Age of parties and duration of marriage

13.026 Section 20(2)(d) refers to:

the age of each spouse, the duration of the marriage and the length of time the spouses lived together.

---

13 [1975] 6 Fam. Law 242.
14 *Michael v Michael* [1986] Fam. Law 374, where there was uncertainty as to whether the wife would succeed under her mother's will.
15 See *R.H. v N.H.* 24 October 1985, unreported, Supreme Court, and **8.015**.
15aSee *L.B. v H.B.* [1980] ILRM 257 and **8.024**.

These matters may well be considered in conjunction with other headings. A spouse's age may, for example, be relevant to the question of her earning capacity; the duration of the marriage and period of cohabitation will usually have a bearing on the contribution which a dependent spouse has made to the welfare of the family.

13.027 Where the marriage has lasted only a short time and the wife is young and capable of earning her own living and she has not contributed in any significant way to the home, the order made in her favour may be modest.[16] On the other hand, where the wife is an older woman, even though the marriage may not have lasted long, the court may balance her needs, bearing in mind her age and earning capacity, against the husband's resources, and attempt to leave her in the position she might have enjoyed had the marriage continued.[17] Even in the case of a short marriage between young persons, the birth of a child or children is likely to make a difference to the award in favour of the wife who, regardless of her earning capacity, would be regarded as having made a significant contribution to the family.[18] Again, if the marriage, no matter how short, has caused the wife financial loss, the award to the wife is likely to reflect that fact.[19] Under the Act of 1976, the courts have refused to allow a maintenance order to be used to compensate a spouse for losses arising out of the marriage. See *J.S.J. v R.S.J.*, at **8.009**.

13.028 The reference to the length of time the spouses have lived together suggests that a long marriage, in which the couple cohabited only for a short time, may attract a lower order. In the English case of *Krystman v Krystman*[20] where a couple who had been married for 26 years lived together for only a fortnight, the court made no order in favour of the wife. On the other hand, it is possible that the court may take into account a long period during which the spouses cohabited preceding their marriage. Even if the expression, "the length of time the spouses lived together", is interpreted strictly as the length of time they were living together "as spouses", it would still be possible for the court to take account of pre-marriage cohabitation by virtue of the court's duty to have regard to all the circumstances of the case. Against this, it may be argued that, where a couple have chosen cohabitation rather than marriage, it would be contrary to public policy to treat the period of cohabitation as giving rise to rights and duties similar to those which arise from marriage.

13.029 The English courts have been more prepared to take into account pre-marriage cohabitation where the parties were unable to marry because

---

16 See *Khan v Khan* [1980] 1 All ER 497.
17 See *S. v S.* [1977] 1 All ER 56.
18 See *Cumbers v Cumbers* [1975] 1 All ER 1. See also section 20(2)(g).
19 See *Whyte-Smith v Whyte-Smyth* [1974] 119 Sol. Jo. 46, and *Abdureman v Abdureman* [1978] 122 Sol. Jo. 663.
20 [1973] 3 All ER 247.

one of them could not obtain a divorce. In *Kokosinski v Kokosinski*[21] the parties cohabited for 24 years before marrying because the husband a Polish refugee had been unable to obtain a divorce from his first wife in Poland. The second wife had been loving, faithful and hardworking and had brought up their child. In the circumstances, Wood J. took the view that it would offend a reasonable person's sense of justice not to take account of the period of cohabitation in making an order.[22] Where cohabitation is brief or irregular, the courts are highly unlikely to take account of it.[23]

Physical or mental disability of either spouse

13.030 Section 20(2)(e) provides that the Court must have regard to "any physical or mental disability of either spouse."[24] Clearly, these matters are relevant also in the context of financial needs under section 20(2)(b).

Contributions by each spouse

13.031 Section 20(2)(d) provides that the Court must have regard to:

the contributions which each of the spouses has made or is likely in the forseeable future to make to the welfare of the family, including the contribution made by each spouse to the income, earning capacity, property and financial resources of the other and any contribution by looking after the home or caring for the family.

This heading is of particular importance because it indicates that the court, when making financial and property orders under the act, is not merely concerned with meeting the needs of a dependent spouse, but has the additional function of deciding upon a fair distribution of capital assets based on the contributions, in money and in kind, of each of the spouses to the family and its assets. It seems clear, for example, that a court may, under this heading, take into account the contribution made by a dependent spouse as a home-maker in awarding that spouse an interest in the matrimonial home. (Whether this is possible in proceedings brought under section 12 of the Married Women's Status Act 1957 is, as has been explained, still a matter of controversy see **10.042**). The matter was expressed thus by the English Court of Appeal in *Wachtel v Wachtel*.[24]

. . . [T]he wife who looks after the home and family contributes as much to the family assets as the wife who goes out to work. The one contributes in kind, the other in money or money's worth. If the court considers that the home has been acquired and maintained by the joint efforts of both, then, when the marriage breaks down, it should be

21 [1980] 1 All ER 1106.
22 See also *Chaterjee v Chaterjee* [1976] 1 All ER 719, where a long period of post-divorce cohabitation was taken into account.
23 See e.g. *Hayes v Hayes* [1981] 11 Fam. Law 208.
24 [1973] 1 All ER 829.

regarded as the joint property of both of them, no matter in whose name it stands.

The reference, under this heading, to contributions likely to be made "in the foreseeable future", no doubt refers principally to any continuing obligations of support or caretaking which each spouse has in relation to any dependent child of the family.

Effect on earning capacity

13.032 Section 20(2)(g) provides that the Court must have regard to:

> the effect on the earning capacity of each spouse of the marital responsibilities assumed by each during the period when they lived together and, in particular, the degree to which the future earning capacity of a spouse is impaired by reason of having relinquished or foregone the opportunity of remunerative activity in order to look after the home or care for the family.

The court already, under section 20(2)(a), is required to have regard to the present and likely earning capacity of each of the spouses and, in doing so, will no doubt recognise the extent to which a spouse's earning capacity has been diminished by marriage. It is difficult to see how this section adds anything of substance to section 20(2)(a). It seems unlikely that section 20(2)(g) is intended to provide some form of compensation for loss of expected or potential earnings at the time of marriage; it would seem unfair to distinguish between two wives, living in a similar family situation and making an equal contribution, merely on the basis that prior to marriage, one was destined for stardom while the other had limited prospects. If there is to be a difference in treatment, differences in present and future earning capacities would appear more relevant than pre-marriage earning potential.

13.033 The reference to marital responsibilities assumed "during the period when [the spouses] lived together" is puzzling. The responsibility which typically inhibits a spouse from pursuing a career outside the family is the rearing of children; yet this responsibility is not necessarily confined to the period during which the spouses live together.

Statutory benefits or income

13.034 Section 20(2)(h) provides that the Court must have regard to: "any income or benefits to which either spouse is entitled to by or under statute". This would include child benefit and other social welfare payments.

Conduct of each spouse

13.035 Section 20(2)(i) refers to:

the conduct of each of the spouses, if that conduct is such that in the opinion of the court, it would in all the circumstances be repugnant to justice to disregard it.

The relevance of misconduct, or indeed exemplary conduct, by either spouse has been discussed fully in the context of maintenance proceedings under the Family Law (Maintenance of Spouses and Children) Act 1976. (See **8.035–8.048**). The above formula, introduced by the Act of 1989, is now applicable to such proceedings.

13.036 Most of what was said in the context of maintenance proceedings is also applicable to financial provision and property orders made pursuant to a judicial separation. The respective conduct of the spouses (with the exception of desertion) is likely to be ignored as a general rule. The court is, however, required to have regard to it where it would be repugnant to justice to disregard it. But, even where there has been conduct (good or bad) which cannot be disregarded, it is only one of the circumstances to be taken into account alongside all other relevant considerations set out in section 20.

13.037 In determining what conduct "it would in all the circumstances be repugnant to justice to disregard", there may be reason for some difference of emphasis between proceedings under the Act of 1976, where the only available order is for periodic maintenance payments, and proceedings under the Act of 1989, where the objective is broader than merely to meet the current needs of the dependent spouse. For example, where a wife is seeking an order requiring her husband to provide her with continuing maintenance, the court might take the view that it would be repugnant to justice to ignore a flagrant adulterous relationship on her part which is continuing at the time of her application. On the other hand, if the wife is seeking a share in matrimonial property, based on her undoubted contributions to the family over a lengthy period of time, her recent "misconduct" may be of less relevance. It is arguable that a spouse who has contributed to the welfare of her family during a long marriage and who has for that reason sacrificed personal career ambitions, deserves a share in the family assets regardless of recent misconduct, even though she may have forfeited her right to continuing maintenance.

The accommodation needs of either spouse

13.038 These needs must be taken into account by the court by virtue of section 20(2)(j). Consideration of the accommodation needs of either spouse may be relevant to the question of financial provision; it may also influence the making of orders relating to property. The power to order the sale of the family home is likely to be used in some cases to make available capital for the spouses to purchase separate accommodation.

Desertion

13.039 The court is not entitled to make an order under section 13 (maintenance pending suit), 14 (periodical payments and lump sum orders), 15 (property adjustment order) or 16(a) or (b) (occupation order or order of the sale of the family home), for the support of a spouse where that spouse has deserted and has continued to desert the other spouse up to the time of the institution of proceedings for judicial separation. The only exception is where, as set out in section 20(3), having regard to all the circumstances (including the conduct of the other spouse), the court is, of the opinion that it would be repugnant to justice not to make an order. By section 20(5) "desertion" includes conduct by a spouse which results in the other spouse, with just cause, leaving and living apart from that spouse, that is "constructive" desertion. The same rules apply to maintenance proceedings under the Family Law (Maintenance of Spouses and Children) Act 1976, and have been fully discussed in that context. (See **8.035–8.038**). The case law relating to desertion was discussed at **7.035–7.078**.

13.040 It is important to note that the desertion bar operates only where one of the above orders is made "for the support of a spouse". There may be instances where an order is made for a purpose other than support. The term "support" is not defined in the Act of 1989, nor is it used to define the general objective of the court in making financial or property orders; the word "provision" is preferred.[25] The term "support" is, however, used in section 5(1)(d) of the Family Law (Maintenance of Spouses and Children) Act 1976 to describe the purpose of a maintenance order made under that Act. In the context of that Act, the provision of "support" has come to be identified with an order whose purpose is that of meeting the current needs of a dependent spouse or child.[26] Although many ancillary orders made under the Act of 1989 will be for the purpose of meeting such current needs, there will be others which, in whole or in part, have other objectives. We have seen that the courts discretion under the Act of 1989 is wide enough to allow it to make lump sum or adjustment orders which have, as their object, not only support for dependents, but a fair distribution of family assets on the breakdown of marriage. Arguably, therefore, where (or insofar as) an order is made for the latter purpose, the desertion bar does not apply.

Provision for a dependent child of the family

13.041 The definition of "dependent child of the family", in section 10 of the Act of 1989 is the same as that contained in section 3(1) of the Family Law (Maintenance of Spouses and Children) Act 1976 as amended by section 16(b) of the Status of Children Act 1987. The definition is set out,

---

25 In section 20(1), maintenance pending suit is described (section 13) as being for the "support" of a spouse or dependent child of the family.
26 See *H.D. v D.D.* 8 May 1978, unreported, Supreme Court, and **8.008–8.009**.

and commented upon at **8.005–8.007**. The court may, on the application of either spouse, make any one or more of the following orders for the benefit of a dependent child of the family:

(a) An order for maintenance pending suit. (Section 13)
(b) A periodical payments (secured or unsecured) or lump sum order. (Section 14)
(c) A property adjustment order. (Section 15)

In the case of (a) above, payments are made to the applicant spouse for the support of dependent children of the family. In the case of (b) payments are ordered to be made to such person as may be specified in the order, for the benefit of the child. In the case of (c) above, a property transfer order may require transfer directly to the child or to a specified person for the benefit of the child; a settlement of property for the benefit of a child may be made on terms, and to trustees, determined by the court.

13.042 In exercising its powers under sections 13, 14 and 15, in relation to a dependent child of the family, by virtue of section 20(4) of the Act of 1989 the court must in particular have regard to the following matters.

(a) the financial needs of the child;
(b) the income, earning capacity (if any), property and other financial resources of the child;
(c) any physical or mental disability of the child;
(d) any income or benefits to which the child is entitled by or under statute.
(e) the manner in which he was being, and in which the spouses expected him to be, educated or trained;
(f) the considerations mentioned in relation to spouses in subsection 2(a), (b), (c) and (e) of [section 20];
(g) the accommodation needs of the child.

13.043 The court may not refuse to order maintenance for the support of a dependent child by reason of the desertion or other misconduct of the applicant spouse. Nor may such conduct be a ground for varying or discharging any part of a maintenance order providing for the support of a dependent child. Section 23(1) provides that every maintenance or variation order must specify what payments under the order are for the support of a dependent child. It should also be recalled that, while orders relating to occupation or sale of the family home under section 16 are not made specifically in favour of dependent children, the court must, under section 19(b) in making such orders, take into consideration, *inter alia*, the need to provide proper and secure accommodation for such children.

Order extinguishing succession rights

13.044 The court has power under section 17(1) on the application of either spouse, at any time after granting a decree of judicial separation, to consider making an order extinguishing the share that either spouse would otherwise be entitled to in the estate of the other spouse, as a legal right or on intestacy, under the Succession Act 1965. The court is obliged to make an order extinguishing such share in each of the following circumstances:

(a) Under section 17(2)(a) where the court is satisfied, having regard to the provisions of section 20, that adequate and reasonable provision of a permanent nature has been made to provide for the future security of the spouse whose succession rights are in question,

(b) Under section 17(2)(b) where the court is likewise satisfied that the case is not one where provision of a permanent nature needs to be made for the future security of such spouse or

(c) Under section 17(2)(c) where such spouse is not a spouse for the support of whom the court, having regard to the provision of section 20, made an order under section 14 (periodic payment and lump sum orders), section 15 (property adjustment orders) or section 16(a) (occupation orders), or

(d) Under section 17(2)(d) where the court is satisfied that such spouse is not a spouse for the support of whom the court would, likewise, have made an order under the same sections if an application had been made to it.

13.045 The old rule whereby a spouse, against whom a deceased had obtained a decree of divorce *a mensa et thoro*, was automatically precluded from taking any share in the estate of the deceased as a legal right or on intestacy[27] has been abolished. A "guilty" party will not, therefore, automatically lose succession rights. However, where it would be repugnant to justice to ignore it, "misconduct" may be taken into account by the court (under section 20) in deciding that it should not, or would not, make an order for the support of that spouse; in such case, the court would be bound, on application by the other spouse, to order the extinguishment of that spouse's succession rights. Similarly, where a spouse has been, or would be, refused support because of that spouse's desertion, extinguishment of succession rights must, on application, be ordered. If an application is not made, the deserting spouse's succession rights remain secure. The decree of judicial separation itself terminates any pre-existing desertion. Therefore, section 120(2) of the Succession Act 1965, which precludes a spouse from enjoying succession rights under the Act, where he has been in continuous desertion for a period of 3 years before the death of the other spouse, would not apply. Section 17 is ambiguous in one respect. It makes clear the circumstances (described above) in which the court must order the extinguishment of succession rights; it is unclear whether the court may order their extinguishment in other circumstances. It is possible that the court may regard itself as having a general discretion, under section 17(1), to consider whether it is just and reasonable to order extinguishment in circumstances not covered by section 17(2).

27 Succession Act 1965, section 120(2).

Variation and discharge of financial and property orders

13.046 The court has power under section 22 of the Act, on the application of either spouse, to vary or discharge certain orders, and to suspend temporarily or to revive any provisions of such orders. The orders concerned, set out in section 22(2), are:-

(a) An order for maintenance pending suit.
(b) A periodical payments order (secured or unsecured).
(c) Any part of a lump sum order requiring payment by instalments or requiring such instalments to be secured.
(d) An order relating to the occupation of the family home.
(e) An order for the sale of property.

The power to vary, discharge, suspend or revive is to be exercised subject to the provisions of section 20, and having regard to any change in the circumstances and to any new evidence.

13.047 In the case of an order for secured periodical payments, an application pursuant to section 22(6) of the Act for variation or discharge may be made following the death of the liable spouse, either by the other spouse or by the personal representatives of the deceased spouse. In either case however the application may not, except by permission of the court be made more than twelve months from the date on which representation in respect of the deceased's estate was granted. Where the personal representatives of the deceased distribute any part of the deceased's estate after the period of 12 months has elapsed, they are not liable on the ground that they should have anticipated the possibility that the court would permit an application to vary or discharge; (section 22(7)).

13.048 An order or any part of an order providing for the support of a dependent child, stands automatically discharged when the child ceases to be a dependent child of the family, by virtue of reaching the age of 16 or 21, as the case may be. The court, on application pursuant to section 22(3) of the Act is required to discharge the order if it is satisfied that for any other reason the child has ceased to be a dependent child of the family.

General considerations

13.049 The Act of 1989 has for the first time given the courts wide discretionary powers in relation to family provision and the distribution of family assets, where a judicial separation has been granted. There is, as yet, no case law to indicate the manner in which the courts will use their powers. The emphasis is likely to be on flexibility. Lord Justice Ormrod, commenting on the similar provisions of the English Matrimonial Causes Act 1973 said[28]

---

28 In *Martin v Martin* [1977] 3 All ER 762.

The rules are not very firm . . . It is the essence of such a discretionary situation that the court should preserve, so far as it can, the utmost elasticity to deal with each case on its own facts. Therefore, it is a matter of trial and error and imagination on the part of those advising clients. It equally means that the decisions of this court can never be better than guidelines. They are not precedents in the strict sense of the word.[1]

13.050 A particular word of caution is needed in relation to English precedents. Although many of the provisions of the Irish Act of 1989 are similar or identical to those contained in the English Act of 1973, the context is different. In England, the powers of the court are usually exercised in a divorce context, and the court will often be aware of the possibility that one or both spouses may re-marry. That possibility is not available in Ireland where the marital relationship will, in most cases, continue until the death of one of the spouses. It is therefore less possible in this country than in England for the courts to help the parties to achieve a "clean break", or in the words of Scarman J. "to encourage each to put the past behind them and to begin a new life which is not overshadowed by the relationship which has broken down."[29]

13.051 Even in England, the courts have recognised that the principle of the clean break is not always appropriate, particularly where dependent children require support, or one of the spouses is not in a position to become self-sufficient.[30] This situation arises more frequently in Ireland, where the participation rate of married women in the work force is lower than in most other European countries. The financial and property orders made under the Irish Act are, therefore, likely to be more strongly influenced than in England by the possibility that the period during which one spouse remains dependent, may be substantial.

13.052 In most cases, the principal concern of the court will no doubt be that of providing, in the fairest way possible, for the needs of family members, in relation to support and accommodation; and where the needs of children are involved, it may be anticipated that these will be accorded some priority. The decision for example as to which spouse should remain in occupation of the family home is likely in many cases to depend on which spouse has custody of the children.

13.053 Note — Section 29 of the Act gives the court jurisdiction to make a variety of orders in respect of transactions entered into with the intention of defeating a claim for financial relief. In *O'H. v O'H.* 22 June 1990, unreported, High Court, Barron J., held that the court had no power to set aside (under section 29(2)(b)) a disposition made before the coming into operation of the Act. An appeal is pending.

---

29 In *Minton v Minton* [1979] AC 593 at 608.
30 See for example *Moore v Moore* [1980] 11 Fam. Law 109.

Chapter 14

CHILD CUSTODY AND ACCESS DISPUTES

This chapter deals principally with disputes between married parents over the custody of or access to their children. It is not intended to deal with child custody or access disputes between unmarried parents or between parents and third parties, to which different legal and constitutional principles apply.

Private arrangements and court involvement

14.001 Inter-parental child custody and access disputes in the courts generally arise when a marriage breaks down and the parents are unable to agree on their own private arrangements relating to the care and custody of their children. The law allows the parents a great deal of autonomy in making appropriate arrangements for their children. These arrangements, as will be explained in chapter 16, may be embodied in a separation agreement. It is highly desirable that parents should try to agree upon arrangements and avoid litigation; agreed custody and access arrangements are more likely to afford satisfaction and be adhered to by parents than solutions imposed by a court.

14.002 As a general principle, provided that the children are not at risk,[1] the courts will not become involved in resolving custody or access issues unless one of the parents invites the intervention of the court; if the children are at risk care proceedings under the Children Act 1908 may be appropriate. Once an application for custody or access is made to the court the welfare of the child becomes the first and paramount consideration, and a court is entitled on that basis to set aside any pre-existing agreement between the parents.[1a] The Judicial Separation and Family Law Reform Act 1989 (section 3(2)) has for the first time introduced a procedure

1 In which case, care proceedings under the Children Act 1908 may be appropriate.
1a*Cullen v Cullen* (8 May 1970, unreported, Supreme Court).

whereby, before granting a decree of judicial separation, the court is required (whether the parents wish for it or not) to review provisions made for the welfare of the children. However for reasons of principle and of practicality the courts are unlikely except on rare occasions to disturb arrangements which have been freely negotiated and agreed between the parents.[2] The reasons of principle derive from Article 42.1 of the Constitution in which the State guarantees to respect the inalienable right and duty of parents to provide for the education (in the broadest sense) of their children. It would also usually be impractical for the court to make an order which goes against the wishes of both parents.

Guardianship

14.003 Because of its importance in custody and access disputes, the term "guardianship" requires explanation. It is a term used to denote a collection of rights and duties which a person—usually a parent—enjoys in respect of an infant. Although guardianship rights may be limited, and often have to be exercised jointly, they generally include the right to make decisions about, or at least to influence, all aspects of the upbringing of an infant, including education, health, religion and general welfare. Section 10(1) of the Guardianship of Infants Act 1964 describes every guardian as "a guardian of the person and of the estate of the infant unless, in the case of a guardian appointed by deed, will or order of the court, the terms of his appointment otherwise provide." Guardians have a corresponding duty to act for the welfare of the infant and, in the case of parental guardians, to maintain their dependent children and to provide according to their means for their education[3] and general welfare.

14.004 A parental guardian also usually enjoys the right to have custody of an infant—that is, the right to physical care and control of the infant. However this right like all guardianship rights is subject to limitation. In particular, where parents separate, one may lose custody of an infant by order of a court. In such a case, the non-custodial parent remains a guardian and continues to be subject to duties, including the duty to maintain the infant. The non-custodial guardian also has the right to be made aware of and consulted in relation to, major decisions and events affecting all aspects of the infant's upbringing. As stated by Walsh J. in *B. v B.*:

> If one parent is given custody of an infant to the exclusion, whether total or partial, of the other parent, that does not mean that the parent who loses custody is deprived of the other rights which accrue to him (or her) as guardian of the infant. A parent so deprived of custody can continue to exercise the rights of a guardian and, in my view, must be consulted

2 This has been the experience in England, Wales and Scotland. See J. Eekelaar: *Family Law and Social Policy* 2nd ed, 1984, chapter 4.
3 See Article 42.1 of the Constitution.

on all matters affecting the welfare of the child which . . . comprises the religious, moral, intellectual, physical and social welfare of the infant.[4]

14.005 Section 6(1) of the Guardianship of Infants Act 1964 provides that married parents are joint guardians of their infant children. The implications of joint parental guardianship are discussed at **14.014–14.016**. In the case of unmarried parents, the general principle is that the mother is during her lifetime the sole guardian of the infant[5] unless an order has been made by a court appointing the father to be a guardian.[6] The subsequent marriage of the natural parents will also result in the father becoming a guardian.

14.006 Special rules apply to the children of void or voidable marriages.[7] In the case of a voidable marriage which has been annulled, the parents will continue to be treated as joint guardians, provided that the nullity decree was granted after (or at some time during the period of ten months before) the birth of the infant. In the case of a void marriage, the parents will be joint guardians provided that the father reasonably believed that the marriage was valid at "the relevant time". The relevant time is either, (1) where the ceremony occured before the infant's birth, at some time during the period of ten months before the birth, or (2) where the ceremony occurred after the birth, at the time of the ceremony.[8] Unless the contrary is shown, under section 2(3)(b) it is presumed that the father had such a reasonable belief. An example would be where a party to a marriage which has been annulled by an ecclesiastical tribunal, but which remains valid at civil law, "re-marries" in a ceremony which is void at civil law. If the male partner in the "re-marriage" reasonably believes at the relevant time that that marriage is valid, then he becomes automatically a joint guardian of a child of that marriage. Because of the presumption of reasonable belief there is now in effect a presumption that all fathers in such situations are joint guardians of their children. It is irrelevant, in the context of a book which focusses on marriage breakdown, to detail the various ways in which non-parental guardians may be appointed. It should however be noted that a parental guardian may appoint by deed (or will) a person to be guardian after his (or her) death.[9]

---

4 [1975] IR 54 at 61.
5 Section 6(4), as amended by the Status of Children Act 1987, section 11.
6 Under section 6A of the Act of 1964, as inserted by the Status of Children Act 1987, section 12.
7 See the definition of "father" in section 2(1) and (3) of the Act of 1964, as amended by section 9 of the Act of 1987.
8 Section 2(3)(a)(ii) of the Act of 1964, as amended by section 9 of the Act of 1987.
9 See Act of 1964, section 7.

The statutory framework

Guardianship of Infants Act 1964

14.007 The involvement of a court in custody or access disputes usually arises from an application made under section 11 of the Guardianship of Infants Act, which provides:

> 11–(1) Any person being a guardian of an infant may apply to the court for its direction on any question affecting the welfare of the infant and the court may make such order as it thinks proper.
>
> (2) The court may by an order under this section—
>
> (a) give such directions as it thinks proper regarding the custody of the infant and the right of access to the infant of his father or mother; . . .

14.008 The court referred to is the District or Circuit Court, and possibly in exceptional cases the High Court (see **15.029.**). The applicant must be normally a guardian which, in the case of a child born within marriage, usually means the father or the mother. A natural father who is not a guardian may also apply for an access or custody order.[10] In *Oxfordshire County Council v J.H. & V.H.*[11] Costello J. allowed the local authority to make application under section 11 on the basis that, under the law of the domicile of the children who were the subjects of the proceedings, the County Council was their guardian. An infant, for the purposes of section 11(1) and (2)(a), is a child below the age of 18.[12] The child must be one in relation to whom the applicant is guardian, except where the applicant is the natural father. In the case of a married applicant section 6(1) provides that this includes a child of the marriage, or a child adopted in the State or abroad under an adoption order which is entitled to recognition within the State.[13] It does not include a child in relation to whom the applicant is only *in loco parentis*, unless the applicant has been appointed guardian of the child, for example, where the applicant has been appointed as a testamentary guardian by a deceased parent under section 7 of the Act of 1964, or has been appointed by the court under section 8. An application for directions under section 11(1) may be made, and may become effective, whether the parents are living together or apart. Directions relating to custody and access, applied for under section 11(2)(a), may be given while the parents are still residing together, but they are not enforceable until a separation occurs, and will cease to have effect if the parents continue to reside together for three months after the directions are given.[14]

---

10 Section 11(4) of the Act of 1964, as amended by the Status of Children Act 1987, section 13.
11 19 May 1988, unreported, High Court.
12 Age of Majority Act 1985, section 2.
13 See Act of 1964, section 2(1), as amended by the Status of Children Act 1987, section 9.
14 Section 11(3) of the Act of 1964, as amended by the Age of Majority Act 1985, section 6(a).

Judicial Separation and Family Law Reform Act 1989

14.009 The Judicial Separation and Family Law Reform Act 1989 contains a number of provisions relating to the making of custody, access and other orders relating to children in the context of, or following, proceedings for judicial separation. The relevant courts are the Circuit and High Court.

14.010 Section 11(a) of the Act of 1989 provides for the making of such orders after an application for judicial separation has been issued but before the determination of the case. The order must be sought by one of the parties, but it is unnecessary to institute separate proceedings under the Act of 1964.[15]

14.011 Section 3(2)(a) provides that a court may not grant a decree of judicial separation under the Act of 1989, where there are dependent children of the family, unless either it is satisfied that proper provision has been made for the welfare of those children, or it intends upon the granting of the decree to make provision for their welfare. Dependent children under this provision may include children of whom the spouses are not guardians. The term "dependent child of the family" includes for example a child in relation to whom both spouses are *in loco parentis*, and a child in relation to whom one spouse is *in loco parentis* where the other spouse, being aware that he is not the parent of the child, has treated the child as a member of the family.[16]

14.012 Section 3(3) of the Act of 1989 allows a court of its own motion, upon the granting of a decree of judicial separation to give directions under section 11 of the Act of 1964, as it thinks proper regarding the welfare or custody of, or right of access to, an infant. In this context the term "infant" takes its meaning from the Act of 1964. Although the matter is not clear beyond doubt, the reference to section 11 of the Act of 1964 and the use of the term "infant" suggest that only children of whom one of the spouses is a guardian (or natural father) may be made the subject of an order under this provision. This would appear anomolous in the light of the broader category of children in respect of whom the court has duties under section 3(2). As already indicated, it seems unlikely that a court will make much use of this power to act on its own motion where the parents have agreed their own arrangements. In some cases no doubt the court may think it proper to embody the parents' agreement in an order.

14.013 It is open to either spouse, on or at any time after the grant of a decree of judicial separation, to apply for any order under section 11 of the Act of 1964 "concerning any dependent child of the family."[17] Presumably such an application, because it is made under section 11 of the Act of 1964, is limited to a guardian or natural father of the child.

---

15 Act of 1989, section 12.
16 Act of 1989, sections 3(2)(b), and 10.
17 Act of 1989, section 16(g). For the meaning of "dependent child of the family", see above.

The principle of joint parental guardianship

14.014 Fundamental to the resolution of custody and access disputes is the principle that under the Constitution and statute law, married parents begin with equal rights and duties in respect of their children. They are guardians of their children jointly and neither can claim to have a stronger right than the other to determine matters such as the religious upbringing, schooling or medical treatment or any other matter affecting the welfare of their children.

14.015 The statutory basis for the principle of joint parental guardianship, where the parents are married, is to be found in section 6(1) of the Guardianship of Infants Act 1964. The Constitutional basis is Article 42 which, in describing parents' rights and duties, refers throughout to "parents" in the plural. It was in the context of religious upbringing that the principle of joint parental responsibility was first clearly articulated. In *re Tilson, Infants*[18] Murnaghan J. stated for the majority in the Supreme Court:

> Where the father and mother of children are alive . . . [Article 42.1] recognises a joint right and duty in them to provide for the religious education of their children. The word "parents" is in the plural and naturally should include both father and mother. Common sense and reason lead to the view that the mother is under the duty of educating the children as well as the father and both must do so according to their means.

14.016 In cases involving religious upbringing the decision in *re Tilson Infants* which pre-dated the Guardianship of Infants Act 1964, has been consistently followed.[19] Since the passing of the Guardianship of Infants Act the Supreme Court has confirmed that the more general principle of joint parental guardianship embodied in it reflects the constitutional norm implicit in Article 42. In *B. v B.* Walsh J. stated:

> The main purpose of the Guardianship of Infants Act 1964 was to give both parents of an infant equal rights in guardianship matters. In doing so it provided a statutory expression of the rights already guaranteed by the Constitution . . .[20]

The principle that married parents have joint and equal parental rights and duties also has the consequence that, in disputes between them over

---

18 [1951] IR 1, at 32. The decision was one of great importance, overruling as it did a long line of decisions which had supported paternal supremacy in determining a child's religious upbringing. See *re Frost, Infants* [1947] IR 3, and *re Corcoran, Infants* (1950) 86 ILTR 6.
19 See *re May, Minors* (1957) 92 ILTR 1, and *H. v H.* (4 February 1976, unreported,) High Court.
20 [1975] IR 54, at 61. See also the judgment of O'Dálaigh J., ibid., at 58.

custody and access, the one set of constitutionally guaranteed parental rights cancels out the other. As a result the court is able without fear of breaching any parental rights, to regard the welfare of the child as the first and paramount consideration. The court does not have the same freedom in determining a custody or access dispute between a married parent and a third party, where the same equality of constitutional rights does not prevail.[21]

The welfare principle

14.017 Section 3 of the Guardianship of Infants Act 1964 states:

> Where in any proceedings before any court the custody, guardianship or upbringing of an infant, or the administration of any property belonging to or held in trust for an infant, or the application of the income thereof, is in question, the court, in deciding that question, shall regard the welfare of the infant as the first and paramount consideration.

Section 2 of the Act of 1964 defines welfare, in relation to an infant, as comprising "the religious and moral, intellectual, physical and social welfare of the infant."

14.018 Although the welfare of the child is the first and paramount consideration, it is not something which is considered in the abstract but rather in the context of the options for the child which are made available by the two parents. This is particularly so where the dispute relates to custody. The court uses the welfare principle as the criterion to decide which of two options to prefer. If the court is of the opinion that neither option is ideal in terms of the child's welfare, it is not open to it to order that neither parent should have custody. (In an extreme case the Circuit or High Court could use the ward of court jurisdiction to protect a child at risk; the District Court could recommend care proceedings). The court may impose conditions on an award of custody, including an element of supervision, but its choice is basically limited to one of two alternatives. As Henchy J. stated in *MacD. v MacD.*,[22] "The problem for a court . . . is to determine which custody—with the father or with the mother—is more likely to accord with the child's welfare . . ."

14.019 In the same judgment Henchy J. considered the meaning of the principle that welfare is to be treated as "the first and paramount consideration." He approved Lord MacDermott's approach to similarly worded English legislation in *J. v C.*:[23]

---

21 See *K.C. v An Bord Uchtála* [1985] ILRM 302.
22 (1979) 14 ILTR 60.
23 [1970] AC 710, at 711.

Reading these words in their ordinary significance . . . it seems to me that they must mean more than that the child's welfare is to be treated as the top item in a list of items relevant to the matter in question. I think they connote a process whereby, when all the relevant facts, relationships, claims and wishes of parents, risks, choices and other circumstances are taken into account and weighed, the course to be followed will be that which is most in the interests of the child's welfare . . . That is the first consideration because it is of first importance and the paramount consideration because it rules on or determines the course to be followed.

14.020 Although the Act of 1964 defines different aspects of welfare—religious and moral, intellectual, physical and social—it has been stressed by Walsh J. that it is necessary to take a "global" view of an infant's welfare. In *O'S. v O'S.* he stated:[26]

All the ingredients which the Act stipulates are to be considered . . . globally. This is not an appeal to be decided by the simple method of totting up the marks which may be awarded under each of the five headings. It is the totality of the picture presented which must be considered. The picture is to be viewed and judged as a whole and not as a sum of the values of each of the constituent parts of the picture because, unless together they all form an acceptable composition, the picture is a bad one. The word "welfare" must be taken in its widest sense.

Relevant factors in custody disputes

14.021 Because each case is unique and is judged on the total picture presented to the court, and because the different elements of welfare have not been put in any order or priority, analysis of the decided cases can produce no more than an approximate guide to the factors which may be considered relevant in future cases. A list of factors which have influenced past decisions on custody is set out below. Most of the cases cited originated in the High Court, and were decided before the changes in jurisdiction brought about by the Courts Act 1981.

The "tender years" principle

14.022 In the case of young children, there is a marked preference for awarding custody to the mother. This appears to derive from two considerations. First there is the assumption that for biological reasons a mother is better able to respond to the physical and emotional needs especially of a very young child. Second, there is the fact that in many of the cases only the mother has been in a position to care for the infant on a full-time basis.

---

26 (1974) 110 ILTR 57. The quotation is taken from the original judgment at page 6.

14.023 In *B. v B.*[27] Budd J. agreed with the trial judge's view "that young children are notoriously nearer to their mother than their father," and referring to a six-year-old boy, he said that he was "of an age when he requires the care that a mother can give to his physical needs, and he needs her maternal affection." In the same case Fitzgerald J. stated (at 72) that where separated spouses are equally suited to have custody of a child "it seems to be generally accepted that children of tender years should be left in the custody of the mother while they are of an age where they naturally turn to their mother for the care and attention which she naturally provides for them, and which the father cannot so readily supply." In *MacD. v MacD.*[28] Henchy J. spoke of a mother "having regard to the ties of nature," as the person who is usually "primarily and uniquely capable of ministering" to the welfare of very young children. In that case the father's absence from home during the day, compared with the mother's ability to care full-time for the children, was a critical factor in the decision to award custody to her. There are numerous other cases in which the tender years principle has been influential.[29]

14.024 The fact that the father is now living in a relationship with another woman who is in a position to care for a young child may weaken the influence of, but will not displace the tender years principle, which applies only to the natural mother. In *O'S. v O'S.*[30] Walsh J. stated that ". . . the relationship of a mother to her very young children is something that cannot be replaced or usurped by any other woman; however well intentioned . . ." However, the majority of the Supreme Court preferred to grant the father custody. See **14.031–14.046** and **14.043–14.050**. In *P.G. v C.G.*[31] a similar argument was used by Finlay P. in transferring custody of a 19-month-old child from his paternal grandmother to the mother, despite the upset which it was admitted the child would suffer as a result of the move.[32]

14.025 Although the tender years principle is not a rule of law, it is sometimes stated in strong terms. In *H. v H.*[33] Parke J. referred to the proposition "for which there is ample judicial support, . . . that a child of tender years should be entrusted to the custody of his mother unless she

27 [1975] IR 54.
28 (1979) 114 ILTR 60.
29 See, e.g., *Cullen v Cullen* (8 May 1970, unreported) Supreme Court (5½-year-old boy left in custody of mother); *J.W. v M.W.* (July 1978, unreported) High Court, (girl of 4 and boy of 7 given to custody of mother who was then living in a refuge in London); *J.C. v O.C.* (10 July 1980, unreported) High Court (5-year-old child regarded as clearly within the tender years category, 9-year-old son described as "just outside". Both awarded to custody of mother); *E. v E.* (3 February 1977, unreported) High Court (three boys aged 13, 11 and 8 and a 9-month-old girl given into custody of mother).
30 (1974) 114 ILTR 59, at 62.
31 March 1982, unreported, High Court.
32 See also *O'N. v O'B.* (22 January 1980, unreported, High Court) 7½-year-old girl transferred from custody of grandparents to mother on a probationary basis.
33 4 February 1976, unreported, High Court.

has so gravely failed in her duty as a mother as to forfeit such right . . ." However, there have been some cases in which young children have been placed in the custody of fathers.[34] There is also an increasing awareness that fathers have the capacity to parent young children. In *T.O'G. v Attorney General*,[34a] MacMahon J. stated (at 64):

> The culture of our society has assigned distinct roles to father and mother in two parent families in the past . . . but this is a feature of our culture which appears to be changing as the younger generation of married people tend to exchange roles freely.

There is no hard and fast rule as to what constitute the "tender years", though the benefit of maternal contact is usually assumed to be more important for girls than for boys as they approach their teenage years.[35]

Capacity to care for the child

14.026 A parent's capacity to provide a reasonable standard of care for a child will always be relevant. The physical and mental health of the parent, the time which he has available to devote to the child[36] and his ability to provide basic material requirements (proper accommodation, schooling, etc.) may each be taken into consideration. The fact that one parent has less resources than the other is not of itself important, unless the lack of resources is such that the child's basic requirements cannot be met. In most cases, where a marriage breaks down, the wife finds herself in the less favourable financial situation; this will not in general prejudice her claim for custody, and her financial position relative to the husband may in any case be improved by a maintenance order.

14.027 Physical or psychological illness may occasionally incapacitate a parent from performing the parental role. However, the courts tend to be reluctant to deny custody to a parent (where other factors point in that parent's favour) on the basis only of ill health. In *A.H.S. v M.S.*[37] custody of a 7-year-old son was given to a mother who was suffering from "manic depressive psychosis". Barron J. accepted that there was a danger to the child's welfare if the mother had a further acute recurrence of her mental illness; but the mother's condition was under control and a recurrence seemed unlikely. In *E. v E.*[38] custody of four children was given to a mother who at the time of the proceedings was an in-patient in St. Patrick's hospital following successful treatment for depression. There was medical

---

34 See, e.g., *J.J.W. v B.M.W.* (1971) 110 ILTR 45 (three young girls aged 9, 7 and 3); *A.H. v B.H.* (11 January 1982, unreported) High Court (three children aged 7, 6 and 5); *A.O'B v C.O'B.* (12 November 1985, unreported) High Court (11-year-old daughter).
34a [1985] ILRM 61.
35 See, e.g., *B. v B.*, supra, where, Fitzgerald J. at 72, as an approximate guide suggests the ages of 8 for a boy and 12 for a girl.
36 See *MacD. v MacD.*, supra, and **14.031–14.036**.
37 12 November 1982, unreported, High Court.
38 3 February 1977, unreported, High Court.

evidence that the mother would be capable of looking after the children provided she continued to receive psychological and psychiatric help. The order was made subject to review, particularly with regard to the mother's health. However, in *C.O'B. v A.O'B.*[39] custody of an 11-year-old daughter was transferred to her father from the mother, who was an alcoholic for whom treatment had been unsuccessful. The daughter and mother had reversed roles, so that the daughter felt responsible for her mother. They have been living in unsatisfactory circumstances from the point of view of the daughter's welfare, and there was a risk of her becoming delinquent. Custody was transferred to the father who had also been an alcoholic but had been successfully treated.

14.028 A court may also regard a parent as unfit, by reason of character or conduct, to have custody of a child. It is very unusual for a court to make a specific finding of unfitness, because in the words of O'Dálaigh J. in *B. v B.* (at 59) "the welfare of children will rarely be advanced by a verdict of condemnation on one or other of the parents." The conduct or character of the parent may, however, be relevant when considering specific aspects of the child's welfare, such as moral, social (**14.043–14.050**) or physical welfare (**14.040–14.042**).

Maintaining family unity

14.029 There have been many cases in which judges have expressed a preference not to separate siblings, based on a belief that the companionship of brothers and sisters is nearly always beneficial for a child. In *B. v B.* O'Dálaigh C.J. (at 60) described the "spirit of comradeship" which existed between an eight-year-old sister and her elder brother as "a valuable asset in the present broken state of their parents' marriage," and was of the opinion that "nothing should be done to waste or squander it." In *J.C. v O.C.*[40] a father sought custody of his two sons (aged 5 and 9), but not of his daughter (aged 11). He was unsuccessful. One "by no means insignificant" factor favouring their existing custody with the mother was, according to Finlay P., that it enabled them to stay together, which from the point of view of "their social development as a family" would in the future be of "considerable importance."[41] On the other hand, there are cases where split custody orders have been made. In *Cullen v Cullen*,[42] for example, the Supreme Court gave custody of two boys (aged 15 and 11) to the father, and a girl (aged 17) to the mother. In *P.G. v C.G.* (No. 2)[43] Ellis J. refused to order the return of a 13½-year-old son to live with his mother who had custody of his sister (aged 16) and brother (aged 2). The

39 2 November 1985, unreported, High Court.
40 10 July 1980, unreported, High Court, at pages 4 & 5 of Finlay P.'s judgment.
41 Other cases in which the unity principle was considered important include *E. v E.* (3 February 1977, unreported) High Court, at page 8 of McWilliam J.'s judgment; *A.H. v B.H.* (11 January 1982, unreported) High Court, at page 16 of Barrington J.'s judgment; and *M.K. v P.K.* (November 1982, unreported) High Court.
42 8 May 1970, unreported, Supreme Court.
43 July 1983, unreported, High Court.

son had an exceptionally good relationship with his father, and did not wish to return to the mother.

14.030 As well as preferring an arrangement which maintains unity between siblings, judges may also be influenced, in making a custody order, by any potential it has for helping to effect a reconciliation between the parents. This is based on the assumption that it is in general in the long-term interests of a child that his parents should remain united. As stated by Budd J. in *B. v B.* (at 6) "Anything which gives some hope for the reconciliation of husband and wife is of outstanding importance from the point of view of the welfare of the children." (The same argument had been made by Kenny J. in the High Court. Though the particular method of achieving this objective proposed by Budd J., namely to split custody of the children between the parents, has little to recommend it.) In *E.K. v M.K.*[44] Walsh J., favouring the father's custody of two young children, pointed out that the father and mother were still young, and "whatever prospect may exist of an ultimate reconciliation of this family, it is more likely to be advanced by stabilizing the children's position than leaving them in the present more unstable and uncertain position." The difficulty in this approach lies not with the objective, which, if the reconciliation is genuine, may well be in the interests of a child, but rather with the means. It is difficult to envisage circumstances in which a particular custody disposition is likely to be an effective means of bringing about a reconciliation between a child's parents. Arguably a custody order should not be employed as a vehicle for promoting something which may be no more than an aspiration.

Continuity of care and the stability of relationships

14.031 The need to provide stability in the life of a child is often emphasised. For this reason a court will usually be reluctant to disturb a custody arrangement which has been in place for a substantial length of time. The importance of continuity in the care of a child derives from two considerations. The first is more relevant in relation to a very young infant, and has to do with the child's psychological need to identify and attach himself to a parent figure who has a regular presence in his life. The second is the disturbance, and sometimes distress, which may result from a change of custody, particularly where the change involves a move to a different area, to a new school and away from established friends.

14.032 In *B. v B.*[27] O'Dálaigh J. believed it to be in the interests of a 10-year-old boy "that he should not be disturbed from the home in which he has grown up". In *O'S. v O'S.*[46] it was principally for reasons of continuity and stability that the Supreme Court, by a majority, decided to leave three children in the custody of their father, despite the fact that he had formed a relationship with another woman. The children (a boy aged 5, and two girls

44 31 July 1974, unreported, Supreme Court; at page 18 of Walsh J.'s judgment.
45 [1975] IR 54.
46 (1974) 110 ILTR 57.

aged 6 and 7) had been living with the father for four years. They were happy and being well looked after by the father and stepmother. If custody were given to the mother, they would have to move to live in a different town. This would, according to Henchy J., have resulted in adverse consequences for their intellectual and social development. Their intellectual development "would be retarded by the emotional disturbances that the change would cause and by the rupture of the continuity of their schooling." As to their social welfare,

> They lead an active, normal and well integrated existence. In their young lives, this is the third home they have known. To sunder them from it and to thrust them into a fourth, this time with their grandparents, who are probably strangers to them, in a large, old house, would be a change fraught with the problem of fitting into new schools and making new friends and settling into a new domestic and social environment. All this would be apt to inflict a trauma that might have permanent ill-effects on them.

14.033 Griffin J. reached the same conclusion as Henchy J. and for similar reasons, but both judges noted that, if the application for a change of custody had been made at an earlier date, before the children had set down roots, the decision might have been different.

14.034 The importance of stability of relationships in a child's life was also emphasised in *J.J.W. v B.M.W.*[47] Three children (aged 8, 7 and 3) were in the custody of their father, though two of them had to spend most of each week in a special school, described as an "orphanage" for children from broken families. Nevertheless the children saw their father regularly and had good relationships with both sets of grandparents. The mother was living in England with another man and was in a position to offer the children a home environment. Apart from the issue of the children's moral welfare, an important factor in Walsh J.'s opinion (at 54) was the greater stability offered by the father's custody.

> . . . having regard to the melancholy events affecting their parents' marriage over the last few years, it is very much in the interests of the children to be brought up, as they are being brought up, in close proximity to their four grandparents and their father, all of whom are to the children recognisably stable elements in their lives. The present position of their mother offers no such stability and there is nothing to suggest that in the immediate future any such stability will be available.

Chief Justice O'Dálaigh and Budd J. concurred.

14.035 *J.J.W. v B.M.W.* should, however, be contrasted with *MacD. v MacD.*[48] where the Supreme Court (Griffin J. dissenting) accepted that a

47 (1971) 110 ILTR 45.
48 (1979) 114 ILTR 59.

mother who was living in a stable relationship with another man was, in the circumstances, better able than the father to provide the children with a secure and emotionally satisfying environment. The father was a busy executive who was away from home all day, and would have to leave the children in the care of a housekeeper, whereas the mother was living in comfortable circumstances which allowed her to devote her time to the children. Henchy J. emphasised the importance, from the point of view of the children's physical, social and intellectual welfare, of having a mother constantly present to minister to their needs. The difference between the decision in *J.J.W. v B.M.W.* and *MacD. v MacD.* can be explained in part by a difference in the degree of stability which life with the two mothers offered. However, the two cases also reveal divergences of judicial opinion about the danger to a child's moral welfare of living with a parent who is engaged in an adulterous relationship. See **14.043–14.050**. The decision in *E.K. v M.K.*[49] is similar to that in *J.J.W. v B.M.W.* The greater stability offered by the father, combined with the bad moral example provided by the mother, were the principal reasons for the Supreme Court deciding to favour the father's custody.

14.036 A parent's irresponsible or unpredictable behaviour prior to the breakdown of a marriage may lead a court to conclude that he or she cannot offer a child the required stability. In *B.H. v A.H.*[50] the mother had left the matrimonial home on a number of occasions without notice in an irresponsible way and admitted to having had an extra-marital affair. Barrington J. gave custody of the three children to the father, who was not himself blameless, on the basis that he had "in the children's day-to-day life shown himself the more practical and caring parent". This offered the best chance of the children "enjoying a modicum of stability" (at page 16 of the judgment).

Educational arrangements

14.037 A court will examine, sometimes in great detail, the appropriateness of the educational arrangements proposed for a child as an aspect of the child's social and intellectual welfare. The element of continuity has already been referred to. In *J.C. v O.C.*[51] the three children (aged 11, 9 and 5) were in the custody of their mother. The father applied for the custody of the two younger children to be transferred to him. His principal argument was that there had been a continuous decline in their academic standards. Two of the children's teachers gave evidence. Finlay P. rejected the father's claim, being satisfied that the children were getting on well enough at school. "I think inevitably the family dispute will have retarded them at school; children do not do as well if they are from a broken family, but I don't think transferring them to the father would make any change in their educational progress" (at page 7 of the judgment). He went on to give

49 31 July 1974, unreported, Supreme Court.
50 11 January 1982, unreported, High Court.
51 10 October 1980, unreported, High Court.

detailed directions to ensure that one of the children, who played the violin, should receive a more sophisticated and formal musical education than she had so far received. The father was to make the arrangements.

Conduct of parents towards each other

14.038 "An award of custody is not a prize for good matrimonial behaviour."[52] The primary and paramount concern of the court is to secure the future welfare of the child, rather than make a judgment as to which of the parents bears the greater responsibility for the breakdown of the marriage. In *E. v E.*[53] McWilliam J., referring to the allegations and counter allegations made by each parent with a view to fixing responsibility for the breakdown of their marriage, stated:

> This is both unfortunate and unnecessary because, once it has been established, as it has been here, that the marriage has completely broken down, I am mainly concerned with the welfare of the children and, except in so far as it gives one an insight into the attitudes of the parents to the children, am not greatly concerned with the behaviour of each to the other.

14.039 In *B. v B.* Fitzgerald J. stated that evidence relating to the relative responsibility of the parties for the breakdown of a marriage "was relevant only to the character of the respective parents" with a view to deciding which custody would best serve the welfare of a particular child. These principles have been repeated on numerous occasions, for example in *E.K. v M.K.*[54] where Walsh J. at page 10 of his judgment stated "The question of doing "justice" between the husband and wife is . . . an extraneous factor." A similar case is *J.C. v O.C.*[55] Nevertheless evidence of misconduct may be introduced for the purpose of demonstrating that a particular parent has an irresponsible attitude to family commitments and would be less likely to provide a child with a secure and stable environment, or that the misconduct is such that it puts at risk the child's moral welfare.

Parental conduct towards the child

14.040 Instances of cruelty, neglect or abuse by a parent towards the child whose custody is an issue may clearly be relevant to the issue of welfare. As has been stated (**14.026–14.028**) a court will be reluctant to characterise a parent as unfit to have custody, but it will not ignore misconduct. In *J.O'C. v M.O'C.*[56] the issue of corporal punishment arose. There were four children (two boys aged 12 and 6, and two girls aged 9 and 8), on whom the mother consistently inflicted severe corporal punishment. She humiliated them before each other, and the children were very frightened of her.

52 Per Kenny J,. in *J.J.W. v B.M.W* (1971) 110 ILTR 45 at 47.
53 3 February 1977, unreported, High Court, at pages 2 and 3 of McWilliam J.'s judgment.
54 31 July 1974, unreported, Supreme Court.
55 10 July 1980, unreported, High Court.
56 August 1975, unreported, High Court.

Kenny J. placed the children in the father's custody and observed (at page 7) that

> severe corporal punishment administered consistently to young children and particularly to girls is certain to cause emotional trouble. The parents who use corporal punishment on young children may think that it is for their good but civilised human beings have long since abandoned this barbaric practice.

14.041 If one parent leaves the family home, abandoning the children to the care of the other, this may be seen as relevant to the question of whether that parent can be trusted to act responsibly in the future (see **14.036.**) In *MacD. v MacD.*[57] Griffin J., in a dissenting judgment, regarded the fact that a mother had originally conceded control of two young children to the father, while she pursued a relationship with another man, as indicating where the mother's priorities lay. When custody had been transferred to her at a later stage, she had been prepared to jeopardise her position by bringing the children into contact with the other man in breach of the custody conditions. However, the same emphasis was not placed on these matters by the majority of the court who for reasons mainly related to the emotional needs of the children, awarded custody to the mother.

14.042 Allegations of sexual abuse by one parent against the other are, it seems, becoming more frequent in custody and access disputes. It is unlikely that a court will accept that abuse has in fact occurred unless it is proved "on the balance of probabilities." On the other hand, in considering a child's welfare, a court may well feel obliged to take account of any real possibility, or risk of abuse in the future, even where the fact of abuse in the past has not been proved. This has been the approach adopted by the English courts. See *H. v H. and C.*, and *K. v K.*[58]

Second relationships and moral welfare

14.043 Not infrequently, following the breakdown of a marriage, one of the parties will enter into a second relationship which, in the absence of divorce, will usually not be based on marriage. The effects of such a relationship on that parent's claim to the custody of children of the marriage is a matter on which divergent views are held among judges and justices. The prevailing judicial view is that the existence of a second "adulterous" relationship, because it represents a rejection of conventional moral principles, poses certain risks, by the bad example it sets, for a child's moral welfare. However, judicial opinion differs on the questions of how serious that risk is, and how prominently it should feature in the context of other factors relevant to the child's welfare. These differences of opinion exist at all levels of the courts, including the Supreme Court.

57 (1979) 114 ILTR 66.
58 [1989] 3 All ER 740.

Indeed, Supreme Court decisions on the issue are not easy to reconcile, as the following cases show.

14.044 In *J.J.W. v B.M.W.*[59] the wife had left her husband and gone to England where she lived with another man. She had obtained a decree nisi of divorce, and was planning to marry the other man. There were three daughters aged 9, 7 and 3. Custody of two of the children had changed hands but, at the time of the proceedings, all three were in the custody of the father, who was now living in his parents' house. Because of the inability of the grandparents to cope, two of the children were placed in a special school. The father visited them at weekends and they spent their holidays with their father and grandparents. In the High Court Kenny J., while recognising "the corrupting example" set by their mother, gave custody of the children to her on the basis that, having regard to the sex and ages of the children, they would be happier growing up together in a home environment. The father's appeal to the Supreme Court was successful. Fitzgerald J. (at page 52) emphasised the children's moral welfare, McLoughlin J. concurring:

> The fact is . . . that the home which she [the mother] has to offer to her children is one in which she continues an adulterous association with a man who has deserted his own wife and his two children. A more unhealthy abode for the three . . . children would be difficult to imagine.

14.045 Nor did he think that the wife's plans to divorce and marry the man with whom she lived in any way advanced her status in relation to the children. In his judgment, Walsh J. (O'Dálaigh C.J. and Budd J. concurring) took a more global view of the children's welfare, placing some emphasis on the greater stability and continuity which the father's custody offered. He agreed with Kenny J.'s view that the mother's relationship was a "corrupting example" for the children, and that they would not be able to reconcile it with the tenets of the Roman Catholic religion in which they were being brought up.

14.046 In *O'S. v O'S.*[60] a father who was living in a stable relationship with another woman was allowed by the Supreme Court to retain custody of his three young children. An important factor was that the children had been out of the mother's custody for four years, and had been living contentedly with the father and his new partner for two years. The decision was by a majority, and what divided the court were the different attitudes towards the question of moral and religious welfare. Henchy J., while accepting that the father's relationship with the "stepmother" was a bad example for the children, pointed out that it was an established fact in the children's lives which would not be obviated by a change in custody. There was no evidence to suggest that the children were not in other respects living in a

59 (1971) 1109 ILTR 49.
60 (1974) 110 ILTR 57.

healthy moral atmosphere. The children's need for continuity and emotional security were the principal factors favouring the father's custody. Griffin J., while accepting that the "ménage" in which the children had been brought up left "much to be desired from a moral point of view," shared Henchy J.'s concern for continuity. But Walsh J., in a dissenting judgment, placed much greater emphasis on the moral risks. Referring to the support given by the Constitution to the family based on marriage, and its recognition of such a unit as "the keystone of the social structure which the Constitution undertakes to maintain," he described (at 61) the present atmosphere in which the children were found "in spite of every good intention on the part of their father and the woman he is living with", as being "a manifest repudiation of the social and religious values with which they should be inculcated at this stage of their lives."

14.047 Similar terminology was used by Walsh J. in *E.K. v M.K.*[61] in which, by a majority of three to two, the Supreme Court withdrew custody of two young children from a separated mother who was involved in a relationship with another man and who had engaged in sexual intercourse with him on a number of occasions in her home after the children had gone to bed. The father had also become concerned that the relationship between the children and the other man was becoming intimate. Fitzgerald C.J., in the same case, concentrated exclusively on the mother's conduct, and described her claim for custody at page 1 of his judgment as "a claim for a licence from this Court to have custody of the children while she carries on adulterous intercourse with another man." There were however other reasons which favoured the father's custody, in particular the greater stability which he could provide, which are brought out in the judgments of Walsh J. and Griffin J. The two dissenting judges, Henchy and Griffin JJ., disagreed with the majority's refusal to admit, on appeal, certain medical evidence relating to the possible harm that might arise for the 3-year-old girl from a change of custody.

14.048 In *MacD. v MacD.*[62] the Supreme Court, again by a majority, confirmed custody of two children (a girl aged 6 and a boy aged 4) in a mother who was living in a settled relationship with another man. Henchy J. described the mother's relationship as "a bad example and a cause of scandal to the children," but again emphasised that, even if custody were given to the father with access to the mother, the children would grow up in the knowledge of her circumstances. The deciding factor in giving custody to the mother, was the emotional and psychological well-being of the children. Kenny J. spoke of the "deplorable" example provided by the mother's behaviour, but regarded the strong emotional links of young children to their mother as the decisive factor. Griffin J. dissented for reasons explained in **14.041**.

61 31 July 1974, unreported, Supreme Court.
62 (1979) 114 ILTR 60.

14.049 In *A.H.S. v M.S.*[63] Barron J. deduced the following principle from the decisions of the Supreme Court:

> [In] . . . cases in which one of the parties was living in a permanent adulterous association, and *a fortiori* where the association was less than permanent, the Supreme Court has essentially regarded the moral danger to the child as being more important than its physical and social welfare unless it can be shown that it would be harmful to its latter welfare to remove it from a settled home.

In *A.H.S. v M.S.*, the evidence given by a child psychiatrist suggested that the 7-year-old boy whose custody was in issue would obtain a more normal experience of growing up if he remained with his father, but that a transfer of custody to the mother would not harm the child. The mother had suffered a psychiatric illness which was then under control. The father was living with another woman. Barron J. concluded (at page 14) that "the benefits of remaining with his father are overborne by the danger to his moral welfare if he remains with him," and ordered a transfer of custody.

14.050 The above principle enunciated by Barron J. accurately reflects the general emphasis in the case law. Other cases, in which the existence of an adulterous relationship influenced the court's decision, included *W. v W.*[64] *J.C. v O.C.*[65] *and H. v H.*[66] in which Parke J. stated at page 17 of his judgment that "In general . . . the courts will not grant custody to a parent who has abandoned the matrimonial home and lives in an adulterous establishment." Nevertheless, the series of divided judgments in the Supreme Court shows that, in the application of that principle, judicial approaches can and do vary. The very language employed by different judges reveals differing views as to the moral censure attaching to second non-marital relationships, and therefore different opinions about the level of risk which they present to a child's moral welfare.

Religious upbringing

Choice of religion

14.051 The determination of a child's religious upbringing is a matter for both parents. In *Re Tilson, Infants*[67] (see **14.015**) the Supreme Court rejected the old common law doctrine of paternal supremacy, and decided that Article 42 of the Constitution recognised a joint right and duty in married parents to provide for the religious education of their children. The court further decided that an agreement made between the parents, before or after marriage, concerning religious upbringing would bind the parents, and that neither could subsequently, against the will of the other, revoke the joint decision. The mother and father in Tilson were respec-

---

63 12 November 1982, unreported, High Court.
64 8 December 1974, unreported, Supreme Court.
65 10 July 1980, unreported, High Court.
66 4 February 1976, unreported, High Court.
67 [1951] IR 1.

tively Roman Catholic and Protestant and the father had signed an undertaking, before their marriage in a Roman Catholic ceremony, that any children of the marriage would be raised as Roman Catholics. When differences arose between the parents, the father removed three of them to a Protestant institution. The High Court order for their return to the custody of the mother was confirmed on appeal to the Supreme Court.

14.052 In the subsequent case of *In Re May, Minors*[68] the same principles were applied in a case where the agreement between the parents was implied rather than express. Both parents at the time of their marriage were Roman Catholic and the five children of the marriage were initially brought up as Roman Catholics. When the father became a Jehovah's Witness he attempted to interfere with the children's religious upbringing. Davitt J. decided that the father was not entitled to depart unilaterally from the implied agreement that the children be raised as Roman Catholics.

14.053 Where there is no agreement, express or implied, between the parents and a dispute over the religious upbringing of their children is referred to the court, the position is unclear. *In Re May* suggests that in such a case the father's view prevails. It seems unlikely that this view would be accepted today. On the one hand in the words of Parke J. in *H. v H.*[66] (at page 15) "the Court is not one of comparative religions," and will not engage in theological debate about the relative merits of different religions; on the other hand, the principle of joint parental rights and responsibilities would appear to preclude the court from favouring the views of one parent over the other. In such a case the court may consider the social implications for a child of his being brought up in a particular religion, as for example where the child would become an "odd man out" if he were brought up in one of the two religions advocated by the parents. In *H. v H.* the mother who was living with a partner of the Jewish religion and was herself undergoing conversion to that religion, wished to bring up her son, a baptised Roman Catholic, as a Jew. Parke J., following *Re May, Minors*, held that the mother had no right to depart from the agreement implied between her and her husband that the child be brought up as a Roman Catholic. He also discussed the social problems for the child if the mother's proposal were carried into effect.

14.054 The parents' right to determine religious upbringing is not absolute. There will come a point in a child's life when his own wishes may take priority over those of his parents. Section 17(2) of the Act of 1964, which is part of a section dealing with religious education, states that "Nothing in this Act shall interfere with or affect the power of the court to consult the wishes of the infant in considering what order ought to be made or diminish the right which any infant now possesses to the exercise of his own free choice." The infant's wishes and rights are discussed further in the next section.

68 (1957) 92 ILTR 1. Followed in *H. v H.* supra.

Religion as a factor in custody disputes

14.055 Custody may be awarded to a parent who does not practise the religion in which the child is being brought up. In such a case the court will generally give directions to ensure that proper arrangements are made to see that the child continues to receive appropriate instruction in his religion and that the child has the opportunity to attend worship in that religion. The feasibility of making such arrangements will be a factor in determining which parent should in fact have custody.

14.056 In *MacD. v MacD.*[69] custody of children who were being brought up in the Roman Catholic faith was given to a mother who was a Protestant living with another man, also a Protestant. The mother had undertaken in evidence to bring the children up as Roman Catholics, to see that they would receive proper religious instruction, to ensure that they would say their prayers, and to take them to Mass on Sundays. Henchy J. accepted these undertakings as genuine and hoped that, in granting the father who was a Roman Catholic generous periods of access, particularly at weekends, any necessary supplement or corrective, especially in matters of religion and morals, would be supplied. Griffin J., at pages 10–11 of a dissenting judgment, thought that "with the best will in the world, it would be an extremely difficult, if not insuperable, task for the mother to bring up the children in the Catholic faith," when neither she nor her partner were members of or familiar with the tenets of that faith. In *Cullen v Cullen*[70] a mother whose religion had lapsed, was given custody of the youngest son on the basis of her undertaking to see to it that he would be taught his religion and say his prayers. The access arrangements to the father also took into account the need for the child to be associated with his father's and his brothers' attendance at Sunday Mass. In *A.H.S. v M.S.*[71] the father was Moslem while the mother and child were Roman Catholics. The child was being brought up as a Roman Catholic. Barron J. was satisfied that in either home he would be brought up as a Roman Catholic. Although the mother was in a better position than the father to attend to his religious upbringing, this was not a major factor in awarding her custody.

The wishes and rights of the child

14.057 Section 17(2) of the Guardianship of Infants Act 1964 provides that the wishes of the child may be taken into account by the court and in order to ascertain these wishes the court may interview the child usually in an informal setting. In the case of an older child in particular, his wishes may have a decisive influence on questions of custody and access.

14.058 In *Cullen v Cullen*[70] a seventeen year old daugher was interviewed and expressed a wish to remain with the mother. This appears to have had

69 (1979) 114 ILTR 60.
70 8 May 1970, unreported, Supreme Court.
71 12 November 1982, unreported, High Court.

a considerable influence on the decision. In *W. v W.*[72] the Supreme Court confirmed a decision of the High Court to give custody of two boys (aged 14 and 11) to the father, principally on the basis that the boys expressed a strong preference for living with the father and threatened to run away if placed in the custody of their mother. Other cases where an interview took place are *B. v B.*,[73] where the Supreme Court, on appeal, interviewed the children; *N.O'D. v M.O'D.*;[74] *M.K. v P.K.*;[75] *N.A.D. v T.D.*;[76] and *O'S. v O'S.*[77] where Kenny J. took the children to see the boat show at the Royal Dublin Society.

14.059 The court has a discretion whether or not to interview a child; it is not obliged to do so. There is a reluctance to do so where it is feared that an interview might upset a child,[78] or where there is a danger that the child may have been coached in what to say. In *J.C. v O.C.*[79] Finlay J. declined to interview the three children (aged 11, 9 and 5) before deciding custody. There was some risk that the mother would persuade them to take up a particular attitude. He decided, however, that he would interview them at a later stage after the decision about custody had been made, when they would know that nothing hinged upon their answers. And in *F.M. v J.M.*[80] the same judge thought it unnecessary to interview the children (aged 18, 16 and 11) because the mother had disqualified herself for the time being as a person to whom custody should be entrusted.

14.060 It should be noted, in this context, that children have "imprescriptible" though undefined rights under Article 41.5 of the Constitution, and that section 17(2) of the Act of 1964 states that nothing in the Act shall "diminish the right which any infant now possesses to the exercise of his own free choice." Arguably there comes a point in a child's life when a court is no longer entitled to compel him against his wishes to live with either parent. In *The People (Attorney General) v Edge*,[81] the consent of a 14½-year-old boy was successfully pleaded as a defence to a charge of kidnapping. The boy had been removed without the parents' consent. The general question was raised as to whether at the age of 14 a boy has discretion to choose his own home, but the discussion was inconclusive.[82] It may be that the courts will be prepared to accept a right to self-

---

72 xx June 1975, unreported, High Court. There was no written judgment in the Supreme Court.
73 [1975] IR 54.
74 16 November 1977, unreported, High Court.
75 Noted in [1984] ILRM 311.
76 [1985] ILRM 153.
77 10 July 1973, unreported, High Court.
78 See *B. v B.* (January 1969, unreported) High Court, where Kenny J. declined to interview the children.
79 10 July 1980, unreported, High Court.
80 November 1983, unreported, High Court.
81 [1943] IR 115.
82 *In re Connor* [1919] IR 361 was cited in support of the proposition, Articles 41 and 42 of the Constitution against it.

determination as one of the unspecified rights of an older child, though it would appear unrealistic to set a specific age at which the right is acquired. Its acquisition arguably should depend on the court's judgment as to whether the particular child has sufficient capacity and intelligence to exercise the right.[83] If and when such a right is held to exist it would seem, *a fortiori*, improper for a court to make an order for custody without consulting the wishes of the child.

Access to the non-custodial parent

14.061 If parents cannot agree on the matter of access to their child by the non-custodial parent, the court may, under section 11 of the Act of 1964, on the application of either parent, make such order as it thinks proper. The court may determine, not only entitlement to access, but also the conditions under which it is to take place. The welfare of the child is again the first and paramount consideration, and many of the factors already mentioned which are relevant to the issue of custody, including the wishes of the child, may have a bearing also on the question of access.

14.062 There is a strong presumption that a child's welfare will be promoted by maintaining contact, and having the opportunity to develop some relationship, with the non-custodial parent. It has also been suggested that access to the non-custodial parent is a right of the child.[84] A court will be particularly anxious to ensure adequate access in cases where the non-custodial parent is able to supplement, or make up for any deficiencies in, the care provided by the custodial parent. Thus, where the custodial parent is not of the same religion as the child, access to the non-custodial parent may be seen as an important guarantee of the child's religious and moral welfare.[85] In *W. v W.*[86] arrangements for weekend and vacation access to their father by two boys aged 14 and 11 were such as to enable them to have "the benefit of their father's outdoor interests and his ability to bring them to sports, football matches and other forms of entertainment suitable to boys of their age."

14.063 The reluctance of the courts to refuse access is illustrated by the following cases. In *B. v B.*[87] the father at first had custody of the children. He used them to spy on the mother and tried to turn them against her. Despite his misconduct, in subsequent proceedings in which custody was transferred to the mother, the father was allowed access, limited to once a

---

83 See e.g. the approach of the House of Lords to the question of a 16-year-old girl's autonomy in relation to contraceptive advice and treatment in *Gillick v West Norfolk Area Health Authority* [1985] 3 All ER 402.

84 Per Parke J. in *H. v H.* 4 February 1976, unreported, High Court, citing *M. v M.* [1973] 2 All ER 8.

85 See *MacD. v MacD.* and *Cullen v Cullen*, discussed at **14.055–14.056**.

86 8 December 1974, unreported, Supreme Court, per Walsh J. at page 9 of his judgment.

87 July 1974, unreported, High Court.

month. In *A.MacB. v A.G.MacB.*[88] the father was living in Tipperary, and the mother in Derry. The mother, who had custody of the three children, objected to the children staying with their father in Tipperary and wanted access to be in Derry. A consultant psychologist gave evidence that the chidren were, in varying degrees, afraid of their father, a "withdrawn character" who had been guilty in the past of malicious damage to property. Barron J. refused the mother's request, on the basis that it would place a barrier between the children and their father stating at page 13: "It is essential that the children know that they have a father and it is essential that their father is able to take the place of a father in their lives."[89]

14.064 Nevertheless, in exceptional circumstances access may be refused, particularly where an older child is set against it. In *N.A.D. v T.D.*[90] the mother had deserted the family and had no contact with her five children for nine years. When a meeting was arranged, she attended bringing with her a child of her second relationship of whose existence the five children had been unaware. The access application was made four years later, by which time the five children were aged 20, 19, 18, 17 and 14. The children were living in Galway, and the mother in Dublin. Barron J. decided that no practical benefit would accrue from arranging infrequent meetings between the mother and the children at some town between Galway and Dublin. There was no realistic hope of producing a better relationship between the children and their mother, and "even now the youngest is too old to be forced to see her mother with whom her older brothers and sisters may have no communication."

14.065 The court may attach conditions to an access order. In a case where the non-custodial parent is living with another partner, the court has sometimes imposed a condition that the child should not be brought into contact or associate with the partner. In *B. v B.*[91] the mother, who was living with another man, became pregnant and was unable to meet her two children at a hotel under the original access arrangement. She applied for a variation of access conditions to enable the children to visit her in her own home. Kenny J. permitted this on condition that the children had no contact with her partner. There have, however, been cases in which this stipulation has not been made. There may be little purpose served by it, particularly where the non-custodial parent's relationship is already an established fact in the minds of the children.[92] In *J.C. v O.C.*[93] no such stipulation was made in relation to access to the father, who had established a second relationship. Finlay J. (at page 4) stated that the children would have to understand that their father was living with someone to whom he was not married and had two children of that union. The

---

88 6 June 1984, unreported, High Court.
89 See also *D.C. v A.C.* May 1981, unreported, High Court.
90 [1985] ILRM 153.
91 December 1973, unreported, High Court.
92 See the remarks of Henchy J. in *MacD. v MacD.* (**14.048**).
93 10 July 1980, unreported, High Court.

situation was one which they would have to live with and treat with understanding and compassion.

International aspects

Removal of a child from the jurisdiction

14.066 If there is a dispute between parents as to whether a child may be removed from the jurisdiction, the court may, on the application of a parent under section 11 of the Act of 1964, determine the matter. There is no rule against the removal of a minor,[94] nor against an award of custody to a parent who resides outside the jurisdiction. For example in *A.McB. v A.G.McB.*[95] the mother, who had obtained custody under a consent order in earlier proceedings, was living in Northern Ireland. The matter will be determined on the basis of the child's welfare. A court may be reluctant to allow a child to be removed to live abroad, where as a result access to the non-custodial parent would become impossible or impractical. This was one factor relevant to the mother's unsuccessful claim for custody in *H. v H.*, supra. She wished to take the child in question to live in England. If appropriate, the court may give directions, under section 11, designed to prevent the removal of a child. Where the removal of a child from the jurisdiction by one parent, without the other's consent, appears imminent, an injunction may be sought on an *ex parte* basis in the Circuit or High Court prohibiting the removal of the child (see chapter 6).

Removal of a child to the jurisdiction

14.067 The courts occasionally are required to make orders in cases where children have been bought to Ireland from abroad by one parent, without the consent of the other parent and/or in breach of a custody order made by the foreign court. In such a case, as a general rule, the court will order that the child be returned to the jurisdiction in which he ordinarily resides. In *O'D. v O'D.*,[96] the father had, without the consent of their mother, brought his children from Alberta to Ireland. The Alberta Supreme Court had some time previously made a custody order in favour of the mother. The father, who had been living in New Mexico, had obtained a divorce there, with an order for joint custody which stipulated that the children should have their principal residence with the mother. Hamilton J. ordered that the children be returned to Alberta on the basis that the proper forum for determining their custody was the Supreme Court of Alberta.

14.068 Judges have differed in their preparedness to entertain arguments against returning the child based on considerations of the child's welfare. If there are obvious dangers for the child, then the court, treating the child's

---

94 See, e.g., *In re Molloy, a Minor* (1871) IR 6 Eq. 339, and *In re Westby Minors* (No. 2) [1934] IR 310.
95 6 June 1984, unreported, High Court.
96 July/August 1979, unreported, High Court.

welfare as the first and paramount consideration, will not ignore them. It is significant that in *O'D. v O'D.*, the court ordered a psychiatric examination of the child and the parents to determine whether any direct harm would be done by returning the child. On the other hand, there is sometimes a reluctance in the court to embark on a general review of the child's welfare.[99] In *Kent County Council v C.S.*[99] a father had brought his two-year-old son from England to Ireland in breach of an English High Court order placing the child in the care of Kent County Council with leave to place the child with the mother. Finlay P., having satisfied himself that no Constitutional rights were at risk, refused to conduct a full hearing into the merits of the case and ordered the return of the child to the custody of Kent County Council. The reason for the peremptory order was "the fundamental importance" of the principle that "the appropriate forum for the determination of the future welfare of the child [is] . . . the courts in the country in which it was born and intended to be brought up." The fact that relevant English witnesses were not ordinarily amenable to the Irish courts was a further consideration. (Contrast *Re C. Minors*,[98] a decision of the English Court of Appeal, in which Ormrod L.J. criticised the trial judge for confining his review to obvious moral or physical dangers, and insisted that the "best interests of the children" principle should be applied without gloss.[99])

14.069 In *Sanders v Mid-Western Health Board*[1] the parents had brought their three children to Ireland in breach of an order of the High Court in England placing the children in the care of the Hampshire County Council. The parents had no previous connection with Ireland. Finlay C.J. upheld the decision of the High Court in favour of the Hampshire County Council, and said at page 3 of his judgment which was assented to by the four other members of the Court.

> As a general principle, subject to exceptions in the interest of justice, the comity of the Courts and the questions of the welfare of children requires or demands that disputes and matters affecting their custody and upbringing when they fall to be determined by the Courts, should be determined by the Court at the jurisdication in which they ordinarily reside and in which they were intended to be brought up.

14.070 The order of the Supreme Court was not, however, a peremptory one. Evidence had been given in great detail before the High Court, and before the Supreme Court in the form of affidavits. The Chief Justice decided that no exceptional circumstances nor any special concern with regard to the children's welfare existed which would justify setting aside the ordinary rules. The decision was reached only after careful consideration of the evidence. The case indicates that, while arguments relating to

97 [1984] ILRM 292.
98 [1978] 2 All ER 230.
99 *Report on the Hague Convention on the Civil Aspects of International Child Abductors* . . . (LRC 12–1985), page 9, where Ormrod L.J.'s approach is supported.
1 23 June 1987, unreported, Supreme Court.

welfare will be entertained, there will be a strong presumption that a child's welfare is best secured by ordering his return to the country of his ordinary residence.

A similar approach was adopted by Costello J. in the earlier case of *Oxfordshire County Council v J.H. and V.H.*[2] While emphasising that the welfare of the child is the first and paramount consideration in proceedings under the Act of 1964, and that the existence of a foreign order relating to custody does not necessarily determine the issue, he nevertheless stressed that the comity of courts is a powerful doctrine in all cases.

14.071 The approach of the courts has not been uniform. In *D.A.D. v P.J.D.*,[3] more emphasis was placed on the paramount importance of the child's welfare than on the importance of the appropriate forum. The case demonstrates that the courts will be very reluctant to make a peremptory order for a child's return where the child has remained within the jurisdiction, living with the parent who has removed him, for a substantial period of time. The facts were that a father, in breach of a custody order made pursuant to divorce proceedings instituted by the mother in England, had removed a five-year-old daughter to his parents' home in Ireland where he had been living with her for thirteen months. Indeed, the child had first been brought to Ireland eighteen months previously, but had been taken back to England for a brief period pursuant to an earlier order of the English court. The mother's application for a peremptory order for the return of the child was refused by Blayney J., who decided that there would have to be a full investigation of every aspect of the case before a final order could be made. He distinguished this case from *Kent County Council v C.S.* on the basis of the longer residence of the child in Ireland, (in the latter case the period was only three months), but went on to express a general principle that the welfare of the child remains the paramount consideration regardless of the circumstances in which the infant happened to come within the jurisdiction.

14.072 In doing so he followed the decision of the English Court of Appeal in *Re L. Minors*[4] *and Re C. Minors*.[98] In the former case Buckley L.J. stated, at 925 that, "The action of one party in kidnapping the child is doubtless one of the circumstances to be taken into account, and may be a circumstance of great weight; the weight to be attributed to it must depend on the circumstances of the particular case." It is not easy to reconcile the emphasis here with the approach adopted by Finlay P. in *Kent County Council v C.S.*, nor with the approach later adopted by the same judge, this time as Chief Justice, in *Sanders v Mid-Western Health Board*. Possibly the approach adopted by Blayney J. should be confined to cases where the child in question has been within the jurisdiction for a prolonged period.

2 19 May 1988, unreported, High Court.
3 7 February 1986, unreported, High Court.
4 [1974] 1 All ER 913.

14.073 Cases may be further complicated by a claim by the parents that their rights under the Constitution are in issue. In *Northampton County Council v A.B.F. and M.B.F.*[5] the father had brought his three-year-old daughter from England to Ireland and placed her in the care of the defendants. The child had been placed by an English juvenile court in the care of Northampton County Council with a view to adoption. The mother was willing for the child to be placed for adoption, but the father was not. Hamilton J. stated that in the ordinary course he would have granted the County Council's application for the return of the child, without considering the merits of the case. However, under Irish law the adoption of a legitimate child in the circumstances of the case would not have been permissible, and the father was entitled "to rely on the recognition of the family contained in Article 41 for the purpose of enforcing his rights as the lawful father." The child's natural rights had also to be considered. Consequently it was necessary to order a full plenary hearing "for the purpose of ascertaining whether the child's rights are being protected," before any final order could be made. Despite being unconnected with Ireland before bringing his child here, the father was entitled to rely on constitutional rights founded on natural law which had universal application. In *Oxfordshire County Council v J.H. and V.H.*, supra, Costello J. also thought that reliance could be placed on constitutional guarantees. However, he doubted whether parents, who had ceased to be guardians under the law of their domicile, could advance rights which the children have. Also the court may under the Constitution refuse custody to parents where there are compelling reasons for so doing.[6]

(The decision was upheld on appeal to the Supreme Court (no judgment is available.) While upholding the decision, the Supreme Court referred to its earlier judgment in *Sanders v Mid-Western Health Board*[7] to which no reference had been made by Costello J).

14.074 However, in *Sanders v Mid-Western Health Board*, the Supreme Court held that Constitutional rights may not be claimed in such circumstances. Finlay C.J. stated

Where, as has happened in this case, parents having no connection with Ireland bring their children unlawfully from the country in which they are, into the jurisdiction of this court, in breach of an order made by the court in the jurisdiction in which they were domiciled and in which the children were being reared, I do not accept that they can by that act alone confer on themselves and their children constitutional rights under Articles 41 and 42 of the Constitution.

Some uncertainty remains, in that it is not clear what form of connection with Ireland would justify reliance on Constitutional protections. For

5 [1982] ILRM 164.
6 See *J.H. (an infant)* [1985] ILRM 302.
7 23 June 1987, unreported, Supreme Court.

example, would the fact that one parent is an Irish national be sufficient, even though all parties are domiciled and ordinarily resident in the country from which the child has been unlawfully removed?

The Hague Convention on International Child Abduction

14.075 The Convention on the Civil Aspects of International Child Abduction was adopted by the Hague Conference on Private International Law on 24 October 1980. Fourteen States are now parties to the Convention. These are the U.S.A, Canada, Australia, the U.K., Austria, France, Luxembourg, Norway, Portugal, Spain, Sweden, Switzerland, Germany and Belize. A number of other States, including Greece, the Netherlands and Finland will soon ratify the Convention. Its purpose is to protect children below the age of 16 from the harmful effects of their wrongful removal or retention across international borders, and to establish procedures for their prompt return to the State of their habitual residence, as well as to secure protection for rights of access. The main features of the Convention are (a) the principle that, where a child has been removed or retained in breach of custody rights under the law of the State of the chid's habitual residence, the requested State is bound, with very limited exceptions, to order the immediate return of the child, without conducting an inquiry into the child's welfare, and (b) the establishment of central authorities within contracting States to co-operate with one another, to assist in locating children and to facilitate the return of abducted children. The Department of Justice is currently preparing legislation which will incorporate the Convention.

The basic rule—a peremptory order for the return of the child

14.076 Article 12 requires the authorities in a requested State to order the return of a child forthwith to the State of his habitual residence, where he has been wrongfully removed or retained, and where that removal or retention occured within one year of the commencement of proceedings in the requested State. It is not clear whether time begins to run from the date of the actual wrongful removal or retention or, if it is later, from the date when the child is taken out of the State of his habitual residence. Where proceedings are commenced after the one year period, an order for return must be made "unless it is demonstrated that the child is now settled in its new environment". Article 3 provides that the removal or retention of the child is wrongful where:

(a) it is in breach of rights of custody attributed to a person, an institution or any other body, either jointly or alone, under the law of the State in which the child was habitually resident immediately before the removal or retention; and

(b) at the time of removal or retention those rights were actually exercised, either jointly or alone, or would have been so exercised but for the removal or retention.

14.077 "Rights of custody" include those which arise by operation of law. To avail of the Convention, therefore, it is not necessary for a parent who had actual custody of his child prior to removal, to obtain a custody order from a court in the State of the child's habitual residence. A non-custodial parent who remains a joint guardian may, it seems, avail of the Convention to secure the return of a child who has been removed by the custodial parent without the consent of the non-custodial parent. In *C. v C.*[8] the English Court of Appeal ordered the return to Australia of a child who had been taken from Australia by his mother, who had custody, without the consent of the father who was joint guardian. An Australian court had ordered that neither parent should remove the child from Australia without the consent of the other.

Grounds for refusing an order for the return of the child

14.078 Article 13 provides that the authorities in the requested State are not bound to order the return of the child where it is established:

(a) that the person . . . having care of the person of the child was not actually exercising the custody rights at the time of removal or retention, or had consented to or subsequently acquiesced in the removal or retention; or

(b) there is a grave risk that his or her return would expose the child to physical or psychological harm or otherwise place the child in an intolerable situation.

14.079 Return of the child may be refused where the child objects to being returned and has attained an age and degree of maturity at which it is appropriate to take account of its views. Return may also be refused under Article 20 "if this would not be permitted by the fundamental principles of the requested State relating to the protection of human rights and fundamental freedoms." Given that the philosophy underlying the Convention is to secure the swift return of children to the State of their habitual residence save in exceptional circumstances, it is likely that these provisions will be interpreted strictly. It should, nevertheless, be borne in mind that a parent seeking to resist an order for the return of a child who has been abducted to Ireland may, under Article 20, invoke rights under the Constitution, provided that he is sufficiently "connected" with Ireland to justify their invocation: see **14.067–14.073**.

The Central Authority

14.080 The Central Authorities in the contracting States play a central role in achieving the Convention objective of securing the prompt return of abducted children. Apart from co-operating with one another, the Central Authorities must, under Article 7, take all appropriate measures—

(a) to discover the whereabouts of a child who has been wrongfully removed or retained;

8 [1989] 1 WLR 654.

(b) to prevent further harm to the child or prejudice to interested parties by taking or causing to be taken provisional measures;

(c) to secure the voluntary return of the child or to bring about an amicable resolution of the issues;

(d) to exchange, where desirable, information relating to the social background of the child;

(e) to provide information of a general character as to the law of their State in connection with the application of the Convention;

(f) to initiate or facilitate the institution of judicial or administrative proceedings with a view to obtaining the return of the child and, in a proper case, to make arrangements for organizing or securing the effective exercise of rights of access;

(g) where the circumstances so require, to provide or facilitate the provision of legal aid and advice, including the participation of legal counsel and advisers;

(h) to provide such administrative arrangements as may be necessary and appropriate to secure the safe return of the child;

(i) to keep each other informed with respect to the operation of this Convention and, as far as possible, to eliminate any obstacles to its application.

The European Convention

14.081 It is likely that Ireland will also ratify in the near future the European Convention on Recognition and Enforcement of Decisions concerning Custody of Children and on Restoration of Custody of Children, which was signed (subject to ratification) on behalf of Ireland on 20 May 1980. Unlike the Hague Convention, which is based on the principle that abducted children should be returned forthwith to the State of habitual residence, the European Convention provides for the recognition and enforcement of custody decisions made in other countries. Although its use will, in many cases, achieve the same results as the Hague Convention, its operation appears to be more cumbersome and, unlike the Hague Convention, it does not protect custody rights which arise by operation of law in the absence of a court order. The Convention also appears to offer the abducting parent greater scope to challenge an application for the return of a child. The grounds on which an application for recognition and enforcement may be refused are as follows:

(a) that the defendant was unrepresented and had not been served with the document instituting proceedings in sufficient time to enable him to arrange his defence (article 9.1.a.);

(b) that the decision was given in the absence of the defendant or his legal representative, and the competence of the authority giving the decision was not based on habitual residence of the defendant or the child or on the last common habitual residence of the child's parents (article 9.1.b.);

(c) that the decision is incompatible with a decision relating to custody in the State addressed (article 9.1.c.);

(d) that the effects of the decision are manifestly incompatible with the fundamental principles of the law relating to the family and children in the State addressed (article 10.1.a.);

(e) that by reason of a change in circumstances since the original decision, its effects are no longer in accordance with the welfare of the child (article 10.1.b);

(f) that the child is a national of the State addressed or was habitually resident there, and no such connection existed with the State where the decision was given; (article 10.1.c.);

(g) that the child, being a national of the State of origin and of the State addressed, was habitually resident in the State addressed (article 10.1.c.);

These grounds are not all available in every case. In some cases of improper removal, the grounds are limited by the Convention. But individual States may reserve their position in relation to such limitations. Further elaboration must await the passing of the relevant legislation.

Chapter 15

CHILD CUSTODY AND ACCESS DISPUTES: PRACTICE AND PROCEDURE

District Court procedure

Jurisdiction

15.001 The relevant Rules are District Court (Guardianship of Infants Act 1964) Rules 1982, SI No. 141 of 1982. Rule 4 provides that the proceedings may be brought at any sitting of the court for the District Court area (or in the case of the Dublin Metropolitan District, the district), where any party ordinarily resides or carries on any profession, business or occupation. The proceedings are heard otherwise than in public. The most common application is under section 11 on a matter affecting the welfare of an infant usually custody or access. Rule 10 provides that the application is by "Notice" (this term is used rather than summons) in Form 11, and must be served on all other guardians of the infant. The form only provides for a guardian to apply for the court's direction. This overlooks the right of a natural father to apply for access to his non-marital child. However, the summons can be amended by deleting guardian and inserting father. Rule 14 provides that the age of the child may be proved by a certified extract from the register. In practice, this is often not done. The nature of the application must be specified for example, by inserting "to wit, custody or access or an application for a passport where the other guardian does not consent" etc.

Service

15.002 Rule 13 provides for twenty one days notice by registered post to the respondent. The usual statutory declaration, and the original summons with service endorsed, must be lodged at least seven days before the hearing.

Custody/access and the Health Board

15.003 If a child of a married couple, who have separated is in the care of the health board, on foot of a "fit person" order under the Children's Act 1908,[1] it is possible to issue section 11 proceedings and name the Health Board as respondent. Such application, in Dublin, is usually taken in the Family Law Court in Dolphin House rather than the Children's Court in Smithfield. This is on the basis that the Children's Court has jurisdiction to deal with children in care under the Children's Act 1908. However rule 4 of the 1982 Rules allows proceedings under the 1964 Act to be taken in *any* court, in the area where any party resides.

15.004 The general rules of the District Court provide for service out of the jurisdiction of the State in specified ciurcumstances.[2] In proceedings in respect of custody or access it is permissible to serve outside the jurisdiction if the respondent is domiciled or ordinarily resident within the jurisdiction, (rule 4(e)) or if the respondent is a necessary or proper party to an action brought against another person duly served within the jurisdiction (rule 4(f)). This might arise where the relevant children are in the care of a Health Board, and one spouse is residing and served within the jurisdiction, and the other spouse is served out of the jurisdiction.

Orders under Section 11 of the Guardianship of Infants Act 1964

15.005 If an application *for access only* is before the court, the court may exercise its discretion to order custody to the other spouse. That spouse may have had *de facto* custody for some time. Because an order of access cannot be granted except to a non custodial parent, the court may take the view that an order of custody should be made also. If there is likely to be a problem of non compliance with the order of access, it is essential that custody be indicated on the face of the order. This is helpful if the Gardaí are called to enforce the order. The consequences of breach of the order should be explained to the spouses before they leave the vicinity of the court. A warning of the consequences of a breach of such order (that is, prosecution under the Courts Act 1986) is incorporated into the order in the Dublin Metropolitan District: the penalties, under section 5 of the Courts Act 1986, are a fine of £200 or/and six months imprisonment. The 1982 Rules do not have a draft order under section 11, though there is a draft order for every other relevant section. (See **15.070**)

Variation and discharge of orders

15.006 An application to vary an order made under Part II of the Act of 1964 can be made at any time, as the order is regarded as interlocutory. (A spouse with immediate objections to an order may appeal within the usual fourteen day limit.) Rule 11, Form 12 of the 1982 Rules deals with

---

1 See also section 1 of the Childrens Act 1989 which authorises a Health Board to act (retrospectively, and prospectively) as a fit person.
2 S.I. No. 7 of 1962. District Court Rules (No. 1) 1962.

applications, under section 12 of the Act to vary or discharge an order made under Part II of the Act. The grounds of the application to vary or discharge are to be set out in the application. For example, "to vary the order of the —day of —— 1990, as follows; to reduce access by the respondent to once per month, instead of once per week". The procedure is the same as for a section 11 application—see Rule 13 of the 1982 Rules.

15.007 An application for variation or discharge may be accompanied by a summons under section 5 of the Courts Act 1986 for a prosecution. This may arise when an order is breached by the children not being returned. The custodial spouse may prosecute, and seek to discharge the order of access. (see **15.022**) The court may, on an application to discharge the order, ask the parties to amend the summons to a variation, and order reduced access rather than discharge the order. Or it may discharge the order temporarily in preference to making a committal order.

15.008 It is surprising that there are not more applications to vary or discharge orders of access. A common situation is where the non custodial spouse, who may have a drink problem, regularly fails to collect the children. If the custodial spouse, instead of returning to court to discharge or reduce the access, refuses to allow access, the non custodial spouse may apply to court to prosecute the custodial spouse for breach. Since it is a criminal offence to breach the order, the custodial spouse may end up with a conviction. In such case the solicitor for the custodial spouse should issue a discharge or variation summons to be listed on the same date as the prosecution. The court will then hear the full history, and may opt to vary the order to a reduced number of visits and dismiss the prosecution.

15.009 Variation and discharge are of importance in cases of child sexual abuse. If such abuse is disclosed, and there is a pre-existing access order, an emergency application to discharge the order may be issued. The court can abridge the time for service and order substituted service. Whether the court is prepared to list the discharge before the next date of access is at the discretion of the court. The lists may be full, or the court may feel that there is insufficient notice to the other spouse. In those circumstances, it may be more appropriate to seek an injunction in the Circuit or High Court to restrain further access pending a hearing of an application to discharge the order in the District Court. This may seem like forum shopping, but there should be an imaginative use of the emergency procedures to protect a child, provided there is full disclosure of all facts to the court, and there is no abuse of process.

Appeals

15.010 One feature of a District Court hearing is that an appeal operates as a stay on the order, provided a recognizance is entered into.[4] The

3 Rule 190, of the District Court Rules 1948, as amended by SI 84 (No. 2) of 1955.
4 Rule 192 of the 1948 Rules.

practicalities of the suspension need to be clarified before the parties leave the vicinity of the court. If for example, the wife obtains an order of custody and plans to leave the family home and return to her parents, with the children, there may be repercussions at a later stage if she takes the children after her husband has entered into a recognizance to appeal.

15.011 If, on the other hand, a wife with custody appeals the making of an access order, and enters into a recognizance, the husband cannot enforce his right to see the children in the interim, as the order in his favour is suspended. The solicitor for the husband should try and ensure that the appeal is listed as soon as possible. If the summer vacation intervenes he should, if necessary, make application to the court to have the appeal listed during a vacation sitting. In most family law cases, the recognizances are waived. In a case where a child is thought to be at risk in the hands of the appellant, it may be considered unwise to agree a waiver.

Other orders under the Guardianship of Infants Act, 1964

Death of guardian

15.012 In the context of marriage breakdown, the custodial spouse may have made a will nominating a third party to act as testamentary guardian of the children in order to prevent the other spouse taking custody of the children. The third party will have consented to so acting. On the death of the custodial parent, the testamentary guardian may take physical custody of the children. If there is a dispute as to which guardian is to have custody, or the surviving parent objects, or the testamentary guardian considers that the surviving parent is unfit to have custody, the testamentary guardian may issue an application under section 7(4) of the Act. Rule 6 of the District Court Rules provides for the notice to be in Form 1, and to be served on any other guardians including the surviving parent. The will may have nominated more than one testamentary guardian, and the surviving parent may only be objecting to one of the guardians. Rule 13 deals with service of the forms.

15.013 There are separate forms of orders available in the Rules, depending on whether the order is made under section 7(5)(a), (b) or (c). Section 7(5)(a) provides that the court may refuse to make the order, on an application by the testamentary guardian. Section 7(5)(b) provides that the court may make an order that the testamentary guardian shall act jointly with the surviving parent, and section 7(5)(c) provides that the court may make an order that the testamentary guardian shall act as guardian of the infant, to the exclusion (so far as the court thinks proper) of the surviving parent. Form 2 provides for the court refusing to make an order, on the application of the testamentary guardian. However, section 5(a) states that where the court refuses to make the order, the surviving parent remains sole guardian. This is not stated on the face of the order and the respondent may apply to have that fact stated on the face of the order.

15.014 In the case of an order under section 7(5)(c), the solicitor for the surviving parent needs to clarify with the court whether the order (that the testamentary guardian shall act to the exclusion of his client) excludes him from being consulted on all matters relating to the upbringing of the infants, or obtaining school reports, or being notified if any of the infants is hospitalised. These are other rights of a guardian which are not included under the heading of "access". If these can be itemised in the order, conflict at a later stage between the testamentary guardian and the surviving parent may be avoided.

15.015 Also requiring clarification is the question of a maintenance order made against the surviving parent in favour of the testamentary guardian. Section 7(6) provides for maintenance to be granted to the testamentary guardian for the maintenance of the infants having regard to the means of the surviving parent, as the court considers reasonable. Form No. 1 in the Rules does not make provision for the surviving parent to be notified in advance of the hearing that, in the event of the court making the order under section 7(5)(c), maintenance will be sought. The surviving parent it would appear, has a right to know exactly what orders are being applied for, and this should be stated by way of amendment to the standard form. This avoids an application for judicial review on the basis that the rules of natural justice were not complied with. A prosecution can be initiated for a breach of an order relating to custody or access by either the surviving parent or the testamentary guardian. It should be noted that Section 5 of the Courts Act 1986 applies to any person, and not only to a guardian under section 11.

Application to appoint a guardian

15.016 An application to appoint a guardian has limited relevance to marriage breakdown. However if a spouse has left the jurisdiction and cannot be found, or the estranged spouse has died without nominating a testamentary guardian the infants may be left without a guardian. An application may be taken by relatives of either spouse for the appointment of a guardian under section 8(1) or (2) of the Act. Section 8(1) provides that where an infant has no guardian, the court may, on the application of any person, or persons, appoint the applicant or applicants or any of them, to be the guardian or guardians of the infant. Section 8(2) provides that if no guardian has been appointed by a deceased parent or if a guardian so appointed dies or refuses to act, the court may appoint a guardian or guardians to act jointly with the surviving parent.

15.017 An example of the former would be an application by a grand-parent to be appointed guardian, where a mother has died, who had a child born outside marriage after separation from her husband, and the natural father has not been appointed a guardian under section 6a of the 1964 Act. The application is made *ex parte* in Form 5 under rule 7 of the 1982 Rules and the order is drawn up in Form 6. The section and rule 7 do not envisage a contested application between disputing relatives. The District Court Clerk will expect some notice so that a date can be fixed to hear the application.

15.018 An application, in accordance with section 8(2) of the Act may be made on an *ex parte* basis by the surviving parent. Rule 8 does not provide any form for such application, though the rules do provide Form 5 for the *ex parte* application under section 8(1). An amended form 7 should be lodged with the District Court Clerk. The surviving parent may want his cohabitee to be appointed as guardian. Or he may wish to delegate custody to a relative, who would act jointly with him as guardian. The court would use the guidelines of section 3 (which states that the welfare of the infant is the first and paramount consideration) to assist it in making an order. Welfare comprises the religious and moral, intellectual, physical and social welfare of the infant. Rule 15 provides for the court to direct service of any notice on any person not already served. In theory, the court could adjourn such an application, and order the maternal or paternal grand-parents or other relatives to be served. Form 7 may be used. The court may appoint them guardians instead. They would then act jointly with the surviving parent (section 3(3)), and the court could also make orders of custody and access.

15.019 If a testamentary guardian dies, or refuses to act, section 8(2) provides that any person may apply to be appointed as guardian. This application must be on notice to the surviving parent (rule 8). Rule 9 provides for the issue of a notice under section 8(4) or 8(5). Section 3(4) provides that the court may remove from office any guardian appointed by will or deed or order of the court; section 8(5) provides that the court may appoint another guardian in place of a guardian so removed or in place of a guardian appointed by any such order who dies. It is in Form 9 and should be served on each guardian, including the surviving parent. The surviving parent may use this procedure to remove a guardian, or to appoint a new guardian. The order of the Court is drawn up in form 10.

Part III of the Guardianship of Infants Act 1964

15.020 Part III of the Guardianship of Infants Act 1964 deals with disputes between third parties (including Health Boards) and parents as regards custody of infants. Parent is defined in section 13 as including a guardian of the person and any person at law liable to maintain an infant or entitled to his custody. It is relevant where a marriage breaks up and a child is left with a grandparent or other relative, or is placed in the voluntary care of the Health Board. One of the spouses may then seek the return of the child, and the person looking after the child may refuse to comply. "Person" in this context includes any school or institution.

15.021 The parent issues a notice in Form 14, in accordance with rule 12, and it is served on the person who has custody of the infant. This may be on the senior social worker, or other official nominated by the health board, as the infant may be in the custody of foster parents, where the health board is not prepared to disclose their address. The form seeks an order for the production of the infant in court. Section 14 provides that a court may decline to enforce the parental right to custody, where the court is of opinion that the parent has abandoned or deserted the infant. See *S. v Eastern Health Board and others*.[5] If the court does grant the order of production, it will be served on the person having custody of the infant. The court will then proceed to hear the merits of the application, and decide whether the parent is a fit person to have custody, taking account of the welfare of the infant. If the court grants custody to the parent, the order is drawn up in Form 16. If the court, in addition, decides to order that the parent repay the costs of bringing up or providing assistance for the infant, the order is drawn up in Form 18. There are no guidelines as to how the court is to deal with this issue. It is questionable whether the court could award a sum in excess of the limit of the District's courts jurisdiction.

Enforcement of District Court orders of custody or access

15.022 The most commonly held view is that it is not possible for a person to be committed for contempt of the District Court, unless it is in the face of the court. When the Courts Act 1981 introduced custody and other related proceedings into the District Court, it failed to include a provision relating to enforcement of its orders. Section 5 of the Courts Act 1986 now makes it an offence for a person "having the actual custody of an infant" to fail or refuse to comply with a custody or access order made by the District Court. Section 5 is limited to the District Court and the maximum penalty is a fine of £200 and/or 6 months imprisonment. A person having *de facto* custody by a deed of separation would not be able to use the section.

15.023 The respondent must have been given or shown a copy of the order (see **15.078**). He is deemed to have seen it if he was present in court when the order was made. If he was not in court, the service of the order should be proved, as part of the necessary proofs in the prosecution. Where breach of a custody order is alleged, a proper request for delivery of the child should have been made. This could be orally by the custodial spouse, or by registered letter (or letter delivered personally) sent by the solicitor for the applicant. If the Gardaí made the request they should be present in court to so state. The refusal or failure to return the child should be proved by giving evidence of the exact response of the respondent to the request for return.

15.024 Where breach of an access order is alleged, equally strict proofs are necessary, as the case must be proved beyond reasonable doubt. The request for access must have been made on or behalf of the person entitled

5 February 1979, unreported, High Court.

to access. The custodian, whether it be a spouse or a relative or "any person having actual custody" is guilty of the offence if he fails or refuses to comply with the requirement to exercise access in accordance with the terms of the order. "Any person having actual custody" includes a case where a child is placed in a foster family, or some other form of voluntary care, or where a fit person order is made in favour of a health board. Arguably such custodians take the place of the custodial spouse, and are liable to prosecution if they fail to comply with the order. If it is not possible for them to obey the terms of the original order, they should apply for its discharge. This also applies to a testamentary guardian. The existence of such strict sanctions shows the importance of having clear access orders, setting out exact dates, delivery and collection points, and times.

15.025 There are no rules under the Courts Act 1986 but the courts have adopted a form of summons, and the offence may be prosecuted summarily, as there is no power of arrest for breach of a custody or access order. One difficulty arises with teenage children who, despite being informed of the court order, may decline access to the non custodial parent. The custodial spouse in this case should apply to discharge the order rather than risk conviction. The court may take the view that the parent is encouraging the teenager to disobey the order, or is not doing enough to persuade him to comply. If a respondent spouse is not represented by a solicitor, and there has been a blatant breach of either the custody or access order, the court may assign a solicitor under the Criminal Legal Aid Scheme as it can be argued that the offence is serious enough to warrant legal aid. Alternatively, the court may adjourn the prosecution, and encourage the respondent to apply for civil legal aid at a law centre. If this is the case, the respondent will have to fulfil the criteria for civil legal aid which include the requirement that he has a reasonable chance of success in defending the proceedings. He will also have to pay a contribution, whereas criminal legal aid is free. Encouraging the respondent to apply for legal aid reduces the chance of judicial review on the basis that he was not advised of his right to apply for such aid.

15.026 There is a time limit of six months within which the prosecution should be brought. The prosecution is heard in the family law court, or at family law sittings. The Gardaí generally leave it to the parties to deal with the prosecution, and do not issue the summons. In any event, they do not have a power of arrest. The respondent may appeal against the conviction. The applicant may not appeal against a dismissal of the prosecution, nor may she appeal to seek an increase in the penalty imposed. Recognizances should be fixed immediately after the conviction, especially if a sentence of imprisonment has been imposed. The offender will be held in custody until the recognizance is entered into. The court, on appeal by the accused has the right to increase the sentence or suspend or reduce it, or substitute a fine, or uphold the appeal, and discharge the order.

Circuit Court procedure

Jurisdiction

15.027 The relevant rules are Circuit Court (No. 6) Rules 1982, SI No. 158 of 1982. The Circuit Court was given jurisdiction over all proceedings under the Guardianship of Infants Act 1964 by section 15 of the Courts Act 1981. Section 15 of the Courts Act 1981 substitutes a new section 5 into the 1964 Act, and also amends the definition of "court". The Circuit Court may vary or revoke an order made by the High Court before the commencement of the 1981 Act (12 May 1982), if the circumstances to which the order of the High Court related have changed other than by reason of such commencement. The Circuit Court may not make an order where the High Court has already made an order, subject to the right to vary or revoke. Section 16(1) of the Act of 1981 provides for the jurisdiction to be exercised by the judge of the Circuit Court where any party to the proceedings ordinarily resides or carries on any profession, business or occupation. This is also provided for in rule 4 of the Rules of 1982.

15.028 Rule 6 provides for the application to be brought in accordance with form 2, or such modification as may be appropriate. The dates of birth and the full names of each child must be stated. The procedures for the issuing of the application and service are the same as for maintenance (rules 10–18 of the 1982 Rules) and indeed an application for maintenance is normally consolidated with an application for custody. An application for interim custody or interim access is made by the issue of a notice of motion, grounded on the facts justifying the application. This is particularly important if the hearing date is likely to be after the long vacation. The notice of motion is normally listed for the mention date in Dublin, and the date for hearing can also be granted. Outside Dublin, the practice varies from circuit to circuit. If the case is not to be given a hearing date for some considerable time, an application within the circuit can be made by way of emergency to have interim orders made. An answer will be filed (rule 15) in the usual way. Rule 19 provides for costs which may be measured as between party and party by the judge. In practice this is never done because of the complexity of the average custody or access battle. Costs may be taxed in default of agreement.

High Court procedure

Jurisdiction

15.029 General problems concerning the jurisdiction of the High Court have been discussed at **1.022–1.029**. For reasons explained therein the great majority of custody and access applications are made in the Circuit Court or the District Court. Proceedings are still issued in the High Court in cases of child abduction, where they are usually combined with *habeas* *corpus* applications.[6] They are also issued where they are combined with an application for an injunction to restrain serious misconduct towards a spouse, particularly by a cohabitee. These proceedings will be issued more usually in vacation, particularly outside Dublin, where the Circuit Court is less accessible in vacation time. Also, as explained in Chapter 1, where the High Court has made an order under the Guardianship of Infants Act 1964, prior to the coming into force of the Courts Act 1981, it is possible to re-enter such proceedings in the High Court. This is because such orders are interlocutory in nature. Some High Court judges have remained seised of custody and access cases of a particularly complicated or protracted nature. Liberty to apply to the particular judge may have been given to the spouses.

15.030 The High Court procedure for an originating application is the special summons, and grounding affidavit. A replying affidavit is filed while the matter is before the master. When the documentation is in order, the master sends the case into the judge's list. There will then be submissions to decide whether the case should be heard in the High Court. If there is an emergency hearing, by way of *habeas corpus*, or an injunction has been granted, interim orders will most likely have been granted by the time the case comes into the judge's list. This may render any submissions as to whether the High Court should hear the matter academic. The proceedings as outlined are in accordance with the practice direction issued on 7 May 1982 which reads as follows:

Practice direction

Guardianship of Infants Act, 1964

Family Law (Maintenance of Spouses and Children) Act, 1976

Family Law (Protection of Spouses and Children) Act, 1981

> Having regard to the decision of Mr Justice Gannon in *R. v R and The Attorney General*, delivered on 16 February 1981 the notice of practitioners is drawn to the following practice direction.
>
> In any case where relief is sought in The High Court under any of the above-named Acts, the summons shall be returnable before the Master in the ordinary way and thereafter shall be put in the list before the judge sitting for Family Law on a Friday Motion day.
>
> The parties must on that occasion attend and submit such evidence or arguments as they see fit as to whether the case is one appropriate for The High Court to exercise its jurisdiction under one or other of the above Acts or whether it is a case which should be remitted to the Circuit Court or District Court. A decision will then be made on that issue and depending upon the nature of that decision the case will be listed for hearing, but such listing will not determine the appropriate scale of

6 See Article 40.4 of the Constitution, and Order 84 of the Rules of Supreior Courts.

costs, if any, to be awarded which will be subject to the provisions of section 17(4) of Courts Act, 1981.

Taking instructions in a dispute under the Guardianship of Infants Act 1964

Preliminary guidelines

15.031 It is important to clarify to the client the distinction between guardianship, custody and access. The custodian frequently assumes that custody gives her total rights over the child to the exclusion of the non-custodial parent. The non-custodial parent may assume that he can have the same relationship as before with his children, and call to the family home or telephone them at his convenience.

15.032 Instructions must be taken bearing in mind that the welfare of the children is the first and paramount consideration. If the solicitor stresses this constantly to his client, he may succeed in keeping the focus on the interests of the children, rather than on the behaviour or misbehaviour of the other spouse.

15.033 Instructions are best taken under each item of welfare[7] in the first place. These may later be combined to form a global picture of the welfare of the children. Otherwise, important facts may be overlooked. The existing arrangements under each heading are noted, followed by future arrangements under each heading. Next, similar instructions should be taken in relation to the role played by the other spouse by way of existing arrangements and likely future arrangements. The client may resist this exercise, but it is a useful way of ascertaining weaknesses, or allegations that will be made by the other spouse and also of seeing if some compromise can be reached.

15.034 The role of the extended family must not be overlooked. It may offer a supportive network to the separated spouse, or one of the extended family may be influencing the client against acceptance of reasonable proposals put forward by the other spouse. One must bear in mind that the courts are reluctant to disturb the status quo. It may be more helpful to see if present arrangements can be improved, or modified, rather than to suggest novel arrangements which may be impractical.

Welfare aspects

Religious and moral welfare

15.035 A solicitor must act sensitively in asking questions on the religious and moral welfare of children. The client may become defensive if he thinks that the solicitor is putting questions in a disparaging way. If neither

---

7 See sections 2 and 3 of the Guardianship of Infants Act 1964.

spouse attends worship regularly, the matter may not be an issue in a court. If, however, one of the spouses has strongly held views or has taken up with an unusual religion since the marriage, this is likely to give rise to conflict. Instructions on the tenets of that religion should be taken. Any documentation that will explain its beliefs is helpful to the court especially if it is known that the judge or justice himself has strong religious views. If the *de facto* custodial parent has a different religion from the children, the court will expect detailed practical arrangements to be put to it as regards how the children will be educated religiously. Some clients who have lapsed in the practice of their religion underestimate the seriousness with which the judiciary view the question of religious welfare. This point should therefore be stressed.

15.036 In relation to moral welfare, the client should be asked if he is going out with a member of the opposite sex. The relevance of this has been discussed in chapter 14. The question of whether the relationship is stable or casual should be explored. Clients do not always understand why a judge or justice might take issue with the fact that they have another relationship. They need to be well briefed on this important aspect of welfare. The court may take a more serious view of a client who engages in a homosexual relationship, whether the client is male or female. This may lead to loss of custody or restrictions on access, particularly overnight access. The solicitor will have to try to establish that all the other aspects of welfare operate in favour of the client and that these far outweigh any risk to moral welfare, particularly if the client is as discreet as possible. The client should be advised that the judge or justice may raise the question of whether custody of the children is more important to her than continuance of the relationship with the third party.

Educational welfare

15.037 The names of the schools, and the level of each child, should be noted. School reports should be inspected as should details of any particular problems at school. The level of schooling of each spouse may be relevant. If it is likely to be a contested custody dispute, then the school teachers should be contacted for fuller reports with a view to being summonsed as witnesses. If it is proposed to move the children from their schools, in the event of a change of custody, details of the children's involvement with school activities, extra curricular activities, and friends at school should be taken.

Physical and social welfare

15.038 The daily routine of each parent and the children should be noted. This may be seem tedious but it often elicits surprising information that is helpful to the case. The children's roots in their community, and their social network of friends, neighbours and colleagues in sports and related activities are relevant to the question of whether they should be moved out of their present environment. The accommodation and sleeping arrangements proposed by each spouse should be noted, whether in the context of a custody or an overnight access dispute. If any of the children suffer from any disability up-to-date reports from whatever special facilities the child is attending should be obtained. If the child has been attending a child guidance clinic, a report should be requested. The method and source of referral will affect whether the clinic is prepared to furnish a report to one spouse. The clinics generally prefer to receive a joint letter of request, and then the report is sent simultaneously to both solicitors. It may be possible, if a child is not already attending such a clinic, but is manifesting signs of psychological upset or disturbance, for the solicitor to refer the child for assessment. It is more appropriate to obtain the other spouse's consent, via his solicitor, as the clinic will usually not want to proceed without seeing both spouses and all the children.

15.039 If a client is accompanied by a neighbour or relative or friend, it may be useful to interview that person separately, to elicit further information. If the parents' relationship is acrimonious it may be helpful to find out if this person is prepared to collect and deliver the children to the other spouse, or allow delivery or collection at their address. If supervised access is to take place, the details can be worked out at an early stage. This may result in agreement. This can be more practical than suggesting supervision by a social worker, which usually cannot take place at weekends as the social workers attached to the Health Boards in the community care service do not generally operate at weekends (or evenings). They are overstretched during working hours and are rarely available to supervise access. If the solicitor feels that the full picture of the children's welfare is not being elicited, or that a report from the Probation and Welfare Service attached to the court will help the court decide a complex case, then the client's consent to the solicitor making that request should be sought at an early stage. The solicitor for the other spouse may be asked to consent prior to the date for hearing, and the case adjourned by agreement.

Preparing for court

Preparation for hearing in the District Court

15.040 Because there are no pleadings, it is difficult to know what allegations are likely to be made against the client. Problems may be encountered if the other spouse is not legally represented. If this is the position, the solicitor for the applicant should write to the respondent explaining the claim, and seeking to clarify what the respondent's intentions. Since the respondent does not have to file any replying document, the solicitor may find himself on the date of the hearing not knowing what case he has to meet. In those circumstances, it may be helpful to ask the respondent to consent to an order for a report from the Probation and Welfare Service. This service is attached to the Department of Justice, and it provides a social work service to the courts. Its role is usually that of supervising those placed on probation for offences, but it has provided an investigation and reporting function to the courts on family law matters, although this function has no strict basis in statute. The use of the Probation and Welfare Service will lessen a prolonged hearing where the unrepresented spouse may raise irrelevant evidence and possibly focus on the behaviour of the other spouse. If he subsequently fails to cooperate with the officer, the court will see this as contempt. The District Court may not commit except if the contempt is committed in the face of the court. However, since a probation and welfare officer is an officer of the court, if one of the spouses refuses to cooperate, and indicates such to the Justice in court, he may be committed. There is little to be gained by committing in these circumstances.

Section 40 of the Judicial Separation and Family Law Reform Act 1989, has inserted a new section 11(5) in the 1964 Act allowing the court of its own motion to procure a report on any question affecting the welfare of the infant. This section is very similar to the Australian Family Law Rules Order 30 rule 5(i). This new power should improve the quality of information available to the Court in many cases.

15.041 Witness summonses should have been served on any professional witnesses. They usually prefer this option, as it reduces the impression that they volunteered to give evidence for one party only, thus leading to accusations of bias. Copies of reports should be available for the opposing solicitor and the justice. The District Court lists are usually so crowded that the court often cannot set aside sufficient time to hear a protracted custody or access dispute. This is not to say that the Court, certainly in the Dublin Metropolitan District, may not sometimes devote considerable time to hear complex individual cases.

Preparation of reports for the hearing

15.042 Certain details should be included in a report no matter whether it is from a social worker, psychologist or psychiatrist. These are: the general background of the case, an outline of the family history, details of the present home situation of the children the antecedents of the children who are at the centre of the dispute, the allegations and concerns of each spouse and the children, an assessment of the children, their school records, medical histories if relevant, conclusions and recommendations. Hearsay should be clearly noted as such in the report, and avoided if possible. If it is included, it should be by way of corroboration of the author's findings of facts in relation to the child. The report should draw a distinction between facts and the impressions or expressions of opinion of the author. The qualifications of the author should be set out in the report. If possible, it should be written in language intelligible to lay persons. If reports from other clinics or agencies are used, these should be clearly identified. If recommendations are made based on certain psychological theories, for example "bonding", the theory should be briefly explained and, if necessary, the author and reference should be quoted. If a report presents one of the spouses in glowing terms, without referring to any good points of the other spouse, the court may assume that the author of the report is biased. The professional should maintain objectivity to retain credibility.

15.043 A child guidance clinic may decide that the team of professionals who are already giving treatment to the child should not prepare a report to the court. It may then arrange for a separate team to assess the child for the purpose of the court proceedings. This is done where the parents originally agreed to the child being referred specifically for treatment, although the procedure can delay matters. The ultimate report may be based on a series of long interviews with the child separately from the parents, with each parent separately, perhaps with the other children of the family separately and together, and several sessions with the whole family together. A consultant child psychiatrist generally takes charge of the team, and has responsibility for preparing the report. The team itself is interdisciplinary.

15.044 It is preferable if the parents agree to a joint referral, and a joint report. This saves the children from the ordeal of assessment by a second child psychiatrist. The courts may frown on children being seen by different psychiatrists, particularly where only one spouse is seen, and where it is only one consultation. The Circuit Court does not use the probation and welfare service as much as the District Court. The High Court relies more on the parties obtaining reports from child psychiatrists. In both of these courts it is possible to serve a notice for further and better particulars if reference is made in the pleadings to an expert's report. A notice to produce for inspection can also be served, to obtain the report prior to the hearing. If there is no cooperation with a notice to produce, an application by way of motion and affidavit can be made for an order of discovery.

15.045 A problem may arise where the report requested by one spouse is unfavourable to that spouse. A solicitor is not entitled to dictate or edit a doctor's report. In *Noble v Thompson and Partners*[8] a doctor successfully sued a firm of solicitors for payment of the fee for a report. The solicitors had sought a report in relation to court proceedings on access. The doctor included a statement that the wishes of the four children should be taken into account and the solicitor objected to this. The judge considered that the doctor was entitled to insist that his report should not be edited. The doctor was not entitled to put into his report anything he thought fit, merely what was relevant to the purpose of such report. If the other spouse is aware that "editing" may have occurred he may summons that witness to attend court and the spouse who requested the report may cross examine the maker of the report, as he is no longer his witness. However, if a report

---

8 A County Court decision reported in the *Irish Law Times and Solicitor's Journal* ot 21 June 1980.

is delivered *after* an expert has already been summonsed to attend court the person who summonsed him cannot cross examine his own witness. He may seek to serve a notice to cross examine that witness, but it is open to the court to decide whether to allow this. In certain cases, even before the amendment to section 11, the court adopted a flexible attitude, and asked questions itself to clear up any discrepancy.

15.046 Social work evidence is under-used in custody disputes. The social worker has the advantage of seeing the family in the home setting. Some of the visits are made without appointment. Also, a public health nurse who is concerned about a child being at risk of abuse or neglect will inform the community care social workers, to see if action is needed. If there has been a history of marital disharmony, there may be an extensive file with community care relating to the spouse who is looking after the children. Individual or family counselling sessions may have been conducted. Information from such sources may be useful to the court.

Mediation

15.047 If the only dispute between the parties is access or custody, consideration should be given to recommending that the parties attend a Mediation Service. (see **18.010–18.018**) Access often becomes a symbolic fight between the spouses as both may unwittingly want or need a focus to continue their struggle. Some sessions with a mediator, who may also talk to the children, may help the spouses to do what is best for the children, instead of having a solution imposed by a court. There is less chance of access arrangements breaking down where the parties have themselves agreed those arrangements.

Children attending at court

15.048 Generally, the courts do not like children to be brought into the vicinity of the court, or made to attend court on behalf of one of the parents. The impression may be given that the parent, who calls the child in evidence, has pressurised the child to do so. In some rare cases the High Court has allowed older or adult children to give evidence which was relevant to a dispute in respect of younger children. This was done in court, in the presence of solicitor and counsel, but in the absence of both clients, and on undertakings by the lawyers not to disclose the evidence to their clients.

15.049 Alternatively, the court may hear the children, either separately or together, in the presence or absence of the lawyers, but always in the absence of the clients. In *B. v B.*[9] D'Arcy J. ruled that because the interests of the children were paramount, he could see the children in the absence of counsel. Counsel had objected on the basis that a judge might hear charges from the children made against one or other of the parties, where they had no opportunity to refuse these. If children are ordered to give evidence,

9 Reference unknown; information supplied by T. Egan B.L.

the parents should be warned not to coach them, or put pressure on them. If such pressure is imposed, it may be treated as an interference in the court process, and punishment by way of committal is possible.

Hearing of disputes over children

15.050 The courts may hear the evidence of the experts before the evidence of the spouses or at special times, to facilitate busy professional staff in attending court. If the case is likely to take a day or more, an application may be made to the judge at the outset for the experts to be heard first or at some other suitable time. If there is time on the morning of the hearing it may be possible to agree the admissibility of reports in whole or in part.

15.051 Efforts to settle or agree the practicalities of access, if this emerges as the only matter in dispute, should be made. The patience of the court may be stretched by trivial fighting over whether access should be on a Saturday rather than a Sunday, or whether collection should be in town, at the family home, or at the nearest bus stop. It facilitates the hearing if the lawyers have tried in advance to identify areas of agreement and disagreement on these points.

15.052 Where proceedings have been consolidated into one hearing, some Circuit Court judges take the view that the application for judicial separation or/and barring should proceed first, because questions of maintenance, custody and access may depend on the decision on the status of the parties, or who is to live in the family home. When the court has made the decision to bar, it is unlikely that custody will be granted to the barred spouse. The dispute will then be reduced to access. Advance instructions should be taken from the applicant on the access arrangements that she would find agreeable, in the event of her husband being barred. It may also be helpful for the lawyers to discuss the matter in advance on a "without prejudice" basis. If the court declines a barring order on the ground of insufficient evidence, any further evidence called should not repeat the evidence already heard, but should focus on the welfare of the children.

15.053 It is difficult for a spouse who is guilty of violence or mental cruelty towards the other spouse to obtain custody. Clients often have unrealistic views as to their chances of success. A client should be forewarned of these problems, and should be advised in a sensitive way to face up to the risk of losing custody well before the hearing. Otherwise there may be emotional outbursts in court towards the other spouse or worse still the Judge.

15.054 If both spouses have been violent or cruel to each other, the task of the court is more difficult. In some cases the courts have indicated that, if they had power to do so, they would have ordered the children to be committed to the care of the Health Board. In such cases the court does have power to order the monitoring of custody the Probation and Welfare Service, or by community care social workers, and/or continuing assessment by a child guidance clinic. In *O'N. v O'B. and others*[10]

Finlay J. ordered that if the child psychiatrist or any of her team became alarmed at the way the child was being looked after he should be informed directly and the case would be re-entered on the judge's own motion.

Access arrangements

15.055 Court orders that deal with access only should record, on the face of the order, who is the person having sole custody as enforcement is easier if custody and access is clearly set out. Access arrangements should be set out in detail, particularly if the access has been bitterly fought. The weekly access, delivery and collection points, access on birthdays, Christmas and Easter holidays and summer vacation should be specified. Whether access is to be overnight and if so, any special provisions on accommodation should be set out. All access orders should have a provision that, in addition, there shall be such further or other access as may be agreed between the parties. The parties should be advised that, if they vary the arrangements by consent, they should notify the solicitors. Otherwise, at a future date, it may suit one of the parties to allege a breach of the order.

15.056 Sometimes there is a gap of three to five years before there is an application for access. If a spouse who has not seen his children for some time wants to withdraw his application for access to a particular child, it should not be assumed that the court will allow it, even if there is consent. It may require evidence, including evidence from an expert, as to whether it is in the child's welfare *not* to see the spouse. If witnesses are available in the precincts of the court, they should wait until the court rules on the application.

Prisoners

15.057 If the spouse applying for access is a prisoner, the probation and welfare service, the prison governor's office, and the prison chaplain should all be consulted. If a solicitor is opposing access, or representing a prisoner, he should ask to inspect the proposed visiting area. Otherwise embarrassment may be caused in court, when there are arguments as regards the facilities in the prison. The probation and welfare service may agree to supervise the visit, depending on resources. They may agree to visit the opposing spouse, who has custody and invite her to see the visiting area. Arrangements can be made for relatives of the prisoner to collect the children and deliver them to the prison, remain in the visiting area, and return the children. Special arrangements have been made in Dublin for visits to take place at the probation and welfare service offices at Marlborough Street, where space is less restricted, and more facilities exist for play with children. The prison service will facilitate visits if they are

10 22 January 1980, unreported, High Court.

consulted in advance about arrangements, and security and staffing levels permit. The nature of the offence for which the prisoner has been sentenced may be relevant to the question of whether access will be ordered. The past history of the marriage, including any violence to the other spouse, will be given in evidence, though it may be possible for access to take place without the prisoner and the custodial spouse coming into contact with each other.

15.058 The prison authorities may decline to bring the prisoner to the court unless there is a body warrant granted by the court in advance, or the court registrar or clerk contacts them, and verifies that the case is listed for the particular court and time. The District Court has a standard form for a body warrant, which is signed by the Justice, and posted or hand delivered to the prison office. The Circuit Court can be asked, by way of an *ex parte* docket, for an order to produce the prisoner. There is a similar procedure in the High Court—an *ex parte* application—though there is no reason why the application cannot be made when the case comes into the list for a date for hearing. The prison officers usually insist on remaining on in the court during the hearing for security reasons. The court usually accedes to this request, but may order that any evidence given is confidential and is not to be repeated to anyone else. A copy of any court order should be sent to the Governor's office and the Probation and Welfare Service.

Evidence on appeal

15.059 A problem should not arise over the introduction of new expert evidence, or updated evidence, in an appellate court, except perhaps in the Supreme Court. Because the Supreme Court relies on the transcript of the High Court evidence, an application by way of motion, setting out the grounds for applying for admission of the new evidence should be issued, with a grounding affidavit. In *B. v B.*[11] the new evidence was heard orally. However Walsh J. stated that it would be undesirable for the Supreme Court, except in the most exceptional circumstances, to delay the other business of the court by conducting a time consuming examination of oral evidence. In *E.K. v M.K.*[12] new evidence was not admitted by the majority of the court. Henchy J., dissenting, criticised this refusal on the basis that the Court would be determining the issue of custody in the absence of medical evidence which might have an important bearing on the welfare of one of the two children concerned.

15.060 Guidelines were laid down in *J.M. and G.M. v An Bord Uchtála*,[13] an adoption case, on the role of an appellate court. For the purpose of an appeal from a judgment of the High Court, the facts may be divided into two categories. First there are primary facts which are determined by the

11 [1975] IR 54.
12 July 1974, unreported, Supreme Court.
13 [1988] ILRM 20.

judge after assessment of the credibility and quality of the witnesses. As *Northern Bank Finance v Charleton*[14] shows, it is only when the findings of primary facts cannot be held to be supported by the evidence that the Supreme Court will reject them.

15.061 The second category comprises secondary or inferred facts. Henchy J. stated that these are facts which are not determined directly from an assessment or evaluation of the credibility of the witnesses, or the weight to be attached to their evidence, but which derive from inferences drawn from the primary facts. The Supreme Court is free to draw its own inferences, if it considers that those drawn by the High Court were not correct.

Child abduction

Checklist: Taking instructions where there is a threat to take a child out of the Republic of Ireland

15.062 It is helpful if there has been a prior court order granting the client custody, with no provision allowing access outside the jurisdiction. The following is a check list for taking instructions:

1. The names, and any nicknames of the children, and their dates and places of birth.
2. The full name, birthplace, date of birth, maiden name, or other aliases commonly used by the respondent.
3. Full descriptions and photographs of the children.
4. Full description and photograph of the respondent.
5. Check if passports have been issued for the children in their own names, or whether they are included in the parents' passports. Check if a passport of any foreign country has ever been obtained by the respondent or, if not so obtained, whether he was entitled to apply for one, depending on his domicile, nationality or place of birth. Check if he holds a second passport, and whether this was issued on the basis that he surrendered his first passport, or whether he was entitled to retain the two passports. Check if he ever made a report of a passport being stolen or lost. This is in case the report was false, and the passport has been retained with a view to leaving the country undetected.
6. Addresses of relatives or friends abroad.
7. If he is likely to go to the United Kingdom or France by ferry with a car, which exit he is likely to use, and what is the car's registration? If he has no car, what exit is he likely to use, depending on the home address, location of relatives or friends.
8. The country that he is likely to go to, based on whether he has a passport or not.
9. Current addresses within the jurisdiction where he may take the

14 [1979] IR 149.

children initially, with a view to removing them from the jurisdiction when things have quietened down.

10. Addresses of schools, so that they can be notified immediately not to allow the children to be collected by anyone other than the custodial parent.

Checklist: Action to be taken where there is a threat to take a child out of the Republic of Ireland

15.063 Where there is a threat to remove a child from the jurisdiction the following steps should be taken:

1. If passports have not already been issued to the children, or they are not on either parent's passport, then notify the Passport Office by telephone, to be confirmed in writing, that passports are not to be issued for the children, and that the custodial spouse does not consent to their issue. This is because the non custodial parent may present a form, with a forged signature of the custodial parent, to the Passport Office. Try to ascertain, if the respondent has no passport, whether he has made a recent application for a passport, or whether one has recently issued.

2. If the respondent is holding a passport from another jurisdiction, either because he has dual nationality, or because he is a foreign national, notify the nearest embassy of any court orders in existence, and that objections are being made to any proposed application for passports for the children, or to including the children on his passport. Even if he is a naturalised citizen of this jurisdiction, he may still be entitled to obtain a passport of his country of origin, or the country of his habitual residence or domicile.

3. If passports are in the custodial parent's home, have them locked in the bank or solicitor's safe in case there is an attempt to remove them.

4. Make application to the Circuit Court, or the High Court, for an injunction restraining the respondent spouses from removing or attempting to remove the children from the jurisdiction. If possible, obtain an order suspending the access order, pending an application to the originating court to discharge the order or to attach supervisory conditions to it. If the court is not prepared to make such an order, then an order restraining any contact or communication or any attempt to collect them for access should be sought. Also, seek an order requiring the respondent to surrender his passport to the registrar of the court forthwith.

5. Notify the airport and port authorities of all places of exit from the jurisdiction that an unauthorised attempt to remove the children from the jurisdiction is feared, and that application is being made for an injunction, or that a temporary injunction has been granted. The airport and port or harbour police have their own powers. If they are not cooperative, it is possible to contact the local Garda Station to the airport or port as they usually have a member present

at entry and exit points. So, for example, in Dublin, the Santry police would be contacted for Dublin Airport, and Store Street Garda Station in relation to the ferry in Dublin City, and Dun Laoghaire Garda Station in relation to the ferry from there. A photograph of the respondent and the children is essential, and should be given to the relevant authorities. This can be transmitted electronically to all exit points. Indicate the country to which he is likely to take them.

6. If a visa is about to issue for entry to countries such as the United States or Australia, notify the relevant embassies. They are likely to suspend the issue of the visa until a court order clarifies the position.

7. Obtain permission of client to ask the court to lift restrictions on reporting the case by the Press. This may help in the tracing of children abroad, particularly in the United Kingdom. In *B.D. v T.D.*[15] extensive press publicity led to the tracing of a child in Scotland.

8. *District Court* Proceed to issue summons under section 11 of the Guardianship of Infants Act 1964 to discharge the access order or if no orders under the Act are in force, issue custody proceedings (using rule 10, form 11) and seek an order of no access. Note that Part III of the Guardianship of Infants Act 1964 is not relevant here; the rules applicable to seeking an order for the production of the infants cannot be used. An application to abridge the time for service, and an order of substituted service, should be obtained. The advantage of using the District Court is that the respondent can be prosecuted (using section 5 of the Courts (No. 2) Act 1986) for breach of the original order or for an attempt to breach the new order of no access. The prosecution, in the case of the former, can be listed at the same time as the application to discharge the access order. The Gardaí can be enlisted to warn the respondent that he will be prosecuted if he does not hand over the children to the parent accompanying them. The Gardaí have no power of arrest under section 5 of the 1986 Act, and some officers will not be readily familiar with the section.

OR

9. *Circuit Court* The advantage of the Circuit Court is that an injunction may be obtained *ex parte* without notification to the respondent. The element of surprise is important. Proceedings by way of an application for custody and an order forbidding access may be issued or, if an order is already in existence, a motion to attach and commit the respondent to prison, and an application to discharge the access order, may be issued. They may be served with the interim injunction order.

If the custodial spouse has to await a District Court hearing which is on notice, even if the time is abridged to the absolute minimum, the respondent may leave the country before the hearing. Ob-

15 21 October 1976, unreported, High Court.

viously, if he already has taken the children in breach of a District Court order, a District Court application to discharge the access order is of no use unless the children have already been returned to the custodial spouse. However after the obtaining of an *ex parte* injunction in the Circuit Court, a summons to prosecute him for breach of the District Court order can be served with the Circuit Court order, so that the maximum penalties can be imposed although this can only be done if the original order *was* a District Court order. In this way the respondent may be committed for contempt if he disobeys the injunction, and also (possibly) prosecuted for breach of the original order. This is important where a respondent is prepared to continue breaking the order, and is not influenced by the committal powers of the Circuit Court.

Action by a non-custodial spouse

15.064 It is more difficult for a non-custodial spouse, who has an access order in his favour, to prevent the custodial spouse from leaving the jurisdiction. A solicitor acting on his behalf may have to apply for custody or/and an order preventing the other spouse from leaving the jurisdiction. He may not bring a prosecution for an anticipated removal from the jurisdiction. The prosecution must be based on failure or refusal to comply with the access order. If the custodial spouse has already refused him access in contemplation of leaving the country, a prosecution may be initiated but, by the time the summons is served, the custodial spouse will probably have left the jurisdiction. The best remedy lies in the Circuit or High Court. An injunction may be sought on the basis that the removal of the children would deprive the applicant of access and guardianship rights, and be in breach of the access order. If it was originally a District Court order, it will probably have included an express clause prohibiting removal of the children from the jurisdiction without an order of the court or the consent of the other spouse. The higher courts are more likely to grant an injunction where an order of another court has been disobeyed. The applicant spouse may not have a sufficient case to obtain custody of the children. He may therefore have to apply for very strict conditions attaching to the custody order to ensure that further attempts to leave the jurisdiction are not made. He may be granted further access, or overnight access, or telephonic access to try to maximise his contact with the children.

Where child is removed (or retained) within the jurisdiction, or removed here from another jurisdiction

15.065 An application by way of *habeas corpus* may be made in the High Court, to seek the production of the child in court, on the basis that he/she is unlawfully detained.[17] Jurisdiction in *habeas corpus* rests on the presence

16 See District Court (Guardianship of Infants Act 1964) Rules 1982, rule 11, form 12.
17 See Order 34 rule 3 of the Rules of the Superior Court 1986, and Article 40 of the Constitution.

in the jurisdiction of the person being detained as well as the person who is detaining him. It does not therefore provide a remedy where an offending spouse abducts a child and takes him abroad. An injunction may be applied for seeking, *inter alia*, the return of the child to the sole custody of the applicant spouse. There is a duty to make full disclosure in the grounding affidavit, of *every material fact*. In *D. v D.*[18] Blayney J. set aside an *ex parte* order requiring the father to hand over the child to the mother, on the basis that he was not satisfied that the affidavit grounding the wife's application had disclosed every material fact to the court. There may be a problem locating the respondent to serve the order on him, and his servants or agents. If it is known that he is receiving assistance from specific relatives or friends, it may be more appropriate to join them as defendants. In *B.D. v T.D.*[19] costs were awarded against a grandfather and aunt for prolonging the proceedings by not making full disclosure of what they knew about the location of the child who had been abducted. The court may order the attendance in court of such people to state where the infants are being detained. If they fail to cooperate they may be committed for contempt.

15.066 The court may also order that the Gardaí give active assistance to try to trace the children, or grant liberty to the applicant to obtain the services of the Gardaí for the purposes of enforcing the interim order, and serving the court documents. There is no specific power given to the courts or the Gardaí to get involved in these custody matters. However, individual judges have made such orders and, in a case where the Gardaí refuse to assist, the court's assistance may be asked for, or alternatively the commissioner's office may become involved. It would, however, make the task of the court much easier if the powers of the Gardaí were clarified in legislation. Even if such an order is not made, the local Gardaí can be advised that a breach of the peace is likely when the solicitor or someone on his behalf goes to serve the order as the Gardaí do have powers of arrest where there is a breach of the peace. If the original order of custody or access was made in the District Court, the Gardaí can be advised of their powers of prosecution, though they do not have a power of arrest. They may arrest if they are assaulted, resisted or obstructed, while in the course of their duty. If they accompany the custodial parent and her solicitor when the conditional order of *habeas corpus* is being served, and the respondent commits a breach of the peace or one of the above mentioned crimes, he can be arrested and brought to the station. The respondent may more readily cooperate in the return of the child if the Gardaí are involved.

Where both spouses are ordinarily resident outside the jurisdiction

15.067 If both spouses reside outside the jurisdiction and one of them brings the children into the jurisdiction in breach of a foreign court order,

---

18 7 February 1986, unreported, High Court.
19 21 October 1976, unreported, High Court.

an application may be made to make the children wards of the Circuit or High Court and in addition, an application for *habeas corpus* or an injunction can be made. The application for the child to be made a ward of the Circuit Court can be included in the application under the Circuit Court Rules (No. 6) 1982 SI No. 159 of 1982. For the High Court, Order 65 of the Rules of the Superior Courts 1986 is applicable. Proceedings under the Guardianship of Infants Act 1964 should be issued. It must be stated in the grounding affidavit that the applicant is a citizen of a named country. The court may order the applicant to surrender his passport to his solicitor pending a hearing as to whether the children should be allowed return to the foreign jurisdiction with the applicant. This was done in *K.F. v E.F.*[20]

15.068 There are certain difficulties in the gathering of evidence for such a hearing. Any court orders made in the foreign jurisdiction should be furnished together with the grounding summons and affidavit. It may be possible, depending on the distances and time involved, to file an affidavit of a social worker or other professional involved with the children. Alternatively, the solicitor in Ireland may swear an affidavit, seeking the liberty of the court to admit the reports of the social workers or other professionals, which he exhibits in his affidavit. On the question of whether or not a court will allow a full hearing on the merits, see section 15.

Emigation

15.069 If a parent wishes to emigrate to a country like Australia, the court may be reluctant to approve on the basis that the other parent may not be able to afford to travel there and will effectively be denied access. The court will weigh up all the aspects of welfare, including the right of the child to access to the non custodial parent. Also, if the custodial parent has not made detailed provisions with regard to schooling and religious welfare, the provision of accommodation or employment or maintenance to support the children the court may decline the order. It is essential that the parent has made practical provisions for the welfare of the children, and these should be set out in detail in the grounding affidavit. If the court has declined the order, it may also take the precaution of ordering the surrender of any passports in the possession of the person who has been refused the order.

Forms and precedents

15.070 Circuit Court: Draft application

Take Notice, (insert the first page of Form No 2, of the Circuit Court (No. 6) Rules 1982).

1. An order granting the applicant sole custody of the infants named in the title herein.

20 10 November 1982, unreported, High Court.

2. An order restraining the respondent from in any way whatsoever interfering with the care custody and control exercised by the applicant over the said infants and each of them.

3. An order providing for and regulating access by the respondent to the infants named in the title herein. OR

   An order pursuant to section 11 of the Guardianship of Infants Act 1964, giving custody of the infant to the plaintiff on such terms and conditions, and subject to such right of access by the defendant as to this Honourable court may seem just—OR

   An injunction restraining the defendant from threatening molesting assaulting or coming near the plaintiff or the infant of the marriage.

And take notice that the applicant will rely upon the following matters in support of the application:

1. The applicant is of opinion that, having regard to the respondent's total disregard for the welfare and well being of the children of the marriage, it is in their best interests that they should continue to reside with her and under her care and control. OR

   The applicant is of opinion that, having regard to the history of her marriage and the age of the infants named in the title herein, the said infants should continue to reside with her and under her care and control.

2. The respondent has failed adequately to maintain the applicant and the children, in that he spends any money available to him on drink. OR

   The children of the marriage frequently witnessed these assaults and were extremely frightened by the respondent's behaviour. The children have become extremely distressed and disturbed after the drunken rows of the respondent. The husband has threatened violence and this form of mental cruelty has had a severe effect upon the welfare and safety of the applicant and the infants.

Clauses when sexual or physical abuse on the children is alleged

1. The infants have disclosed that the respondent subjected them to sexual assault and abuse during their childhood. This behaviour has had a serious effect on each of them and they have become withdrawn and nervous. Each of them requires professional counselling.

2. As a result of examination by medical doctors and the attendance of the infant with Dr. —, a specialist in child sexual abuse, attached to — Sexual Assault Clinic, it became apparent to the applicant that the said abuse had become committed by the respondent. The said infant is greatly distressed and has suffered physical and mental anguish, as has the applicant. As a result of the respondent's behaviour, it is necessary for the infant to receive ongoing treatment.

15.071 Circuit Court: Answer

Insert the headings of Form No. 9 of the 1982 Rules

1. The respondent denies that the main burden of looking after the children of the marriage has fallen on the applicant, or that she is in the best position to look after the said children. He further denies that he is not a suitable person to be given custody of the said children.

   OR, in the case of child sexual abuse—

   I say that I, this deponent, categorically and absolutely deny that I have sexually abused my daughter. It is the respondent's belief that the applicant's dislike for him is such that she makes these false allegations in order to remove any contact he may have with the infants, the subject matter of this dispute. If, which is denied, the infant is suffering from any psychological difficulty, the respondent proposes to the court that the infant be assessed by an independent child psychiatrist, to be appointed by the court.

2. The respondent reserves the right to give further evidence at the hearing of the application.

   Answer in a cross application

   It is not in the best interest of the infants that a custody order would be made in favour of the applicant. The grounds for so stating are set out in the Application filed by the respondent on the — day of — 1990.

Types of order

It is ordered that the parties do continue to have joint custody of the infant but that the said infant should remain in the care and control of the wife. The access is to be under the supervision of Ms K, social worker. **OR**

It is ordered that the plaintiff have custody of . . ., and the defendant undertake by his counsel to stay away from the family home, save for access to the said infants, as agreed between the parties. **OR**

It is ordered that the respondent be restrained from removing or attempting to remove the infant from the custody of the applicant.

15.072 Circuit Court: Notice of motion for stay on appeal pending the hearing

. . . An order staying the access to be enjoyed by the respondent to the infant, pursuant to the Circuit Court order, dated the — day of — 1990, pending the hearing of the appeal in these proceedings.

[In the alternative . . . that the access be supervised in such manner as to this Honourable Court may seem just and equitable, pending the full hearing of the appeal.]

15.073 Grounding affidavit

The motion is grounded on an affidavit, which may include clauses similar to the following:

I say that evidence was heard in the Circuit Court relating to the sexual abuse by my husband of my child. I beg to refer to a copy of my solicitor's notes of the evidence in the Circuit Court in these proceedings, which I believe constitutes an accurate note of the evidence then produced.

I beg to refer to a copy of the report of the child psychiatrist, who was called to give evidence on behalf of my husband. I beg to refer to a copy of the said report upon which marked with the letter "A" I have endorsed my name prior to the swearing hereof. I also beg to refer to the new report, which reveals that the extent of the abuse committed on the said child was far greater than realised at the time of the first report. I beg to refer to a copy of the said report, upon which, marked with the letter "B", I have endorsed my name, prior to the swearing hereof. In the light of the matters disclosed in the new report, I am now of the view that such continued access is not in the best interests of the infant. The second report reveals that access is having an adverse effect on the said child. I believe that it is in the best interests of the infant that no access should take place prior to the full hearing.

I say and believe that the team of professionals involved in the assessment and treatment have advised me that, pending further assessment, no access should take place. I say and believe that the sexual abuse committed by my husband on the eldest child, has put the welfare of that child, and the younger child, seriously at risk.

15.074 Circuit Court: Notice of appeal to the High Court

Take Notice that the applicant hereby appeals to the High Court sitting in Dublin, at the next sittings thereof after the expiration of 10 days from the date of service hereof, against so much of the order of the Circuit Court, made herein on the — day of — 1990, as awarded access to the respondent.

Ground of appeal

1. That the learned Trial Judge is wrong in law, in holding that the welfare of the children was best served by having them in the care of the Plaintiff.
2. The learned Trial Judge is wrong in law in holding that the conduct of the Plaintiff was merely a factor, and not a decisive factor, in determining with which parent the children should live. The determination by the learned Trial Judge that the welfare of the children is best served by being in the care of the Plaintiff is against the evidence and unsustainable.

15.075 Supreme Court: Notice of motion seeking liberty to adduce further evidence

TAKE NOTICE that upon the hearing of this matter, on the — day of — 1990, the Defendant will apply to this Court for liberty to adduce fresh evidence of facts and events which have taken place since the Order of the High Court, made on the — day of — 1990, which said application will be grounded on the Affidavit of the Defendant filed herein, the pleadings had herein, the nature of the case, and the reasons to be offered.

15.076 Notice of motion in relation to breach of an access order

1. . . . an order of attachment against the above named defendant directing, that the defendant be brought before the said Court to give reasons why he should not be committed, OR
2. an order for committal, for contempt of this Honourable Court, of the defendant, in his failure to comply with an undertaking made by counsel on his behalf and in his presence before this Honourable Court on the — day of — 1990, and pertaining to the defendant's access to the above named infant pending the determination of these proceedings.
3. Such further or other order pursuant to section 11 of the Guardianship of Infants Act 1964, or otherwise, as may seem just.

15.077 District Court: Application under Guardianship of Infants Act 1964 Section 11

Rule 10.

GUARDIANSHIP OF INFANTS ACT 1964
Section 11.

NOTICE OF APPLICATION FOR DIRECTION ON QUESTION
AFFECTING WELFARE OF INFANT.

District Court Area   District No.—
Dublin Metropolitan District.

_____ Applicant.
_____ Respondent.

TAKE NOTICE that the above named applicant of — address, in the court area and district aforesaid, being a guardian of — an infant, intends to apply at the sitting of the District Court to be held at — on the — day of — 1990, at —, for the court's direction under section 11 of the Act on a question affecting the welfare of the infant, to wit, — insert, "custody or access or maintenance".

Dated this — day of — 1990.

Signed._____
Applicant/Solicitor for Applicant.

15.078 District Court: Order

ORDER OF THE District Court.

On the hearing of an application of X. of x address in the court district aforesaid, she being a guardian of a, b and c infants, for direction under section 11(i) of the said Act, the justice then sitting at Court No. 11 Dolphin House, East Essex Street, in the City of Dublin, on the — day of — 1990, being satisfied that the welfare of both infants so requires, ordered custody of a, b and c, to the mother, and access by the father to the said children, each Sunday from 10 a.m. to 6 p.m., the husband to collect and return the children, to outside of the Garda station at Blanchardstown, and at such further or other times as may be agreed

Provided that the party hereby granted custody of the said child/ren shall not be at liberty to remove the said child/ren from the jurisdiction of this Court without having obtained the prior consent in writing of the other party, or the leave of this Court, or of any other Court of competent jurisdiction.

Dated this — day of — 1990.

Signed: Justice of the District Court.

Warning:

A person having the actual custody of the infant/s who, having been given or shown a copy of the order, or who was present in Court at the making of the order, shall, on failure to comply with the said order, be liable on summary conviction to a fine not exceeding £200, or to imprisonment for a period of 6 months or to both.

15.079 District Court: Prosecution for breach of custody or access order

Guardianship of Infants Act 1964, as amended by the Courts Act 1981, and the Age of Majority Act 1985.

Summons

Whereas a complaint has been made to me that you, the said defendant, did on the — day of — 1990, fail to comply with an order of the District Court to wit, that on the day of — 1990, you did fail to give custody of the infant x to the said plaintiff in accordance with the order of the said Court dated the — day —, contrary to section 5 of the Courts (No. 2) Act 1985.

This is to command you to appear at a sitting of the District Court to be held at — on the — day of — 1990 to answer the said complaint.

Dated
Signed by District Court Clerk.

15.080 Circuit Court: Application where child abducted

Application, as per Form No. 2 of the Circuit Court (No. 6) Rules 1982.

Take Notice etc.

1. for an Order pursuant to section 11, granting sole custody of the infant to the applicant,
2. an Order compelling the respondent to return the said infant to the custody of the applicant,
3. a mandatory Order compelling the respondent to return the infant to the jurisdiction of the court.

Grounds of the application

1. It was an express term of the said Separation Agreement that the applicant should have sole custody, and have sole discretion in determining the infant's maintenance, education and place of residence and that the respondent should not interfere with such rights in any way or by any means whatever.
2. It is understood that the respondent will bring the applicant to the courts in England, on the — day of — 1990, seeking custody of the infant, and for an order making the infant a ward of the courts in that jurisdiction.
[If the applicant and the children are foreign, but the children have been removed into this jurisdiction, recite in the first paragraph that the applicant and the infants are citizens of that country.]

15.081 Circuit Court or High Court: Affidavit grounding an ex parte application for an injunction and interim orders pending a full hearing

I say that it is not in the child's best interest that he be removed from jurisdiction to jurisdiction and that, since he is a citizen of Canada, that his permanent home is Canada.

With regard to the foregoing averments, I am anxious and willing to supplement this affidavit with oral evidence at the hearing of this Motion should this Honourable Court so require.

15.082 High Court: Conditional order of Habeas Corpus

It is ordered, in accordance with Article 40.4.2 of the Constitution, that the respondent do produce before this Court at — in the afternoon of this day the body of the said infant and do certify in writing the grounds of his detention. It is ordered that the said respondent be restrained from taking the said infant out of the jurisdiction and it is ordered that this order be served forthwith on him.

[When the absolute order is made, it recites:]

It is ordered that the plaintiff do have custody and do have liberty to take the said infant out of the jurisdiction of the Court.

[Where the child has parents of a different domicile, the applicant, who is seeking to invoke the Irish jurisdiction, should specifically plead that the infant is an Irish citizen and is of Irish domicile.]

15.083 Order for the return of a child unlawfully removed from the jurisdiction

1. The Court doth order that the said infant be taken into the wardship of this Honourable Court.
2. The court doth order interim custody to the applicant, pending the further hearing, upon the applicant undertaking to serve the respondent with a copy of the application. The applicant is at liberty to serve by prepaid ordinary post and by registered post the proceedings herein on the

respondent, at [addresses].

3. . . . that the respondent return the infant to the jurisdiction of this Honourable Court forthwith and thereafter refrain from removing the said infant from the jurisdiction pending the determination of these proceedings.

4. . . . that the respondent lodge into the Court the passport of the said infant, and that the said husband do notify the wife of any arrangement to take the said infant outside the jurisdiction of this Court.

Liberty to apply

15.084 Application to stop a child being removed out of the country

1. An injunction restraining the defendant by himself his servants or agents from taking the said infant out of the jurisdiction pending the hearing of the issues between the plaintiff and the defendant.

2. The welfare of the said infant is best served by continuing in the custody of the plaintiff.

3. The respondent is likely to attempt to return the child to England against the wishes of the applicant.

4. The applicant seeks liberty to notify the Garda Siochána, the port and airport authorities of the making of the orders.

15.085 Application to prevent a foreign spouse removing the child from the Irish jurisdiction

An Application may be issued together with an Affidavit grounding a Notice of Motion, seeking an order to serve the proceedings out of the jurisdiction, and interim orders based on the orders sought in the Application;

The Application will set out the usual averments, and seek the following orders:

1. An order restraining the Respondent, his servants or agents, or anyone acting in consort with the Respondent, from interfering or attempting to interfere with the custody of the children, exercised by the Applicant.

2. An order restraining the Respondent, his servants . . ., from removing or attempting to remove the infant from his jurisdiction of this Honourable Court, without the consent of this Honourable Court.

[The Notice of Motion may seek interim custody of the child, if there is no pre-existing order, and an order restraining the Respondent in the terms of paragraph one and two, and an order restraining the Respondent from exercising access to the infant, pending an order of the court. It may also seek liberty to notify the Garda Siochána of the making of the order.]

15.086 Affidavit grounding the application to serve proceedings out of the jurisdiction

1. I beg to refer to a true copy of the intended Application in the above entitled matter upon which, marked with the letter "A", I have endorsed

my name prior to the swearing hereof. I say that the matters therein referred to insofar as they are within my actual knowledge are true, and in relation to matters which are not within my actual knowledge, I say that they are true to the best of my information and belief.

2. I say that the said Application seeks Orders, *inter alia*, of custody of my daughter who was born on the — day of — 1990. I say that I am the mother of the said infant, and that I am a citizen of Ireland, and that the said infant is also a citizen of Ireland.

3. The intended Respondent has threatened to travel to Ireland from France, and remove the said child. I say that it would be more convenient and involve less expenses if the Application were determined by this Honourable Court.

4. I say that the said intended Respondent resides at —— France, and that he is a French citizen. I pray this Honourable Court for an Order granting liberty to issue and serve this intended Application, together with Notice thereof, out of the jurisdiction, by sending same to the intended Respondent, at his address, together with such further or other Order, including such interim orders as to this Honourable Court shall seem proper.

15.087 Application by a spouse residing abroad for the return of a child wrongfully removed to Ireland

[The Application is best made in the High Court using *habeas corpus* proceedings. In addition orders under the Guardianship of Infants Act 1964 may be sought.]

1. The Plaintiff seeks an order granting him custody, for the purpose of removing the said infant to the jurisdiction of the High Court of Justice in London, England, pursuant to Orders of the Family Division of the said Court.

2. . . . an order directing the Defendant to produce the said infant before the High Court, forthwith,

3. The Plaintiff seeks liberty to notify the Garda authorities of the making of any order of this Honourable Court, and that the Court direct that the said order be served on the Defendant in the presence of the Gardaí and a social worker from the Eastern Health Board, if necessary.

4. An order restraining the Defendant, his servants or agents from molesting or interfering with the Plaintiff and the said infant in any manner whatsoever.

15.088 Motion seeking the court's permission to emigrate

. . . an order granting liberty to take the said infant outside the jurisdiction of this Court for the purpose of establishing residence outside the jurisdiction of this court.

15.089 Affidavit grounding opposition to a request to emigrate

I say and believe that if an order is granted by this Honourable Court giving liberty to the said applicant to take the said infant outside the jurisdiction for the purpose of establishing residence, I will lose my rights of access and may never see my child again. I say that all ties with my son will be relinquished.

15.090 Hague Convention on the Civil aspects of Child Abduction

Model request for return form

Requesting central authority of _____

Requested authority of _____

Concerns the following child ——,[21] who will attain the age of 16 years on the — day of — 19—.

Child

> 1. Identity of child and its parents:
> 2. Child-name and first names:
> 3. Date and place of birth:
> 4. Habitual residence before removal or retention:
> 5. Passport or Identification number, if any:
> 6. Description and photograph if possible:

Mother

> 7. Mother-name and first names:
> 8. Date and place of birth:
> 9. Nationality:
> 10. Occupation:
> 11. Habitual residence:
> 12. Passport or Identification number:

Father

> 13. Name and first names:
> 14. Date and place of birth:
> 15. Nationality:
> 16. Occupation:
> 17. Habitual residence:
> 18. Passport or identification number:
> 19. Date and place of the marriage:

Requesting individual or institution[22] (who actually exercised custody before the removal or retention)[23]

> 20. Name and first names:

---

21 It may be more appropriate to complete a separate form for each child to lessen confusion, especially if there is a risk that the children will be kept at separate locations.
22 This could be a Health Board, who have had the child in voluntary care, or under a court order.
23 The remaining part of C relates to an individual applicant.

21. Nationality of individual applicant:
22. Occupation:
23. Address:
24. Passport or identification number:
25. Relation[24] to the child:
26. Name and address of legal adviser if any:

Place where the child is thought to be

Information concerning the person[25] alleged to have removed or retained the child:
27. Name and first names:
28. Date and place of birth, if known:
29. Nationality:
30. Occupation:
31. Last known address:
32. Passport or identification number:
33. Description and photograph if possible:

Address of the child

Other persons who may be able to supply additional information relating to the whereabouts of the child

Time, place, date and circumstances of the wrongful removal or retention

Factual or legal grounds justifying the request

Civil proceedings progress

Child to be returned[26] to

Name and first names:
Date and place of birth:
Address:
Telephone number:
Proposed arrangements for return of the child:

Other remarks

List of documents[27] attached

Dated this — day of —.
Signed and/or stamp of requesting civil authority or individual applicant.

24 It could be that a relative is acting as agent for the custodial parent, because of his familiarity with the country to which the children have been removed.
25 This may have been a friend or relative who removed the children at the behest of the parent.
26 The child may be returned to a friend or official in the foreign country, before being brought back to this jurisdiction.
27 An example of the documents that may be attached are certified copies of the relevant court orders of custody or access, a certificate or affidavit as to the law of this jurisdiction, reports on the child's background from social workers, doctors, school teachers, and an authorisation giving permission to the central authority to act on behalf of the applicant.

Chapter 16

SEPARATION AND MAINTENANCE AGREEMENTS

General principles of law

Introduction

16.001 By a separation and maintenance agreement estranged spouses are able, without the need for litigation, to resolve in a legally enforceable way many of the issues which are likely to arise on the breakdown of marriage, including in particular financial and property arrangements. It is now well accepted that separation agreements are enforeable in the same way as other private contracts. Doubts which had, for reasons of public policy, existed as to their enforceability were resolved for the Irish courts by Palles C.B. in *McMahon v McMahon and Purser v Purser*:

> Contracts for immediate separation are not against the policy of the law; and . . . the reason . . . is that the rights of the spouses in respect of co-habitation have since the Reformation been no more than private rights which the spouses can validly renounce.[1]

However, a contract made in contemplation of a separation which may occur at some future date, and which is not inevitable, probably remains unenforceable.[2] The assumption is that such a contract might tend to encourage or too readily facilitate the breaking of the marriage vows. It seems, therefore, that it is void for reasons of public policy.

16.002 As a general principle, separation agreements are regarded by the law like other private contracts. They are "formed, construed and dissolved and to be enforced on precisely the same principles as any respectable commercial agreement, of whose nature indeed they some-

---

1 [1913] 1 IR 428, following the decision of the House of Lords in *Wilson v Wilson* (1848) 1 HLC 538. See also *Courtney v Courtney* [1923] 2 IR 31.
2 See *Fender v St. John-Mildmay* [1938] AC 1.

times partake."[3] However, in the public interest and in order to protect dependent family members, some special rules apply to separation agreements which on the one hand place limits on what the parties may agree upon and on the other hand supplement the usual remedies for enforcing contracts. These special provisions, which overlay the ordinary contractual rules, will become apparent below.

The form of the agreement

16.003 It is usual for the parties to draw up their separation and maintenance agreement in the form of a deed which is signed by both parties and sealed, and which thereby becomes legally enforceable. Less formal, even oral, agreements are possible, but if they are to be enforced, they must have the ingredients necessary for a binding contract. In particular, each spouse must provide valuable consideration. In *Courtney v Courtney*[4] the spouses, in the presence of a priest, agreed orally to live separately in consideration of the husband paying the wife £150. She also gave back a watch and a ring, and later signed a receipt for the £150 "in full discharge of all claims of every nature" that she might have against him. The agreement was upheld on the basis that the consideration from the wife was her implied promise not to bring proceedings against him for separation or alimony. It is possible that a spouse's agreement to cease cohabitation is itself sufficient consideration. In *Courtney v Courtney*, this proposition was rejected by Dodd J. (at 37), but supported by Ronan L.J. (at 42). When the agreement is not under seal, it is necessary also to show that the parties intended to create a legally binding obligation, not simply to enter into an informal domestic arrangement binding in honour only.[5]

Consent

16.004 Frequently where spouses negotiate a separation and maintenance agreement they occupy unequal bargaining positions; the dependent spouse may feel under some pressure to conclude arrangements quickly so that her immediate needs, and those of the dependent children, may be met. If she can prove duress, fraud, misrepresentation or in some cases mistake, the contract may be set aside. She may also be able to rely on the equitable doctrine of unconscionable bargains, if it can be shown that there was something intrinsically unconscionable about the agreement.[6] It is clearly advisable that both spouses should seek independent legal advice before signing a separation agreement. But the absence of independent legal advice will not of itself provide grounds for setting the agreement aside. In *V.W. v J.W.*[7] the wife sought to have her separation agreement declared void. The agreement had been proposed by the husband and

---

3 Per Lord Atkin in *Hyman v Hyman* [1929] AC 601, at 625.
4 [1923] 2 IR 31.
5 See *McGregor v McGregor* (1888) 2 QBD 424, and *Balfour v Balfour* [1919] 2 KB 571.
6 See *Grealish v Murphy* [1946] IR 35. See also *Lloyds Bank v Bundy* [1975] QB 326, and *Edgar v Edgar* [1980] 1 WLR 410.
7 10 April 1978, unreported, High Court.

handed to the wife who signed it in the presence of a neighbour. The wife had deliberately not obtained legal advice. She claimed that, at the time, she was an alcoholic, and was acting under the influence of drink and drugs. Costello J. did not accept this claim, and rejected on the facts (a) a plea of *non est factum* based on alleged mistake as to the nature or content of the document which was signed, (b) a plea of undue influence, and (c) the wife's submission that the agreement was unconscionable.

16.005 The unequal bargaining position of the dependent spouse is, to some extent, redressed by the principle, discussed at **16.012** that any agreement which purports to exclude or limit a spouse's right to seek maintenance under the Family (Maintenance of Spouses and Children) Act 1976, is void, by virtue of section 27 of that Act.

The agreement to live apart

16.006 The agreement by spouses to live separately and apart has the effect of releasing them from their normal legal duty to co-habit. It will normally bring to an end desertion by either of the spouses. For this reason a deserted spouse may prefer a form of words which preserves any claim or right which she has by virtue of desertion by the other spouse. This is provided for in the model agreement. Desertion may affect the succession rights of the deserting spouse in that a spouse whose desertion (actual or constructive) has continued for a least two years prior to the death of the other spouse is precluded from taking any share in the estate of the deceased either as a legal right or in intestacy. Desertion may also affect the maintenance rights of the deserting spouse under the Family Law (Maintenance of Spouses and Children) Act 1976 (see **8.035–8.038**), the rights of the deserting spouse to various protections afforded by the Family Home Protection Act 1976 (**11.024–11.031**) and the right of the deserting spouse to certain ancillary remedies in proceedings for judicial separation (**13.039**).

16.007 The agreement to live separate and apart, and the usually allied non-molestation clause, may be enforced by injunction. The bringing of a "*bona fide* matrimonial action," such as a petition for a judicial separation, does not constitute molestation,[9] but an agreement not to bring such action may be implied or expressed elsewhere in the agreement.[10]

Provision for maintenance, and review and variation of maintenance

16.008 Various options in relation to maintenance payments are set out in the model agreement. The principal matters which the spouses need to decide are as follows: Who is to pay maintenance? What amount is to be paid? How are payments to be apportioned as between the dependent

8 Succession Act 1965, section 120(2).
9 Per Dodd J. in *Courtney v Courtney* [1923] 2 IR 31, at 42.
10 See *K. v K.* 12 February 1988, unreported, High Court, discussed at **16.012**.

spouse and dependent children? Is maintenance to be secured? If so, by what means? At what intervals is maintenance to be paid, on what dates and by what means? For how long is maintenance to last for the dependent spouse and for the dependent children respectively? Under what other conditions, if any, are maintenance payments to cease? The taxation implications of maintenance provisions need also to be considered (**16.038** et seq).

16.009 It is advisable that provision of some sort be made for review and variation of maintenance arrangements. Inflation may reduce the real value of the agreed maintenance, making periodic reviews essential. Equally, the earnings of the liable spouse may decrease, or he may become unemployed; if a review is not provided for, he may find himself contractually bound to pay a sum which he cannot afford. Again, various options are set out in the model agreement. If it is not possible for the court to interpret the meaning of a variation clause and it appears that the parties were not *ad idem* as to its meaning or effect, the court will not enforce it.[11]

Effects where there is no provision for review or where review is unsatisfactory

On the dependent spouse

16.010 Unlike the position in many other jurisdictions, the courts have no express statutory powers to review, vary or add to the terms of a privately negotiated maintenance agreement. However, the court probably does have power to vary a maintenance agreement in the context of proceedings for judicial separation.[12] Regardless of the terms of a maintenance agreement, a dependent spouse is always entitled to apply for a maintenance order under the Family Law (Maintenance of Spouses and Children) Act 1976. (See **8.010–8.012**) If, as a result of the absence of a review and variation clause in a maintenance agreement, or as a result of a review provision that proves to be unsatisfactory, or for any other reason, a dependent spouse is not receiving such maintenance as is proper in the circumstances, the court may under the Act of 1976 order the liable spouse either (a) to pay an amount by way of maintenance in addition to that which he is contractually obliged to pay under the agreement, or (b) to pay the full amount of maintenance which is proper in the circumstances, in which case maintenance paid under the order is treated as satisfying *pro tanto* the contractual obligation arising from the agreement.[13] In proceedings under the Act of 1976 the existence of the maintenance agreement, and the record of the liable spouse's payments under it, will be treated as relevant only in determining whether proper maintenance is being paid and, if not, how much should be ordered.[14]

11 *R.H. v N.H.* 20 June 1983, unreported, High Court. See **8.028**.
12 See Judicial Separation and Family Law Reform Act 1989 section 15(1)(c) and (d), and **13.010**.
13 See *O'S. v O'S.* 18 November 1983, unreported, High Court, **8.027**.
14 See *H.D. v P.D.* 8 May 1978, unreported, Supreme Court, discussed at **8.026**.

On the liable spouse

16.011 In *D. v D.*[14a] Barron J. held that a spouse who is liable to make higher payments than he can afford under a maintenance agreement containing no provision for variation, is entitled to apply to the court for a downward variation. The decision is based on the Judge's view that "there must be a mutuality of rights" as between the creditor and debtor. The precise legal basis for the decision is not clear, and it is in conflict with *J.D. v B.D.*, below. However, whatever be the strict legal position, as a matter of practicality the creditor cannot rely on the agreement. As Barron J. points out, if the debtor spouse is put in a worse position than the creditor as a result of paying the agreed maintenance, he may himself apply for a maintenance order against the creditor under the Act of 1976. It may in any case be impossible to enforce the debt.

In *J.D. v B.D.*[15] the agreement provided for an annual increase in maintenance in line with the increase in the Consumer Price Index. It did not provide for any review in the event of changes in the circumstances of the parties. When the agreement was entered into the wife was not working, nor were any of the children. The husband was living with his father. Subsequent to the agreement, the wife obtained employment and also began receiving money from some of the children who were earning. The husband's father died and his free accommodation ceased. By 1984 the husband's maintenance obligation had increased to £80 per week, an amount which he was unable to pay. The wife brought a motion for committal of her husband or alternatively for an attachment of earnings order. She was entitled to seek enforcement by these means because the agreement had been made a rule of court under section 8 of the Act of 1976. (**16.018–16.019**) The husband, on a counter motion, applied for a variation in the maintenance. Carroll J. held that, even though the agreement had been made a rule of court under the Act of 1976, she had no power to vary its terms. Nevertheless, she refused to commit the husband to prison "for failing to observe an agreement which in view of the changed circumstances is unjust." Nor would she make an attachment of earnings order for the full amount because the husband's net earnings would then fall below the protected earnings rate, which the court is bound (by section 10(4)(b) of the 1976 Act) to fix having regard to the resources and needs of the maintenance debtor. The wife had not sought the standard contractual remedy of damages. If she had, there is little doubt that she would at the end of the day have experienced the same difficulty in enforcing any order made in her favour. However, although Carroll J. did not refer to the matter, the husband's contractual liability probably remained and, had his circumstances subsequently changed for the better, it might then have been possible for the wife to recover the full arrears.

14a 19 December 1989, unreported, High Court.
15 6 September 1984, unreported, High Court.

Agreements not to apply for maintenance, or other financial or property orders

Maintenance orders under the Act of 1976

16.012 As has already been emphasised, any agreement, no matter how strongly worded, which purports to exclude or limit the right of a spouse to apply for maintenance under the Act of 1976 is made void by section 27 of that Act. The same is true whether the agreement was made before or after the Act of 1976 came into force.[16] Thus a general statement to the effect that a spouse accepts the benefits provided for in a separation agreement in full satisfaction of all claims against the other spouse, does not preclude her bringing proceedings for maintenance under the Act of 1976, even where that agreement has been made part of an order of the court, as was the case in *H.D. v P.D.* It should be noted that under section 27, an agreement is void only "in so far as" it excludes or limits rights under the Act. The remainder of the maintenance agreement, including a promise to pay maintenance, remains valid and enforceable.[17]

Orders made under the Judicial Separation and Family Law Reform Act 1989

16.013 Under the old law, the only ancillary remedy available pursuant to a decree of divorce *a mensa et thoro* was an order for the payment of alimony. Whether or not it was possible to waive rights to proceed for alimony became, after 1976, of little practical concern because the right to proceed for maintenance under the Act of 1976 was in any case guaranteed. Now that a much wider range of ancillary financial and property orders has become available under the Act of 1989, the question of whether a spouse can expressly or by implication waive his or her right to proceed under the Act is of great importance. The Act itself offers no answer. There is no equivalent to section 27 of the Act of 1976. If it were possible to waive the right to proceed for ancillary orders under the Act of 1989, it could presumably be done in one of two ways. The first would involve an agreement not to institute proceedings for judicial separation; because the ancillary remedies are available only on foot of such proceedings, this would effectively preclude their use. The second would be to agree to preserve the right to institute proceedings for judicial separation and to waive only the right to apply for ancillary financial or property orders. The question is whether either of these devices is permissible.

16.014 Decisions made in the context of divorce *a mensa et thoro* support the proposition that a spouse will, as a general rule, be bound by an express or implied agreement not to proceed for a divorce *a mensa et thoro* or for alimony pursuant to such a decree. In *Ross v Ross*[18] the acceptance by the

---

16 Per Walsh J. in *H.D. v P.D.* (8 May 1978, unreported) Supreme Court, at page 7 of his judgment.
17 Cf. *Bennett v Bennett* [1952] 1 KB 249.
18 [1908] IR 339.

by the wife of certain specified chattels plus £100 in full discharge of all further claims against her husband for maintenance or support precluded her from obtaining permanent alimony after she had obtained a decree of divorce *a mensa et thoro*. In *Courtney v Courtney*[19] the wife, who received £150 from her husband "in full discharge of all claims of every nature and kind" against him, was held to have agreed implicitly not to bring proceedings for divorce *a mensa et thoro*, and was bound by that undertaking. Dodd J. stated (at 40):

> It is said that there is no express covenant not to sue, no agreement not to sue to be implied. But if parties who are free to contract do, in fact, contract for the settlement of an action or for the abandonment of claims which might terminate in legal proceedings, can it be contended that the settlement having been entered into and completed by one party complying with it, the other party can keep the money and go on with an action? . . . When . . . the tribunal is satisfied that the transaction was a binding contract, parties to it who agree so to settle a matrimonial controversy must be taken to contract that they will not go behind the settlement, and cannot be listened to saying that they did not make an express stipulation not to sue. The decision . . . is not to be taken to extend to contracts that are against public policy."

16.015 The decision in *Courtney v Courtney* was followed in *K. v K.*[20] where the fact that the parties had entered into a separation agreement was held alone sufficient to bar the husband from proceeding for a decree of divorce *a mensa et thoro*. The husband had wished, by obtaining a decree on the basis of the wife's adultery, to deprive her of succession rights under section 120(2) of the Succession Act 1965. McKenzie J. at page 3 of the judgment took the view that the husband was in effect attempting to vary the terms of the separation agreement, and that, once the wife had entered into the agreement, "she was entitled to consider that subsequent proceedings such as an action for divorce would not be contemplated. . ." He took *Courtney v Courtney* as deciding that, where there is a separation agreement without an express covenant not to sue, it will still bar subsequent proceedings for divorce "if that can be shown to have been the real character of the agreement entered into by the parties."

16.016 Despite this line of authority, it may yet be possible to argue that, in some circumstances, a covenant not to proceed for judicial separation should be held void as being contrary to public policy. Indeed the last sentence of the dictum of Dodd J. in *Courtney v Courtney* citing the judgment of Palles C.B. in *McMahon v McMahon*[21] (which deals with contracts which are against public policy) envisages this possibility. In *Hyman v Hyman*[22] the House of Lords held that no agreement can

19 [1923] 2 IR 31.
20 12 February 1988, unreported, High Court.
21 [1913] 1 IR 428.
22 [1929] AC 601.

preclude a spouse from applying for financial relief in divorce (*a vinculis*) proceedings. The court's jurisdiction to grant such relief is, per Lord Hailsham (at 614) "conferred not merely in the interests of the wife, but of the public." The public interest includes the avoidance of a situation in which a dependent spouse becomes a liability on the taxpayer as a result of not receiving proper support from the other spouse. In the Irish context, it could be argued that this particular public interest is largely secured by the fact that a dependent spouse may always, regardless of any agreement to the contrary, apply for maintenance under the Act of 1976. However, there may be cases where maintenance alone is not sufficient to secure the position of the dependent spouse and dependent children. In some cases an order for the payment of a lump sum or an order for the sale or transfer or property by the liable spouse may offer the best and most appropriate means of providing for the needs of dependants; and those orders are only available pursuant to proceedings for judicial separation. There is therefore a public interest in ensuring that the wide range of ancillary orders in judicial separation proceedings remain available to the spouses, and this may justify a decision to treat as void, in a particular case, an agreement which has the effect of barring access to them. The argument becomes even stronger when it is remembered that the ancillary orders exist to make provision, not only for a dependent spouse, but also for dependent children. Children are not parties to separation agreements, and there would appear to be a strong case, based on public policy, for not enforcing a parental agreement which has the effect of depriving children of appropriate provision on the breakdown of their parents' marriage.

Maintenance orders under the Guardianship of Infants Act 1964

16.017 Although there is no authority on the point, it is arguable that an agreement between spouses not to sue for maintenance would not be effective to bar proceedings brought under section 11 of the Guardianship of Infants Act 1964, to secure maintenance for a dependent child. The public interest in preventing parents from avoiding their obligations to support dependent children, combined with the general principle that the welfare of the child is the first and paramount consideration under section 3 of the Act of 1964, suggest that an agreement between parents not to apply for maintenance under the Act would be void. It is true that in most cases the child's welfare and the public interest may equally well be served by the alternative of proceeding for maintenance under the Act of 1976; section 27 of that Act makes void any agreement to waive the right to proceed. Indeed, the great majority of applications for maintenance for the support of dependent children are made under that Act. However, in certain cases the Act of 1964 may provide a more convenient basis to apply for a child support order, as for example where the parents have been divorced abroad by a decree which is entitled to recognition in this country. A parent may prefer not to employ the procedure provided by the Act of 1976 for obtaining maintenance for a *non-marital* child, although this would also be available in such a case.

Making an agreement a rule of court under section 8 of the Act of 1976

16.018 Section 8 of the Family Law (Maintenance of Spouses and Children) Act 1976 permits either spouse to apply to have an agreement made a rule of court. Application may be made only in the Circuit Court or High Court. The practical and procedural aspects of such an application are discussed in the next section. The conditions which must be met are as follows:

1. The agreement must be in writing and made after 6 May 1976, the commencement of the Act of 1976
2. The agreement must include either or both of the following provisions:
   (a) an undertaking by one spouse to make periodical payments towards the maintenance of the other spouse and/or any dependent child of the family;
   (b) a provision governing the rights and liabilities of the spouses towards one another in respect of the making or securing of payments (other than those specified in (a) above), or the disposition or use of any property.
3. The court must be "satisifed that the agreement is a fair and reasonable one which in all the circumstances adequately protects the interests of both spouses and the dependent children (if any) of the family." In *J.D. v B.D.*[23] Carroll J. expressed the opinion, *obiter*, that an agreement is neither fair nor reasonable if it does not contain a provision enabling application to be made to the court to vary it in the same way as if it were a maintenance order. A material change in the circumstances of the parties since the agreement was concluded may be relevant to the question of whether it is fair and reasonable, but will not necessarily preclude the agreement from being made a rule of court, particularly if the court is satisfied that review is possible.[24]
4. The agreement must not contain any clause which is contrary to public policy. In *Dalton v Dalton*[25] a separation agreement between a husband and wife, who were resident and domiciled in the Republic of Ireland, contained a clause making provision for the wife to obtain, with the consent of the husband, a foreign divorce (*a vinculis*). There was no evidence that either party intended to acquire a domicile abroad. O'Hanlon J. refused to make the agreement a rule of court because to do so would be "to lend [the court's] support to a, course of conduct which is contrary to public policy." The judgment of Kingsmill Moore J. in *Mayo-Perrott v Mayo-Perrot* was cited in support of the proposition. It is difficult to see how the parties' plan to divorce would in any way have been assisted by the agreement becoming a rule of court.

23 [1985] ILRM 688. See **16.012** for the facts of the case.
24 See *J.H. v C.H.* (25 July 1978, unreported) High Court. Though see below for doubts as to whether variation was in fact possible.
25 [1982] ILRM 418.

16.019 The effect and advantage of an agreement being made a rule of court is that its provision for maintenance is thereby deemed to be a maintenance order for two purposes:- (1) the provisions relating to the payment of maintenance through the District Court under section 9 of the Act of 1976 and (2) the provisions relating to enforcement by attachment of earnings under Part III of the Act of 1976. The agreement to provide maintenance is not treated as a maintenance order for any other purpose.[27] *Quaere* whether it is open to the court subsequently to entertain an application under the Act of 1976 to vary the agreed maintenance.[28] In *J.H. v C.H.* Keane J. appears to assume that an application, under section 6 of the Act of 1976, to vary maintenance does become possible. However, it is not clear from the judgment whether the separation agreement itself provided for variation. As has been explained, the absence of a clause within the agreement itself to provide for variation by the court may in any case result in it not being made a rule of court. While the agreed maintenance becomes enforceable, in the event of default, through the attachment of earnings procedure, the income of the liable spouse cannot be reduced below his protected earnings rate which must be fixed by the court having regard to his resources and needs. If his resources and needs do not permit him to pay the agreed amount, enforcement of the full amount by attachment of earnings will not be ordered (see **16.012**).

Section 8 applications: Agreed procedure

16.020 The statutory instrument that implemented the Courts Act 1981 in the Circuit Court[29] did not include any provision for making a deed of separation a rule of court. However, following representations to the Dublin Circuit Court Office, the following procedure was agreed:

A notice of motion is issued and served in the usual way. The court then, in the motion list, proceeds to make a deed of separation a rule of court. The assumption is that both parties consent. No provision was made for the case of a spouse who wishes to object to the deed being made a rule of court. Strictly speaking, where the rules are silent on a procedure, order 5 rule 1 of the 1950 Rules of the Circuit Court[30] applies. This provides that civil proceedings shall be instituted by the issue of a civil bill, unless otherwise provided for by statute or by the Circuit Court Rules. Obviously, where there have been prior proceedings, a motion can be issued in accordance with order 51. This procedure was endorsed by a practice direction made by the former President of the Circuit Court in December 1982, but as far as the authors are aware no amendment to the relevant statutory instrument was ever made.

---

26 [1958] IR 336.
27 Per Walsh J. in *H.D. v P.D.*, supra, at page 8 of his judgment.
28 See **16.011**.
29 SI No. 158 of 1982, Circuit Court Rules (No. 6) 1982.
30 SI No. 179 of 1950.

In any event, the motion is to include the following wording:

TAKE NOTICE that on the———day of———1990 an application will be made to have the settlement/Deed of Separation agreed/entered into made a Rule of Court under the provisions of Section 8 of the Family Law (Maintenance of Spouses and Children) Act 1976. Dated this——— day of———1990.

16.021 On the hearing, the deed and counterpart must have been duly stamped in the Stamping Office of Dublin Castle. The counterpart, or original, is taken in by the registrar for the judge to read. However, it is kept as a record by the office. Therefore a certified copy of the original should have been retained prior to attendance at court for the respondent. If proceedings have already been issued it is usual to adjourn these with liberty to re-enter.

Where the respondent spouse is not legally represented

16.022 It is fairly common for a respondent to agree to enter into a deed of separation but to refuse independent legal advice. He may wish to avoid litigation or, if proceedings have already been issued, he may be anxious to avoid a hearing. The court in the latter case will adjourn and advise the respondent to go to his solicitor or to apply for civil legal aid. The respondent may not do so.

16.023 It is easier in some ways to conclude a deed if there are already proceedings out. The court can put the respondent into the witness box and confirm that he understands the nature of the deed and its implications. It can also confirm that he was not put under any pressure to sign it. However, the courts have made an agreement a rule of court in the absence of the respondent where satisfied that he was properly served with a summons. It helps if he has been in communication with his spouse's solicitor before the hearing. Where there are no proceedings, all correspondence should remind the respondent of the importance of obtaining proper advice.[31] Each clause may have to be explained in writing, in simple English.

16.024 If it is intended to negotiate with an unrepresented respondent, it is advisable that he is asked to confirm his views, in writing if possible, or if he is unable to do so, he can be asked to sign an acknowledgement when he comes in to sign the deed. It may be helpful to have him come into the office with a friend or relative and have them witness the deed. Alternatively it can be posted to him, and he can be asked to sign it and have it legally witnessed. Each case depends on the particular circumstances, the level of education and experience of the respondent, and the history of the marriage.

---

31 See *V.W. v J.W.* (10 April 1978, unreported) High Court, **16.004**.

The acknowledgement is as follows:

"I, Joe Bloggs, of [here insert address] hereby acknowledge that I have notified [name of the solicitor] of [solicitor's address] that I do not wish to consult or instruct a solicitor in respect of the drafting and entering into of the deed of separation between myself and my wife, Mary Bloggs. I confirm that [name of solicitor] has urged me to obtain independent legal advice, but I have declined to do so because [if prepared to do so, insert the reason]. I am entering into this deed having been fully informed of its practical and legal consequences. I give my fully free and informed consent to entering into this deed. I confirm that I have read the deed [or the Deed has been read to me by————(name of solicitor)————or my relative———— ————(name of relative)————] and that I fully understand the contents of same. I undertake to abide by the terms and conditions of the deed of separation.

Signed: Joe Bloggs
Witnessed by: Solicitor
and: Bloggs.
                     [Insert full name of relative of Joe Bloggs.]

Settlements entered on the record of the court

16.025 Where proceedings for matrimonial relief are settled between the parties by agreement, the terms of that "consent" may be entered on the record of the court. The consent is in effect a form of separation agreement[32] and is enforceable as such. In the past, in the context of proceedings for divorce *a mensa et thoro*, the recording by the court of a consent which contains a maintenance provision has added a new dimension to the agreement. The recording of the agreed maintenance has been held[33] to constitute an "allotment" of alimony for the purposes of order 70 rule 55 of the Rules of the Superior Courts. Once an "allotment" was made, it was open to the wife to seek an increase, and to the husband to seek a reduction, in alimony, on the basis of the increased or reduced "faculties" of the spouses.

The Judicial Separation and Family Law Reform Act 1989 (section 22) provides for either spouse to apply for a variation of financial or property orders made under the Act on the basis of changed circumstances or new evidence. It is not, as yet, known whether rules will provide for the variation procedure to apply to consent orders.

The effect of adultery and co-habitation on agreed maintenance

16.026 The parties are free to decide for themselves the conditions under which agreed maintenance will cease to be payable. The agreement may

32 See, e.g., *H.D. v P.D.* 8 May 1978, unreported, Supreme Court. The facts are set out at **8.011**.
33 *M.C. v J.C.* [1982] ILRM 562.

contain a clause (known as a *dum casta* clause) making payment of maintenance to the dependent spouse conditional upon her not committing adultery. More commonly, payment may be made conditional upon the dependent spouse not co-habiting with, and/or being supported by, another partner. In either case it is usual to exempt from the condition payments for the support of dependent children. Although breach of either condition will discharge a spouse's contractual liability to pay maintenance for the support of the dependent spouse, the latter remains entitled to apply for a maintenance order under section 5 of the Family Law (Maintenance of Spouses and Children) Act 1976. The implications of adultery and co-habitation in such proceedings have already been discussed at **8.039–8.046**.

16.027 Where no *dum casta* clause is expressed in the agreement, none will be implied.[34] An argument, based on Article 41 of the Constitution, that it would be contrary to public policy to enforce a contract requiring an innocent spouse to support an adulterous spouse, has been rejected by both the High Court (in *Lewis v Lewis*[35]) and Supreme Court (*Ormsby v Ormsby*[34]). The position is less clear where, in the absence of a co-habitation clause, the dependent spouse begins living with, and being supported by, another partner. The judgment of Hanna J. in *Lewis v Lewis* (at 52) suggests the possibility that in such a case the agreement may be set aside on equitable grounds:

> It would seem to me, on the one hand, to be unjust to leave a wife, who is living by agreement separate from her husband, destitute in consequence of an isolated act of adultery, and probably drive her to an immoral life, but, on the other hand, it would seem to me to be a monstrous state of the law if her husband is bound to pay her alimony while she is being supported by someone with whom she is openly living as his wife.

Fearon v Aylesford[36] is cited in support, in which Cotton L.J. stated: "There may be circumstances of such a character as will prevent the guilty wife from insisting upon the deed, and which will enable the husband in a Court of Equity to set up an equitable defence." He excluded mere adultery as such a circumstance.

Succession rights

16.028 Section 113 of the Succession Act 1965 provides that "The legal right of a spouse may be renounced in an ante-nuptial contract made in writing between parties to an intended marriage, or may be renounced in writing by the spouse after marriage and during the lifetime of the testator." The "legal right" refers to a surviving spouse's statutory right to

34 (1945) 79 ILTR 97.
35 [1940] IR 42.
36 (1884) 14 QBD 792.

a share in the estate of a spouse who has died leaving a will. The right is to one-third of the estate, if there are surviving children; and one-half if there are no surviving children. Although there is no similar provision governing the waiver by one spouse of rights of succession on the death intestate of the other, it is generally assumed that this is permissible. If the intestate leaves no "issue," the surviving spouse is entitled to the whole estate; if there are surviving "issue", the entitlement is to two-thirds of the estate. Where a waiver clause is included, it often refers to all rights of succession under the Act of 1965.

16.029 Where a testator has during his lifetime (and before 1 January 1967) made permanent provision for his spouse, for example, by the transfer of property under the terms of a separation agreement, section 116(1) of the Succession Act provides that the property is regarded as having been given in or towards satisfaction of the legal right share of that spouse.

Covenant not to proceed for judicial separation

16.030 In theory, a covenant in a separation agreement not to proceed for judicial separation would appear unexceptionable. The agreement itself achieves the same object as a judicial separation; it releases the spouses from their normal duty to co-habit. Therefore nothing is lost by waiving the right to obtain a judicial separation. This certainly was the approach taken by the courts in relation to covenants not to proceed for a divorce *a mensa et thoro*.[37]

16.031 However, with the passing of the Judicial Separation and Family Law Reform Act 1989, the situation has changed. A waiver of the right to proceed for judicial separation, if effective, would result not only in stopping the grant of an order for judicial separation, but also in preventing the spouses from taking advantage of the range of ancillary financial and property orders available under the Act. For this reason it is possible that a waiver of the right to proceed for judicial separation might in some circumstances be held void (see **16.012–16.016**).

Custody of and access to children

16.032 Separation agreements usually contain detailed provisions relating to the custody of, and access to, children. Section 18(2) of the Guardianship of Infants Act 1964 states:

A provision contained in any separation agreement made between the father and mother of an infant shall not be invalid by reason only of its providing that one of them shall give up the custody or control of the infant to the other.

---

37 *Courtney v Courtney* [1923] 2 IR 31, and *K. v K.* 12 February 1988, unreported, High Court. See **16.015**.

Although agreements relating to custody and access are not void[38] neither are they strictly binding, in the sense that either parent may, if he or she considers that the arrangements agreed upon are not working in the best interests of a child, apply to the court for a custody or access order, or an order for directions, under section 11 of the Act of 1964. In dealing with such an application the court will naturally take account of the agreement but without being bound by its provisions. The welfare of the child is the first and paramount consideration, and "the Court's duty, in considering the interest of the child, transcends the agreement of the parents as to the custody of the children."[39]

Discharge of the agreement

Discharge by agreement

16.033 The parties may subsequently agree to discharge their agreement, or the agreement itself may specify the conditions under which it, or any part of it, is to come to an end.[40] For example, the agreement may provide that it shall cease to have effect if the parties resume co-habitation.

Resumption of co-habitation

16.034 Whether a resumption of co-habitation terminates an agreement will depend on the wording of the agreement itself. If there is no express reference to the matter, it may still be possible to infer, from the wording of the agreement, that the parties intended it to lapse on resumption of co-habitation. Early cases, suggesting the existence of a presumption that co-habitation terminates an agreement[41] have been superseded by cases in which the emphasis has been on the need to interpret each agreement according to its own wording.[42]

Discharge by breach or repudiation

16.035 Breach of a condition in the agreement may result in the loss of specific rights under the agreement as, for example, where a *dum casta* clause, upon which payment of maintenance is conditional, is broken. Breach of a specific covenant will not however justify the other party in regarding the agreement as a whole as discharged, unless the breach is of a fundamental nature.[43] The repudiation of the entire agreement by one party entitles the other to treat it as discharged. A court may be reluctant to discharge a parent from a contractual obligation to support a dependent child by reason only of breach of the agreement by the other parent. In

---

38 Presumably an agreement between parents not to make application under the Act of 1964 would be regarded as contrary to public policy and void.
39 Per O Dálaigh C.J. in *Cullen v Cullen* 8 May 1970, unreported, Supreme Court, at page 5 of his judgment.
40 See *Newsome v Newsome* (1871) LR 2 P & D 306.
41 For example *Bateman v Ross* (1813).
42 *Negus v Forster* (1882) 46 LT 675; *Nicol v Nicol* (1886) 31 Ch.D. 524 (both Court of Appeal).
43 *Besant v Wood* (1879) 12 Ch.D. 605.

O.C. v T.C.[44] the mother had committed "flagrant breaches" of a separation agreement. In fact, while the agreement provided for the father to pay educational fees for the son, McMahon J. held that the parties never contemplated that he should be liable for fees and expenses at an American university. The father was therefore under no contractual liability in the particular circumstances.

Effects of nullity and divorce

16.036 Where a marriage is absolutely void, a separation agreement entered into by the parties as husband and wife will also be void, being based on a mistake of fact.[45] The annulment of a voidable marriage does not, it seems, discharge any obligation to pay maintenance under a separation agreement.[46] Similarly, a separation agreement is not necessarily discharged by a decree of divorce (*a mensa et thoro*[47] or *a vinculis*[48]) or of judicial separation.

Remedies for breach

16.037 The usual contractual remedies are available for breach of a separation agreement: damages, specific performance and injunction. Specific performance may be sought to compel performance of a positive obligation under the agreement, such as the transfer of property. An injunction may restrain breach of a negative obligation including, for example, a non-molestation undertaking, or a promise not to remove a child from the jurisdiction. Where an agreement is made a rule of court, its breach constitutes contempt, and the remedies of attachment and committal to prison apply. Where an agreement is made a rule of court under section 8 of the Act of 1976, maintenance payments under it may be enforced by attachment of earnings (see **16.018**); the normal contractual remedies must be applied for to enforce other provisions in the agreement, even though they may relate to financial provision.[49]

Taxation aspects of separation

Maintenance agreements after 8 June 1983

16.038 A married couple living apart under a deed of separation are taxed as two separate single persons, unless, as explained below, they have opted for joint assessment under section 4 of the Finance Act 1983. The same principles apply where a couple are living apart by a less formal agreement, or with no agreement, provided that their separation is likely to be permanent. As a single person, each completes a separate tax return,

44 December 1981, unreported, High Court.
45 *Galloway v Galloway* 30 Times LR 531 (1914).
46 *Adams v Adams* [1941] KB 536 (Court of Appeal). The decision relied on an analogy between a nullity decree and a decree of divorce.
47 *Grundy v Grundy* (1882) 7 PD 774168.
48 *May v May* [1929] 2 KB 386 (Court of Appeal).
49 *J.H. v C.H.* 25 July 1978, unreported, High Court.

computes income separately and claims relevant allowances and reliefs separately.

16.039 Finance Act 1983, section 3(2) provides that maintenance payments which are made by one separated spouse for the support of the other, under a legally enforceable agreement or covenant, are deducted when computing the payer's income for the tax year in which the payments are made. The payments are treated as income in the hands of the recipient spouse, chargeable to tax under Schedule D Case IV. By contrast, payments made in the same circumstances for the benefit of a child of the spouse who makes the payment, may *not* be deducted in computing the income of the payer, and are not treated as income of the child or of the other spouse. The payments are in effect made out of the payer's after-tax income.

16.040 These rules apply to legally enforceable maintenance obligations entered into after 8 June 1983. In addition, they apply to maintenance arrangements entered into up to and including that date where either (a) both spouses, by notice in writing, jointly elect that the provisions of section 3 of the Finance Act 1983 shall apply or (b) the maintenance arrangement is varied or replaced by another arrangement after 8 June 1983. In pre-1983 agreements maintenance was often expressed to be "such sum as, after the deduction of income tax, amounts to . . ." Such a clause will cease to be operative where the spouses elect that section 3 should apply. The provisions of the Act of 1983 apply regardless of the country in which the maintenance arrangement is made, and regardless of whether the arrangement has been made a rule of court.

16.041 Where a legally enforceable maintenance obligation exists between separated spouses, they may, under the Finance Act 1983 section 4, elect to be assessed jointly. The option of joint assessment is only available where both spouses are resident in the State for the year of assessment. It is not available where the marriage has been annulled or validly dissolved by a foreign divorce. Where they do so opt any maintenance payments, whether for the benefit of a spouse or a child, are ignored in computing the joint income of the spouses. The payer is not entitled to deduct maintenance payments from his income, and the payments are not regarded as income in the hands of the other spouse. The advantage of joint assessment is that it enables separated spouses to continue to derive full benefit from the double-rate bands, allowances and reliefs applicable to married couples, as for example, where one of the spouses is making substantial mortgage repayments on the family home. On the other hand, joint assessment precludes separated spouses from claiming the single parent allowance, to which each may be entitled if they are being taxed separately. Whether joint or separate assessment is preferable will depend on the particular circumstances of the spouses which may vary from year to year. Transfer from one form of assessment to the other from year to year is possible with prior notice to the inspector, that is, before the end of the tax year in which the new regime is to apply. A move from separate to joint assessment requires the consent of both spouses; a move from joint to separate assessment may be made at the request of either spouse.

16.042 Provisions relating to children in a separation agreement should be carefully drafted. There may be a temptation for the dependent spouse to attribute a disproportionate share of maintenance to the support of children. This has the short term benefit, where separate assessment applies, that less maintenance is taxable in the hands of the recipient spouse. However, when maintenance for the children ceases, the dependent spouse may find herself with a disproportionately small amount to live on. Where responsibilities for maintaining a (handicapped) child are shared between the spouses, this should be clearly expressed in the agreement so that any tax allowance in respect of the child can be divided *pro rata*. Where separate assessment applies, it should also be borne in mind that each parent will be entitled to the single parents' allowance, provided that he or she maintains the child at his or her own expense for at least part of the tax year. Provisions relating to maintenance and access should be drafted with these conditions in mind. The residence condition may for example be satisfied, in respect of the non-custodial parent, by a provision for access at weekends on an overnight basis or for holidays.

Maintenance agreements before 8 June 1983

16.043 The pre-1983 regime still applies to separation deeds and to certain other agreements (approved by the court or made a rule of court) before 9 June 1983, provided (a) that the spouses have not jointly elected to have section 3 of the Finance Act 1983 apply, and (b) that the maintenance arrangements have not since been replaced or varied. Under this regime, maintenance payments made by one separated spouse for the support of the other are treated as annual payments from which tax is deducted at source by the payer. The payments therefore represent taxed income in the hands of the recipient, who may be able to claim tax credit for some part of the tax deducted, depending on her other income and her allowances and reliefs. Where the deed provides that the maintenance payable should be "such sum as after the deduction of income tax at the standard rate then in force shall leave the wife with a clear weekly sum of £..." and the husband fails to deduct tax at the time of payment, he has no right to deduct the amount at a later date. In contrast with payments to a spouse, payments made for the support of a child may not have tax deducted at source and are not treated as taxable income in the hands of the child.

16.044 In practice, it seems unlikely that the pre-1983 regime will apply to many maintenance arrangements. Many such arrangements will have included variation clauses under which, since 1983, maintenance will have been increased, thus making the post-1983 regime applicable. Under a pre-1983 separation agreement, which has been made a rule of court under section 8 of the Family Law (Maintenance of Spouses and Children) Act

1976, payments are made without deduction of tax. The maintenance payable is ignored for the purposes of assessing the payer's liability for tax, and is not income assessable for tax purposes in the wife's hands.

Model deed of separation

16.045 This model deed of separation will incorporate a variety of clauses to meet as many fact situations as possible. Lawyers are traditionally conservative in drafting these deeds, incorporating standard clauses that have changed little in the wording over the last one hundred years. However, if standard clauses are used, they are less likely to arouse suspicion from the lawyers on the other side. The paragraph numbers and headings (which have been included in square brackets) are *for guidance only* and they do not form part of the deed.

THIS INDENTURE made the — day of — 1990,
BETWEEN Mary Soap of 11 Separated Road in the County of the City of Dublin, (hereinafter called "the wife") of the one part, and Joseph Soap of 13 Separated Hostel, St Jude's Row, in the City of Dublin, (hereinafter called "the husband") of the other part.
OR (in a case where nullity proceedings are likely to be issued, or the grounds of nullity apply)[50]
. . . hereinafter, for the purposes of this Deed referred to as the husband, and a similar clause for the wife.
WHEREAS

1. The husband and the wife were lawfully married to one another on the 14th day of June 1974.

   OR
   (if there are grounds for nullity) The husband and the wife were party to a marriage ceremony performed on the — day of —.

2. AND WHEREAS there are two children of the marriage, and no more, namely
Josephine born on the 11th day of September 1985,
and John born on the 16th day of May 1980.
3. AND WHEREAS Unhappy differences have arisen between the husband and the wife and they have agreed to live apart from each other upon the terms and conditions hereinafter contained.[51]

---

50 It may be queried why the parties do not proceed for nullity, instead of entering into a deed of separation. One spouse may be aware of the right to proceed for nullity, but still want to sort out the practicalities of breakdown. If the rider is not put in, the parties may be estopped from later issuing nullity proceedings.
51 The agreement to live apart is a standard one. The agreement to live apart may prevent one party alleging that the other party has deserted. It therefore has implications for deserted wife's allowance benefit.

OR

AND WHEREAS the husband and the wife are living apart from each other and they have agreed that while living apart and until they make other provisions for the matters hereinafter set forth or the terms hereof are superseded by any Order of the Court the following provisions shall have effect and shall regulate their mutual rights and obligations.[52]

OR

AND WHEREAS the husband deserted the wife on the — day of — 1989.[53]

OR

The husband/wife does not consent to the wife/husband living apart and nothing herein contained shall prejudice such rights (if any) as he/she may have in relation to his/her claim that he/she has been deserted by her/him.

OR

Neither the husband or the wife admits to blame for the fact of separation and nothing herein contained shall prejudice such rights . . .

OR

Nothing herein shall prejudice such rights (if any) that the wife may have in relation to her claim under section 195 of the Social Welfare (Consolidation) Act 1981, as amended.[54]

NOW THIS INDENTURE WITNESSETH AS FOLLOWS:

In pursuance of the said agreement and in consideration of the premises the husband and wife hereby mutually covenant and agree with each other as follows:

[16.046 Standard separation clause][55]

1. The husband and the wife shall each live separate and apart from and free from the marital control (if any) of the other and neither the husband nor the wife shall in any manner annoy, molest disturb or otherwise interfere with the other in his or her manner of living, or in his or her profession or business or with the others friends, relations or acquain-

---

52 This is where the parties are already living apart when the deed is entered into. It avoids dealing with the question whether one party deserted the other at the time that they ceased to cohabit. If this clause is inserted it is strictly a maintenance agreement, rather than a deed of separation. However, in practice, solicitors and their clients regard such a deed as a formal recognition that the marriage relationship is over.

53 The clause whereby one party accepts he has deserted is rarely agreed to. This is because of its implication for maintenance and successions rights. Note that a husband is now entitled to apply for a deserted husband's allowance, if he fulfils the regulations, under the Social Welfare Act 1989.

54 For deserted wife's allowance.

55 This separation clause is designed to prevent interference with the parties, and their cohabitees. Specific performance proceedings can in theory be issued for its breach, but in practice, a barring order is more likely to be sought. Note the case of *Fearon v Aylesford* [1884] 14 QBD where Brett M.R. stated that the husband's covenant to pay maintenance, and a wife's covenant not to molest her husband were not interdependent. She could enforce her obligations, though she had failed to observe her own.

tances, or use any force, violence or restraint on the person of the other, and each may live as if he or she were unmarried without restraint or correction of the other.

2. Neither the husband nor the wife shall visit or be or stay in any place in which the other is for the time being resident save at the express invitation of the other.

> OR
> "for the time being resident."
> OR
> . . . for the time being resident and the wife shall have sole right of residence in the family home at 11 Separated Road in the County of the City of Dublin, and the husband shall not enter or approach the said home save at the express invitation of the wife
> OR
> . . . save for the purposes of collecting or returning the children from access.

[16.047 Custody and access]

3. The husband and the wife shall remain as joint guardians of the children of the marriage.[56]

3(a) The wife shall have custody of the children, and the husband shall have access to the children as follows:

(b) On every Saturday/Sunday between the hours of 12 p.m. and 8 p.m., the husband to collect the children from — the gate of the family home, OR from the no. 27 bus stop at the end of Salkey Road,

> OR at the terminus of the no. 27 bus at Middle Abbey Street, in the City of Dublin.
> OR
> on every alternate Saturday and Sunday . . .
> OR
> Provided that in the event of the husband arriving more than 20 (or 30 minutes) late, the wife will not be obliged to wait at the — bus stop with the children, and no access will take place on that day, without arrangement with the wife, and a satisfactory explanation offered for the delay.[58]

56 Strictly there is no need to insert this clause as, under the Guardianship of Infants Act 1964, he is a joint guardian, with the right to be consulted on all matters affecting the upbringing of the children (**14.003**).
57 Definite access arrangements are beneficial for the children, as they reduce misunderstandings and disagreements. There is still flexibility built in, as there is the right to change or increase the access, with the agreement of the parties, and in default, a summons under section 11 can be issued, seeking the court's direction.
58 The lateness clause may seem off putting, but it is designed to reduce the disappointment caused to children, by a spouse who is constantly late, or who frequently does not turn up, without warning. Courts have used similar clauses for those with such dilatory habits. It is especially relevant to alcoholics.

OR

The child named — may have access to the father, as she wishes, and he may accompany [name of child] on his access visits.[59]

OR

The access arrangements made by the spouses in connection with the child named — shall take account of his wishes.

OR

The access arrangements may be varied as the children get older, and the father shall have the right to take each child out for access, on his or her own, provided that same shall not interfere unduly with the home routine, or school commitments.[60]

In addition the husband shall have access to the children from the hours of 4 p.m. to 8 p.m. inside the family home on every Wednesday, or on such other weekday as is agreed between the parties.[61]

(c) The husband shall be entitled to have the children stay at the home of his sister Grace Joy at — or the home of his mother Mary Soap at — on the first Saturday of each month, for the weekend, and shall return them to the family home at 6 p.m. on the Sunday.[62]

OR every second weekend from Friday at 5 p.m. to Monday morning at 8.45 a.m. the husband to collect the children and return them to school at St Francis School.

OR

on the first Saturday of every second month. . . .

OR

The husband shall be entitled to have the children stay with him for six weekends during the year. The husband shall give reasonable notice of the weekends he wishes to take the children, and shall ensure that the accommodation is suitable.

(d) The husband shall have holiday access on two consecutive weeks during the summer, provided that the husband shall give three weeks (or reasonable notice) to the wife, of the exact dates upon which he wishes to

59 The view is taken that teenage children are old enough to decide whether to go with the non-custodial parent or not. As they get older, and want to be with their peers, they may want to reduce or cease access. The non-custodial spouse may feel that the reduced access is at the instigation of the custodial spouse. Referral to a child guidance clinic or mediator may resolve the problem.

60 This is designed to deal with a family, which has large age gaps between the children. It also makes possible exclusive attention for a problem child. However, if there has been a confirmed allegation of sexual abuse, or a serious risk of such abuse, obviously such a clause would not be inserted.

61 The weekday access should not interfere with school homework. In fact, it gives the non custodial spouse the opportunity to help the children with it.

62 There is often objection to weekend access, on the basis that it will upset the children. It depends on the ages of the children, the animosity of the parents to each other, and the suitability of the accommodation for the children. Mothers may seem over protective at insisting on a bed for each child, while the children themselves may welcome a "camping expedition" in their father's flat.

exercise holiday access. He shall advise the wife of the address of the place in which the children shall reside during the holiday access.

OR

In every year commencing on the — day of — 1990, the husband shall be entitled to have access to the children for two weeks holidays upon the following conditions:

a. the period of two weeks may be continuous or broken into two periods of one week each.

b. the holiday period or periods during school holidays and if taken at Christmas or Easter, shall consist of one week not including Christmas Day or Easter Sunday and

c. notice in writing setting out full particulars of the holiday arrangements, including the address of the place in which the children shall reside with the husband during the said holiday periods, to be given to the wife by the husband not later than six weeks prior to the holiday period.

OR/AND

(e) The husband shall also have access during the three days of Christmas and at Easter.

OR

At each Christmas, either Christmas Day or Christmas Eve, or St Stephen's Day (Boxing Day), to be arranged between the parties.

OR

At Christmas, commencing on the 24th day of December 1990, the husband shall be entitled to access between the hours of 11 a.m. and 7 p.m., and in the year 1991, he shall have access on Christmas Day, between the same times, and in the year 1992, he shall have access on St Stephen's Day, and thereafter, in the same sequence over the following three years.[63]

(f) Such further or other access as may be agreed between the parties.

OR

Save that in the event of the said weekly access proving inconvenient to either spouse, on a particular Saturday, that alternative access arrangements may be arranged between the spouses, provided that advance notice of at least 24 hours is given to the other spouse.

(g) Access may take place on the birthdays of the children. The husband shall have access to the said children as school hours permit, if the birthday falls during the school week, or he shall be entitled to have access for an additional day, falling on the following weekend.

---

63 The tax implications of holidays and overnight access (re eligibility for single person's allowance) need to be examined: See **16.042.**

(h) The wife shall notify the husband if the children become seriously ill, and in particular, if the children are admitted to hospital. The party for the time being having care and control of the children, shall have the right, independent of the other, to acquire and provide such medical attention, including hospitalisation, as may be deemed necessary for any of the children.

(i) Neither the husband nor the wife shall remove the children or any of them outside the jurisdiction of the Irish Courts, without the prior written consent of the other (such consent not to be unreasonably withheld).

(j) The husband and the wife agree to sign any application forms necessary for passports for the children, and the wife shall retain custody of the said passports.

OR

The wife may apply for a passport for each of the children, to be held by each child in his/her name, and the husband hereby consents to each of the children obtaining a passport.

OR

The children shall be placed on the passport of the wife, and the husband hereby consents to the children being so placed.

(k) Each of them the husband and the wife shall foster and encourage the love, affection and respect of the children for the other of them, and shall not do or omit to do any act or thing which would tend to lower the other of them in the esteem of the children.

(l) The wife undertakes not to interfere with such postal or telephonic communication, as is reasonable, that the husband may wish to have with the children.

OR

The husband shall have access to the children, every second Friday, between the hours of 2 p.m. and 4 p.m. at the Happy Valley Health Centre in the County of the City of Dublin, under the supervision of — senior social worker, or some other social worker authorised by her. In the event of circumstances beyond the control of the wife, whereby the husband fails to have access on a particular Friday, due to the unavailability of the social worker, the wife will use her best endeavours to organise alternative access, for the following week, or additional hours on the following Friday.

(m) The husband undertakes not to bring the children into a public house, or a betting shop. The wife reserves the right to refuse to allow the children to accompany the husband, if the husband is under the influence of intoxicating liquor (or is intoxicated).

(n) The husband and wife shall jointly request any school that any of the children may attend, to send copies of school reports to both the husband and the wife.

OR

The wife undertakes to furnish the husband with copies of any school reports, whether term or annual reports.

(o) The husband undertakes that he will not bring the children into contact with Jane Jolly or any other woman with whom he may cohabit, or with any of the relations or friends of any such woman.

OR

Whereas the parties acknowledge the order made by the Circuit Court on the — day of — 1988, providing that the wife shall have sole custody, and that the husband shall exercise access, the husband shall be entitled to seek access while the child remains in the jurisdiction of the Republic of Ireland, or having left the said jurisdiction, when he returns to the said jurisdiction and in accordance with any order of the Circuit Court.[64]

[16.048 Maintenance]

4. In consideration of the premises, the husband hereby covenants with the wife as follows:
(a) That he will pay to the wife the sum of £— per week/per month, for the support of the wife and the children (being £— for the wife and £— for the children, or £— for the support of — (named child) and — for the support of — (named child).[65]
The first payment shall be paid on the — day of — 1990, and shall be paid on each subsequent Friday/Thursday thereafter, by Standing Order/ Direct Debit/personally/by cheque sent by registered post/prepaid ordinary post, or by postal orders, into the wife's bank account at — current account no. 12345.[66]

OR

payable in advance on the 1st day of every month, the first payment to be made on the first day of December 1990,
OR
payable on a four weekly basis, commencing on the first Friday of December 1990.
OR
The husband shall pay the said sums of maintenance to the wife, through the office of the District Court Clerk, at — address, on each Friday, by cheque made payable to the wife.[67]

---

64 Where there is already a court order relating to access, the order should be accurately incorporated into the deed.
65 The named child can be inserted where it is decided to allow a greater sum of money for an older child or a handicapped child.
66 It is most important to clarify the details of the method of payment. There is nothing more upsetting for a client than to receive payments in an irregular manner.
67 The payments may be made through the District Court Clerk only where there is a pre-existing maintenance order.

4(b) AND IT IS FURTHER AGREED AND DECLARED that the said weekly payment shall be annually increased in accordance with any increase in the cost of living as set down in the consumer price index issued by the Central Statistics Office, using the 10th day of November 1990 as a base date[68] and the first such increase shall be payable on the first day of January 1991, and on the first day of January thereafter.[69]

OR

The parties also hereby undertake to consult on a revision of the amount of maintenance payable hereunder every 12 months. Such revision shall take into account but shall not be based upon the percentage rise in the consumer price index.

OR

In the event that, on such review, the parties fail to agree on a revision of the amount of maintenance payable hereunder, either party may serve notice by registered post, on the other, to refer the said dispute to mediation.[70] The other party has twenty one days to accept or reject the said offer. If the parties fail to agree, either to attend at mediation, or to agree on the revision, either party may apply to the court under the provisions of the Family Law (Maintenance of Spouses and Children) Act 1976 (as amended or repealed or replaced) or under the Guardianship of Infants Act 1964 (as amended or repealed or replaced).

OR

The husband may serve notice on the wife informing her of his intention to reduce the sum of maintenance, or, in the alternative, the wife may serve notice on the husband informing him of her need for a greater sum, in excess of that which is provided herein. On service of the notice, the other party is entitled to obtain full details of the other's financial circumstances, and when six weeks have elapsed, if no agreement has been reached, the husband shall cease to be liable to pay maintenance, in accordance with the provisions herein. The wife may apply for an order of maintenance.

---

68 The base date is the date last issued with the consumer price index. It does not really matter what date of the month is inserted, as the actual index is not published until approximately six weeks later, though the increase should then be backdated to the date it was due to commence.

69 A variation clause must be inserted in a deed. See *J.D. v B.D.* [1985] 5 ILRM 688, at page 690, where Carroll J. stated, "It is my opinion that unless there is such a provision for variation, the agreement is neither fair nor reasonable". It may be helpful if it is agreed that P60's be exchanged every year, to help assess a variation. In some cases, a C.P.I. clause is objected to, and instead, the variation is linked with net increase in the husband's salary.

70 The parties may have reached agreement, through mediation, which agreement was incorporated into the deed of separation. The mediator usually arranges a follow-up session, six months after mediation, to see if there are problems. It is better if agreement can be reached, through the solicitors, or a mediator, rather than to go to court on a variation. If there is a pre-existing order, then a consent variation can be applied for, so that the court record is correct.

4(c) AND IT IS FURTHER AGREED AND DECLARED that the maintenance payable in respect of the children shall cease to be payable upon each child attaining the age of 18 years or if the child has attained that age and is still attending at a full time course of education or instruction at any university, college, school or other educational establishment, upon the child completing his/her education or attaining the age of 21 years whichever be the earlier.[71]

4(d) In the event of a fundamental (or material) change in the circumstances (financial or otherwise) of either the husband or the wife, or that the parties fail to agree on a revision of the amount of maintenance payable hereinafter, either party may apply to the court, under the provisions of the Family Law (Maintenance of Spouses and Children) Act 1976 (as amended or repealed or replaced) or under the Guardianship of Infants Act 1964, (as amended or repealed or replaced).

OR

In the event of a change in circumstances in the financial position of either the husband or the wife, then either party will be at liberty to apply to the other for an increase or a decrease, in the amount of maintenance payable under this agreement, as appropriate in the circumstances and, failing agreement being reached by the husband and the wife, then either party hereto shall be at liberty to apply to the court under section 5 of the Family Law (Maintenance of Spouses and Children) Act 1976, or otherwise have the matter determined by the court.

4(e) In the event of the wife taking up full time employment, the maintenance for the wife shall be reviewed, in the light of these changed circumstances.

OR
The husband and the wife mutually agree and acknowledge that the provisions in relation to maintenance, may be enforced and/or varied in accordance with the Family Law (Maintenance of Spouses and Children) Act 1976, as amended or repealed or replaced.
OR
While (or if) the husband becomes (or remains) unemployed, (or if the husband is in receipt of disability or invalidity benefit) the husband agrees and consents to such portion of the benefit or allowance, payable under the Social Welfare (Consolidation) Act 1981 (as amended or repealed or replaced) which is attributable to and payable in respect of

71 The Family Law (Maintenance of Spouses and Children) Act 1976 provides for maintenance ceasing at the age of 16 years (unless there is further education, or a child is handicapped). Since there may be problems with maintenance of teenagers who are unemployed, but not in receipt of social welfare payments, it is recommended that maintenance should be stated as continuing until 18 years, provided that the child is not employed.

the wife and children, to be paid directly to the wife, by the persons, body or authority, by whom such benefit or allowance shall be payable to the husband.[72] The clause shall also apply, in the event of the husband obtaining monies under a FAS scheme,[73] or Social Employment Scheme, or any other such scheme for the relief of unemployment. The husband also consents in the event of him obtaining pay related benefit, to give 60% (or 75%) of such benefit[74] to the wife and children.

OR

The wife reserves her right to seek maintenance from the husband, in the event that the husband ceases to be unemployed (or secures steady or full time regular employment).[75] If the husband and the wife fail to reach agreement on the amount of maintenance, either party may apply to the court, under the provisions of the Family Law (Maintenance of Spouses and Children) Act 1976 (as amended or repealed or replaced) or under the provisions of the Guardianship of Infants Act 1964 (as amended or repealed or replaced).

OR

The husband is in receipt of unemployment benefit (or assistance). Upon the resumption of gainful employment by him, the husband undertakes to pay to the wife a sum to be agreed, for the support of herself and the children, or if it is not agreed, the amount to be determined pursuant to the provisions of the Family Law (Maintenance of Spouses and Children) Act 1976 (as amended or replaced).

OR

The wife acknowledges that at the present time her circumstances are such that she will not require personal maintenance, alimony or support from the husband. She further acknowledges that, at present, she does not anticipate circumstances in the future in which it would be necessary for her to seek personal maintenance, alimony or support from the husband pursuant to the Family Law (Maintenance of Spouses and Children) Act 1976 or any subsequent statutory substitution, amendment or modification thereof or otherwise.[76] PROVIDED ALWAYS that nothing in this agreement shall constitute an acknowledgement by the husband that the wife is entitled to any personal maintenance, alimony or support from him and on the other hand shall not constitute a waiver by the wife of any right she may have to claim personal maintenance from the husband.

72 The social welfare authorities may need his consent to her obtaining separate payments of his benefit or allowance, if she is not eligible for her own allowance or benefit.

73 FAS is the national training authority, and the social employment scheme is a work experience programme.

74 Pay related benefit is a percentage of earnings, which the employee can claim when he ceases working. His spouse is not entitled, if on separate payments, to any share of this amount.

75 Strictly, she does not need to reserve her right to seek maintenance, but the Department of Social Welfare may be happier if she does, so as to preserve her continued entitlement to deserted wife's benefit or allowance.

76 Section 27 of the Family Law (Maintenance of Spouses and Children) Act 1976, makes an agreement, which purports to exclude the operation of any provision of the Act void. See also *H.D. v P.D.* (May 1978, unreported, Supreme Court).

4(f) The husband shall insure the wife and children with the Voluntary Health Insurance Board and, if at any time the wife or the children requires hospitalisation, and/or medical care, if the hospital or medical fees relating thereto, exceed the sum recoverable from the Voluntary Health Insurance Board, the husband shall pay the difference. The husband shall in addition, discharge reasonable dental expenses incurred by the wife and children.

OR

The husband shall pay all subscriptions necessary to insure the wife and children with the Voluntary Health Insurance Board, for in-patient semi-private hospital treatment, at the Board's recommended premium, in respect of such treatment.

4(g) The husband shall discharge all accounts for school fees and books, for the children, and all reasonable expenses incurred in their education.

4(h) The wife shall be entitled to receive all social welfare allowances in respect of the children, and in particular child benefit.

4(i) The husband agrees to continue paying the premiums on the life assurance policy held with the — Company, and further agrees that the wife will continue to be the named beneficiary.[77]

4(j) The husband shall provide that on his death, during the infancy of the children, or until the children shall have completed their education, the proceeds of his policies of life assurance shall be made available for the benefit of the children, and the husband therefore covenants to maintain the said policy, by the payment of the monthly premiums (or in an amount of not less than £15,000 with the child as beneficiary).

OR

The husband will endorse over to the wife any interest which he has in the following insurance policies presently held with X company. The wife shall assume total responsibility for the payment of all premiums due, as and from the date on which the husband relinquishes any interest in the said policies, and the wife shall be exclusively entitled to all benefits and payments under the said policies.

4(k) The husband will pay and discharge the mortgage on the said family home, and the water rates. He shall in addition insure the contents and the structure of the home, and discharge all premiums payable in respect of same. He agrees to discharge all reasonable bills relating to the proper maintenance and decoration of the said home.

---

77 It is worthwhile checking the actual life policies. Clients rarely understand their implications. The wife may find herself paying premiums on the life of her husband, or policies taken out, where he is the beneficiary.

OR

The wife undertakes to maintain the said family home, and to pay all outgoings in relation thereto.

4(l) The husband and the wife agree that the figure of maintenance agreed, is on the basis of full disclosure of all assets.

4(m) Maintenance will cease on the happening of the following events:

(i) The death of the husband.
(ii) The death of the wife.
(iii) The maintenance for the wife shall cease to be payable if the wife goes through a ceremony of marriage with another, at any future time, regardless of whether the ceremony does or does not give rise to a valid marriage according to Irish Law.[78]
(iv) The maintenance for the wife shall cease if she cohabits with a person who is supporting her financially.
OR
if the wife openly cohabits with another man as if they were husband and wife.[79]
(v) in the event of a court making a maintenance order, which supersedes the maintenance provided for in this deed.[80]

[16.049 Property]

5. The husband undertakes to transfer the tenancy of the family home situate at — into the sole name of the wife. The husband agrees to sign any documentation required to complete the said transfer.

OR

The husband and the wife hereby agree that the family home at — which is presently held in the joint names of the husband and the wife (or held in the sole name of the husband or the wife), shall be sold by way of private treaty (or auction), for a minimum reserve figure of £—. Any offer received below this sum shall be considered by the husband and the wife, and they shall take into account the recommendation of the auctioneer, and it is hereby agreed that no reasonable offer shall be refused. The solicitor for the wife and the solicitor for the husband shall have joint carriage of sale.
The wife hereby consents[81] to the sale of the family home at — pursuant to section 3 of the Family Home Protection Act 1976 and the wife covenants to sign all legal documents to give effect to the sale.
The net proceeds shall be divided between the husband and the wife in equal shares, one half share to each, after deduction of the following;

---

78 For the effect of a foreign divorce on maintenance rights see **8.002**, **8.005** and **8.052**.
79 The cohabitating clause is not always inserted. It may be insisted upon by a husband who suspects the wife of having a boyfriend.
80 This goes without saying, but some clients may prefer to put it in explicitly.
81 Section 3 of Family Home Protection Act 1976 deals with the consent of the other spouse.

(a) all legal costs and auctioneer's fees incurred in respect of the sale.

(b) the costs of discharging the mortgage on the family home in favour of — Building Society (or Bank).

(c) any outstanding utilities or other household debts incurred up to the date that the parties vacated the family home.

OR

The husband shall forthwith, upon the execution of the deed, transfer the family home situate at — into the joint names of the husband and the wife, subject to the existing charge (or charges), or burden (or burdens). The husband undertakes to complete any documentation required to complete the said transfer.

IT IS HEREBY AGREED AND DECLARED that until the said family home shall be formally placed into the joint names of the husband and the wife, in accordance with the provisions herein, the husband shall hold the said family home as trustee for himself and the wife jointly.

IT IS HEREBY AGREED AND DECLARED that on the completion of the transfer aforesaid, the husband and the wife will hold the said family home subject to and with the benefit of the charge in favour of — County Council (or — Corporation, or — Building Society, or Bank), set out in Folio — of the County of —,

TO THE INTENT that on any future sale of the family home, the husband and the wife shall share equally in the net proceeds of such sale, after discharge of the mortgage, and the expenses of the sale.

OR

The family home, at —, presently held under a Tenant Purchase Scheme,[82] shall remain the joint property of the husband and the wife. The wife shall assume total responsibility for payment of the mortgage repayments, as and from the date of this Deed, and shall at all times indemnify the husband against all claims for arrears with regard to the repayments falling due after this date, provided that the husband continues to make the maintenance payments as aforesaid.

OR

The husband hereby agrees with the wife to release and assign unto her, the beneficial ownership of all his estate and interest in the family home at — (hereinafter called "the family home") freed and discharged from all claims which he may have in respect of the same, whether under the Family Home Protection Act 1976 or otherwise howsoever, and the wife hereby agrees that in consideration of the husband executing and delivering such release and assignment to her, she will indemnify and keep indemnified the husband from and against all claims thereafter arising on foot of the mortgage of the — Building Society at present secured on the family home.

AND the husband shall, at or prior to the execution of these presents, duly execute and deliver to the wife such deed of release and assignment, AND ALSO shall at any time hereafter, at the request of the wife or any

---

82 The Tenant Purchase Scheme allows local authority tenants to purchase their homes. The local authority consent to the transfer is required.

person claiming through or under her, execute any deed, document, or consent, that may be required, whether for the purpose of sale or otherwise, for the confirmation of this agreement or the giving of full legal effect thereto.

OR

The husband shall transfer to the wife his one half interest in the family home situate at — for a consideration of £20,000, payable by the wife to the husband on the execution of the transfer by the husband. The husband acknowledges that the sum £20,000 represents fifty per cent of the value of the said home, after deduction of the present mortgage of £—. The husband shall accept same in full settlement of any rights or claims which he may have in relation to the said home, and any other premises in which the husband and the wife have resided during the marriage, and will on request, execute and deliver any further specific consents sought by the wife.

The wife will arrange for the — Building Society to furnish their consent to release the husband from the obligations arising under the mortgage relating to the said home, insofar as it affects the husband. This agreement is conditional on the said consent being obtained. If the said consent is subject to a condition or conditions, which the husband is unable to comply with, the consent shall be deemed not to have been obtained, until the wife is in a position to obtain the consent, on terms which can be reasonably complied with.[83]

5(A) The wife as the spouse of the husband acknowledges that any house or premises which might subsequently be purchased by the husband, at any time in the future, are not to be held to be a "family home" within the meaning of the Family Home Protection Act 1976, and further to the extent that same is required, consents for the purposes of section 3 of the said Act of 1976,[84] to the sale (or other disposal) by the husband at any time hereafter, at his absolute discretion, without any notice to her, of any property which the husband might own at any time in the future, and acknowledges to the husband that this indenture shall constitute her written consent such as may be required by the said Act of 1976 (or any statutory amendment or modification of that Act) to any such sale or sales.

5(B) The husband as the spouse of the wife acknowledges that any house or premises which might subsequently be purchased by the wife at any time in the future are not to be held to be a "family home" within the

---

83 The building society will probably insist on arrears being discharged before consenting to a transfer. It is helpful to agree that if the husband is to continue paying the mortgage in the event of the house not being transferred, the wife will be given the right to contact the building society to check from time to time that the mortgage is being paid. This is where the house remains in his sole name. The building society will also probably insist on the wife having a guarantor, unless she is in full time employment outside the home.

84 Strictly, the consent under the Family Home Protection Act 1976 should be inserted at the end of the deed, to make it easier to copy that portion, to be included in the title documents. A statutory declaration form, under the Family Home Protection Act 1976, can also be signed.

meaning of the Family Home Protection Act 1976, and further to the extent that same is required consents for the purposes of section 3 of the said Act of 1976, to the sale (or other disposal) by the wife at any time hereafter, at her absolute discretion, without any notice to him, of any property which the wife might own at any time in the future, and acknowledges to the husband that this indenture shall constitute his written consent such as may be required by the said Act of 1976 (or any statutory amendment or modification of that Act) to any such sale or sales.

OR

The wife (or the husband, as the case may be) hereby consents to the sale or transfer by the wife/husband of any house or property or premises which he/she now owns or in the future may purchase or acquire by inheritance or otherwise obtain should such consent be deemed necessary by virtue of the provisions of the Family Home Protection Act 1976, or any Act of the Oireachtas amending or extenting the said Act.

OR

The husband and the wife hereby agree to execute a separate deed of waiver giving up any rights they may have in relation to any other properties which are not a "family home", within the meaning of the Family Home Protection Act 1976, which may be obtained by either party either now or in the future.

6(a) The husband acknowledges that the household chattels as defined[85] in section 9 of the Family Home Protection Act 1976 shall remain within the confines of the family home at —.

OR

The husband acknowledges that the household chattels contained in the family home are the sole property of the wife.

OR

The husband acknowledges that he has received or will take with him, when he vacates the family home on the — day of —, the items listed in the annexed schedule, and the husband shall accept same, in full and final settlement of any claim he may have in relation to the contents of the family home.

OR (in the event of the sale of the home)

The wife shall purchase the husband's half share of the contents of the said premises, on the basis of the agreed valuation of the said contents, and in default of agreement, the contents shall be sold by way of auction, and the proceeds divided equally between the husband and the wife,

85 Section 9 of the Family Home Protection Act 1976 defines household chattels as "furniture, bedding, linen, china, earthenware, glass, books, and other chattels of ordinary household use or ornament and also consumable stores, garden effects, and domestic animals". Chattels cannot be disposed of where matrimonial proceedings have been issued.

after discharge of auctioneer and valuer's fees, and any other charges or taxes.

OR

The husband and the wife agree that on the sale of the family home, the contents shall be divided in the following manner;

(a) All engagement or wedding presents from the friends, relations, or acquaintances of the wife shall be returned to her.

(b) All engagement or wedding presents given by the husband's friends, relations or acquaintances shall be returned to him.

(c) All items of personal apparel, and items of sentimental value belonging to each spouse shall be given to that spouse, insofar as it is possible to identify the ownership of each item.

(d) All the belongings of the children, including beds, bedlinen, toys shall be given to the wife.

(e) The electrical appliances shall be divided as equally as possible between the spouses, and in default of agreement shall be sold.

OR

6(b) The husband and the wife hereby covenant and agree with each other that they will execute and deliver such further assurances, authorities, and things as may be reasonably required for the purpose of carrying out and giving full effect to the covenants, agreements and provision herein contained.

OR

The husband and the wife hereby covenant that each of them and their respective executors or administrators will execute and do all such assurances, acts or things as the other of them or his or her executors, administrators, and assigns may at any given time reasonably require for the purposes of giving effect to this deed and the covenants and conditions herein contained.

7. The husband and the wife shall at all times hereafter keep the other indemnified against all such debts and liabilities as he or she may contract, hereafter and from all such costs, damages, expenses, charges, losses, claims and demands that may be incurred by the other on account thereof.

OR

The wife, her heirs, executors, administrators and assigns shall at all times hereinafter keep indemnified the husband, his heirs, executors, administrators, and assigns against debts and liabilities heretobefore or hereinafter to be contracted or incurred by the wife, and from all actions, proceedings, claims, demands, costs, damages and expenses whatsoever in respect of such debts, liabilities, or any of them. (insert a similar clause for the husband).

449

8. The wife shall be entitled to carry on any business without any interference from the husband[86] and all profits therefrom and any property purchased or money saved by the wife out of the allowance payable to her by the husband, in accordance with the terms of this deed, shall belong solely to the wife, and section 21 of the Family Law (Maintenance of Spouses and Children) Act 1976 shall not apply thereto.[87]

9. The wife hereby covenants with the husband that during the continuance of this agreement, and in consideration thereof, the wife will at all times support and maintain herself and support and maintain the children, and will make all such payments as may be necessary for that purpose and she will at all times keep the husband indemnified against all debts heretofore or hereafter contracted and incurred by her, and against all liability whatsoever in respect of the children, and against all actions, proceedings, claims, demands, costs, damages, losses and expenses in respect of or on account of any matter aforesaid.

PROVIDED ALWAYS and it is hereby agreed and declared by and between the husband and the wife that if the husband shall at any time be called upon to make or shall in fact make any payment in respect of which he is entitled to indemnity under the covenant in that behalf herein contained, he may in every such case deduct the same from the payments falling to be made hereunder and retain the amount of every such payment made by him together with the amount of all costs, damages and expenses incurred by him in relation thereto, but without prejudice to his rights under this clause.[88]

The husband and the wife shall sign any such certificates and do all such things as may be required to enable either party to obtain such relief in respect of the payment of income tax as he or she may be entitled to.

(if applicable) The wife hereby agrees that the husband shall be entitled to such tax relief as is allowed by law in respect of herself and such of the children as the husband is for the time being maintaining. The husband and the wife acknowledge that they are jointly assessed for tax purposes and that the husband has the benefit of all the tax free allowances at present obtained under the joint tax assessment, and that the maintenance payable under this deed has taken the joint assessment[89] into account.

[16.050 Succession rights]

The husband and the wife hereby mutually surrender and renounce all rights under the Succession Act 1965 (or any other Acts of the Oireachtas, which may extend or amend[90] the said Act), to the estate of the other, and

---

86 There is no need to put this in, unless there was harassment, which might occur more frequently in a small town.

87 Section 21 provides for any property acquired out of a household allowance to belong jointly to the spouses, unless there is an express or implied agreement to the contrary.

88 This clause is rarely inserted.

89 See **16.038** et seq.

90 Note the relevance of section 17 and section 42 of the Judicial Separation and Family Law Reform Act 1989.

furthermore, hereby renounce their respective rights to the extraction of a grant of probate or administration or (as the case may be) to the estate of the other and hereby undertake not to interfere in any way with the extraction of a grant of probate or administration to the estate of the other, provided that none of the foregoing shall deprive either the husband or the wife from taking any legal action on behalf of the children, in protecting or defending the children's interests in the estate of either the husband or the wife or from taking any action on behalf of the said children under the Succession Act 1965 (or any other Acts of the Oireachtas which may in the future extend or amend the Succession Act 1965).[91]

OR

The husband and the wife hereby renounce and surrender all or any rights he or she may have to any share in the estate of the other in pursuance of the provisions of the Succession Act 1965 (or any other Acts of the Oireachtas which may in the future extend or amend the Succession Act 1965) to the intent that, on the death of either the husband or the wife, his or her estate shall pass to the person or persons who may be entitled thererto as if the husband or the wife had never been married. (optional) — And provided always that the rights of the children as provided for by section 67 subsection 3 or section 117 of the Succession Act 1967 shall not be abrogated.[92]

[16.051 Pensions]

10. The husband agrees that the wife shall benefit from his pension rights arising out of his employment with — company, and any other future pensionable employment which he may take, insofar as same shall consist of a widow's pension and any payment to be made by an employer or ex employer on his death.[93]

11. In the event of either the husband or the wife becoming redundant, and his or her pension contributions being refunded, he or she shall invest such sum as shall be received in respect of pension contributions (after all taxes thereon have been discharged), and the sum shall remain invested at compound interest, until he or she shall attain the age of 65 years, at which stage the annual income of the accumulated fund shall be payable to him or her as and for a pension. After his or her death, the survivor shall receive the annual income from the said fund for a period of five years from the

---

91 When dealing with waiver of succession rights, it may be helpful to ask the client to initial her confirmation of instructions on a separate instructions sheet. This can be confirmed later in writing. Be wary of a spouse being too eager to waive, where she is only being granted maintenance but no property rights, and especially where the family home remains in his sole name and he consents only to giving her a right of residence until the eldest child reaches the age of 18 years. A will should be made immediately after a deed is entered into.

92 There is really no need to put in a clause in relation to the children's rights. It may be needed for the purpose of reassurance.

93 Pensions are a very complex subject. Clients should make full disclosure of their pension entitlements. Often clients are not familiar with the pension scheme at work, and seem reluctant to make inquiries in case this draws attention to their marital breakdown.

date of the other party's death, and the accumulated fund shall form part of the estate of the other party to be disposed of, as he or she shall see fit, subject only to the aforementioned five annual instalments to the surviving party (subject to amendment to suit the situation).[94]

12. The costs of the preparation and execution of the deed shall be paid by the husband.

OR

The husband shall, upon signing this deed, discharge all legal costs incurred by the wife in respect of legal advices given to the wife concerning her matrimonial difficulties, and in respect of all proceedings brought by the wife against the husband, and in respect of the negotiation and conclusion of this deed, and together with the stamp duty payable therein.

13. If the husband and the wife shall, at any future time, live together as husband and wife for a period of 12 months, then this deed shall thereupon become null and void without prejudice to any rights which may have previously accrued to either party hereto against the other.

Nullity clause [if relevant]

For the purposes of the law of nullity, the husband and the wife hereby agree that this deed shall not be regarded as an approbation or a ratification of a void or voidable marriage.[95]

IN WITNESS WHEREOF the parties hereto have hereunder set their hands and affixed their seals the day and year first herein written.

SIGNED SEALED AND DELIVERED
by the said —
in the presence of: client to sign here.
(witness — the solicitor to sign here)

A similar clause is to be inserted for the other spouse.

---

94 If there is a considerable redundancy payment, this may be the subject of negotiation. It could, for example, be used to reduce the mortgage, or to purchase another home, allowing the previous family home to be transferred to the dependent spouse.
95 See **2.130** et seq.

Chapter 17

RECOGNITION AND ENFORCEMENT OF JUDGMENTS

This chapter deals with the recognition in the Republic of Ireland of foreign divorces, the enforcement in the Republic of Ireland of financial provision orders made abroad, whether or not pursuant to a foreign divorce, and the enforcement in European Community countries of maintenance and other financial provision orders made in the Republic of Ireland. It does not deal with the recognition of other foreign decrees affecting status, such as nullity decrees and decrees of judicial separation.[1]

The recognition of foreign divorces

Introduction

17.001 Article 41.3.3 of the Constitution of Ireland states:

No person whose marriage has been dissolved under the civil law of any other State but is a subsisting valid marriage under the law for the time being in force within the jurisdiction of the Government and Parliament established by this Constitution shall be capable of contracting a valid marriage within that jurisdiction during the lifetime of the other party to the marriage so dissolved.

After a period of uncertainty[2] the case law[3] now establishes that this sub-article does not prevent the recognition of foreign divorces, but rather

---

1 On these and other conflict of laws matters see W. Binchy, *Irish Conflicts of Law.* (Butterworth (Ireland), 1988).
2 See *Mayo-Perrott v Mayo-Perrott* [1958] IR 336 (Supreme Court), in which Maguire C.J. claimed that the sub-article prevented the recognition of foreign divorces. It was the opposing view of Kingsmill Moore J. which found favour in subsequent cases.
3 *In re Caffin (Deceased); Bank of Ireland v Caffin* [1971] IR 123, *Gaffney v Gaffney* [1975] IR 133, *M.T.T. v N.T.* [1982] ILRM 217, *L.B. v H.B.* [1980] ILRM 257, *M.C. v K.E.D. (orse K.C.)* (13 December 1985, unreported) Supreme Court.

confirms the right of the Oireachtas to vary the recognition principles from time to time. It is only when a foreign divorce is not entitled to recognition, under current recognition principles, that the "dissolved" marriage remains "a subsisting valid marriage" within the meaning of the sub-article. Where the divorce is entitled to recognition, whether under principles opperating before or after the enactment of the Constitution in 1937, the sub-article has no effect.

17.002 Before 1937 judges were prepared to recognise a foreign divorce where it had been granted by the court of the jurisdiction wherein both parties were domiciled at the time of the commencement of divorce proceedings.[4] This practice continued, once the Constitutional question had been resolved after 1937. It was not until 1986 that legislation was passed affecting the issue. The Domicile and Recognition of Foreign Divorces Act 1986, having abolished prospectively the rule that a wife's domicile is dependent on that of her husband (in section 5(1)) broadened the law to allow recognition of a divorce granted in the country where either spouse is domiciled.

17.003 Before looking at the rules in more detail, two preliminary points should be made. The first is that recognition principles are primarily concerned with jurisdiction. Where the validity of foreign divorce is in issue, the principal question is not whether the substantive law applied by the foreign court is acceptable. Indeed, it has been held that the grounds upon which a foreign divorce is granted are not relevant.[5] The Irish court is primarily concerned to determine whether the foreign court had jurisdiction to grant the divorce. The second point is that the test of jurisdiction is that laid down by Irish law. It is not a question of deciding if the foreign court exercised jurisdiction properly according to its own rules of jurisdiction. It is a matter of deciding whether the foreign court was exercising jurisdiction in circumstances which are acceptable to Irish law. This is a matter of some importance, given the wide range of jurisdictional rules applying to divorce cases in different countries. For example, in England and Wales, Scotland and Northern Ireland, the courts are entitled to grant divorce where, at the commencement of proceedings, the petitioner or respondent is either domiciled, or has been habitually resident for one year, in one of those jurisdictions.[6] However, as will be seen, the Irish courts do not regard "habitual residence" as a sufficient basis of jurisdiction, and will not recognise a foreign divorce on a basis other than

4 See *Sinclair v Sinclair* [1896] 1 IR 603, following *Le Mesurier v Le Mesurier* (1895) AC 517.
5 *In re Caffin*, supra, in which Kenny J. rejected an argument that an English divorce grounded on desertion should not be recognised because desertion had never been accepted as a ground for divorce *a mensa et thoro* under Irish law. In an extreme case, grounds may be relevant in considering whether recognition would be contrary to public policy.
6 For England and Wales, and Scotland, see Domicile and Matrimonial Proceedings Act 1973. For Northern Ireland, see the Matrimonial Causes (Northern Ireland) Order, SI 1978/1045 (NI 15) art. 49.

"domicile". It should also be stressed that the definition of domicile in the context of divorce recognition is governed by Irish law, and not by the law of the jurisdiction where the divorce is obtained.[7]

The concept of domicile

17.004 Because the concept of domicile is centrally important to divorce recognition, some attention must be given to a few of its more important features.[8] All persons receive at birth, by operation of law, a domicile of origin.[9] Except in the case of a foundling, the domicile of origin is determined, not by the location of the birth, but by the domicile of the relevant parent. A legitimate child with a living father takes his domicile of origin from the domicile which his father has at the time of the child's birth. A non-marital child or a legitimate child whose father is dead takes his domicile of origin from the mother's domicile at the time of the child's birth. As a general rule, a child's domicile changes with any change in the domicile of the controlling parent.[10] This generally means the father's domicile, though under section 4 of the Domicile and Recognition of Foreign Divorces Act 1986 the rules are modified where the father and mother are living apart. Section 2 of the Age of Majority Act 1985 provides that a child ceases to have a dependent domicile when he reaches the age of 18.

17.005 An independent person of full age may acquire a new domicile, known as a domicile of choice, by a combination of actual residence in, and the formation of an intention to reside permanently or indefinitely in, a new jurisdiction.[11] The proof required to establish that a domicile of choice has been acquired is in practice considerable. In *M.T.T. v N.T.T.*[12] the Supreme Court held that the husband, who had a domicile of origin in England, had not acquired a domicile in the Republic of Ireland after moving to Cork to take up permanent and pensionable employment. His wife and children had subsequently joined him in Cork, and he had been living there for three years when he instituted proceedings for divorce in England. The Supreme Court found that the husband had not formed the intention necessary to abandon his domicile of origin and acquire a new domicile; he remained domiciled in England, and his divorce was therefore entitled to recognition. The issue was expressed by Griffin J. as follows:

> Unless . . . the plaintiff (the wife) can show that the proper inference to be drawn from the established facts in the case is that the defendant has shown unmistakably by his conduct that he had formed the settled purpose of residing indefinitely in Cork and that he had an intention to

7 For the general principle, see *Re Adams Deceased* [1967] IR at pages 434–5 and *In Bonis Rowan Deceased: Rowan v Rowan* [1988] ILRM 65, at 67.
8 For a full treatment, see W. Binchy, *Irish Conflicts of Law*, op. cit., chapter 6.
9 See *Udny v Udny* LR 1 HL (Sc.) 441 (1869).
10 See *Spurway v Spurway* [1894] 1 IR 385.
11 See, e.g., *In re Joyce: Corbet v Fagan* [1946] IR 277, *In re Adams Deceased* [1967] IR 424.
12 [1982] ILRM 217.

abandon his former domicile, the plaintiff will not have discharged the onus of proof on her.[13]

17.006 The same heavy onus rests on a spouse who has a domicile of origin in the Republic of Ireland and who seeks to prove that he has acquired a domicile of choice in the foreign country where he petitions for a divorce. Unless the evidence is clear that the petitioner, at the time of the institution of the divorce proceedings, formed a settled intention to remain in that jurisdiction indefinitely, he will retain his domicile in the Republic of Ireland and the divorce may not be recognised.[14]

17.007 A domicile of choice is lost where the individual ceases to reside, and ceases to intend to reside, in the jurisdiction where he had his domicile of choice.[15] It is, in fact, much easier to prove loss of a domicile of choice than loss of a domicile of origin. Where a domicile of choice is lost, it may be replaced by another domicile of choice. However if the requirements for the acquisition of another domicile of choice are not met, the domicile of origin revives and remains the individual's domicile until such time as a new domicile is acquired.[16]

17.008 The rules for determining the domicile of a married woman are as follows. According to section 1 of the Domicile and Recognition of Foreign Divorces Act 1986, where the domicile of a married woman is to be determined at any time after the commencement of the Act (2 October 1986) she is to be regarded as having an independent domicile determined by reference to the same factors as in the case of any other person capable of having an independent domicile. She may therefore have a domicile different from that of her husband, and this may occur even though they are living together. An example would be where a man with an English domicile of origin marries a woman who has a domicile in the Republic of Ireland, and they establish their matrimonial home in Dublin. The wife retains her domicile in the Republic of Ireland; but the husband will not acquire a domicile of choice in the Republic of Ireland unless and until he forms the requisite intention to remain in the Republic permanently or indefinitely.

17.009 The determination of a wife's domicile prior to 2 October 1986 is more problematic. It used to be thought[17] and in a number of cases it was assumed[18] that on marriage a woman became dependent for her domicile on her husband. His domicile was automatically hers, and any change in his

---

13 Id., at page 221. The phraseology is that of Budd J. *in Re Sillar: Hurley v Wimbush* [1956] IR 344, at page 350.
14 See e.g., *M.C. v K.E.D. (orse K.C.)*, supra.
15 *Revenue Commissioners v Matthews* (1958) 92 ILTR 44 (Supreme Court).
16 See *Udny v Udny*, supra.
17 See, e.g., *Gaffney v Gaffney* [1975] IR 133 per Kenny J. (at page 138) in the High Court, citing *Lord Advocate v Jaffrey* [1921] 1 AC 146, and *Attorney General for Alberta v Cook* [1926] AC 444.
18 *In Re Caffin*, supra, *M.T.T. v N.T.*, supra.

domicile automatically effected a change in hers. However in *Gaffney v Gaffney*, Walsh J. raised the possibility that "some day" the dependency principle might be challenged on constitutional grounds "in a case where the wife has never physically left her domicile of origin while her deserting husband may have established a domicile in another jurisdiction".[19] Similar reservations were expressed by McCarthy J. at page 5 of his judgment in *M.C. v K.E.D. (orse K.C.)* in the Supreme Court. More emphatically in *M.(C.) v M.(T.)*[20] Barr J. described the dependency principle as "potentially unconstitutional . . . unjust and unreal in its application." He referred to the principle as "a relic of matrimonial female bondage which was swept away by the principles of equality before the law and equal rights in marriage as between men and women which are enshrined in the Constitution".[21] If Barr J.'s opinion is correct, the domicile of a married woman, whether before or after 1986, must be determined by reference to the same factors as in the case of any other independent person.

Domicile and recognition: the position before 2 October 1986

17.010 It is well established that a foreign divorce granted before 2 October 1986 is entitled to recognition where the parties to the divorce had their domicile in the divorce jurisdiction at the time of the institution of the divorce proceedings. In *Re Caffin*[22] for example, Kenny J. recognised an English divorce granted in 1956 to parties who were at the relevant time domiciled in England.

17.011 Although the matter has never been addressed by the Irish court, it is possible that a pre-1986 divorce, though not granted by a court of the parties' common domicile, may be recognised if it would be recognised in the country of the parties' common domicile.[23] This is supported by the general principle that the country of the domicile should determine matters of personal status.

17.012 A more difficult question is whether recognition can be given to a pre-1986 divorce granted by a court in a country where only one party was domiciled. This situation can only arise if it is accepted that the principle of the wife's dependent domicile was inoperative, for constitutional reasons, even before 1986. Some judicial pronouncements appear to insist that both parties should have been domiciled in the relevant jurisdiction. In *Gaffney v Gaffney*,[24] Walsh J. stated at 150 ". . . The Courts here do not recognise decrees of dissolution of marriage pronounced by foreign courts unless the

19 [1975] IR 133, at page 152.
20 [1988] ILRM 456.
21 Id. The Articles of the Constitution referred to were Articles 40.1 and 40.3, and Article 41. These views were confirmed by Barr J. in later proceedings in the same case (30 November 1989, unreported) High Court, at pages 5 and 6 of Barr J.'s judgment.
22 [1971] IR 123.
23 The principle was accepted in England in *Armitage v A.G.* [1906] P 135.
24 [1975] IR 133.

parties were domiciled within the jurisdiction of the foreign court in question."

17.013 Other decisions also assume the requirement of a common domicile in the divorce jurisdiction.[25] However, such decisions are based on the further assumption that the wife's domicile is necessarily tied to that of her husband. Now that serious doubt has been expressed about that assumption, it may be unwise to interpret earlier *dicta* too literally. The safest course is to regard as novel and undecided the issue of recognition of a pre-1986 divorce based on one party's domicile. No doubt in determining the issue, the courts will take account of the legislative preference in favour of recognising such divorces where granted after October 1986.

Domicile and recognition: the position after 2 October 1986

17.014 The Domicile and Recognition of Foreign Divorces Act 1986, section 5(1), provides for the recognition of a divorce granted in the country where either spouse is domiciled. Section 5(7) provides that "domiciled" means domiciled at the date of the institution of the proceedings for divorce. The new rule applies (by virtue of section 5(3)) only to a divorce granted on or after 2 October 1986, the date on which the Act came into operation. Where proceedings were commenced before the Act came into operation, but the divorce was granted afterwards, the Act still applies even though the new statutory rule conferring an independent domicile on a married woman only operates where her domicile is to be determined after 2 October 1986.[26]

17.015 In the case of a divorce granted in England and Wales, Scotland, Northern Ireland, the Isle of Man, or the Channel Islands, by section 5(3) the divorce will be recognised if either spouse is domiciled in any of those jurisdictions. Section 5(4) provides that: "In a case where neither spouse is domiciled in the State, a divorce shall be recognised if, although not granted in the country where either spouse is domiciled, it is recognised in the country or countries where the spouses are domiciled." Thus, while a divorce *granted* in a country where only one party is domiciled will be recognised, a divorce which is merely *recognised* in such country will not be recognised in the State.

Other bases for recognition

17.016 Domicile-based divorce recognition principles are restrictive, particularly in view of the difficulty in proving the acquisition of a domicile of choice. From time to time, consideration has been given to the possibility of judicial development of the rules. In *Gaffney v Gaffney*, in the context

25 See, e.g., the judgments of Kenny J. *in Re Caffin*, supra, and in *C. v C.* (27 July 1973, unreported) High Court.
26 See *M(C.) v M(T.)* [1988] ILRM 456, where the apparent anomaly was resolved by Barr J. holding that the dependency principle was in any case unconstitutional and therefore invalid even before 1986.

of divorce recognition, Walsh J. emphasised that the two Constitutions of 1922 and 1937 were not to be construed as freezing common law principles in their pre-1922 condition.[27] In *Re Caffin*, Kenny J. expressly reserved the question of whether "residence" might be a basis for recognition.[28]

17.017 However, in those cases in which opportunities to expand the rules have presented themselves, the courts have not in fact responded positively. In *C. v C.*[29] Kenny J., refused to recognise an English decree of divorce granted to an Irish-domiciled wife on the basis of three years residence in England. In *M.C. v K.E.D. (orse K.D.)*[30] the Supreme Court rejected an argument that an English divorce granted to a couple who were domiciled in the Republic of Ireland should be recognised on the basis that the parties had a real and substantial connection with England.[31]

17.018 The Domicile and Recognition of Foreign Divorces Act 1986 does not prevent judicial extension of the recognition principles in the future. The rule which it introduces relating to domicile-based divorces is not expressed to be exclusive. According to section 5(1), the new single-domicile rule is a substitute for the previous common-domicile rule. However, there is at present no indication of judicial willingness to consider new bases of recognition.

Grounds for refusing recognition

Apart from lack of jurisdiction, there are a limited number of additional grounds for refusing recognition to an apparently valid foreign divorce.

Fraud as to the jurisdiction of the foreign court

17.019 It seems that where the parties deliberately mislead the foreign court in relation to that court's jurisdictional requirements, a divorce subsequently obtained may be refused recognition even though the parties in fact satisfy the domicile test. In *Middleton v Middleton*[32] an English court refused to recognise an Illinois divorce granted on the basis of a false claim to residence despite the fact that the parties were, at the time of the proceedings, domiciled in a State (Indiana) which would have recognised their divorce. In *Gaffney v Gaffney*[33] an English decree based on a false residential claim was refused recognition by the Supreme Court. Although it was clear that the domicile test was not satisfied, the defect in the jurisdiction of the English court, brought about by the husband's fraud, was an independent reason for not recognising the decree. However, dicta

---

27 [1975] IR 133, at page 151.
28 [1971] IR 123, at page 131.
29 27 July 1973, unreported, High Court.
30 13 December 1985, unreported, Supreme Court.
31 The Supreme Court declined to follow the English House of Lords decision in *Indyka v Indyka* [1969] 1 AC 33.
32 [1967] P 62.
33 [1975] IR 133.

in *Pemberton v Hughes*[34] suggest that not every jurisdictional defect in a foreign court will justify non-recognition, but only a defect which gives rise to substantial injustice or one which would make recognition contrary to natural justice.

Fraud inter partes

17.020 Fraud or deceit *inter partes* has occasionally justified non-recognition of a foreign divorce because, despite the jurisdictional competence of the foreign court, recognition was contrary to public policy or natural justice. There are not many examples of the application of these principles. In *Kendall v Kendall*[35] a Bolivian decree was refused recognition in England as being "manifestly contrary to public policy", under the Recognition of Divorces and Legal Separations Act 1977 section 8(2).[36] The English wife had been deceived into signing documents in the Spanish language which she thought would enable her children to leave Bolivia, but which in fact related to divorce proceedings. In *McAlpine v McAlpine*[37] an English court refused, on grounds of natural justice, to recognise a decree where the petitioner had withheld from the foreign court knowledge of the defendant's whereabouts.

Duress

17.021 It is not clear whether, in this jurisdiction, duress constitutes an independent ground for refusing to recognise a foreign divorce. The issue arose in *Gaffney v Gaffney* where there was evidence that the wife had been compelled by her husband to initiate English divorce proceedings. In fact the divorce could not be recognised because both parties were at all material times domiciled in the Republic of Ireland. But in the High Court, Kenny J. expressed the opinion that a divorce obtained under duress was not entitled to recognition.[38] In the Supreme Court, however, Walsh J. said that "it might well be that in such a situation it would be incumbent upon the plaintiff to have the decree of dissolution, made by the court having jurisdiction, set aside before she could successfully assert the status of wife".

Collusion

17.022 In *L.B. v H.B.*[39] a certain level of collusion between the parties in establishing the grounds for their divorce was viewed by Barrington J. as an independent reason for refusing recognition. The husband and wife, who were domiciled in France at the relevant time, had obtained a French

---

34 [1899] 1 Ch. 781. The relevant dicta are referred to at length by Griffin J. in *Gaffney v Gaffney*, supra.

35 [1977] Fam. 208.

36 See also *Joyce v Joyce and O'Hare* [1979] Fam. 93.

37 [1958] P 35.

38 Relying on *Re Meyer* [1971] P 298.

39 [1980] ILRM 257. *Shedden v Patrick* 2 Sw. and Tr. 170 (House of Lords) was cited in support.

divorce following an exchange of letters, written on the advice of their lawyers, which was clearly designed to secure a divorce on equal terms. The divorce was refused recognition first because "there was a substantial defeat of justice for which the parties, and not the court, bear the responsibility," and second because it would be hard to reconcile the recognition of the divorce with the constitutional duty of the State to uphold the institution of marriage. It is, however, clear that Barrington J. did not think that all forms of collusion would be fatal. He expressly excluded collusion "about peripheral matters". He also referred, without dissent, to the judgment of Cairns J. in *Middleton v Middleton*[40] which in fact minimises the importance of collusion and suggests that a decree based on false evidence (usually the product of collusion) may be recognised.[41]

Estoppel

17.023 In *Gaffney v Gaffney* a wife (who had been subjected to duress) had nominally petitioned for an English divorce and, in so doing, had claimed to have a domicile in England. In the Irish proceedings, in which she contended that the divorce should not be recognised, it was argued that she should be estopped by the record from denying what she put on record in the English proceedings, namely that she had an English domicile at the relevant time. The Supreme Court decided that estoppel by record could not operate where "the record arose in proceedings . . . which the court in question had no jurisdiction to adjudicate on" (per Henchy J. at 155). In other words, it must be established that, in the eyes of Irish law, the foreign court is competent to exercise jurisdiction before any question of estoppel arising from the record of the court can be considered.

17.024 It is also clear that a doctrine of estoppel by conduct may not be invoked to determine a matter of marital status.[42] If, for example, a husband and wife co-operate in obtaining a foreign residence-based divorce when they are both domiciled in Ireland, the divorce, which is clearly not entitled to recognition under normal principles, cannot be rendered valid by the argument that the parties are estopped from denying the validity of a decree which they willingly sought and obtained.

17.025 A more difficult question is whether a spouse who has sought and obtained a foreign divorce may later claim that it should not be recognised in order to gain some pecuniary or other advantage. The issue here is not one of status; it is rather a question of whether, for reasons of equity, a person should be denied specific advantages which would normally result from the non-recognition of his divorce. A willing party to a foreign divorce might, for example, argue against its recognition in order to obtain a maintenance order against the other party, or in order to benefit as a

---

40 [1967] P 62.
41 For further analysis of *L.B. v H.B.*, see W. Duncan "Collusive Foreign Divorces—etc" (1981) Dublin Univ. L.J. 17.
42 *C. v C.*, supra, and the judgment of Walsh J. in the Supreme Court in *Gaffney v Gaffney*, supra, at page 152.

surviving spouse under the estate of the other party when deceased. A husband who has remarried on foot of a foreign divorce, may claim that the divorce should not be recognised, in order to avoid a maintenance claim by his second wife. The question in each of these cases is whether for equitable reasons the divorced spouse should be estopped by conduct from denying the validity of a divorce which he willingly obtained and from which he may already have gained advantage. Despite foreign authority to the contrary[43] the Irish cases[44] demonstrate an unwillingness to entertain estoppel-based arguments in such circumstances. A striking example is *L.B. v H.B.*, in which Barrington J. conceded the right of a "wife", who 22 years before had, in collusion with her husband, obtained a French divorce, to obtain a maintenance order against him, on the basis that the divorce was not entitled to recognition in Ireland.[45]

Effects of recognition

17.026 Where a divorce is entitled to recognition, the parties cease to have the status of spouses. They are entitled to re-marry. Should one of the parties subsequently die, the other is not entitled to claim rights in the deceased's estate as a surviving spouse under the Succession Act 1965.[46]

17.027 It appears unlikely that a divorced spouse is entitled to apply *de novo* for maintenance under the Family Law (Maintenance of Spouses and Children) Act 1976, for a barring or protection order under the Family Law (Protection of Spouses and Children) Act 1981, or for the various remedies made available to a spouse under the Family Home Protection Act 1976. In *M.(C.) v M.(T.)*[47] Barr J. considered the doctrine of "divisible divorce", whereby a spouse who takes no part in foreign *ex parte* divorce proceedings, may be regarded as retaining separable personal rights despite the recognition of the divorce.[48] If the doctrine were accepted, it would mean that such a spouse might be able to apply *de novo* for the above remedies. In the circumstances of *M.(C.) v M.(T.)*, there was no question of the doctrine applying because the wife had participated in the foreign (English) divorce proceedings. It therefore remains uncertain whether the doctrine applies in Irish law. Its scope would in any case be narrow, being confined to cases where the non-petitioning spouse has not entered an appearance or been personally served in the jurisdiction where the divorce is granted.

17.028 The effect of a recognised foreign divorce on an *existing* order

43 See, e.g., the decision of the Supreme Court of Alberta in *Re Plummer* (1942) 1 DLR 34, and the decision of the Canadian Supreme Court in *Downton v Royal Trust Co.* (1972) 34 DLR, 12 (3d.) 403. See also the U.S. Restatement, *Conflict of Laws* 2d. s74.
44 *C. v C.*, supra, *Gaffney v Gaffney*, supra, and *L.B. v H.B.*, supra.
45 For further analysis of the estoppel doctrine, see W. Duncan, *Foreign Divorces obtained on the Basis of Residence, and the Doctrine of Estoppel* 9 Ir. Jur (n.s.) 59.
46 In *Re Caffin* deceased, supra.
47 30 November 1989, unreported, High Court. See above, 9.2.
48 The doctrine is supported in *Estin v Estin* 334 U.S. 541, and has been applied in England. See *Wood v Wood* [1957] P 254.

made under the above Acts is a separate question. In *M.(C.) v M.(T.)* Barr
J. held that a foreign divorce does not have the effect of terminating a
maintenance order made under the Family Law (Maintenance of Spouses
and Children) Act 1976, at least in a case where the creditor is domiciled in
the Republic of Ireland. It also remains open to either party to apply for a
variation in the maintenance order in the light of changed circumstances;
see **8.052** et seq. There seems no reason why the same principle should not
apply to a barring or protection order, a periodical payments order made
under the Judicial Separation and Family Law Reform Act 1989, or a
protective order (for example, one restricting disposal of household
chattels under section 9) made under the Family Home Protection Act
1976.

Orders for financial provision

Enforcement of foreign orders under common law

17.029 Under general principles of common law, a foreign judgment *in
personam* may be enforced[49] in the State if the defendant was present in
the originating jurisdiction at the time of the action, or if the defendant
submitted to the jurisdiction of the originating court. These principles are
still applicable to financial provision orders made abroad in non-E.C.
territories.

17.030 One major proviso to these common law principles is that a
judgment will not be enforced if it is not final and conclusive. Most
maintenance orders, being subject to the possibility of variation, are not
final and conclusive, and may not therefore be enforced at common law.[50]
This was why it was necessary to provide by legislation for the reciprocal
enforcement of maintenance orders between the Republic of Ireland and
the United Kingdom.[51] An order for the payment of arrears in maintenance is generally final and conclusive and may be enforced.[52] The same is
true of a lump sum order made by way of financial provision for a spouse.[53]

17.031 A second proviso to the general common law principles is that a
foreign order may be refused recognition on grounds of public policy. For
some time, it was uncertain whether the prohibition on divorce in Article
41.3.2 of the Constitution might render unenforceable, for reasons of
public policy, a financial provision order made pursuant to a foreign
divorce. In *Mayo-Perrott*[54] the Supreme Court refused to enforce an order
for costs arising out of English divorce proceedings on public policy
grounds. However, an order for costs is a special case because its

49 See generally W. Binchy, *Irish Conflicts of Law*, loc. cit., chapter 33.
59 *Leake v Douglas* (1952) 88 ILTR 4.
51 Maintenance Orders Act 1974. See below, **18.13**.
52 *Beatty v Beatty* [1924] 1 KB 807, *G. v G.* [1984] IR 336.
53 *Sachs v Standard Chartered Bank (Ireland) Ltd.* (18 July 1986, unreported) Supreme
Court.
54 [1958] IR 336.

enforcement can be seen as facilitating the bringing of divorce proceedings by providing the petitioner with the "sinews" of battle. An order for financial provision has a different purpose, that of making appropriate provision for dependent family members following the breakdown of marriage. As such, it is now clearly established that there is no public policy reason for refusing its enforcement, even though it is made pursuant to a divorce.[55] In *Sachs v Standard Chartered Bank (Ireland) Ltd.*, the Supreme Court approved the enforcement of an English lump sum order for £35,000 made pursuant to a divorce decree, in favour of the former wife. Finlay C.J. stated:

> The provision of maintenance arising from the obligation of a spouse in a marriage to a dependent spouse is something recoverable within the law of this country and something for which ample provision has been made by relatively modern legislation. In these circumstances, it seems to me that not only should public policy not be deemed to prevent the enforcement of this judgment, but . . . the requirements of public policy seem clearly to favour it.

Maintenance Orders Act 1974

17.032 The Act of 1974 provides for the reciprocal recognition and enforcement of maintenance orders as between the State and Northern Ireland, England and Wales, and Scotland. Only an outline of some of the Act's principal provisions is given here.[56] As will be seen the Jurisdiction of Courts and Enforcement of Judgments (European Communities) Act 1988 provides inter alia, for the mutual enforcement of maintenance orders throughout the European Community. The Act of 1974 in effect provides, in relation to England and Wales, Northern Ireland and Scotland, an alternative system of enforcement to that provided by the Act of 1988.

17.033 Under the Act of 1974, a maintenance order includes an order providing for periodical money payments "towards the maintenance of any person, being a person whom the person liable to make payments under the order is, in accordance with the law of the jurisdiction in which the order was made, liable to maintain" (section 3(1)(a)). It includes "such an order which is incidental to a decision and to the status of natural persons" (section 3(2)(a)), for example, a decree of divorce. It also includes a written maintenance agreement between spouses "which has been embodied in or approved by a court order or made a rule of court" (section 3(2)(c)). It does not include an order for the payment of a lump sum. Such an order, as has been seen, may be enforceable in the State at common law.

17.034 Part II of the Act provides a detailed mechanism for the enforce-

---

55 See *N.M. v E.F.M.* (11 July 1978, unreported) High Court. *G. v G.*, supra, and *Sachs v Standard Chartered Bank (Ireland) Ltd.*, supra.

56 For a more detailed description, see W. Binchy, *Irish Conflicts of Law*, loc. cit., pages 310–317.

ment in the State of maintenance orders made in the reciprocating jurisdictions. Requests for enforcement are made to the Master of the High Court. Under section 8(4), the Master considers the request privately and decides whether, on the basis of the documents submitted,[57] to grant an enforcement order or to refuse such order on grounds set out in section 9. Section 10 provides a right of appeal by either party to the High Court.

17.035 Under section 9, recognition and enforcement may be refused if:

(a) recognition and enforcement would be contrary to public policy,[58]

(b) where the order was made in default of appearance, the person in default was not served with notice of the institution of the proceedings in sufficient time to enable him to arrange for his defence, or

(c) it is irreconcilable with a judgment given in a dispute between the same parties in the State.

Section 10 provides that in recognition and enforcement proceedings under the Act, the jurisdiction of the originating court may not be examined, nor may there be any examination of the order as to its substance. The District Court is given jurisdiction (by section 14) to enforce an enforceable maintenance order. The order, if made in favour of a spouse, is deemed to be an order made by the District Court under section 5 of the Family Law (Maintenance of Spouses and Children) Act 1976.

17.036 Courts within the State are given jurisdiction by section 17(1) to make a maintenance order against a defendant who is residing in a reciprocating jurisdiction. Provision is made for transmission of documents (section 17(3)) as well as the order itself (section 19), to a reciprocating jurisdiction to make possible its enforcement there.

Jurisdiction of Courts and Enforcement of Judgments (European Communities) Act 1988

Introduction

17.037 The Act of 1988 brings into force in the State the 1968 E.E.C. Convention on Jurisdiction and the Enforcement of Judgments in Civil and Commercial Matters.[59] The principal purpose of the Convention is to create (1) common rules governing the jurisdiction of the courts in civil and commercial matters in the countries of the E.C., and (2) a system whereby a judgment, in a civil or commercial matter, made by a court in one E.C. country will be virtually automatically enforceable in all other E.C. countries. The rules relating to jurisdiction are confined to cases where the defendant is "domiciled" in a contracting (i.e. E.C.) State. The

---

57 The documents are listed in section 13(1). The maintenance debtor may not at this stage make any submission on the request. (Section 6(2)).

58 The fact that the order was made persuant to a divorce decree does not make its enforcement contrary to public policy. See *N.M. v E.F.M.*, supra.

59 For a more detailed analysis, see Irish Centre for European Law, *The Brussels Convention on Jurisdiction and the Enforcement of Foreign Judgments* (Eds. G. Moloney and N.K. Robinson, 1984).

rules relating to mutual enforcement apply to all civil and commercial judgments given in a Contracting State whether or not they are given against a person "domiciled" in that State. No more than a general outline of the effects of the Convention can be attempted here.

Scope of the Convention

17.038 The Convention does not apply to "the status or legal capacity of natural persons, rights in property arising out of a matrimonial relationship, wills and succession." (Article 1.1) It does not, therefore, affect existing rules governing the recognition of foreign divorces or other decrees affecting status. On the other hand, it does cover maintenance orders and certain lump sum payment orders (provided that the lump sum order does not constitute a division of property, whether or not such orders are made pursuant to a decree (such as divorce) affecting status. An argument that an order made ancillary to proceedings which are outside the scope of the Convention should be excluded, even where its subject matter falls within the Convention, was rejected in *DeCavel v DeCavel (No. 2).*[60]

17.039 The meaning of "rights in property arising out of a matrimonial relationship" was considered by the European Court in *DeCavel v DeCavel (No. 1).*[61] In the course of divorce proceedings brought in France by a Frenchman against his German wife, the French court made interim orders preventing the wife from dealing with joint property (situated in Germany), pending judgment. The question was whether these orders could be enforced in Germany under the Convention. The Court held that rights in property arising out of a matrimonial relationship include not only property régimes which can be created only by marriage—such as the community of property systems found in Continental law—but also any property relationship resulting directly from the marriage or its dissolution. This has interesting consequences in relation to some of the financial and property orders which may be made by an Irish court in the context of marriage breakdown. An order made under the Married Women's Status Act 1957, determining that a spouse has acquired an equitable interest in matrimonial property on the basis of "contributions" will, it appears, come within the Convention where made on the basis of general equitable principles which are not applied exclusively to married couples. Where, however, a wife's interest is calculated on the basis of her contribution as a home-maker,[62] the order in her favour will not come within the Convention because the wife's rights arise out of the matrimonial relationship. Similarly, a property adjustment order made under section 15 of the Judicial Separations and Family Law Reform Act 1989 (see chapter 13) would be outside the Convention.

---

60 [1980] ECR 731; [1980] 3 CMLR 1.
61 [1979] ECR 1055; [1979] 2 CMLR 547.
62 As in *B.L. v M.L.* [1989] ILRM 528. See above, **11.7.**

17.040 The concept of a "maintenance order" requires explanation. According to the Official Report on the Convention, the essence of a maintenance order is that it is intended to provide for the support of a spouse or child and is based, in part at least, on need. Whether the order is for periodic payments or for a single payment is of secondary importance. Consequently a lump sum order made pursuant to a judicial separation, (under section 14 of the Act) with the primary purpose of providing support for a dependent spouse or child, may be regarded as a "maintenance order". Where, however, a lump sum order is made exclusively to recompense a spouse for past contributions to the marriage, rather than to provide for current needs, it may be seen as constituting a division of property and hence falls outside the Convention. It might even be argued that an order for periodic payments if it is clearly not made for the purpose of meeting current needs, should not be regarded as a maintenance order under the Convention.

The jurisdictional principles

17.041 The Convention's basic jurisdictional principle (Article 2) is that a person "domiciled" in a Contracting State may be sued in the courts of the State. An Irish court, in determining, for the purpose of assuming jurisdiction, whether a party is domiciled in Ireland, must (under Article 52) apply Irish law. And in this context, under the Act of 1988, "domicile" is taken to mean ordinary residence.[63] In determining whether a party is domiciled in another Contracting State, the court must apply the law of that State.

17.042 In regard specifically to maintenance proceedings, a court has jurisdiction, under the above general principle, if the defendant is "domiciled" in its jurisdiction. In addition, under Article 5.2, a court has jurisdiction:

(a) if the maintenance creditor is domiciled or habitually resident within the court's jurisdiction, or
(b) if the matter is ancillary to proceedings concerning the status of a person, if the court has jurisdiction according to its own law to entertain those proceedings, unless jurisdiction is based solely on the nationality of one of the parties.

Recognition and enforcement

17.043 A judgment given in a Contracting State is entitled to recognition in other Contracting States without any special procedure being required (Article 26). A judgment given in a Contracting State which is enforceable in that State is generally enforceable also in other Contracting States (Article 31). Section 7 of the Act of 1988 lays down procedures for the enforcement in the State of maintenance orders made in other Contracting

---

63 See Part 1 of the Fifth Schedule to the Jurisdiction of the Courts and Enforcement of Judgments (European Communities) Act, 1988.

States. The provisions are generally the same as those used in the Maintenance Orders Act 1974.

Under Article 27, a judgment may be refused recognition on the following grounds:

1. if such recognition is contrary to public policy in the state in which recognition is sought;
2. where it was given in default of appearance, if the defendant was not duly served with the document which instituted the proceedings or with an equivalent document in sufficient time to enable him to arrange for his defence;
3. if the judgment is irreconcilable with a judgment given in a dispute between the same parties in the State in which recognition is sought;
4. if the court of the State in which the judgment was given, in order to arrive at its judgment, has decided a preliminary question concerning the status or legal capacity of natural persons, rights in property arising out of a matrimonial relationship, wills or succession in a way that conflicts with a rule of the private international law of the State in which the recognition is sought, unless the same result would have been reached by the application of the rules of private international law of that State;
5. if the judgment is irreconcilable with an earlier judgment given in a non-Contracting State involving the same cause of action and between the same parties, provided that this latter judgment fulfils the conditions necessary for its recognition in the State addressed.

Article 34 provides that enforcement may be refused on the same grounds.

Chapter 18

PRACTICAL MATTERS

Civil legal aid

The scheme

18.001 This section deals with the practicalities of the civil legal aid and advice scheme. Details of the scheme, which has no basis in statute, are available in booklet form from the Government Publications Office, Molesworth St, Dublin 2. This chapter does not purport to analyse the many inadequacies of the scheme, or the need for comprehensive reform of the system as detailed in the annual reports of the legal aid board and the free legal advice centres. The civil legal aid scheme commenced in 1980. It operates out of law centres which are staffed by full time salaried solicitors. It should not be confused with the criminal legal aid scheme, which is staffed by private practitioners on a panel, who represent persons charged with criminal offences who fulfil a means test. The proposed family law client should attend in person at the nearest law centre. There are 12 full time centres, some of which are a considerable distance apart, and 15 part time centres, staffed once or twice a month from the full time centres.

Periodically the centres close to new applicants, for weeks or months, due to the shortage of staff, and the huge volume of family law cases, in addition to the other legal work. However, special provision is made to deal with emergencies arising from physical violence, sexual or physical abuse of children, and child abduction.

One centre cannot represent two spouses who are in conflict with each other. This may result, for example, in a Donegal client being represented by Sligo Law Centre, while the other spouse is represented by Athlone or Galway Law Centre.

18.002 The client will not be given an appointment to see a solicitor until it is determined that he is eligible for legal advice or aid. Eligibility is tested by a clerical officer who will assist the applicant to complete a means test form. Alternatively the applicant may obtain the form by post, complete it, and post it back to the clerical officer, who will check whether the applicant is eligible for legal services. Financial eligibility is dealt with in Part 5 of the scheme. Schedule 5 sets out in detail how the assessment of means is made, and how financial contributions are computed. It is easier to assess the applicant's means if he has proof of income and outgoings, such as rent, mortgage, payslip and P60. The maximum disposable income, after deduction of certain "allowable" items, such as rent, social insurance deductions, V.H.I., must not exceed £5500 per annum. A spouse who is in receipt of housekeeping money, which has not been incorporated into a maintenance order, has that sum disregarded for the purposes of assessing income. It is not easy to estimate in advance whether a person will be eligible for legal services, as each applicant's circumstances are different. Suffice is to say that a person in receipt of social welfare as their source of income will be eligible for legal services, on a minimum contribution of £1 for advice and £15 for legal aid.

An applicant for legal aid who has considerable capital assets, even though he may have quite a low income, may find that he is assessed for a contribution based on the capital.

Legal advice

18.003 The clerical officer makes the appointment for the prospective client to see a solicitor on a later date which may be a number of weeks or months ahead. A solicitor may give advice on any family matter, with three exceptions. Property disputes are excluded under the scheme, but Ministerial Policy Directive No. 1 of 1980 directed that this was not to extend to proceedings under the Married Women's Status Act 1957, the Family Home Protection Act 1976 or otherwise with rights in relation to the property of spouses as such. This does not mean that the solicitor will be authorised to undertake conveyancing transactions in respect of the family home or farm. The costs of such conveyancing, if authorised, will be charged for, at a certain hourly rate, and will be deducted from the proceeds of sale. Authorisation may be forthcoming if the family home is being transferred into the dependent spouse's sole name, as part of a court settlement or Deed of Separation, rather than if the home is going to be sold. The Board can exercise its powers to claw back its costs, under section 8.4. Criminal proceedings are excluded in practice even though the scheme provides for advice to be given if the criminal matter arises out of the same circumstances as gave rise to the family law matter. Legal advice is limited to advice on the application of Irish law. This may exclude assisting a client to defend proceedings for a divorce in a foreign jurisdiction. Even though a solicitor may assist a client in preparing for a social welfare appeal, legal aid does not extend to representation at the hearing of the appeal. The scheme excludes legal aid for "test" cases, and for representative actions.

Legal aid

18.004 Legal aid will only be granted if it meets the criteria laid down in 3.2.3 of the scheme, as follows

1. It would be in conformity with the purpose (1.2.1) and terms of the scheme to grant it, and
2. the applicant has as a matter of law reasonable grounds for taking, defending or being a party to proceedings, and
3. the applicant satisfies the financial eligibility criteria, and
4. the applicant has made a case for his being granted a certificate which is such as to warrant the conclusion that he is reasonably likely to be successful in the proceedings, assuming that the facts put forward by him in relation to the proceedings are proved before the court, and
5. there is no available method other than court proceedings, which is satisfactory (having regard to all the circumstances, including the cost to the applicant), by which the result which the applicant hopes to derive, or a more satisfactory one, could be achieved, and
6. having regard to all the circumstances of the case, including the probable cost of taking or defending the proceedings, measured against the likely benefit to the applicant, it is reasonable to grant it.

18.005 A certifying committee may decide whether legal aid will be granted. A certifying committee is composed of three members of the Board, one of whom must be a lawyer. The Board itself has twelve members, of whom two are practising barristers and two practising solicitors. The chairman is usually a senior counsel, and there is a representative from each of the Departments of Finance, Social Welfare and Justice, and three other persons. In practice, in straightforward cases, a decision may be made by certain senior staff, though this decision may be reviewed by a committee, if the applicant is dissatisfied by the refusal to grant legal aid. The power to grant legal aid has been delegated in most District Court family law matters to the solicitor in charge of the relevant law centre. His decision is also reviewable. If legal aid is refused by a committee, an appeal may be lodged to an Appeals Committee of the Board. Section 4.7.3 provides for two lawyers and two other members in addition to the chairman to sit as the appeals committee. If it upholds the refusal to grant legal aid, there is no further right of appeal. The refusal cannot be appealed to a court, though it may be subject to judicial review. The only challenge to a refusal to grant legal aid (which was rejected as the applicant was still awaiting an appeal) was made in *E. v E.*[1]

18.006 If aid is granted, once the legal aid contribution is fully discharged, counsel can be briefed in the usual way. Delays can be experienced in the processing of an application for legal aid. This may result in a spouse who is privately represented having his case adjourned pending a decision on legal aid. There are also cases which are adjourned because, at a late stage, a client fails to pay a private solicitor, who then refers the case to a law

1 [1982] ILRM 497.

centre. The courts may be reluctant to entertain an application from a private solicitor to come off record in these circumstances. Costs can be awarded against a legally aided client, but these costs are not paid by the Board. Costs awarded against the respondent spouse will be pursued as a matter of policy by the Board.

18.007 Addresses of legal aid centres

The following are the addresses and telephone numbers of the main legal aid centres.

	Address	Telephone
Dublin	Legal Aid Board Head Office, 47 Upper Mount St, Dublin 2	615811
	45 Lower Gardiner St, Dublin 1	787295
	9 Lower Ormond Quay, Dublin 1	724133
	Aston House, Aston Place, Dublin 2	712177
	517 Main St, Tallaght, Dublin 24	511519
Cork	24 North Mall, Cork	(021) 300365
	96 South Mall, Cork	(021) 275998
Galway	5 Mary St, Galway	(091) 61650
Limerick	Lower Mallow St, Limerick	(061) 314599
Waterford	5 Catherine St, Waterford	(051) 55814
Kerry	6 High St, Tralee	(066) 26900
Westmeath	Northgate St, Athlone	(0902) 74694
Sligo	1 Teeling St, Sligo	(071) 61670

Criminal legal aid

The scheme

18.008 The criminal legal aid scheme is run by the Department of Justice. It was introduced by the Criminal Justice (Legal Aid) Act 1962. The important decision of *The State (Healy) v Donoghue and Ors.*[2] stated that there was a constitutional right to be informed of the entitlement to legal aid. It consists of a panel of private lawyers who agree to be paid on a case by case basis. It is free, but subject to a means test. It is relevant to family law in that, for example, a spouse who is accused of assaulting the other spouse, or of sexually abusing the children, can be represented under the scheme. The local District Court Clerk has a list of the solicitors who are registered under the scheme. It is not available to those who are the victims of crime. In theory, a victim who wishes to prosecute the other spouse privately, may apply for civil legal aid. In practice, such prosecutions are rarely brought, as the spouse prefers to rely on the civil remedies.

18.009 The criminal prosecution brought against the respondent spouse by the Gardaí may be adjourned, pending an assignment of legal aid. Solicitors employed by the Legal Aid Board cannot defend a criminal matter. Clients who have been victims of a crime need to be advised of this, and that another solicitor or representative from the Director of Public Prosecutions office will advise them. That is not to say that the solicitor for the victim cannot perform a liaison role with the prosecution.

Mediation

The nature of mediation and the mediation service

18.010 Mediation is a process whereby those who have agreed to separate enter into negotiations with the assistance of a third party, with a view to agreeing arrangements relating to such matters as maintenance, property, custody of, and access to, children. It is usually a prerequisite that they have agreed to separate. However, if one party is ambivalent, and the other party has made up his mind, this may be sufficient for them to commence mediation. If the ambivalent party does not come to terms with the separation, and does not cooperate in making decisions, then the mediation will come to an end. It must be distinguished from marriage guidance counselling, which may be more directed towards reconciliation. It is not the same as settlement negotiations conducted by lawyers. Both sides will usually have lawyers representing them separately who may become involved in giving formal expression to the agreement and in advising on its legal implications. A client approaching a solicitor may have already seen a mediator, or have made an appointment to see one. If the client does not want to continue with mediation, the solicitor should advise him carefully of the implications. The court may ask why the parties

2 [1976] IR 325.

stopped going to mediation. The court will view with disfavour any conduct of a solicitor which can be interpreted as an attempt to dissuade the client from continuing to attend without good cause. This is particularly so in view of the obligation now placed on a solicitor under section 5 of the Judicial Separation and Family Law Reform Act 1989. There may be difficulty in complying with the requirement of section 5(1)(b) to supply a list of mediators to a client, particularly outside Dublin, as there are so few mediators.

18.011 The solicitor should advise a client who is continuing with mediation that, when the mediation agreement is concluded, the client should bring the agreement back to the solicitor for advice on its legal implications, and with a view to drawing up a deed of separation, incorporating its terms. It may well be that the solicitor will advise the client to renegotiate some terms, where it appears that the client has accepted far less than his legal entitlement. In those circumstances, it may be best to try to persuade both spouses to go back to mediation, rather than litigate the matter.

18.012 The mediation services generally advise clients not to keep referring back to their respective solicitors during the course of mediation. Some services obtain the client's written agreement not to resort to court while the mediation process is ongoing. If proceedings were already issued prior to referral to mediation, the clients will be advised to tell their solicitors to adjourn the proceedings for a minimum of three months. Mediation is especially helpful in relation to those child custody and access disputes in which the parents' mutual animosity is the real cause of disagreement. Litigation may only serve to exacerbate the situation. The parties may then try to subvert the court's order, and they may begin a process of returning to court, on various applications to vary or discharge acess. In those circumstamnces, before the parties get to the stage of threatening proceedings, it may be best to consider recommending that they attend a mediator. A mediator usually has a background in social work or psychology, and is far better placed to deal with the emotional issues, and if necessary, to refer the parties for appropriate counselling.

18.013 Most solicitors are reluctant to refer a property dispute alone to a mediator. However, in practice, it rarely is the only matter in issue. It may be that one spouse is making unrealistic proposals in relation to property in order to delay settlement, not having come to terms with the fact that the marriage has irretrievably broken down. Some cases are unsuitable for mediation, as, for example, where one of the spouses is suffering from severe alcoholism or a psychiatric disorder. This also applies to cases of chronic physical violence, or physical or sexual abuse of children. In cases where one of the parties has unequal bargaining power, or is so frightened or intimidated by the other spouse, that she is likely to concede too much for the sake of making any agreement, then it is not appropriate to refer to mediation.

The mediation agreement

18.014 Some mediation services call the mediation agreement a "separation agreement". This is confusing to clients who have been told by their solicitors that a separation agreement or deed of separation will be entered into after they conclude with mediation. Mediation agreements usually specify that the agreement is not legally binding, that the mediator has not advised on legal matters, that the negotiations have been conducted on a "without prejudice" basis, and that anything disclosed by the parties is confidential. As long as there is no intention to create legal relations, the mediation agreement is not binding. However, if one party proceeds to act on foot of it by substantially performing some of its terms, the other party may be estopped from denying that the mediation agreement was to be acted upon.

18.015 The agreement goes on to deal with very similar matters to a deed of separation, with the exception of a non molestation clause. The non molestation clause is in practice always included in the legal agreement, even if the spouses have not molested each other. It is regarded as a safeguard against future deviant behaviour. However, it does carry connotations of past misconduct, and this is something that mediators seek to avoid. Custody and access provisions are included, usually with the emphasis on joint decision making, and as much participation as can be agreed on by the non custodial parent. Maintenance and tax issues, and entitlement to any social welfare allowances are dealt with. The responbility for debts and life assurance premiums is allocated. Mediation agreements in this jurisdiction attempt sometimes to resolve what may be complex family property issues, such as who is going to remain on in the family home and when it is to be sold. Quite frequently it is agreed that the family home is to be sold when the youngest child reaches the age of 18 years. Most lawyers adopt a conservative view of such a clause, and resist its insertion into a deed of separation. This is partly because they fear a client claiming in the future that they were not properly advised in signing away a right to remain on in the family home indefinitely.

18.016 Consents are sometimes inserted in the same terms as a consent under the Family Home Protection Act 1976. The lawyers for the spouses may not be happy about the insertion of a clause resembling the consent under the Family Home Protection Act with regard to a future sale of the family home. If there is a future dispute, and the parties have not committed the agreement to a deed of separation, one of them may attempt to rely on the mediation agreement. The agreement may provide for the allocation of furniture. Other assets like pensions and bank accounts may also be included. The spouses may agree to consult their respective solicitors in relation to the drawing up of wills. Some agreements have gone so far as to provide that the surviving parent will be guardian of the children of the marriage. Such a clause cannot be regarded as binding, as it is not possible to interfere with the freedom of a testator to make arrangements for his children, even though after the testator's death, a court may interfere with such arrangements.

18.017 One of the advantages of the mediation agreement is that provision is usually made for review of the agreed arrangements, in approximately six months. This may help avoid future litigation. It also acts as an incentive to both parties to keep to the terms of the agreement, knowing that the agreement may be varied to their detriment. The agreement may have provided for weekly access. If a non custodial spouse were to turn up infrequently for access, then the variation may reduce access to every fortnight, or a lesser frequency. In the event of one spouse not retaining a solicitor, it may make the task of the solicitor for the party who draws up the Deed of Separation easier, knowing that the other spouse has already agreed to matters with the mediator and the spouse. A solicitor is placed in a dilemma where his client is anxious to enter into a Deed of Separation based on a mediation agreement which the solicitor in conscience feels is not in his client's best long term interests. The solicitor may decide to proceed if the client signs a form of indemnity, whereby he clearly instructs the solicitor to draw up the Deed in the same terms as the mediation agreement, despite the fact that some legal rights have been surrendered. Or the solicitor may decline to act and advise the client to seek legal advice elsewhere.

18.018 If a client has been referred to a mediator in the first place by the solicitor, the solicitor should have obtained his client's written consent to doing so. The client should have been warned not to act on the mediation agreement until he has discussed it in full with his solicitor, with a view to having it incorporated into a Deed of Separation. If mediation breaks down, and one party has recourse to litigation the mediator will claim privilege and refuse to act as a witness. Mediators have a practice of not discussing the progress of mediation, or the proposed contents of the mediation agreement, with solicitors. This practice is helpful in securing the trust of the parties.

Privacy

The *in camera* rule

18.019 A matrimonial dispute often involves disclosure of the most intimate details of each spouse's life. It is important that these personal details be kept away from the prurient, and that the parties feel protected enough to reveal the necessary details in a sensitive private atmosphere. As against that, there have been allegations from time to time that justice, if it cannot be seen to be done, is justice denied. However, if a hearing held in private, is not in accordance with the rules of justice, the parties have a remedy by way of judicial review or appeal.

18.020 Article 34(1) of the Constitution provides that "Justice shall be administered in courts established by law . . . and save in such special and

limited cases as may be prescribed by law, shall be administered in public".
Section 45(1) of the Courts (Supplemental Provisions) Act 1961 sets out
that matrimonial matters come within the "special and limited cases"
prescribed by law. It provides that "Justice may be administered otherwise
than in public in . . . matrimonial causes and matters . . . and minor
matters". In this context "minor" refers to children. The term "matrimonial causes and matters" is not defined in the Act. It must be assumed
that the courts will adopt a strict interpretation of what matters come
within its scope.

18.021 Section 45 of the 1961 Act was judicially considered in the case of
In Re R Limited.[3] This concerned an appeal against an order of the High
Court, that a petition under section 205 of the Companies Act 1963 be
heard in camera. The Supreme Court allowed the appeal. Walsh J. stated
that the specified exceptions to the rule that justice should be administered
in public were matters in respect of which the judges had a discretion prior
to the enactment of the Constitution. The Constitution had removed any
judicial discretion to have proceedings heard, other than in public, save
where expressly conferred by statute. However, in deciding whether to
exercise a discretion conferred by statute, the court had to keep in mind
the overriding consideration of doing justice. Before ordering that proceedings be heard other than in public, the court had to be satisfied that a
public hearing of all or part of the proceedings would fall short of the doing
of justice, it being a fundamental principle of the administration of justice
in a democratic State that justice be administered in public.

18.022 The language of the statutory provisions, and the rules made
thereunder, vary, stating that the proceedings shall be heard in camera, or
in chambers, or otherwise than in open court. Rule 17 of the Circuit Court
Rules (No. 6) 1982[4] provides that, in applications under the rules (that is,
applications under the Guardianship of Infants Act 1964, Family Law
(Maintenance of Spouses and Children) Act 1976, and Married Women's
Status Act 1957) shall be heard otherwise than in open court. Proceedings
for a divorce *a mensa et thoro*, under Order 69 rule 4, were heard in
camera. Section 25 of the 1976 Act provides that proceedings under the
Act were to be conducted in a summary manner and shall be heard
otherwise than in public.[5] Subsection 2 provided that cases heard in the
High Court and Circuit Court were to be heard in chambers.

18.023 Section 14(1) of the Family Law (Protection of Spouses and
Children) Act 1981 makes similar provision, with the addition that an
appeal from the Circuit Court to the High Court, will be heard in

---

3 [1989] ILRM 757.
4 SI No. 58 of 1982.
5 See Rule 5 of the District Court [Family Law (Maintenance of Spouses and Children) Act
   1976] Rules 1976, SI No. 96 of 1976.

chambers. The Circuit Court rules[6] relating to this Act do not make any special provision for the implementation of this section. However the District Court rules do provide for privacy. The court, allows, *inter alia*,[7] witnesses to be present. However, it is good practice to exclude all witnesses until they are to be individually heard.

18.024 Property disputes are also heard in private. Section 12(4) of the Married Women's Status Act 1957 allows a discretion to hear the case in private. The Family Home Protection Act 1976 has a mandatory provision (section 10). There is no provision in the Status of Children Act 1987 for hearing cases in private. In practice, the courts will exclude the public.[8] The sections relating to disputes under the Succession Act 1965 also allow proceedings to be heard in chambers.[9] Proceedings under the Judicial Separation and Family Law Reform Act 1989 (section 34) are to be heard otherwise than in public.

The press and publicity

18.025 The press may report criminal prosecutions concerning a family, for example, an assault on a spouse or children, incest or other charges of a sexual nature against a spouse. In the latter type of case, they may not report the names of the victim or the accused. Restrictions on reporting have been specially lifted in some cases of child abduction cases, where the assistance of the press is required to trace the child. This has resulted, sometimes, in photographs of children and parents and details of family law proceedings being published. In sexual abuse prosecutions, there may be allegations that the accusations are connected with a family law dispute between the spouses. This may result in the press reporting certain details of the dispute.

18.026 The relevant provisions are contained in the Censorship of Publications Act 1929. The first restraint imposed on publication is based on the protection of public morals; section 14(1) forbids publication of any indecent matter. Second, it is not lawful to print any report in relation to divorce, nullity, or judicial separation, except the names and addresses of the parties and witnesses, and, inter alia, a concise statement of the charges and defences given, points of law and the findings of the jury (now largely irrelevant) or the decision of the court (section 14(2)). However, the practice of the courts has been to exclude the press, making it impossible for them to publish to the limited extent allowed by the Act. The restraints imposed do not restrict the publishing of any transcript or

---

6 Circuit Court Rules (No. 3) 1982, (Family Law (Protection of Spouses and Children) Act 1981) SI No. 152 of 1982.
7 Rule 5 of the District Court [Family Law (Protection of Spouses and Children) Act, 1981] Rules, 1981, SI No. 246 of 1981.
8 There was such a provision in section 3(5) of the Illegitimate Children (Affiliation Orders) Act, 1930, as amended by section 28(1)(d) of the 1976 Act.
9 See section 56(11), 119 and 122.

other document for use in connection with any judicial proceedings or the communication thereof to persons concerned in the proceedings.

18.027 The printing of law reports is not prohibited. In practice, the names of the parties, their addresses and other distinguishing features are erased from all reports, as well as unreported judgments. If a publisher or editor contravenes any of these provisions, he is guilty of an offence, punishable by a fine of £500 or six months imprisonment.

In *Re McCann v Kennedy*[10] the editor and a journalist were found guilty of contempt, and fined. They had published details of a family law case, which they had obtained from one of the spouses, and which was inaccurate. They also published photographs of the children and mother. The Supreme Court took a strong view against such contempt. O'Higgins C.J. stated, "Orders providing for the hearing of such cases in camera are made in order to preserve, for the sake of the children and their welfare, a decent privacy in relation to the disputes which have arisen between the parties".

Discovery and inspection

Procedure

18.028 Discovery and inspection are important procedural aids in family law litigation. In the first instance, a notice to produce for inspection, may be served on the opposing party, seeking production of any document referred to in the affidavit (or application or summons) filed.[11] If the party served does not comply with the notice, then an application to court may be made for an order for inspection.[12] This is grounded on an affidavit setting out the documents sought to be inspected, and stating that the documents are in the possession or power of the other party. The court may reserve making the order, if any issue between the parties needs to be determined first.[13] It may order that copies or extracts from business books be produced for inspection, instead of the original books. The copies can be verified by the affidavit of a named person, for example, the company secretary. Despite this, the court may still order inspection of the original book.[14]

18.029 A party may object to production for inspection on the basis of a claim of privilege.[15] There is extensive case law on the nature of a claim of privilege, most of it concerning objections raised by Ministers or local

10 [1976] IR 326.
11 High Court R.S.C. Order 31 rule 15, where the notice is in Form 10, in Appendix C. The similar Circuit Court Rule is contained in Order 29 rule 4.
12 Order 31 rule 18, R.S.C. Order 29 rule 5 of the Circuit Court Rules.
13 Order 31 rule 19 of R.S.C. The Circuit Court does not have an equivalent rule, but Order 29 rule 4 does state that the defendant can show cause or an excuse for not complying with the notice.
14 Order 32 rule 20 of the Rules of the Superior Courts. There is no equivalent rule in the Circuit Court.
15 Order 31 rule 20(2) of the Rules of the Superior Courts.

authorities or other public bodies.[16] In summary, once the document sought is shown to be relevant, the onus of establishing that it should not be produced is borne by the person objecting. The objection must be in respect of each individual document and not in respect of the class of documents to which the documents are alleged to belong. The court reserves the right to inspect each document in which there is a claim of privilege.

18.030 An application for inspection implies knowledge of the existence of the particular documents to be inspected. The essence of an order for discovery is that it requires the person to whom it is directed to list documents of which he is aware, but of which the applicant for the order need not necessarily be aware.[17] An application for discovery is made by notice of motion, seeking an order that the other party make discovery on oath of all specified relevant documents.[18] The court has wide powers to order discovery, or to limit it to a certain class of documents, or it may refuse to make the order on the ground that it is not necessary.[19] The court may order either an affidavit to be filed of the documents, or a list of documents to be delivered.[20]

18.031 A claim of privilege may also be made to oppose an application for discovery. In *S.M. and M.M. v G.M.*[21] the Adoption Board relied on such a claim in opposing an application for discovery by prospective adopters. An order requiring the Adoption Board to make further and better discovery was appealed by the defendants in the case of *P.C. v An Bord Uchtála*[22]. The applicant had sought the birth certificate and the natural mother's consent. The Adoption Board claimed privilege on the basis that the information would allow the applicant to trace the adoptive parents. McWilliam J. refused to make the order on the basis that it would not be in the best interests of the child for the information to be disclosed.

Section 3 of the Adoption Act 1976 prohibits an order for discovery, inspection, production or copying of any document, unless the court is satisfied, that it is in the best interests of any child concerned to do so. It was held that the confidentiality of the Board's papers should be maintained, unless it was established, to the satisfaction of the court, as a matter of probability, that the best interests of a child required their discovery or production. The best interests of the child would normally require

16 *Murphy v Dublin Corporation* [1972] IR 215. *Geraghty v Minister for Local Government* [1975] IR 300. *Folens Co Ltd. v The Minister for Education, and Ors.* [1981] ILRM *Av Minister for Industry and Commerce* (11 March 1988 unreported, High Court).
17 *Holloway v Belenos Publications Ltd. and Others* [1988] ILRM 685 at page 687, per Barron J.
18 Order 31 rule 12 R.S.C. Order 29 rule 1 of the Circuit Court Rules provides for a four day notice of motion.
19 Order 31 rule 12(1) of Rules of the Superior Courts. Order 29 rule 1 of the Circuit Court Rules.
20 Order 31 rule 12(2) of the Rules of the Superior Courts.
21 [1935] ILRM 186.
22 25 April 1980, unreported, High Court.

discovery of documents necessary to enable all parties to present their case to the full. However, in the circumstances, Lynch J. refused discovery on the ground that the various documents sought constituted a form of hearsay and were not capable of being used for the purpose of securing witnesses who could give admissible evidence, as the applicants had claimed.

18.032 In the course of a marital dispute, information may be given to a professional involved, that children have been put at risk by the behaviour of one or both of the spouses. A reference to such allegations may be made in a report from a social worker, or public health nurse. One of the spouses may seek discovery of the identity of the informant. In *D. v R.S.P.C.C.*[23] the mother of an infant sought to obtain damages for false accusations that she had neglected her child. She sought discovery against the society, to establish the identity of the informant. The order was refused. The House of Lords relied on the rule relating to immunity accorded to police informants. The public interest required that those who gave information about child abuse to the society should be immune from disclosure of their identity in legal proceedings. This was despite the fact that the society was not under a legal duty to bring care proceedings, and was not a department of central government. *Per curiam*, it was held that the fact that information had been communicated by one person to another in confidence is not of itself a sufficient ground for protecting from disclosure, in a court of law, the nature of the information or the identity of the informant if either of these matters would assist the court in ascertaining facts which are relevant to the issue on which it is adjudicating. This decision was discussed in *R. v Bournemouth Justices Ex Parte Grey, and Ex Parte Rodd.*[24] In that case, a social worker was refused a claim of privilege, and was ordered to produce a single document which was with the adoption agency, which concerned an admission of paternity from a putative father. The mother had applied for maintenance after not proceeding with the adoption. There was no public interest in the social worker refusing to give the evidence, as the evidence was going to be given by the mother. The courts have power to order production of documents at any time while any cause or matter is pending, and can deal with the documents in such manner as shall appear just.[25]

18.033 As regards what documents can be disclosed, the Irish courts have referred to the principle laid down in *Campagnie Financière du Pacifique v Peruvian Guano Co.*[26] where Brett J. stated

any document which, it is reasonable to suppose, contains information which may enable the party applying for discovery, either to advance his

---

23 [1977] 1 All ER 589.
24 23 May 1986, QBD.
25 Order 31 rule 14 of the Rules of the Superior Courts and order 29 rule 3 of the Circuit Court Rules.
26 [1882] 11 QB at page 65.

own case or to damage that of his adversary, if it is a document which may fairly lead him to a train of inquiry which may have either of these two consequences must be disclosed.

This principle was adopted in *Golden Vale Co-operaticve Creameries Ltd. v Barrett*.[26a] The correct procedure to adopt where a subpoena has been issued, in which documents that are privileged are sought to be produced, is to seek to set aside the subpoena.

Discovery against a third party

18.034 The right to seek an order for discovery or inspection, or to answer interrogatories before trial against a non party was introduced in Order 31 rule 29 of the Rules of the Superior Courts 1986. Interrogatories in practice are not used in family law cases. The new rule has not been formally introduced into the Circuit Court, but one could argue that Order 59 rule 14 may apply. This provides that where there is no rule to govern practice or procedure, the practice and procedure in the High Court may be followed. The applicant must indemnify the non party in respect of costs reasonably incurred. If a party is legally aided, the Legal Aid Board would have to bear the costs of such an application.

18.035 The new rule has been judicially considered in *Holloway v Belenos Publications Ltd. and others*.[27] The validity of the rule was upheld. Barron J. stated that the right to discovery against a non party does not create an independent enforceable right against such person. It imposes an obligation on such person in the same way as a subpoena. If the applicant can establish the existence of specific documents, then an order for inspection may be made. If he can establish that there must be other documents, but is unable to be precise as to them, then an order for discovery is appropriate. An order under rule 29 has the same attributes and consequences as an order under rule 12 (which deals with the application for discovery against one of the parties). In an earlier judgment[28] concerning the same plaintiff and defendants, Costello J. had refused the order on the basis that it was not to be used for the purposes of issuing a licence to explore the files of a notice party in the hope of discovering a relevant document, and there must be evidence before the court that relevant documents do exist.

18.036 The rule was challenged again in *Fitzpatrick v Independent Newspapers plc and Martin*.[29] In this case an order was made against the third party. The fact that the documents were private and confidential was not relevant. Witnesses are frequently required to produce private and privileged documents to the court. However, the court did agree that it should not make an order if the documents sought are otherwise available to the

26a 6 June 1986. unreported. High Court.
27 [1988] ILRM 685.
28 3 April 1987, unreported, High Court.
29 [1988] ILRM 707.

party seeking the order. This rule is useful to obtain documents that are in the possession of the employer of a respondent, or that have been left with a relative or friend or accountant. The advantage is the ability to obtain documents in advance of the trial, rather than serving a subpoena and seeing the documents on the morning of the hearing. The other advantage is that the third party is required to swear an affidavit verifying what documents are in his possession and if they are no longer in his possession, to whom where they given. If the third party fails to cooperate he, like one of the parties to the action, could be liable for attachment.[30] An imaginative use of this rule, together with the general right to obtain inspection discovery or to deliver interrogatories can greatly aid an applicant in seeking a remedy before the court. Costs of any application for discovery may be ordered, provided the judge certifies that discovery was reasonably requested.

Evidential matters

The competence and compellability of spouses

18.037 At common law a spouse was regarded as generally incompetent to give evidence for or against the other spouse in both civil and criminal proceedings. The principal exception was in criminal cases where one spouse was accused of violence towards the other, in which case the alleged victim was competent but not compellable. The common law principles have been modified by legislation and affected by Constitutional principles relating to fair procedures and the due administration of justice in the courts.

Civil cases

18.038 The rule of incompetency in civil cases was abolished by the Evidence Amendment Act 1853 which made spouses competent and compellable witnesses for any party to a civil action. An exception was provided for in section 3 in relation to questions tending to show that a spouse has been guilty of adultery, but this has now been abolished by section 47 of the Status of Children Act 1987, subsection (1) of which renders a spouse's evidence admissible in any proceedings to prove that marital intercourse did or did not take place. Earlier, in *S. v S.*[31] O'Hanlon J. had declared unconstitutional the rule which prohibited the admission of evidence of a spouse to prove that a wife's child was not that of her husband. The rule, which was known as the rule in *Russell v Russell*,[32] was regarded as contrary to the constitutional guarantee of fairness in procedures—Articles 34.38.1 and 40.3.

---

30 Order 31 rule 21 of the Rules of the Superior Courts and order 21 rule 7 of the Circuit Court Rules.
31 [1983] IR 68.
32 [1924] AC 687.

Criminal cases

18.039 The Criminal Justice (Evidence) Act 1924 section 4(1) provides that a spouse is a competent witness for the prosecution against the other spouse in relation to certain listed offences. The spouse is not compellable in such circumstances, and the listed offences are at any rate limited in scope. Offences such as rape, abduction and indecent assault are listed but not incest, murder or bigamy. Offences under the Prevention of Cruelty to Children Act 1904 were included.[33] A spouse of an accused is competent, but not generally compellable to give evidence on the application of the accused (section 1(e)). The Married Women's Status Act 1957 section 9 makes a spouse a competent witness for the prosecution in criminal proceedings against the other spouse brought to protect and secure the former's property.

18.040 The Law Reform Commission has recommended that spouses should be competent witnesses against each other in all criminal proceedings, but should not be compellable.[34] In *D.P.P. v T.*,[35] the Court of Criminal Appeal decided that, where one spouse is charged with a sexual offence against his or her child, the common law rule precluding testimony from the other spouse is unconstitutional having regard to the State's obligation to protect the family under Article 41. The Court's judgment supports compellability in such cases.[36]

Privilege

Communications between spouses

18.041 Section 1(d) of the Evidence Amendment Act 1853 provides that neither spouse may be compelled in civil or criminal proceedings to disclose any communication from one to the other made during the marriage. The privilege is that of the spouse giving evidence and may be waived unilaterally. Subject to the rules relating to the admission of hearsay, third parties are entitled to report in evidence the content of spousal communications.

Communications with marriage counsellors, mediators, etc

18.042 Communications between a spouse or spouses and a priest acting as a marriage counsellor made on a confidential basis are privileged. This was decided by Carroll J. in *E.R. v J.R.*,[37] relying on the principle in *Cook v Carroll*[38] (that a communication made to a priest acting in his pastoral

---

33 For offences under the Children Act 1908, see *McGonagle v McGonagle* [1951] IR 123.
34 *Report on Competence and Compellability of Spouses as Witnesses*. Report No. 13, July 1985.
35 (27 July 1988, unreported) Court of Criminal Appeal.
36 Contrast the decision of the House of Lords in *Hoskyn v The Metropolitan Police Commissioner* [1979] AC 474.
37 [1981] ILRM 125.
38 [1945] IR 515.

capacity is privileged) and Article 41 of the Constitution. The provision of confidential marriage counselling by a priest to help couples overcome problems in marriage was viewed as a practical means of securing the Article 41 objective of protecting marriage and the family. The privilege is that of the married couple and may be set aside where there is a clear and unequivocal waiver by both. Carroll J. reserved the question whether the privilege extended to marriage counsellors other than priests. Arguably it should extend to them and to other persons, such as mediators, who seek on a basis of confidentiality to assist in resolving marital disputes.

18.043 There is clearly a public interest in fostering such activity, and this has been underlined by the status accorded to counselling and mediation in the provisions of the Judicial Separation and Family Law Reform Act 1989. If privilege were claimed, it would be necessary to show that the counselling or mediation was entered into on the basis of confidentiality. To the extent that privilege does exist, it is not clear how absolute it should be regarded. There may be certain cases (for example, where disclosure is sought with the object of protecting a third party, such as a child, from serious abuse) where the public interest in fostering counselling or mediation may be outweighed by the need to protect a vulnerable third party.

18.044 Where proceedings for judicial separation have been adjourned under section 7 of the Act of 1989, for the purpose of giving spouses the opportunity to consider a reconciliation or to reach agreement on the terms of separation, section 7(7) provides that any oral or witten communication between either spouse and any third party giving the spouses assistance towards these ends, is inadmissible as evidence in any court. The rule covers all communications, whether or not made in the presence of the other spouse, and any record of such communications.

Expert witnesses and reports

18.045 A witness may not in general offer an opinion unless he or she is expert in the relevant area. Expert evidence is admissible "wherever peculiar skill and judgment, applied to a particular subject, are required to explain results, or trace them to their causes".[39] On the other hand, the opinion of an expert is not in general admissible on matters that are within the normal range of observation and experience. In family law cases, the expert evidence of such persons as doctors, psychiatrists, psychologists amd social workers is frequently admitted to assist the court both in determining the facts and in predicting likely patterns of behaviour in hypothetical situations. This is especially so in child custody and access disputes where the court's primary and paramount concern is the future welfare of the child. It is sometimes forgotten that opinion evidence is not admissible unless it can be established that the expert is an expert and competent in a specialised area. It is helpful in family law cases, if the

39 Per Pigot C.B. in *McFadden v Murdock* (1867) IR 1 CL 211, at page 217.

qualifications and specialised practical knowledge of the expert are given in any report and in the court. This may be particularly relevant to social workers, who rarely describe their expertise and who therefore find their evidence does not carry the same weight as that of child psychiatrist or a doctor.

18.046 Under section 40 of the Judicial Separation and Family Law Reform Act 1989 (which amended section 11 of the Guardianship of Infants Act 1964) a court may now of its own motion or by application in guardianship proceedings "give such directions as it thinks proper to procure a report from such person as it may nominate on any questions affecting the welfare of the infant". Such report must be made available to the parties' legal representatives and may be received in evidence in the proceedings. The court or either party to the proceedings may call the person making the report as a witness. In the past the courts in family law cases have frequently ordered reports from the probation and welfare service by consent of both parties and have allowed the parties to introduce their own reports.

18.047 Principles of natural justice, in particular the *audi alteram partem* rule, are applicable when the court relies on reports. In the *State (D.) v G.*[40] the Supreme Court set aside a "fit person" order made by the District Court in a case of alleged child abuse partly on the basis that the pre-trial procedures were defective. The solicitor for the prosecutors (the parents of the child made subject to the order) was, prior to the hearing, not given a copy of one medical report and only given a loan of another shortly before the hearing. These reports formed part of the case made by the Health Board for a fit person order. Nor was the solicitor given a copy of the video recording of an interview between a doctor and the child which had formed the basis of certain conclusions made in a report given to the court. Finlay C.J., disapproving these procedures, stated at page 6 of his judgment that "for a lawyer acting on behalf of the parents and therefore joining issue on the question of abuse, to be in a fully prepared position to cross-examine the witnesses dealing with such evidence, it would be necessary for him to have had in good time before the trial reports or summaries of the evidence which was to be given and, in addition, an examination of any video recording by him and by any medical witness he proposed to call". Procedural requirements relating to the admission of reports in criminal cases are more stringent.[41]

Proof of previous convictions

18.048 This has relevance to barring cases, and custody/access disputes, where it may be material that the respondent had previous convictions of a violent or sexual nature. Under section 18 of the Prevention of Crimes Act

---

40 27 July 1989, unreported, Supreme Court.
41 See *State (M.D.) v District Justice Kennedy* (23 July 1979, unreported, High Court) and *State (Slattery) v Judge Roe* [1986] ILRM 511.

1871, a previous conviction may be proved by producing a certificate signed by a court officer (in the case of an indictable offence) or copy conviction order signed by a justice or court officer.

18.049 In order to trace the record, the name of the prosecuting Garda, the station, the date of the arrest or conviction and, if possible, the charge sheet number, is required. If the name of the Garda is already known he should be contacted and he will furnish the charge sheet number and the date of conviction. An application is then made, in the chief clerk's office in the Dublin metropolitan district, and elsewhere that of the local clerk, for a copy of the order. The office of the county registrar is contacted for a conviction for the Circuit Criminal Court, and Green Street Court office, for the Central Criminal Court. There is a separate Court of Criminal Appeal office in the Four Courts. Proof of the identity of the convicted person is required to be given in court. It is usual for the Garda who prosecuted to be present in court, and he formally identifies him. The Garda will normally produce a printout from the criminal record office, setting out all previous convictions. The criminal record office will not give details to any person other than a Garda. The Gardaí may not have a record of any private prosecutions for assault or binding to the peace. It is up to the solicitor who has successfully prosecuted a respondent to send a copy of the court order to the criminal record office. If the respondent objects and disputes any conviction, then the case should be adjourned, and the court office contacted for a certified copy of the conviction.

Res judicata

18.050 *Res judicata* is a defence whereby a respondent argues that there has been a judgment which has already determined either the cause of action or one of the issues between the same parties. The decision must have been given by a court of competent jurisdiction, and must have been conclusive. Either party is then precluded from trying to litigate the dispute again. The rationale for this principle is that it is in the public interest that there should be an end to litigation between parties, and that no one should be sued twice on the same grounds. The two corresponding Latin maxims are *Interst rei publicae ut sit finis litium* and *Nemo debet bis vexari pro eadem causa*. The question of *res judicata* is raised in many family law cases, but the courts have sometimes adopted a more flexible attitude than they would in other civil litigation. One of the difficulties with the law on marriage breakdown is the multiplicity of court jurisdictions and causes of action. Some proceedings concern the parties only, and others concern the children only.

18.051 There have been very few judgments on how *res judicata* should apply to family law proceedings. The most important exposition of the law was in the nullity case of *D. v C.*[42] The petitioner had already obtained

42 [1984] ILRM 173.

orders in the High Court barring the respondent from the family home, and custody orders with regard to the children. At the time of the High Court original proceedings, the plaintiff was not aware of her right to seek a nullity decree. If she had been, it is submitted that she should have sought an injunction instead of a barring order. She had recited the fact that she was married in issuing those proceedings. Costello J. rejected a plea of estoppel per *res judicata* and in doing so, discussed at length the law applicable to such a defence. He defined a judgment *in rem* as a judgment of a court of competent jurisdiction, determining the status of a person or thing, or the disposition of a thing, as distinct from a particular interest in it, of a party to the litigation. It was held in *Razelos v Razelos (No. 2)*[43] that a county court's findings in judicial separation proceedings are binding on the High Court in later proceedings under the Married Women's Property Act 1882, section 17 (as amended). It has been the view that it is not possible to consent to a decree of judicial separation, which suggests that it is a judgment *in rem*. This is because a judgment *in rem*, made by consent, reduces the decision to a judgment *inter partes*. Whether section 3(2) of the Judicial Separation and Family Law Reform Act 1989, which provides for a consent application to rescind the decree will change this view is open to question. An example of a judgment *in rem* is an order of nullity, or divorce. Such an order is binding on all persons, and not just the parties. Therefore all persons are estopped from denying or disputing the order of the court. A declaration of parentage (granted under sections 35–36 of the Status of Children Act 1987) is binding on the parties, and on the State, if the Attorney General is made a party to the action. On the other hand, a judgment *in personam* (or *inter partes*) includes all other judgments which are not judgments *in rem*. It determines the rights of parties between one another, and does not affect the status of the person or make any disposition of property. Costello J. held that the judgment with regard to custody and barring was a judgment *inter partes*.

18.052 He next turned to the distinction between a cause of action estoppel and an issue estoppel. A cause of action estoppel arises where the same cause of action was determined, between the same parties, in a previous action. However, the questions of whether the safety and welfare of the spouse or children required the making of a barring order, and whether the welfare of the children required that they be given into the custody of the mother, was different from the question of determining the validity of the marriage. Even when there is not the same cause of action, an estoppel may arise where a matter which came directly in issue in the first action, and which was embodied in the decision of the court, is regarded as conclusive between the same parties, and thus cannot be raised again. This is known as issue estoppel.[44] Costello J. held that the validity of the marriage was not put directly in issue in the first set of proceedings, and was not determined in those proceedings.

43 [1970] 1 All ER 336.
44 See also *Thoday v Thoday* [1964] P 181 (at 197) which was cited with approval by Costello J.

18.053 An interlocutory order cannot create an estoppel. There must have been a final judgment. It seems that, because custody or other orders under section 11 of the Guardianship of Infants Act 1964 are interlocutory orders, no matter how definitive they appear to be, an estoppel cannot be pleaded. However, this does not mean that the court process can be abused by frivolous or vexatious proceedings. If one of the spouses seeks to have a custody or access issue litigated again, he should establish that the court's jurisdiction is being invoked because the welfare of the child is at risk due to some change in circumstances.

18.054 A judgment that is final, though made by consent or by default, may raise a plea of *res judicata*.[45] Generally speaking, there must have been a decision on the merits. If the proceedings are struck out on the basis that the court has no jurisdiction, this does not create an estoppel nor if the proceedings are withdrawn. If the subject matter of the two sets of proceedings is different, it may be possible to adduce evidence which was rejected in the first proceedings in the second proceedings.

18.055 *Res judicata* was successfully raised in an earlier case of *Downey v Downey*.[46] It was held that where a summons for maintenance had been heard and dismissed, the matter was *res judicata*, and a justice of the District Court had no jurisdiction to hear a second summons founded on the same cause of complaint. The wife's first summons was dismissed in September 1942. She brought an identical summons in February 1943, and it was brought on the same ground (of desertion). The husband's solicitor made a preliminary objection based on *res judicata*. The court dismissed her application. Her appeal was also dismissed, after her solicitor submitted no further arguments. She should have appealed against the first dismissal. Repeated frivolous allegations may be an abuse of the court. The court has power to make an order prohibiting any further applications to court without leave of the judge.[47]

18.056 The time factor may be important in deciding whether there are different issues between the parties. In *O'B. v O'B.*[48] the plea of *res judicata* was not entertained by the Supreme Court. The Circuit Court, on appeal, had refused a barring order to the plaintiff. Two days before the appeal was due to be heard, proceedings seeking (inter alia) a permanent barring order in the High Court were issued. The hearing in the High Court did not proceed, though they were re-entered some time later. Costello J. in the High Court held that the circumstances prevailing at the time of the hearing before him were completely different from those of June 1981 when the proceedings had been issued. The wife relied at the

---

45 *Halsbury's Laws of England* 4th ed. Volume 16 paragraph 1520, states that a judgment which would be final, if it resulted from judicial decision after a contest, is not prevented from being so by the fact that it was obtained by consent or default.
46 [1943] Ir. Jurist Rep. 72.
47 See *Grepe v Loam* [1887] Ch. 168.
48 [1984] IR 316.

hearing on events prior to June 1981, but also on events after 1981. Lord Denning in *Thompson v Thompson*[49] took the view that, since estoppel does not bind a court, as distinct from the parties, a divorce court could investigate a matrimonial offence again, if not satisfied that there has been a full and proper inquiry in the previous litigation. Once the court does so, either party is no longer bound by the estoppel.

Settlements and consent orders

18.057 The term "settlement" in the following discussion is used to include a compromise. Strictly speaking, a "compromise" involves a settlement of the issues in the proceedings before the court. A settlement may however include matters not before the court in the instant proceedings. It is fundamental to family law practice, more than in any other area, that efforts be made to settle cases, to avoid them going for full trial. One is often dealing with a vulnerable client, who may feel bitter towards the other spouse, but who is also in fear of giving evidence. He or she may never have given evidence before, and the experience may be very traumatic, even if there is a sympathetic judge or justice. It is also usually in the interests of children to avoid litigation concerning their custody or access. That is not to say that family law cases should be settled by the surrender of important rights or protections. Some cases may not be suitable for settlement, as where there has been serious violence against a spouse or children, sexual abuse of a child or spouse. If there are areas of potential agreement, these should be isolated and consolidated by both solicitors. This may reduce costs, and help the parties in negotiating outstanding matters. Unfortunately, it is often the case that failure to reach agreement on all points results in those areas agreed upon also being left to be fought out in court.

18.058 It is important that settlement efforts be made before the date for hearing. If possible, a joint consultation should be arranged at a suitably neutral venue, and a time limit imposed. It is not fair to expect a client to make lifelong decisions on the morning of the hearing, when about to give evidence on intimate matters. A settlement reached to compromise the issues listed before the court may later collapse if the parties have neglected to discuss other outstanding issues that were not directly before the court. This is another reason why an exchange of correspondence on all outstanding issues, however trivial, is important, so that if settlement discussions are left to the last minute the parties and their solicitors and counsel know exactly what has or has not been settled.

18.059 In *Mespil Limited & Aramaic Ltd. v Capaldi & Capaldi and Bowes*[50] there was a mutual mistake as to whether the written terms put into a memorandum of settlement had settled all items of dispute between

---

49 [1957] P 19.
50 10 February 1984, unreported, High Court. A summary of the case is available in the Law Society, Gazette of January/February 1985.

the parties in the two sets of proceedings. The High Court held that the settlement was not vitiated by ambiguity or uncertainty. The defendants were held bound by the settlement which had been signed by their counsel.

18.060 If a settlement is reached at the door of the court, or a few days beforehand, it should be reduced to writing, and signed by both parties and their respective legal advisers. In *Barrett and Barrett v Lenehan & Co.*[51] the court upheld an agreement reached at the door of the court, though it had unfortunately not been reduced to writing. The court held that, since the plaintiffs authorised their legal advisers to negotiate on the issue of compensation, this implied authority to negotiate on collateral matters. Barrington J. also commented: "What did cause me some concern is whether the plaintiffs might have been so upset by the happenings of the morning, and by the atmosphere of the courthouse, that they did not fully appreciate what was going on".

18.061 It is usual for counsel to draw up the consent document. It may include matters that are not strictly before the court, but which are capable of being subject to a court's ruling for example, the contents of the family home, are often not included in the pleadings though they are a common source of dispute between the spouses. The court's ruling should preferably be written out on a separate page. If a client seems ambivalent, or very distraught, he or she may not be fit enough to give rational clear instructions. Such a client may allege at a later date that the solicitor or counsel forced him to sign the agreement. If a settlement document is drawn up, there should be duplicate and each document should be signed by both spouses and their respective legal advisers. The court should inspect same, though it may allow the plaintiff's solicitor to take back the handwritten document to be engrossed and signed again by the clients. Legal advisers should not leave the precincts of the court, without having clarified what their client has agreed to, and without being satisfied that the client has fully understood the agreement. It may be helpful to have written headed notepaper on which the agreement is recorded. It can be useful, with a difficult client, to ask him to sign a note on the headed notepaper, stating that he fully understands what has been agreed and that he has not been put under pressure by either his own or the other party's solicitor or counsel. If it is felt that the client is too upset, or is becoming confused, it is best to adjourn the case for a short "cooling off period" before making the final settlement.

18.062 If a consent document has been signed, the proceedings may be adjourned for a number of weeks, so that a proper deed of separation may be drawn up and made a rule of court. If the parties sign this deed in their respective solicitor's offices, it is unlikely that they will succeed in a subsequent application to set aside the deed.

---

51 [1981] ILRM 207.

18.063 Liberty to apply (i.e. to the court) is usually incorporated into an agreement filed in court. This may lead a client to think that the settlement can be subsequently changed. In *Gallagher v Sloan*[52] it was held that the words "liberty to apply" in the order referred to the working out of the actual terms of the order. The court would not try an entirely new claim, which ought to be the subject of a fresh action.

Costs

18.064 Order 70, rules 74–78 of the Rules of the Superior Courts 1986 (and Order 58 of the Circuit Court Rules 1950) govern costs in matrimonial causes and matters. The High Court's powers derive from section 27 of the Matrimonial Causes and Marriage Law (Ireland) Amendment Act 1870 which allows the Court to make such order as to costs as "may seem just". Much of the law relating to costs has been developed on the assumption that a wife will usually have no means of her own and will be powerless to bring proceedings unless her husband provides her with the means of doing so. (See *Flower v Flower*[53] and *Bradley v Bradley*.[54]) The rule in the past, therefore, has been that a wife with no separate estate[55] was entitled as of right to have her costs provided by her husband. The rule applied whether the wife was petitioner or respondent and whether she won or lost her case, but not where proceedings were brought without any justification. Furthermore, in *Bradley v Bradley* Murnaghan J., relying on *Sullivan v Sullivan*[55] and *Flower v Flower*,[53] held that the wife's necessary legal costs were recoverable from her husband by virtue of the wife's agency of necessity.

18.065 In *F. v L.*[56] Barron J. reviewed the above practice relating to costs and concluded that times have changed.

> In particular since the passing of the Married Women's Status Act 1957 any fetters which may have existed in relation to a married woman's rights to own property were removed. In my view the justification for allowing a wife her costs as against her husband in all circumstances is no longer justified. In each individual case, it is the duty of the Court to make such order as is just in the circumstances.

In the particular case (a successful nullity petition grounded on psychological impotence), both parties were working and neither would have been able without hardship to pay the costs of the other. Each was therefore ordered to bear his or her own costs.

52 [1983] NI 76 (Ch. D).
53 (1873) LR 3 P & D 132.
54 January 1971, unreported, High Court.
55 In *Sullivan v Sullivan* [1912] 2 IR 116 it was held that, where solicitors obtained a judgment for costs against a wife with a separate estate, they could not subsequently sue her husband for their unrecovered costs.
56 25 May 1990, unreported, High Court.

18.066 In practice it is recommended that the issue of costs be determined at the first interview. This may be difficult with a client who is upset, but it avoids problems for the solicitor and the client at a later date. If the case is a protracted one the client should be furnished with monthly accounts at a minimum. It should be made clear at the outset what are the difficulties likely to be encountered in recovering costs from the respondent. The client should not be under a misapprehension that her case will be subsidised by the solicitor.

18.067 The client will have to be consulted about whether the husband is financially capable of paying costs. If property is being sold, the solicitor for the applicant may ask the court to order that the proceeds be lodged in a joint account of the respective solicitors, and that the taxed costs be deducted, or that a reasonable sum be kept in the account until the costs are taxed.

18.068 A legal accountant normally prepares a detailed item by item bill of costs. It is in the interests of the respondent to pay at this stage, rather than to allow the matter proceed to taxation, where considerable stamp duty may be payable. The principles laid down in *Dunne v O'Neill* as regards the taxing master's role are relevant. It was made clear that each item of the claim should be assessed on the basis of what a practising solicitor, being reasonably careful and prudent, would consider a proper and reasonable fee to offer counsel for that item, in the light of the solicitor's day to day experience in his practice.

18.069 The High Court, in *The State (Gleeson) v Minister for Defence and the Attorney General*[57] relied on *Dunne v O'Neill*.[58] It was not the function of the taxing master to assess the nature or value or quality of the work done, or required to be done by counsel, in preparing for the hearing or in the conduct of cases in court. A legal accountant, with experience of drawing up and taxation of solicitors costs, should be able to advise the taxing master of the current standards of the reasonable careful and prudent solicitor.

18.070 In *The State (Gallagher, Shatter & Co.) v The Taxing Master*[59] the Supreme Court considered the basis of the taxing master's power in family law cases. It was held, in allowing the appeal of the solicitors, that the taxation by the taxing master, regulated by Order 99 rule 15(e), derived from the Attorneys and Solicitors (Ireland) Act 1849, and not from the Superior Court Rules Committee, or from any provision of the Courts (Supplemental Provisions) Act 1961.

18.071 The position of a solicitor handling a family law action at a higher court level was considered in *H.P. v W.P.*[60] It was held by Finlay J. that

57 23 June 1980, unreported, High Court.
58 [1974] IR 180.
59 [1986] ILRM 3.
60 [1985] ILRM 527.

while a solicitor acting without counsel is not entitled to a separate and specific fee, there should be an increase in the instruction fee to reflect the additional work for example, in advocacy in researching and preparing legal points, and in considering the approach to and pleadings of the case. The court also made clear that, if a plaintiff has in total paid to a solicitor more than the costs eventually taxed against another party, and more than the costs which would, in addition, be taxed on a solicitor and client bill, such a person has a right to recover excess monies from the solicitor concerned. If, on the other hand, a party has made to his or her own solicitor a payment on account of costs, which is less than the aggregate of the party and party costs taxed against an opponent and the additional items of solicitor and client costs properly payable, such party receives the costs awarded, and out of them pays the balance due to the solicitor.

18.072 The position of costs in a Circuit Court family law application were considered in *O'G. v O'G.*[61] The wife applied in the Circuit Court for interim costs and further costs on a *de die in diem* basis pending the hearing. She applied under Order 70 rule 75 of the Rules of the Supreme Courts, relying on Order 5a rule 14 of the Rules of the Circuit Court. O'Halley J. refused the application. He doubted if the relief sought was available and, if it were available, it should be granted on rules analogous to those which apply to an application for security of costs.

Contempt of court

18.073 Criminal contempt consists of conduct calculated to prejudice the due course of justice. In the context of family proceedings, it would include, for example, contempt in the face of the court or publication of in camera proceedings.[62] Civil contempt features more prominently. Because of the highly emotive content of much family litigation, civil contempt in the form of persistent failure to obey an order of the court is not uncommon. Breach of access, custody and barring orders, as well as injunctions, are familiar problems, as is persistent and wilful failure to obey a maintenance order. Contempt may be punished by fine or imprisonment. In the case of civil contempt, imprisonment may last indefinitely, until the court's order is obeyed, or until the applicant waives his rights.

18.074 Section 9 of the Petty Sessions (Ireland) Act 1891 provides that District and Circuit Courts have jurisdiction to punish contempt in the face of the court. The District Court has no jurisdiction to punish other[63] forms of contempt, such as breach of a custody or access order. This problem led to the introduction of section 5 of the Courts (No. 2) Act 1986 which makes it an offence not to comply with orders of the District Court made under section 7 or 11 of the Guardianship of Infants Act 1964. The Circuit Court

---

61 Irish Law Times, September 1988, page 219.
62 *Re Kennedy and McCann* [1976] IR 382.
63 *R. v Lefroy* [1873] LR 8 QB 134.

in practice does exercise such jurisdiction. The High Court has power to punish all forms of contempt, and may punish contempt of an inferior court which is not committed in the face of the court.[64]

18.075 Contempt proceedings should be viewed as a last resort in seeking compliance with a court order.[65] If it is possible to proceed to enforce a court order by other civil proceedings or by prosecuting for a specific criminal offence, this may be more appropriate (or example, an application to vary the original access order, which has become the focus of the dispute). If a respondent has assaulted a spouse or child, it may be more appropriate to have him charged with assault, actual bodily harm or grievous bodily harm, rather than to have him committed for breaking an injunction. The criminal process should be speedier if the Gardaí are willing to prosecute. With a persistent or psychopathic offender, or someone with a prior criminal record of assault against the spouse or other persons, an application for contempt may not be sufficient protection for the applicant. Judges are sometimes reluctant to commit, as they are afraid of the respondent becoming vengeful.

18.076 A solicitor must always advise a client to obey a court order, no matter what his personal feelings are with regard to the decision of the court. If a client is unhappy with a decision, an appeal can be lodged, and a stay on the order sought. A client should be urged orally and by letter, in simple non-legal language, to obey the order, and advised what the penalties are for non compliance. Sometimes, wrong advice is given. For example, it is sometimes suggested that the client does not need to comply with a District Court order once an appeal is lodged. This only applies where recognisances have been entered into. The practice in family law cases is to waive recognisances as a matter of form; a special application has to be made to fix recognisances.

18.077 There is sometimes a long delay before an applicant decides to act in response to breach of a barring, custody or access order. Such delay makes it more difficult to proceed with a contempt motion. Applicants should be advised at the earliest possible stage that if there is a breach of an order the solicitor should be contacted. The solicitor can write to the solicitor for the respondent warning that contempt proceedings will be issued if he does not obey the order.

18.078 Access provisions cause particular problems. They are often used by separated spouses as the ground upon which to continue a power struggle. Minor breaches of access orders occur frequently and often give rise to strong feelings of resentment or insecurity in the custodial parent,

---

64 See *A.G. v O'Ryan and Boyd* [1945] IR 70, and *A.G. v Connolly* [1947] IR 213.
65 *Ross Co Ltd v Swan* [1981] ILRM 416 held, in applying *Danchevsky v Danchevsky* [1974] 2 All ER 5612, that the power to commit is a jurisdiction that should not be exercised when it is unlikely to produce the desired result, and when there is a reasonable alternative available.

who may react by making access more difficult. A court's decision to use its contempt jurisdiction will be influenced by considerations of the child's welfare. It may ignore or tolerate minor breaches in the hope that the anger may dissipate or heal over time. There may be particular problems with older children who decline to go for access. The non custodial spouse may believe that this has been orchestrated by the custodial spouse. He may apply to commit her for contempt. The custodial spouse may decline to force a teenage child to go for access on the basis that he is old enough to make up his own mind. The court may not agree with this view.

18.079 Before issuing contempt proceedings, the precaution should be taken of serving the respondent directly with the order, if that has not already been done. If the breaches persist, it may be appropriate, at an early stage, to seek a variation of the original orders, and include an application for contempt. The court may vary the order more readily as an alternative to committing the respondent for contempt. If there is a practical way of ensuring or encouraging compliance with the orders, then it should be explored. For example, with regard to an access order, the venue for collection and delivery can be changed to a centre city location, in a public place, where the applicant will feel safer, or arrangements may be made that the respondent's named relative or friend, and not the respondent himself, collect and deliver the children. When the applicant eventually applies for contempt, if he has himself complied with the order and been reasonable about trying to obtain compliance, this will make it easier to persuade the court that contempt proceedings have been issued as a last resort.

Miscellaneous practice notes

18.080 It is assumed that the reader is already familiar with the rules applicable to all the courts, and the statutory instruments made under the various Family Law Acts. It is also assumed that the reader keeps up to date with the various practice directions, both generally and in family law. However, the following points are of particular relevance to the family law practitioner.

Drawing up of orders in the Dublin Circuit Court

18.081 In Dublin, the Circuit Court family law office have adopted a practice in relation to the drawing up of orders. When the original order is engrossed by the solicitor, he must type, on the back of the draft drawn up by the registrar, that "I certify that the order has been engrossed as of the terms of the original draft order herein". It is dated and signed. In non family law cases, the orders may not be drawn unless a request is made to the registrar. The registrar should be asked to draw up an injunction order before the solicitor leaves the precincts of the court.

Stenographers

18.082 A stenographer is not generally available in a family law case. There is an exception in custody cases, and in nullity cases. If a stenographer is required, then the Irish Stenographers Ltd. of Hillcrest House, Dargle Valley, Bray, should be contacted. If a case is likely to be appealed from the High Court to the Supreme Court, it is particularly important to have a stenographer. This also applies to protracted cases. Alternatively, the solicitor will be expected, in consultation with counsel, to type up all the attendances. This is then submitted to the trial judge for his comments. The final agreed transcript is then submitted to the Supreme Court.

List of helpful agencies

18.083 This list is not exhaustive.[66] It may be helpful in an emergency. It may also be useful where the client needs ongoing support. Solicitors or barristers are not trained to act in a counselling capacity, and should not hesitate to recommend a client to go for such support. This suggestion should not be made in a brusque manner, but by gently explaining the role of the lawyer, and how he or she can work best with a client who is receiving support from properly trained counsellors. Lawyers should not underestimate the depth and range of human emotion encountered in dealing with those who are the victims of marital strife. There is sometimes a risk of a nervous or physical breakdown, or even suicide, by a client. This is all the more reason why the lawyer, particularly the solicitor, needs to build a network of colleagues from different professional backgrounds, who can be called on in times of difficulties, and to whom to make appropriate referrals.

Marriage guidance counselling

18.084 The following agencies provide help for those needing advice and counselling as to whether to separate.

	Telephone
Catholic Marriage Advisory Council (CMAC), Main Centre: All Hallows College, Drumcondra, Dublin 9	375649
See phone directory for local centres	
Marriage Counselling Services, 24 Grafton St, Dublin 2 This is a non denominational service	720341

---

66 See *Directory of Voluntary Organisations*, published by the National Social Services Board, or the *Women's Diary*, published annually by Attic Press. Or the *I.P.A. Diary*, published annually.

AIM Group for Family Law Reform,
64 Lower Mount St,
Dublin 2
Mornings only   616478

Gingerbread,
Top Floor,
12 Wicklow St,
Dublin 2   710291

Clanwilliam Institute,
Clanwilliam Terrace,
Grand Canal Quay,   761363
Dublin 2   762881

Mediation

18.085 The following agencies provide mediation help:

Family Mediation Service,
Block 1, Floor 5, Irish Life Centre   728277
Abbey St,   728708
Dublin 1   728475

Michael Williams,
14 Charleville Road,
Dublin 6   978402

Clanwilliam Institute: see above

Gingerbread: see above

Alcoholism

18.086 The main agency involved in combatting alcoholism is Alcoholics
Anonymous, which has branches all over Ireland. Al Anon is a separate
branch for the spouses of alcoholics, and Al Ateen is for teenage children
of alcoholics. In addition, there are alcoholic units attached to most local
psychiatric hospitals.

Alcoholics Anonymous,
100 South Circular Road,
Dublin 8   538998

Rutland Centre Ltd,
Knocklyon House,
Templeogue,
Dublin 16   946358

Stanhope Alcoholism Centre,
Stanhope St,
Dublin 7   773965

Drugs

18.087 The following agencies provide help for drug addiction:

Drug Treatment Centre,
Trinity Court,
30 Pearse St,
Dublin 2   771122

Coolmine Therapeutic Centre,
19 Lr Edward St,
Dublin 2   793765

also: Clonsilla,
Dublin 15

Gambling

18.088 The main agency which helps those with gambling problems is:

Gamblers Anonymous,
31 Dominick St,
Dublin 7   300993

Financial problems

18.089 Those who cannot afford an accountant may obtain free financial advice from the Financial Information Service Centre, where officers sometimes attend at local community centres. Advice regarding social welfare may be obtained from the nearest Free Legal Advice Centre.

Financial Information Services Centre (FISC),
87/89 Pembroke Rd,
Dublin 4   682044

Free Legal Advice Centre (FLAC),
Head Office: 49 South William St,
Dublin 2   794239

Emergency situations of violence

18.090 In such a situation, the victim should contact the local doctor, or if the injuries are serious, attend the casualty unit of the hospital on call and ask the casualty consultant to note the bruises or marks. The local police station should then be contacted, and a written complaint should be made, with a view to prosecution.

Women's Aid,
PO Box 791,
Dublin 6   971370

This agency helps battered wives; addresses of local hostels for battered wives may be found in the phone book or by using directory enquiries.

If there has been sexual violence, contact:

The Rape Crisis Centre,
70 Lower Leeson St,
Dublin 2   614911

There are local rape crisis centres in most large towns—see phone book for details.

For medical advice and examinations, contact:

The Sexual Assault Treatment Unit,
Rotunda Hospital,
Parnell St,
Dublin 1   730700

In the case of violence to a child (under 18), in addition to contacting the nearest Women's Aid Refuge, contact the social worker at the local health clinic, or the local children's hospital.

If there has been sexual abuse of a child, contact:

Children's Hospital,
Temple St,
Dublin   (Northside)
or
Children's Hospital,
Crumlin,
Dublin   (Southside)

Outside Dublin, contact the area headquarters for the Health Board, in the front pages of the phone book. Each Health Board now has a specialist team to deal with this problem. Although the Health Boards have a statutory responsibility to care for children under 16 years old, a client may prefer to deal with a voluntary agency. In such a situation, the client and child should be referred to the local rape crisis centre.

The Irish Society for the Prevention of Cruelty
to Children has a Childline telephone advisory
service for sexually abused children and
teenagers.   793333

Appendix A

Inability to enter into or sustain a normal marriage relationship

The Supreme Court's decision in *H.F. (orse H.C.) v J.C.* 11 July 1990, unreported, came too late to be incorporated in the main text. The respondent was at the time of the marriage a practising homosexual, a condition which he concealed from the petitioner, who was completely unaware of this side of his nature. Shortly after the marriage the respondent resumed his homosexual practices and the marriage as a result broke down irretrievably. In the High Court Keane J. refused to grant a decree of nullity and questioned the right of the courts to introduce new grounds of nullity. In particular, he rejected the idea that a decree could be granted on the ground that one spouse, by reason of emotional disability or incapacity at the time of the marriage, was unable to enter into and sustain a normal marriage relationship. The reasons for Keane J.'s decision are set out at **2.064–2.066**.

It soon became apparent, following Keane J.'s judgment, that other High Court Judges favoured the new ground for nullity. (See, for example, *P.C. v V.C.*, 7 July 1989, unreported, High Court, O'Hanlon J. (**2.051**), *R.T. v V.P. (orse T.)* 30 July 1989, unreported, High Court, Lardner J., and *C.(G.) v C.* October 1989, unreported, High Court, MacKenzie J.) The Supreme Court has now added its imprimatur by overruling Keane J.

Finlay C.J. allowed the appeal and granted a decree on the ground of the respondent's incapacity, by virtue of his homosexual nature, to form or maintain a normal marital relationship with the petitioner. The following are the main features of Finlay C.J.'s judgment:

1. Kenny J.'s statement in *S. v S.* 1 July 1976, Supreme Court, unreported, to the effect that nullity law should not be regarded as fossilised in the state it was in in 1870 (see **2.002**) is cited with approval.

2. In exercising their jurisdiction in nullity, under section 13 of the Act of 1870, and in framing new rules judges are not confined, as Keane J. suggested, to having regard only to advances in psychological medicine. Advances in knowledge concerning sexual orientation and development are also relevant.

3. The judgments of Barrington J. in *R.S.J. v J.S.J.* (**2.040**), and of Costello J. in *D. v C.* (**2.041**), which laid the foundations for the new ground, are cited with approval.

4. The analogy drawn by Barrington J. in *R.S.J. v J.S.J.* between sexual impotence and incapacity to enter a caring or considerate relationship is approved.

5. The analogy applies "not only in cases where that incapacity arose from psychiatric or mental illness so recognised or defined but also in cases where it arose from some other inherent quality or characteristic of an individual's nature or personality which could not be said to be voluntary or self-induced". (At page 14 of the judgment).

6. In certain circumstances "the existence in one party to a marriage of an inherent and unalterable homosexual nature may form a proper legal ground for annulling the marriage at the instance of the other party to the marriage in the case, at least, where that party has no knowledge of the existence of the homosexual nature". (At page 17 of the judgment).

In a judgment agreeing with the Chief Justice, McCarthy J. expressly approved the principles laid down by Costello J. in *D. v C.* (**2.041**), and stated (at pages 4 and 5), that:

> The marriage contract requires a particular capacity, both mental and physical. The understanding of such mental capacity did not cease to develop after 1870. Along with the progression and change in diagnosis and treatment of physical incapacity there have been advances in the diagnosis and treatment of mental incapacity.

On the question of the onus of proof in nullity proceedings (**2.011–2.014**), Finlay C.J. took the view that the matter was not in issue, and reserved it for future decision. McCarthy J. agreed that the matter was not in issue, but confirmed the view he had expressed in *N.(K.) v K.* (**2.013**), that the "balance of probabilities" standard should apply.

McCarthy J. also made certain observations *obiter* implying that the case raised an issue of consent. "It is, in my view, unthinkable that one of the parties who is totally ignorant of that [homosexual] proclivity in the other should be held to have entered into a valid contract of which one of the implied but most important terms is the commitment to physical consummation and mutual satisfaction." (At page 6).

Appendix B

Practice and Procedure under the Judicial Separation and Family Law Reform Act 1989[1]

The practice and procedure under the Act of 1989 is not yet well settled or established. Indeed, it may very well remain so until the superior courts have considered the provisions of the Act at length.

Statutory instrument number 97 of 1990[2] came into force on the 1st May 1990. This establishes a procedural framework for the Act when proceedings are commenced in the High Court. In addition, it encompasses changes regarding applications under a number of other Acts and related matters.[3] Rule 1 of the statutory instrument refers to The Rules of the Superior Courts[4] and has the effect of deleting from those rules references to legal remedies abolished, expressly or by necessary implication, by the 1989 Act.[5] Rule 2 inserts a new Order into the R.S.C., Order 70A. This sets out a list of proceedings and applications which a new term of "family

---

1 It had been intended to include a comment on the rules enacted for the Circuit Court in this part. Unfortunately at the time of going to print these rules are not yet finalised. The comments concerning the procedure in the High Court is largely restricted to the Statutory Instrument enacted under the Act as the majority of cases have been taken in the lower court and there is as yet no substantial body of practice enunciated in the higher court. Various Circuit Court Judges have taken differing views on the substantive law involved and there does not appear as yet to be any significant development or interpretation of the procedural matters. Readers are referred in addition to chapter seven which deals with some of the procedural provisions set out in the Act itself.
2 Rules of the Superior Courts (No. 1), 1990; P1 7237.
3 The other legislative provisions are: Married Women's Status Act, 1957; Guardianship of Infants Act, 1964; Adoption Act, 1974; Family Law (Maintenance of Spouses and Children) Act, 1976; Family Home Protection Act, 1976; Family Law Act, 1981; Family Law (Protection of Spouses and Children) Act, 1981; and the Adoption Act, 1988. This discussion deals principally with the position under the 1989 Act and only incidentally with the other legislation where the present position is materially affected.
4 SI No. 15 of 1986. Hereinafter R.S.C.
5 I.e. "permanent alimony" and "divorce *a mensa et thoro*".

law proceedings" shall include. Rule 1 of Order 70A specifically refers to the 1989 Act at sub-rules 6 and 7.

Rule 2 of Order 70A provides that all family law proceedings, with one exception,[6] shall be commenced by a special summons which shall be a family law summons. The matters distinguishing this family law summons from other special summons are, as far as the drafting is concerned, slight. As the new rule itself outlines, the endorsement of claim shall state specifically with all necessary particulars the relief sought and the grounds upon which it is sought, and a sufficient statement of the facts alleged to establish the right to such relief, together with all such ancillary relief and the grounds upon which such is sought. In any proceedings pursuant to the 1989 Act an affidavit verifying such proceedings shall contain detailed particulars of a number of matters.[7] These particulars comprise information about all the matters to be in issue between the parties together with details of the specific ancillary relief sought. This rule goes on to provide that the certificate required under section 5 or section 6 as the case may be of the Act shall be exhibited in the form set out in the table to the Order.

Rule 4 of this new Order allows the court to adjourn proceedings to allow such amendments as may be necessary to the summons where any relief is sought which has not been specifically claimed. The court may so adjourn on such terms and conditions as it sees fit. Any party to such action or proceedings[8] commenced in the High Court may apply to the High Court to have the matter transferred or remitted to the Circuit Court or District Court.[9] The High Court has a discretion whether or not to accede to this application and must consider the interests of justice in this regard. The High Court is empowered to so order upon such terms and subject to such conditions as to costs or otherwise as may appear just. The application to transfer or remit may be made at any time after an appearance has been entered.[10]

Certain of the provisions of Order 49, R.S.C., which concern the Hearing, Transfer and Consolidation of causes and matters are applicable to any proceedings commenced under rule 2 of Order 70A.[11] Rule 9 of Order 70A allows a respondent in family law proceedings to counter-claim in like manner as if he were an applicant and subject to the provisions of the Order. The Master of the High Court or the Court is empowered at any stage of the proceedings to direct such service of notice of the proceedings on any person not already a party in such manner as the court shall direct having regard to the nature and effect of the relief claimed and its effects if

6 This is pursuant to rule 16 of Order 70A. This covers an application to court under section 6A(3) of the Guardianship of Infants Act, 1964 as inserted by the Status of Children Act, 1987.
7 Rule 3 of Order 70A.
8 This includes all the matters covered under the Statutory Instrument, not merely those under the 1989 Act.
9 Rule 5 of the new Order.
10 Rule 5(2).
11 Rule 6.

granted.[12] Where proceedings are transferred to the High Court pursuant to section 31(3) of the 1989 Act the applicant and the respondent are ordered, within fourteen days of the making of the order or such further time as may be allowed, to file in the Central Office an affidavit or supplemental affidavit and to deliver amended pleadings as shall appear necessary to conform to the requirements of Order 70A.[13]

Where a spouse desires to apply pursuant to section 22 of the Act for an order varying or discharging a financial or property order the application is to be by a Motion on Notice to the other party supported by an affidavit verifying same and setting out fully when and in what respect the circumstances have changed or what new evidence exists.[14] Rule 13 deals with applications under sections 11 and 29(2)(a) of the Act for interim relief. Sub-rule 1 provides that such applications may be made *ex parte* where the urgency of the matter requires the making of the order. Sub-rule 2 includes applications under section 13 of the Act for maintenance pending suit and all applications under section 29. These are by motion on notice grounded upon an affidavit which sets forth details of the relief which has been claimed or granted and where applicable details of the disposition or transfer or other dealing with property which is being impunged. The court may direct service of notice of such application on such other parties to any such disposition, transfer or dealing as in the circumstances seems proper.[15]

Application for rescission of the grant of a decree of judicial separation shall be preceded by a notion of re-entry grounded upon an affidavit sworn by each of the spouses.[16] The nature and extent of the reconciliation must be included and must state whether they have resumed cohabitating as husband and wife. The provisions of Order 119, rules 2 and 3, R.S.C., relating to the robes of Judges and Counsel do not apply to any cause, action or proceeding under Orders 70A or 71.[17] The rules under this Statutory Instrument are to be construed together with the R.S.C. and may be cited as the Rules of the Superior Courts (No. 1), 1990.[18]

Sections 27 and 28 of the Act make appropriate amendments to two statutes relevant to the enforcement of orders under this Act. Section 27 amends the Defence Act, 1954 to provide that an order for the payment of alimony shall be construed as including references to an order for maintenance pending suit, a periodical payments order and a secured periodical payments order. Section 28 makes a similar amendment to section 8 of the Enforcement of Court Orders Act, 1940, as amended. However, this amendment does not refer to a secured periodical payments order. There does not appear to be any particular reason for this

---

12 Rule 10.
13 Rule 11.
14 Rule 12.
15 Rule 13(3).
16 Rule 14.
17 Rule 17. Order 71, R.S.C. concerns applications under the Legitimacy Declaration Act (Ireland), 1868.
18 Rule 18.

difference. Section 32 of the Act in summary lays down that the Circuit Family Court shall hear family law proceedings separate from ordinary sittings of the Court. This provision is causing difficulties in the Circuit Court sitting outside Dublin. With a heavy case load in the courts and sittings being held in any particular venue on an infrequent if regular basis, court officials appear reluctant to set aside a day or time specifically for family law proceedings. This reluctance is grounded upon the fact that such proceedings are often settled at or before hearing, are adjourned or are very lengthy. The provision in respect of a different place appears impracticable due to lack of resources.

Section 33(1) and (3) refer to the informality of proceedings in the Circuit Family Court and High Court. Section 45(1) is in similar terms with respect to the District Court. Differing attitudes have been detected to these provisions already. These involve differing approaches being adopted by the judiciary and also depend upon the relief sought. Some judges have not altered the manner in which they approach family law cases as a result of the Act, dealing with such matters with the formality prescribed for other areas of law. On the other hand other judges always approached family law matters with a degree of informality and have continued to do so. Differences in the relief sought and the extent of the argument against such relief have produced differing degrees of informality. Applications in respect of barring orders, "exclusion orders" under section 16(a) of the Act and in respect of custody of children are still generally treated very strictly and formally.

Section 33(2) and (4) deals with the wearing of wigs and gowns by judges, counsel and solicitors in the Circuit Family Court and High Court. There is a difference in the phraseology used in the two subsections. In relation to the Circuit Family Court it appears to be an absolute requirement on all occasions that judges and lawyers are prohibited from wearing wigs or gowns. However, in relation to the High Court the prohibition is framed in terms of proceedings being heard and determined in the court. In practice there are different attitudes among the High Court Judiciary. Some of the judges continue to wear wigs and gowns at all times. Others wear these during call-overs of the list and for the determination of motions, dispensing with same if there is a hearing or determination of any proceedings. One anomaly in relation to the prohibition on wigs and gowns is that it does not apply at all to petitions for nullity. Section 45(2) in relation to the District Court is framed in terms similar to those applicable to the High Court rather than the Circuit Family Court. Again different attitudes to this are apparent among District Justices.

Section 40 of the Act amends section 11 of the Guardianship of Infants Act, 1964. Five subsections are added to section 11.[19] These provide in effect for the ordering of reports on the welfare of children and for the availability of such reports for court. Such reports may be ordered by the court on its own motion or on the application of a party. In deciding whether or not to request a report under the section the court is obliged to

---

19   These become subsections 5 to 9 of section 11.

have regard to the wishes of the parties before the court where ascertainable but is not bound by them. It is not entirely clear if this provision applies to applications by a party requesting a report or where the court acts on its own motion. Experience to date shows that the judiciary as a whole are familiar with the new power of the court to order a report of its motion and on occasion reports have been ordered notwithstanding the wishes of the parties to the contrary.

Lastly, it appears now to be the case that, upon a property transfer order being made under the Act, the Registrar of Titles is requesting that the order of the court expressly recite that the folio is to be rectified in accordance with the order. This appears at first sight to be a somewhat cautious approach. However, in light of the powers of the court under the Act subsequently to amend, vary or revoke orders already made on the application of either or both spouse, it is probably a wise and advisable development.

Index